ROMANS
in a New World

*Classical Models in Sixteenth-Century
Spanish America*

David A. Lupher

THE UNIVERSITY OF MICHIGAN PRESS
Ann Arbor

First paperback edition 2006
Copyright © by the University of Michigan 2003
All rights reserved
Published in the United States of America by
The University of Michigan Press
Printed and bound by CPI Group (UK) Ltd, Croydon, CR0 4YY

2009 2008 2007 2006   5   4   3   2

A CIP catalog record for this book is available from the British Library.

Library of Congress Cataloging-in-Publication Data

Lupher, David A., 1947–
    Romans in a new world : classical models in sixteenth-century
Spanish America / David A. Lupher.
        p.   cm. — (History, languages, and cultures of the Spanish and
Portuguese worlds)
    Includes bibliographical references and index.
    ISBN 0-472-11275-9 (cloth : alk. paper)
    1. Mexico—History—Conquest, 1519–1540.   2. Spaniards—Mexico—
History—16th century.   3. Indians—First contact with Europeans.
4. Spain—History—To 711.   5. Romans—Spain—History.   6. Iberians.
I. Title.   II. Series.
FI230.L953   2003
972'.02—dc21   2002005408

ISBN 0-472-03178-3 (pbk. : alk. paper)
ISBN 978-0-472-03178-8 (pbk. : alk. paper)

Praise for *Romans in a New World*:

"This is a fine and careful study: deeply learned and beautifully written."
—Arthur M. Eckstein, *International History Review*

"*Romans in a New World* contains the most lucid and straightforward account of the complex uses of 'Rome' and a Roman model in the Spanish colonization of the New World."
—Patricia Seed, Professor of History, University of California Irvine

". . . original and highly productive. . . . Not since J. H. Elliott's too brief but sagacious analysis of the mindset of Cortes have we had such a revealing look at where the Spanish, as one says in California today, 'were coming from.' Well researched, straightforwardly written, this book is well worth reading slowly and carefully. It contributes to history of colonization and control and to the history of education and the history of religion."
—L. R. N. Ashley, *Bibliothèque d'Humanisme et Renaissance*

"[This] study will prove to be a fundamental point of reference for anyone considering the classical tradition in this sphere."
—William Stenhouse, *Renaissance Quarterly*

"This monumental work . . . begs for superlatives. It is sprawling and sweeping, yet disciplined and consequential, elegantly written and enormously erudite, but approachable and relevant. David A. Lupher's thrust is clear. He means to portray these past scholars' often negative views about the impact of Spain on American cultures by comparing that impact to what the Roman conquest had done to Iberia's own pre-Latin culture a millennium and a half earlier. Thus Lupher's work is ultimately as much about an emerging Spanish identity in Europe as it is about the creation of America's own native and Creole identities."
—Richard C. Trexler, *American Historical Review*

"Lupher provides a rich introduction to sixteenth century Spanish writers to whom ancient Roman echoes were second nature . . . . *Romans in a New World* will serve as a valuable resource for undergraduate courses on the classical tradition or on Roman culture and its aftermath. For teachers at any level, the book adds a dimension to the array of reasons for the study of Greco-Roman civilization. It yields an excursion across the southern border and a glimpse of the influential role played there historically by Rome. For this reason alone, it will amply justify the attention of Latinists and classicists in the English speaking world."
—Edward V. George, *Classical Outlook*

". . . essential reading for those who would understand the political language and culture of the early modern transatlantic world. The complex paths that Lupher traveled to unravel remote references are unequaled in the literature. It is cogent, thorough, and convincing—a major work of intellectual history."
—S. Elizabeth Penry, *Society for Spanish and Portuguese Historical Studies Bulletin*

"Lupher has written a complex work of wide learning and profound scholarship, a substantial contribution not only to the study of Spanish and Latin American intellectual history but to the reception of the classics, above all to understanding the remarkably complex and changing image of Rome in early modern Europe. . . . Would that we all had the courage to embark on such complex and difficult new fields; would that we all had the patience, ability, and intelligence to master them as well as Lupher has. This is one of the most sustained and intelligent pieces of serious scholarship and interpretation that I have read in a long time."
—James Zetzel, *Bryn Mawr Classical Review*

History, Languages, and Cultures of the Spanish and Portuguese Worlds

*This interdisciplinary series promotes scholarship
in studies on Iberian cultures and contacts from the premodern
and early modern periods.*

Acknowledgments

Readers of this book should be warned that it was written by a classical scholar inspired to invade the foreign territory of colonial Latin American studies by the happy accident of finding himself assigned to teach Bernal Díaz's engrossing chronicle of the Spanish conquest of Mexico. This means, of course, that this project could not have been completed without the kind and patient assistance of specialists in fields far distant from Greek tragedy.

Thanks to peculiarities of late-twentieth-century scholarly behavior, my deepest debt is to three scholars I have never met. William McCuaig, a Renaissance intellectual historian, was the first person to read a complete draft of this book, and I am deeply grateful to him for his early and persistent support. Patricia Seed, a Latin Americanist from whose work I have learned much, also read a complete draft, and her suggestions and encouragement have been profoundly welcome. And finally, the Greek historian Debra Hamel read the manuscript with meticulous care, making hundreds of suggestions, nearly all of which I have adopted. My debt to her is immense.

I am grateful as well to colleagues at the University of Puget Sound who have read portions of the manuscript at various stages of its evolution: Molly Pasco-Pranger, John Lear, Jack Roundy, and Alix Cooper (currently of SUNY, Stony Brook). Other UPS colleagues have also given me welcome assistance and encouragement, especially Bill Barry, Rob Garratt, Michael Curley, and Ili Nagy. But it was Florence Sandler whose initial encouragement nourished the conference paper that eventually metamorphosed into this book. And Lina Bloomer has unfailingly come running with expert and patient technical assistance, and she has aided me skillfully and unstintingly in the formatting of the manuscript.

George Pesely of Austin Peay State University has given me much valuable help on the eccentric Dalmatian Dominican Vinko Paletin. I have learned much about Las Casas, Peter Martyr, and Polydore Virgil from Geoffrey Eatough of the University of Wales, Lampeter. Thomas

Izbicki of Johns Hopkins helped me on questions of canon law, and Brian Ogilvie, then a graduate student at the University of Chicago, came swiftly to my aid on questions of Renaissance antiquarianism. Another young scholar, my nephew Brian Cope, helped me with iconographic issues. I am also grateful to Richard Boyer (Simon Fraser University) and to Richard Unger (University of British Columbia) both for their own suggestions and for the opportunity to present portions of this project to their colleagues and students. And I have profited much from suggestions by Sabine MacCormack and the two anonymous readers for the University of Michigan Press.

I am particularly grateful for the assistance of the staffs of several libraries. First and foremost, there is the staff of the Collins Library of the University of Puget Sound—above all Christine Fisher of Inter-Library Loan. In addition, I could not have written this book without the help of the libraries of the University of Washington, the University of British Columbia, and the Bancroft Library of the University of California, Berkeley. Barbara Tenenbaum of the Library of Congress has given me invaluable assistance on more than one occasion. And the staff of the Lilly Library of Indiana University were most helpful in giving me ready access to the Latin version of Vinko Paletin's fascinating treatise. Finally, I wish to thank Daniel Riaño Rufilanchas of the Instituto de Filología, CSIC, Madrid, for archival investigations at the Real Academia de la Historia, Madrid.

I regret that my book will not be seen by two people who had expressed a strong interest in it: my mother, Lucretia Lupher; and my Doktorvater, A. E. Raubitschek. I am pleased, however, that it will be hefted at long last by the three wonderful descendants of Spaniards and Indians (and perhaps Romans) who have given so much encouragement to a project that has competed with them for my attention long enough: my wife Norma Ramírez and our children, Antonio and Sonia Lupher.

Contents

Introduction

In an arresting fantasy in his essay "Of Coaches," Michel de Montaigne improved upon history by imagining a Mexico conquered not by the savage and unscrupulous Spaniards of brutal reality, but by the ancient Greeks or Romans. Mexico would thus have experienced the birth of a mestizo population blessed with both the natural virtues of the Indians and the more polished manners of the classical world. "What an improvement that would have been, and what an amelioration for the entire globe, if the first examples of our conduct that were offered over there had called those peoples to the admiration and imitation of virtue and had set up between them and us a brotherly fellowship and understanding!"[1]

It is the aim of the present study to demonstrate that the Greeks and the Romans—especially the Romans—were, in fact, on hand for the conquest of Mexico, packed securely in the mental baggage of both the conquistadors and their critics. Contrary to Montaigne's historical reverie, however, the Romans were not in Mexico to conquer, but to be conquered. Indeed, in the ideological skirmishes that swirled around the actions of the conquistadors in the New World, the Roman Empire fell three times over. While the conquistadors themselves and their admiring publicists proudly challenged the reputation of the ancient Romans for incomparable military genius and daring, Spanish critics of the conquest launched an impassioned assault upon two other prominent uses of ancient Rome as a model: as an exemplar of imperial motives and behavior fit for Christians to emulate, and as a yardstick against which to measure the cultural level of the natives of the New World. If Montaigne's dream of a utopian extension of the classical world to Mexico seems a characteristic Renaissance fantasy, no less distinctive of the Renaissance was the desire of many Spaniards to transcend or outgrow classical models as they coped with the challenges of America.

Not only did the conquest of the New World inspire Spaniards to reevaluate the model of ancient Rome; that reevaluation in turn led some of them to reflect more deeply on their own ethnic ancestry and identity, as Spanish treatment of the American natives awakened the slumbering memory of Rome's subjugation of the Iberian tribesmen whom modern Spaniards were increasingly embracing as their truest ancestors. The exploitation and rejection of the model of ancient Rome in the discourse of the conquest of the New World thus played a significant, if hitherto relatively neglected, role in that vigorous debate about Spanish identity—*hispanidad*—that has raged unabated from the Middle Ages to the post-Franco era.[2]

Our exploration of attacks upon the "Roman model" in the conquest of the Indies begins with a campaign launched by the conquistadors themselves and by their publicists (chapter 1, "Conquistadors and Romans"). The target of this self-promotional assault was the reputation of the ancient Romans for martial courage and strategic intelligence supposedly unmatchable by future conquerors. Not only was Cortés declared a far greater general than Julius Caesar, but even an ordinary conquistador in the ranks, Bernal Díaz del Castillo, could claim that he personally had surpassed the exploits of that celebrated Roman. This agonistic stance toward classical antiquity, far transcending in intensity conventional Renaissance "topping" of the ancients, was partly the by-product of the disappointment and wounded pride that many conquistadors felt over the paltry honors and privileges they received from a Spanish Crown decidedly disinclined to encourage the growth of a potentially unruly colonial nobility. But the "anti-Romanism" of the conquistadors also reflected their persistently vivid sense that they were operating in a profoundly unfamiliar world, one where the models of European antiquity required bold reassessment. Even the very distances that Spaniards had to travel in order to reach this "New World" widened the gap between themselves and their classical rivals, a point developed especially by a latter-day rival of Pliny the Elder, the industrious chronicler and natural historian Gonzalo Fernández de Oviedo.

The second chapter initiates an exploration of the use to which the ancient Romans were put in the so-called controversy of the Indies, an impressive examination of the justice of the conquest. Seldom, if ever, in history has an imperial power encouraged or permitted so intense a questioning of its own imperial motives, rights, and behavior during the very height of its conquests. The classical world played two main roles in this debate: in the form of Aristotle's concept of the "natural slave," and in the much less fully studied precedent of Rome's acquisition of a supposed "world empire." The Roman question became especially prominent during the years when the Spanish conquest of the New World was presided over by the "Roman emperor," Charles V (1519–56), and we shall accordingly begin with the propagandistic tradition of Charles as "Emperor of the Romans and Lord of All the World." But for the bulk of this chapter we shall be taking our seats in the lecture halls of the Universities of Salamanca and Alcalá, for it was there that the validity of the "Roman title" for Spanish dominion in the Indies first came under vigorous attack, above all in the widely influential semipublic lectures known as "relections." Of special interest will be the neglected status of Domingo de Soto as pioneer both of the academic debate over the justice of the conquest and of the challenge to the use of the Romans as imperial models. The ambiguous role of the Romans in the influential "Indian relections" of the celebrated Salamantine theologian and pioneer of international law Francisco de Vitoria will then be analyzed, as well as the attempts of Vitoria's students, colleagues, and successors to counteract their revered master's disconcertingly positive assessment of the virtues of ancient Roman imperial rule.

The famous debate in Valladolid in 1550–51 between the Aristotelian Juan Ginés de Sepúlveda and the fiery Dominican bishop of Chiapas Bartolomé de las Casas is the central concern of the third chapter. In this dispute, ancient Rome figured more as a positive or negative model for imperial behavior than as a foundation in civil or canon law for Spanish dominion in the Indies. Unlike the subjects of the second chapter, neither Sepúlveda nor Las Casas was a university professor, and neither was a trained theologian or jurist. Nevertheless, their clash has always been recognized as the climactic event in the controversy of the Indies. Accordingly, the radically divergent views that the contenders expressed about the model of ancient Rome are inevitably of considerable interest.

Despite Las Casas's vigorous assault on the prestige of the Romans, the question of a Spanish title to the New World derived from the dominion of the Roman Empire did not disappear from the controversy of the Indies after the great debate in Valladolid. The fourth chapter explores four treatments of this question conducted outside Spanish university circles in the decade after the debate. Three of these attempted to defend the Roman model—and one of them, indeed, went so far as to argue that the current Spanish claim to dominion in the Indies was circuitously derived from a circumstance that no other contributor to the debate seems to have dared to imagine: a specific ancient Roman dominion in the Antilles and adjacent mainland! On the other hand, a relection delivered by Alonso de la Vera Cruz in the first academic year of the University of Mexico demolished the "Roman title" at exhaustive length before an audience of young clerics soon to be faced with the currently sensitive question of whether or not to administer the sacraments to conquistadors eager to assert their credentials as "emperor's men." This chapter closes with a brief discussion of Juan Solórzano Pereira's influential early-seventeenth-century "postmortem" on the controversy of the Indies and on the role of the ancient Roman Empire in that debate.

The last two chapters of this book explore two extraordinarily bold strategies pursued in the controversy of the Indies: the comparison of the Spanish conquest of the New World with the Roman conquest of Spain, and the juxtaposition of the native cultures of America with the cultures of the ancient Mediterranean, especially Roman civilization. Though Las Casas employed both of these strategies in his celebrated debate with Sepúlveda in Valladolid, versions of both surfaced repeatedly well outside the walls of the formal debate. Furthermore, both strategies offer powerful evidence for the impact of events in the New World upon the changing perceptions of Europeans about their own cultural identity.

The fifth chapter explores the intriguing claim that the Spanish conquest of the Indies disturbingly recapitulated the horrors of the Roman conquest of Spain in the second century B.C. This analogy owed its power to a growing but by no means widely self-evident assumption that the ancient Iberians whom the Romans subjugated were fundamentally the same people as modern Spaniards. In turn, the deployment of this parallel in the discourse of the conquest of the New World contributed to the intensification of that "Iberian patriotism" in the first place. Thus, an argumentative strategy designed to induce Spaniards to empathize with the sufferings of their New World subjects contributed to a sharpening perception of the European past. But though this appeal to the distant past of the Iberian Peninsula was most deftly employed by the Dominicans Melchor Cano and Bartolomé de las Casas in their polemical struggle against the conquistadors and their chroniclers and apologists, we shall see how "Iberian patriotism," a powerful identification with the pre-Roman Iberian peoples, also found expression in the writings of others who discussed or alluded to the conquest of the Indies—most notably, in the "anti-Romanism" of the prolific chronicler Gonzalo Fernández de Oviedo. We shall also be detecting New World resonances in the account of the Roman conquest in the very influential history of Ambrosio de Morales, who was in close contact with Cano at the very time the Dominican employed this analogy. And finally we shall be looking at tantalizing evidence that in the years just before the debate in Valladolid certain Franciscan friars in New Spain were teaching Aztec youths that the ancestors of their conquerors had once themselves been not only heathens, but also recalcitrant victims of a foreign imperial power.

The last chapter of this book investigates the surprisingly powerful tendency of sixteenth-century Spaniards to compare the cultures of the New World with those of classical antiquity, especially Roman civilization. It will once again prove to be Las Casas who made the boldest and most startling uses of this kind of "comparative ethnology," employing it to demonstrate the surprising superiority of the Indians to the Romans in all the areas of social life listed by Aristotle as prerequisites for true civilization. From this cultural agon it was the New World "barbarians" who emerged as exemplars of civilized behavior, while the Romans "far outdistanced all other nations in insensitivity of mind and barbarism." Thus, Las Casas's comparison of the Indians with the Romans was fueled both by his mission to neutralize the slanders against the Indians and by the passionate anti-Roman bias that his encounter with the classical enthusiasms of Sepúlveda had enkindled in his mind.

But Las Casas was by no means the only Spaniard in this period to compare Romans and Indians in ways that unexpectedly dignified the latter. It will perhaps surprise those accustomed to hear references to "the racist historian Oviedo" that this complex and diligent chronicler made extensive use of classical and especially Roman parallels for New World phenomena. Though his reasons for doing so differed sharply from those of Las Casas, he, too, was convinced that the juxtaposition of Romans and Indians was illuminating and not at all to the disadvantage of the supposedly primitive newly "discovered" peoples.

We shall conclude with the contest between Romans and Indians as warriors, as patriotically courageous and militarily skilled fighters. Here, too, a motif central to the controversy of the Indies escaped the confines of the academic debate and surfaced in the chronicles of conquistadors—perhaps most powerfully in an epic poem written by a man who experienced the martial qualities of the Indians at close quarters, Alonso de Ercilla's *La Araucana.*

The comparison of Indians and Romans, whether expressed in documents of the controversy of the Indies or in the writings of the conquistadors and their publicists, resembles the comparison of the Spanish conquest of the Indies with the Roman conquest of Spain in that it, too, contributed to a new sense of the European past. First and most obviously, it had the inevitable effect of qualifying faith in European cultural uniqueness and in the exemplarity of that supposed cultural apogee of European civilization, the Greco-Roman world. Each employment of the comparison of Romans and Indians was a blow to European cultural pride, even if the manifest purpose of such a comparison might happen, at times, to be to dignify the Spaniards who had prevailed over enemies worthy of comparison with the Romans. But Las Casas devised yet another way to make this cultural comparison open the eyes of his fellow Spaniards to unexpected glimpses of their own supposedly familiar world. As a counterblast to those who accused the Christianized natives of the New World of persisting in their ancestral paganism, Las Casas showed how an investigation of ancient Roman religious beliefs and practices, conducted in the first instance to provide a foil for the superiority of precontact New World religion, inevitably revealed the disturbing persistence of Greco-Roman paganism in the daily lives of modern Europeans. Just as comparison of Indians with Romans raised doubts as to who were the true "barbarians," so a heightened alertness to survivals of ancient Roman rituals in modern Europe could cause one to wonder who were the true latter-day "pagans."

Several studies of the first European perceptions of the New World have properly emphasized the distortions and limitations that the classical tradition imposed upon what Europeans saw—or thought they saw— and did and wrote in the course of the discovery and conquest of these lands.[3] This book attempts to make its own contribution to this theme, but it seeks also to explore less familiar dimensions of the intellectual history of the conquest. Thus, it emphasizes how the appeal to ancient texts and events could deepen and sharpen, not just deform, discourse about the New World. Specifically, debate over the nature of Roman civilization and especially over the ways Rome acquired and maintained an empire provided a stimulating and productive framework for assessments of Spain's presence in the Indies and of the native societies the Spaniards encountered there. At the same time, however, this book will demonstrate how the largely unprecedented ethical and cultural challenges raised by the Spanish encounter with the New World precipitated a powerful and sustained reevaluation of Europe's Greco-Roman heritage. As we shall see, the controversy of the Indies has a strong claim to be regarded as the first chapter in a recurrent American "anti-classical tradition."[4] Above all, however, this study is a contribution to the growing scholarly interest in the intellectual impact of the experience of the New World upon the Old, for it explores the influence that reports of remarkable events and peoples in the Indies exerted upon the way at least some influential Europeans came to regard their own past and present.[5] Both for the conquistadors and their critics, the political and cultural achievements of the ancient Greeks and Romans, a numinous element of early modern European cultural self-awareness, underwent startling and complex transformations when set alongside the disorienting strangeness of lands and peoples undreamed of by the ancients and the unprecedented deeds performed, for good or ill, by the adventurers who brought these new lands within the orbit of European dominion and discourse.

CHAPTER ONE

Conquistadors and Romans

"The greatest event since the creation of the world, apart from the Incarnation and death of its creator, is the discovery of the Indies; and that is why they call it the New World."[1] So begins the dedicatory epistle to Charles V, "Emperor of the Romans, King of Spain, Lord of the Indies and the New World," that Francisco López de Gómara, secretary and chaplain to Hernán Cortés, placed at the beginning of his *Historia general de las Indias* (1552). Gómara's proud proclamation of the world-historical significance of the Spanish enterprise in America is a conveniently arresting introduction to the mental world of the conquistadors and their publicists. As we shall see, it was the fall of the Aztec empire to Cortés and a handful of obscure adventurers that inspired the chroniclers of Spanish deeds in the Indies to launch their boldest and most sustained challenges to the prestige of those exemplary European culture heroes, the great generals of Greece and Rome. Julius Caesar, conventionally regarded as the institutional ancestor of the reigning king of Spain, was the favorite defeated rival of Cortés and his men, but the model of Titus also exerted a powerful attraction, for the destruction of the great city of Tenochtitlan in 1521 insistently called to mind— and, Spanish chroniclers would claim, dwarfed—the Roman siege and sack of Jerusalem in the year A.D. 70. The frequency and intensity of these challenges to classical exempla transcended the boisterous emulation of the ancients that was a commonplace in Renaissance writings. As the ringing tone of Gómara's orchestral pronouncement implies, unprecedented experiences, trials, and exhilarations shaped the view of the distant past of the "Old World" expressed by those Spaniards who were struggling to come to terms with their bracingly disorienting "New World."

*"The Most Famous Romans Never Performed Deeds Equal to
Ours": Conquistadors and Their Publicists Challenge the
Prestige of the Romans*

It was a fitting coincidence that the venture in which Cortés was to challenge the prestige of the ancients should begin with a mandate to track
down some refugees from classical mythology. When Diego Velázquez,
the governor of Cuba against whom he promptly rebelled, named him
caudillo of an expedition to Yucatán on October 23, 1518, item 26 of the
formal instructions ordered him to find out "where the Amazons are,
who, according to the Indians you are taking with you, are in that vicin-
ity."² Cortés had other things on his mind than Amazons over the next
few years, but news of a society of warrior women did reach his ears at
last, and he assumed that Charles V would be eager to hear the report.³
Accordingly, he dispatched an expedition to the Pacific coast to search
for them, assuring its leader, his cousin Francisco Cortés de Buenaven-
tura, that "these women follow the practices of the Amazons described
in the *istorias antiguas*."⁴ But while these eagerly sought classical adversaries displayed their customary propensity to recede into the distance
(this time northwards to a long "island" soon christened California,
after the land of the Amazon queen Calafia in Rodríguez de Montalvo's
romance *Sergas de Esplandián*), the conquistadors repeatedly grappled
with classical warriors even more vividly present to their minds than the
Amazons. These imaginary competitors were the celebrated generals
and conquerors of classical antiquity.⁵

At first glance, the eagerness of the conquistadors to compete with
the fame of classical, especially Roman, heroes might seem nothing
more than the familiar emulation of ancient models so characteristic of
the Renaissance—and indeed of the medieval and classical periods as
well. As both Julius Caesar and his rival Pompey had emulated Alexander the Great, so Cortés was presented by the conquistador-chronicler
Bernal Díaz del Castillo as a man in the mold of all three of those
ancient conquerors, as well as more recent models such as the heroes of
the Reconquest of Spain from the Moors. But what is especially arresting about such passages in the writings of the conquistadors and their
champions is an unmistakable note of defiance fueled by the nervous
megalomania of many of these adventurers, particularly those
embarked on expeditions as dangerous and as shakily authorized as
that of the quasi-renegade Cortés. Against a constant undertone of such

insecurity one might have expected Bernal Díaz to emphasize his caudillo's sufficiently respectable hidalgo origins ("a gentleman by four lines of descent," he termed him) and more especially his eventual title of Marqués del Valle de Oaxaca. Instead, he insisted upon referring to him as simply Hernán Cortés, for that name by itself "was as honored both in the Indies and Spain as that of Alexander in Macedon, and those of Julius Caesar, Pompey, and Scipio among the Romans, and that of Hannibal among the Carthaginians, and that of Gonzalo Hernández, the 'Great Captain,' in Castille."[6] Thus the deeds of Cortés allowed the stark simplicity of his name to transcend the complications, the indignities, and the inadequate honorifics of its particular historical reality to join the great names of the heroes of antiquity. From cattle rancher and debt-plagued alcalde in Cuba to neighbor of Julius Caesar in the pantheon of historic conquerors, the self-charted trajectory of Cortés's career streaked serenely beyond the ken of jealous governors, nervous royal councilors, or even the shrewd emperor himself.

But did Cortés himself concur with Bernal Díaz's ranking of him with the likes of Julius Caesar? It is true that such classical comparisons are utterly lacking in his four surviving *Cartas de relación* to Charles V, but that is scarcely surprising. In reports to an "invictísimo César" and a "cesárea majestad," references to one's own emulation of Caesar would be tactless, to say the least. Bernal Díaz, however, claimed that Cortés invoked precisely this comparison as he announced his famously bold decision to scuttle the ships to prevent defections to Cuba: "he uttered many other comparisons and heroic deeds of the Romans. And we all answered that we would do as he ordered, and that the die was cast for good fortune, as Julius Caesar said at the Rubicon."[7] (No less an authority than that connoisseur of exemplary heroes, Don Quixote de la Mancha, similarly linked these actions of Caesar and Cortés in an epideixis on fame delivered to Sancho Panza.)[8] Intriguing hearsay evidence that Cortés did see himself as a second Caesar is Bernardino Vázquez de Tapia's charge in the *residencia* of 1529 that Cortés had been in the habit of repeating Cesare Borgia's motto *aut Caesar aut nihil* and also of uttering a Machiavellian maxim from Euripides (*Phoen.* 524–25) that Cicero claimed was constantly on the lips of Julius Caesar.[9]

To compare a nonroyal adventurer with Julius Caesar was bold enough, to be sure, but Cortés's admirers—and perhaps the man himself—did not stop there. They insisted that Cortés must in fact be rec-

ognized as *superior* to the great conquerors of antiquity. The most sustained example in Bernal Díaz's narrative is his account of Cortés's handling of a near mutiny during the campaign in Tlaxcala. Seven leading
grumblers came to the *capitán's* hut and observed, inter alia, that,
according to the history books, "both those about the Romans and
those about Alexander, as well as those about others of the most
famous leaders who had ever existed in the world, no one had dared to
scuttle his ships and attack with such a small force such large populations containing so many warriors." Cortés's alleged response to this
history lesson was this: "And as for your claim, gentlemen, that never
did a Roman *capitán*, not even one of the most famous, accomplish
such great deeds as we have performed, you speak the truth. And from
now on, with God's help, they will say in the history books that people
will make far more mention of this deed than of those of men in the
past."[10] Elsewhere, in the process of correcting Gómara's ascription to
Cortés of an action rightly belonging to Juan de Salamanca, Bernal Díaz
insisted that he meant no disrespect to Cortés, for "while the Romans
granted triumphs to Pompey and to Julius Caesar and to the Scipios,
our Cortés is more worthy of praise than the Romans."[11] In the same
vein, Gómara himself claimed that Cortés's capture of Moctezuma elevated him well above the heights scaled by classical worthies: "Never
did Greek or Roman, or man of any nation, since kings have existed, do
what Cortés did in seizing Montezuma, a most powerful king, in his
own house, a very strong place, surrounded by an infinity of people,
while Cortés had only four hundred and fifty companions."[12] (In a
briefer but similar aside in his *Historia general de las Indias,* Gómara
noted that "ninguno romano" had ever equaled Balboa's feat of not losing a single man in the battles he fought on his famous expedition of
discovery to the Pacific.)[13]

A more sustained testimony to Cortés's habit of making classical
models obsolete is to be found in Francisco Cervantes de Salazar's dedication to him of his continuation of Pérez de Oliva's *Dialogue on the
Dignity of Man,* published in Alcalá in 1546, the year before the conquistador's death.[14] At the time, Cervantes de Salazar was a professor at
the University of Osuna, but the depth of his fascination with the New
World can be gauged by the fact that in 1551 he left for Mexico, where
he became rector of the university and author of a chronicle celebrating
Cortés's deeds, the *Crónica de la Nueva España,* written 1558–66. In his
dedication to Cortés of the earlier work, he presented the *magnánimo*

capitán as a paragon of human *dignidad* who took second place to no one—least of all to any Greek or Roman. To begin with, there was the obvious point that the conquistador had acted on a stage untrodden by earlier Europeans, for "none of the ancients knew the existence of that which Your Excellency has conquered and subjected to the Royal Crown." Then there was the fact that Cortés had "more speedily than Alexander or Caesar defeated so many thousands of men and conquered such a great expanse of land." His shrewdness in the field was another challenge to the prestige of the Greeks and Romans, for "Your Excellency has shown so many new stratagems in matters of war that it cannot be said that in any of them you have imitated the ancients."[15] But the most dazzling triumph over Alexander and Julius Caesar that Cervantes de Salazar ascribed to Cortés was founded upon the paradoxical basis of his inferiority to them in one self-evident respect: his lack of comfortably commanding social status or sweeping political power.

> Alexander with the Macedonians, as their king, and Julius Caesar with the Romans, as their emperor, conquered the territories of which we read, but Your Excellency, attended solely by your own valor *(virtud)*, without any other advantage, came to equal them—and I'm not sure I shouldn't rather say that you came to surpass them. Hence it is clear that your valor ought to be illustrious and marvelous, for it has proved strong enough that you have come by yourself alone *(con sola su persona)* to be lord of so many caciques and lords.

Thus it was the lonely striving of Cortés, conquering vast territories "without the help of any king" [sin ayuda de rei alguno], that most spectacularly elevated him above the more politically powerful, socially prominent, and hence more efficiently supported heroes of antiquity.

Cervantes de Salazar's encomium of Cortés as a magnificent loner, dwarfing the ancients as conqueror "by himself alone" of a vast world unknown to them, would have infuriated Bernal Díaz del Castillo. For the old soldier never tired of reminding his readers that it was not Cortés alone who put the Romans to shame; he may not have had a king's help, but he had the strong arms and stout hearts of men like Bernal Díaz himself. We may recall that the old soldier proudly remembered Cortés as casting in the first-person plural his boast in the "mutiny scene" in Tlaxcala: "Never did a Roman *capitán*, not even one of the most famous, accomplish such great deeds as we *(nosotros)* have performed." A similar celebration of the rank and file by means of classical exempla occurs in his account of the defeat of the numerically superior expedition sent by Diego Velázquez under the command of Pánfilo de Narváez to put down the freebooting "rebel." Not only did Bernal Díaz proudly record the words of Guidela, Narváez's black jester, that "the Romans never did such a deed," but he also put into the mouth of Narváez himself, in conversation with another Cortesian victim, Francisco de Garay, a sweeping classical encomium of "every single one" [cada uno] of Cortés's followers:

> I want you to know that there has not been a more fortunate man in the world than Cortés, and he has such captains and soldiers who could be named who are each and every one of them as fortunate in his undertakings as Octavian, as fortunate in conquering as Julius Caesar, and more fortunate in toiling and engaging in battles than Hannibal.[16]

In attributing these words to the defeated Narváez, Bernal Díaz was not only claiming for himself and his companions a dignity equal to that of the Romans, he was also appropriating words originally intended for a major figure of the Reconquest and the civil conflicts of mid-fourteenth-century Castile. For in one of the most famous poems in Spanish literature, the *Coplas por la muerte de su padre,* Jorge Manrique (1440–79) celebrated his late father Don Rodrigo as

En ventura, Octaviano;	[In luck, Octavian;
Julio César en vencer	Julius Caesar in winning
e batallar; and	giving battle;
en la virtud, Africano;	in virtue, (Scipio) Africanus;
Aníbal en el saber	Hannibal in wisdom
e trabajar.[17]	and toiling.]

With these words Jorge Manrique began a pair of stanzas of Roman comparisons characterized by Ernst Robert Curtius as "the monumental conclusion and highpoint" of a "national Spanish historical tradition" that had for at least two centuries sought to equate medieval Spain with ancient Rome.[18] Indeed, it is tempting to imagine that the great poem that Bernal Díaz was here quoting and paraphrasing was securely lodged at the back of his mind as he wrote his *Historia verdadera.* Just after the "Roman stanzas," Jorge Manrique had declared that his father "did not leave behind great treasures, nor did he gain great riches," but, as the concluding lines of the poem note, "though he lost his life, he has left us as ample consolation his memory."[19] Similarly, Bernal Díaz lamented in his preface: "I have no riches to leave my sons and descendants other than this truthful and important account of mine."[20]

Audacious though Bernal Díaz may have been in usurping, along with his companions, a great Moor-slayer's place alongside Roman heroes, a reader may still be forgiven for being taken aback by the defiant boldness of the following words near the end of the *Historia verdadera*:

> And furthermore I want to say something to let you see that I deserve more praise than I give myself, and that is that I have been in far more battles and engagements than the 53 battles writers say Julius Caesar was in. Also, though he had fine chroniclers, he didn't rest content with what they wrote of him, but he wrote with his own hand in his *Commentaries* about the fighting he had done personally, and so it's not out of line for me to write the heroic deeds of the brave Cortés— and my own deeds and those of my companions who found themselves fighting alongside one another.[21]

Thus the celebrated Julius Caesar, though he may have been a "great emperor, whose chroniclers say he was very prompt in arms and mighty in giving battle,"[22] was surpassed a millennium and a half after his death by one among many valiant young conquistadors in the ranks. So, at least, it appeared to that conquistador's octogenarian older self, who grandly proceeded to bury Caesar's 53 battles under the crushing weight of a catalog of the 119 "battles and encounters in which I found myself," an astonishing climax to these latter-day *Commentaries*.

Bernal Díaz's boast that the Romans had been surpassed not only by the larger-than-life Cortés but also by his less conspicuous soldiers might seem a personal eccentricity of one whom Juan Gil has labeled "el más pródigo en reminiscencias clásicas" of all the chroniclers of New Spain.[23] But this same boast was regretfully recalled by one of his companions, Francisco de Aguilar, who likewise wrote his memoirs in old age, though in his case from the unusual and repentant perspective of conquistador-turned-Dominican. Recording the lightning return of Cortés's party to Tenochtitlan to relieve the beleaguered Pedro de Alvarado, Aguilar recalled that "all of them went around very proud" at having achieved "an exploit and labor so great, greater than those of the Romans."²⁴ True enough, Aguilar looked back upon this boast as the dangerous folly of men who failed to give due thanks and credit to God, thereby inviting the epic sufferings of the subsequent Noche Triste. As we shall soon see, he thus shared the jaundiced view of classical models for New World conquests taken by his fellow Dominicans. But for the moment the importance of Aguilar's recollection is its support for Bernal Díaz's testimony that ordinary conquistadors felt that they had *all* surpassed the ancient Romans.

While Bernal Díaz's claim to have surpassed Julius Caesar may thus have had roots in the original campaign itself, in the kind of boasting in the ranks that Francisco de Aguilar penitently recalled in later life, megalomania of this magnitude needed years of disappointment and resentment to achieve its full luxuriant growth.²⁵ It was the fruit of the very same feelings of slighted worth and failed hopes that fertilized the growth of the *Historia verdadera* as a whole, for this great chronicle may be considered the bloated supplement to its author's petition to the Council of the Indies for due recognition, his *probanza de méritos y servicios* of 1539. In strict point of fact, that *probanza* proved successful in eliciting a royal *cédula* to restore to the conquistador the two *encomiendas* of which he had been deprived, despite the opposition of the *fiscal* (public prosecutor) Villalobos, who complained that "Bernal Díaz had not been such a conquistador as he claimed." Indeed, Cortés himself wrote in support of Bernal Díaz's petition, declaring that "in everything he has labored and served very well, as I am a good witness."²⁶ Despite some difficulty in getting the *cédula* put into effect, Bernal Díaz generally proceeded to live the life of a substantial *encomendero* and perpetual *regidor* (alderman) of the town of Santiago de Guatemala, where a fellow townsman testified that he lived "with much splendor and abundance of arms and horses and servants, like a very fine knight and servant of His Majesty."²⁷ But despite his neighbors' assessment of his prosperity and local prominence, Bernal Díaz himself consistently seems to have assumed that his rewards and honors markedly failed to match his merits. "I have no other wealth to leave my children and descendants but this true and notable account"—these bitter "last words," placed at the beginning of the chronicle, establish for the reader its persistent undertone of loss and disappointment.²⁸

In perfect accord with this mood, Bernal Díaz's personal agon with Julius Caesar serves as the climax of a chapter (212) dominated by a

tone of resentment and hurt pride. If earlier in the chronicle, as we have
seen, he was willing to extol Cortés as Caesar's superior, his appropriation of that superiority for himself at this retrospective moment reveals
the true festering sore point in the old soldier's soul. It was not really
Julius Caesar whom Bernal Díaz resented and envied; it was the capitán
whom he himself, first by sword and later by pen, had helped surpass
Caesar. Despite Cortés's unequivocal support for Bernal Díaz's
probanza in 1539, the resentment was clearly planted at least as early as
the publication of Cortés's *relaciones*. Of his reaction to reading the
writings of Gómara, Illescas, and, last but not least, Cortés himself,
Bernal Díaz wrote:

> What I see in those writings and chronicles is nothing but praise of
> Cortés, and they hush up and conceal those glorious and famous deeds
> of ours by which we exalted that same captain to become a marquis
> and to have the great income and fame and renown that he has. . . .
> And I maintain that when Cortés wrote in the beginning to His
> Majesty, always instead of ink there flowed pearls and gold from his
> pen, and all of it in his own praise and not that of us valiant soldiers.[29]

To right this wrong, Bernal Díaz had devoted chapters 205 and 206
to a catalog of those unsung fellow heroes, followed, at the beginning of
the next, by a plaintive expression of his own social insecurity and
unstable compound of self-doubt and self-importance:

> I have now listed the soldiers who came over with Cortés and have
> told where they died. And if one really wants to know about us: all
> the rest of us were hidalgos, though some not of especially distin-
> guished lines, for it is well known that not all men are born equal in
> this world, neither in social status nor virtues. Besides our ancient
> claim to nobility that we earned by our heroic deeds and great
> exploits in the wars, fighting day and night, serving our king and lord,
> exploring these lands and winning this New Spain and the great City
> of Mexico and many other provinces, all at our own expense, being
> so far from Castile and having no help whatever except that of Our
> Lord Jesus Christ, who is our succor and true help, we achieved much
> more glory than we had before.[30]

This 207th chapter proceeds with an explosion of bitterness over the
paltriness of the honors and titles granted the conquistadors, compared

with the inflated prestige accorded less remarkable men, both in Spain and elsewhere, about whom Bernal Díaz had read in "las escrituras antiguas." In particular, it was the warriors of Spain's Reconquest who aroused his envious ire—men who engaged in lesser campaigns than his, and then only when paid handsomely in advance, but who nevertheless received "villas and castles and great estates and perpetual privileges with exemptions, which their descendants now possess."

Distance and time are powerfully charged concepts here. The services rendered by the conquistadors of the New World "to our lord the king and to all of Christianity" (chapter 207 still) exalted them to a worth at least equal to that of Spanish "caballeros y soldados" in Europe. But the fact that the New World heroes performed their deeds "so far from Castile" had a double-edged effect. On the one hand, this distance was a further source of glory, for it left them "with no other aid than Our Lord Jesus Christ." On the other hand, this distance removed them from the close and appreciative gaze of the Spanish Crown, thus ensuring their eventual disappointment and sense of slighted worth. Hence Bernal Díaz's compensatory strategy. From his distanced and marginalized perspective, it was *Europe* that risked becoming distanced and marginalized, as the deeds of the conquistadors took center stage and dwarfed past history back through the Reconquest all the way to the battles of Julius Caesar. In an audacious appropriation of the prestige of earlier heroes celebrated in "las escrituras antiguas," Bernal Díaz characterized the distinction merited by the recent exploits of himself and his fellow conquistadors as "nuestras antiguas noblezas." Thus, what his compatriots in Spain considered the distant and the new became for the bitter conquistador the central and the "old."

This reversal of perspective helps account for the peculiar power of the old conquistador's surprisingly sympathetic portrayal of a monarch who, unlike Charles V and Philip II, *did* direct a close and appreciative gaze upon Bernal Díaz and his fellow *soldados:* none other than Montezuma himself. Just as Jaime of Aragón had the discernment and the justice to reward both "caballeros y soldados" with land and honors, so Montezuma, upon his very first visit to the Spaniards' quarters in Tenochtitlan, had the grace not only to give the *capitanes* little gold objects and three loads of cloaks with rich featherwork, but also to distribute "to every single one of us soldiers two loads of cloaks with a festive air *(alegría)*, and in everything he quite acted the part of a great lord *(y en todo bien parecía gran señor).*"[31] But the true proof of Montezuma's princely quality was his dignified deportment during his astonishing captivity in the midst of his own city. Here, in this complex and ambiguous social drama, the captive king came paradoxically to act the part of model prince to jailers who half assumed (at least in Bernal Díaz's retrospective view) the role of duly grateful vassals. "He got to know all of us well, and learned our names and even our qualities, and he was so good as to give some of us jewels, and others of us cloaks and Indian girls." When Bernal Díaz himself delicately conveyed to the king his desire for "una india muy hermosa," Montezuma was delighted to oblige. No less treasured a memory was the report that the Aztec king had declared that "Bernal Díaz seems to me to be of noble birth."[32] In this wonderfully disorienting passage, the Spanish conquistador implicitly held up an Indian monarch as a mirror for the king of Spain. *There* stood a great lord capable of recognizing and rewarding true worth. While Spanish kings consistently failed to confer nobility upon Bernal Díaz and his comrades, the Aztec king, a finer judge of true worth, assumed that our worthy conquistador must already be "de noble condición." It is in this context of the conquistadors' reversal of European and New World arbiters and models of excellence that I would locate their exploitation and expansion of the topos of "besting the ancients." Bernal Díaz's deflation of the classical world joins his exaltation of the Aztec monarch at the expense of Charles V and Philip II as a foretaste of that "creole patriotism" that David Brading has traced back to the end of the sixteenth century.[33]

The centrality of the social ambitions of the conquistadors as driving forces behind their actions was recognized and excoriated by their most passionate critic, the Dominican friar Bartolomé de las Casas, who frequently linked ambition with greed as their chief motivations and accused their defenders of pandering to "those who desire and endeavor to become rich and to rise to ranks which neither they nor their ancestors possessed."[34] In fact, as Stuart B. Schwartz has shown, despite the great expectations of many of the conquistadors, "few titled nobles *(títulos de Castilla)* were created as a result of the conquest and exploration of the New World."[35] Even those who did receive titles, even the celebrated Marques del Valle de Oaxaca himself, could easily persuade themselves that suspicious and envious officials and grandees in Spain were determined to deny them the full measure of honor, wealth, and power to which they believed their deeds and their sufferings had enti-

tled them. Conquistadors who felt insufficiently appreciated could find
some consolation, then, in a proud assertion of hard-won superiority
not only to those Spanish warriors in the past who *had* received adequate—or more than adequate—rewards, but even to the greatest conquerors of classical antiquity. It is easy enough to mistake this competition with the classical world for the familiar medieval and Renaissance
rhetorical device of "topping" classical precedents, a topos E. R. Curtius labeled "Überbietung."[36] Conventional rhetorical instances of such
"outdoing" are indeed there to be found. For example, writing while
the news from Mexico was still fresh, the Milanese humanist and Spanish publicist Pedro Mártir de Anglería (Pietro Martire d'Anghiera, d.
1526) had declared of the portage of the prefabricated brigantines from
Tlaxcala to Texcoco for the siege of Tenochtitlan: "Behold a deed that
would not have been easy for the Roman people, even when their affairs
were flourishing gloriously."[37] But the challenges to the Romans offered
by later chroniclers, notably Bernal Díaz, have a sharper edge to them,
a profounder emotional investment. When Bernal Díaz goes *mano a
mano* with Julius Caesar and wins, what we have witnessed is a remarkable instance of "Renaissance self-fashioning" fueled by disappointment and wounded pride.

Gonzalo Fernández de Oviedo: Outdistancing the Ancients

Around the time that Bernal Díaz del Castillo was showing visitors to
Santiago de Guatemala early drafts of his vivid chronicle, the *alcaide*
(commandant) of the fortress of Santo Domingo on the island of Hispaniola died clutching the keys of the fortress, having some eight years
earlier deposited in a Spanish monastery the unfinished and unfinish-
able manuscript of an equally remarkable and much more massive and
influential literary monument.[38] Gonzalo Fernández de Oviedo y Valdés
(1478–1557) was better born, better educated, better connected, and
generally (though not spectacularly) more successful in life than Bernal
Díaz. Having served as page to the Infante Don Juan, he spent a number of years in Italian courts, before sailing to the New World in 1514 in
the entourage of the infamous Pedrarias Dávila as *Veedor de las fundi-
ciones de oro de la Tierra Firme* (inspector of gold mines of the mainland). Despite six journeys back to Spain, he spent most of the rest of
his life in the fortress of Santo Domingo, surrounded by a library of

Spanish, Italian, and (mostly translated) classical volumes, and visited by a constant stream of informants as he composed, on royal commission, his monumental *Historia natural y general de las Indias.* Only the first of its three parts was published in his lifetime (1535; reprinted 1547), but that substantial first part was widely circulated and translated. A testimony to its impact was López de Gómara's claim in 1548 that "Fray Bartolomé de las Casas, Bishop of Chiapas, is trying to block the General History of the Indies that the chronicler Gonzalo Fernández de Oviedo showed to the Council of Castile in order to print it."[39] Though book 20, the first book of part 2, was published in 1557, the year of Oviedo's death, the rest of part 2 and all of part 3, as well as very extensive additions to part 1, were not published until 1851–55. In a later chapter we shall consider the fiery Dominican's objections to Oviedo's project. At the moment, what concerns us is its contribution to the contest between Spaniards in the New World and the Greeks and Romans—especially the Romans—in the Old World. We shall see that Oviedo to some extent confirms what we have seen in Bernal Díaz, but also offers a new dimension, a suggestion of a further incentive for Spaniards in America to dethrone classical exemplars.

It is, in fact, in the pages of Oviedo that we find the fullest and most considered formulation of the superiority of Hernán Cortés over Julius Caesar. As his narrative of the conquest of Mexico in book 33 entered a crescendo with the second march on Tenochtitlan, Oviedo paused to compare the Spaniard and the Roman:

> Hernando Cortés reminds me of the military prowess of that mirror of chivalry *(espejo de caballería)* Julius Caesar the Dictator, as portrayed in his *Commentaries,* and in Suetonius and Plutarch and other authors who wrote of his great deeds. But those of Hernando Cortés, performed in a new world or in provinces so distant from Europe, with so many hardships and deprivations, with such scanty forces, among such innumerable, barbarous and warlike people, who eat human flesh—considered an excellent and savory dish by his enemies—he and his men the while lacking bread and wine and all the other foods of Spain, and being in such diversified regions and climates, and so remote or far from help and from their prince—all these are things to fill one with astonishment. Caesar waged his wars in provinces and places that were well peopled and provisioned, among the best in the world, attended by his own men and by many Romans and natives and other civilized people. . . . But here in these

lands the smallest danger to men may grow very big indeed, because of the adverse effect of the airs and climate and difficult regions upon the health of those unaccustomed to them, so different from those of Spain, in a strange country and under stars unseen except from over here, drinking-water of many kinds and different flavors, and so with the other things by which human bodies must be sustained, quite unlike the foods that our stomachs were used to, in taste as well as in their digestion, lacking physicians and surgeons and beds, and other things necessary to life.[40]

This extended comparison of Caesar and Cortés is clearly indebted to Francisco de Jerez's exaltation of the Spaniards at the expense of the Romans in the prologue to his *Conquista del Perú* (Seville, 1534), a work Oviedo openly exploited for his own account of the conquest of Peru in book 46.[41] Jerez's more general comparison runs,

When have been witnessed among ancients or moderns such great undertakings by so few people against so many, and through such climes of heaven and gulfs of the sea and such distances to traverse to conquer that which had never been seen or known? And who could equal the men of Spain? Not, certainly, the Jews or Greeks—or Romans, of whom more is written than of all the rest. For if the Romans subjugated so many provinces, it was with an equal or only slightly smaller force, and in lands which were known and supplied with familiar provisions, and with captains and armies who received pay.[42]

Expanding the hint from Francisco de Jerez, Oviedo based his assessment of Cortés's superiority to Caesar squarely upon that proclamation of the startling and daunting *newness* of the New World that repeatedly found eloquent expression in his massive "general and natural history of the Indies." It is not so much that Cortés was in and of himself the superior of Caesar; it is that the stage upon which he had to operate was so much more challenging. The superiority of Cortés's deeds was provoked by the greater challenges that he had to overcome. Without assigning undue weight to the historian's resentment over Cortés's neglect of his request for copies of certain documents, we may nonetheless suspect that for Oviedo the real "hero" of this ancient-besting comparison was not a man but a landscape.[43] And it is here that we start to sense Oviedo's main contribution to the fall of Rome in the Indies.

It is tempting to exaggerate Oviedo's fascination with the newness and strangeness of the Indies, but in a later chapter we shall see the justice of Antonello Gerbi's insistence upon the chronicler's belief in the "oneness of the terraqueous globe."[44] In particular, we shall examine the frequent pains Oviedo took to place the human phenomena of the New World within a classical armature of interpretation. Even the non-human data of America Oviedo was glad to assimilate to classical models, where possible. For example, when discussing even so quintessentially an American product as maize, Oviedo declared: "Since I delight in reading Pliny, I will say here what he says about the millet of India, and I think that it is the same thing which in our Indies we call maize."[45] Nevertheless, it is impossible to deny that Oviedo was in fact often overwhelmed by the "shock of the new." "Marvelous are the works of God, and very different in kinds are the animate creatures in diverse provinces and parts of the world."[46] And on the level of human society, Oviedo promised to record "such great kingdoms and provinces with such strange peoples and diversities and customs, ceremonies, and idolatries unlike what has been recorded from the beginning to our own day."[47] But not only was the New World often full of surprises for European visitors, its wonders—and terrors—often surpassed those recorded by classical writers. Thus, Oviedo claimed that had the ancients known the volcanoes Masaya, Maribio, and Guajocingo, they would have had less to say of Etna and the like.[48]

If, according to Oviedo, Cortés surpassed Caesar because the New World's challenges surpassed those of the Old, the key factor that allowed it to do so, that allowed it to be called a New World in the first place, was distance. Cortés's deeds, unlike Caesar's, were performed "in a new world or in provinces so very distant from Europe" [en un mundo nuevo o tan apartadas provincias de Europa]—language anticipating Bernal Díaz's emphasis upon the fact that the conquistadors performed their noble deeds "tan apartados de Castilla" (chap. 207). Not only was there the daunting and disorienting distance from home—"so remote or far from help and from their prince" [tan desviado o lejos de socorro e de su príncipe], a phrase again reminiscent of Bernal Díaz's boast: "ni tener otro socorro ninguno, salvo el de Nuestro Señor Jesucristo"—but there were the vast distances that the conquistador and his men had to cover within the New World itself, distances embracing "such diversified regions and climates."[49] For Oviedo, the New World was entitled to its name largely because it was so far from Europe and because its mainland opened vast vistas of lands unseen by Europeans before, "under stars unseen except from over here." While the individual phenomena of the New World might not in themselves have startled Pliny, the formidable distances a Spanish conquistador or official had to traverse in order to experience them automatically elevated him above the ancients. (Perhaps one should admit here that Oviedo was somewhat loading his dice by choosing to compare Cortés's exploits with Caesar's campaigns in Gaul rather than with the grander sweep of Alexander's conquests.)

The ennobling and heroizing effect of traversing vast distances and enduring the resulting sufferings constitutes a frequent theme in Oviedo's history. But it was not only a capitán, an eventual recipient of a noble title, whom he considered exalted by endurance of the challenges of an epic journey. Immediately after declaring Cortés's superiority to Caesar, Oviedo hastened to add that the caudillo's men were "all equal to Cortés in similar inconveniences, and his soldiers endured them even more completely than he did, for it is the custom that when people are faring badly the captains have more opportunity to endure the inconveniences."[50] Here, then, at last was a chronicler whose account of Cortés's expedition, had it been published, would have brought a glow to the heart of the less socially distinguished Bernal Díaz, who complained in chapter 207 of the *Verdadera historia* that encomiasts of Cortés ignored his men's "ancient claim to nobility, which we earned by our heroic deeds and great exploits in the wars." But whereas Bernal Díaz was content to fashion his own nobility by engaging Julius Caesar in a simple battle-counting contest, Oviedo founded the superiority of Cortés's followers not on the fact that these Spaniards fought more battles than the famous Roman, but on the unprecedented distances they traveled in order to fight them and on the epic sufferings that those journeys inevitably inflicted to a greater degree upon ordinary soldiers than upon their leaders. Thus, for the hidalgo Oviedo, as for the socially more humble Bernal Díaz, an ordinary foot-soldier in the Indies was entitled to more glory than the celebrated Roman conqueror of Gaul.

Thus we see that what Jaime González has called the "antiromanism" of Oviedo resembled that of Bernal Díaz in the way it intersected with and intensified what Ramón Iglesia termed the "popularism" of sixteenth-century chronicles of the Indies.[51] While Iglesia correctly focused on Bernal Diáz as the most complete example of this "process of democratization," he aptly cited Oviedo's attribution of Spain's conquest of the Indies to her "rare and precious gift of nature": whereas in other countries only the nobles were trained for war, "in our Spain it seems that all are commonly born to, and principally dedicated to, arms and their exercise."[52] But as the encomium on Cortés and his followers shows, Oviedo's "popularism" or, better, his revised definition of true nobility rested less upon native Spanish social practices than upon the bracing and dignifying encounter with the remote challenges of the New World. Thus, in the proem to book 18, after a catalog of horrors like the one that he would later devise for book 33, he declared that such sufferings made those who faced them "more worthy than many who are born with great inheritances and who live at their ease, not knowing more than their neighbors do, and who in great comfort give themselves up to learn what they can learn from their beds without working."[53]

We need to admit at once that in other moods—and we are dealing here with a man of many moods—Oviedo was perfectly happy to give vent to the aristocratic biases one would expect from a man of his class, especially one who never felt that he had fully attained his initial hopes and deserts. Thus, in the proem to book 33, his account of the conquest of Mexico, he complained that, just like "los escriptores antiguos," he had had to endure more than his fair share of detractors, for a very mixed bag of people had come over to the New World, in particular "more people of base blood than hidalgos and distinguished men."[54] Similarly, the sufferings of those who plundered Castilla de Oro, far from ennobling them, were the condign punishment of these "ministros de Satanás," a mongrel mob composed of "such different types and mixed peoples and nationalities and such odd classes," a menace not only to the natives but also to "the good and virtuous hidalgos."[55] And a few pages later, in the proem to book 30, he sarcastically commented that "the majority of those who come over here do so because they don't have in their homeland what they need in the abundance that their fine desires and their personal merits demand."[56] The pretension of such glory-seekers came in for derision also in the *Quinquagenas*, the lengthy moralizing work of Oviedo's last years, where he ridiculed "the vanity of some in these our Indies, who shamelessly dare to say that they are relatives of lords and members of prominent and ancient houses, and they tell it to me, who know for certain the opposite."[57] It was as an antidote to the prominence of such bogus nobles that Oviedo unsuccessfully lobbied the emperor in 1519 for a New World chapter of the Order of Santiago, so that the land of Tierra Firme might be settled "by men of honor and good lineage" [de honra e de buena casta].[58]

Such expressions of aristocratic sentiment, scarcely surprising in a man of Oviedo's class and time, offer a sharp contrast not only to his celebration of Cortés's ordinary soldiers, but also to one of his most arresting challenges to the Old World's respect for classical exemplars. This is the account in book 31 of an exploit of Francisco Hernández, an "honorable merchant" [mercader honrado] of Santo Domingo. The proem of this book devoted to Honduras and Yucatán is largely an attack on the inexplicably hardy respect Oviedo's contemporaries persisted in bestowing upon the achievements of the Greco-Roman world. For Oviedo, the Achilles heel of the prestige of the classical world was the fame of its seagoing heroes. The expedition of the Greeks to Troy, the voyage of Aeneas to Italy, and the return of Ulysses to Ithaca collectively struck Oviedo as "cosa ridícula" in comparison with the exploits of modern Spaniards. Here an alert reader of conquest chronicles will expect what was becoming a commonplace in the period: a declaration that the voyage of Magellan's *Victoria* had withered the laurels of Jason's *Argo*.[59] Oviedo had himself helped develop this motif in his account of Magellan's voyage in book 20, the last part of his history to be published in his time, where he declared that "the *Victoria* is much more worthy of being painted and placed among the stars . . . than the *Argo*, which sailed from Greece to the Black Sea."[60] And in fact Oviedo did duly trot forth this topos here in the proem to book 31: "Let the *Argo* be still, for we have recently seen the ship *Victoria*," and so on. But our chronicler delayed this expected *Überbietung* by telling first of a pointedly much less spectacular voyage. After summarizing the story of wandering Ulysses and the weaving wiles of "la casta Penélope," Oviedo proceeded:

> All the sailing Ulysses did in his life is much less than the journey from Spain to our Indies; and in spite of the length and difficulty and danger and expense of this voyage, I say that in this city of Santo Domingo there lived an honorable merchant by the name of Francisco Hernández, a man who was such a good friend to his friends that he and his wife were invited to be sponsors at the wedding of a friend who wrote him from Seville saying that he was waiting for them to celebrate the wedding and receive the benedictions of the church with his wife; and they departed from here in a ship and arrived in Seville. The couple they sponsored held their wedding, and

then the sponsors returned home to this city. And at this time there
still lives here the wife of this Francisco Hernández, herself a native of
Seville. This would seem to me a vastly longer voyage than the Greeks
or Trojans sailed, since, no matter what good weather they may have
had, this neighbor of ours and his wife sailed a round trip of three
thousand leagues, more or less.[61]

This anecdote casts a pure and intense light upon what Oviedo
deemed the decisive index of the superiority of the Spaniards in the
Indies to the ancient Greeks and Romans: the distances they had to traverse to arrive in America in the first place. Quite literally, modern
Spaniards had *outdistanced* the heroes of the ancient world. To make
his point as ruthlessly as possible, Oviedo carefully selected a kind of
laboratory specimen of a modern "hero," one whose prize was neither
the Golden Fleece nor, for that matter, the gold of the Indies (at least,
not on *this* voyage!), but rather the quaintly ordinary honor of serving
as best man at a friend's wedding. He also shrewdly chose a decidedly
uneventful journey to deflate the wanderings of Ulysses, one that failed
to present its voyager with the epic sufferings of many modern
Spaniards—men such as Pánfilo de Narváez and Cabeza de Vaca,
whose woes, Oviedo elsewhere assured us, surpass the "ficciones e
matáforas" of Ulysses, Jason, and Hercules, or the unlucky protagonists
of the final, "shipwreck book" of Oviedo's history (bk. 50), such as the
licenciado Alonso Zuazo, whose story beat anything found in "los nov-
elas de los fabulosos griegos" or Ovid's *Metamorphoses*.[62] But above
all, observe the status of the "hero" himself: neither a classical demigod
nor a modern Spanish hidalgo adventurer, but a "mercader honrado"
matter-of-factly sustaining his reputation as "amigo de sus amigos." A
prosaic endurance of distance alone earned such a man a place in
Oviedo's history alongside Magellan—and well above the likes of
Ulysses and Jason. Once again, as with his praise of the men who followed Cortés, we see that "process of democratization" to which
Ramón Iglesia has drawn attention in Bernal Díaz, and in both chroniclers this process was facilitated by a deflation of the classical models
that had been a staple of aristocratic encomia.[63]

Not only does the proem to book 31 declare this remarkably unre-
markable merchant of Santo Domingo a greater hero than Ulysses, its
opening words are an only slightly more restrained insinuation that
Ulysses' great epic publicist, Homer, had himself been surpassed—or at

least challenged—by another less than obvious modern Spanish candidate, none other than Oviedo himself. The proem opens with a quotation of Cicero's famous anecdote of Alexander's envy of Achilles for having had Homer as the herald of his virtues. After offering Petrarch's poetic paraphrase of Cicero's words, Oviedo proceeded to demonstrate his classical learning by adding Plutarch's fuller version of the story. Finally he revealed that he was ostensibly citing this anecdote as a modesty topos, conceding that "the style and eloquence of the author of a famous history" confers considerable dignity upon his subject matter, and lamenting the corollary that great deeds tend to suffer when related by less skillful authors. Professing to number himself among the latter, Oviedo affected to regret the lack of a greater writer than himself to tackle such impressive and diverse subjects as he was here assembling. "Still, it suffices for my consolation and for the satisfaction of the reader that the authority granted to Homer over there *(acullá)* compensated for his subject matter, while over here *(aquí)* the subject matter compensates for the inadequacy of my pen and talent."[64] Note how the spatial dichotomy "over there" (Homer) / "here" (Oviedo) prepares us for the ensuing contest between the voyages of "those Greeks" and the much more impressive journey of the honorable merchant of "this city of Santo Domingo." Here again Oviedo enlisted space and distance to do much of the work of rendering the classical world irrelevant. But no less important was the dichotomy between the style, talent, and authority *(pluma, ingenio, auctoridad)* of Homer and the subject matter *(materia)* of Oviedo. The fox Homer may have known many tricks, but the hedgehog Oviedo knew one, a good one. Denied Homer's golden voice, Oviedo did not at least have to settle for Homer's second-rate material, his humdrum heroes. Armed with this confidence in the superiority of his subject matter to that of classical writers, the commandant of the fortress of Santo Domingo was ready to place the laurels of Ulysses on the brow of his humble townsman Francisco Hernández.

Homer was not, however, the classical author against whom Oviedo most consistently measured himself. That role was taken by a Roman, Pliny the Elder, a writer whose material Oviedo *did* respect—up to a point.[65] Not only did the *Naturalis historia* of Pliny supply Oviedo's *Historia general y natural de las Indias* with hundreds of parallels, near parallels, and significant contrasts for the vegetable, animal, and human phenomena of the New World, but Oviedo cheerfully professed a desire "to imitate him whenever I can."[66] Nevertheless, already in the first book, which is an introduction to the whole work addressed to Charles V and itself an imitation of Pliny's dedicatory epistle to Titus, Oviedo had boldly announced a claim to surpass the renowned Roman natural historian. Of the material which he was about to present, Oviedo wrote:

> I have not gathered it from two thousand volumes that I have read, as Pliny writes in the passage mentioned above [i.e. the preface to Titus, 17], . . . but everything I write about here I have accumulated from two thousand million toils and deprivations and dangers in the more than twenty-two years in which I have seen and personally experienced these things, serving God and my king in these Indies, and have eight times crossed the great Ocean Sea.[67]

We find here yet again the crossing of the wide sea as a decisive means of putting a distance between oneself and the ancient authorities. These sea crossings inspired Oviedo to an ironic dig at Pliny when the subject turned to New World whales. Pliny offered the measurement of whales at the beginning of book 9 of his natural history, and Oviedo with mock humility bowed to the Roman's authority, "for I have not measured or seen them on land; but I have seen many of them on the sea," and from that adventurous perspective the New World varieties appeared no smaller than the Old.[68] Like many other Spaniards in the Indies, notably his bête noire Las Casas, Oviedo was immensely proud of his privileged status as a writer with an astonishing variety of firsthand information, and this autoptic authority enabled him not only to abash modern Spaniards who never dared that heroic ocean crossing, but also to surpass his principal classical model, Pliny.[69]

Not only did Oviedo imply that he had surpassed the bookish Roman by traveling thousands of leagues to view distant wonders with his own eyes, he also suggested that he had bested the Roman in the heroic sufferings he had undergone in order to gather, to *experience* his material. (True, Oviedo was perfectly aware that Pliny had in fact lost his life in pursuit of "natural history," becoming what one might label an "autoptic martyr." But he was careful not to mention this fact in that part of his history where it would have been most apposite as a classical parallel: in his elaborate and vivid account of one of his proudest achievements, the ascent of the Nicaraguan volcano Masaya.)[70] Anthony Pagden has recently drawn attention to the care with which "the narrator fashions himself as a sufferer" and has suggested that in Oviedo's view suffering "authenticates and ennobles the text he will finally be able to write." Indeed, Pagden goes so far as to suggest that Oviedo viewed his tribulations in gathering his material as "a secularized, scientific analogue" of Christian martyrdom, a willingness to suffer in order to "bear witness" to the wonders of the New World. Pagden aptly adduces the proem to book 18, where Oviedo wrote:

> Those who have been busy (as I am now) in recording and informing the world and its many nations of several natural things (things known, not to those who are absent, but to those who have set forth to investigate and discover them) have exposed themselves to many dangers until they can see and contemplate them, dangers that he who takes on such a task must undergo on sea and on land, not only passing through diverse regions with different qualities . . . but also enduring the inconveniences that they must necessarily find in such lands and provinces and seas: e.g., the different foods, waters, airs, temperatures of the mountains and plains they traverse, unhealthy and unpleasant; the animals, like tigers, lions, snakes; and other dangerous situations and countless other trials that cannot be expressed in a few lines.[71]

Oviedo proceeded to complain of carping critics *(murmuradores)* and also of empty-headed readers who preferred the tales of Amadís and Esplandián, but he also could not resist a dig at the classical world, ridiculing earlier writers who had written in comfort "from Greece or from hothouses and gardens." He then ran through another list of tribulations endured by conscientious chroniclers of the Indies ("wounded without a doctor or medicines, hungry without food, thirsty without water, tired without being able to sleep," etc.). At this point, Oviedo's chronicle of the woes of authorship in the Indies widened out to an encomium of toilers in the New World generally, natural aristocrats ennobled by suffering—a passage that we have discussed above in the context of Oviedo's "popularism." One cannot help but note the close similarities between the catalog of authorial sufferings quoted above and those epic sufferings that, according to Oviedo, earned Cortés and his men their place above Julius Caesar in the pantheon of valiant "knights." While Oviedo, unlike that rougher-edged conquistador Bernal Díaz, chose not to declare himself the superior of Julius Caesar, his insistence on the ennobling power of long-distance travel and monumental sufferings allowed him to enjoy a "glory by association" that implied a besting of even more impressive classical competitors than Pliny the Elder, distinguished as Pliny's own fame was in the Renaissance.

Another passage late in Oviedo's history poignantly reinforces this solidarity of warrior and chronicler as fellow heroes of modern "epic" sufferings more impressive than those of the ancients. The sixth chapter of book 47, continuing an account of Diego de Almagro's futile incursion into Chile in 1536–37, begins with an extended denunciation of the "metáforas y vanidades" of the accounts by Ovid and others of the voyage of the Argonauts in quest of the Golden Fleece, excoriating in particular their fascination with the "whoredom and witchcraft" of the fratricidal Medea.

> Listen, then, you who take no pleasure in empty and fanciful books, you who wish to be informed of true histories, listen to the further account of this unhappy journey and unhappy army and its unhappy captain and the unhappy chronicler who tells you about it; and you will learn how deeply involved I was in these toils, and you will see that these are not metaphors but a history that comes so close to home that it suffices to leave me for the rest of my days an inconsolable father, weighed down with the death of the only son I had, for my sins allowed him to die there.[72]

Thus the young *veedor* Francisco González de Valdés, drowned in a disastrous river crossing in a failed expedition, surpassed Jason's epic labors, and, in turn, his loss became itself one of those ennobling tribulations that helped ensure the superiority of his father, "infelice cronista," to his avowed classical model, Pliny the Elder.

Thus we see that the contest against the ancients waged by the conquistadors and their chroniclers was given its special intensity by the convergence of two overmastering emotions: a frustrated or only partially satisfied social ambition, and a powerful—and not unjustified—sense of themselves as acting upon a stage both vaster than any the ancients had trodden and also, quite simply, impressively *distant* from the Mediterranean world. "If you are to stay," a fresh ship-lagged arrival in Cuzco is told in a 1555 dialogue by Pedro de Quiroga, "you must forget everything you thought you knew at home."⁷³ It is true that near the end of his second letter to Charles V, dated October 30, 1520, Cortés explained that he had given his freshly conquered territory the name of Nueva España because of "the similarity between this land and Spain, in its fertility and great size and the cold and many other things."⁷⁴ But near the end of his fourth letter, dated October 15, 1524, Cortés implied that what Anthony Pagden has christened "the principle of attachment" no longer sufficed,

> for the great size and diversity of the lands which are being discovered each day and the many new things which we have learnt from these discoveries make it necessary that for new circumstances there be new consideration and decisions. . . . A new fact elicits a new opinion.⁷⁵

"Nuevo caso me hace dar nuevo parecer." Tzvetan Todorov has argued that these words of Cortés elevate "the art of adaptation and innovation" to the "very principle of his conduct," and he contrasted this flexible improvisation with the Aztecs' "submission of the present to the past." While the Aztecs' cyclical conception of history left them "reluctant . . . to admit that an entirely new event can occur," Cortés and his men were free to see—or driven to see—the past as irredeemably past, and to declare their fiercely independent superiority to it.⁷⁶ While it may be unwise to accept Todorov's "Eurocentric" view as a fully adequate account of the military success of the conquistadors, the eagerness of some Spaniards in the New World to challenge, transcend, or even discard some of the most potent exemplary figures in their cultural heritage, the Greeks and the Romans, does testify to an awareness that a new world had indeed been found—and that a new world, with new standards both of heroism and of literary achievement, was currently in the making.

The Romans at the Fall of Tenochtitlan: Models from the Jugurthine War and the Jewish Revolt on the Last Day of the Aztec Empire

Sixteenth-century Spanish chroniclers of the conquest of the New World manifestly wrote the first chapter in the "anticlassical tradition" in the Americas. Still, there is no denying that the agonistic stance against classical models taken by Bernal Díaz and Fernández de Oviedo was itself a tribute to the enduring and ineluctable power of those very same ancestral cultural patterns. Only a still numinous model could attract such passionately emulous hostility. Bernal Díaz might rout Julius Caesar, and an "honorable merchant" of Santo Domingo might scuttle wandering Ulysses; yet those defeated classical models survived as valuable, even necessary frames of reference for the lives and activities of Europeans who found themselves in a dauntingly *new* world. Whether besting the Romans or searching for Amazons, the Spaniards in America were actively keeping the classical tradition alive as a framework for their own sense of mission, for their sense of themselves as historical actors. To paraphrase Lévi-Strauss's popular *mot* on the Amerindians' use of animals in myth, Spaniards in the New World found Romans "good to think with." Even as they were being marked for dismantling, classical models served as familiar props on the disorienting new stage across which the conquistadors strode. To bring this point home, this phase of our investigation concludes with a look at a pair of Roman analogies that helped bring into European focus that most transcendent of all New World events in the first decades after the discovery: the fall of Tenochtitlan.

The climax of the epic siege of the Aztec capital occurred when Gonzalo de Sandoval deputized García Holguín, captain of an especially swift brigantine, to set off in pursuit of the fleeing king Cuauhtémoc. Efficiently accomplishing his mission, Holguín wasted no time in hastening directly to Cortés with his royal prize, much to the irritation of his commander and erstwhile friend Sandoval. When both men appeared before Cortés to advance their claims of honor, the commander, according to Bernal Díaz, lowered the temperature by means of a deft classical allusion.

> Cortés told them a story about how the Romans had a dispute, neither greater nor lesser than this one, between Marius and Cornelius Sulla. It was when Sulla brought in as a prisoner Jugurtha, who had been with his father-in-law Bocchus. When they entered Rome to celebrate a triumph for the deeds and exploits they had performed, it looked as though Sulla was going to put Jugurtha in his triumph with an iron chain around his neck. But Marius said that it was for him, not Sulla, to put Jugurtha in the triumph, and now that Sulla was putting him in he needed to declare that he, Marius, had given him

the authority and had sent him to bring Jugurtha captive in his name, and King Bocchus handed him over in Marius's name, for Marius was the commander in chief, while Sulla served under his authority and standard. Now, Sulla, since he was one of the patricians of Rome, had much support, but Marius did not have the support Sulla had, since he was from a town near Rome called Arpinum and was a newcomer, even though he had been consul seven times. And it was over this that the civil wars between Marius and Sulla occurred, and the question of the one to give the honor of Jugurtha's capture was never settled.[77]

How likely was Cortés to have uttered such a learned and leisurely anecdote on such an intense occasion? Modern opinions differ. Hugh Thomas, for example, accepts the Roman exemplum as the legitimate contribution of Cortés, "ever anxious to show off his humanistic education," and he observes that "the conversation between these three Extremeños in the ruins of Tenochtitlan about Jugurtha, Marius and Sulla, in the presence of the uncomprehending Cuauthémoc, adds a final bizarre if certainly classical note to the history of the conquest."[78] W. H. Prescott, on the other hand, declared that "this piece of pedantry savors much more of the old chronicler than his commander."[79] One must grant that, even if the old chronicler was in fact recalling an authentic utterance of Cortés, he manifestly eked out his memory of the Roman story by consultation of a written source, though it does not appear to have been a classical or late antique work.[80]

But what function did either chronicler or commander intend this classical (or pseudoclassical) anecdote to accomplish? To a certain extent, of course, the Roman *cuento* served to dignify an incident in the history of the New World by asserting its fundamental equivalence to a key event in ancient history. But a closer look liberates a subtler and shrewder point. Viewed on its own terms, the Roman anecdote seems designed to account for the relatively trivial origin of a disastrous rivalry between two warlords, a rivalry resulting in the first of a series of civil wars ultimately destined to prove the ruin of the Roman Republic and to pave the way for the imperial autocracy. The Cortés of Bernal Díaz's account provocatively declared that this momentous Roman quarrel was precisely equivalent *(ni más ni menos)* to a quarrel of honor between Sandoval and the lesser capitán Holguín (for whom this story constitutes virtually his sole "claim to fame"). There are two striking analogical imbalances here that call into question this claim of classical-modern equivalence. One obvious imprecision exposes the New World "recapitulation" of the classical event as markedly less momentous, as farce replaying tragedy (to invoke Marx on the 18th Brumaire). Not only were Sandoval and especially Holguín far less consequential actors in the grand theater of the world than Marius and Sulla had been, but there was also little danger that their quarrel was likely to shake the known world, be that world either the "old" or the "new."

But another imprecision serves to shift our perspective, allowing us to view the New World incident as ultimately, if ambiguously, superior to its Roman *comparandum.* The key elements here are the casts of characters. The explicitly proposed equivalences are these: Jugurtha equals Cuauhtémoc; Marius equals Sandoval; Sulla equals Holguín. But these equations are skewed the moment we recall that in the Jugurthine War Marius was commander in chief, and Sulla was his lieutenant, while in the siege of Tenochtitlan it was *Cortés* who was commander in chief—provided that one discounts for the moment *his* superior, the king—while Sandoval was subordinate to him, and the distinctly minor figure Holguín was acting under Sandoval's orders. But the sequel efficiently repaired this imprecision in the Roman-Spanish equation. Bernal Díaz proceeded to record that Cortés asked the king to decide which man, Sandoval or Holguín, should receive the right to put the captured Aztec monarch on his coat of arms. Some two years later, the royal reply arrived that *Cortés* had the right to put seven kings on his banner, the seventh being "this Cuauhtémoc over whom the quarrel had occurred."[81] Thus, the Sandoval-Holguín/Marius-Sulla quarrel was subtly displaced onto a higher level. Neither Bernal Díaz in his chronicle nor Cortés in his *relaciones* ever completely disguised the subterranean tension implicit in Cortés's initial status as quasi rebel angling for royal approval. After all, the very months in which the upstart caudillo's status was most dubious coincided precisely with the spectacular Comunero Revolt back in Spain. (It is jolting to recall that Bernal Díaz's own *noble e insigne villa* of Medina del Campo, to which he compared Tenochtitlan's twin-city Tlatelolco, was destroyed in the Comunero Revolt almost exactly a year before Tenochtitlan and Tlatelolco themselves fell.)[82] By selecting the capture of Cuauhtémoc as the strategic occasion to jump two years ahead to the symbolically charged moment when the king conferred upon Cortés his coat of arms, Bernal Díaz deftly suggested that the New World incident had strikingly surpassed its Roman model. Not only had the resolution of the tension between Charles and Cortés dwarfed and in fact annulled that between Sandoval and Holguín, it had established itself as an impressive modern "topping" of a Roman model. While the Marius-Sulla quarrel not only had remained unresolved but even had proved disastrous for the Roman world, the Charles-Cortés tension, like the Sandoval-Holguín quarrel that it subsumed, ended innocuously. And yet, no alert reader of Bernal Díaz's chronicle can miss the lurking irony that this superficially satisfactory besting of the Romans only served to reinforce one of the chronicle's obsessive themes: Cortés's harvesting of honors whose seeds had been sown by his subordinates. Thus, this appeal to classical antiquity serves simultaneously to inscribe a New World incident into a numinous Old World context and to establish an ambiguous superiority of the new to the old.

The moment Bernal Díaz concluded his elaborate attempt to "Romanize" the climactic capture of Cuauhtémoc, he immediately attempted to add resonance to his account of the aftermath of the final battle by invoking an event in Roman history that exerted an extraordinary fascination upon the Spanish mind: the Roman siege and destruction of Jerusalem in A.D. 70.[83] Recalling the eerie silence that succeeded to the nerve-wracking "belfry din" of the final battle, Bernal Díaz recorded that in the streets and courtyards of Tlatelolco where the last bitter struggles had taken place

we could only walk among the bodies and heads of dead Indians. I have read of the destruction of Jerusalem, but I doubt that there was greater loss of life there than here, for in that city there had not been so many people as here, warriors who had gathered from all the provinces and subject peoples, the greater part of whom died, so that, as I have said, the ground and the lake and the stockades were full of dead bodies, and the stench was unbearable.[84]

But Bernal Díaz was not the first to compare the fall of Tenochtitlan to Titus's sack of Jerusalem. When Cortés's second *relación* to the emperor was published in Seville in 1522, a note was appended reporting that the receipt of this letter had been followed by news "of how the Spaniards had taken by storm the great city of Temixtitan [Tenochtitlan], in which there had died more Indians than Jews in Jerusalem during the destruction of that city by Vespasian and, even so, there were more people in it than in the Holy City."[85] These words appear to have been written by Cortés's publisher, Jacopo Cromberger, but Anthony Pagden has suggested that Cromberger apparently had access to a now lost letter of the conquistador.[86] By around 1540 the comparison with the fall of Jerusalem appears to have become standard, for the Franciscan friar Toribio de Motolinía recorded in his *Historia de los Indios de la Nueva España* that "as for the large numbers who died on both sides in this war, they compare the number of the dead and say that it was more than died in Jerusalem when Titus and Vespasian destroyed it."[87]

Once again, though, it is Fernández de Oviedo who offers us the fullest development of this topos of Spaniards surpassing Romans. In the account of the conquest of Mexico in book 33 of his massive chronicle he wrote,

> In his *De Bello Judaico* [5.13.7] Josephus records concerning the destruction of Jerusalem that Annius [Mannaeus], son of Eleazar, testified that 115,080 [in fact 155,880] corpses were found of those who perished in the city from the time the emperor Titus besieged it on April 13 until the first of July. This man was not the guardian of the gate, but the one who disbursed for the city the wages of those who removed the dead bodies, and thus he of necessity counted them. And many others were buried by their close relatives. For burial, the dead bodies were cast outside the walls. In addition to this man, other nobles who deserted to the Romans said that all the dead bodies cast out of doors amounted to 600,000, and that the number of the others could not be calculated in any way. And since there were not enough poor people to carry so many, they gathered together many of the dead and buried them in large houses, as in tombs. All the above is from Josephus. The author of this our *History of the Indies* [i.e. Oviedo himself] declares that in his view the destruction and loss of human life among the Indians of Temistitán [Tenochtitlan] was greater than that recorded of the Jews in Jerusalem, for quite apart from the numbers of the dead that the general Hernando Cortés mentioned in his *relación* to our lord the emperor (which is the number recorded in this history), there remained unknown and incalculable the larger number that he saw in the streets of that city when he found himself its conqueror. For missing were the innumerable ones who drowned, and the even greater numbers sacrificed and eaten, whose tombs were the bodies and bellies of those who remained alive and also of those dead men stinking in the streets, or even the stomachs of those allies who found human flesh no less tasty—as they victoriously ate it for their enjoyment and spiteful gluttony—than had those oth-

ers who were besieged, who ate out of necessity, to satisfy their
hunger. I have seen many gentlemen and others who were in this business of Temistitán whom I have heard say that they believed that the
number of the dead was more uncountable and excessive than at
Jerusalem, at least according to the account of Josephus.[88]

Oviedo's juxtaposition of the fall of Jerusalem with that of Tenochtitlan is worth quoting at full length for a number of reasons. For one
thing, like his extended comparison of Cortés with Caesar earlier in
book 33, this passage allows us to gauge the degree of Oviedo's investment in the strategy of inserting New World actions and actors within
a classical framework, even if it was his contention that this insertion
shattered that framework. Furthermore, consideration of the whole
passage allows us to confirm what we have earlier learned about
Oviedo's classical negotiations. Oviedo saw the agon between the
Spaniards and the Romans as conducted on two levels: on the level of
action, where Cortés surpassed Caesar; and on the level of discourse,
where Oviedo himself surpassed Pliny and other classical authorities.
(These two levels must not, of course, be rigidly segregated. While earlier we saw Oviedo making much of his own travels and labors, so here
we see him acknowledging his debt to Cortés the writer.) In this passage, just as Cortés surpassed Titus, so Oviedo, thanks to his superior
subject matter, has implicitly surpassed Josephus. The curt phrase
"Josephus records" [cuenta Josefo] is neatly countered and "topped"
by the proud proclamation "the author of this our *History of the Indies*
declares" [Dice el auctor desta nuestra *Historia de Indias*]. But Oviedo's
pride in outdoing a respected ancient historian did not hinder him from
disclaiming originality for his classical-modern juxtaposition, for he
noted that the Jerusalem-Tenochtitlan parallel was standard among
"muchos hidalgos e personas." This is a valuable hint that the "Roman
model" was not merely a piece of chroniclers' pedantry, but a living formula of the oral tradition of the conquistadors.
    The Roman siege and destruction of Jerusalem was a multivalent
model for the siege and destruction of Tenochtitlan. To begin with, in
the context of the familiar topos of "besting the ancients" Titus served
as yet another now superseded model of Roman *virtus*. His military
operation had been enshrined in two enduring ancient monuments
widely known in the Renaissance—Josephus's *Jewish War* and the Arch
of Titus in the Roman Forum. Thus, the higher body-count in Cortés's

siege of Tenochtitlan was a spectacular deflation of a celebrated demonstration of Roman military might. The brief note that Cromberger appended to the first publication of Cortés's *Segunda relación* developed this point effectively from the perspective of curious stay-at-homes, for a few words after the Jerusalem parallel one finds this conclusion: "These are great and wonderful things and it is without doubt like another world *(es otro mundo sin duda)*, which we who live beyond are most envious merely to see."[89] True, Cortés had himself brought that *relación* to a close with an insistence upon the *similitud* that justified his bestowal of the name New Spain upon his conquest. But the editor Cromberger clearly wanted to leave the reader with the impression that this was truly an *otro mundo*—not only in its human, animal and plant life, but also (the actual focus of the brief appendix) in the *cosas grandes y extrañas* that the Spaniards had performed there, deeds culminating in a siege more momentous than the most famous of all the sieges conducted by the Romans.

But Titus was not invoked simply to be bested and thereby to dignify the Spanish enterprise; he also implicitly served to justify it. For the destruction of Jerusalem was not merely an event in the secular history of the Roman Empire; unlike the quarrel of Marius and Sulla, it was also a central event in sacred history. Not only had this Roman military operation been foreshadowed in the Gospels by Jesus' prediction of the destruction of the Temple (e.g. Matt. 24:2); it was, for the medieval and Renaissance Christian, a divinely ordained act of vengeance against infidel Jews who had rejected and killed the Savior. In fact, the locus classicus of this idea, in the early-fifth-century Hispano-Roman Orosius, neatly balanced the dual aspect of Titus as triumphant Roman general and as deputy of God: "When the city of Jerusalem had been overthrown . . . and the Jews wiped out, Titus, who had been ordained by the judgment of God to take vengeance for the blood of Lord Jesus Christ, in company with his father Vespasian shut the temple of Janus as a victor in triumphal procession *(victor triumphans)*" (7.3.9, 9.9). These words inspired Dante to place in the mouth of Statius a celebration of how "the good Titus, with the aid of the Highest King, avenged the wound whence issued the blood sold by Judas" (*Purg.* 21.82–84; cf. Justinian in *Par.* 6.93 on "la vendetta del peccato antico"). Sixteenth-century Spaniards were most likely to have imbibed this interpretation of the Roman destruction of Jerusalem from the very popular late-fifteenth-century theological romance *La estoria del noble Vaspasiano enperador de Roma,* which was in turn based upon the twelfth-century French verse text *La vengeance de nostre Seigneur.* The fall of Jerusalem was the subject not only of a popular sixteenth-century Spanish auto (sacramental play), but also, remarkably, of a Mexican play in Nahuatl that survives in a late-seventeenth-century manuscript.[90] It is also intriguing that the native inhabitants of Tlaxcala, no doubt with the assistance of Franciscan friars, chose to stage an elaborate spectacle of "la conquista de Jerusalén" at the feast of Corpus Christi on June 5, 1539.[91] From the detailed account of this production offered by Fray Toribio de Motolinía (though perhaps drafted by another friar), we can see that it combined elements of the traditional Christian view of the Roman siege of Jerusalem with neo-Crusading motifs in a bizarre and vertiginous mixture. The emperor who was camped outside Jerusalem (erected over the still unfinished plaza of the new provincial capital) was Charles V, his army was largely composed of Spaniards (impersonated by Tlaxcalteca) and contingents of all the major peoples of New Spain (as well as the Caribbean), and the besieged enemy were led by the "Sultan," who, amazingly, just happened to be "El Marqués del Valle don Hernando Cortés," assisted by his captain general Pedro de Alvarado—that is, again, Indians impersonating them! This bizarre pageant was probably designed to outdo the *Siege of Rhodes* staged in Mexico City in February of that year, in celebration of the treaty of Aigues-Mortes between Charles V and Francis I, and like that earlier production its main scenario embodied a "prediction" of a crusade led by Charles V against the Turks, though one in which the decisive role would be played by the emperor's native allies from New Spain. But this future fantasy was evidently conflated with elements of the Roman siege of Jerusalem, for the inhabitants of the besieged city were "Moros y Judíos," and though the sultan Cortés's troops wore bonnets "such as the Moors wear," the people of Galilee and Judea flocked into the city to help them.[92] Several scholars have suggested that the Tlaxcalteca actors and spectators savored the subversive thrill of watching Indian troops, albeit serving as Christian allies of Charles V, attack and defeat a "Moorish sultan" who was played by a Cortés impersonator.[93] Perhaps memories were awakened of the initial resistance of the Tlaxcalteca to Cortés in 1519. But it is also likely that this dazzlingly complex festival was electric with the Tlaxcalteca's recollection of how they were taught to interpret their decisive participation in the fall of Tenochtitlan.

The dominant Christian interpretation of the Roman siege of

Jerusalem suggests the subterranean potency of this event as a classical model for the Spanish siege of Tenochtitlan. Spaniards worthily vied with Romans on this analogical field, it is implied, because their respective enemies were fundamentally similar. Both Jews and Mexica were infidels—obstinate infidels who had thrown away their scrupulously proffered opportunity to accept the Way of Christ. It is true that Spanish apologists for the conquest could also claim that the destruction of Tenochtitlan was a secular *recompensa* for the Aztecs' supposed betrayal of their oath of vassalage to the emperor—this is the point to which Oviedo proceeded immediately after his juxtaposition of Jerusalem and Tenochtitlan.[94] But the popularity of the Jerusalem-Tenochtitlan parallel reveals the eagerness of the conquistadors to transcend the role of merely secular avengers and don the shining armor of divine agents.

In one remarkable passage early in his *Historia verdadera*, Bernal Díaz in fact suggested that the parallel between the Mexican Indians whom he himself battled and the Jews punished by Titus may have been more than merely a resonant analogy. When the mortally wounded captain Francisco Hernández de Córdoba led home to Cuba the remnants of the first expedition to Yucatán in 1517, the golden objects they brought back aroused considerable comment and speculation. While some pundits declared these little golden ducks and fish to be the work of "pagans" [gentiles], "others said that they were the work of the Jews whom Titus and Vespasian exiled from Jerusalem and had cast forth onto the sea in boats that had come to port in that land."[95] Now, this identification of the Mexican Indians with ancient Jews was not unparalleled in the sixteenth century.[96] For example, the mestizo Dominican Diego Durán, basing his arguments on a manuscript signed by a certain Doctor Roldán, began his *Historia de las Indias de Nueva España* (ca. 1580; first published 1867–80) with the confident boast that "we can almost positively affirm that they [the Mexican Indians] are Jews and Hebrews," a claim that he proceeded to support with an appeal to parallel customs and to supposed biblical echoes in Indian legends.[97] But Durán, like other supporters of the Israelite-Indian hypothesis, identified the Indians with the so-called lost tribes displaced during the Assyrian conquest of the Northern Kingdom in the late eighth century B.C. The hypothesis that the Mexican Indians were descended from survivors of Titus's siege of Jerusalem is decidedly "unorthodox," but it adds a special force to Bernal Díaz's much more "orthodox" comparison of the fall of Tenochtitlan to that of Jerusalem.

This implied assimilation of Spaniards to divinely guided Romans and of Aztecs to deicidal Jews collaborated efficiently with another, more pervasive historical model for the conquest. For if the conquistadors saw themselves as spectacularly successful emulators of the Romans, they also persistently measured themselves against their more immediate heroic forerunners—indeed, often their literal ancestors—the warriors of the Spanish Reconquest. Thus, they often viewed the conquest of the New World as virtually an extension of the *Re*conquest of Spain from the Moors, coreligionists of those Turks who, like the Jews punished by the Romans, unjustly occupied the Holy City of Jerusalem. The conquest of the Indies was thus a marvelously unexpected opportunity for these epigonoi to give their fathers' war-cry of *Santiago y a ellos* ("Saint James—and let them have it!"—Santiago Matamoros, St. James the Moor-slayer, being the patron saint of the Reconquest) as they attacked heathen armies and dismantled their "mosques" (as Cortés called Aztec temples).[98] Cortés tapped effectively into this energy when he told dissident followers that "as Christians we were obliged to wage war against the enemies of our Faith; and thereby we would win glory in the next world, and, in this, greater honor and renown than any generation before our time."[99] And López de Gómara, in the dedication of his *Historia general de las Indias* to Charles V, declared that "the conquests of the Indians began when that of the Moors was finished, so that Spaniards might always war against infidels."[100] Indeed, the pedigree of this topos goes all the way back to Columbus himself, for he saw the hand of Providence in the fact that his mission began at the very moment when the Reconquest was consummated by the fall of Granada (and the expulsion of the Jews!), and he urged the Catholic Monarchs "to spend all the profits of this my enterprise on the conquest of Jerusalem."[101]

Thus, the natives of the New World were recast in the mold of both of the Old World's two most persistently offensive populations of unbelievers, Jews and Muslims, while the Spaniards projected themselves as simultaneously super-Romans and latter-day Crusaders. But we shall soon discover that many other influential Spaniards passionately rejected this interpretation of the conquistadors' "mission." In fact, the Jerusalem parallel's implicit boast of a preeminence in slaughter would soon come back to haunt these self-styled deputies of God.

These two Roman models deployed for the climactic events of the

capture of Cuauhtémoc and the destruction of Tenochtitlan demonstrate the versatility of classical exempla not only as ways of inscribing
New World events into the most numinous pages of the history of the
Old World, but also as superseded benchmarks that allowed the doings
of geographically and socially marginalized Spaniards to usurp center
stage in the grand theater of the world. These Roman "ghosts" who
marched alongside the conquistadors at one and the same time enabled
them to feel culturally "at home" in a New World and, thanks to their
accommodating inferiority, emboldened them to accentuate the very
newness of that New World and the uniqueness of those who dared to
face its challenges. This versatility—and ambivalence—of the Roman
model was to persist in the roles that the Romans found themselves acting in the debates over the justice of the conquest and the nature of the
inhabitants of the New World.

CHAPTER TWO

The Model of Roman Imperialism in the Controversy of the Indies, First Phase

Vitoria and His Disciples

If the conquistadors both emulated and rejected such classical exemplars as Julius Caesar, other sixteenth-century Spaniards found themselves even more deeply and persistently engaged with the numinous power of a related classical model. While the conquistadors' ancient rivals were individual fellow conquerors who had faced similar, if purportedly lesser, challenges, it was the entire imperial project of the ancient Romans that helped intensify the judgment these other Spaniards passed upon their compatriots' conquests in the Indies. For these deeply engaged observers, Roman imperial motives and methods exerted a fascination that was either attractive or repellent, providing for Spanish behavior in the New World either stimuli and dignifying parallels or warnings and object lessons. While much attention has been paid to another classical contribution to this sixteenth-century "controversy of the Indies," Aristotle's doctrine of the "natural slave," the role of the dispute over the nature of ancient Roman imperialism has been relatively neglected—which is surprising, given its intensity and extent.[1]

The Roman Imperial Glory of Charles V, "Rey de Romanos y Emperador del Mundo"

But before turning to the role of ancient Rome in the vigorous Spanish debate about imperial policy in the New World, we need to consider the particular historical circumstances that made the Roman Empire so appealing a model—or so formidable an obstacle. With the election in 1519 of Charles I, king of Castile and Aragon, as Charles V, Holy Roman emperor, there occurred a confluence and an intensification of three long-developed traditions of attempts to revive ancient Roman imperial glory. These traditions, sometimes distinct, sometimes over-

43

lapping, had been developing within three contexts: the court of the Hapsburgs, the monarchies of the Iberian Peninsula (especially Castile), and the offices of bureaucrats and civil jurists in the orbit of the court of the "German" Roman empire.

Well over two centuries before Charles's paternal grandfather became a purported institutional successor to Augustus by his election as Emperor Maximilian I in 1493, Hapsburg propagandists, like those of many other European princely houses, had crafted for his line a supposedly direct genealogical descent from the Julio-Claudian dynasty. This claim was bolstered by his marriage in 1477 to Mary of Burgundy, a direct descendant of Charlemagne, and in turn Charlemagne's own fabricated Trojan-Roman pedigrees were well established. At the behest of Maximilian, a stable of Northern Renaissance humanists elaborated and propagated this claim to Roman descent—with various connections to Greek heroes and Jewish kings and prophets added for good measure.[2]

When Maximilian's grandson Charles of Ghent acceded to the thrones of Castile and Aragon in 1516, his Austro-Burgundian claims to Roman imperial descent were able to mingle comfortably with a native Iberian tradition of pretensions to Roman imperial dignity, fantasies that could even envision a Hispano-Roman world monarchy. Though it had undergone a recent intensification, this predominantly Castilian tradition had been developing for at least four centuries. After his conquest of Toledo in 1085, Alfonso VI of Castile reinforced his claim to supremacy over other Spanish monarchs by assuming the title of emperor, and his grandson Alfonso VII celebrated his more secure overlordship of the West Spanish kings by likewise taking the imperial title in 1135 in a grand ceremony in León that was repeated in Toledo, henceforth called the Imperial City. Pope Innocent II, perhaps intending a slap at the Holy Roman emperor, confirmed Alfonso's right to the title "King of Kings."[3]

While Spanish pretensions to Roman imperial grandeur normally maintained a proud distance from the Holy Roman Empire, and Spanish jurists like Vincentius Hispanus (d. 1248) loftily asserted the entire peninsula's exemption from the jurisdiction of "the Germans," the imperial ambitions of Alfonso X el Sabio of Castile (reigned 1252–84) defied this pattern, as the learned but maladroit monarch made an unsuccessful bid for election as Holy Roman emperor.[4] His Roman imperial dream may, as Charles Fraker has persuasively argued, account for the way in which the history of the Roman Empire tends to dwarf the history of Spain in the influential, though unfinished, *Estoria de Espanna* that he commissioned and oversaw.[5] Though the various imperial claims of these medieval Castilian monarchs proved ephemeral, R. B. Merriman noted that "the imperial tradition had been too firmly planted in mediaeval Castile to be entirely forgotten."[6] Thus, in the reign of Juan II (1407–54), Juan de Mena, royal secretary of Latin correspondence, celebrated his master in the Dantesque poem *Laberinto de Fortuna* as a "novel Agusto" whose bearing makes him appear king "not of Spain alone, but of the whole world."[7] Such talk of a new Spanish Roman empire intensified after the marriage of Isabel of Castile and Ferdinand of Aragon in 1469. The defeat of the Portuguese in the battle of Toro in 1476 inspired Alonso Palma to look forward to the day when "the kings of the Spains will have the monarchy of the world," and Fray Juan de Padilla declared that her new rulers made Spain worthy of a "mayor monarquía" than that of Caesar.[8]

So Charles inherited pretensions to Roman imperial glory both from his Hapsburg-Burgundian paternal grandparents and from his Spanish maternal grandparents, the Catholic Monarchs. His election as Roman emperor on June 28, 1519, whatever difficulties it caused him in Spain initially, added yet a third incentive for those in the orbit of the monarch to activate the model of imperial Rome.[9] This propagandistic exploitation of the prestige of the ancient Roman Empire on behalf of the modern emperor was orchestrated initially by Charles's neo-Ghibelline chancellor Mercurino de Gattinara, whose enthusiasm for the Roman model may be gauged by his peculiar attempt in 1527 to persuade the distinctly unsympathetic Erasmus to edit the first printed edition of Dante's celebration of Roman imperial rule, *De Monarchia*.[10] But the numinous power of the ancient Roman Empire had been memorably invoked, manifestly at Gattinara's instigation, as early as 1519. For it was during the Spanish crisis over the question of Charles's acceptance of the imperial throne that Pedro Ruiz de Mota, bishop of Badajoz, told the Cortes at La Coruña, in words John M. Headley has suggested were actually composed by Gattinara himself, that

> those who wrote in her praise say that while the other nations sent tribute to Rome, Spain sent emperors. She sent Trajan, Hadrian, and

Theodosius, to whom Arcadius and Honorius succeeded, and now the empire has come again to seek the emperor from Spain, and our king of Spain is made, by grace of God, king of the Romans and emperor of the world *(Rey de Romanos y enperador del mundo)*.[11]

Intensifying the continuity regularly asserted between the Roman emperors of antiquity and the "German" Roman emperors of modern times, Mota thus established a special kinship between the (partly) Spanish "Roman emperor" Charles and the distinguished company of Spanish-born Roman emperors of antiquity. At the same time he forged a flattering link between Charles's modern Spanish subjects and their Hispano-Roman forefathers as fellow "exporters" of Roman universal monarchs. This was a deft way of "selling" that rather dubious product, the "German" Roman empire, to a wary Spanish audience.

Six years later, in 1525, the Navarrese jurist and royal counselor Miguel de Ulzurrum (or Ulçurrum or Ulcurrunus) printed a substantial treatise promoting Charles's claim to world dominion by virtue of his election as "emperor of the Romans." This taxing and clotted *Catholicum opus imperiale regiminis mundi,* dedicated to Gattinara, does not seem to have won many scholarly readers in recent centuries, but we shall eventually be seeing that its potentially baleful importance was nervously recognized by at least two distinguished champions of the natives of the New World, Bartolomé de las Casas and Alonso de la Vera Cruz.[12] Two aspects of Ulzurrum's argument deserve special attention here: his celebration of ancient Roman imperialism as the foundation of Charles's claim to world dominion, and his insistence that this "Roman" imperial authority needed to be extended *de facto,* not merely recognized *de iure,* among unbelievers everywhere on the face of the globe.

Ulzurrum placed the Roman Empire, both ancient and modern, in the last phase of a tripartite historical schema. The first era of history was a primordial "Golden Age" when the unity of the human race was assured by its members' generally virtuous willingness to abide by agreements and live in harmony. The "imperial" authority at this period was simply the "law of nations," that body of customs and values which Roman law assumed all human communities shared—hence Ulzurrum sometimes referred to this period as the "regimen iurisgentium."[13] As sin abounded, however, it was necessary that the increasingly fractious inhabitants of the world fall under the sway of "universal empires," of which Ulzurrum supplied only two examples: the Assyrian and the Roman—the latter at this point meaning the Roman Empire as a *territorial* concept, the lands under the sway of the Roman people during what we are accustomed to call the Roman Republic. "But finally the Romans themselves, who then ruled the nations, acting on behalf of the whole human race *(vice totius generis humani),* chose one man, so that in him might be complete power. . . . But now by the statute and approbation of the church, that power of election is in the hands of those electors of Germany, who on behalf of the whole society of the world *(vice totius universitatis mundi)* choose the emperor."[14] According to Ulzurrum, the jurisdiction of the emperor as world monarch was confirmed by "evangelical authority," for the Gospel of Luke records that Christ chose to be born not only during the Augustan Peace (a point pioneered by the fifth-century Hispano-Roman Orosius) but also in the course of his parents' compliance with a worldwide tax census issued by the emperor Augustus. Furthermore, Christ ordered us to "render unto Caesar," so we cannot help acknowledging that we owe loyalty to the Roman emperor "non solum exemplo Christi, sed etiam eius praecepto."[15] Accordingly, anyone who resists the emperor "resists God's ordination, and so he who resists brings damnation upon his own head."[16]

While in his main discussion of these points Ulzurrum tended to speak of the ancient Roman Empire rather vaguely, in an appended response to the fourteenth-century canon and civil lawyer Oldradus da Ponte he indulged in a remarkably fulsome encomium of Augustus as "imperator optimus," a complete exemplar of virtue in both public and private life ("humilitatis, civilitatis, clementiae, patientiae, disciplinae . . . exemplar"). Indeed, he accepted the popular medieval legend that Augustus was the first to erect an altar to Christ, in accord with a personal vision of the Virgin and Child.[17] But if Christ willed to be born under the reign of such an emperor, what of the succeeding "Caesar" to whom he ordered his followers to "render"? So enthusiastic a "Romanist" was Ulzurrum that he was prepared to accept the remarkable consequence that Tiberius was "vir magnarum virtutum."[18] True enough, further on in this addendum he was willing to admit that Caligula was an unworthy successor to the excellent Tiberius, that Nero was "sceleratissimus," and that the three emperors who disastrously vied for the imperial throne in the chaotic year after Nero's death provided a negative demonstration of the fact that God detests a splintered empire. But his breathless history of the early empire quickly jumped to a neutrally presented Domitian—inexplicably omitting those nobler Flavians, Vespasian and Titus, popularly considered chastisers of the killers of Christ—and concluded with Nerva and "that most excellent Trajan, and so after him the empire by Divine Will always rests in one man"— a bold suppression of the divided empire of late antiquity.[19]

Not only did Ulzurrum contribute to the respect for the ancient Roman Empire during the reign of Charles V, but he also advanced a particular imperial claim that had manifest implications for a "Roman" title to the Indies. In these years of escalating tension between emperor and pope, Ulzurrum was determined to distinguish sharply and decisively between their respective claims: not only were their jurisdictions separate, but they were separate in two distinct ways. First, there was the traditional distinction between the pope's plenitude of power in spiritual matters and the emperor's supreme authority in temporal matters. Given the obvious superiority of the spiritual to the temporal, this division of authority naturally made the pope the greater of the world's "two lights." But Ulzurrum's principal interest lay in another distinction between pope and emperor, one that tipped the scales in the latter's favor: a distinction between the subjects over whom their authority extended. The pope was the "head of the Church Militant, which is the congregation of the faithful." As shepherd of the flock of all the world's Christians, he had nothing to do with the unbelievers, who belong to the flock of the Devil. "Since therefore the unbelievers are not part of the Church, . . . the pope is not their head. But the power of the emperor may be extended and *is* extended to all human beings, be they believers or unbelievers."[20] True enough, Innocent IV in his decretal *Quod super his* (1250) had maintained that "lordship, possession and jurisdiction can belong to infidels licitly and without sin, for these things were made not only for the faithful but for every rational creature."[21] While Ulzurrum grudgingly acknowledged that this might indeed be so, "nevertheless since the emperor is the one sole lord of the world, as has been said and proved above, if there are rebels against him, I say that it is permitted that he deprive them of their goods."[22] And it is the main thrust of the "Third Principal Question" of the second part that anyone, Christian or infidel, who resists the authority of the Roman emperor is nothing more or less than a rebel and a traitor. This lengthy question concludes with a ringing conclusion focusing directly upon the imperial mandate of the current emperor:

And so those laws [cited from Roman civil law], with divine authorities added, prove the conclusion that, while there may now be many
kings, especially unbelievers, who are rebels against the empire, nevertheless Charles, the most powerful and holy king of the Romans,
may by right—and with divine aid *shall*—reduce whatever rebels
there may be in the whole world to obedience to his empire.[23]

Now, it is true that Ulzurrum nowhere specifically mentioned the
infidels of the New World, and his words here surely apply as much to
the dreaded Turks as to the distant Indians. Still, it is perfectly understandable that Las Casas and Vera Cruz would find in his argument
serious consequences for the natives of the Indies.

A reflection of Ulzurrum's thesis was soon produced in the 1528
Castillo inexpugnabile defensorio de la fe of the Benedictine chronicler
Gonzalo Arredondo y Alvarado. Here we find the claim, speciously
based on Augustine's *City of God,* that the Romans had "looked not to
their own good, but to the common good." Following in their imperial
footsteps, Charles had been granted, by direct gift of God, the "Empire,
kingdoms, dominions, and lordships, and universal monarchy of all,
and by His hand will be guided."[24] A poetic echo of Ulzurrum's arguments may be found in the verses Ariosto added to the *Orlando Furioso*
in 1529, declaring that God had decreed that Charles "have not only the
diadem that Augustus, Trajan, Marcus, and Severus had, but that of
every furthest land in either direction. . . . and he wishes that under this
emperor there be one sheepfold only and only one shepherd."[25]

But surely the most impressive and memorable expressions of
Charles's attempt to revive ancient Roman glory were the pageants
staged for his entries into the great cities of Europe, most spectacularly
his entry into Bologna in 1529 to receive at last his imperial crown from
the hands of the pope. Designed to evoke the sights and mood of
Roman triumphs and imperial *adventus,* the festal architecture, cos-
tumes, iconography and oratory that greeted Charles, Roy Strong
notes, "enabled Renaissance humanists and artists to apply to a living
individual the whole rediscovered repertory of classical antiquity. . . .
More vividly than any emperor since antiquity was Charles depicted as
a Roman *imperator* in antique armor, his brow wreathed in laurel."[26]
Even in the New World, where we have seen it was often the fashion to
consider Roman glory passé, Roman imperial splendor was evoked in
an elaborate festival staged in Mexico City in 1539 to celebrate

Charles's recent visit to France. Bernal Díaz assures us that this festival
was distinguished by games "like those they used to perform in Rome
when the consuls and captains who had won battles used to enter in triumph." Indeed, this festival had a special claim to classical authenticity,
for "the man who devised these things was a Roman knight named Luis
de León, a man said to be a descendant of the patricians, a native of
Rome"—a fleeting near-fulfillment of Montaigne's dream of ancient
Romans in Mexico![27]

   This "neo-Ghibelline" tradition of revived Roman imperial dignity
cohabited comfortably with both the Hapsburg and the native Spanish
versions of the Roman model during the reign of Charles. The Hapsburg strand is nicely epitomized by the *Historia imperial y cesárea*
(Seville, 1545) of the official chronicler and humanist Pedro Mexía, a
celebration of Roman glory running all the way from Julius Caesar to
Maximilian I.[28] The native Spanish strand may be detected in the enduring popularity in manuscript form of the Rome-heavy Alphonsine *Estoria de Espanna* and its publication in 1541 by another official chronicler,
Florián de Ocampo, who then embarked on his own, also unfinished,
generally Rome-friendly *Crónica general de España*.

   The convergence of these propagandistic appropriations of the prestige of the ancient Roman Empire for the reign of Charles V remarkably
failed to inhibit the composition and wide dissemination of a sustained
and eloquent denunciation of Roman imperialism, a classic of Spanish
prose that impressively foreshadowed the attacks on the Romans soon
to be launched in the controversy of the Indies. Popularly known as "El
villano del Danubio" (The Danubian peasant), this ringing protest of a
German victim of Roman imperialism was the work of the Franciscan
Antonio de Guevara, a chaplain of the emperor and a writer whose
influence, especially for his "euphuistic" style, soon spread far beyond
the boundaries of Spain. Ironically, Guevara embedded this denunciation of Roman imperialism in a work designed to offer Charles V a suitable ancient Roman imperial exemplar. *El libro aúreo del emperador
Marco Aurelio* was a fictional biography of the great pagan philosopher-
emperor designed as a handbook for the reigning Christian emperor. "It
has been my intention, Serene Highness, to persuade you to imitate and
follow, not all, not many, not a few, but one man—Marcus Aurelius
alone, whose virtues few or none have equaled."[29] Guevara began work
upon the *Libro aúreo* in 1518 and presented an unfinished manuscript of
it to the emperor, at his urgent request, in 1524.[30] Against the author's

wishes, this manuscript was widely copied, and parts, including the "Villano," were plagiarized in printed works. When Jacopo Cromberger issued an unauthorized edition of the book in Seville in February, 1528, Guevara hastened to produce his own "official" printed edition with the Valencian printer Juan Joffre at the end of that same year. Though other editions were to follow, Guevara had by then reworked and expanded the "Villano" and the other material of the *Libro aúreo* for incorporation into the *Reloj de príncipes*, a statesman's guide first printed in April of 1529, frequently reprinted, and widely translated.[31] Thus the "Villano del Danubio" achieved a very wide circulation, both in manuscript and in print, in the very years when the Roman trappings of Charles's reign were most splendidly unfurled.

Not only was the speech of the "villano del Danubio" embedded in two books that held up an ancient Roman emperor for the edification of his modern successor, but Guevara also shrewdly re-routed the speech through the mouth of Marcus Aurelius himself.[32] As a plague ravaged the city of Rome, the emperor in his Campanian retreat found himself surrounded by a learned company of philosophers and doctors who lamented "how changed Rome was now, not only in its buildings, but even more in its customs, and how full of flatterers it was and how empty of men who would dare to tell the truth."[33] In confirmation of this sentiment, Marcus told the gathering of the visit to the Roman Senate of "a poor peasant from the banks of the Danube" during the year of his first consulship. Though rude, even bestial in appearance, his words caused the future emperor to deem him a veritable god among men.

The peasant boldly predicted that the glory the Romans had won from their military victories would in future ages be transmuted into infamy because of the atrocities *(crueldades)* against innocent victims that had sullied those triumphs. The driving forces behind Rome's empire were "greed to seize others' goods" and "pride at giving orders in foreign lands." But Rome's victims had at least the consolation of trusting that the gods are just and would in time repay their oppressors in their own coin. The peasant lingered lovingly on this comforting dream of future vengeance before turning again to greed as a principal motivation of Roman imperial expansion, a hunger for wealth at the expense of their own good name. Vergil was wrong when he declared that the mission of the Romans was "to war down the proud and spare the conquered"; rather, it was "to plunder the innocent and disturb the peaceful."[34] And why harass such distant victims, peoples who are difficult to get at and, accordingly, no threat to the Roman homeland? Again, warned the fearless peasant, the Romans had to expect an inevitable future retribution at the hands of the angry gods.

In the expanded version of the *Reloj de Príncipes,* the eloquent peasant turned next to a demolition of the Romans' claim that they had earned their empire by bringing civilization and the rule of law to a backward race, "saying that we are a people without law, without reason and without a king, whom you are allowed to seize as slaves like unknown barbarians."[35] On the contrary, the peasant insisted, the Romans brought a lawless chaos of corruption and greed to peoples who had surpassed them in justice. "With much more reason might we call *you* a people lacking reason, for, not content with sweet and fertile Italy, you go shedding blood throughout the whole world." True, the Germans had no army and no senate, but that was because, content with little, they had no need of such "advanced" consequences and correctives of corrupt natures.

Both printed versions of the "Villano del Danubio" proceed to allude to the (utterly fictitious) catastrophic demographic consequences of the Roman occupation of Germany. So depressed were Rome's Danubian subjects over their exploitation by their Roman imperial masters that they steadfastly refused to continue reproducing, lest they simply breed more slaves for the Romans.

> Do you know what you have done, o Romans? You have made us swear not to approach our wives and to kill our own children, lest we leave them in the hands of such cruel tyrants as you are, for we prefer that they die with liberty than that they live in servitude. Like desperate men, we have decided to endure the brute movements of our flesh for what remains to us of our lives in order that not another woman becomes pregnant, for we would rather endure being continent for twenty or thirty years than to leave our children slaves forever.[36]

In closing, the peasant deplored the decadent luxury he had witnessed in the city of Rome during the fifteen days he had waited for a chance to address the Senate and declared his willingness to face death on the spot if his words had proved too offensive to his listeners' ears.

Guevara's Marcus Aurelius followed his reproduction of the bold peasant's speech with a gushing encomium of this "hombre tan heroico" and his "razones tan altas." He claimed that the Senate, having endured this remarkable tongue-lashing, not only voted to investigate the peasant's complaints of provincial mismanagement, but also enrolled this bold critic as a Roman patrician and ordered that a permanent record be kept of his indictment of Roman imperialism. Thus, the Franciscan chaplain offered his imperial addressee a model of how those who preside over a "world empire" can, paradoxically enough, endorse and co-opt the forthright criticism of the motives, methods and consequences of that very empire.

As several scholars—most fully, perhaps, Agustín Redondo—have pointed out, it is impossible to read this remarkable document denouncing Romans on the Danube without repeatedly thinking of Spaniards in the Indies.[37] First, there is the insistence upon a greed-driven venture to distant peoples whom "the sea with its depths could not help."[38] Then there is the final version's extensive explosion of a title to imperial rule based upon the supposed inferiority of a people fit only for slavery. While the fictive Romans' contempt for these barbarians reflects the view of some Spaniards that the New World natives were a race of lesser humans, the peasant's celebration of his countrymen's "Golden Age" way of life reflects the other pole of early reactions to the Amerindians, a view of "soft primitivism" in the New World expressed, at moments at least, by Columbus, Peter Martyr, and Vespucci.[39] Any lingering doubt that Guevara was thinking of the Indies must be dispelled by the reference to Rome's German subjects refraining from procreation—or even killing their own children. The Dominican Pedro de Córdoba, arriving in Santo Domingo in 1510, observed that the native women "have given up conceiving and bearing children . . . and others, who have already given birth, kill their children with their own hands."[40]

But we do not need merely to guess that readers of the "Villano" would have interpreted this account of Romans and Germans as an allusion to Spaniards and Indians, for two contemporaries obligingly recorded their perception of this parallel. The first was Guevara's fellow Franciscan, the celebrated bishop of Michoacán, Vasco de Quiroga, writing in 1535. His addressee has sometimes been assumed to be the emperor himself, though Marcel Bataillon has argued that it was Bernal Díaz del Luco of the Council of the Indies.[41] Speaking of an Indian interpreter *(naguatato)* of an embassy of the Indians of Michoacán to the Audiencia in Mexico, Quiroga wrote:

If I knew how to relate here the complaints and valid arguments which he uttered and set forth, perhaps Your Majesty [or Your

Grace] would enjoy hearing them here and would have as much reason to praise them as the argument of "The Danubian Peasant,"
which once upon a time I heard you praise before it was printed,
while you were progressing with the court from Burgos to Madrid,
for in truth it [the Indian's speech] resembled it a good deal, and it
was expressed almost in the same words; and perhaps he had no less
cause or reason to say it.[42]

Indeed, Quiroga claimed that the similarity of the Tarascan's words to
those of Guevara's Danubian peasant struck more than one listener
("algunos de los que allí estábamos"). Similarly, the eccentric and med-
dlesome Sevillan nobleman Don Alonso Enríquez de Guzmán, looking
back on the conflict between Francisco Pizarro and Diego de Almagro
in Peru in 1537, wrote: "When the governor [Almagro] came to the
aforesaid place, an Indian captain came out to him with two thousand
Indians and made him a speech better than I could relate to you, which
resembled that of the Danubian peasant to the Senate."[43]

The passage just cited from Vasco de Quiroga's *Información en
derecho* not only confirms the powerful New World resonances of Guevara's "Villano"; it also tells us that this denunciation of Roman imperialism was "enjoyed" and praised in the entourage of the latter-day
"emperor of the Romans." It seems, too, that the political situation had
been ripe for the high-level encomium Quiroga heard. The royal
progress from Burgos to Madrid in which Quiroga had heard the "Villano" praised took place from February 20 to March 7, 1528. This was
less than a year after the most distressing "public image crisis" of
Charles's reign: the sack of Rome by imperial troops, both Spanish reg-
ulars and German Lutheran mercenaries, in May of 1527. This catastrophic event at first evoked only an "embarrassed silence in official
Spanish circles. . . . Charles abstained from comment."[44] In the summer
of that year, however, Alfonso de Valdés, the emperor's secretary,
penned his *Diálogo de las cosas occurridas en Roma,* a vigorous attack
on the papal perfidy and meddling that, according to Valdés, inevitably
and deservedly precipitated the disaster. Valdés proposed to demonstrate that, not only was the emperor blameless of the atrocities of the
sack, but "everything which has happened has been through the manifest judgment of God, in order to punish that city where reigned, to the
great disgrace of the Christian religion, all the vices human malice could
invent. . . ."[45] The manuscript of this dialogue soon made the rounds of

government officials and censors, and Valdés told Erasmus that it circulated widely throughout Spain.[46] Predictably, the Curia protested, via
the papal nuncio, none other than the famous authority on courtly life
Baldassare Castiglione, whose attempts to suppress the dialogue greeted
Charles shortly after his arrival in Madrid in the spring of 1528, and the
dialogue was not in fact published until the end of 1529 or the beginning
of 1530.

In this context, enjoyment and praise of Guevara's "Villano" by
members of the emperor's court in the spring of 1528 makes superb
sense. Like Valdés's dialogue, Guevara's declamation harped at length
on the theme of the inevitability of divine punishment for the misdeeds
of "Rome." Someone who read the "Villano" not long after the 1527
sack of Rome would have been especially struck by the peasant's warn-
ing to the Senate that "that which you acquired in 800 years you might
see lost in eight days," for the most virulent phase of the sack did indeed
last eight days.[47] Though it is possible that this uncanny anticipation of
the 1527 sack was already present in the manuscript Guevara lent the
emperor in 1524, it was apparently after 1527 that Guevara expanded
this passage to include the Danubian's threat that "just as now you treat
us like slaves, someday you will recognize us as masters."[48] While the
most immediate event foreshadowed here is the fall of the Western
Empire to the northern barbarians, a pro-imperial reader at the end of
the decade would be more than apt to think here of the Sack of Rome
by German troops under the ultimate command of an emperor whose
Hapsburg family was most at home on the banks of the Danube. Perhaps inspired by this suggestion, Pedro Mexía, an author often
influenced by Guevara, claimed in his 1542 *Silva de varia lección* that
the sack of Rome was carried out by "the imperial army, Spaniards and
Germans, through the secret judgment and ordination of God," albeit
without the emperor's explicit desire, as a kind of belated revenge of the
formerly oppressed, showing that "there will be almost no nation or
people of all those subjugated by Rome in ancient times that will not
have subjugated and humbled her."[49] Some forty years later, Miguel de
Cervantes, in his patriotic drama *El cerco de Numancia* had the River
Duero prophesy the 1527 sack of Rome as belated retribution for the
Romans' siege and destruction of Numantia![50]

Guevara's "Villano del Danubio" and Quiroga's testimony to its
reception in the circle of the emperor demonstrate that the propagandistic appropriations of the model of ancient Roman imperialism by the

court of Charles V, "emperor of the Romans," did not in the least hinder the composition and wide dissemination of a ringing indictment of ancient Roman imperial motives, pretensions, procedures and consequences. Furthermore, we see in the "Villano" the ease with which Roman imperialism could be established as an anticipation of the theory and practice of Spanish dominion in the Indies. In addition, by "recycling" the imperial victim's complaint through the mouth of the exemplary emperor Marcus Aurelius, Guevara devised a shrewd strategy for "selling" a rejection of imperial expansion to none other than the reigning Roman emperor himself. Guevara repeated this strategy in the fourth letter of the "Epistolario," the second part of the *Libro aúreo*. Here the philosopher emperor denounced "our such foolish folly" [nuestra locura tan loca] in seeking triumphs by troubling distant peoples, and suggested that the Romans had been misled by the belief "that the Emperor of Rome is lord of all the world."[51] In reworking this passage for the *Reloj de príncipes,* Guevara wrote that "they tell him that at the moment they elect him emperor of Rome, he may freely conquer the whole world."[52] It is true that elsewhere in the *Reloj* Guevara, the emperor's chaplain after all, claimed that God "desires that one sole emperor be monarch and lord of the world," but he emphatically rejected the notion that this divine desideratum constituted a justification for imperial wars of conquest.[53] Thus, in his denunciation of ancient Roman imperial behavior, his implied equation of that behavior to Spanish ventures in the Indies, and his rejection of the reigning Roman emperor's supposed right as "lord of the world" to launch wars of conquest, the eloquent Franciscan Antonio de Guevara strikingly anticipated the great Dominicans who would soon launch the major phase of the controversy of the Indies.

The Beginning of the Controversy of the Indies

The very years that witnessed the most industrious construction of this "Romanization" of the image of the Spanish monarchy and of the Spanish Empire also saw what is perhaps the most remarkable internal debate ever conducted by an imperial power still actively embarked upon an ambitious program of overseas conquest. A wide array of priests, theologians, jurists, conquistadors, government officials, and royal councilors engaged for some decades in a vigorous, often bitter, dispute over the justice of the New World conquests and over the proper treatment and the true nature of the subjugated natives. Commenting on the debate's climactic event, David Brading asks, "Where, in all the long centuries of European imperialism was there a scene to equal the public debate staged at Valladolid between Juan Ginés de Sepúlveda and Las Casas?"[54] Similarly, Lewis Hanke remarked that "probably never before or since has a mighty emperor—and in 1550 Charles V, Holy Roman emperor, was the strongest ruler in Europe with a great overseas empire besides—ordered his conquests to cease until it was decided if they were just."[55] But despite an impressive and ever-mushrooming bibliography in all of the major European languages, including English, this astonishing controversy of the Indies has not yet earned a secure place in the "cultural literacy" of most educated Anglophones, who tend to be surprised to learn that the Spaniards, of all people, publicly aired and argued profound doubts about their own acquisition of American territory, wealth, and human labor. Ironically, the controversy's very success in publicizing the horrors of the conquest may have obscured the fact that there had been such a controversy in the first place. For the luridly powerful "Black Legend" of the Spanish conquest, so potent in Protestant Europe and America and still so influential today, owes a deep debt to the most passionate piece of writing to emerge from the controversy, the *Brevísima relación de la destrucción de las Indias* of the Dominican friar Bartolomé de las Casas (1542; first English translation, 1583). Las Casas's intense and tireless role in this controversy has generated a controversy of its own among modern scholars. Was Las Casas, as the eminent Spanish historian Ramón Menéndez Pidal claimed, "the bitterest man in the world" and a cultural traitor to Spain?[56] Or is he to be celebrated as the "apostle to the Indians" and the first true practitioner of "liberation theology," a movement whose leader, the Peruvian theologian Gustavo Gutiérrez, has recently written a large, rich book on Las Casas.[57] But as we shall soon see, Las Casas not only contributed mightily to the Black Legend of the contemporary Spanish conquest of the Indies; he also strove to project back onto the past a strikingly similar "black legend" of Roman imperialism. For the controversy of the Indies not only temporally coincided with the fullest development of the Roman model in Spanish statecraft, it also explosively engaged with it.

Appropriately enough, the controversy of the Indies burst into life with a dramatic—and carefully staged—scene of confrontation. In the

years 1510–11, a contingent of Dominican friars, freshly arrived on the
island of Hispaniola, was shocked to witness the colonists' brutal
exploitation of nominally free Indian "vassals" of the Crown whose
labor was extracted, in exchange for minimal sustenance, under the system euphemistically known as the *encomienda* (commission, trust).
Accordingly, they drafted a fiery sermon and assigned it to Fray Antonio de Montesinos, "whose talent lay in a certain sternness when
reproaching faults and a certain way of reading sermons both choleric
and efficient" (Las Casas), to read on the Fourth Sunday of Advent,
1511.[58] Mounting the pulpit before the assembled Spanish population of
Santo Domingo, "including the admiral Diego Columbus, and all the
jurists and royal officials, who had been notified each and every one
individually to come and hear a sermon of great importance,"[59] Montesinos launched into an exhortation based on the Gospel reading of the
day, *Ego vox clamantis in deserto:*

> This voice says that you are living in deadly sin for the atrocities you
> tyrannically impose on these innocent people. Tell me, what right
> have you to enslave them? What authority did you use to make war
> against them who lived in peace on their territories, killing them cru-
> elly with methods never before heard of? How can you oppress them
> and not care to feed or cure them, and work them to death to satisfy
> your greed? And why don't you look after their spiritual health, so
> that they should come to know God, that they should be baptized,
> and that they should hear Mass and keep the holy days? Aren't they
> human beings? Have they no rational soul? Aren't you obliged to love
> them as you love yourselves? . . . You may rest assured that you are
> in no better state of salvation than the Moors or Turks who reject the
> Christian faith.[60]

We have noted the habit of the conquistadors of viewing their enterprise as a continuation of the Crusades and the Reconquest of Spain,
with the Indians serving as latter-day Moors and Turks. Montesinos
here initiated a countermodel that, as we shall see, was to play an active
role in the clash of ideologies his sermon initiated: it was the present-
day Spaniards, not their native victims, who resembled the Moslem foes
of their ancestors. (We do need to admit the possibility, however, that
this topos is a retrojection by Las Casas, who reconstructed our sole
version of Montesinos's sermon in his *History of the Indies* in 1559.[61]
Las Casas was demonstrably fond of the Spaniard-Moor equation.)

The uproar ignited by Montesinos's Advent sermon could not be contained in the tight little island community of Hispaniola; both sides sent representatives to Spain to attempt to resolve the dispute over the issues so forcefully raised by the friar. King Ferdinand, sensing an insult to the royal decision to grant the settlers *encomiendas,* ordered the Dominicans expelled from the island and brought home to their provincial in Spain "to explain what induced them to do a thing so unheard of and lacking in any foundation."[62] But upon their arrival in Spain the Dominicans proved unwilling to soften their position, and Montesinos himself powerfully argued their case in the royal presence. Accordingly, Ferdinand set up a commission of royal officials and theologians to debate the issue and draft a set of ordinances. In the course of the commission's more than twenty sessions, the *licenciado* Gregorio, a royal preacher, introduced a classical contribution destined to vigorous life in the subsequent career of the controversy. Gregorio, anticipated a couple of years earlier by the Scottish theologian John Mair at the University of Paris, suggested that the American Indians could best be conceptualized as "slaves by nature," in accord with the teaching of Aristotle in the first book of the *Politics.*[63] Eventually, however, the commission produced a document confirming the late queen Isabel's insistence that the Indians "be treated as free men," while at the same time endorsing the *encomienda* system. On this basis a further council soon produced an extensive set of royal ordinances known as the Laws of Burgos (December 1512, with amendments added the following July). These laws regularized and in some respects actually intensified the *encomienda—* notably in their instruction that, for the purposes of more efficient conversion, the natives be moved to settlements near their fields or mines and that their original villages be destroyed. But the Dominican campaign revealed its effect in the provisions for humane treatment of the "entrusted" natives, including fixed periods of rest, medical care, better food, extensive "maternity leave" for women, permission to retain their customary dances *(areitos),* and, above all, active encouragement to convert to the faith. Remarkably, not only must a Spaniard who beat an Indian pay five gold pesos, but "if he should call an Indian 'dog,' or address him by any name other than his own, he shall pay one gold peso."[64]

We are entitled to doubt that such humanitarian provisions had as much effect in the Indies as did the document's emphatic renewal of the *encomienda* system as a whole. Certainly they had little practical effect

on the rapidly diminishing native population of Hispaniola, whose vulnerability to Old World viruses was intensified by the forced removal to
Spanish-built settlements. There is also much to be said for Patricia
Seed's contention that the Dominicans' insistence upon the rationality,
full humanity, and hence convertibility of the Indians served ultimately
to justify Spanish dominion in the Indies (as well as the Dominicans'
own presence there), for the papal "donation" of the Indies in 1493 was
predicated upon the Spaniards' willingness to spread the faith, and so
"upon the foundation of the Indians' 'capacity for conversion' rested
the entire edifice of Spain's political control over the New World."[65]
Seed also reminds us that the Dominicans did not enter an ecclesiastical
vacuum in 1510—"they had been preceded on the island by the Franciscan friars who had effectively monopolized the conversions on Hispaniola," and Montesinos's stunning Advent sermon may have been in part
a blow at that monopoly.[66] In support of this interpretation, one might
observe that the Dominican Las Casas drew invidious attention to the
encomienda granted the head of the Hispaniola Franciscans, Alonso del
Espinal, whom the settlers chose as their delegate to the king in the
Montesinos affair.[67] Still, this "Gray Legend" that scholars like Seed
and Daniel Deckers have recently attempted to interpose between the
notorious Black Legend and the pro-Spanish "Rose Legend" it predictably provoked cannot ultimately diminish our respect for the vigor
and frankness of the controversy that began that Advent Sunday in
Santo Domingo.[68]

But the most impressive effect of Montesinos's "voice of one crying
in the wilderness" was not in the drafting and administration of royal
ordinances; it was in helping to precipitate the awakening, in 1514, of
the conscience of a secular priest who had received an *encomienda* during the brutal subjugation of the island of Fernandina (Cuba). "He slays
his neighbor who deprives him of his living; he sheds blood who denies
the laborer his wages"—with these words of Sirach (34:22) echoing in
his mind, Bartolomé de las Casas freed his Indians and set forth upon a
lifelong mission to seek justice for his Indian "neighbor." With the
enthusiastic support of the Dominicans, whose order he was to enter in
1522, Las Casas returned to Spain in 1515 and spent six years—years
that saw Charles of Ghent become Charles I of Spain and Charles V
emperor of the Romans—tirelessly lobbying the Spanish court to support projects of enlightened settlement. Alas, his eventual success
brought humiliating failure in its wake: the disastrous venture at

Cumaná on the Venezuelan coast. Subsequently Las Casas lay low in Hispaniola for some years, to emerge again into an increasing spiral of activity and writing beginning in 1534. But before we meet him again and explore his obsession with the model of Roman imperialism, we must turn to a remarkable group of Dominican theologians in Spain who boldly probed the justice of the Spanish conquest before academic audiences at Salamanca, Valladolid, and Alcalá—even, before long, in the face of the emperor's prohibition. As we shall see, the model of Roman imperialism played a central role in these discussions from the very start.

Roman Empire and Spanish Dominion in the Indies in Domingo de Soto's Relectio de dominio

This most intense phase of the controversy of the Indies is usually said to have been inaugurated by two extremely influential lectures delivered by the celebrated neo-Thomist theologian Francisco de Vitoria in Salamanca in 1539. Given their striking and problematic use of the model of ancient Roman imperialism, Vitoria's lectures will soon demand our close scrutiny. But there is a strong case to be made for dating the beginning of the academic controversy—and the role of the Roman model in it—four years earlier, with the delivery of an unjustly neglected lecture by Vitoria's prize pupil, Domingo de Soto (1495?–1560), then Vespera (i.e. afternoon) Professor of Theology at Salamanca.[69] Soto was destined for a very distinguished career, marked most notably by his prominent participation in the Council of Trent and by the publication of his massive and extremely influential treatise De iustitia et iure in 1553. He was also to achieve prominence in the climactic event of the controversy of the Indies as one of the board of theologians appointed to preside over the debate between Las Casas and Sepúlveda in Valladolid in 1550–51, and it was Soto who was assigned the task of summarizing for publication the arguments of the disputants. But when Soto delivered his Relectio de dominio in the spring of 1535, he was near the beginning of his career, in the third year of his professorship at Salamanca.[70] Despite his relative lack of prominence at that time, however, his relection did circulate widely in manuscript—at least four contemporary copies survive to this day—and we shall see that later participants in the controversy of the Indies were indeed influenced by Soto's early contribution. Nevertheless, unlike the relections of Vitoria, Soto's remained unpublished until relatively recently, and this fact has undoubtedly contributed to its neglect. Its relative obscurity even since Jaime Brufau Prat's *editio princeps* of 1964 may be partly due to the assumption—only partly true, as we shall see—that the relection is in effect only an early draft for the first five questions of the fourth part of *De iustitia et iure*. In fact, however, this relection deserves to be considered in its own right as a bold challenge to the legitimacy of Spanish dominion in the Indies. But it was also a frontal assault upon the prestige and legitimacy of the ancient Roman Empire as precedent and juridical foundation for the overseas empire of Charles V. It was Domingo de Soto who established the Roman model at the very heart of the controversy of the Indies. Though fellow Dominicans such as Melchor Cano, Bartolomé de Carranza, and Bartolomé de las Casas built upon and extended Soto's assault upon the Roman model, we shall see that his own revered teacher, Francisco de Vitoria, carefully distanced himself from this position, thereby creating a difficulty and a challenge for these other prominent members of his "school."

Soto began his lecture with a definition of *dominium,* a complex term that played a central role in the debate over the Spanish presence in the New World.[71] After noting that *dominium* was of two main kinds, the power of lordship over subjects *(dominium iurisdictionis),* and the power to use and to alienate things *(dominium rerum)*—Soto devoted more than half of the lecture to a consideration of this second form of *dominium,* which he succinctly defined as "the power or capability of taking up some object for our use" [potestas seu facultas assumendi rem aliquam in usum nostrum].[72] Many of the issues Soto discussed here were highly relevant to the Indies, especially the legitimacy of slavery, which Soto accepted but illustrated only with a reference to "those Africans *(aethiopes)* who hand themselves over to the Portuguese when compelled by hunger." In fact, however, Soto reserved the New World—and the ancient Romans—for an extended discussion of the question "whether the emperor is lord of the whole world," a inquiry inevitably bringing into play the other sense of *dominium:* "the power of jurisdiction, which is lordship or sovereignty" [potestas iurisdictionis, quod est dominatio seu dominatus].[73]

The emperor's supposed claim to world dominion would have to rest, Soto argued, on at least one of three possible legal foundations: natural law, divine law, or human (also known as positive) law. The fact that all humans are of the same nature, thus ensuring that natural law is equal for all, implies that by natural law "no one is lord of others" [nullus est aliorum dominus]—though Soto was quick to add that this fact does not invalidate the institution of slavery, which is an instance of *dominium rerum,* not *iuirisdictio!* Furthermore, "if someone were by nature lord of the world, it would follow that there had always been such a one in the world." But history revealed that there never had in fact been a true world empire. None of the great monarchies of Daniel's vision of the statue (Dan. 2) had really ruled the whole world— for example, Alexander the Great had never ruled Spain.[74]

Next Soto turned to the Romans: "But if you say that in the time of Octavian everything was at last united, this is false, for many nations were not then subjugated, as is attested by Roman historical writing itself; and this point is most obvious with regard to the other hemisphere and the lands across the sea recently discovered by our countrymen."[75] Soto here inaugurated a clever reversal destined to appear frequently in the controversy of the Indies. The contention that the Romans' "world empire" supplied the current "Roman emperor" with a legal foundation for his overseas conquests was turned inside out as Soto employed the Romans' ignorance of the Indies to explode their claim to world dominion in the first place. The Indies thus undermined that very "Roman model" that imperial publicists were invoking to justify their seizure.

Soto proceeded to argue that Scripture showed that God had set up only certain limited kings, such as Saul and David. After all, since world rule does not square with the law of nature, "God did not concede it to anyone." He then went on to offer briefly two other arguments against the emperor's world dominion. One was simply the impracticability of one ruler dominating the whole world either directly or even through agents. Since *dominium* exists only to be actually used, the practical impossibility of world dominion rendered any theoretical legality moot. Thus, both divine and natural law failed to support world rule, for "God and nature make nothing in vain." Next, he argued that each state possessed, by right of nature, sovereignty over itself, unlike the divinely ordained centralized power structure of the Church. Hence, if one person were lord of the world, he would have to have been duly elected by the whole world, each state making over to him the autonomy that the law of nature had originally bestowed upon it. Since there had obviously never been a worldwide assembly to conduct such an election, the emperor's claim to world dominion was rendered invalid by human (positive) law as well as by divine and natural law.

"But there remains," Soto went on, "a very powerful difficulty *(difficultas potissima)* here. For there are those who say that God handed the empire of the world over to the Romans on account of their virtues *(propter eorum virtutes)*, and subsequently the Romans handed it over to the emperor." This, of course, would constitute a foundation in divine law for the Roman Empire, and hence for the claim to the Indies of the current "Roman emperor." Supporters of this claim appealed first and foremost to book 5, chapters 12 and 15, of St. Augustine's *City of God,* "where Augustine wrote that, since there had long been famous kingdoms in the Orient, God wished there to be a western one, and he granted it to the Romans on account of their excellence so that they might control the serious evils of many peoples."[76] Given that the Romans were not destined to a share in eternal blessedness, God's grant of secular empire to them was a suitably generous earthly reward. Supporters of this position proceeded to cite Thomas Aquinas, who in book 3 of *De regimine principum* claimed that God granted empire to the Romans on account of three virtues: "a most powerful love of their country, a love of civil benevolence, and a zeal for justice."[77] In fact, this portion of *De regimine principum* was not by Aquinas at all, but by his continuator Ptolemy of Lucca, but this fact was unknown to the Spanish neo-Thomists, and these chapters of the treatise thus constituted a formidable obstacle to those who rejected the positive valuation of ancient Roman imperialism.[78] Both the Augustine and the "Aquinas" passage it inspired were to play a vigorous role in the controversy of the Indies, as we shall see. Further support for the Romans' divine right to world rule was offered by the early history of the Christian Roman Empire. Constantine, though "a great friend of Christ," did not renounce imperial rule, nor did Pope Sylvester advise him to do so. Nor did Ambrose urge Theodosius to repudiate his claim to empire. "It is not likely, however, that God would allow such holy men to persist in so great an error; hence it appears that those emperors had a right to empire." This concludes Soto's presentation of the contentions of those who argued for a divine grant of world dominion to the ancient Romans.

Soto then launched his attack upon this encomiastic interpretation of ancient Roman imperialism:

I do not dare to make any assertion contradicting the opinion of Augustine and the authorities concerning Sylvester and Ambrose. But nevertheless I do not know what right *(ius)* the Romans had to the lands they conquered. From their own historians we learn that their right was in force of arms *(ius erat in armis)*, and they subjugated many unwilling nations through no other title than that they were more powerful, and one can't find where God gave them such a right. And granted that the Romans had a right over some nations, nevertheless Julius Caesar, as one learns in his *Commentaries*, obtained the empire tyrannically and by means of civil discord.[79]

Soto unmistakably felt uneasy leaping over the rampart of unimpeachable authorities thrown around the pro-Roman thesis. Augustine, "Aquinas's" main source, was his most formidable obstacle here. We shall see later that Soto eventually was to confront directly Augustine's apparent claim that God ordained and favored Roman imperial rule—for this obstacle continued to rankle him. But at this early date Soto was reduced to the expedient of claiming to be unable to contradict Augustine and then proceeding to do precisely that. The Romans' claim to their empire was, in Soto's view, a purely human claim, and not even a sound one at that. The starkly paradoxical phrase *ius erat in armis* is not at all equivalent to the claim of the Romans and their latter-day champions that, quite apart from divine dispensation, their empire was based on the laws of war *(ius belli)*. No, Soto coolly reduced the Romans' claim to dominion over other nations to a question of brute military superiority—a point he may have owed to the Neapolitan jurist Marinus da Caramanico (d. 1288).[80] Turning to the constitutional sense of *imperium*, Soto located the tainted origins of the Roman imperial autocracy in Julius Caesar's tyrannical and opportunistic seizure of power. In support of this interpretation of the behavior of Augustus's adoptive father and monarchical forerunner, Soto offered a sterling authority to counteract the apparently pro-Roman arguments of Augustine: Julius Caesar's own *De bello civili*.

But let us suppose, Soto went on, "that Augustine meant that many nations willingly handed themselves over to the Romans on account of the zeal for justice they recognized in them." And let us further suppose "that the Roman people handed the empire over to Octavian or to some other successor to whom the current emperor succeeds." Even if we grant these dubious propositions, the Romans' claim to world dominion still collapses.

For the Romans could not give to the emperor something they did not possess. But the Romans never possessed the empire of the whole world, for it has never been recorded that Romans came to the antipodes or to these lands that have just been discovered. Therefore, the Romans could not hand over the rule of these nations to anyone, because they did not possess it, any more than the French can create a king of Spain. Furthermore, in Asia, Africa, and Europe there were peoples who were never subject to the Romans.

Once again we see the circular trap that Soto spread for those who would base Charles V's title to the Indies on the supposed right of his Roman imperial "ancestors" to world dominion. The very fact that the Romans did not know the Indies invalidated precisely that claim to world dominion upon which the current Roman emperor's claim to the Indies supposedly rested.

Next Soto released a barrage of citations of both canon and civil law that implied that the Romans themselves did realistically acknowledge that there were solid geographical limits to their dominion, that there were lands that manifestly lay beyond their borders and beyond their imperial reach. On the other hand, Soto admitted, supporters of the emperor's world dominion had their own favorite passages to cite as well, above all the famous "Lex Rhodia," in which Antoninus Pius boldly declared "ego mundi dominus." True enough, Soto granted, it was the custom of the Romans to call themselves lords of the world, just as the city of Rome was called the head of the world *(caput orbis)*. This was because (1) they knew no superior power in the world, and no province could withstand them, (2) they did in fact harbor the desire to subjugate the whole world, and (3) they had subjugated the greater part *(maiorem partem)* of the world then known to them. "And this point is clear, for when Augustus issued an edict that the whole world should be counted, he did not decree that the antipodes be counted, nor those who have just been discovered in Peru, but he termed 'the whole world' the lands subject to the Roman people." Yet again the New World serves to bring out sharply the limitations of the pretensions of the most numinous of the Old World empires.

But Soto's conclusion to the question of the emperor's right to world dominion shows that the New World was not introduced repeatedly in this section solely to undercut the claims of the Roman emperor, both ancient and modern. Rather, Spanish dominion in the New World stands at last revealed as nothing less than Soto's central underlying concern—understandably so, given the recent shocking events in Peru that had also, as we shall see, been troubling the mind of Soto's great teacher, Vitoria:

> From these things it follows that the emperor has no right or domin-ion over the lands of infidels, except for those lands that were for-merly ours, as is said of [Northern] Africa, or unless by right of war in the event that they invade us, as the Turks do. But in the case of these islanders who have just been discovered these two conditions are lacking. For they do not on the basis of their being infidels forfeit their goods or the dominion of jurisdiction which they have, just as this is not lost because of more serious sins, as St. Thomas proves.

Soto's preoccupation with the justice of the New World conquests resurfaces very soon after this, following a brief dismissal of the pope's supposed power to transfer to kings and emperors a secular dominion he purportedly inherited from Christ (whose dominion, Soto insisted, was not of this world). In this remarkable passage, Soto's eloquent fail-ure to reach a satisfactory answer in fact constitutes a powerful claim for him as the true public initiator of the great phase of the controversy of the Indies:

> We hold that the emperor in no way possesses empire in the whole world. By what right, then, do we retain the overseas empire that has just been discovered? The fact is, *I don't know. (Re vera ego nescio).* In the Gospel we read, "Go preach the Gospel to every creature" (Mark 16), which gives us the right of preaching everywhere in the world, and consequently we have also been given the right to defend ourselves against those who would hinder us from preaching. There-fore, if we are not safe, we may defend ourselves against them at their own expense. But to take their goods over and above this and to sub-ject them to our rule—I do not see whence we have such a right.

After all, Christ sent his disciples forth "not as lions but as sheep in the midst of wolves, not only without arms, but without staff, without bag, without bread, without money." In addition, he did not ask them to preach to the unwilling, but to leave them to God's judgment. Soto then concluded with a forlorn hope: "I haven't said these things to condemn everything that is happening among those islanders; for the judgments of God are a great abyss, and perhaps God wishes so many peoples to turn to him through a path unknown to us."

While Domingo de Soto's questioning of the Spanish title to dominion in the Indies thus ended on an ambiguous note, no such equivocation marked his treatment of the ancient Roman Empire and its status as a precedent and justification for the overseas conquests of vassals of the contemporary "emperor of the Romans," Charles V. Soto diminished the status of the ancient Romans in two ways. To begin with, their claims to world rule were dismissed on strictly factual grounds: not only did they not conquer or even know of the Indies, they did not even conquer all of the world that was then known to them. Then there is the moral question: their "right" to those territories that they did subjugate was purely the "right" of the mighty. Even the constitutional position of Augustus was dubious, for his path to autocracy was paved by the tyrannical usurpation of power by his adoptive father Julius Caesar, and it is unclear that the Roman people in fact explicitly consented to his rule. Soto's assault on the Roman model was thus sustained and thorough. He left open no scope for a Roman "title" to the Indies. Indeed, his attack on Roman imperialism had the subtle effect of calling into question the aims and behavior of the Romans' Spanish successors and imitators. Had the Spaniards any stronger right to their imperial conquests than had their Roman models? Or must it be said of them, as Soto said of the Romans, that "their right was in force of arms" [ius erat in armis]?

The Roman Empire in Francisco de Vitoria's *Indian Relections of 1539*

Though the great Dominican theologian Francisco de Vitoria (ca. 1485–1546) joked that his decision not to publish anything was an act of mercy toward students who already had more than enough to read, he nevertheless proved "one of the most influential political theorists in sixteenth-century Catholic Europe."[81] As Prima (i.e., morning) Professor of Theology at the University of Salamanca for the last two decades of his life, he slowly dictated his explications of Thomas Aquinas and Peter Lombard to devoted students, some of whom (notably Domingo de Soto and Melchor Cano) subsequently promulgated many of Vitoria's views in classrooms and on the printed page, while many others were to rise to key positions in the ecclesiastical hierarchy of both Spain and the New World.[82] Particularly influential were the lectures Vitoria delivered to wider academic audiences, the genre to which the *Relectio de dominio* of his Sorbonne student and Salamanca colleague Domingo de Soto also belonged. Though focused on topics or passages touched on during the yearly courses, Vitoria's *relectiones* also addressed political or social questions of considerable current interest, and so it is not surprising that they had circulated widely in manuscript form well before thirteen of them were first published in Lyon in 1557.

In our century, Vitoria's fame has been recharged, for he has been widely hailed as a forerunner of Grotius and Pufendorf, both of whom frequently cited him, in the evolution of international law.[83] It may seem odd that a theologian best known in his own time for his central role in the revival of Scholastic theology could acquire a legitimate, if sometimes exaggerated, reputation as a pioneer of modern international law. In fact, however, this "modernity" of Vitoria had sturdy medieval roots, for it grew from Aquinas's insistence that all human political and social systems derive their legitimacy not from direct divine institution but from natural law, though of course natural law itself ultimately derived its own validity from divine law. If natural law served as the immediate foundation for each society's human ("positive") laws, its influence was most strikingly evident in those laws and customs shared by all peoples, a body of practices known to Roman law as *ius gentium*. Vitoria's powerful formulation of the *ius gentium* as a direct expression of natural law accounts for his recent status as a "father" of international law. But viewed in the context of his own time and place, Vitoria's Thomistic arguments would have had two consequences of particular interest to his fellow Spaniards. For one thing, they offered a stern rebuke to the Lutheran and Calvinistic position that religious infidelity and mortal sin abolished the legitimacy of a political system and of the authority of that system's ruler. And more specifically, they opened the disturbing prospect of the essential legitimacy of "barbarian" societies hitherto lying far beyond the ken of Christian Europe.

The discovery and destruction of the startlingly complex civilizations of the Aztecs and the Incas intensified the urgency of the debate over the nature of the natives of the New World and hence also over the legitimacy of Spanish dominion over such unexpectedly civilized peoples. It appears to have been the second of these astonishing events that first drew Vitoria's attention to America. Writing apparently in November 1534 to Miguel de Arcos, Dominican provincial of Andalusia (to whom, incidentally, we owe one of our manuscript copies of Soto's *De dominio*), Vitoria expressed his revulsion at the events of the recent conquest of Peru, specifically the massacre at Cajamarca and the murder of Atahualpa: "Their very mention freezes my blood." Vitoria declared that the conquistadors could "allege no title other than the law of war" for the wealth and land they had seized, but he proceeded vehemently to deny them even that title. For though he was willing at this point to posit "the emperor's right to conquer the Indies" as an axiom, he could detect no injury done to these particular Spaniards that could make their Peruvian *entrada* a just war. Indeed, the very premise of the emperor's dominion over the Indies meant that this brutal campaign was "not against strangers, but against true vassals of the emperor, as if they were natives of Seville."[84] In this same academic year of 1534–35 Vitoria made his first public pronouncement on the Indies in his lecture "On the Evangelization of Unbelievers," part of his regular lecture course on Aquinas. Here he argued that forcible conversion of foreign unbelievers was generally impermissible, and he also insisted that "unbelievers cannot be deprived of their goods on the grounds of their unbelief . . . because they possess true right of ownership *(dominium rerum)* over their own property." Still, there is one title by which "the emperor is empowered to coerce the *insulani*": the existence among them of "some sins against nature which are harmful to our neighbors, such as cannibalism or euthanasia of the old and senile," for "the defence of our neighbors is the rightful concern of each of us."[85]

In November or December 1535, again in his regular course on Aquinas, Vitoria offered an argument to which Reginaldo Di Agostino Iannarone first drew attention as an anticipation of the celebrated lectures on the Indies that he was to deliver four years later.[86] What seems to have passed unnoticed, however, is the fact that this remarkable passage strongly echoed the reflections that Domingo de Soto had offered on the Spanish title to the Indies in his *Relectio de dominio* several months earlier. Like his pupil and colleague, Vitoria maintained here that Christians have no prima facie right to occupy the lands of infidels, unless those lands had been taken from Christians by force, as (Northern) Africa had been. But this was not the case with the Indies, nor did the pope have temporal jurisdiction there. Again like Soto, Vitoria proceeded to grant that Christians did have the right—indeed, the duty—to spread the Gospel among those people. But whereas Soto had simply added that, if impeded in this evangelical task, "we may defend ourselves against them at their own expense," Vitoria seemed to offer a freer scope for military action: "if they impede us from spreading the teaching of Christ, we may reduce them by right of war in order to spread the Gospel, and, likewise, when we meet with some imminent danger it will be allowed us to take some of their possessions for our security, in accord with *ius gentium*." Unlike Soto, Vitoria neglected to remind his listeners that Christ sent his apostles "not as lions but as sheep in the midst of wolves." Nevertheless, the master's echo of the student's pronouncements on the Indies is remarkable.

At last, in 1539, Vitoria chose the more public format of the *relectio* for two systematic investigations of the Spanish claim to dominion in the Indies: the *De Indis* in January, and the *De iure belli* in June.[87] The primary question that he designed his *Relectio de Indis* to address was "by what right the barbarians came under the rule of the Spaniards."[88] This investigation, in turn, entailed a pair of anterior questions that in fact dominated the entire lecture: "whether those barbarians were true possessors *(domini)* before the arrival of the Spaniards, both privately and publicly—that is, whether they were true possessors of private property and possessions, and whether there were among them some true princes and lords *(domini)* of other men."[89] In the first section Vitoria assaulted the claim advanced by the thirteenth-century canon lawyer Hostiensis (Enrico de Segusio), as well as by the Protestants of more recent years, that either mortal sin or lack of Christian faith is sufficient to annul a people's civil *dominium*. Vitoria countered, in good Thomistic fashion, that *dominium* is directly rooted in natural law, not divine ordinance. Irrationality, being a severe natural defect, *would* annul a claim to civil *dominium*, but Vitoria insisted that this was irrelevant in the present case, for the Indians "are not irrational, but have the use of reason, after their fashion" [non sunt amentes, sed habent pro suo modo usum rationis].[90] In support of this claim he listed several widely attested indications of rational behavior among the Indians, in particular their orderly mode of life and genuine political communities *(civitates)*. When they present the appearance of irrationality, it is the result of "a bad and barbarous upbringing," a phenomenon that can be paralleled by many European peasants. For good measure, Vitoria concluded the first section with a rejection of the relevance of Aristotle's doctrine of "natural slavery" to the case of the Indians.

Having established that the Indians were by natural law true lords of their own domains when the Spaniards arrived, Vitoria proceeded at the beginning of the second part to introduce the Spanish newcomers and their claims to *dominium* in the Indies. "For, even if it be granted that it is true that they [the Indians] are true lords, yet they may have superior lords."[91] From here on, the *relectio* is an examination of both the illegitimate and the legitimate titles (parts 2 and 3, respectively) of Spanish overlordship of the Indian polities.

It was in his refutation of the first of the illegitimate claims that Vitoria first brought the Roman model into play. This false title was that the emperor is lord of the whole world—precisely the proposition that brought modern Indians and ancient Romans into joint focus in Soto's *De dominio* four years earlier. As we have seen, the status of the current Spanish king as reigning "Roman emperor" gave the emperor's supposed world dominion a special power and interest for a Spanish audience. We recall that the royal counselor Miguel de Ulzurrum had devoted his 1525 *Catholicum opus imperiale regiminis mundi* to this thesis. Accordingly, Vitoria chose to tackle this "title" first, giving it pride of place even before the pope's supposed right to assign secular dominion to secular rulers. He argued that the Roman emperor's claim to worldwide dominion was vulnerable on the level of both natural and divine law. Apart from a father's power over his children or a husband's over his wife, Aquinas did not recognize a *dominium* based directly upon natural law. Civil *dominium*, while indeed ultimately rooted in natural law, was the immediate product of human law. Therefore, strictly speaking, "no one can be emperor of the world by natural law"—precisely Soto's conclusion four years earlier.[92] Nor could the lordship of the world be conferred by divine law. True, the great civil jurist Bartolus of Sassoferrato (1314–57), whose "opinions had the force of law in Spain and Portugal,"[93] had adduced the supposed precedent of Nebuchadnezzar as lord of all men by divine election, but the God-given sovereignty of the people of Israel refuted the claim of the Babylonian monarch. Vitoria then turned, as had Soto, to the ancient Romans' more plausible claim to divinely ordained lordship over the whole world:

> And although St. Thomas (*De regimine principum*, bk. 3, chaps. 4 and 5) seems to say that the Roman Empire was handed over by God on account of their justice and love of the country and the most excel-

lent laws that they used to have, this must not be understood to mean that they possessed their empire through a divine grant or institution, as even Augustine says (*De civitate Dei*, bk. 18), but because it was brought about through divine Providence that they acquire the empire of the world—not in the manner in which Saul and David had their kingdom from God, but through some other right, i.e., that of just war or another title.[94]

Like Soto before him, Vitoria here disputed the claim that the Roman Empire acquired its dominion through divine law as a supposed reward for its patriotism and passion for justice. He also shared with Soto the embarrassment that Augustine and "Aquinas" appeared to lend support to those who made this claim. But it is remarkable that Vitoria proved much less bold in disputing the Romans' claim than had his student. Not only did he not draw explicit attention to the politico-geographical reality that the Roman Empire was in fact quite limited, but he also shied away from challenging the Romans' claim to being worthy rulers of those territories that they did in fact come to possess by right of war. Vitoria offered no challenge at all to the reputation of the Romans as patriotic and just imperial rulers. True, he did suggest that *ius belli* was apparently the Romans' only secure title to imperial dominion, but even this was a far more favorable judgment than Soto's harsh formula for Roman *Machtpolitik:* "ius erat in armis." Thus, in the very act of denying to the Roman emperor, both ancient and modern, an explicit and direct "divine entitlement" to world dominion, Vitoria did not hesitate to affirm the virtues of ancient Roman imperial rule, the human justice of the means by which it was acquired, and God's providential favor in creating the conditions for its extensive sway.

Vitoria's other appeal to ancient Roman imperialism in the *Relectio de Indis* was even more emphatically positive, for he deployed it to confirm one of the *legitimate* titles of Spanish intrusion into the New World. This seventh just cause that Vitoria accepted was "for the sake of allies and friends" [causa sociorum et amicorum]:

For since the barbarians themselves sometimes wage legitimate wars among themselves, and the party that has suffered an injury has the right to wage war, it may call in the Spaniards for help and may share with them the spoils of victory. This is how they say the Tlaxcalteca *(Talcathedani)* acted against the Mexicans. They made an agreement with the Spaniards that the latter help them and possess whatever might come their way by the law of war. For the fact that aid to allies and friends is a just cause of war is not in doubt, as Cajetan declares (*Secunda Secundae*, quaest. 40, art. 1). . . . And this is confirmed by the fact that it was indeed especially by this method that the Romans expanded their empire, that is, when they offered aid to their allies and friends; and by undertaking just wars upon this opportunity they came by right of war into possession of new provinces. And yet the Roman Empire is approved as lawful by Saint Augustine (bk. 5, *De civitate Dei*) and by St. Thomas (*Opusculum* 21 [i.e., *De regimine principum*]). And Sylvester considered Constantine the Great as emperor, as Ambrose did Theodosius. Yet it does not appear that the Romans came into possession of the world by any other juridical title than right of war, the greatest occasions for which were the defense of allies and the taking of revenge for them.[95]

Note here the full barrage of authorities in support of the legitimacy of Roman rule whom Soto had had to confront—and evade—four years earlier: "Aquinas" and Augustine, and also the imperial-ecclesiastical teams of Constantine-Sylvester and Theodosius-Ambrose. But utterly unlike his pupil, Vitoria was here perfectly happy to accept these authorities as formidably buttressing the right of the Romans to their territorial conquests. After this relatively full consideration of the Roman precedent, Vitoria concluded his discussion of the seventh just title with a brief biblical instance: Abraham's military aid to Melchizedek, king of Salem (Gen. 14).

Vitoria's positive application here of the model of Roman imperialism to the case of Spanish dominion in the Indies is immediately arresting for its historical specificity. Nowhere else in his discussion of the legitimate and illegitimate titles did Vitoria appeal to actual, rather than hypothetical, events and circumstances from either recent or ancient history. It is, of course, the recent example that has struck most readers of this treatise, though few seem to have fathomed its true power. Vitoria's citation of Cortés's alliance with the Tlaxcalteca against their Aztec oppressors, surely the decisive factor in the eventual fall of the Aztec empire, is in fact the sole reference to a specific New World event in either of his relections on the Indies. We need to recognize that this fact in itself confers a special weight upon this generally neglected Vitorian title, for it is here and only here that Vitoria accorded explicit legitimacy to a specific Spanish war of conquest—and an extraordinarily momentous war at that, not least because it was directed against an

Indian society that could make an impressive claim to what the Spaniards understood as "civilization." This point seems to have been obscured by the eagerness of so many modern scholars to hail Vitoria as a consistent champion of the victims of Spanish aggression. But if the citation of the procedure of Cortés in Tlaxcala is of greater consequence than is usually acknowledged, its power communicates itself also to the model of Roman imperialism by which Vitoria claimed it was "confirmed" *(confirmatur)*. For his appeal to the Roman Empire in support of what he accepted as a powerful Spanish title to dominion in the New World reestablished the Roman model in a potently strategic position in the controversy of the Indies. Vitoria's reluctance to adopt his pupil's critical stance toward Roman imperialism was destined to haunt his students and admirers (including, naturally, Soto himself).

But there is another, deeper anomaly in the seventh "just title" and hence in the appeal to ancient Rome supposedly confirming it. Not only do the other "just titles" lack the seventh's appeal to specific historical events or institutions; they are also founded on a strikingly different premise, a premise that makes this third section of the *Relectio de Indis* Vitoria's most persuasive claim to recognition as a pioneer in the evolution of the modern concept of international law. This pathbreaking premise is Vitoria's conception of the *ius gentium* as not only a body of customs shared by the majority of human societies, but also as a force generating a strong sense of universal human solidarity and "neighborliness"—a point that we have seen that Vitoria had anticipated some four years earlier in the lecture "On the Evangelization of Unbelievers." Thus, all of the "just titles" save one—the seventh—rest upon a fundamental harmony or even identity of the interests of any two societies that may on any given occasion come into contact—specifically, in this instance, the Spaniards and the Amerindians.

Thus, the first title is founded upon the principle of *naturalis societas et communicatio,* which promotes and protects the right of free travel and free trade, provided always that the incoming foreigners intend and commit no injury.[96] The second just title is an extension of this "free travel, free trade" principle, for it affirms the unobstructed right of the Spaniards to travel throughout the Indies to offer a spiritual "commodity," the Christian faith. After all, this will be for the "benefit of the barbarians themselves" [commodum ipsorum barbarorum].[97] Once this process has generated native converts, their mistreatment by their own lords would constitute the third just title for military intervention. Vito-

ria insisted that this is "a title based not on religion, but on human
friendship and sociability *(amicitia et societas humana)*."[98] Then, if a
considerable percentage *(bona pars)* of an Indian population becomes
converted (no matter by fair means or foul), the pope might have the
power to assign the whole people, whether or not they so request, to a
Christian prince—the fourth "just title."[99] True enough, Vitoria
justified this shelving of a native prince's natural right to *dominium*
principally on religious grounds *(ad conservationem religionis Chris-
tianae; in favorem fidei*—this latter phrase occurs three times here). But
even here he did not lose sight of the worldly and spiritual welfare of the
Indians themselves, for this step would also be taken "to obviate danger" [ad vitandum periculum]—that is, the danger of persecution of
converts by a heathen ruler. Even without the pope's mandate, however, the Spaniards might intervene to annul the dominion of native
rulers who abuse their subjects with tyrannical customs, especially
human sacrifice and cannibalism.[100] This fifth "just title"—the sole title,
we recall, of "On the Evangelization of Unbelievers"—seems at first
flatly to contradict Vitoria's earlier rejection of the fifth "illegitimate
title" in the second section, for there he had denied that "the sins of the
barbarians themselves," even such "unnatural" practices as cannibalism, incest, or sodomy, constitute just cause for intervention. But while
such acts viewed in and of themselves indeed do not authorize intervention, they may do so when they are viewed as injustices committed
against our neighbors—"and all those people are our neighbors" [et illi
omnes sunt proximi].[101] A similar acknowledgment of the wishes of our
"neighbors" animates the sixth just title: "true and voluntary choice"
[vera et voluntaria electio], a fully informed transfer of *dominium* by at
least a majority of an Indian population itself—firmly to be distinguished from the kind of uninformed pseudoelection that constituted
the sixth "illegitimate title."[102] Even the notorious eighth just title, hes-
itantly advanced by Vitoria as *dubius,* rests on the principle of human
sociability. This doubtful title is the relative (not absolute) imbecility of
the natives, which implied that the Spaniards might have to step in and
act *in loco parentis* for the natives' own good ("pro utilitate eorum").
"And this could indeed be based upon the principle of charity *(in praecepto caritatis),* for those people are our neighbors and we are constrained to look after their own good." What must be vigilantly
guarded against here, Vitoria insisted, was any primary consideration

of "the profit of the Spaniards, for in this lies the whole danger for our souls and salvation."[103]

We are now able to grasp the full oddity of the seventh "just title" *(causa sociorum et amicorum)*, which associates the legitimacy of Cortés's conquest of Mexico with that of the ancient Romans' acquisition of "world empire." As Vitoria himself indicated, the appeal here to *ius belli* would not have been at all out of place in the context of patristic or medieval theology or canon law. In addition to the authority of Cardinal Cajetan on the legitimacy of resorting to arms to aid allies in a just war, he could have cited such luminaries as Aquinas, Gratian, and Ambrose.[104] No, it is in the context of Vitoria's own premises and emphases in the exposition of the "just titles" that the seventh title, the Roman model, and, by extension, the Spanish conquest of Mexico are all problematized. For there is not the slightest pretence here that either Cortés and his conquistadors or the Romans before them were assuming dominion over their purported neighbors for their own good *(pro utilitate eorum)*, that their actions were based "on the principle of charity" [in praecepto caritatis]. The *dominium* acquired here over goods, territory, and political systems is frankly designated as *praemia victoriae*—"spoils of war." While it is one thing to justify this, as Vitoria candidly did, simply in terms of traditional *ius belli*, it is astonishing to witness the attempt of Venancio Carro, the great modern Dominican historian of the controversy of the Indies, to subsume the seventh just title, to which he devotes precisely half a sentence of his lengthy discussion of the relection, under "la idea de la sociabilidad universal de todos los hombres."[105] But Carro's gambit—like James Muldoon's more economical expedient of quietly omitting the seventh "just title" from his analysis of the *relectio*—offers striking testimony to the ambiguities of this title and hence of the Roman model in Vitoria's influential lecture.[106]

We have seen that the two appeals in Vitoria's *Relectio de Indis* to the precedent of Roman imperialism for Spanish dominion in the Indies both present the Romans in a favorable light, even though the first of these Roman citations is disqualified from offering corroboration to the first of the "illegitimate titles" of Spanish dominion, the emperor's supposed divine grant of lordship over the whole world (sect. 2.1). We have also seen that both citations of the Roman Empire locate the Romans' title to imperial dominion in the traditional concept of the right of war ("non . . . ex traditione aut ex institutione divina . . . sed alio iure scilicet iusti belli vel alia ratione," sec. 2.1; "non . . . alio iuridico titulo nisi iure belli," sec. 3.17), rather than in the more characteristically Vitorian principles of *societas, amicitia,* or *caritas.* Accordingly, we would expect to find the Romans' "just title" by right of war invoked yet again when Vitoria offered a "sequel" in the form of a relection *On the Law of War (De Indis, sive de iure belli Hispanorum in Barbaros, relectio posterior).* We shall not be disappointed. But first we need to come to terms with those peculiar features of the *Relectio de iure belli* that have no doubt led to its relative neglect in comparison to *De Indis.*

For a sequel to *De Indis, De iure belli* is an oddly "distanced" production. To begin with, it is distanced from Vitoria's own most characteristic principles. The first sentence tells us that the subject of this relection is dictated by the fact that "the possession and occupation of the provinces of those barbarians whom they call Indians seems in the final analysis capable of defense principally through the law of war *(videtur tandem maxime iure belli posse defendi)."*[107] This may seem a startlingly retrograde assertion after the more "modern" principles of intervention that constituted the "legitimate titles" of part 3 of *De Indis.* But it is, after all, supported by the seventh "legitimate title," to which we have devoted so much attention—the title that was not only confirmed by the Roman model, but that also offered the only specific reference to a New World event in these two relections. It also rather eerily echoes the words of Vitoria in 1534 to Miguel de Arcos concerning the conquistadors in Peru: "they can allege no title other than the law of war"— though in that letter Vitoria had vehemently denied them that title. Now, it is true that Vitoria did at last return to his principle of "neighborliness" in the three "canons and rules of warfare" appended as a virtual afterthought at the very end of *De iure belli.* Here we are told that a prince should seek peace not war, for he should know that "other peoples are his neighbors" [alii sunt proximi]; he should not intend the ruin of his enemy; and, should he win, he should act the part of merciful judge, not vindictive victor.[108] In a rhapsodic celebration of the "beauty and importance" of these words, J. B. Scott declared "they stand alone in Vitoria's Reading."[109] They do indeed, and that is precisely what is so odd about these "reglas de oro" (as L. Pereña has labeled this section)— and about the relection that they conclude. They are a sudden and startling reminder of the remarkable third section of *De Indis,* and they are thus distinctly out of place in a lecture that breaks little new ground in its exposition of the medieval theory of just war.[110]

Even more surprising, *De iure belli* is distanced from the New World.[111] The specific hypothetical cases Vitoria constructed here were usually built around war between Spain and France, and while he did make much of the distinction between wars among Christian states and wars against unbelievers, the hypothetical unbelievers are Turks or Saracens—a shift in focus that helps account for the harsher views about the treatment of "infidels" dominating this disconcerting sequel to *De Indis*.[112] A year before the delivery of this relection, Spain and France had attempted to defuse their long hostility with the Treaty of Nice, one provision of which was a league against the Turks. But Vitoria obviously harbored grave fears for the fragile unity of Europe in the face of the ever-present and quite active Turkish threat.[113] Thus, when striving to "bring home" the medieval doctrine of the "law of war" to an academic audience in 1539, Vitoria turned instinctively to the potentially explosive European situation rather than to his proposed subject, the remote Indies. Indeed, after the opening sentence we have just examined, the Indians virtually dropped from sight as Vitoria turned to a rather arid survey of four main questions: "(1) Are Christians allowed to make war at all? (2) With whom does the authority for waging or declaring war rest? (3) What could and should be the causes of a just war? (4) What is the nature and extent of the treatment accorded to enemies in a just war?"[114] Now, it will be evident that the debate over the legitimacy of the Spanish conquests of the Indies directly engaged only the last two questions here—though, again, Vitoria never once specifically alluded to the New World even here. But Vitoria's discussion of the third question is highly abstract and offers none of the legitimating principles or scenarios presented in the earlier relection. It is the final question, concerning the treatment of the enemy, that would have had the deepest resonance for an audience that had assumed that it was hearing the case for the Spaniards' right to dominion in the Indies *iure belli*. Here, in unsettling contrast to the *Relectio de Indis,* a listener would have heard Vitoria affirm a Christian prince's right to enslave pagans in a just war—though, characteristically, the specific example of pagans offered is "Saracens."[115] Indeed, even a war of extermination may be permitted, for "sometimes security cannot be obtained by any other means than elimination of all the enemy, and this seems especially true in a war against unbelievers, from whom a fair peace cannot ever be expected on any terms."[116] In addition, the dethronement of enemy rulers and the seizure of their sovereignty may be justified by the circumstances—and, again, Vitoria here offers no clear hint that this was *not* justified in the Indies.[117]

It is in this context that Vitoria again offered the Roman Empire as a divinely sanctioned model of imperial expansion. Arguing that immovable property (i.e., land, forts, etc.) may be occupied as compensation for losses, in self-defense, and in revenge for injuries received (a point anticipated in his comments on Aquinas in late 1535), he added:

> In this way and by this title the Roman Empire was enlarged and extended—that is, by taking over by law of war the cities and provinces of enemies from whom they had received an injury; and yet the Roman Empire is defended as just and legitimate by Augustine, Jerome, Ambrose, St. Thomas, and by other holy doctors. In fact, it may be seen as approved by our Lord and Redeemer Jesus Christ in that famous passage: "Render therefore unto Caesar the things which are Caesar's, etc.," and by Paul, who appealed to Caesar (Acts 25:10) and advised us (Romans 13) to be subject to the higher powers and to be subject to the princes and render them their tributes—all of which princes at that time had their authority from the Roman Empire.[118]

Though Vitoria did not here, as he had in *De Indis,* explicitly use the Romans' right to their empire *iure belli* to confirm the Spaniards' claim to New World territory by the same title, it would be hard to counter a listener's natural tendency to assume that a resurrection of that parallel was being strongly implied. And, again, we should emphasize that Vitoria was marshaling the Roman precedent here to illustrate the power of *ius belli* to legitimate an act that was one of the most contentious aspects of Spanish policy in the New World: the seizure of territory.

So Vitoria called upon the precedent of Roman imperialism three times in his influential 1539 relections on the Indies. Despite the extended and uncompromising attack on the Roman precedent launched four years earlier by his pupil and colleague Domingo de Soto, Vitoria couched each reference to the Roman Empire in positive terms, even when he was rejecting the empire of the Romans as support for the "illegitimate title" of the emperor's dominion over the whole world. Equally important, however, is the fact that in each passage Vitoria founded Rome's dominion squarely and solely on traditional *ius belli,* never on those more radical principles central to all but one of the "legitimate titles" of dominion in the Indies: *amicitia et societas humana*—or, more succinctly and biblically, *caritas.* While Vitoria, unlike Soto, never chose to deny the Romans their right to their empire, he never pretended that they derived or exercised their imperial rule on the basis of the best interests of those "neighbors" [proximi] whom they brought under their sway. Not even his pseudo-Aquinian reference to the Romans' "justice and patriotism and excellent laws" in the second section of *De Indis* strongly suggests Vitoria's belief in Roman imperial altruism.

Thus we are left—or, more to the point, Vitoria's students and intellectual inheritors were left—with a characteristically Vitorian ambiguity. For this powerful and suggestive teacher was, we need at last to admit, a paradoxical intellectual guide.[119] Though celebrated as a pioneer of modern international law, he could slip easily back into the traditional confines of medieval *ius belli*, and we have noted that even his most "modern" internationalist sentiments have a soundly Thomistic foundation. There is also the incompletely resolved tension between his unsurprising belief in the superiority and desirability of Christian polities and his rather more arresting insistence that natural law grants even infidel "barbarians" the full right to possession of their lands, their goods, and their political systems. More specifically, we have been experiencing the frustrating difficulty of pinning Vitoria down on the question of the justice of Spanish dominion and behavior in the Indies. Thus, after decades of scholarly consensus that Vitoria was offering a powerful challenge to the legitimacy of the conquest of the Indies, it should not be profoundly shocking that such recent scholars as Luciano Pereña, Eberhard Straub, Luis Rivera, Daniel Deckers, Rolena Adorno, and Gustavo Gutiérrez have offered an equally plausible reading of Vitoria as a subtle or even open apologist for Spanish imperialism in the New World.[120]

To these Vitorian ambiguities we may now add the Salamantine master's view of Roman imperialism and the role that he believed that it should play in the controversy of the Indies—a view emphatically rejected four years earlier, as we have seen, by Vitoria's own most devoted pupil and colleague, Domingo de Soto. Was Vitoria genuinely impressed by the Romans' claim to what they themselves (on occasion, at least) and their eager emulators regarded as "world empire?" Was he influenced by—or at least content to make his accommodations with—the aura of ancient Roman dignity still clinging to the reigning "Roman emperor" even after the death of his neo-Ghibelline chancellor Gattinara?[121] Qualified support for this hypothesis might be found in his first surviving relection, the 1528 *De potestate civili,* where the thesis of the superiority of (Spanish) monarchy was supported by an appeal to the superiority of the system instituted by Octavian to replace the more chaotic tyranny of the Roman Republic.[122] Thus, Vitoria's apparent pro-Roman sentiments might be an example of what Gustavo Gutiérrez has called "Vitoria's famous prudence"—or what Las Casas claimed was his willingness to "temper" his analysis of Spanish dominion so as not to offend the "emperor's people" [Caesariani].[123] Or was Vitoria subtly suggesting that the Romans in fact resembled Pizarro and his men in being able to "allege no other title than the law of war?" For though he granted that the Romans had a more legitimate claim to that title than did the butchers of Cajamarca, they still could be faulted for lacking those deeper, Christian principles (seven of the eight "legitimate titles" of *De Indis*) that potentially constituted Spain's most profound claim to imperial dominion—and that definitely constituted Vitoria's own claim to have founded, in the words of J. A. Maravall, "a new universalism, transcending the limitations of medieval civilization."[124]

The Valladolid Lectures of Bartolomé de Carranza (1540)

Though Vitoria's relections on the Indies in 1539 fell far short of an assault on the legitimacy of Spanish dominion in the New World, they clearly disturbed the king, who wrote in November of that year to the prior of the Dominican faculty at Salamanca expressing his irritation that "certain religious teachers" there had been both privately and publicly discussing "the right which we have to the Indies, the islands and mainland of the Ocean Sea." In light of the "prejudice and scandal, the disservice and harm which may redound to the Crown from the treating of such themes without the knowledge and authorization of the court," Charles ordered that the prior demand from these teachers an account of their pronouncements, that he collect and forward to a royal deputy all offending manuscripts, and that he see to it that "neither now nor in the future, without our express permission, will they treat or preach or dispute about the aforesaid matter or print any writing touching upon it."[125]

But no mere royal ban could blunt the stimulus of Soto's and Vitoria's demonstration that the Spanish claim to the Indies could and should be subjected to probing examination. A few months after

Charles wrote his stern letter to the Dominican prior at Salamanca, Bartolomé de Carranza y Miranda (1503–76), a theologian destined for dangerous and fleeting eminence as archbishop of Toledo before he fell spectacularly afoul of the Inquisition in 1559, insinuated into a lecture course on Aquinas in the Colegio de San Gregorio in nearby Valladolid some startling extensions of Soto's and Vitoria's views on the "matter of the Indies."[126] While Vitoria seems to have made the realistic assumption that the Spaniards were in the Indies to stay, Carranza seriously proposed that they leave after sixteen or eighteen years, after their missionary work was sufficiently advanced and a generation of young converts had grown to maturity.[127] Carranza also offered a striking extension of Soto's and Vitoria's insistence that the Indians had a right to dominion over their own goods and polities. He argued that "if Christians initiate an unjust war against infidels, as sometimes happens against the Indians, then they may be justly despoiled and enslaved by the unbelievers, and the unbelievers will have just dominion over them."[128] In support of this unusual argument, Carranza offered the precedent of the tribute that the Jews owed to the Romans, a tribute legitimized by the principle that "we are not exempt from the natural power due even to a tyrannical prince."[129] This is an arrestingly ambivalent invocation of the Romans to bring home a point about the Spanish presence in the New World. True enough, the validity that natural law conferred upon the Roman Empire was taken for granted here, for Carranza's point depended upon the assumption that the Romans were justified in demanding tribute money from their Jewish subjects. But it was also implied here that the Roman emperor was a *princeps tyrannus*, even if that fact failed to invalidate his right to tribute from the Chosen People. Carranza's analogy would have especially struck those who were aware of the conquistadors' habit of viewing themselves as latter-day Romans conquering latter-day Jews. Carranza's hypothetical case of Spaniards whose initiation of an unjust war might place them under the dominion of Indian lords had inspired here an exemplum in which the Romans were equated with the *Indians* as "infidel overlords," while the Jews stand in for Spaniards, both fancying themselves, in their respective periods, as God's people.

Carranza's other reference to the Romans in his lecture notes of 1540 was rather more "orthodox," for it was offered in support of one of Vitoria's main points. But even more emphatically than the precedent we have just examined, it revealed an attitude toward the Roman

Empire that departed markedly from that of his mentor—and reached back to that of Vitoria's student Domingo de Soto. Taking up Vitoria's first "illegitimate title," Carranza agreed emphatically that the Spanish claim to the Indies could not be based on the Roman emperor's presumed lordship over the whole world. We don't even know the greater part of the globe, he observed, so how could the emperor rule the whole of it? Besides, history reveals that there never has been a world monarchy in the past. "Even if you say that the Romans governed the whole world, the answer is that this is false: they didn't govern the whole world; no, rather they governed the greater part of it tyrannically *(imo maiorem partem tyranice gubernarunt)*."[130]

In this passage, precisely as in Soto's 1535 relection, we witness a double shrinkage of Roman imperial glory. The first diminishment was one of simple fact: the ancient Roman Empire was simply too geographically constricted to be counted as a true "world empire." Recognition of Carranza's manifest debt here to Soto's relection in fact solves a difficulty in the interpretation of these rather sketchy notes of his 1540 course lecture. Since Carranza had just pointed out that even modern Spaniards did not know the "greatest part of the world" [maximam partem mundi], is there not a contradiction in his claim immediately afterwards that the Romans, while not lords of the whole world, ruled "the greater part" [maiorem partem] of it? Accordingly, Pereña, in his 1956 edition of the text of Carranza's relection, suggested the translation "the greater part [of their empire]" *(la mayor parte [de su imperio])*. This would presumably imply that, however brutally the Romans might have exploited a province like Spain, some parts of their empire—Italy, for example—were not governed tyrannically. But when we look back at Soto's unjustly neglected 1535 relection, we find in this very context precisely that phrase *maiorem partem* complete with the supplement that gives it what is clearly its required sense in Carranza also: "qui tunc erat cognitus," "which was then known." But Carranza's second diminishment of the Roman model in this passage, likewise indebted to Soto, was a matter of *ius* rather than *factum*: over that greater part of the world known to them, the Romans' rule was tyrannical. So much for Vitoria's apparent endorsement of Augustine's and "Aquinas's" references to the Romans' "justice and patriotism and excellent laws." Far from an empire favored and rewarded by God's benevolent Grace, the Roman polity did not even meet minimal standards of human justice.

The fact that the Roman precedent managed to find a place in these very sketchy student notes implies that Carranza probably placed considerable emphasis upon it in his lecture, as had Soto and Vitoria before him. But it is also clear that Carranza had no patience with his master Vitoria's respect for the Romans. Bartolomé de Carranza chose to circumvent his mentor and join his fellow Vitorian disciple Domingo de Soto in helping to shape what one may call the Dominicans' "black legend of Roman imperialism."

Melchor Cano's Relectio de dominio Indorum

It was another distinguished Dominican theologian, Melchor Cano (1509–60), who took the next step in countering Vitoria's surprisingly positive view of Roman imperialism and in sustaining Soto's harsh attack on the Roman Empire as a fit model for Spanish dominion in the Indies. In 1527–31, Cano had been one of Vitoria's first students at Salamanca, and he was destined to succeed him as Prima Professor of Theology there upon his death in 1546, following a three-year tenure at the University of Alcalá. In the 1544–45 school year at Alcalá he presented, in a lecture course on Aquinas, a faithful summary of his master's *Relectio de iure belli,* complete with its positive Roman model.[131] But Cano's first major contribution to the controversy of the Indies was his *Relectio de dominio Indorum,* delivered in Alcalá in 1546, shortly before he moved to Salamanca to succeed his dead master, and here the Roman model came under heavy fire.[132]

A superficial reading of this trenchant document may not reveal a serious gulf between the positions of master and disciple. Vitoria would have found no fault with Cano's negative answers to the three main questions here: (1) Does possession of a fully developed political system *(vera politia)* entitle a ruler to subject the Indians to his rule? (2) May a ruler invade the Indies by "right of empire" [iure imperii]? (3) May a ruler do so through a mandate of the pope? But a deeper look at Cano's treatise reveals striking departures from his Salamantine master's positions. For instance, in his treatment of the first question, he categorically stated,

The barbarians may not be oppressed by any prince through open force for the barbarians' own good *(propter utilitatem barbarorum),* although some legal experts *(iurisperiti)* have denied that conclusion because of certain frivolous arguments *(ob quaedam argumenta frivola)*. For to procure the good of other people is the task of charity and not of justice, unless it coincides with duty. . . . But charity has no coercive force, as is clear from almsgiving and fraternal correction, in which there can be no coercion, unless someone should kill himself, for he does not have dominion over his own life. But in other matters, while one may have dominion, coercion has no place. As for driving out tyrants, I say that if the people themselves call for aid, then that is acceptable; but if the people themselves are willing to suffer, we can't [help them]. Likewise, we are not entitled to occupy their lands on the ground that we have offered them aid.[133]

Against whose "frivolous arguments" were these sharp words directed? Luciano Pereña has asserted that "Melchor Cano is no doubt alluding here to Sepúlveda."[134] True enough, that eloquent apologist for the conquest did argue that Spanish dominion in the Indies should and did have benevolent motives, that *Christiana caritas* demanded that Spaniards guide "men who are comrades and neighbors" [homines socios ac proximos nostros] to the true path.[135] But it is nonetheless difficult to escape the rather startling conclusion that Cano's true target here was none other than Vitoria, a man who, unlike Sepúlveda, was genuinely entitled to be called *iurisperitus*. We recall that a fundamental principle of Vitoria's "legitimate titles" of conquest was "the benefit of the barbarians themselves" [commodum ipsorum barbarorum].[136] Vitoria's doubtful eighth title, the relative imbecility of the Indians, derived all of what power it possessed from the assumption that Spanish tutelage of the Indians would be exercised "for those people's benefit" ("pro utilitate eorum"; cf. Cano's "propter utilitatem eorum"), and this whole title "could be founded on the principle of charity *(in praecepto caritatis),* a principle Cano emphatically rejected as fundamentally incompatible with the use of force.[137] We note also that Cano singled out "fraternal correction" as a species of *caritas* incapable of legitimizing coercive intervention, while Vitoria had specifically proposed *fraterna correctio* as a basis, sanctioned by natural law, for his second just title, the freedom to evangelize.[138] Furthermore, Cano's insistence that the native victims of Indian tyrants must themselves explicitly call in outside help flatly contradicted Vitoria's words in his fifth title: "And it doesn't matter if all the barbarians consent to laws and sacrifices of this sort and do not wish to be freed by the Spaniards. For in these matters they don't have so much power over themselves as to be able to hand themselves or their children over to death."[139] Comparison of these words of Vitoria with those of Cano quoted above leaves little doubt about the main target of Cano's attack, however difficult it may be to adjust to the fact that Cano dared to label his distinguished master's words as *argumenta frivola*.

At the end of his relection, Cano again turned a critical gaze on Vitoria's *Relectio de Indis*. Here, having concluded his discussion of the three main questions, Cano examined six "other special titles" [alii tituli speciales]. These were all drawn from Vitoria's "legitimate titles." The first is Vitoria's first, cited in the master's own formulation: *naturalis societas et communicatio*. While Cano did not in fact dispute Vitoria's claim that freedom of travel is guaranteed by *ius gentium*,[140] he did do what his teacher generally avoided doing: he attempted to test the abstract principle against what he could glean of real events in the Indies and thus to determine if the "title" was indeed met by the facts of the particular case at issue. Granted that those who hinder travelers do them an injury, he said,

> it is unclear that the Indians have done any injury, unarmed and timid as they are, nor is it clear that they have ever acted in an inhuman way, especially since the Spaniards [have entered] not as travelers but as invaders—unless one were to label Alexander a traveler. For the Spaniards themselves wouldn't endure this at the hands of the French.[141]

These terse sentences, manifestly only a summary of Cano's actual spoken words, offer us a more vivid glimpse of a mind attempting to grasp the true meaning of a war of conquest than anything in the printed relections of Vitoria, for all of their estimable injunction of *caritas* toward our "neighbors." Not only did Cano devise here the memorably ironic counterfactual image of Alexander, a favorite model-competitor of the conquistadors, as a harmless tourist or merchant—indeed, his word *peregrinus* fleetingly suggests the even more piquant fancy of the Macedonian conqueror as pilgrim!—but he also undermines the applicability of this Vitorian "just title" by the bold device of inviting his Spanish audience to project themselves into the position of the Indians by imagining themselves the unwilling hosts of armed French "visitors." In his stimulating book on Las Casas, Gustavo Gutiérrez devotes a chapter entitled "If We Were Indians" to Las Casas's attempt "to understand things from a point of departure in the Indian," a procedure that Gutiérrez claims was "in his time . . . unheard of" and that helped mark him as "so different from others of the time." To illustrate this claim Gutiérrez offers a passage from a late treatise, *De thesauris*, in which Las Casas ridiculed the supposed right to travel freely and engage in commerce by vividly imagining an armed French mining expedition in Spain.[142] But we can now see that Las Casas was here borrowing a theme already sounded by his friend Melchor Cano in Alcalá in 1546 and preserved for us in the laconic summary sentence: "Id enim nec hispani a gallis sustinerent."

Cano also alluded to Vitoria's seventh "just title," the acquisition of dominion *iure belli* as a species of booty *(praeda)* earned in aiding allies—this becomes his sixth "other special title." The surviving summary of Cano's remarks makes no mention either of Vitoria's Roman model or of his reference to Cortés's acquisition of dominion over the Aztecs. What does emerge from the summary of Cano's words, however, is a much more powerful insistence that the war to which one is being invited be in fact just. True, Vitoria did presume that the wars in question would be *legitima* and that the inviting party had suffered that *iniuria* without which no war could be considered just. But the summary of Cano's discussion falls far more heavily upon the question of justice, suppressing or at least soft-pedaling Vitoria's stark reference to *praeda*: "A sixth title is to render aid to justice *(opem ferre iustitiae)*; hence, if two parties wage war, it is permitted to support the party of justice and, in accord with an agreement with them, to receive" (no specific direct object stated).[143] In Cano's formulation, the role of justice is less an underlying assumption about the war to which one happens to be invited than it is the explicit end to which one should be directing one's energies: not the reaping of opportunities offered by traditional *ius belli*, but the liberation of the oppressed from the shackles of tyrannical enemies.

Cano's greater emphasis here on justice than on alliance was soon reflected in a relection delivered in 1547–48 by Diego de Covarrubias (1512–77), professor of canon law at Salamanca. In the same spirit as Cano, Covarrubias supplemented the bare assumption that the natives are engaged in a just war *(iustum gerunt bellum)* with the nobler claim, missing in Vitoria, that "the Spaniards may justly come to the aid of the oppressed *(subvenire . . . oppressis)* and hence, a just occasion of war having been seized, to vanquish those tyrants *(tyranos illos debellare)* and exercise against them other things that the right of war permits."[144] Unlike the record of Cano's discussion, however, that of Covarrubias's relection did proceed here to cite Vitoria's defense of the ancient Roman Empire.[145] Indeed, the Roman model seems implicit also in his phrase *tyranos illos debellare*, an echo of Anchises' famous celebration of the Roman civilizing mission "to vanquish the haughty" [debellare superbos] (Verg. *Aen.* 6.853).

Cano's first direct attack on the Roman model in his *Relectio de dominio Indorum* came in his treatment of the question of whether a politically and culturally "superior" state has by virtue of that superiority the right to conquer an "inferior" people. One argument often offered in support of this proposition was, of course, the doctrine of Aristotle that Cano formulated thus: "By nature a slave and a barbarian are the same thing" [idem est natura servus et barbarus].[146] But close on the heels of this classical "natural law" argument came what Cano labeled "the second principal argument": "The Romans legitimately acquired the lordship of the whole world on account of their political system *(politia)*; for they could have no other title than the fact that they made use of just laws. Accordingly, by the same title, a wise prince may subject barbarous nations to his laws."[147] Cano then dutifully cited the expected authorities for this position, the same ones evaded by Soto and embraced by Vitoria: Augustine (*De civ. D.* 5.12, 15, 17, "where he says that the Romans earned their empire through their customs and laws"), "Aquinas" (*De regimine principum)*, and the implicit approval of Sylvester and Ambrose. Cano then appended the biblical passages approvingly cited by Vitoria in *De iure belli:* Paul's injunction of obedience to Roman authority in Romans 13, and Jesus' "render unto Caesar" dictum of Luke 20:25.

Cano's attack upon this use of the Roman Empire as a model for the imperialist projects of other "superior" states was, if anything, even more emphatic than Soto's had been eleven years earlier:

> To say that the Roman state was just on the basis of those passages from Augustine and Thomas has no plausibility. For the Gospel says that the hypocrites have received their reward—not, however, because of their good works. In the same way, then, the Romans in their pursuit of temporal things merited them through a certain appropriateness; nor do we deny that some provinces were justly cap-

tured. But most of them they invaded because of avarice or ambition. For they invaded the Spaniards for the sake of the gold that they got from them, as we read in the book of Maccabees. Likewise, Judaea was not attacked because of any defect in government, for they had received from God a government better than that of the Romans.[148]

Cano's focus on the Roman conquests of Spain and Judaea proved extremely influential, as we shall see. In particular, the brutal and greedy Roman conquest and exploitation of Spain proved a rich theme in the controversy of the Indies. Like Cano's hypothetical case of armed French "travelers" in Spain, this was a powerful strategy designed to force Spaniards to view the conquest of the New World from the perspective of the victims.

Proceeding to respond directly to the pro-Roman party's citations of Augustine and Aquinas, Cano pointed out that these distinguished doctors viewed the Romans as scourges of a wrathful God *(virga furoris)*, like the Assyrians and other infidels, whose divinely directed punishment of the sins of God's people constituted no claim to any merit of their own. Accordingly, the Jewish people were given over into the power of the Romans to be punished *(in vindicta illorum)*. This in no way contradicts Cano's contention, a few lines above, that the Romans had no claim to Judaea by right of their enjoyment of a "superior" form of government. The Romans were tools, not paradigms.

As he brought this part of the question to a close, Cano drew a distinction between an empire's violent and unjust beginnings and its subsequent legitimacy. As had been the case with the Babylonian and Persian empires, so too with the Romans: "for in the time of St. Luke it was already a legitimate empire."[149] This, then, accounted for Paul's urging that his followers be dutiful subjects of Roman rule, for "at that time they were legitimate [subjects]." When Jesus endorsed "rendering unto Caesar," on the other hand, he wasn't so much praising Roman rule as he was trying to evade a trap set by wily opponents by pointing out that what we owe God does not conflict with what we owe an earthly prince. Cano's argument here is not very fully developed, at least in the form in which his relection has come down to us. It does appear to dilute somewhat the bolder anti-Roman stance with which he had begun this refutation of the Roman model. Clearly a major stumbling block for Cano, as for Soto before him, was Augustine's supposedly favorable view of Roman rule. This problem was destined to remain in

place another seven years, until Soto tackled it directly in his authoritative *De iustitia et iure,* though some chopping at its foundations did
occur in the great debate at Valladolid in 1550–51, as we shall see in the
next chapter.

Having disposed of the appeal to the Roman Empire as a paradig-
matic "higher" civilization that might serve as an inspiration and validation to latter-day imperialist powers, Cano needed to attack the
Romans yet again in their even more familiar theoretical habitat of the
ius imperii. If Charles V had no title to dominion in the Indies as the
head of a "superior" civilization akin to that of the Romans, did his
juridical status as heir to the Roman "lords of the whole world" entitle
him to this transatlantic territory? Cano had to admit, of course, that
"many jurists hold that the emperor is lord of the world," notably
Enrico de Segusio (Hostiensis) and Bartolo de Sassoferrato—the latter
declared, Cano noted, that "he who denies this errs against sacred
Scripture and the Gospel." One basis for this contention was simply the
common custom *(usus communis),* in both ancient and modern times,
of calling the emperor "lord of the world," a usage reflected in Roman
law. Here Cano, like Soto, cited the Lex Rhodia, in which Antoninus
Pius declared, "Ego mundi dominus." Then there was Augustus's biblically attested (if historically improbable, as we now know) order that
the "whole world" be counted. Cano supplemented these appeals to
Roman claims with general arguments for universal dominion: granted
Aristotle's principle that monarchy is the best form of government, it
follows that the "author of nature" must have intended this principle
for the whole world; on the analogy of God's status as sole lord in the
world, there should be but one ecclesiastical head and one secular head
(together forming *duo luminaria*); also, it is not fitting that the emperors should hold less power in the Christian era than they had before the
coming of Christ.

Having presented the case for the Roman emperor's worldwide
dominion, Cano declared,

> But this opinion is false. For never did one man rule the whole world.
> The desire to attribute to our emperor that which has never fallen to
> anyone's lot from the beginning of the world is stupidity or sloppy
> thinking *(stultitia vel inconsideratio).* That is shown by the fact that
> the Armenians in Asia were not subjugated, nor were princes of
> Africa, nor [did the Romans control] the bulk of Germany. Also,

there was that endless war with the Persians. Also, Augustine says
(*De civitate Dei,* bk. 4) that a state is well governed when its authority is contained within proper boundaries, and for this reason Aristotle says, "A state is not better because it is bigger, for this would
impede mutual communication, nor would it be possible to take adequate precautions." This would be precisely the case with a world
empire, for no one person could conveniently govern it.[150]

Both of Cano's arguments here—the factual point that the Romans did
not control the whole world known to them, and the theoretical point,
supported by Aristotle, that a true world empire would be impracti-
cal—were fully anticipated in Soto's 1535 *Relectio de dominio.*[151] Neither point was to be found in Vitoria's 1539 refutation of the thesis that
the emperor is lord of the whole world.

After briefly arguing against imperial world dominion on the basis
of natural law, Cano addressed the difficulty that the emperor's lordship of the whole world seemed to be sanctioned by "common usage"
[usus] and by statements in Roman law and even in Christian Scripture
(Luke 2). Here Cano shrewdly turned to the origin and purpose of such
speciously impressive language. If the Lex Rhodia quoted Antoninus
Pius as calling himself "lord of the world," Cano dryly noted that "we
would be able to say that the prince spoke in his own favor, or others
spoke in adulation of him. . . . Therefore that manner of speaking has
derived from the Romans, who used to employ that title by way of
flattery *(ambitione).*"[152] By turning a harshly revealing light upon the
circumstances under which Roman emperors originally enjoyed the title
of universal monarchs, Cano deftly countered the power this claim
seemed to derive from its insinuation into passages in Roman law and
Christian Scripture. Simultaneously, of course, he tacitly impugned the
motives of imperialist jurists and propagandists of his own day. A title
concocted by the fawning *adulatio* and *ambitio* of a servile imperial
court in classical antiquity could not help communicating its tainted
purpose to those who chose to apply it to Charles V, even if the emperor
did himself on occasion choose personally to deprecate the claim.[153]

Thus we see that on the question of the proper use of the model of
Roman imperialism in the controversy of the Indies Melchor Cano
reached back past his teacher Francisco de Vitoria to join Vitoria's
other protégé, Domingo de Soto. Interesting—and apparently
neglected—evidence exists to testify to the immediate impact made by

Cano's tacit criticism of Vitoria's positive treatment of the Roman Empire. This appears in the form of another Alcalá relection apparently delivered within two years of Cano's *De dominio Indorum* of 1546 by two Dominican theologians, Domingo de las Cuevas and Juan de Salinas.[154] Cuevas appears to have been a close associate of Cano's, for when the latter attended the Council of Trent in 1551, Cuevas was selected to be his substitute at Salamanca—and he then substituted for Domingo de Soto when *he* went off to Trent the following year.[155] The relevant portion of the *Relectio de insulanis* of Cuevas and Salinas is an extensive summary of Vitoria's arguments in the *Relectio de Indis* of 1539, a summary directed in part against the arguments of yet another Alcalá professor, Domingo de Santa Cruz, who had delivered a relection defending the emperor's dominion in the Indies apparently between 1536 and 1539.[156] A look at the Cuevas-Salinas version of the two passages where Vitoria offered a positive assessment of the Roman Empire in the *De Indis* demonstrates at once the impact of Cano's anti-Roman bias. True enough, the first passage, Vitoria's response to the claim that the emperor is lord of the whole world, was reproduced virtually word for word, complete with the approving citations of "Aquinas" and Augustine.[157] But this Vitorian passage was immediately supplemented by a qualification manifestly derived from Cano's recent *De dominio Indorum*: the justice of Roman imperial rule was true only "in some places; for in others they dominated tyrannically" [et hoc in aliquibus locis; nam in aliis dominabantur tyrannice]. If here Cuevas and Salinas neutralized Vitoria's positive reference to Roman imperialism by means of a Canoesque revision, their treatment of Vitoria's other Roman precedent in *De Indis* was more economical: for they simply excised altogether Vitoria's reference to Roman imperial practice as a precedent for acquisition of territory as booty in wars of alliance— though they did retain Vitoria's reference to Cortés's alliance with Tlaxcala.[158] Both strategies converged on the same result. After Cano's 1546 relection, even an otherwise scrupulously faithful summary of Vitoria's *De Indis* needed to have its pro-Roman references corrected or purged.

Domingo de Soto Rereads Augustine on the Roman Empire: *De Iustitia et Iure (1553)*

Soon after Melchor Cano delivered his relection *De dominio Indorum* in 1546 he became enmeshed in the controversy over the proposed publication of Juan Ginés de Sepúlveda's dialogue defending the justice of the wars against the Indians, *Democrates secundus*. Cano's energetic attempt to suppress Sepúlveda's book helped precipitate the most famous event in the entire controversy of the Indies, the debate between Sepúlveda and Las Casas in Valladolid in 1550–51. The Valladolid debate involved as judges the three most important disciples and associates of Vitoria whom we have met so far: Cano, Soto, and Carranza. It also shared with the academic lectures that we have been examining a preoccupation with the appropriateness of ancient Roman imperialism as a model for Spanish behavior in the Indies. Nevertheless, since neither of the two principal contestants was a professional theologian or jurist teaching in a Spanish university, and also since the Valladolid debate deserves a chapter of its own, we shall pass over that famous landmark for the moment and consider two subsequent contributions to the Roman question by members of the "School of Salamanca."

The first of these "post-Valladolid" contributions to the academic discussion was offered by the man who, as we have seen, deserves at long last the credit for having started it all in the first place: Domingo de Soto. Busy though Soto had been as judge and official reporter of the Valladolid debate and then as delegate to the Council of Trent, he managed to find the time to bring to completion and, in 1553, to see through the press the massive *De iustita et iure*, a distillation of his teaching and reflection on political theory A revised edition appeared three years later, and it was reprinted twenty-seven times in the sixteenth century alone, for it quickly became "a standard manual on rights which could have been found on the shelves of every scholarly library in Europe."[159] Within the wide range of questions Soto explored in this influential work, the issues that he had discussed in his 1535 *Relectio de dominio* naturally found a place, in the form of the first five questions of book 4. His treatment here of the question of the emperor's lordship of the world is manifestly a mature statement of the earlier discussion in *De dominio*, with some striking new arguments and emphases.[160] Someone familiar with the early relection would, however, be struck by one de-emphasis in the later treatise. Though at first the Indies had seemed literally peripheral in the relection, serving as that corner of the globe whose overlooked existence undercut the Romans' claim to be genuine "lords of all the world," the new professor's lecture increasingly revealed that his treatment of the question of the emperor's universal *dominium* was fueled by his doubts over the justice of the conquest of the New World. In the *De iustitia et iure*, on the other hand, references to America are relatively sparse in what is, nevertheless, a rather fuller discussion of the "world empire" question than that of the 1535 relection. When such references do appear, they perform their traditional "peripheral" function of undercutting the ancient Roman title to world dominion.[161] And yet we learn at the end of this discussion that Soto believed in 1553, precisely as he had in 1535, that the sifting of the Roman claim to world dominion seemed "to demand that a question be raised concerning the particular dominion that Catholic Kings have over those infidels who were discovered fifty years ago."[162] And now we also learn the simple reason why Soto had not been suggesting or building up to that question in the course of this argument: "But the question would take too long; and anyway I have set it aside to be argued in a little book *(libellus)* 'On the Means of Spreading the Gospel,' which I have ready for the press." Alas, this treatise *De ratione promulgandi Evangelium* was apparently never in fact printed, nor has a manuscript copy survived.[163] But at least we know that for Domingo de Soto the link between the question of the legitimacy of the Roman Empire and that of the Spanish title to the Indies remained indissoluble.

Perhaps the most impressive contribution of Soto's *De iustitia et iure* to the "Roman question" was his handling this time around of the formidable authority of Augustine. We have seen that for every member of the "School of Salamanca," beginning with Soto himself in 1535, the bishop of Hippo's apparent claim that the Romans received their empire as a divine reward for their civic virtues proved an awkward impediment to an assault upon ancient—and hence modern—Roman imperialism. Indeed, it seems likely that it was in part Vitoria's respect for the powerful authority of Augustine that led him to cast so benign an eye upon Roman imperial practice. In addition, we saw that Soto, at the beginning of his career as theologian and political theorist, had been incapable of devising any better expedient than that of simply nodding respectfully to Augustine and moving directly on to the stark claim that the Romans' "right was in force of arms" [ius erat in armis]. By 1553, however, this evasion no longer satisfied Soto. What he did now—and what he said he had been doing for a while *(saepe adnotavi)*—was to point out a fact that should have been obvious to any attentive and unprejudiced reader of book 5 of the *City of God*: that Augustine had been misinterpreted, that his apparent celebration of Roman civic virtue was in fact profoundly ambivalent, to say the least. Soto wrote:

For he scarcely intended to assert that God assigned empire to the
Romans as a reward for their virtues. For in both chapters [5.12 and
15] he manifestly strove to show that whatever those people did they
did under the inspiration of earthly glory and for the sake of magni-
fying their reputation. Therefore he judges that none of them—or at
most one or two—was truly devoted to virtue, in view of the fact that
that hunger [for glory] was a sin, albeit a venial one. Hence it might
be, he says, that the virtue of Cato was closer to true virtue than was
the virtue of Caesar; nevertheless, neither was, accurately speaking,
virtue. But God grants no reward for a sin. Rather, he says that God
allowed it by a just judgment, just as Christ says that those who perform their justice before the eyes of men have received their reward—
that is, at the hands of men, God himself permitting it and the course
of nature arranging events. Thus, after the words I have just cited at
the end of chapter 12, he says, "Because for the sake of that one vice,
that is, the love of praise, they suppressed the love of money and
many other vices, God granted that empire to them." If, therefore, it
was for a vice, he cannot have granted it in any other way than by
simply letting it happen. And finally, to the same purpose, he concludes chapter 15 in this way: "The Romans have no grounds for
complaint against the justice of the supreme and true God, for 'they
have received their reward.'"[164]

True enough, Soto chose to overlook Augustine's inconvenient phrasing
in chapter 17, where he urged Christians to be inspired to outdo for
godly aims the secular zeal of the Romans, who endured so much to win
glory and in fact "deserved to receive it as a kind of reward for such
virtues" [tamquam mercedem talium virtutum]. Still, there is no fault-
ing Soto's insistence that Augustine rooted the Roman imperial achievement securely in the pursuit of worldly glory, a vice he unequivocally
condemned as a *pestis* (chap. 13) and an *immundia* (chap. 14) that
would be eradicated from human hearts in a better world than this one.
   With Augustine as ally at last, no longer opponent or obstacle, Soto
was able in 1553 to attack the prestige of the Roman Empire even more
confidently than he had in 1535. God had not granted dominion to the
Romans in the way that he had conferred kingship upon Saul or David;
rather, he had "permitted it through right of war or through their
tyranny." The flicker of concession to his teacher Vitoria's approval of
the Romans' title *iure belli* was here immediately and mercilessly undercut by the phrase "vel per suam tyrannidem." Further undercutting fol-

lowed at once as Soto lumped the Roman Empire in with the other great "world empires" mentioned by the Bible, empires both geographically limited and unjust—"For no one can doubt that they had their strongest right in force of arms *(ius potissimum . . . in armis),*" a clear echo of the claim in the 1535 relection that the Romans' own historians revealed that "their right was in force of arms" [ius erat in armis].[165] In fact, these great empires "supplied terrified peoples with imperial dominion rather than with justice." For even if these imperial powers had a specious ground in *ius belli* because of a broken treaty, they had themselves unjustly extorted such treaties in the first place, and so it was no crime for their victims to break them. Singling out the case of the Romans, Soto repeated his 1535 dig at Julius Caesar, who "insinuated his private authority through the entire state and then wrongly obtained power over it, for which he paid with his life." But Soto did join Cano in conceding that the Roman Empire subsequently acquired a certain legitimacy, either in the reign of Augustus or in the time of his Christian successors, and so there legitimately reigned in contemporary Europe "unus Christianorum Imperator felicissimus et invictissimus," but no true "world emperor."

But what of the widely cited claim of the great civil lawyer Bartolus of Sassoferrato that it would be downright heretical to ignore the "biblical" argument that the emperor's world dominion was supported by the edict recorded in the second chapter of the Gospel of Luke? Here again Soto blamed hermeneutical sloppiness for the bogus authority of a standard prop of "world empire."

> For the Evangelist simply recorded it as an unadorned historical fact that an edict went forth from Caesar Augustus that the whole world be counted; he by no means went so far as to affirm that Augustus published it legitimately. . . . Nay, rather, if you meditate on the hidden meaning, it will be evident that the Evangelist condemned that edict. For he obviously mentioned that frothy arrogance of Augustus *(spumosam illam Augusti insolentiam)* in order to remind us that it was not he, as he boasted, but rather the one who was being born who was Lord of the world, the whole of which he had bound to his laws and which he was going to summon at last to judgment.[166]

Confirmation of the "frothiness" of Augustus's boast was the fact that it was obvious that he was not mandating a census for "the antipodes or for those other peoples who lie so far from him and of whom he had never heard." The Lex Rhodia of Antoninus Pius was yet another piece of imperial self-puffery that, Soto observed, "reeks of arrogance" [arrogantiam redolere], for it belonged to God alone to proclaim "ego mundi dominus." These assaults on the supposed authority of Luke and the Lex Rhodia repeated and extended Melchor Cano's anchoring of the Romans' claim to world dominion securely in the self-serving propaganda of the ancient imperial court, in the *ambitio* and *adulatio* of imperial tyrants.

The Ambivalence of Juan de la Peña (1559–60)

The attacks on the authority of the model of Roman imperialism launched by Cano, Carranza, and especially Soto clearly constituted an impressive counterweight to the *adulatio* of modern imperial propagandists—the most recent and annoying being the eloquent Sepúlveda, to whom we shall turn in the next chapter. But the urgency of their anti-Roman project undoubtedly owed much also to the apparent blessing conferred upon the Roman Empire by their revered mentor Francisco de Vitoria. Even so, in spite of these impressive and emphatic challenges, the power of the model could still be registered, even within the boundaries of the "neo-Thomistic" school itself. Evidence of this lingering ideological potency is intriguingly offered by a lecture questioning the legitimacy of wars against the Indians delivered by one of the leading lights of the "second generation" of the "School of Salamanca," Juan de la Peña (1513–65). Peña, who had been a student of both Cano and Carranza in the Colegio de San Gregorio of Valladolid, delivered this lecture during the 1559–60 course on Aquinas at Salamanca, while he was substituting for Domingo de Soto in the *prima* chair of theology, the chair previously held, we recall, by Vitoria and Cano.[167]

Like his teachers and associates, Peña emphatically argued in this lecture *De bello contra insulanos* that the *potestas imperatoria* did not furnish a title to compel the *insulani* to observe natural law or to deprive them of their dominion. As had Vitoria in *De Indis*, Peña maintained that "our emperor did not succeed to the full right of the Roman emperors, nor is he the heir of the Romans or of the Roman Empire; for had he so succeeded, he would have power over Spaniards, Italians, and

Frenchmen, just like Constantine and others of his successors."[168] Peña's automatic dependence on Vitoria here appears to have blinded him to the anachronism of this argument, for Charles V had not only resigned the imperial crown in 1556 but had in fact died in 1558! In addition, it will be noted that Peña's contention here, like that of Vitoria, implied no challenge to the *ius* of the ancient Roman emperors; it merely denied that their later successors inherited the geographical fullness of that *ius*. Next, he observed that the second chapter of Luke referred to a "worldwide" taxation order issued "not by God, who cannot err, but by Caesar, who could have issued this edict through arrogance and pride *(per arrogantiam et superbiam)*, since Caesar had not himself subjugated the whole world either de jure or de facto, since [the Romans] hadn't subjugated the Indians." This will at once be recognized as a clear reflection of Soto's attack on Bartolus's appeal to the Gospel passage and thus another contribution to Cano's rooting of the imperial claim in Roman propaganda. But the doubtful *poterat* ("who *could* have issued this edict") offers a further hint that Peña's anti-Romanism was not as passionate as had been that of his teachers and colleagues.

Peña's debt to his teacher Melchor Cano on the Roman question is evident in the third part of the second question, where he attacked the claim that natural law confers upon a king the right to compel infidels to observe natural law and abandon their infidelity. This is essentially the position Cano had refuted when he denied that a politically "superior" state had the right by natural law to subjugate an "inferior" state. Accordingly, Peña followed Cano in considering the historical example of the Romans directly after the theoretical issue of Aristotle's claim that "by nature a slave and a barbarian are the same thing." Yet again Augustine and "Aquinas" were duly trotted forth as the warhorses of the pro-Roman champions.[169] When at last Peña was ready to refute this position, he again drew upon Cano's *De dominio Indorum*.[170] We recall that Cano had made a somewhat perfunctory distinction between the violent and unjust origins of the Roman Empire and its subsequent achievement of legitimacy, and even Soto was willing to accept this in *De iustitia et iure*. Peña built an interestingly ambivalent expansion of this idea around a distinction between two kinds of tyrant: one *(tyrannus in iurisdictione)* "who unjustly and violently *(contra ius per violentiam)* dominates some other region," and another *(tyrannus in guber-*

natione) "who is truly lord of a region but who nevertheless rules his subjects with wicked laws and oppresses them with unjust exactions." Peña then proceeded to locate the ancient Romans on this grid.

> Now that these premises have been laid down, I say that the Romans were in some kingdoms tyrants in the first sense, for they subdued them through violence, since the Romans used to suppose that right lay in might and arms. The Romans were also tyrants in the second sense, but not as much as other nations, because even though the Romans had some wicked laws, they nevertheless governed well and with good civic order *(politice)* among many peoples, the Jews excepted. And for this reason that Roman Empire is praised by Augustine and by Thomas. For they say that it was for this reason that God permitted them to rule over so many nations and to have so many kingdoms in the whole world *(in universo orbe)*—and above all because they were great observers of divine worship, though it is true that that worship was false and wicked. But it does not follow from this that the Romans justly conquered many nations. Were that so, it would follow that the kings who often, with God's permission, sub-jugated the people of God because of the latter's sins were acting justly. Yet, nevertheless, it is true that the Romans very often waged wars justly. For this see Plutarch, in his life of Flamininus, and also Livy in his account of the life of the same Flamininus, where it is recorded that the Romans were called in by the Greeks to aid them, and after they defeated the Greeks' enemies, they left the Greeks free, even though they could have ruled over them.

This splendidly confused passage is powerful testimony both to the enduring power of the example of Roman imperialism and to the impressive attacks that that model had sustained at the hands of Peña's mentors Soto, Carranza, and Cano—and also, as we shall soon see, Peña's friend Las Casas. Particularly striking is the charge that the Romans used to assume that "right lay in might and arms" [ius erat in potentia et armis], a manifest echo of formulations occurring both in Soto's 1535 relection and in his 1553 treatise. But no less striking is Peña's tacit refusal to follow Soto in recognizing that Augustine had been far more critical of the Romans than was commonly allowed. Indeed, Peña even foisted upon Augustine and "Aquinas" a respect for Roman religiosity that is in fact utterly lacking in both texts—and that must have jolted Peña's friend Las Casas, for whom, as we shall see, the

Romans' religious life provided the richest evidence of their cultural degradation. Furthermore, Peña's tellingly careless phrase "ut . . . haberent tot regna in universo orbe" shows how lukewarm was his commitment to his mentors' campaign to deflate the Romans' claim to lordship of the "whole world."

Indeed, Peña could not even abide by his initial Sotoesque condemnation of the Romans' wars of conquest, wars that seemed to assure their status as "tyrants of the first type," that is, those who achieved dominion *contra ius per violentiam.* For Peña quickly proved willing to grant that the Romans waged these wars justly—not merely occasionally, but "very often" [saepissime]. The particular case in point that he supplied has a double interest in the controversy of the Indies. For one thing, Titus Quinctius Flamininus's activity in Greece in the early second century B.C. served as a fine specific example of what Vitoria may have had in mind when he cited the Romans in support of his "seventh just title" of Spanish dominion in the Indies: dominion acquired through aid to allies who have called in the imperialist power. Then there is the intriguing fact that Las Casas himself, in his *History of the Indies,* offered precisely this parallel for the New World event to which Vitoria had appealed to illustrate his seventh just title: Cortés's alliance with the Tlaxcalteca against the Aztecs.[171] But Las Casas put far more weight upon a much less seemly Roman precedent for this opportunistic alliance: Pompey's astute exploitation of Jewish factions in Jerusalem in order "to attack the city and enter it by force of arms and subjugate it tyrannically and make it tributary to the Roman Empire; and from then on and by that unjust and tyrannical method Judaea and its inhabitants, the Jews, lost their liberty." In sharp contrast, Peña's single-minded focus on the more edifying tableau of Flamininus proclaiming the "freedom of the Greeks" in 196 B.C. recalls and even intensifies Vitoria's rosier view of the process of Roman imperialism.

Juan de la Peña's inability to make up his mind about the Roman Empire may serve as a fitting close to this survey of the career of the Roman model in the school of Salamanca's contributions to the controversy of the Indies. As we have seen, he was not immune to the anti-Romanism of his associates Cano, Carranza, Soto, and Las Casas. Yet at the same time he shared with Vitoria—not to mention Sepúlveda!— a lingering respect for the Roman imperial achievement. His very confusion demonstrates the numinous fascination of the Roman model for those Spanish academics who strove to find an illuminating context within which to understand and judge the behavior of their compatriots in the New World. Writing in 1772, the brilliant English agricultural economist Arthur Young compared the British Empire of his day with the heyday of Spain's overseas empire: "We, at present, have her example to guide our reckoning; she had none by which to frame her conduct."[172] As we can see, Young's elegant and rather generous pronouncement is slightly inaccurate. Conquistadors and Dominican theologians alike had the example of Rome, if not to "frame their conduct," then at least to serve as a bracingly or depressingly familiar imperial alter ego.

CHAPTER THREE

The Model of Roman Imperialism in the Controversy of the Indies, Second Phase

Las Casas versus Sepúlveda

The climactic event in the controversy of the Indies was a debate in which the principal contestants not only never appeared together in the same room at the same time, but never even read each other's most substantial expositions.[1] This debate between Bartolomé de las Casas and Juan Ginés de Sepúlveda in Valladolid in 1550–51 was not only oblique; it was also inconclusive, for the failure of some of the judges to submit an opinion left the final verdict in doubt. True, this did mean that Sepúlveda never secured permission to publish his defense of Spain's wars in the Indies—the *Democrates secundus* remained unpublished until 1892. And yet the judges' dereliction of duty also meant that Las Casas was engaging in wishful thinking when he declared, in the preface to the Latin version of the text he had earlier read aloud in Valladolid, that the commission "judged that the expeditions, which in Spain we call conquests, are evil, unlawful, and unjust, and, therefore, ought to be altogether outlawed in the future."[2] In fact, the king's moratorium on future conquests pending the debate's outcome quickly fell into abeyance. And yet the Valladolid junta has never lost its fascination as an evidently unparalleled instance of an imperial power at its height sponsoring a probing and often passionate public disputation about the legitimacy of its own overseas conquests.

Part of the enduring impact of this debate derives from the forceful personalities and colorful backgrounds of the contenders. For their passionate contempt for each other could not obscure the fact that Sepúlveda and Las Casas were in one way impressively alike: they both brought to the debate the atmosphere of a wider and livelier world than that inhabited by the Dominican academics who precipitated and supervised the debate in Valladolid and whose pronouncements on the Indies we have explored in the last chapter. By 1550 Las Casas had spent some thirty-five of his sixty-six years in the New World, and this conferred upon his views an authority that clearly impressed his listeners. It was one thing to say, as Domingo de Soto had said in his *Relectio de dominio* sixteen years earlier, that peaceful methods of evangelization were preferable to violent ones, for Christ had sent his disciples to preach "not like lions but like sheep in the midst of wolves."[3] It was quite another thing for Soto to be able to write in his précis of the Valladolid debate that the wars of conquest waged by the Spaniards in the New World made the natives "abhor and spit upon the kind of God who would allow such men to be, and hate the law that permits such behavior, and consider false the faith that they preach—as the bishop says, who has displayed his experience in the Indies."[4] Sepúlveda shared his judges' lack of firsthand American experience, but he too came from another world than they, and they were acutely and uncomfortably aware of this. In an acerbic exchange of letters with Melchor Cano a year before the debate, Sepúlveda launched into an encomium of Italy, where he had passed over twenty years of his life and where his writings received a warmer reception than they did in Spain. To this Cano testily responded, "Now it wearies and disgusts you to have been born in Spain! Those blessed Italians whom you praise so much would settle the case of the disputed book to your liking. But what can *I* say—a simple Spaniard who has scarcely been to Italy once?"[5] If the judges and audience of the Valladolid debate found Las Casas in many ways an intriguingly "Americanized" Spaniard ("más americano que europeo," Angel Losada has claimed), Sepúlveda was himself relatively exotic as, in Marcel Bataillon's phrase, "un Espagnol italianisé."[6]

Sepúlveda and the Romans before the Valladolid Debate

Born on his father's estate in Pozoblanco near Córdoba around 1490, Juan Ginés de Sepúlveda studied at Alcalá and Sigüenza (1510–15) before leaving Spain at the age of twenty-five upon being elected to a scholarship at the Colegio de San Clemente, the Spanish college at Bologna.[7] Here he encountered two mentors who decisively shaped his mental outlook. One was the celebrated, if theologically suspect, philosopher Pietro Pomponazzi, who, though Greekless himself, inspired in his more linguistically gifted Spanish pupil a love of Aristotle destined to result in the Latin translations of Greek philosophical texts upon which Sepúlveda's chief claim to scholarly distinction came to rest. The other mentor whom he met in these years was a patron and frequent visitor of the Spanish College, Alberto Pio, prince of Carpi, nephew of Pico della Mirandola and tutee and later patron of the great Venetian humanist scholar and printer Aldus Manutius (Aldo Manuzio). An industrious collector of intellectuals and writers, Pio was delighted to "acquire" Sepúlveda, who spent much of the period from 1522 to 1525 in the court of Carpi. There his training as a Hellenist was deepened by association with the prince, who had been trained in Greek scholarship not only by Aldus but also by the distinguished Cretan scholar Marcus Musurus, who had helped oversee the court's collection of nearly 150 Greek codices.[8] Accompanying Pio to Rome in 1526, Sepúlveda received from Clement VII the commission to translate into Latin Alexander of Aphrodisias's commentary on Aristotle's *Metaphysics* (or, to be more precise, the commentary of Alexander on the first four books and the spurious commentaries on the last eight). An unwelcome break from this formidable task was his experience of the 1527 sack of Rome by imperial forces, when he found himself, as a Spaniard, expelled from his refuge in the Castel Sant' Angelo on the orders of Cardinal Orsini. Not long after this, Sepúlveda decamped to Naples, where he soon had to be rescued from the famine of the 1528 siege by none other than the celebrated commentator on Aquinas and general of the Dominican Order, Tommaso de Vio, Cardinal Cajetan (Gaetano), who brought him to Gaeta to assist him in interpreting passages in the Greek New Testament.

In August 1529 Sepúlveda was one of a distinguished party sent by Clement VII to greet the emperor upon his landing at Genoa. He then took part in the emperor's splendid and elaborately staged *adventus* into Bologna for his papal coronation—an event we have cited in the last chapter as the most impressive of Charles's ceremonial evocations of ancient Roman glory. As his contribution to the occasion, Sepúlveda composed an eloquent *Exhortation to Charles V to Make War upon the Turks,* which he published in Bologna at the end of the year. He spent the next few years in Rome, where in 1535, after the death of his papal patron, Clement VII, he accepted the emperor's offer of the post of official chronicler, with the additional honorary benefice of "chaplain" (Sepúlveda had been ordained as a priest by at least 1529). He returned to Spain the next year in the emperor's company, after an absence of two decades. Here, dividing his time between Valladolid and his beloved native Pozoblanco, he devoted himself to a number of ambitious projects: a chronicle in thirty books of the reign of Charles V, an elegant Latin account of the conquest of Mexico *(De rebus Hispanorum ad novum terrarum orbem Mexicumque gestis,* also called *De orbe novo),* a translation into Latin of Aristotle's *Politics,* and a number of shorter treatises, one of them the notorious *Democrates secundus.*

Sepúlveda's long immersion in Italian humanist culture would in itself lead us to expect that his view of classical antiquity in general and of ancient Rome in particular would be more enthusiastic than that of the Spanish Dominican professors whose views we have explored in the last chapter. Such a predisposition would have been intensified by his eventual association with the court of Charles V and his incorporation into the imperial propaganda establishment.[9] But a third factor appears to have invigorated Sepúlveda's enthusiasm for the ancient Romans from the beginning of his career as a writer. This was his consistent opposition to the views of Erasmus and his associates, a hostility he shared with—and presumably imbibed from—the distinguished biblical exegete Diego López de Zúñiga, whom he had known at Alcalá, and also his first patron, Alberto Pio. Zúñiga and Pio both devoted much of the time and energy of their last years to increasingly bitter controversies with Erasmus, and Sepúlveda was deeply involved in these quarrels.[10] On his deathbed in 1530, Zúñiga sent for Sepúlveda and entrusted him with his final criticisms of Erasmus, bidding him not to publish them but to send them directly to their target. Sepúlveda gladly complied, taking the opportunity to correct some geographical errors Erasmus had committed in his writings, thereby earning from the great man the title of "the most boastful of the Spaniards."[11] His involvement in Pio's quarrel with Erasmus was even deeper. Upon the posthumous publication of Pio's final volley in March 1531, Erasmus dashed off a lengthy and bitter *Apologia,* in which he claimed, apparently erroneously, that much of Pio's tract had been in fact written by Sepúlveda. Exactly a year after his late patron's polemic appeared, Sepúlveda answered Erasmus's *Apologia* with his own *Antapologia pro Alberto Pio Principi Carpensi in Erasmum Roterodamum.* Though later ridiculed by Las Casas as a maladroit attempt to help his late patron's "hunt for glory from an attack on Erasmus," this work displayed a moderation of tone that the final writings of the protagonists had conspicuously lacked, and Sepúlveda and Erasmus in fact managed to sustain a civil correspondence, usually on questions of Greek philology, until the latter's death in 1536.[12] The objections that Zúñiga and Pio raised in print to the views of Erasmus were primarily theological. Both saw him as essentially crypto-Lutheran, though Zúñiga was also critical of his biblical scholarship. Still, it is plausible that Sepúlveda's deep and early association with prominent anti-Erasmians would have influenced his views on other issues. In particular, the pacifism of Erasmus and his distinguished Spanish associate Juan Luis Vives seems to have stimulated a sharp counterresponse in Sepúlveda, and it is in this context that the Roman model came into play.[13]

Erasmus considered the imperial phase of ancient Roman history a prime example of the dangers of unlimited autocracy and wars of territorial expansion, and he was profoundly distrustful of the Roman legacy in modern Europe, particularly in the form of the "Holy Roman Empire," despite his general respect for Charles V in the first decade of his reign. In the lengthy essay on the adage *Scarabaeus aquilam quaerit* ("The grub pursues the eagle"), which he added to his *Adagia* in 1515, he alluded to Maximilian's fiscal demands in the Low Countries by referring to "Roman eagles, who plunder the people without end and without measure." In the same essay he objected to the common practice of indoctrinating young princes with "childish fables, or histories worse than these, from which the youthful spirit . . . imbibes an admiration of and a zeal . . . to emulate some pestilent leader, such as Julius Caesar."[14] James D. Tracy has noted that, "in contrast to many humanists"—and Spanish conquistadors, we might add—"Erasmus regarded Caesar not as a glorious but as a 'most pestilent' leader."[15] During the papacy of Julius II (1503–13), he frequently drew parallels between the two Julii, the warlike pope and the Roman warlord: Caesar "too was once *pontifex maximus*," he wrote in a satirical poem; "he too arrived at tyranny by a path of crime."[16] In his 1504 *Panegyricus* addressed to Philip the Fair, archduke of Austria and father of Charles V, "of seven references to Caesar," Tracy has noted, "only one reflects something of the conventional admiration for this hero of antiquity."[17] Erasmus's later works—including the *Institutio principis christiani* addressed to the future Charles V—sustain this negative image of Caesar.

Juan Luis Vives eloquently contributed to this vilification of Julius Caesar in a peculiar declamation, the *Pompeius fugiens*, composed in April 1519 in the midst of the intense maneuvering destined to secure Charles's election as emperor two months later. Here the defeated Pompey lamented, in the quasi-Christian language of a Republican martyr, that the little birds, the nightingales, the ants have their nests, but the

once great Pompey has no place of refuge, not even any safe haven to
send his wife to escape the clutches of "that Caesar . . . so impure and
ugly, adulterer of all the women of Rome!"[18] Much of this declamation
was given over to intense invective against "Caesar, universal pestilence
of the world," who had handed his country over "to the insatiable
greed of his pirates."[19] Not only was Caesar characterized here as a lust-
ful and grasping warlord, but his triumph was also implicitly identified
as a fatal turning point in Roman history. Passing in review the great
deeds of Republican worthies, Pompey asked, "Did those heroes do this
so that the state should finally fall into the servitude of Caesar?"[20]
Though Vives had declared in his preface that this work was devoted to
the theme of *contemptus mundi* and the ill will of fortune, it clearly had
political as well as moral implications, deflating as it did the Roman
imperial rhetoric of the court of the late Maximilian as well as the
laudatory hyperboles no doubt already beginning to be heard in the
entourage of the grandson who was maneuvering to succeed him. Fittingly enough, the same year that Vives composed this passionate
rhetorical attack upon Roman imperial autocracy he began work, at
Erasmus's request, on what proved to be upon its publication in
1521–22 a very widely circulated edition of Augustine's *City of God*,
with a commentary that extended Augustine's bitter assessment of the
violence and hunger for glory of the ancient Roman Empire to the
plight of a contemporary Europe "bathed in floods of mutual blood."[21]

In stark contrast to these pacifistic and anti-Roman views of Erasmus and Vives, Sepúlveda composed in the court of Carpi and published in Rome in 1523 his dialogue *Gonsalus* in defense of the pursuit
of glory *(De appetenda gloria dialogus, qui inscribitur Gonsalus)*.[22]
This elegant conversation among three Spanish warrior nobles had a
double polemical aim. On the one hand, it was designed as an answer
to "those who have written books to show that glory ought to be condemned," who contended that "through the quest for glory there have
often arisen wars more pernicious for the human race than any
plague."[23] Such people, who after all were themselves seeking glory as
writers, needed to be shown that the pursuit of true glory is virtually
synonymous with public service and is in fact a step on the path to the
summum bonum.[24] Though Sepúlveda seemed to be referring to recent
critics of worldly glory, among them pious inculcators of *contemptus
mundi* (a declared theme, we recall, of Vives's *Pompeius fugiens*), it is
hard to escape the suspicion that his most formidable target here was

none other than Augustine, whose attacks upon glory in general and Roman glory-seeking in particular had achieved renewed currency with the publication of Vives's edition and commentary the year before. In addition, the dialogue served the patriotic purpose of celebrating Spanish military glory as worthy of taking its place alongside that of the ancient Romans. Thus, the speakers regularly paired incidents from Roman antiquity with recent Spanish parallels: if glory incited Regulus to a spectacular demonstration of his *fides,* the very same could be said of García Gómez Carrillo, while the *temperantia* of Scipio was matched by that of the dialogue's eponymous Cordoban hero Gonzalo Fernández.[25] It is true that Sepúlveda confined himself here to heroes of the Roman Republic, and he was willing to link Caesar with Sulla and Marius as examples of the decline that sets in when "hatred, greed, or some other pleasure" usurps the place of that pure quest for glory which strengthens and expands a state.[26] But this brief and understated concession to Erasmus and Vives did little to dim the bright colors in which the dialogue painted the model of Roman military glory for the benefit of Spanish prestige in a Europe that often looked upon Spanish ambitions with fear or contempt.

Six years after the publication of Sepúlveda's *Gonsalus,* Vives renewed his assault upon the destructive effects of the prestige of ancient Roman imperialism and the ancient and modern pursuit of glory in his lengthy treatise *De concordia et discordia in humano genere.* This work was dedicated to none other than Charles V himself and published in the very year (1529) in which he received his imperial crown with full Roman pageantry from the hand of Clement VII in Bologna.[27] This tract passionately denounced discord as the font of human misery and the destroyer of the unity that was the original and still yearned-for state of the human race. In the first book, Vives identified the love of glory as a major source of disastrous public discord, and he singled out the Romans, with their elaborate and all-pervasive cultural celebration of martial virtues, as prominent offenders in the human race's sordid pursuit of glory. "They composed epics and wrote histories, erected triumphal arches and statues with encomiastic inscriptions in the most frequented parts of their cities, and from this came the renown and the nobility that passed from sons to grandsons."[28] Vives was particularly harsh on the pernicious power of exemplary heroes marketed by the poets. Thanks to Homer, Achilles became a model for Alexander the Great, and Alexander in turn inspired Pompey and Julius Caesar to embark upon their disastrous collision course in the pursuit of personal glory.[29]

Especially interesting is Vives's denunciation of the use of treaties and alliances as pretexts for making war. Not only do princes and powerful states weave webs of alliances designed less to defend allies than to invade other states, but they also transform into pretexts for further wars the natural alliances that their enemies have contracted through consanguinity or proximity.

> There was no other pretext for the Roman people to take arms against many peoples of Italy than that they had contributed to the armies of their enemies. This was the same reason they made war against the Numantines, and the same reason they made war against the Britons, even though those peoples' alliances were not made to harm the Romans but, as is often the case, because of neighborliness, as the Britons came to the aid of the Gauls since they were of the same race, and the Numantines came to the aid of the Saguntines.[30]

The harsh light that Vives here casts upon Roman territorial expansion through the manipulation of treaties contrasts sharply with the benign view of Roman expansion via alliances that Vitoria would offer some ten years later in his *Relectio de Indis*. We also see here a foreshadowing of a strategy that we have seen in Melchor Cano and will see also in Las Casas. For Vives's specific historical references here are slyly pointed. The questioning of the Romans' right to conquer the states of Italy was particularly bold in a work dedicated to an "emperor of the Romans" in the very year in which he received amid Roman pomp not only the imperial crown but also the "crown of Italy." The allusion to the Britons' understandable aid to their fellow Celts, the Gauls, would surely have resonated with readers who observed with alarm the recent rapprochement of Henry VIII, unhappily married to the aunt of the emperor (Catherine of Aragon), with the hated French. Even more arresting is Vives's reference to the Numantines and Saguntines. Sepúlveda himself had referred to these Spaniards in his *Gonsalus* of 1523; their honorable fall, he averred, spread the glory of "Hispania nostra."[31] Unlike Sepúlveda, however, Vives emphasized the status of these Iberian cities as victims of Roman imperialism, a topos destined for rich development in future decades.[32] Interestingly enough, shortly after mentioning these victims of Roman imperialism, Vives alluded to the transatlantic victims of contemporary Spanish imperialism. As a specific example of discord arising from the obstacles that geographical distance erects to mutual comprehension, Vives cited "the attitude that the men of our hemisphere display in the recently discovered New World toward those Indians whom they do not consider human."[33] Thus, in the eyes of Vives, wars of imperial conquest, whether conducted by ancient Romans in Italy and Spain or by modern Spaniards in America, were the distressing signs of a fallen world. Only a sincere turning to the teachings of Christ could set the human race back on the path to its primal state of joyous concord.

When Sepúlveda revisited the Colegio de San Clemente at Bologna in the entourage of Clement VII in December 1531, he discovered that pacifist sentiments of this sort were spreading among the students there, several of whom denied that it was possible to be both a soldier and a good Christian. Out of his discussions with these students emerged the dialogue *Democrates primus* (its official name was *De convenientia militaris disciplinae cum christiana religione dialogus qui inscribitur Democrates*), eventually published in Rome in 1535, the only one of his works to achieve a contemporary Spanish translation (Seville, 1541).[34] Conducted in the Vatican Gardens by Sepúlveda's mouthpiece, the Greek Democrates; the quasi-Lutheran student Leopoldus; and the old Spanish soldier Alphonsus, this fictive conversation attempted to establish a harmonization of the *vita activa* and the *vita contemplativa* and at the same time a balance between Christian and pagan (Peripatetic, Stoic, Ciceronian civic humanist) values. "And herein," notes J. A. Fernández-Santamaría, "lies precisely a source of Sepúlveda's uniqueness: his ability to remain a theologian while retaining intact his humanist outlook, and vice versa."[35] And yet, though the *Democrates primus* was, like Sepúlveda's earlier dialogue, the *Gonsalus,* a riposte to the pacifistic ideas of Erasmus and Vives, it generally lacked the earlier dialogue's celebration of classical Rome as a model for contemporary Europeans. In fact, one of its few references to Roman history—a brief encomium of the republican Rome of such honorably poor heroes as Regulus and Cincinnatus before it was "destroyed by the arrogance and riches of Crassus, Pompey, and Caesar"—parallels an equally conventional passage in the third book of Vives's *De concordia et discordia*.[36] It was, rather, the explosively controversial sequel to this dialogue that renewed the celebration of the model of Roman valor that had permeated the *Gonsalus.*

The Romans in Sepúlveda's Democrates secundus

Sepúlveda's composition of the dialogue *Democrates secundus sive de iustis causis belli apud Indos* (also often called the *Democrates alter*) was apparently a product of the uproar generated in the New World and in Spain itself by the passage in 1542 of the imperial legislation known as the New Laws. Profoundly indebted to the tireless petitioning and networking of Las Casas, these laws were simultaneously a drastic limitation of the power of the colonial elites and a forceful assertion of direct royal authority in the Indies. They prohibited the enslavement of even rebellious or recalcitrant Indians captured in war, severely restricted the use of natives as beasts of burden, deprived certain abusive encomenderos of their Indian laborers, and denied encomiendas to prelates and royal officials. Most galling of all to the settlers was Law Number 35: "Henceforth no encomienda is to be granted to anyone, and when the present holders of encomiendas die, their Indians will revert to the Crown."[37] Immediately rendered moot in Peru by the widespread resistance culminating in the revolt of Gonzalo Pizarro, in Mexico the New Laws were passionately opposed by many religious and government officials, and in 1544 the provincials of the religious orders there and representatives of the *ayuntamiento* (city council) of Mexico City set off for the court of the emperor to lodge their protests on behalf of the encomenderos. According to a source close to Sepúlveda, the arrival of this delegation initiated "much talk about the justice of the conquest of the Indies," and this in turn inspired Francisco García de Loaysa, archbishop of Seville and president of the Council of the Indies, to urge Sepúlveda to supplement his reflections on proper Christian warfare in the *Democrates primus* with a more specific and topical defense of the justice of the wars in the Indies.[38] The *argumentum* introducing Las Casas's Latin *Apologia* implied that Sepúlveda was in fact commissioned by agents of the encomenderos to "attack these new laws with all his might."[39] If so, the attack was somewhat oblique, for the *Democrates secundus* failed to mention the New Laws and referred to encomiendas only in passing; it focused squarely upon the justice of the original conquest.[40]

The longer and more systematic first book of the *Democrates secundus* begins with a recapitulation of a principal argument of the *Democrates primus:* just wars are permitted by natural law, and what is permitted by natural law is permitted also by divine law. The behavior of the Romans is cited approvingly in support of the principle that punishment of injuries done to a state constitutes a just cause of war: the Romans declared war on the Corinthians over Corinthian mistreatment of Roman ambassadors, just as the Spartans had avenged the mistreatment of their maidens at a Messenian festival. Such classical precedents as this, "Democrates" claimed, occurred "with the widespread approval of men, whose consensus is thought to be a law of nature."[41] The rest of this first book is devoted to a discussion of four main arguments in support of the justice of Spanish wars of conquest in the Indies: (1) the necessity of subduing by war, if no other means suffice, those "whose natural condition is such that they ought to obey others"; (2) the abolition of abominations such as cannibalism, devil worship, and human sacrifice; (3) the charitable duty of coming to the aid of innocent victims of oppression; and (4) the need to eliminate obstacles standing in the way of the preaching of the Gospel.[42]

It was in support of the first of these just causes of war against the Indians that Sepúlveda made his most impressive use of the Roman model, as a specific instance illustrating a principle derived from another sphere of the classical tradition, Greek philosophy. As readers of Lewis Hanke's arrestingly titled book *Aristotle and the American Indians* will recall, Sepúlveda based his views on the servile nature of the American Indians from the first book of Aristotle's *Politics*. Indeed, it appears that the *Democrates secundus* was in some sense the *parergon* with which, as was his long-standing custom, he relaxed his mind during the labor of translating the *Politics* into Latin—a translation that appeared in Paris in 1548, as the controversy over the dialogue was getting into high gear. We have seen that the *licenciado* Gregorio had introduced Aristotle's doctrine of natural slavery into the Spanish debate of the Indies as early as 1512, during the uproar greeting Montesinos's Advent sermon in Santo Domingo. But the Scottish theologian John Mair (Major), teaching at the University of Paris, had anticipated him in a commentary on Peter Lombard's *Sentences* published in 1510.[43] Vitoria, who had been in Paris at that time as a student at the Collège de Saint-Jacques, later faced—and then evaded—the Aristotelian argument in the first part of his *Relectio de Indis* of 1539.[44] Interestingly enough, Sepúlveda neglected to cite in his *Democrates secundus* the key Aristotelian passage that Mair, Gregorio, and Vitoria all explicitly quoted: "it is clear that some are by nature free and that others are slaves, for whom it is advantageous and just that they do a slave's job"

(1255a1–3). In a deft move, Sepúlveda substituted for this expected Aristotelian passage a biblical analogue, one cited by Aquinas in support of the principle that the conquered serve the victor: "he who is foolish will serve the wise" (Prov. 11:29).[45] In fact, of eighteen references to the *Politics* in the *Democrates secundus,* only three were offered in support of the doctrine of natural slavery. One is a reference to Aristotle's general principle that every composite entity has a dominant and a subordinate part.[46] The other two references are to a single passage, one brutally apt for Sepúlveda's aim of justifying wars against the Indians and the violent seizure of their political dominion and property:

> Therefore, the art of war also will be by nature in some sense an art of acquisition (κτητική)—since the art of hunting is a subcategory of the art of war that ought to be used against both beasts and those men who, though by nature fit to be ruled, prove unwilling, since this sort of war is just by nature.[47]

Whether or not Sepúlveda had before him a copy of Vitoria's *De Indis* when first composing the *Democrates secundus,* his citation of this striking passage constitutes an effective rebuttal to Vitoria's feeble claim that Aristotle did not endorse a violent subjection of "natural slaves" but only imagined a willing submission of the weak to the strong.[48] On the other hand, Sepúlveda was at pains to distinguish the philosophical concept of natural servitude from the legal and civic status of slavery. Cooperative Indians would share the fate assigned to the non-Canaanite enemies of the Israelites in Deuteronomy 20: they would "offer service under tribute" [sub tributo serviant], and they would receive (unspecified) better treatment as in the course of time they became more civilized *(humaniores)*—for the subjection of the natives was, of course, principally for their own good.[49] Only if they resisted the dominion of their "natural masters" would they become chattel slaves *(mancipia)* by right of war.

This, then, was the classical philosophical doctrine that Sepúlveda illustrated and confirmed by the classical historical example of Roman imperialism. Melchor Cano, we may recall, in his Alcalá relection of 1546, similarly juxtaposed Aristotle and the Romans as, in his view, equally specious support for the false doctrine that "a wise prince may subject barbarous nations to his laws." There appears to be no firm evidence that Cano had encountered Sepúlveda's dialogue before 1547, when his opinion as to its suitability for publication was solicited.[50] It is possible, then, that this appeal to the Roman Empire in support of the Aristotelian doctrine of natural slavery was at this time becoming almost as familiar as the Romans' traditional contribution to the argument for the world dominion of the emperor. Be that as it may, here is Sepúlveda's formulation of the general principle and the historical confirmation:

> Let it be established, therefore, with the authority of the wisest men, that it is just and natural for the wise, upright, and humane to rule over those who are unlike themselves. For the Romans had this justification for ruling over many peoples with a lawful and just rule, as Thomas mentions in the book *De regimine principis*.[51]

At this point, Sepúlveda turned to Augustine, the principal authority cited by "Aquinas" (that is, of course, his continuator Ptolemy of Lucca), perpetrating upon Augustine's text an impressively audacious distortion of the bishop of Hippo's actual attitude toward Roman rule. Beginning with a deviously loose quotation of a passage near the beginning of chapter 13 of book 5, he wrote:

> "In order to overcome the serious vices of many peoples, God granted the greatest and most illustrious empire to the Romans, who for the sake of glory restrained the lust for wealth and many other vices"— that is, in order that by means of the excellent laws they observed and the virtue in which they excelled they might abolish and correct the barbaric customs and vices of many peoples.[52]

While Sepúlveda did accurately reproduce Augustine's passing reference to God's use of the Romans as scourges to punish the sins of other peoples ("ad domanda gravia mala multarum gentium"), he suppressed the fact that Augustine's main emphasis here, as in the surrounding passages, centered squarely upon the sinfulness of the Romans *themselves,* in particular their addiction to the vice of the pursuit of worldly glory. If, Augustine wrote, they were able to "rein in their lust for wealth and many other vices" [pecuniae cupiditatem et multa alia vitia comprimentes], they did so only "to favor that one particular vice, i.e. love of praise" [pro isto uno vitio, id est amore laudis]. But Sepúlveda's gloss on his doctored quotation insinuated that Augustine was praising the Romans for restraining, not their own greed and other vices, but those of other nations—Augustine's word *vitia*, originally referring to repressed *Roman* vices, being echoed in Sepúlveda's adjacent gloss by the same word denoting the vices of the "barbarians." Furthermore, Sepúlveda entirely suppressed from the quotation itself Augustine's explicit denunciation of the love of praise as a vice. Augustine had in fact proceeded to devote the rest of this chapter and all of the next to branding love of praise as a vice *(vitium)*, a plague *(pestis)*, an impurity *(immundia)*, while his self-styled follower Sepúlveda proceeded to make precisely the opposite point in an encomium on glory reprising the dialogue *Gonsalus*, which he had composed at Carpi some two decades earlier.

> For if those Romans who were considered upright and prudent—men like men like Curius, Fabricius, the Scipios, Maximus, Metellus, and the Catos—sought glory, they should not be summarily assumed to have shrunk from virtue. . . . Thus, no law forbids us to seek glory—that is, good fame—since it is a worthy and most excellent thing and often a great aid to virtue. For, as the Philosopher says (*Ethics* 10), the hunger for noble things is praiseworthy—though it ought to be sought rationally, not so much as an end of action as a cause of virtue. And this happens best if virtue itself also is referred, in accord with the precepts of Christian philosophy, to God as the supreme good. Therefore, Augustine demonstrates more clearly in another passage [Epistle 138, to Marcellinus, sec. 17] the fact that it was through the virtues of the ancient Romans that their empire grew by the providence of God. He writes back to Marcellinus thus [ibid.]: "We tolerate, if can't correct, those who wish the state, which the early Romans established and expanded through their virtues, to stand with its vices unpunished." And a little later he says, "God thus showed in the case of the most wealthy and famous Romans how powerful civil virtues are, even without true religion."[53]

Despite his game attempt to enlist Augustine in support of the values of the *civitas terrena*, Sepúlveda's celebration of glory and of the Roman heroes who pursued it bears the unmistakable stamp of the Italian humanist circles among which he had spent most of his adult life, and it was bound to alienate the Dominican theologians to whose judgment his dialogue was duly submitted. Indeed, it is perfectly plausible that Sepúlveda's egregious distortion of Augustine's argument in the fifth book of the *City of God* was the irritant that finally induced Domingo de Soto, in his *De iustitia et iure* of 1553, to return at last to Augustine's actual text and finally explode its dubious utility as validation for the Roman model of imperialism.

Predictably enough, Sepúlveda immediately balanced this encomium of the Romans with one extolling their modern counterparts, the Spaniards. After all, he notoriously remarked, the New World natives were as inferior to the Spaniards "as are children to adults, women to men, the cruel and inhuman to the very gentle, the prodigiously intemperate to the self-controlled, and finally"—in a climax erased in the most complete manuscript—"I would almost say monkeys to men."[54] In support of this contention, Sepúlveda offered up a historical medley of Spanish virtues and virtuous heroes. In some cases, his lauded Spaniards were literally identical to certain famous Romans—to wit, the Hispano-Roman writers Lucan, Silius Italicus, and the two Senecas. But his contribution to the hoary genre of the *laus Hispaniae* did not omit the opportunity to cast the Romans in the role of the formidable enemy who had allowed Spanish valor to display itself many centuries back, "in the Numantine war and in those waged under the leadership of Viriathus and Sertorius, when great armies of the Romans were routed by a small band of Spaniards and sent under the yoke."[55] Sepúlveda thus made his own modest contribution to the growing identification that many Spaniards of the mid–sixteenth century felt with the pre-Roman Iberian peoples, a phenomenon whose bearing on the controversy of the Indies we shall be exploring in the next chapter.

Having defended the justice of the wars against the Indians with the help of "the example of the Romans *(Romanorum exemplo)*, whose rule over other peoples was just and legitimate"[56] (in the words of the fictive interlocutor Leopoldus in his concluding summary of the first book), Sepúlveda-Democrates proceeded in the second book of the dialogue to offer the Romans as superb models of restraint in warfare for the Spanish conquistadors, who should bear in mind that it is often better not to exercise their strict legal right to kill and enslave the recalcitrant natives of the New World.[57] Again Sepúlveda cited Augustine as his authority for the claim that the Romans were "in bellis gerendis . . . moderatissimi," contenting himself this time with marginal references to letters from Augustine to Boniface and Marcellinus, as well as, again, to the fifth book of the *City of God*, chapters 12 and 13.[58] The letter to Count Boniface, governor of Africa, was presumably number 189, writ-

ten in 418 as a brief essay on the way for a Christian soldier to achieve
eternal salvation. The author of the *Democrates primus* would have
been especially drawn to a letter built around the encouraging admoni-
tion, "Do not suppose that someone who serves in martial arms cannot
be pleasing to God" (sec. 4). Since peace is the goal of war, Augustine
went on, "be a man of peace even when waging war," for "pity is owed
to the conquered or captured" (sec. 6). This advice to a Christian
Roman general did not, of course, imply that such moderation was in
fact standard Roman practice, though it appears that this is how
Sepúlveda chose to take it. The letter to Marcellinus he had in mind
seems to be number 138, to which he had alluded in his encomium on
glory in book 1. This letter, sent in 412 to the imperial agent sent to settle the Catholic-Donatist dispute, was one of several that Augustine sent
Marcellinus in response to pagan calumnies against the Christians.
These letters eventually led to the writing of the *City of God,* which
Augustine appropriately dedicated to Marcellinus. In section 9 of letter
138 Augustine responded to the charge that the Christians' duty to love
their enemies and to turn the other cheek made them poor defenders of
the empire. His strategy here was to seize upon the moderation in warfare of the pre-Christian Romans. In particular, there was the famous
clementia of Julius Caesar, which had caused Cicero to say, either in
praise or flattery, that he forgot nothing save the wrongs that were done
to him. If the great Roman generals were such gentle souls, Augustine
asks, why fear the supposed pacifism of the Christians? Of course,
Augustine was less offering a considered assessment of Roman military
practice than he was deftly scoring a debating point, but Sepúlveda was
happy to exploit further an Augustinian epistle that had already proved
useful to him in this dialogue.

   Sepúlveda now proceeded to offer a capsule account of Roman
imperial practice as proof of their moderation: (1) some defeated states
were reduced to provinces and subjected to mild tribute; (2) others were
left with their autonomy; (3) others, like Carthage upon the insistence of
Cato the Elder, were utterly destroyed. As the personal embodiment of
Roman moderation in warfare, Sepúlveda offered the same general
whom Augustine had cited in his letter to Marcellinus: Julius Caesar.
Caesar, Sepúlveda claimed, treated his defeated Gallic enemies *perhu-
maniter* in general, though the perfidy and rebellion of the Aduatuci and
Veneti did necessitate harsher treatment. This brief but emphatic
encomium of the bête noire of Erasmus and Vives marked a new depar-

ture for Sepúlveda. While his references to Caesar in the earlier dia-
logues *Gonsalus* and *Democrates primus* had been perfunctorily negative, now that Sepúlveda was royal chronicler and also the Latin historian of the deeds of that modern Caesar Cortés, he was happy to
celebrate the Roman warlord as *imperator prudentissimus.* Finally,
near the end of the second book, he yet again held up the Romans as *viri
prudentissimi* whose moderation in imperial rule should serve as a
model for paternalistic Spanish "caretakers" of the homunculi of the
New World.[59]

The exemplarity of the Romans in the *Democrates secundus* thus
manifested itself in two ways. First, their natural superiority to the peoples whom they conquered constituted, in accord with the Aristotelian
doctrine of natural slavery, a solid title to imperial rule, a title that modern Spaniards shared by right of a similar superiority. Second, Roman
moderation in the conduct of wars of conquest served as a model for
Spaniards in the Indies. If the first Roman-Spanish equivalence was presented as a simple datum of cultural history, the second was offered
with at least a hint of exhortation, the Spaniards being implicitly urged
to emulate the moderation that their fellow "natural masters" the
Romans had displayed in the conduct of their imperial conquests. But
while Sepúlveda's Romans provided modern Spaniards with the reas-
surance of a kindred cultural preeminence and with the stimulus of
exemplary moderation, what they most strikingly did *not* provide was
the basis of a legal claim to the Indies. Imperial chronicler though he
may have been, Sepúlveda scrupulously avoided the attractive but powerfully contested claim that the emperor was lord of the whole world, a
claim traditionally bolstered by an appeal to God's purported bestowing of world dominion upon the ancient Romans as a reward for their
virtues. In fact, the emperor was a far dimmer figure in the *Democrates
secundus* than was that unsettlingly independent Caesar-emulator
Cortés, whose boldness in the conquest of Mexico was offered as proof
of the innate superiority of Spaniards to the *natura servi* of the New
World.[60] Whether or not it was in fact commissioned by conquistador-
encomenderos rankled by the passage of the New Laws, the dialogue
catered to their interests and self-esteem at least as much as it reinforced
the emperor's own title to the Indies—and his authority over those same
encomenderos. Charles's natural antipathy to any amplification of the
prestige of the conquistadors, particularly in these years of the revolt of
Gonzalo Pizarro in Peru (1546–48), helps to explain his striking reluc-

tance to champion his publicist's eloquent defense of the conquest when it encountered fierce opposition from the disciples of Vitoria.[61]

Though our sources for the sequence of events leading up to the Valladolid junta are not in complete agreement, there is no dispute about the centrality of the Dominicans in the blocking of the publication of the *Democrates secundus*.[62] Freshly arrived from the New World in mid-1547, Bartolomé de las Casas discovered that the Royal Council of Castile was obeying the instructions of a royal *cédula* to determine the fitness of Sepúlveda's book for publication. Apprised of its contents, Las Casas at once forcefully intervened and engineered the referral of the question to the theological faculties of Salamanca and Alcalá. After deliberations carried on between the fall of 1547 and the spring of 1548, the Dominicans at these universities recommended that the dialogue not be published, though they never formally declared their specific reasons for this recommendation. Sepúlveda assumed that the principal orchestrator of this decision was Melchor Cano, Prima Professor of Theology at Salamanca. Adding insult to injury was the rumor that Cano was boasting of his coup in the university *aula*, "amid youthful listeners" [inter adolescentes auditores]. Accordingly, he fired off a bitter missive to Cano in the last days of 1548. After a delay of some months, Cano responded at considerable length, denying the rumor of his boasting, deprecating the assumption that his was the leading role in the affair, and offering a tantalizing indication of his main objection to Sepúlveda's dialogue. "Since Fray Francisco de Vitoria, a doctor scarcely lacking in fame and one not utterly to be held in contempt *(doctor neque incelebris neque omnino contemnendus)*, had argued copiously on the subject, taking a view contrary to yours, it was no wonder that we would take a doubtful view of your opinion, since we had weighty arguments against it."[63]

In a response to Cano's response, Sepúlveda suggested that it was his use of the Aristotelian doctrine of the natural slave that had been the true stumbling block for the theologians of Alcalá and Salamanca. Now, while it is certainly true that Vitoria did deny the applicability of this doctrine to the inhabitants of the Indies at the end of the first part of his *Relectio de Indis*, it is also clear, as Anthony Pagden has sensibly pointed out, that "the fact that Sepúlveda had not read, or not heeded, Vitoria would hardly have been sufficient to refuse a work an *imprimatur*." I would suggest that there is an intriguing possibility that Cano's somewhat puzzling conjuration of the potent name of his late

master had a hidden significance—perhaps even to some extent hidden
from himself. We recall that in the spring of 1546, while still teaching at
Alcalá, Cano had given vent to a harsh criticism of the *argumenta frivola* of certain *iurisperiti* who justified Spanish military intrusion into the
Indies on the basis of the principle of charity. While some scholars (such
as Pereña and Hanke) have assumed that Cano's target here was
Sepúlveda, it is most doubtful that Cano would have been willing to
dignify the Cordoban humanist with the title of *iurisperitus,* for to the
Dominicans he was a rhetorician and man of letters, not a theologian or
jurist. Furthermore, this was well over a year before the *Democrates
secundus* was sent to Cano and his fellow theologians for consideration.
Of course, there is no proving that Cano had not seen a copy earlier, but
given the fact that even Las Casas never secured access to the dialogue,
we should probably not exaggerate the work's availability. As I argued
in the last chapter, the startling fact of the matter is that the man whose
views most closely resembled those that Cano was dismissing as "frivolous" in 1546 was none other than his revered master Vitoria. Indeed,
we have seen that the "frivolous" argument from charity undergirded
seven of Vitoria's eight "legitimate titles." Striking confirmation of the
fact that Dominican critics of the conquest found Vitoria's *De Indis*
something of an embarrassment is offered by the Latin version of Las
Casas's presentation to the Valladolid junta. Responding to Sepúlveda's
disturbing claim that Vitoria's position fundamentally supported his
own, Las Casas did admit that, in consenting to consider certain "legitimate titles" after his powerful denunciation of the false titles, Vitoria
had argued "rather sloppily" [remisius], for he wished "to soften what
seemed to the Emperor's party *(Caesarianis)* to have been too harshly
stated."[64] It is not, then, implausible that Cano, too, had been
sufficiently troubled by certain implications of Vitoria's arguments to
disburden himself of the stinging rebuke in his Alcalá relection. Furthermore, we may recall that Cano sharply diverged from Vitoria's positive assessment of ancient Roman imperialism. Now it was but a few
months later, in August 1546, that Vitoria died, and the disciple swiftly
chosen to succeed him was, of course, none other than Melchor Cano.
Cano was, then, sitting in his late master's chair when called upon to
revisit the "matter of the Indies" by pronouncing upon Sepúlveda's elegant defense of the wars against the Indians. One does not have to be a
Freudian to detect a certain Oedipal guilt in Cano's insistence that the
main sin Sepúlveda had committed was deviation from the teachings of

Cano's late master and predecessor, a *dux optimus,* as Cano would later call him, whose students owe all their own learning, wisdom, and eloquence to their faithful obedience to his precepts.[65]

As his acrimonious exchange with Cano showed, Sepúlveda was not about to endure in silent resignation what he regarded as the outrageously biased pronouncements of Alcalá and Salamanca. Not only did he send a Latin summary of his arguments to Rome for publication— this *Apologia* appeared at last on May 1, 1550—but he also circulated summaries in Spanish.[66] It was to one of these that Las Casas owed his knowledge of Sepúlveda's points; his request to Prince Philip that he be allowed to inspect a copy of the full dialogue was apparently never granted.[67] Las Casas at once set to work to compose a lengthy refutation in Spanish, a work we know most fully through a Latin translation, produced probably in the early 1550s, and also through Domingo de Soto's Spanish summary, published by Las Casas, without license, in 1552. The intensity and widening publicity of this dispute, along with the pressure of the encomenderos' increasingly successful resistance to the New Laws and their campaign to secure the perpetuity of their encomiendas, induced the Council of the Indies to urge the king "to order a meeting of learned men, theologians and jurists, with others according to your pleasure, to discuss and consider concerning the manner in which these conquests should be carried on in order that they may be made justly and with security of conscience."[68] Accordingly, the emperor issued a remarkable series of *cédulas* decreeing a moratorium on further expeditions of discovery and conquest *(entradas)* pending the outcome of the meeting to be held in mid-1550. Both Sepúlveda and Las Casas requested and received permission to address the junta, and so the dispute was brought into focus around the book that had principally precipitated it.

Las Casas and the Romans before the Valladolid Debate

While much attention has been devoted to Las Casas's arguments against Sepúlveda's use of the ideas of Aristotle, "a pagan burning in Hell,"[69] his attacks upon Sepúlveda's exploitation of the Roman imperial model have received less attention than their vituperative intensity merit.[70] For the views that Las Casas expressed about the Romans after his permanent return from the New World in 1547 constitute an impres-

sive chapter in the history of the "anticlassical tradition." But the hostility that Las Casas began to unleash upon the Roman model during
the controversy with Sepúlveda was not only a startling intensification
of the critical attitude of Melchor Cano and Domingo de Soto, it also
contrasted with what we can discern of Las Casas's own earlier views
on the Romans.

In fact, as recently as 1542 Las Casas had himself invoked the
Roman model in a relatively positive way in a memorial to Charles V.
In this bold document Las Casas urged the emperor to confiscate half
the property of the conquistadors and to plow this income into peaceful
colonial ventures in the Indies. "And thus Your Majesty will create the
greatest and most celebrated settlement in the whole world, the like of
which the Romans never managed to create. They neither did nor could
do what Your Majesty will be able to do and will do."⁷¹ This piece of
strategic flattery was probably indebted to a passage (quoted by Las
Casas in his *Historia de las Indias*) from a letter Columbus had sent to
the Catholic Monarchs during his tumultuous third voyage, October 18,
1498. Responding to those who criticized the expense of outfitting his
voyages, the Admiral asked to be told by "someone who has read the
history of the Greeks and Romans if they ever with so little cost
extended their sovereignty as extensively as Your Majesties have
extended that of Spain with the Indies."⁷² But Las Casas's adaptation of
these words in an attempt to stymie the depredations of Columbus's
brutal successors would have taken on a special resonance in light of the
conquistadors' habit of vying with the ancients, for it neatly turns
against them precisely that topos of "besting the Romans" that they
were in the habit of applying to themselves. In Las Casas's deft use of
this motif, it would not be the violent and greedy conquistadors who
would allow Spain in the New World to surpass Rome in the Old
World; it would be peaceful farmers, traders, and, of course, priests
who would do so.

Nevertheless, in this same year of 1542 Las Casas expressed what
one could read as an implicit anticipation of his later anti-Roman position in the form of yet another clever borrowing of the conquistadors'
topos of dwarfing the ancients. In the very beginning of the prefatory
synopsis of his most widely read—and reviled—book, *Brevísima
relación de la destrucción de las Indias*, Las Casas slyly suggested that
the events that had occurred in the Indies since the first settlements had
been "so marvelous and incredible" [tan admirables y tan no creíbles]

that they threatened to put in the shade "all other deeds, no matter how valiant *(hazañosas)* they were in ages past *(en los siglos pasados)*." Not only does this recycle an historian's self-promotional topos that can be traced back to Thucydides (though Las Casas no doubt knew it best from the beginning of Josephus's *Jewish War*), but it also reads like an able parody of the way the conquistadors habitually described their own exploits. But then Las Casas, without missing a beat, proceeded to list a few examples of the kind of "valiant deeds" he had in mind: "the massacres of innocent peoples, the atrocities committed against them and, among other horrific excesses, the ways in which towns, provinces, and whole kingdoms have been entirely cleared of their native inhabitants."[73] While polemically effective enough in itself, this sarcastic subversion of a common boast of the conquistadors would have had even deeper resonance for readers who recalled the note appended to Cortés's second *relación* to the emperor when it was first printed in 1522. This brief appendix affirmed that in the siege of Tenochtitlan there died "more Indians than Jews in Jerusalem during the destruction of that city by Vespasian." We have seen that Fernández de Oviedo indicated that this claim of a higher body-count for the Spanish siege of Tenochtitlan than for the Roman siege of Jerusalem was a commonplace among the conquistadors. In Las Casas's bitter preface, however, we see this "besting" topos turned back upon its would-be beneficiaries. Still, Las Casas was at this point not inclined to single out the Romans explicitly as his fellow Spaniards' chief predecessors in imperialist atrocity.

Impressive evidence of Las Casas's lack of animus against the Romans before his involvement in the *Democrates secundus* controversy is provided by a document that he apparently composed in Mexico City in November 1546, on the very eve of what would be his last farewell to the New World. First published in 1992 by Helen Rand Parish and Harold E. Weidman, this Latin treatise, which they have given the title *De exemptione sive damnatione*, had its origin in an event that had scandalized Las Casas during his journey in the spring of 1546 to attend a conference of the bishops of New Spain in Mexico City.[74] Stopping in Antequera (now known as Oaxaca), Las Casas learned that this town had recently been the scene of a remarkable violation of clerical immunity. A priest who had committed a serious offense—we do not know what it was—had sought sanctuary in a church, only to be dragged off by the constables *(alguaciles)* and condemned to the loss of a hand by a civil court. When Las Casas arrived in Mexico City in the middle of June, still seething with indignation, he at once informed the viceroy, Antonio de Mendoza, that he and all the provincial judges *(oidores de la Audiencia)* stood under the ban of automatic excommunication because of the Antequera affair. Through all of the episcopal conference's deliberations on the sensitive issue of restitution of Indian property as mandated by the New Laws, Las Casas never lost sight of this principle of preserving the clergy's immunity from civil judgment— an immunity he clearly regarded as a powerful weapon in the contest with the encomendero elite. Not content with securing from his fellow bishops a declaration reaffirming the importance of clerical immunity, he devoted several of his final days in the New World to drafting a ringing defense of the threatened principle.

Early on in this treatise Las Casas argued that the principle that secular authorities are forbidden to punish priests and other sacred personnel is supported not only by divine law, but also by natural law, the law "written or implanted naturally in the mind" [vel scripta vel indita menti naturaliter].[75] Not only did Scripture record the regulations that the Israelites observed with regard to special privileges and provisions for the priests, but "the histories of all the peoples of the whole world confirm the same point." In support of this appeal to the *ius gentium,* Las Casas alluded first, and rather briefly, to practices that could have recently been observed "in nostris Indianis populis," where priests were held in remarkable esteem and were often afforded special support by kings and magistrates.[76] Next, and at much greater length, Las Casas turned to priestly privileges among the ancient Romans. For this, he cited and extensively quoted a single text: the famous *relatio* (dispatch) sent to the emperor Valentinian II in 384 by the pagan prefect of Rome, Quintus Aurelius Symmachus.[77] Though Symmachus was petitioning only for the restoration to the Senate House of the Altar of Victory installed there by Augustus and removed by order of the Christian emperor Gratian, Las Casas, with a little exaggeration, claimed that the dispatch was directed "against the Christians, in favor of the restoration of the old worship of the gods." He proceeded to offer verbatim the bulk of Symmachus's complaint about the disabilities to which the vestal virgins had recently been subjected. True enough, Las Casas noted that the Christian emperors had curtailed the vestals' privileges "out of a desire to abolish that false and impious religion," but for the most part he was content to let Symmachus speak for himself with all of his still moving eloquence. Then Las Casas reminded his readers that these words were "false, to be sure, and impious, for they were uttered for the preservation of a false and impious religion and the privileges of its priests, but they would be utterly true *(verissima)* if spoken by Christians on behalf of the true religion's ministers, priests and others devoted to divine worship."

In late 1546, then, Las Casas was happy to appropriate the eloquence and arguments of one of the most impressive leaders of the pagan resistance to the Christianization of the Roman Empire. Roman religion was, of course, "false and impious," but Las Casas cited its champion at such length here because he believed that he was profoundly *right* about a basic principle of religious-secular relations. The law of clerical immunity was "written naturally on the mind" of the eloquent pagan Symmachus. Indeed, Las Casas took so benign a view of this Roman enemy of Christianity that he recommended that the reader look up the complete *relatio* among the works of Ambrose! It is interesting that we see here in this striking passage a foreshadowing of a procedure that would come to dominate Las Casas's massive *Apologética historia sumaria:* the juxtaposition of New World with European, especially classical, customs. But in the later work, as we shall see, Las Casas tended to take a markedly harsher view of the Romans. At the end of 1546, however, he had not yet encountered the incentive to consider Roman civilization a model to be rejected or denigrated.

Las Casas versus Sepúlveda—and the Romans:
Opening Rounds (1547–51)

Having endured what was to be his final Atlantic passage, Las Casas spent the summer of 1547 in Valladolid and the rest of the year in Aranda de Duero, Monzón, and Alcalá, returning to settle into either the Convento de San Pablo or the Colegio de San Gregorio in Valladolid early in 1548.[78] He appears to have hit Iberian soil running, for he was immediately involved in at least three major controversies concerning Spanish policy in the Indies. His most urgent concern was to combat the erosion of the New Laws, an inevitable process that had become especially worrisome with the revocation of certain provisions in 1545. In particular, he labored mightily to oppose the encomenderos' attempt to restore the heritability of their encomiendas. Here he achieved some initial success. Thanks largely to his efforts, our old friend Bernal Díaz del Castillo returned gloomily to Guatemala from a fruitless meeting of encomenderos with the Council of the Indies, viewing the future of his class like that of a "lame mule."[79] Las Casas also found himself embroiled in a controversy of his own making. As bishop of Chiapas he had composed a stern manual forbidding priests to confess or grant last rites to encomenderos who failed to make full restitution of property unjustly appropriated from the Indians. The anguished wails of many of the settlers had preceded him home to Spain, and he found himself under pressure to generate some cogent explanations. And also, of course, he soon involved himself, no doubt with the encouragement of Melchor Cano from nearby Salamanca, in the controversy over *Democrates secundus*. Rising to the bait of Sepúlveda's praise of the Romans and surely encouraged by Cano's—and perhaps also by Soto's—rejection of that model, Las Casas now began to cast a cold eye on Charles V's ancient predecessors on the Roman imperial throne.

In fact, the bishop's new anti-Roman bias impressively manifested itself in two treatises evidently composed shortly before the great debate of 1550–51.[80] Summoned before the Council of the Indies in Valladolid in 1549 to defend his controversial *Confesionario*, Las Casas presented a succinct rebuttal to the charge that he had implied in that document that the kings of Castile have no just title to overlordship in the Indies. These *Thirty Very Juridical Propositions (Treinta proposiciones muy jurídicas)* affirmed that the Spanish title to dominion in the Indies rested securely upon the papal injunction to the Spaniards to carry out the peaceful conversion of the natives of these newfound lands to the Christian faith. Las Casas published this relatively brief work, without license, in Seville in 1552, along with several other treatises, including the notorious *Brevísima relación* and Domingo de Soto's summary of the Valladolid debate. In both the prologue and the conclusion, he promised that a fuller account of some of these points would shortly be in the hands of the council. This was the impressively titled *Treatise in Support of the Sovereign Empire and Universal Principate That the Kings of Castile and León Hold over the Indies (Tratado comprobatorio del imperio soberano y principado universal que los reyes de Castilla y León tienen sobre las Indias)*. Printed in 1553 with a dedication to Prince Philip, this treatise was designed as an extended treatment of the seventeenth and eighteenth of the *Thirty Propositions*. These affirmed, respectively, the Spanish Crown's right to "that whole grand empire and universal jurisdiction over all the Indies" through the "authority, concession, and donation" of the pope, and the right of the native rulers to preserve, under Spanish overlordship, their "administration, principate, jurisdiction, rights, and dominion over their subject peoples."[81]

The Romans played a dual role in these linked treatises. For one thing, they served as impressive examplars of a species of brutal imperialism best avoided by modern Spaniards and most accurately paralleled by the Islamic enemies of Christendom. The twenty-third of the *Treinta proposiciones muy jurídicas* constituted an answer to those who, like Sepúlveda, argued that violent conquest of the Indians was often a necessary precondition for safe and effective proselytization. This, Las Casas declared, "is the natural method used by Mohammed and the Romans, by which they troubled and robbed the world, and it is the method that the Turks and Moors use now."[82] Note that the Romans are brought in somewhat awkwardly here, for Las Casas's point about violent conversion fits Islamic conquests better than Roman ones, for the Romans were more apt to paper their *interpretatio romana* over native religious pantheons and practices than to attempt substantive changes in those native beliefs and rituals. But it is precisely the gratuitous nature of this slur against the Romans that provides a gauge of the new animus Las Casas had conceived against them. Similarly, in the *Tratado comprobatorio,* Las Casas denied that Spanish rule in the New World should be based on force of arms or superior power ("en armas y en poder más"), as was the way of "Alexander the Great, and the Romans, and all those who were famous tyrants, and as today the Turk invades and harasses and oppresses the Christian world."[83] Not only do such passages contradict Sepúlveda's celebration of the supposedly rational and moderate imperialism of the Romans, they also neatly invert the claims of the conquistadors. While the latter may have been correct in seeing themselves as spectacular emulators of the Romans, their imperial models were in fact no better than the Moslem "infidels" to whom they often, as we have seen, tended to assimilate their New World foes.

The other function of the Romans in these paired treatises was more complicated and ambiguous. It was in some sense a juridical function—"very juridical," Las Casas would have claimed—for it was part of his singularly circumscribed attempt to provide a sound and essentially foolproof (or knaveproof) title for the Spanish Crown's dominion in the Indies. The sixteenth of the *Treinta proposiciones* maintained that Pope

Alexander VI had in 1493 invested the kings of Castile and León with the "supreme and sovereign empire and lordship of that whole universal world of the Indies, establishing them as emperors over many kings *(emperadores sobre muchos reyes)*" in order to facilitate the spread of Christianity among the newly discovered multitudes.[84] The striking phrase "supremo e soberano imperio e señorío de todo aquel orbe universo de las Indias" appears simultaneously to challenge and to tap into the power of the claim, so vigorously disputed by Las Casas's fellow Dominicans (and, as we shall soon see, by Las Casas himself), that the emperor was "lord of the whole world."[85] Here, of course, the *emperadores* in question were not the "Roman" emperors—notwithstanding the coincidence that the reigning successor of the Catholic Monarchs was in fact "emperor of the Romans." No, as the fifteenth proposition had made clear, the Spanish title to empire in the Indies was not based on the reigning king's Roman imperial dignity; it was a papal recognition of Ferdinand and Isabella's fitness for overseas dominion by virtue of their conquest of Granada and their sponsoring of the voyage of that *egregio varón* Columbus. Nor was the "whole world" in question the entire globe, but rather "that whole universal world of the Indies"— "that Indian world" [aquel indiano mundo], as he phrased it in the parallel treatment in the *Tratado comprobatorio*.[86] The "principado universal" of the title of the latter treatise was revealed, then, as lordship over "that new world" [aquel otro mundo] of the Indies.[87] The grandiosity of the Spanish kings' *dignidad imperial* was designed to match "the magnitude of that world of the Indies *(la grandeza de aquel orbe de las Indias)*, which has more than ten thousand leagues of coastline and immense peoples and most populous nations that have been discovered and that do not stop being discovered every day."[88] Indeed, it is not just a new world; it is a *larger* world: "another world of pagans, much larger than the world that we possess and know over here, full of many more peoples and very populous kingdoms."[89]

By initially establishing in the *Treinta proposiciones* this notion of papally endorsed Spanish "universal" "emperadores sobre muchos reyes" in another, larger *orbe,* Las Casas appeared to be sidestepping, even as he was flirting with, the attractive but transient juridical potency of the world dominion of the "emperors of the Romans." But in the very next breath he made a shrewdly bolder and perhaps novel use of what one may call the "Roman title." For he proceeded to argue that the pope's power to invest Spain's Catholic Monarchs and their

successors as proselytizing "emperors" of a "new world" was validated
by the precedent of the way "the apostolic seat accepted and approved
the imperial dignity that it found among the infidels in the world—but
not the acts of tyranny by which the Romans had acquired it—so that
when it adopted him as its son, the emperor might be the advocate and
defender of the Church."[90] In his expansion of this argument in the
Tratado comprobatorio, Las Casas forcefully articulated his theory of a
double empire, one for the New World, one for the Old, both of them
endorsed by the pope in order to further the spread of the Christian religion and the authority of the Church. The Spanish New World empire
derived its prestige from the pope's power to "receive, admit, adopt,
arrange, regulate, authorize, and preserve the emperor and the imperial
dignity in that state, dignity, preeminence, and superiority which it
found among the pagans in the Roman people." This allowed the pope
to create in the New World "another emperor over many kings whom
all would accept as their superior, just as in ancient times *(antigua-
mente)* the kings over here *(de por acá)* did with the tacit or express
acceptance and consent of the Holy Church and the vicar of Christ."
Driving the point home yet again, he reiterated that Alexander VI "had
the power to create afresh a supreme and requisite dignity in that new
world on the model of the imperial *(a la semejanza de la imperial)* that
it found over here in this other world."

   This gambit is a remarkable attempt to accept a carefully regulated
dosage of Roman imperial prestige for Spanish royal dominion in the
Indies while at the same time denying or undercutting both the "juridical" appeal to Roman "world dominion" and the kind of respect for
ancient Roman imperial behavior that Sepúlveda expressed so eagerly
and to which even Vitoria had not been immune. Faced with the harsh
necessity of deflecting the charge of lèse-majesté, Las Casas did indeed
see his way to acknowledging Charles V as a "universal emperor"
whose *dignidad imperial* was ultimately inherited from the Romans.[91]
But the strings he attached to this prestige were even more remarkable
than the concession itself. The "whole world" that formed his empire
was not the entire terraqueous globe, but "that Indian world," a vast
realm whose many kings would retain their dominions when they
acknowledged him as their "emperor," just as the independent kings
of Europe retained their dominions when they acknowledged him as
"emperor of the Romans." Furthermore, Charles acquired this new
"empire" not by virtue of his election and papal confirmation as

emperor of the Romans, but by virtue of his succession to the throne of the Catholic Monarchs, the original recipients of this "imperial dignity," and also by virtue of the acceptance of his overlordship by vassal kings in the New World. In addition, the pope's grant of this "imperial dignity" was "modal"; that is, it came with the charge of "introducing the Catholic faith and the Christian religion into those lands and bringing about the conversion of those peoples."[92] In fact, it was this charge that was primary, while the imperial dignity was strictly secondary, in part a practical ideological tool to facilitate the spread of Christianity across the many borders of the New World's kingdoms, in part a glorious incentive for the Spanish monarch himself to put his shoulder to the missionary wheel.[93] In any case, the pope could annul or transfer this new "empire" should it become evident that the charge was being neglected, just as he had transferred the Roman Empire from the Greeks to the Germans seven centuries earlier.[94] True enough, this imperial dignity that the pope had established in the New World had in some sense originally been possessed by the ancient Romans, but when it had passed to "the divine and marvelous power of Saint Peter and his successors" it had become surgically separated from its diseased origins in the "tiranías" by which the Romans had acquired it. Furthermore, the "Roman" essence of this New World imperial dignity was severely attenuated, for while the pope had "transferred" the "Roman Empire" from the Byzantines to the Germans, thereby recognizing and preserving the institutional continuity of the ancient Roman Empire and the "Holy Roman Empire," he had created this New World "empire" afresh *on the model (a la semejanza)* of the Roman Empire—a very different matter. Thus, Las Casas simultaneously offered Charles a crumb of "Roman" imperial dignity in the New World, while firmly denying the Roman Empire any direct and ongoing potency as a continuing source of Charles's dominion in the Indies.

Las Casas's ingenious notion of a Spanish New World *dignidad imperial* conjured into being, by papal "donation," on the model of that of the Roman Empire was echoed by an intriguing suggestion made by none other than that blackest of the bishop's bêtes noires, Hernán Cortés. Beginning his second *relación* to the emperor in October 1520, after his flight from Tenochtitlan in the Noche Triste and during the preparations for his triumphant return, Cortés insisted that he was pained by his inability to send news in a timely manner,

for I wished Your Highness to know all the things of this land, which,
as I have already written in another report, are so many and of such
a kind that one might call oneself emperor of this kingdom with no
less glory than of Germany, which, by the Grace of God, Your Sacred
Majesty already possesses.[95]

Victor Frankl has argued that Cortés was drawing here upon a Spanish
tradition, developed gradually since the ninth century, that proposed
the concept of a Spanish empire, a union of Spanish kingdoms under the
hegemony of León and Castile, which could stand its legally independent ground against the "empire of Germany." Cortés, Frankl claimed,
was adapting this Spanish tradition to his own purposes, carving out a
notional "empire of New Spain" to stand not only alongside the "German Roman empire," but also, implicitly, to stand free of the threaten-
ing proximity of the Antilles (the bailiwick of the Columbus dynasty
and their representative, Diego Velázquez, against whom Cortés had
rebelled), the Spanish title to which rested on the papal bulls. Note that
Cortés, like Las Casas, did not maintain that Charles's title to his
"empire" in the New World was in any sense dependent upon his status
as "emperor of the Romans." The two empires were simply juxtaposed.
Frankl also argued that in the body of the *Segunda relación* Cortés
craftily contrived, through the fabricated words of Montezuma, a sem-
blance of orthodox "Roman" imperial succession for Charles as
emperor of New Spain, by virtue of inheritance (the Aztec king's supposed identification of Charles as the descendant of the leader who had
brought the Mexica to the valley, only to disappear eastwards) and also
election (the affirmation of Charles's lordship by Montezuma's vassals).
Here, too, we find an echo in Las Casas, who, as Anthony Pagden has
noted, "seems always to have assumed that Moctezuma's 'donation' to
Cortés constituted a legitimate political charter."[96] Pagden has more
recently singled out Cortés's imperial language in the *Segunda relación*
as reinforcement of "the image of the western American empire as a
continuation of the older empire in the East."[97] There is some truth to
this, though it is overstated—and indeed Pagden himself warns that "it
would be unwise to place too much emphasis on this." Characteristically, Cortés was as interested here in establishing independence from
the Roman model as in demonstrating a continuation of it. And that is
even truer of his unlikely ideological bedfellow Las Casas, whose theory
of an "otro emperador" Pagden does not discuss.[98]

Still, these attempts of both Cortés and Las Casas to ingratiate them-selves with a potentially suspicious "Roman emperor" strikingly antic-ipate the tendency of many Spaniards in the second half of the sixteenth century, after the "Roman" crown had passed back to the Austrian Hapsburgs, to speak of a Spanish "empire of the Indies."[99] Thus, in 1593 Philip II was to request from Pius IV the title of "emperor of the Indies." Naturally, it would be going too far to suggest that this propa-gandistic program was inspired by Las Casas's notion of a New World empire presented in these two rather eccentric treatises. Still, there is the intriguing fact that in December 1553, the year in which Las Casas had published the *Tratado comprobatorio* with a dedication to him, Prince Philip issued a *cédula* mandating a survey of the tributes that had been levied by Montezuma as the "señor universal" of his territories.[100] The answers were to serve as a kind of legal basis for the tributes that were now to be levied by the man who had inherited the Aztec ruler's "uni-versal señorío," the Spanish "Emperador Rey." Now, it is true that the New World empire that Las Casas envisioned was much more extensive than the territory Montezuma had ruled as "universal señor." In addi-tion, Las Casas does not appear to have made much of the "precedent" of Montezuma's "universal señorío" in determining the legal basis for Spanish dominion in New Spain. Still, the phrasing of the *cédula* of Prince Philip does strikingly echo that of the Lascasian treatises, raising the possibility that someone on the prince's staff—or (who knows?) perhaps Philip himself—did actually read Las Casas's "massive and almost unreadable" *Tratado comprobatorio*.[101]

Las Casas versus Sepúlveda—and the Romans: Valladolid (1550–51)

The junta proposed by the Council of the Indies and endorsed by the emperor convened at Valladolid in the Chapel of the Colegio de San Gregorio in mid-August 1550.[102] Among the "Council of Fourteen" con-voked to judge the deliberations were, not surprisingly, both Domingo de Soto and Melchor Cano. On the first day, Sepúlveda presented a summary and defense of his *Democrates secundus*. The next day Las Casas began a marathon reading of a very substantial manuscript, a task that took him five full days to complete—unless, that is, Sepúlveda (or someone close to him) was correct in asserting that the judges, "tired of hearing him," called a premature halt to the recitation.[103] In any case, the judges requested that a summary be made of this manuscript, and after Domingo de Soto was delegated to draft one, the first session was adjourned.[104] A copy of Soto's summary was supplied to Sepúlveda, who drafted twelve objections to the arguments of Las Casas, who in turn composed twelve replies to these objections. Sepúlveda and Las Casas seem to have presented their objections and replies at the beginning of the second session, which convened in April 1551 (minus Melchor Cano, who had been summoned to the Council of Trent).[105] Sepúlveda presented his last formal rebuttal to Las Casas on or shortly after April 19, emphasizing his view that the bulls of Alexander VI authorized conquest as a preparation for evangelization.[106] The second session concluded at the beginning of May, and the judges went their several ways to ponder their verdicts. These solitary deliberations appear to have been deliberate indeed. At long last, by 1557 all of the judges save Melchor Cano had managed to submit a verdict, and Cano was pressed for his response at once. Whether or not he complied, no collective pronouncement ever emerged, a state of affairs that allowed both Sepúlveda and Las Casas to claim that the board leaned in his own direction.

Though we no longer have the manuscript Las Casas spent five days reading to the first session of the junta in Valladolid, we can probably trust Domingo de Soto to have given us an accurate account of its contents in the summary that he was delegated to draft and that Las Casas published in Seville in 1552. But the lost manuscript may also be reconstructed through two Lascasian manuscripts that do survive. The one more likely to approximate much of the substance and form of the lost 1550 text is a Latin *Apologia* in 253 folio pages in the Bibliothèque Nationale in Paris. This was first published in photographic reprint with Spanish translation by Angel Losada in 1975, though an English translation by Stafford Poole had appeared the year before under the title *In Defense of the Indians*.[107] Since the argument to Soto's summary states that Las Casas composed his refutation of Sepúlveda in Spanish, the Latin version was apparently a later project, perhaps produced with a view to publication, and there are indeed several indications that it is a revision and expansion of that part of the original text which most directly engaged Sepúlveda's arguments.[108]

The concluding sentence of this *Apologia* heralds "the second part of this *Defense*, written in Spanish," a work designed to defend the

"very sincere, docile, moderate and clever people" of the New World
against their Spanish detractors and exploiters.[109] It appears that Las
Casas had read a version of this "second part" in Valladolid in the
course of his refutation of Sepúlveda's argument that the Indians, as
barbarians, needed to be subjected to their natural superiors, for Soto
noted in his summary that "the bishop recounted at length the history
of the Indians, showing that though they had some customs of an
underdeveloped people (gente no tan política), . . . they had attained
sufficient social complexity (policia) that war could not be waged
against them for that reason."[110] Angel Losada has plausibly argued
that this "second part" of Las Casas's defense speech was a draft of
what eventually became the massive Apologética historia, a project that
may well have begun life as an offshoot of his even more massive Historia de las Indias.[111] But just as Domingo de Soto largely passed over
Las Casas's lengthy account of Indian culture in his summary, so shall
we leave aside the Apologética historia in this chapter. Still, when we
return to it later, we should bear in mind that its juxtapositions of classical and New World cultures may not have languished for centuries in
an unpublished (though not entirely unread) manuscript; they may well
have played a role in the celebrated public debate in Valladolid.

The Latin Apologia is divided into sixty-three chapters. The first five
are devoted to the question of the proper definitions of the word barbarian and the dubious or at least very limited propriety of so labeling
the Indians. The next nine chapters argue the point that the idolatry of
unbelievers does not serve as the basis for the Church's jurisdiction over
them. Chapters 15–27 state the positive case for the Church's jurisdiction over unbelievers in five special circumstances—none of them oper-
ative in the Indies. Chapters 28–38, in many ways the most remarkable
of the book, focus on a further special circumstance, one undeniably
present in the New World: human sacrifice. While this practice would
seem to activate the Church's obligation to rescue innocent victims (and
potential converts), Las Casas argued first that the evils inevitably attendant upon war outweigh the lesser evil of allowing human sacrifice to
continue until peaceful conversion would put an end to it. Second, Las
Casas boldly argued that there was a case to be made for human
sacrifice: not only had it been practiced virtually everywhere in the
world at one time or another, but it constituted in itself a rational, if
misguided, expression of proper religious feeling—that is, the thankful
willingness to offer up to that which one recognizes as a supreme deity

"the greatest and most valuable good, that is, human life."[112] Chapters 39–51 expatiate on the advantages of peaceful over violent conversion and on the injustice of war conducted as a means to spread the Christian faith. Chapter 52 is a refutation of Sepúlveda's appeal to the example of the Roman Empire, though we are about to see that the Romans were by no means confined to this chapter. In chapters 53–56 Las Casas turned from Sepúlveda to his main "theoretical" authority, John Mair (Major), the Paris theologian who pioneered the application of Aristotle's doctrine of the natural slave to the case of the Indians. Chapters 57–58 offer an account of Sepúlveda's attempt to get his *Democrates secundus* published and also a vitriolic attack upon his main supposedly "factual" authority, Gonzalo Fernández de Oviedo. The *Apologia* then concludes with four chapters designed to liberate the 1493 bull *Inter cetera* of Alexander VI from Sepúlveda's supposed misinterpretation of it—an attack that Sepúlveda appears to have countered at some length in the second session.

It was in the *Apologia's* discussion of the meaning of "barbarian" that Las Casas first strategically exploited the ancient Romans. There were, he maintained, four possible kinds of barbarians: (1) cruel, wild, merciless people (a category that fitted "our Spaniards" better than it did their Indian victims); (2) people without writing or learning; (3) primitive people with no real states, rulers, or laws; and (4) non-Christians. While the Indians were clearly barbarians in the second and fourth senses, more suitable candidates for barbarians of the third type, the politically and culturally "underdeveloped," were the Iberian ancestors of the modern Spaniards before the Romans took it upon themselves to "civilize" them.[113] It appears that Las Casas's historical argument did not appear in the manuscript he read in the first session in Valladolid, for he offered it in the "Eighth Reply" to Sepúlveda at the beginning of the second session.[114] This appeal to the conquest of Spain by the Romans is of considerable interest and importance, not only for the controversy of the Indies, but also for the history of Spanish historical self-consciousness, and we shall return to it in our next chapter.

Las Casas concentrated more intently upon the Romans in the fifth chapter of the *Apologia,* his discussion of the fourth definition of "barbarians": "all those who do not acknowledge Christ." Here he made a startling departure from the standard Thomistic position that all peoples, be they Christian or infidel, are capable of orderly and virtuous customs and behavior through their possession of reason and their access to natural law—a position that had, after all, implicitly facilitated his argument in the previous chapter that the Indians "wisely administered the affairs of both peace and war justly and equitably, governed by laws that at very many points surpass ours, and could have won the admiration of the sages of Athens."[115] In chapter 5, however, Las Casas chose to argue that "no matter how well governed a people may be or how philosophical a man, they are subject to complete barbarism, specifically, the barbarism of vice, if they are not imbued with the mysteries of Christian philosophy."[116] Lack of Christian faith allows idolatry to flourish, "from which springs the source of all the evils that make both private and public life miserable and unhappy."[117] For a historical example of Christian faith cleansing such an idolatrous people of "wickedness, filth and foolishness," he offered the Christianization of the Romans, a people "who sought to enact laws for all other nations in order to dominate them and who were, at one time, highly praised for their reputation for political skill and wisdom *(politicae prudentiae ac sapientiae nomine)."* Not only was Las Casas optimistically hinting that respect for Roman civilization was largely a thing of the past, for they were a people praised "at one time" (or, better, "back then," *tum temporis),* but he even insinuated that the most influential and durable aspect of that civilization, its legal system, had been designed primarily as a tool of imperial domination. Furthermore, while using the rule of law to dominate other peoples,

> this people itself was ruled by heinous vices and detestable practices, especially in its shameful games and hateful sacrifices, as in the games and plays held in the circus and in the obscene sacrifices to Priapus and Bacchus. In these everything was so disgraceful, ugly, and repugnant to sound reason that they far outdistanced all other nations in insensitivity of mind and barbarism *(mentis stupore et barbarie).*[118]

Las Casas proceeded to appeal to Augustine and Lactantius on the disgusting nature of the religious practices of the Greeks and the Romans, "who wanted to be considered wiser than all the other nations of the world." In particular, he singled out Lactantius's excoriation of the parentally approved and religiously sanctioned pederasty of the *gymnasia,* quoting the church father's outraged question, "Is there anything astonishing in the fact that all disgraceful practices have come down from this people for whom these vices were religious acts, things that not only were not avoided but were even encouraged?"[119] Now, "this people" to whom Lactantius had been referring was of course the Greeks; he even drew attention to the fact that Cicero, his source for the Greek habit of placing images of amatory divinities in the *gymnasia*, implied the superiority of the Romans to the Greeks in this regard by observing that "vices ought not to be consecrated, but virtues." Las Casas, however, was eager to keep the accusatory spotlight principally on the Romans:

> These are they who called all other nations barbarians, though no true barbarians could do anything more absurd or foolish. Perhaps the Romans excelled in quickness of judgment and mental expertise *(iudicii acrimonia et ingenii solertia)* so that they could make themselves tyrants over mankind and subdue foreign territories amid great destruction *(magnis stragibus)*. But even if the Greeks and Romans did refrain from these horrible crimes and foul vices, where is the credit due if not to the splendor of the gospel, which, once it had spread throughout all the nations of the world, came to the notice even of that ambitious nation?

Notice here the glide in the last quoted sentence from the "Greeks and Romans" to "that ambitious nation" [eius . . . ambitiosae gentis]. The bracketed *sic* attached by Stafford Poole to his translation of that phrase does not so much indict Las Casas of stylistic carelessness as it draws attention to his obsession with the Romans as the classical models in most urgent need of demolition.

In this chapter's remarkable tour de force of transvaluation, Las Casas inverted the cultural position of the Romans from the supercivilized to the bestial ("similes animantibus," as he put it), well below the level of so-called true barbarians—that is, presumably, barbarians of the second and third type. Almost immediately in this chapter, these classical barbarians of the fourth type plummet to the level of barbarians of the first type (among whom, inevitably, Las Casas located the Spanish conquistadors), according to which a barbarian is "any cruel, inhuman, wild, and merciless man" who has put aside "decency, meekness, and humane moderation."[120] We should note that Las Casas manifested his polemical genius here not only by lambasting the Romans as tyrants but also by insisting that they revealed their "barbarity" most spectacularly in their religious practices. Since it was in their religious practices that the New World natives most deeply shocked European sensibilities, their champion shrewdly shifted his readers' attention to the religious abominations of the preeminent European culture heroes. (We shall have occasion to see more of this Lascasian strategy when we turn to the *Apologética historia*.) After this concerted onslaught on the Romans, it is remarkable to see how little space Las Casas allowed himself to express his contempt for those contemporary Mediterranean non-Christian "barbarians," the Turks and Arabs, briefly noting their "effeminate luxury" and their tolerance for sexual deviancy, and concluding that "neither the Greeks nor the Romans nor the Turks nor the Moors should be said to be exercising justice," for Augustine argued that justice depends on Christianity.

We should emphasize, however, that our discussion of the Romans as barbarians of the "fourth type" addresses the surviving text of the *Apologia,* not the text Las Casas read in Valladolid, for Soto's summary makes it clear that in the first session Las Casas discussed only his first three species of "barbarians." True enough, he must have developed the fourth category (non-Christians) relatively soon afterward, for in the "Eighth Reply" to Sepúlveda he mentioned that his *Apologia* identified four species.[121] In fact, the three-species version made somewhat better strategic sense, for it allowed the Indians to be considered barbarians only in one sense (peoples without writing), while the addition of the fourth category, non-Christians, implicitly allowed yet another excuse to consider the pre-Columbian Indians barbarians. Indeed, Las Casas offered no clear reason why the nexus of infidelity, idolatry, and private and public vices that manifested itself among the Romans would have failed to do so among the natives of the New World as well. It would appear, then, that Las Casas allowed his eagerness to assault Sepúlveda's beloved Romans to compromise momentarily his project of lifting the stigma of barbarism from his own beloved Indians. Given that his strategy here was to reveal these "type 4" non-Christian barbarians of ancient Rome as in fact virtually "type 1" cruel and savage barbarians (not unlike their Spanish emulators), one might ask: why did he not simply introduce them in the first category and be done with it? Perhaps it was because he saw the advantage of introducing the Romans into the realm of barbarism through a gate that even Sepúlveda could not shut upon them: paganism. Once firmly settled in this one region of the conceptual territory of barbarism, it was a simple enough matter to shunt them over into the province of type 1 savage barbarians. Las Casas carried out this maneuver with sufficient vitriolic panache that an inattentive reader would not be apt to recall the inconvenient fact that the Indians, too, were type 4 barbarians. Further sleight-of-hand on Las Casas's part is his statement in the "Eighth Reply": "And thus we have said that the Indians are barbarians of the second of the four types which we have accurately marked out in the *Apologia*." Manifestly, then, Las Casas added the fourth species of barbarian not to clarify the status of the Indians but to avail himself of an opportunity to vilify the Romans.

The next major appearance of the Roman Empire in the *Apologia* is in chapter 21, part of Las Casas's lengthy argument that the Church has no jurisdiction over nonbelievers who have never accepted Christianity. An embarrassment for this position was a gloss on Gratian, one frequently cited by later canonists, that declared that "aliens are under Roman rule [or empire]" [gentiles esse sub imperio Romano]. To take this gloss absolutely, Las Casas pronounced, was stupid *(stultum)*, for this would mean failing to make requisite distinctions among kinds of unbelievers. Properly understood, the gloss was intended to refer to unbelievers who live within the territories of Christian rulers or in lands that unbelievers had seized from Christians, "since those realms are included within the limits of Roman rule that do not go beyond the limits of the Christian people. For the Roman Empire is and always has been marked by certain boundaries."[122] In support of this observation, Las Casas cited Boethius, *De consolatione Philosophiae* (bk. 2, prosa 7), who in turn cited Cicero's admission that the fame of the Roman Republic had not passed beyond the Caucasus Mountains. "Therefore," Las Casas concluded, "the Roman Emperors were not lords of the whole world, even when Roman power was more widely spread throughout the world. And today the Roman Empire does not extend beyond the boundaries of the Catholic Church."[123] In support of this familiar contention, Las Casas enlisted a most unfamiliar ally: the authoritative decretalist Enrico de Segusio (ca. 1200–1271), bishop of Ostia (hence "Hostiensis"), whom Las Casas quoted as declaring that "the law of the Emperor can bind only those subject to Roman law and the sanction of the Catholic Church, that is, because outside the Church there is no *imperium*." Now, this famous phrase *extra ecclesiam non est imperium* was commonly employed by canonists who maintained that non-Christian rulers could have no legitimate dominion—*imperium* here having the sense of political authority, in particular a ruler's power to make and enforce laws and to declare and conduct just wars.[124]

Hostiensis himself was famous for his insistence that, "since the coming of Christ, all honor, power, dominion, and jurisdiction have been removed from the heathen and transferred to the faithful."[125] Las Casas had excoriated this position in the *Tratado comprobatorio* as "not only a blind, detestable, and sacrilegious error . . . but a formal heresy."[126] But in this impressive display of polemical dexterity in the *Apologia,* Las Casas seized upon one very particular instance of the canonist's use of the famous formula and exploited it to establish the point that the Roman Empire, being essentially coterminous with Christendom, was a severely limited geographical entity—taking *imperium* here in its territorial sense, as the area within which authoritative power is exercised. So Hostiensis, who had vigorously denied dominion to non-Christian peoples, was suborned to help Las Casas make his case for the legitimacy of the dominion of the native communities in a New World of which the canonist had never dreamed.

Las Casas proceeded to assert that the emperors themselves acknowledged that "the kingdoms of aliens *(regna gentilium)* were exempt from the jurisdiction of the Roman Empire. . . , and therefore neither in law nor in fact did they rule over the entire world." He then cast scorn upon those who "most foolishly" [stultissime] advanced the claim that "the Roman Emperor is lord of the world by right though not in fact." (Presumably he was thinking of Bartolus of Sassoferrato and his followers.) While he derided their inability to support this position with "solid arguments," he did not deign to refute any of them explicitly, for he clearly felt that a reiteration of the denial of the emperor's de facto world dominion was in itself a sufficiently destructive explosion of a de jure claim: "For never in any century until now has anyone been lord of the world, nor did the despotic Roman armies *(tyranica Romanorum arma)* subdue the world." An imperial pronouncement in the *Digest* trumpeting "our jurisdiction, on which the sun never sets and which extends to both ends [of the world]" left Las Casas singularly unimpressed: "Any ruler can say the same thing. For there is no kingdom that does not look to east, west, south, and north." Here is that sober resistance to the charms of ancient Roman propaganda that we saw earlier in Soto and Cano. Suddenly and fleetingly, however, Las Casas did acknowledge the contemporary Roman emperor's "universal dominion" in one important respect: "Yet it is true that the Roman emperor is universal lord of Christians," a point that he supported with a reference to the introduction to the *Digest* of

the fourteenth-century canonist Baldo degli Ubaldi. The unstated implication of this admission is that, as the Indians become converted to
Christianity, they would ipso facto find themselves members of the
"Roman Empire"—qua Christians, it will be noted, not only as vassals
of Charles V. But this "Christian-Roman universalism" could offer no
leverage for limiting or abolishing the dominion of the Indian communities, either before or after conversion.

Having just alluded to the ancient Roman propagandistic assertion
of world dominion, Las Casas concluded this chapter with a stinging
denunciation of latter-day imperial ideologues: "To say that the Roman
Emperor is lawful master of the whole world is an utterly vain bit of
nonsense *(vanissimum nugamentum)* and an occasion for involving the
world in strife." (The Erasmian flavor of this passage anticipates a brief
but emphatic defense of Erasmus against Sepúlveda a few pages further
on, in chapter 27.) Next, Las Casas closed in on his main target: "Even
more ridiculous is what Michael Ulcurrunus (among others) writes in
his treatise *On the Rule of the World:* 'All the nations of the world are
obliged to obey the Roman Emperor elected by the seven distinguished
princes of Germany as representatives of the whole world.'" As a sam-
ple of Ulzurrum's unreliability, he offered his attempt to support his
position through a distortion of the views of the fourteenth-century
Bolognese canonist Johannes Andreae. Las Casas then concluded this
attack on Ulzurrum with a promise of more: "But since we hope, with
God's help, to show elsewhere, point by point *(singillatim),* how full of
errors the above-mentioned treatise *On the Rule of the World* is, for the
present we shall forgo saying anything more about it."

Thus a chapter that had bristled with attacks on unnamed champions of the world dominion of the ancient and modern Roman Empire
concluded with an assault on a prominent named authority: the Navarrese jurist whose densely written treatise we have earlier cited as an ideological pillar of the "neo-Ghibelline" imperial ideology of Charles V.
But we cannot help calling to mind a name never mentioned or hinted
at here at all: that of Sepúlveda. For, as we have noted, the Cordoban
humanist was remarkably uninterested in the "juridical" function of the
Roman Empire. The ancient and modern Roman claim to world dominion, be it de jure or de facto, seems to have been a matter of complete
indifference to him. And yet Sepúlveda's celebration of the *cultural*
power of the Roman model no doubt encouraged Las Casas to compose
this apparent digression on the "illegitimate title" of the emperor's lord-

ship of the whole world. Of course, there was also the additional incentive provided by the discussions of this title by his fellow Dominicans Soto, Vitoria, Carranza, and Cano, but even this does not fully account for Las Casas's motivation in addressing the issue in such detail here. His intriguing promise to devote an entire treatise to Ulzurrum's arguments clearly indicates that the question of the Roman Empire had become, thanks largely to Sepúlveda, a burr under Las Casas's saddle, and his attack on the Roman "world dominion" thesis in this chapter was not simply a formulaic act of conformity to what had become, since Soto's 1535 *Relectio de dominio,* an argumentative tradition.

Las Casas's next engagement with the Romans in the *Apologia* was conducted on terrain speciously more congenial to Sepúlveda, for the implicit question here was the cultural level of the Indians vis-à-vis that of, among other peoples, the Romans. Chapters 34–37 constitute a two-pronged attack upon Sepúlveda's assumption that the practice of human sacrifice securely relegated the Indians to the lower rungs of the human cultural ladder, the top rung being occupied by the ancient Romans and the modern Spaniards. While Las Casas's boldest and most famous (or notorious) gambit was to defend human sacrifice as an eminently rational attempt to give thanks to the divine by offering up the most valuable of all possible gifts, he also employed the more predictable strategy of establishing human sacrifice as a prominent feature of the *ius gentium,* a practice familiar to most regions of the known world at one time or another. After all, "Strabo reminds us that our own Spanish people *(Hispani nostri),* who reproach the poor Indian peoples for human sacrifice, used to sacrifice captives and their horses."[127] A triple identity is implied here: modern Spaniards equal pre-Roman Iberians equal modern Indians. We shall be exploring this strategy further in the fifth chapter.

But it was not only the "barbarian" early Spaniards who practiced human sacrifice; so did their culturally superior conquerors, the Romans. For if the Romans at times displayed a tolerance for human sacrifice among their subject peoples, it was because their own hands bore bloody stains. "Plutarch writes that the Romans failed to punish some barbarians who were sacrificing men to the gods, because they knew it was done from custom and law. Plutarch also says that the Romans themselves did the same thing at times."[128] Las Casas proceeded to bolster this point with a substantial quotation from Plutarch's *Roman Questions* (no. 83; 283F–284A), which tells of how the Romans on one occasion refrained from punishing a barbarian tribe for perpetrating human sacrifice when they were reminded that they had themselves recently sacrificed two men and two women in the Forum Boarium in Rome. Las Casas would no doubt have been delighted to learn that it appears that these particular barbarians whom the Romans failed to punish, the Bletonesii, were an Iberian tribe, of Bletisa.[129]

Now, this enrollment of the Romans into the ranks of the world's known human sacrificers was conducted in a sober enough manner, with no hint of that anti-Roman animus that informed Las Casas's other discussions of the Romans in these years and in this manuscript. After all, his entire strategy in these chapters could be summed up as the attempt to make human sacrifice not only rational, but also normal and ordinary. Hence Romans, early Iberians, and modern Indians have all gathered at the same bloody altar. But in chapter 36 Las Casas did manage to suggest an indictment of the Romans—or of their Italian ancestors, at least—though it was an indictment so delicately phrased that it could not sabotage his main point that human sacrifice was an unremarkably common human practice. Here he first paraphrased and then directly quoted a passage in the first book of the *Roman Antiquities* of Dionysius of Halicarnassus that records how in pre-Roman days "the peoples of Italy," when afflicted by drought, were persuaded to institute an annual offering of "the first-fruits of what was most valuable to the gods"—that is, firstborn human beings. This anecdote brings together Las Casas's two main points in these chapters: the fact that human sacrifice was as common to the Old World as to the New and the claim that human sacrifice was a rational and fundamentally appropriate practice, for it offered up (to cite Dionysius a little more directly) "a thing of all others the most precious in the sight of the gods" (χρῆμα παντὸς μάλιστα θεοῖς τιμιώτατον).[130] Indeed, it is tempting to wonder if the words of Dionysius here, in a passage that Las Casas transcribed at much fuller length in his *Apologética historia sumaria*, might have assisted him to his notorious and breathtaking argument in defense of human sacrifice.

But there was a sting in the tail of Las Casas's citation of this incident in the pseudohistory of ancient Italy, for he couldn't resist appending a barbed conjecture of his own: "Possibly the idea of human sacrifice spread from here through the whole world" [Hinc fortassis demanavit per omnes gentes opinio immolandi homines]. A look at the actual text of Dionysius of Halicarnassus reveals a couple of interesting points here. First, there is the fact that the Greek historian had not been talking here about "the peoples of Italy" [Italiae populi] at all, but about "Pelasgian" interlopers in Italy. (The ancients regarded the "Pelasgians" as pre-Greek "aborigines" in Greece, especially prominent in Thessaly and Thrace.) Second, Dionysius nowhere implied that the practice of human sacrifice spread from this Pelasgian practice *per omnes gentes*. He did, however, mention that shortly afterward the Pelasgian nation itself "was scattered over most of the earth" (ἐπὶ πλεῖστον γῆς). Here, it seems, is the germ of Las Casas's diffusionist suggestion. Now, it is perfectly possible that Las Casas, a prodigiously busy man, had been reading carelessly here, but there was nevertheless a certain polemical incentive for him to do so. To substitute the "peoples of Italy"—which would of course include the ancestors of the Romans—for the transient non-Italian Pelasgians, and then to trace the worldwide practice of human sacrifice back to these "peoples of Italy" would be to stick yet another needle into the inflated reputation of Italy, the Old World's supposed cultural capital, the heartland of the Roman Empire. Las Casas did not belabor the point, however, for this diffusionist scenario could have created difficulties for his general assumption in these chapters that the practice of human sacrifice is part of the *ius gentium*, a body of practices found throughout the world not as a result of cultural diffusion but thanks to the entire human race's access to natural law via the use of reason. Still, he could not resist this drive-by volley at the ancestors of his detested—and Sepúlveda's beloved—Romans.[131]

It is the fifty-second chapter of the *Apologia*, the first of four virtual appendices to the whole work, that offers the most direct response to Sepúlveda's encomium on the Roman Empire in the *Democrates secundus* and in the *Apologia* printed in Rome that summarized it. Despite Sepúlveda's appeal to Augustine and "Aquinas," Las Casas insisted that the Roman Empire "did not arise through justice but was acquired by tyranny and violence, as we have proved elsewhere from historians, lawyers, and theologians" (i.e., in chapter 5).[132] True, Augustine did admit that the early Romans had "some moral virtues, specifically love of country and zeal for the public welfare," and they did promulgate "just laws and dealt kindly and gently with the peoples who were subject to their rule by reason of war or some other reason." But these virtues of the Romans were not genuine virtues, for which one needs Christian faith. If God did grant the Romans their empire, it was to fur-

ther his own purposes, not to reward their virtues, though Las Casas
did cite Augustine's suggestion in *City of God* (5.15) that the Romans
received their empire as a "consolation prize" for their loss of eternal
life. Just as God had earlier made good use of Hell-destined potentates
like Nebuchadnezzar and Cyrus, so, according to Gratian, he used the
Romans under Titus to scourge the Jews for their rejection of the Mes-
siah. Las Casas concluded:

> God, then, used the Romans both to dispose that part of the world for
> his gracious and gentle coming and to symbolize the unity of the
> Church (that is, his holy kingdom, which would take in the entire
> world) through the unification of the nations. Furthermore, he chose
> the Romans to be the executioners or executors of his justice in order
> to punish those nations whose crimes angered him. . . . This, then,
> does not allow Sepúlveda to throw up against us the tyranny of the
> Romans as a justification of our tyranny toward the Indians, which
> has been called a *conquista*. For the Romans, the Persians, and the
> Assyrians have perished forever because their wars were not pleasing
> in the eyes of the Lord, as we have proved from the words of the holy
> Fathers and, God willing, shall make clear at greater length.[133]

Las Casas's liberation of Augustine's highly ambivalent view of the
Roman Empire from the common attempt to enlist his services as pan-
egyricist of Rome in many ways anticipated the position Soto was about
to broadcast in the *De iustitia et iure* in 1553. (There is in fact a marginal
reference to a nearby passage in Soto's work in this chapter, though we
cannot be sure that the notation was made by Las Casas himself.)[134]
Soto's arguments were more wide-ranging and more trenchant, but
both Dominicans were clearly engaged in the same project of denying
Augustine to the Roman party, and it is likely that Las Casas owed
some of his points here to consultation with the Salamantine master,
who noted in the *De iustitia et iure* that he had been making this point
often ("saepe adnotavi"). Especially interesting is Las Casas's concluding promise to discuss the case of the Romans, along with other pagan
empires, "at greater length" [latius].[135] This clearly recalls his proposal
at the end of chapter 21 to refute "point by point" Miguel Ulzurrum's
troublesome defense of the universal sovereignty of the Roman Empire.
Presumably Las Casas had in mind one single project here, one that
would decisively demolish the utility of the Roman Empire for the
justification of Spanish rule in the New World. While he apparently

never got around to writing this treatise, the references to Rome in the *Treinta proposiciones muy jurídicas,* the *Tratado comprobatorio,* and, above all, the *Apologia* give us a good indication of the likely flavor of that "ghost" treatise. But even if he did not find time to devote a treatise explicitly to the defects of the Roman model, Las Casas nevertheless was soon to produce even more intense demolitions of the prestige of the ancient Romans in the context of a sustained defense of the cultures of the peoples of the New World. He gave a foretaste of these later assaults in his attack on Fernández de Oviedo in chapter 58 of the *Apologia.* For "a man who wants to be thought to have read the old histories" (despite his ignorance of Latin!), Oviedo was, according to Las Casas, remarkably unaware that "the Persians, the Scythians, the Massagetes, the Derbices, the Tybarenes, and the Hyrcanians, as well as the Romans, the Angles, the Cantabrians, and the other peoples in Spain, far outdid the Indians (whom our opponents defame as cattle) in vices and uncivilized behavior."[136] The sly insertion of the Romans among obscure and unsavory Old World barbarians (including, of course, the ancestral Spaniards!) is a nice touch in itself, but it also prepares us for the strategy that would dominate the work Las Casas at this time still envisioned as part 2 of the *Apologia* (presented in some preliminary form in Valladolid in the 1550 session) and that we know as the massive and often overwhelming *Apologética historia sumaria.* Here, even more single-mindedly than in the *Apologia,* Las Casas would assault the prestige of the Romans in the arena of cultural achievements and behavior, the very sphere in which Sepúlveda assumed that they shared an unquestioned supremacy with their Spanish emulators.

Appended to the Paris manuscript of the *Apologia* is a letter to the Council of the Indies by Las Casas's fellow Dominican Bartolomé de la Vega. Apparently composed around 1562 (for he noted that the "Indian question" was now seventy years old), this letter was a passionate appeal to the council to authorize and encourage the publication of this work that would dispel the last lingering darkness about "the great question of the Indies (which is beyond all doubt the most important in the world)."[137] Determined to spike the cannons of those who were calling Las Casas a traitor to Spain, Vega began his letter with a hyperbolic encomium of the bishop as a wondrous benefactor of his native land, for as the first to discover and announce the truth of what was happening in the Indies, he was offering his countrymen the chance to repent before God's righteous wrath descended upon them. In an attempt to shame the council into giving Las Casas his due, Vega implicitly contrasted this prophet's lack of honor in his own land with a pseudohistorical counterscenario.

> The ancient Romans and the founders of other ancient kingdoms whose states were ruled by just laws used to honor those who attacked some outstanding abuse or who were benefactors of the state by having their likenesses carved in stone. To these images, erected in temples and elsewhere, they paid the highest reverence in order that death might not blot out the memory of men whose lives had been of such great advantage to the state. For these reasons there is no doubt that if those ancient times had had the good fortune to possess the author of the present book, mortal men would have venerated his image. They would have decreed that he be recognized, honored, and loved by all as the discoverer of truth in Indian affairs and as the father of all the inhabitants of that New World.[138]

Given Las Casas's decidedly negative assessment of ancient Rome in the *Apologia,* Vega's vision of him being granted a virtual apotheosis in a utopian Rome is piquantly arresting. It is in fact something of a rarity in the career of the Roman model in the conquest of the Indies and the attendant controversy, for it is predicated upon the *superiority* of ancient Romans to modern Spaniards, at least in one key respect: their purported willingness to honor those who reveal bitter truths.

But Vega's fantasy of a Roman-wreathed Las Casas also intriguingly parallels the historical fantasy of Montaigne with which we began this study, a fantasy that appeared in print less than twenty years later. Both Montaigne and Vega were devising wish-reveries. If only the Romans had conquered Mexico, what a marvelous new society would have come into being. If only Las Casas had lived in ancient Rome, he would have received his due meed of honor. Note, in fact, that Vega even specified, preposterously (in both senses of the word), that the Romans would have celebrated him "as the discoverer of truth in Indian affairs"! But we may be permitted to take both fantasies as emblematic of deeper truths. While no living and breathing ancient Romans ever set foot in the New World (*pace* Marineo Sículo, whose interesting contention we shall be encountering later on), the Romans did, as we have seen, accompany the Spanish conquistadors every league of the way, ghost legionaries who served as frames of reference and as standards of excellence whose greatest utility was their mute willingness to allow themselves to be surpassed by their Spanish emulators. Similarly, while Las Casas in reading Vega's encomium was presumably disconcerted to find himself contemplating his own bust in a Roman temple, it is nevertheless true that in the course of his involvement in the controversy of the Indies he did find himself repeatedly transported to a Roman world he knew exceptionally well, even by the standards of an age much more classically sophisticated than our own. While Sepúlveda's dangerous celebration of ancient Rome provoked in the fiery Dominican a profound reaction against the power of the Roman model, there can be no doubting that Las Casas was "at home" in the Roman world, that he knew his way around this uncongenial terrain with a sureness impressive even in a man of the Renaissance. This familiarity will come into even sharper focus in the last two chapters of this study, as we explore two of the most fascinating classical themes deployed in the controversy of the Indies: the parallels between the Roman invasion of Spain and the Spanish invasion of the Indies, and the comparison of Greco-Roman and New World societies. Neither Las Casas nor his hated conquistadors and their apologists could banish the Romans from their radically divergent attempts to interpret and evaluate the Spanish conquest of the New World.

CHAPTER FOUR

After Valladolid

The Fate of the Roman Model in the Continuing Debate over the Justice of the Conquest

The vigorous attack that Las Casas mounted against the model of ancient Roman imperialism in the great debate in Valladolid in 1550–51 by no means signaled the immediate demise of the role of the Romans in the debate over the legitimacy of Spanish dominion in the Indies. In this chapter we shall first be examining four documents produced within a decade of that debate, all of them, with one possible exception, expressing or reporting the views of clerics who were either then living in the New World or had at least had direct personal experience of the Indies. (None of these documents appeared in print in its own day; one of them has yet to be fully published.) We shall then conclude with a later, much more influential pair of texts by the great colonial jurist Juan de Solórzano Pereira, who in 1629 and 1639 attempted to survey the controversy that had raged nearly a century earlier and to formulate at last a definitive statement of the Spanish title to the Indies, in the course of which he attempted a reasonably dispassionate assessment of the relevance of Roman imperial theory and practice to Spain's claims.

Miguel de Arcos versus a Bishop of New Spain on Caesar, Titus, and Roman Imperialism

Our first document is a short treatise by Fray Miguel de Arcos entitled *My Opinion of a Treatise on the Permissibility of War against the Indians (Parecer mío sobre un tratado de la guerra que se puede hacer a los Indios)*, assigned by its editors, Agustín Millares Carlo and Lewis Hanke, to a date around 1551.[1] Arcos was the Dominican provincial of Andalusia to whom Francisco de Vitoria in 1534 had confided his revulsion against the deeds of the conquistadors in Peru ("their very mention freezes my blood"). In his *Parecer*, Arcos attacked a now lost treatise by an unnamed Mexican bishop sent him by the archbishop of Mexico. Lewis Hanke and Marcel Bataillon have identified this bishop as none other than the celebrated Vasco de Quiroga, Franciscan bishop of Michoacán, still fondly recalled as "Tata Vasco" ("Daddy Vasco") in the region around Lake Pátzcuaro, where he attempted to create communities of Tarascan (Purépecha) Indians inspired by More's *Utopia*.[2] This identification depends heavily upon a letter of 1553 in which Quiroga mentioned a treatise *(De debellandis Indis)* that he had composed a couple of years earlier in defense of the Spanish title to the Indies. We shall be returning to the authorship and date of the document Arcos criticized, for these questions have a bearing on our second treatise, which has also been assigned by its editor to Quiroga.

The treatise that Arcos was attacking addressed a central question of the debate at Valladolid: whether it is permitted first to make war on the Indians in order to subject them to the Castilian Crown and only then to preach them the Gospel. The author came down firmly on the side of Sepúlveda, though there is no evidence that he cited him. In fact, he argued that the king of Castile was not only permitted but in fact obligated by the demands of "spiritual charity" to subjugate the Indians in order to facilitate their conversion. In his rejoinder, Arcos granted that the Spanish Crown did indeed have an obligation to spread the faith, but he joined his fellow Dominicans in proposing the apostles' peaceful conversion of the Gentiles as the proper alternative to the violent methods favored by their fellow Spaniards in the Indies. The true obstacle to conversion, he argued, was not the fickleness of the Indians, but "our cruelties and insatiable hunger for gold." He went beyond his associates, however, when he proceeded to complain of the compliance of the papacy in granting every request that the Spanish monarchs had made concerning the Indies.[3]

In the second part of his treatise, the New World bishop had turned from "spiritual charity" to the secular benefits conferred upon the Indian population by Spanish rule. Like Sepúlveda, he argued that the conquest was "for their own good" [para el bien dellos]—fine sentiments, Arcos dryly noted, "if the Indians lived in our kingdom of Granada." But, again, Spaniards in the Indies were men driven by an "insatiable hunger for gold," and the last thing on their minds was the benefit of the conquered. Next the unnamed bishop turned to the Roman model, by way of an appeal to Ambrose's gloss on Psalm 45:

To wage war on the Indians to subjugate them is not really to wage
war on them, but to relieve them of many bitter wars that they wage
among themselves. Then, in subjugating them a great benefaction is
done to them. He proves this conclusion through what Ambrose says
in the cited passage: that as a result of Julius Caesar's tyranny over the
empire there came a halt to the civil wars that were destroying Rome
in the time of Marius and Sulla, of Caesar and Pompey, and also in
the time of the [Second] Triumvirate, down to the time when the
empire stayed at peace under Augustus Caesar, and furthermore from
this good accruing to the Roman Republic God opened up a path for
the apostles, so that, while everyone was at peace under the empire,
they might preach the Gospel through a large part of the world.[4]

Countering this argument with the Pauline principle that we are not to
do evil so that good may result (Rom. 3:8), Arcos added that while the
establishment of the Roman imperial autocracy may indeed have had
beneficial side-effects, the thanks were due to God "and not to Julius
Caesar, who ruled tyrannically over that which was not his own and is
now paying for it in Hell and will pay for it for eternity."

Having disposed of the bishop's decidedly eccentric approval of the
"beneficial" tyranny of Julius Caesar as a peaceful interlude in the civil
wars before the final achievement of the Pax Augusta, Arcos discussed
at greater length another Roman exemplum of his own that he obviously considered a more challenging instance of Roman imperialism
unwittingly generating worthy results. This was Titus's destruction of
Jerusalem—one of the conquistadors' own favorite Roman precedents,
as we saw in the first chapter. Like Las Casas in the fifty-second chapter
of the *Apologia* (and so perhaps also in the Valladolid debate), Arcos
linked Titus with Nebuchadnezzar as "scourges of God." He shared
with Las Casas the standard assumption that by destroying Jerusalem
the Roman emperor was indeed avenging the murder of Christ, but
both Dominicans also agreed that God's use of Titus shed no sanctity
on the Roman himself or on Roman imperial rule in general. To emphasize this point, Arcos denounced the lies of "a book called *Gamaliel*,
condemned by the Office of the Holy Inquisition."[5] Like the popular
romance *Vaspasiano*, this pseudohistorical potpourri, composed in
Catalan and translated into Spanish by Juan de Molina sometime after
1517, purveyed the popular late medieval legend that the Roman siege
and destruction of Jerusalem was a deliberate act of revenge against the
Jews for the killing of Christ, a relic of whom had saved a Roman

emperor from death. To these fancies Arcos opposed the testimony of "Josepho, nobilíssimo hystoriador," that the Romans' motives were strictly self-interested: "to return [the Jewish people] to subjection to the Roman Empire, from which they had revolted." Furthermore, Arcos claimed, while Titus may have been a relatively good emperor, he nevertheless

> seriously offended God and was a great blasphemer, for, as Hegesippus recounts in his *De excidio hiersolimitano*, when Titus one day came to parley with the besieged Jews, he told them not to trust in the powers of anyone, for even the powers of God could not protect them from his hands. He said this or something like it, for it has been a while since I've had a look at Hegesippus. This most noble emperor said at the time of his death that he had in all his life performed only one deed that ought to weigh on his conscience, though he didn't say what it was. I suspect that it was the blasphemy that he uttered against God. I have no other basis for the suspicion than the great nobility and good nature of this prince, for which everyone called him "the love and darling of the human race." I have expanded on this point so that it might be seen by very clear examples that not everything that has good success and good results is itself good and licit.[6]

There is a certain irony in the fact that in his search for the "historical" Titus Arcos scornfully rejected the fictional *Gamaliel* but gladly embraced another suspect text, the Latin version of Josephus that purported to be the original work of one "Hegesippus." According to Louis H. Feldman (citing an unpublished Yeshiva University dissertation by Esther Sorscher), this work, identification of whose author has been "one of scholarship's favorite indoor sports, . . . portrays the Roman army as *sanctissimi commilitiones,* a veritable precursor of the church militant" and was designed "to prove that the war was a divine punishment inflicted upon the Jews."[7] Reliance on this source no doubt accounts for the difficulty Arcos experienced in presenting a coherent account of Titus. Was he a "gran blasfemo," or was he the "amor et deliciae generis humani?" It is the latter that prevails as Arcos concludes with the picture of the dying emperor repenting his offense to God, thus obscuring the main point—though he quickly became aware of this and helpfully restated that point.

The *Parecer* of Miguel de Arcos on the treatise of the Mexican bishop offers us in miniature a fascinating parallel to the conflicting

views of the Roman model that had been on display in the great debate
in Valladolid. The fact that the parallel is not precise, that it offers idiosyncratic features on both sides, simply reinforces our sense of the versatility and richness of the model of Roman imperialism in the controversy of the Indies. Like Sepúlveda, our unnamed New World bishop
appears to have shown no interest at all in the "juridical" argument that
the Romans, as "lords of the world," supplied the reigning "emperor of
the Romans" with a title to dominion in the Indies. Unlike Sepúlveda,
however, he appears to have been equally indifferent to the "cultural"
argument that the Romans, as spectacular proof of the supposed Aristotelian right of superior peoples to rule over barbarians, served as a
justification and an inspiration for the modern Spaniards in the Indies.
Rather, the bishop's appeal to the Romans was apparently limited to
their usefulness in furnishing a fairly specific Old World historical
model to be imitated in the New World: the simultaneous establishment
of autocracy in Rome and a secure Pax Romana in the Mediterranean
world. At first glance, this precedent seems familiar enough. At least as
early as Orosius, Christian writers had asserted or implied that God had
intentionally synchronized the birth of Christ with the inauguration of
the Pax Augusta. Not only had Dante elaborated upon this at the end of
the first book of the *De monarchia*, but Las Casas himself alluded to it
in chapter 52 of the *Apologia:* "God, then, used the Romans both to dis-
pose that part of the world for his gracious and gentle coming and to
symbolize the unity of the Church . . . through the unification of the
nations." But our Mexican bishop disconcertingly attributed the origin—or at least an anticipation—of this benevolent autocratic tranquil-
ity to Julius Caesar—and he apparently did not even flinch from conceding that Caesar's supposed pacification of the Roman world was in
itself an act of tyranny. We may recall that in his 1535 *Relectio de
dominio* Domingo de Soto had singled out for special opprobrium Caesar's grab for autocracy: "Julius Caesar, as one learns in his *Commentaries,* obtained the empire tyrannically and by means of civil discord."
That is, the short-lived peace that Caesar's triumph brought simply
capped the momentous civil war his own ambitions had precipitated.
Similarly, Melchor Cano, as we saw, was willing to grant a species of
legitimacy to Roman imperial rule only with the accession of Augustus.
Even Sepúlveda, for all his praise of Caesar as a model of moderation in
warfare, did not venture to praise Caesar's pursuit of autocratic

power—indeed, in his earlier works he had explicitly, if unemphati-
cally, condemned it. Perhaps our Mexican bishop's gentler view of Caesar owed something to the popularity of the Roman warlord among the
conquistadors in whose midst he lived and whom he seems to have gone
out of his way to humor. It was in any case a view sufficiently jolting to
Miguel de Arcos (who, by the way, possessed a manuscript copy of
Soto's 1535 relection) to trigger his passionate denunciation of the
"mucha sangre de Romanos" for which Caesar was still paying in Hell
and to inspire him to a further laying of the Roman ghost in his complex digression on Titus. At least as impressive as the Mexican bishop's
appeal to the Romans is the eminent Dominican's palpable eagerness to
explode it.

The Model of Roman Imperialism in a Fragmentary Treatise Attributed to Vasco de Quiroga

We have noted above that Lewis Hanke and Marcel Bataillon argued
that the treatise attacked by Miguel de Arcos was the lost *De debellandis Indis* of Vasco de Quiroga, bishop of Michoacán. In 1988 René
Acuña published what he confidently affirmed was an extensive fragment of Quiroga's treatise.[8] This fragment dates from the reign of
Charles V and argues for the right of the Spanish Crown, on papal
authority, to dispossess and appropriate by force the principalities of
the infidels of the New World. The manuscript forms part of the collection of papers of Bartolomé de las Casas acquired by Juan Bautista
Muñoz around 1784, and it is today in the Muñoz collection in the Real
Academia Española de la Historia, Madrid. Muñoz himself had suggested that this was a fragment of the treatise that Quiroga mentioned
in a letter of 1553 to Juan Bernal Díaz de Luco, bishop of Calahorra, a
letter to be found in this same collection of the papers of Las Casas.[9]
Quiroga there mentioned that around the time of the Valladolid debate
he had sent his treatise to the Council of the Indies, whose president was
very impressed by it, until Las Casas got hold of it and harshly criticized
it. Muñoz's assignment of the fragment to this lost treatise was seconded, after an interval of nearly two centuries, by the Dominican
scholar Benno Biermann, who discovered a copy of both the fragment
and of Quiroga's letter in the British Museum.[10] Accepting and extend-

ing Biermann's arguments, Acuña has printed a very full edition and commentary, boldly bearing the name of Vasco de Quiroga on its cover and title page.

A lively controversy has been sparked by the fact that the arguments of this newly rediscovered fragmentary candidate for Quiroga's *De debellandis Indis* appear to be quite unlike those of the treatise attacked by Arcos. Biermann obviated this difficulty by simply doubting that Arcos was writing about a treatise by Quiroga at all.[11] But Acuña's solution is rather more ingenious. He argues that Arcos's *Parecer* was indeed a critique of a Quirogan treatise—*not*, however, of the *De debellandis Indis* of around 1551, but of a much earlier treatise to which Quiroga had alluded in his *Información en derecho* of 1535.[12] Acuña speculates that Arcos was requested by Fray Juan de Zumárraga, first archbishop of Mexico, to comment on this earlier treatise of Quiroga's at a time when the latter was first being considered for the bishopric of Michoacán (1533–34). This is implausible for at least three reasons.

First, Arcos's *Parecer* shows an unstated but quite unmistakable debt to the *Relectio de Indis* of his friend Vitoria, delivered in 1539. In fact, when concluding his examination of the treatise with a demonstration that the wars against the Indians did not meet the demands of the rules of just war, not only did he adopt most of Vitoria's "just titles," but he discussed them in the very same order in which Vitoria had presented them.[13]

Second, Arcos's main departure from Vitoria's views was his emphatic contempt for the Roman Empire as a model for Spanish behavior in the New World, a tacit "correction" of the Salamantine theologian's respectful treatment of Roman imperialism. It is precisely this "revision" of Vitoria that we have seen Cano and Las Casas developing, with a similar tactful absence of direct criticism of Vitoria, in the middle to late 1540s. It is true that, as we have seen, Domingo de Soto had foreshadowed that assault on Roman imperialism in his relection of 1535, and it is also true that we know that a manuscript of that relection appeared among the papers of Miguel de Arcos. But Acuña's scenario would still place the composition of Arcos's *Parecer* a year or two before Soto's relection.

Third, Arcos's *Parecer* refers to the historical romance *Gamaliel* as having been "prohibited by the Office of the Holy Inquisition."[14] But the *Gamaliel* was not in fact condemned until the Toledo Index of 1551, the first of the Spanish inquisitional indices.[15] Indeed, so far was the

Gamaliel from being prohibited in 1533–34, it was published by the major Sevillan printer Juan Cromberger in 1534 and again by Domenico de Robertis in 1536.[16] It should be noted, moreover, that Silvio Zavala, the most prominent student of Quiroga's life and writings, has vigorously opposed the attempt of Biermann and Acuña to assign the fragmentary treatise to Quiroga at any stage of his career.[17] His principal procedure is to compare Quiroga's known views and favorite authorities with both the fragmentary treatise and the information supplied by Arcos about the lost treatise. On this basis, Zavala denies Quiroga's authorship of the fragmentary treatise, but affirms it for the treatise attacked by Arcos.

Still, no matter who was the author or what was the precise date of the fragmentary treatise that Muñoz, Biermann, and Acuña have attributed to Quiroga, this document has its own contribution to make to the history of the role of the Roman Empire in the controversy of the Indies, for one way in which it does resemble the treatise Arcos criticized is its emphatically positive valuation of Roman imperialism. The bulk of the treatise as we have it defends the general thesis of Hostiensis that the coming of Christ annulled all dominion among the infidels, and also the more specific thesis that the papal bulls of 1493 assigned temporal dominion over the infidels of the New World to the Spanish Crown. The principal targets of the author are Cardinal Cajetan "and his followers," who held firm to the Thomistic principle that divine law does not annul natural or human law. The Romans entered the argument by way of an appeal to the early-fifteenth-century jurist Paolo de Castro, who argued that the *ius gentium* allowed one free people to go to war against another for a good end, with the aim of providing good rule and government for the people to be subjected. If this principle were not accepted, the Bolognese jurist added, then the *principatus et monarchia* of the Romans would have been illicit, and we know that that could not have been the case, "for Christ approved it when he said, 'Render unto Caesar the things which are Caesar's.'"[18] To this our author added the citation by the Bolognese canonist and archdeacon Guido di Baysio (d. 1313) of papal decretals to support the claim that "all men ought to be subject to this Roman Empire." Next followed the inevitable appeal to the beginning of the second chapter of Luke, the worldwide census supposedly commanded by the emperor Augustus, an edict "under which even Christ chose to be born and enrolled, as though under a just empire." This latter interpretation of the significance of the census was shored up by a reference to Orosius, book 6, chapter 22. Finally, he cited Jerome (a dubiously attributed passage he found in Gratian's *Decretum*), Augustine's *City of God*, book 5, chapter 12, and the jurist Luca da Penne (d. ca. 1390) in support of the familiar thesis that the Romans earned their empire through their virtues.

While our author left the precise aim of his barrage of pro-Roman citations somewhat obscure, it appears that he was trying to hit two targets at once. On the one hand, he wanted to suggest that the rule of the Romans was validated by *ius gentium*. As a benevolent imperial power, Rome's conquests were self-evidently justified by worldwide custom and opinion. Implicit here, of course, was the assumption that precisely the same thing could and should be said for the Spanish conquest of the Indies. But our author's insistent appeal to biblical texts, church fathers, and canon (as well as civil) lawyers indicated that the Romans' title to imperial rule did not rest only on the *ius gentium*, but also on divine law, on the will and providence of God. Again, the Spaniards could be assumed to share this imperial grace, this heady "manifest destiny." Thus, even though he chose to sidestep the vigorously contested title of the emperor's world dominion, our anonymous author may actually have given us a better glimpse than did that elegant student of the classics Juan Ginés de Sepúlveda of the kind of "theology of empire" that Domingo de Soto was attempting to demolish both in his 1535 *Relectio de dominio* and in his 1553 magnum opus, *De iustitia et iure*.

Alonso de la Vera Cruz versus the Roman Empire: University of Mexico, 1554

In 1968 Ernest J. Burrus made an impressive contribution to our knowledge of the controversy of the Indies with his publication of the Latin text, with English translation and a learned commentary, of the remarkable work of a remarkable man.[19] Born to a wealthy family of Caspueñas near Toledo around 1507, Alonso Gutiérrez studied first at Alcalá and then at Salamanca, where he became the devoted pupil of Francisco de Vitoria and, upon completion of his studies, a lecturer in philosophy. Recruited by the Augustinian missionary Francisco de la Cruz, he and his impressive library arrived in 1536 at the port of Veracruz in New Spain, where he promptly joined the Augustinian order under the name Alonso de la Vera Cruz. His first years in the New

World were spent in Michoacán among the Tarascan (Purépecha) people, whose language he soon learned and whose education and religious instruction he furthered through the foundation of a number of monasteries with schools, a project for which he received the encouragement and aid of Vasco de Quiroga. When the University of Mexico opened in 1553, Vera Cruz was on the founding faculty, and in his theological course for that inaugural year of 1553–54 he ambitiously expounded upon the rights of the conquerors and the conquered in the New World, delivering at year's end the great relection published by Burrus. Vera Cruz continued to conduct a distinguished academic career, punctuated by an eleven-year stay in Spain during which he became close to Las Casas in the bishop's final years. He published texts on logic and a manual for priests encountering perplexing native marriage practices *(Speculum coniugiorum)*, but he left also a large number of unpublished manuscripts—some of them, our relection among them, apparently having earned the disapproval of the archbishop of México, Alonso de Montúfar. Vera Cruz died in Mexico City in July 1584.

Though it appears to have originally lacked a formal title, in the *Speculum coniugiorum* of 1556 Vera Cruz supplied a convenient name for the relection he had delivered at the University of Mexico in 1554: *Relection on the Dominion of the Unbelievers and on Just War (Relectio de dominio infidelium et iusto bello)*. It is several times longer than the *Relectio de Indis* of his teacher Vitoria—187 pages in Burrus's edition—and must have been read in several sessions, though it was no doubt also expanded for its intended, aborted publication. It is organized into eleven "doubts" [dubia] or questions, which fall in turn into three main groupings. The first six questions concern the rights and duties of Spaniards, especially encomenderos, in the New World. Many of the students listening to this relection were expecting soon to find themselves in the uncomfortably challenging role of confessors to Spaniards who had acquired tribute, labor, and land from Indians, and the doubts raised by the New Laws and also by the controversy over the *Confessionario* of Las Casas lent an electric sense of urgency to much of Vera Cruz's discussion here. This topicality was heightened by Vera Cruz's measured but powerful invocations of his own witnessing of Spanish acts of usurpation of native rights ("testis sum oculatus," he intoned in one such passage) and also by vivid vignettes of the realities of the encomienda system. (For example: since a certain encomendero's renewal of a mining encomienda required that the cacique of the Indian laborers signal his consent to the viceroy, the baffled chief suddenly found himself fawned upon by the very man who normally addressed him as a "scoundrel dog.")[20] While he agreed with the Dominicans' rejection of the argument of Hostiensis that infidelity does not abolish dominion, Vera Cruz did not deny that Spaniards could legitimately receive land, tribute, and labor in the New World. But in those all too frequent cases where their right was dubious they needed to be sternly instructed to make restitution or forgo the sacraments of the Church. What rights the Spanish did have in the Indies rested in large part upon the authority of two supremely important individuals, the emperor and the pope, and so questions 7–9 are devoted to them. Finally, the last two "doubts" concern the familiar question of the legitimacy of the wars against the Indians, first the illegitimate causes, then the legitimate.

As one might suspect, these last two doubts—like, indeed, much of the rest of the relection—betray a profound debt to Vitoria's *Relectio de Indis* of 1539, even though, remarkably, Vera Cruz never once in this entire work mentioned the name of the man whom he later called, in the *Speculum coniugiorum,* "my teacher, easily the prince of theologians in his day."[21] Ernest Burrus believed that, strong Vitorian echoes notwithstanding, the fact that the great Salamantine theologian's relections were not published until 1557 constitutes a serious problem here, but it is hard to see why.[22] Manuscript copies of Vitoria's *Relectio de Indis* circulated widely, as we have noted, and it would be most remarkable if a distinguished former student and colleague of his, planning to discuss many of the same points, had not managed to secure himself a copy, no tricky matter given the well-documented traffic of Salamanca graduates heading for the New World. Consequently, when we turn to Vera Cruz's "legitimate titles" of conquest (doubt 11), we expect to find a version of Vitoria's "seventh just title," "for the sake of allies and friends" [causa sociorum et amicorum], and we are not disappointed. "If some of the savages waged just war against other savages, the Christians might answer the summons of the injured party and wage just war against the evil-doers, and, in consequence, come into possession of dominion in the same way as might the injured party."[23] Though Vera Cruz immediately introduced the case of Hungarians and Poles calling on the king of Spain to help them against the Turks, the examples he proceeded to develop at greatest length were precisely those adduced by Vitoria: Cortés's alliance with the Tlaxcalteca, Abraham's war against the four kings of Genesis 14, and, inevitably, the means by which the

Romans expanded their imperial rule.[24] His appeal to the Roman Empire is virtually identical to that of Vitoria—the wording is somewhat different, but the authorities and the instances are the very same: Augustine, "Aquinas" (i.e., Ptolemy of Lucca), Pope Sylvester's approval of Constantine, and Ambrose's approval of Theodosius.[25]

Suddenly, however, Vera Cruz subverted the entire "causa sociorum et amicorum" by asking a series of devastatingly inconvenient questions about the Mexican instance—Vitoria's only specific New World reference in his entire relection, we recall.[26] Were the Tlaxcalteca in fact engaged in a just war when they called in the Spaniards as allies against the Aztecs? While Vera Cruz left this question suggestively open, he went on to insist that even if they had been fighting a just war, that would not have given them the right to impose on the Aztecs the same treatment that they themselves had suffered at the Aztecs' hands. By the same token, their Spanish allies had no right to go so far as to commit "injuriam de novo." Nor would their waging of a just war have conferred upon either the Tlaxcalteca or their Spanish allies a right to Aztec treasure. This is clear "in lumine naturali"; you don't need divine revelation to grasp this point. Finally, to top it off, there is the awkward fact that when the Spaniards eliminated the dominion of the Aztecs, they proceeded, without missing a beat, to annul that of their so-called allies the Tlaxcalteca as well! How could an ally's aid to the supposedly injured party in a supposedly just war possibly justify the conquest of the injured party itself? Of course, Vera Cruz's principal aim in all of this was to demolish beyond hope of recovery Vitoria's sole citation of a specific instance of a just war of conquest in the New World. Still, it is hard to avoid the suspicion that Vera Cruz assumed that the Roman imperial model would have collapsed along with the Mexican instance that it was supposed to corroborate. After all, every one of the questions he raised about the Spaniards' alliance with Tlaxcala could be applied with ease to the progress of ancient Roman imperialism.

In fact, Vera Cruz had already undermined the ancient Romans' reputation as just and wise imperial rulers in his doubt 7, the perennial question "utrum imperator sit dominus orbis." As he noted at the beginning of this doubt, this was a question that had been lurking beneath all of the first six doubts, and now it could be deferred no longer. To take in doubts 7–9 at a glance, we may note that Vera Cruz's general contention, not fundamentally unlike that of Las Casas, was that while Charles V did indeed enjoy a just title to dominion in the

Indies, he did not receive it by virtue of a universal sovereignty inherited from the Romans; rather, he acquired it by virtue of his selection as an agent of the pope, who in turn possessed a limited power *(potestas indirecta)* in those temporal matters that concerned the propagation of the Catholic faith—though never, it should be emphasized again, to the serious detriment of the dominion of native rulers.

Like his teacher Vitoria, Vera Cruz offered Luke's account of Augustus's supposed decree that "the whole world" be counted as the most formidable support for the false thesis that the Roman emperor, both ancient and modern, was "lord of the world."[27] This argument for the fact of Roman world dominion during the lifetime of Christ was supplemented by an argument *ex silentio* for the justice of that dominion: the Bible's failure to indicate that Christ ever expressed disapproval of Roman rule. He proceeded to offer a daunting list of civil law glosses and both canon and civil lawyers who held that the emperor possessed de jure dominion over all nations, believers or unbelievers—no matter whether said unbelievers are obnoxious (e.g., the Turks) or harmless (e.g. the Amerindians). For these opinions, as for much else in this seventh doubt, Vera Cruz relied on the anti-imperialist, pro-monarchical tract of the French political theorist Barthelémy de Chassaneuz (Chassanaeus), *Catalogus gloriae mundi* (1529). But he was able to supplement Chassaneuz's roster with a recent Spanish imperial theorist of our acquaintance, "a certain Miguel Ulzurrum," who maintained that "one ought to hold and preach and teach" the doctrine that "the emperor is the one supreme head in matters temporal throughout the world."[28] Vera Cruz singled out for special outrage Ulzurrum's extended attack on the *Consilium* of the canon and civil lawyer Oldradus da Ponte (d. 1335), a treatise that extended the arguments of the Neapolitan jurists that Roman world lordship, both ancient and modern, was contradicted by the endorsement of independent monarchies implicit in the *ius gentium*. Vera Cruz denounced Ulzurrum's claim "that Oldradus . . . is to be condemned for heresy and his effigy and opinion are to be burned; and much else does he say poorly thought-out and inaccurately understood."[29] The animus that Vera Cruz unleashed here against Ulzurrum recalls Las Casas's unfulfilled project of demolishing the arguments of this Navarrese jurist and courtier of Charles V. Ulzurrum's crabbed treatise may fail to interest many modern scholars, but it was clearly regarded by these two champions of the rights of the Indians as a formidable obstacle to their program.

Vera Cruz's substantial refutation of the thesis of the world lord-ship of the Roman emperor hinged on the familiar axes of *factum* and *ius*, though the two tended to get rather jumbled in his increasingly diffuse analysis. The central *factum* was, of course, the absence of any compelling evidence in either Scripture or historiography that there ever was a *dominus totius mundi* either before or after the birth of Christ. Drawing heavily upon Chassaneuz and the *Supplementum chronicarum*, a universal history by Philippus Bergomensis (Jacopo Filippo Foresti da Bergamo, 1434–1520), Vera Cruz demolished the claims to de facto world dominion of the empires traditionally identified as the "four monarchies" of Nebuchadnezzar's vision in chapter 2 of Daniel: the Babylonian, the Persian, the Macedonian, and the Roman.[30] In each case, his procedure was to puncture the empire's claim to world lordship by citing independent polities that existed at the same time. For example, the Persian claim to universal dominion was exploded by the peculiar "fact" that "at the time of Darius there held sway as the emperor among the Athenians a ruler named Alcibiades," a delicious bit of fractured history that Vera Cruz found in both of his sources.

Naturally, it was the territorial limitations of the *quarta monarchia,* the Roman Empire, that received the fullest attention here. Though Jacopo Filippo da Bergamo recorded that Julius Caesar, upon obtaining *imperium* in Europe, crossed over to Asia and won the submission of "all the Eastern kings," nevertheless, Vera Cruz observed, native rulers persisted in Gaul, Spain, Greece, Macedonia, Syria, "and in all the regions of the world, even though God wished to greatly enlarge and have the Roman sway prevail, because of both its zeal for justice and its love of fatherland, as our Father Augustine states, as also the holy doctor [Aquinas; in fact, Ptolemy of Lucca] says in book III of *De regimine principum,* chapters 1 and 4."[31] Similarly, when Augustus became emperor on the death of Julius Caesar (an event Vera Cruz dated to 51 B.C.), there were other rulers—Antony in the East and "other kings ruled in Gaul and Spain."[32] So even at its providentially fostered apogee the Roman Empire was a radically limited entity, even if one confined one's glance to the Mediterranean basin. But of course an even more impressive expanse of territory eluded not only the Roman's grasp but even their knowledge: "iste Novus Orbis." Thus, if any property in that New World has been seized and reassigned by the emperor or his viceroys on the basis of the title of Roman world dominion, "the emperor himself would sin, and the one who owns property in virtue of such a grant cannot be secure in conscience."[33]

Interwoven with this refutation of world empire by appeal to scriptural and historical *factum* was Vera Cruz's refutation of the *ius* of such an empire, granting the counterfactual case of one's existence. "Even if there were one ruler he would have been brought into such a position not justly but through violence, as is evident from the wars they waged one against the other solely out of a desire to rule *(libidine dominandi)*."[34] After all, imperial ventures were implicitly forbidden by such biblical injunctions as the Golden Rule, Prov. 22:28 ("Don't pass beyond the ancient boundaries that your fathers set"), and the Tenth Commandment.[35] Turning specifically to the Roman Empire's claim to *ius* as world ruler, Vera Cruz declared that

> we are to note that if the whole world were actually subjected to the Roman Empire—which we will suppose but not admit—it does not immediately follow that it was rightfully so subjected, because it could have happened through violence and force of arms *(violentia et armorum vi)*, and so it does not follow that the world is held in just possession by the ruler. There were many tyrants who obtained their dominion through violence, as is evident from Sacred Scripture regarding Nimrod. . . , and the same is evident in regard to Nebuchadnezzar, Alexander, Antiochus, and others.[36]

Accordingly, neither by *ius* nor *factum* was the Roman emperor ever lord of the whole world. The reigning emperor's right to dominion in the Indies derived strictly and solely from his status as vicar of the vicar of Christ, and while this overlordship inevitably affected the dominions of the native rulers, it did not annul them. Furthermore, should the impediments to the preaching of the Word disappear, the emperor's dominion would evaporate. But this prospect need not alarm Charles, for the likelihood that native converts would be apt to backslide meant that the emperor and his heirs could expect to retain this dominion for a long time to come.[37]

While Vera Cruz's discussions of most of the just and unjust titles of conquest were clearly designed to be variations on themes sounded by his teacher Vitoria, his refutation of the world dominion of the Roman emperor more closely resembles that which Domingo de Soto offered in his *Relectio de dominio* of 1535 than it does that of Vitoria in the *Relectio de Indis* of 1539. This becomes especially clear when we focus on the views Soto and Vera Cruz expressed on both the *factum* and *ius* of ancient Roman imperialism. Both put far more emphasis than did Vitoria on the geographical limitations of the Roman Empire, emphasizing both the Romans' failure to subjugate all of the world then known to them and also their failure even to learn of the existence of the New World. Furthermore, Vera Cruz's rejection of the *ius* of a Roman Empire that grew only "through violence and force of arms" [violentia et armorum vi] strongly recalls Soto's doubts: "I do not know what right *(ius)* the Romans had to the lands that they vanquished. From their own historians we learn that their right was in force of arms *(ius erat in armis)*, and they subjugated many unwilling nations through no other title than that they were more powerful." A further striking echo of Soto occurs near the end of Vera Cruz's seventh doubt, when he returned to the tricky problem posed by the Augustan census in Luke. "If it is claimed that an enrollment of the whole world took place, this refers to the world under the Roman Empire; the greater part receives the name of the whole in ordinary usage; as when we say 'the whole world' when we mean a major portion *(maior pars)*."[38] Similarly, in his early attempt to deal with the obstacle of Luke 2:1, Soto had noted that one reason why "it was the custom among the Romans to call themselves lords of the world" was that "they had subjugated the major portion *(maiorem partem)* of the world then known." Now, the fact is that both Soto and Vera Cruz, fellow students of Vitoria, began to teach at Salamanca in the same year, 1532, and Soto apparently delivered his *Relectio de dominio* at the end of the last of Vera Cruz's three years at Salamanca (after which he left for the New World). Ernest Burrus, who appears at the time to have been unaware of the precise contents of Soto's relection, plausibly suggested that Vera Cruz was probably in Soto's audience that day.[39] On the basis of the echoes just noted, we can add the further suggestion that he packed a copy of his colleague's relection with the rest of his learned luggage and leafed through both it and Vitoria's *Relectio de Indis* when preparing his own bold and ambitious *Relectio de dominio infidelium*. While I have noted in the second chapter that Soto's *Relectio de dominio* has been oddly neglected even since it was published by Jaime Brufau Prats in 1964, it was clearly not neglected in its own time, though it was no doubt superseded by the 1553 publication of Soto's magisterial *De iustitia et iure*, which appears not to have reached Vera Cruz in time for his own relection.

Perhaps the most striking and significant feature of Vera Cruz's demolition of the title of the Roman Empire to lordship of the world is simply the very considerable amount of time he apportioned to this question in his relection, or at least in the version apparently intended for publication. Of course, the question was one that could not be ignored in an examination of the Spanish title to the Indies. All of the Dominicans whose arguments we have surveyed in the second and third chapters dealt with this question, notably Vitoria and Las Casas (whose manuscript *Apologia* does not seem to have been available to Vera Cruz, if indeed it had been completed by 1553–54). But none of these earlier refutations of the emperor's status as *dominus totius mundi* approached the fullness of Vera Cruz's. It is intriguing that this would be the case in a relection delivered, not in the hallowed *aulas* of Salamanca, but in the first academic year of the University of Mexico before an audience composed largely of young men destined to be immersed in the often agonizing practical dilemmas facing clerics in the aftermath of the New Laws (notwithstanding the watering-down to which the laws were soon subjected) and the controversy and doubts generated by Las Casas's disturbing *Confesionario*. However abstract or learned Vera Cruz's relection could often be, it repeatedly returned to the highly topical question of the administration of sacraments to encomenderos and the likelihood that such administration would have to depend on total or partial restitution of land or wealth acquired on the basis of invalid titles. Repeatedly, also, Vera Cruz mentioned in the first six doubts the title of the emperor's lordship of the world as a speciously impressive "master title," underlying all the others and hence requiring the full treatment it received at last as the seventh doubt.

The implication of all of this is clear: the claim of the ancient and modern Roman Empire to world dominion was manifestly a popular argument among the encomenderos and their allies in the New World. Not only did it have the double dignity of supposed classical origin and approval by an impressive roster of canon and civil lawyers, but it would also have allowed those who exploited it to establish their credentials as "emperor's men" (*Caesariani*, in Las Casas's phrase) in good standing—no paltry consideration for this nervous class of settlers angling for the respect and validation of a suspicious monarch. Consequently, Vera Cruz did not view the "Roman title" merely as an opportunity for a sophisticated and learned digression, but as a challenge demanding decisive and ruthless attention. Those who appealed to ancient Rome as the basis for their tenure of Indian land, tribute, and labor in New Spain needed to be told in no uncertain terms by Vera Cruz's contingent of pupils that on *this* title, at least, they "cannot be secure in conscience." Odd though it may seem to us today, in the Mexico of the mid-1550s the views that one harbored about the ancient Roman Empire were assumed to have a bearing on the state and destiny of one's immortal soul!

Did the Romans Have Dominion over the New World? Vinko Paletin of Korčula (Vicente Palatino de Curzola), circa 1557–59

The ancient Romans took one other brief bow in Vera Cruz's *Relectio de dominio infidelium,* in the course of his discussion of the invalid motives of conquest (doubt 10). Here he argued that the modern Roman emperor, as heir to the ancient Roman Empire, had the right to attack those infidels who were Roman subjects de jure in order to transform them into Roman subjects de facto. Roman subjects de jure were those who currently occupied regions once held by the ancient Romans in their, again, territorially *limited* empire. Among the infidels who would fall into this category were many Turks and Saracens. But what of the American Indians? Well, obviously, "because it is by no means agreed *(constat minime)* that they were ever [Roman] subjects, . . . it follows that war against them for this reason would not have been permitted, nor could the emperor rule in those regions on this excuse."[40] Vera Cruz's phrase *constat minime* is a thought-provoking negation. Though at first it seems to trumpet a self-evident denial of an ancient Roman presence in the New World, it is couched in such a way as to leave open the possibility that there may in fact have been some who *would* argue that the New World had been a Roman province. As a matter of fact, Vera Cruz's *constat minime* intriguingly echoes the phrasing of a widely read author and quondam professor at Salamanca who actually did claim that the New World was discovered not by the modern Spaniards but by the ancient Romans. In his *De rebus Hispaniae memorabilibus* of 1535, the Sicilian émigré Latinist and chronicler Lucio Marineo Sículo had claimed that the discovery of a coin of Augustus in Darién robbed the navigators of modern times (the Spaniards, that is) of their glory, "since by the evidence of this coin it is now established *(iam constat)* that the Romans once made it to the Indies."[41] But Marineo Sículo's anecdote was more a fleeting, impulsive indulgence in Italian chauvinism (albeit in a book on the wonders of Spain!) than a serious attempt to contribute to the debate about the Spanish title to the Indies. For him, the issue was less a matter of Roman *ius* than of Italian *gloria*. Nevertheless, it is tempting to wonder if Vera Cruz was aware of more serious attempts to defend the seemingly absurd Roman claim to the Indies.

It so happens that shortly after Vera Cruz delivered his relection an extraordinary treatise expounded precisely this claim. Composed in the late 1550s, this *Treatise on the Right and Justice of the War That the Kings of Castile and León Wage in the Regions of the West Indies, Which Some Call the New World* was the work of a Dalmatian Dominican named Vinko Paletin (1508–ca. 1571), though on his rare appearances in the scholarship on the controversy of the Indies his name appears hispanicized as Vicente Palatino de Curzola.[42] Though he long remained a rather shadowy figure, recent work by Croatian scholars, notably Franjo Šanjek, has cast considerable light on Paletin's life.[43] Born to a shabby genteel family on the Dalmatian island city-state of Korçula (or possibly nearby Zrnovo) in 1508, Vinko (or Vicko) Paletin went to sea as a young man and, around 1530, found himself in Spain. Here he became fascinated with tales of the New World and soon indulged his "wish to see many almost incredible things."[44] According to his own testimony in the treatise, he spent four years in Yucatán, a "young man in secular garb," serving under the *adelantado* Francisco de Montejo and his son during their second unsuccessful attempt to conquer the region (1531–34).[45] Subsequently, Paletin went to New Spain, where he became a Dominican. He returned to Europe in 1546, pursued theological studies at the University of Bologna, and in 1550 published a map of Spain. Four years later he translated into Italian Pedro de Medina's *Arte de navegar*, to which he also supplied an introduction. He then appears to have composed his treatise on the justice of the American conquests while living in the Convent of Saint Nicholas in his native Korçula. He evidently died in the early 1570s, not long after Korçula's successful defense against a Turkish naval assault, the town having been forewarned by a captive "turned Turk" who was none other than Vinko Paletin's nephew Antun, son of his brother Marko Paletin!

Paletin manifestly cherished high hopes for his treatise. Not only did he dedicate it to Philip II, but he also took the trouble to make the manuscript available in both Latin and Spanish versions.[46] He appears

to have sought a publisher for it in Flanders in the spring of 1558, and
he sent a copy to Bartolomé de Albornoz, first professor of civil law in
the University of Mexico, who praised the treatise as "the best of those
written on the subject."[47] It is tempting to wonder if Paletin had shared
his views on the Roman title with Albornoz a few years earlier, inspiring Albornoz's colleague Alonso de la Vera Cruz to issue his denial that
the Indies had ever been part of the Roman Empire. On October 17,
1560, however, a *cédula* was issued in the name of the treatise's royal
dedicatee commanding the confiscation in the Indies of "the book by
Fray Vicente Palavisin [*sic*], native of Dalmatia, whose title is . . . *De
iure belli adversus infideles*."[48] This implies that the manuscript was
enjoying some circulation and attention in the New World. Apparently
undaunted by this royal rebuff, Paletin attempted to have both the
Latin and the Spanish version published in Venice, and he secured
approval from officials at the University of Padova and from the Venetian Council of Ten.[49] But this plan came to naught, and the Spanish
version, represented today by a manuscript in the Muñoz collection of
the Royal Academy of History in Madrid, was not printed in full
before an edition was published, with extensive introductory material
and facing Serbo-Croatian translation, by Franjo Šanjek and Mirjana
Polić-Bobić in Zagreb in 1994. Before that, the treatise was known,
insofar as it was known at all, through the extracts and summary made
by Muñoz in the late eighteenth century and published by Agustín Millares Carlo and Lewis Hanke in 1943 in their valuable *Cuerpo de documentos del siglo XVI sobre los derechos de España en las Indias y las
Filipinas* (reprinted in 1977). The Latin version seems to exist only in a
partial copy, apparently made in the eighteenth century, now in the
Lilly Library of Indiana University.[50] Writing in 1994, Franjo Šanjek
alluded to another scholar's discovery of a copy of the complete Latin
manuscript, but he has since withdrawn this assertion. The incomplete
Indiana copy presents the first four of the six questions handled by the
1559 Spanish version. Questions 1, 2, and 4 are substantially similar in
the Spanish version and the Indiana copy of the Latin version, but the
Spanish tends to offer reduced—sometimes drastically reduced—discussions, an argument for the priority of the Latin version for these
particular questions.[51] But the third question, which happens to be that
on the "title of the Roman Empire," is radically different in these two
versions. As we shall see, there is good reason to assume that the Indiana copy's version of the Roman question represents a radical revision

of Paletin's original argument in the Spanish version—and presumably in the lost complete Latin version as well.

In either version, Paletin's treatise is an unsettling mixture of a scholastic and juridical discussion of *ius belli,* a historical survey of the Spanish conquest, an autobiographical reminiscence, and a compendium of passages from ancient historical and geographical writers. Its central thesis is that the kings of Spain, principally by virtue of the papal donation of 1493, enjoyed *dominium* in the New World in order to preside over the Christianization of the native inhabitants. Paletin claimed that his personal experience in the Indies allowed him to steer a middle course between those who viewed the Indians as irrational slaves by nature, hence fit for conquest, and those who considered them rational, gentle, and pious, hence ineligible for conquest. While the Latin version tends to be coy about whom Paletin had chiefly in mind among the latter group, the Spanish version makes it clear early on that he was thinking of "a bishop" whose writings had slandered the Spanish enterprise, and at one point, well over halfway through, he let slip, to no one's surprise, that the culprit was "bishop of Chiapas," and a few pages later he openly mentioned Las Casas, for once, by name.[52] Though the Latin version avoids identifying Las Casas by name or rank, it does, like the Spanish version, refer explicitly to his *Thirty Propositions*—and we shall be seeing the importance of Paletin's awareness of this treatise.[53] However openly or obscurely he alluded to Las Casas in the two versions of his treatise, Paletin left no doubt that, despite his initial claim to chart a via media, he regarded the Lascasian Scylla as a more profound threat to a true understanding of Spanish dominion in the Indies than the Sepulvedan Charybdis. In the Latin version, indeed, he darkly warned that the damage done by the products of this "certain person's" pen extended beyond the court of Spanish literate opinion; why, his little book (by which he meant the *Brevísima relación*) was being circulated among the Indians themselves, "many of whom know how to read Latin letters and understand the Spanish language in which he wrote."[54]

Paletin's attack upon Las Casas is most intense in the first section of the treatise, where he argues that the inhabitants of the New World egregiously violated the natural law governing proper treatment of strangers, and so the Spaniards who first encountered them were not the cruel "tyrants" Las Casas accused them of being but well-intentioned and egregiously wronged visitors whose ill treatment at the hands of the natives justified—nay, necessitated—conquest of their territories.[55] In support of this thesis, Paletin offered a lengthy historical narrative from the Columbian encounter to Pizarro's conquest of Peru, an account clearly designed as an antidote to the dangerous misrepresentations Las Casas had perpetrated in his *Brevísima relación*.[56] For example, like Bernal Díaz del Castillo, Paletin recognized the vital importance of supplying a detailed counternarrative to discredit Las Casas's devastating indictment of the massacre ordered by Cortés at Cholula on the march to Tenochtitlan.[57] Whereas Las Casas had claimed that the spectacle of the slaughter of the Cholulans inspired Cortés to belt out a ballad about Nero watching Rome burn, Paletin pronounced the conquistador "a man worthy of being lauded not merely with human praise, for this man was easily superior to all his forerunners: he was stronger than Hercules, bolder than Alexander the Great, more prudent than Marius, superior to Scipio Africanus in every virtue."[58] This language, of course, returns us to the "ancient-besting" topos of the conquistadors that we examined in our first chapter. While it is questionable whether Paletin's years in America in fact gave him the balanced perspective on New World affairs of which he bragged, there is no doubt that he managed to master the discourse of the conquerors perfectly. In this respect, Paletin makes an interesting contrast with Francisco de Aguilar, whom we met in the first chapter. Both men became Dominicans after stints as conquistadors, but Aguilar ruefully recalled the pride with which he and his fellows had boasted of "an exploit and labor so great, greater than those of the Romans," while Paletin was happy to keep repeating such boasts a quarter of a century after his ordination. Also intriguing is Paletin's characterization of Cortés as "more prudent than Marius." We may recall that Bernal Díaz claimed that Cortés had related at length the story of a quarrel between Marius and Sulla over the capture of Jugurtha as a parallel for the quarrel between Sandoval and Holguín over the capture of Cuauhtémoc, the last Aztec king. We have noted that in his deft handling of this potentially explosive quarrel Cortés proved himself to be precisely what Paletin called him here: "Mario prudentior/mas prudente que Mario." It is an attractive possibility that Paletin's less than self-evident selection of Marius as a superseded paragon of prudence was indebted to his awareness of this story. Paletin's phrase thus may offer some support to the historicity of a scene for which Bernal Díaz is our only witness on record.

While the writings of Las Casas were the principal irritants goading

Paletin to compose his treatise, another of the Dalmatian's fellow
Dominicans ultimately loomed larger in the framing and execution of
his principal arguments—and in the use he made of the Roman model.
The identity of this other friar will be evident if we survey the six ques-
tions that Paletin addressed in his treatise (of which the Latin version at
Indiana University offers the first four):

1. Could the "barbarians" of the New World be deprived of their
   dominions through "the title of natural human association" [titulo
   naturalis societatis/título dela compañia natural]?
2. Do the kings of Spain enjoy a monopoly in European dominion
   over American territories?
3. "Is it by reason and title of the Roman Empire that the kings of
   Spain have the right to subjugate and conquer those regions as
   their true and supreme lords?"
4. Do the kings of Spain and their generals have the right to wage war
   and acquire dominion over certain New World peoples in the
   name of wars of alliance ("nomine belli socialis/en base a la
   alianza o en base a la guerra civil")?
5. May war be waged against infidels in order to spread the Christian
   religion?
6. May war be waged against a people in order to punish the crimes
   it commits?

The briefest glance at these six questions reveals at once Paletin's debt
to Francisco de Vitoria's discussion of the "legitimate titles" of Spanish
dominion in the *Relectio de Indis,* even if the Dalmatian was ungrateful
enough to omit any explicit mention of the Salamantine master. (We
should recall, though, that Alonso de la Vera Cruz, who was similarly
indebted to Vitoria, his revered teacher, also failed to mention him by
name in the massive relection of 1554 that unmistakably alludes repeatedly to Vitoria's Indian relection.) It so happens that Vitoria's relections
first became available in print and thus reached circles beyond the Sala-
manca-Alcalá network in 1557, a plausible date for Paletin to have
begun his treatise. In whatever manner Vitoria's relection came to
Paletin's attention, its influence upon his own treatise is unmistakable.
Paletin's first question, on the validity of the "title of natural human
sociability" [titulus naturalis societatis], appropriates the principle of
naturalis societas et communicatio that forms the basis of Vitoria's first
"just title"—and the basis also of his claim to be recognized as an
important forerunner of the modern concept of international law. Like

Vitoria, Paletin insisted that this title should guarantee the right of free travel and free trade, provided that the newcomers intend and commit no injury to the natives, though Paletin left Vitoria's largely theoretical discussion far behind in his burning desire to demonstrate that the inhabitants of the New World had repeatedly and brutally violated this "natural law" and thus richly merited the loss of their dominions.

Paletin manifestly saw his contribution to the controversy of the Indies not only as a rebuttal to the annoying slanders of Las Casas but as a helpful grounding of Vitoria's theoretical case for the conquest in the specific realities of the history of the Spanish encounter with the inhabitants of the New World. But Paletin was not only eager to reveal the true nature of the conquest, he was also happy to seize any opportunity to appeal to the prestige of the Roman Empire as a model and precedent for Spanish behavior in the Indies. Thus, when concluding the first question's lengthy survey of the hostile reception accorded the Spaniards by the New World natives, Paletin sought classical confirmation of this title for just war in the history of the Roman Republic. First, he appealed to book 4 of Livy for the just war of the Romans against the neighboring Etruscan town of Veii, whose king Tolumnius had ordered the murder of four Roman ambassadors, an act Livy duly noted as a monstrous violation of *ius gentium* (4.17.4).[59] Then, though only in the Latin version, Paletin turned to Polybius's account of the First Illyrian War (229–228 B.C.), as a result of which the Romans had established their first foothold on his native Dalmatian coast. The antecedent here for the hostile Indians was the Illyrian queen Teuta, who contemptuously spurned a Roman embassy and turned a blind eye when her people assassinated one of the ambassadors.[60]

> In this way the Romans, the justice and legitimacy of whose imperial rule the most serious theologians affirm with one voice. . . , stood forth as guardians of the laws of nature and of nations and as stern avengers of this sort of violation of those laws. Thus, the lands of the criminals were justly and legitimately seized by the Romans. The Indian nations committed similar—or, rather, much more wicked— crimes against the Spaniards.[61]

To this lengthy excursus on Roman history Paletin appended parallels from the Old Testament regarding the just wars of the Israelites against their neighbors.

Vitoria's only specific reference to the actual history of the conquest, we may recall, had been in his discussion of the seventh "just title"—the right to acquire territory through wars fought nominally in support of allies. Here Vitoria cited the momentously decisive pact that Cortés formed with the Tlaxcalteca, longtime enemies of the Aztecs. Asserting that the justice of this title was confirmed by the fact that "it was indeed especially by this method *(hac maxime ratione)* that the Romans expanded their empire," Vitoria reminded his listeners that the justice of the Roman Empire was assumed by Augustine and Thomas. Vinko Paletin, in the fourth question of his treatise, not only echoed Vitoria's argument; he appropriated many of his very words:

> I say that the Romans especially by this method *(hac maxime ratione)*—undertaking wars of alliance and bringing aid to their allies—extended their just rule and conducted just wars, by which right provinces came into their possession. Hence they were made lords of the whole world. Their rule was approved as legitimate by all the sacred doctors, especially by St. Augustine, *De civ. Dei,* bk. 8, and St. Thomas, *De regimine principum,* bk. 3, chaps. 4–6.[62]

Like Vitoria, Paletin offered Cortés's alliance with the Tlaxcalteca as a foundation for a just war of empire on the model of the practice of the ancient Romans.[63] Unlike Vitoria, however, Paletin, at least in the Latin version, fleshed out his defense of the "title" of wars of alliance with several specific instances from Roman history.

When we turn to the third question—"whether through the reason and title of the Roman Empire the kings of Spain have the right to subjugate and conquer the Indian peoples as their true and supreme lords"—we encounter an astonishing discrepancy between the 1559 Spanish version and the Indiana copy of the Latin version. Here, as in the other three questions handled by both versions, the Spanish does indeed read at points like a summary of a longer treatment. But it is not, after the first proposition at least, a summary of the Indiana version. To begin with, the Spanish version divides the question into six sections *(conclusiones),* while the Indiana Latin text presents only two *propositiones.* But even more striking is the fact that these two versions reach precisely opposite conclusions. Since the Spanish translation appears to be an abridgment of a fuller treatment of the Roman question, and since the Indiana Latin version is, as we shall see, most likely a revision of those two earlier treatments, it makes sense to examine the Spanish version first.

When examining these two incarnations of the third question, we need to keep an important consideration in mind. Composing his treatise after Charles V's imperial abdication in 1556, Paletin would have been unable to make very effective use of the argument that the Spaniards held dominion over the Indies as a consequence of the modern Roman emperor's status as "lord of the whole world." Furthermore, even in the days of Charles V there had been an obvious flaw in that argument, for Spain's first discoveries and conquests in the New World had occurred years before Charles's election or even his birth. How, then, could Paletin, writing after the Spanish monarchy's "Roman interlude" and looking back to the years before it, hope to exploit a "title of the Roman Empire" in support of Spanish dominion in the Indies? Though for a certain distance he was willing to follow the ready path of Sepúlveda in hailing the Romans as the Spaniards' fellow Aristotelian natural masters and benevolent imperialists, he did not remain content with this. In the Spanish version of 1559—and presumably in the fuller, earlier version we are positing—he was inspired to advance an argument that may in fact have been that very rare thing in the learned discourse of his time: an original idea. But if it was in many ways original, we shall soon see that he was helped to it by a highly unlikely intellectual benefactor.

The first section ("primera conclusión") of the Spanish version affirms that "the Roman Empire and its monarchy was the most legitimate of all the empires and monarchies of the unbelievers."[64] While the supporting argument is lopped to a mere two sentences, the Indiana Latin version seems here to offer a plausible candidate for the fuller argument.[65] In ten manuscript pages, it presents an encomium of Roman imperial rule, drawing upon such ancient authors as Livy, Sallust, and Valerius Maximus for historical examples and upon the familiar passages from Augustine (here once again presented as an admirer of the Roman Empire!) and Pseudo-Aquinas (Ptolemy of Lucca) for a Christian theological blessing upon the Pax Romana. First and foremost among the virtues by which Rome merited and appropriated her empire was patriotism *(amor patriae),* exemplified by such Republican heroes as Regulus and Manius Curius Dentatus. Next came the Romans' passion for justice *(zelus iustitiae),* upon which St. Paul reposed such impressive confidence when he appealed his case to the emperor. Finally, there was the kindness *(benevolentia)* by which the Romans acquired friends and softened enemies, a gentleness Paletin anecdotally illustrated by the supposed chivalry of Scipio Africanus in his campaigns against the Carthaginians in Spain. Paletin owed his three principal Roman imperial virtues to Ptolemy of Lucca's *De regimine principum,* book 3, chapters 41–44.

Returning to the Spanish version, we encounter in the "segunda conclusión" Paletin's bold contention that "the Roman Empire held jurisdiction both in the east and the west"—that is, that Roman dominion was truly worldwide.[66] But Paletin was by no means content to base the Romans' dominion over the Indies upon their supposed claim to universal jurisdiction as "lords of the whole world." Rather, he was inspired to advance a specific historical scenario supported by a display of classical learning and a most unusual claim to autoptic authority.

Paletin's scholarly argument was designed to establish the preliminary thesis that the New World was discovered and—at least briefly—settled by the Carthaginians. His classical support for this contention was the tantalizing accounts of Carthaginian discoveries in the far west offered by Pseudo-Aristotle (*De mirabilibus ausculationibus,* chap. 84), Diodorus Siculus (5.19–20), and Pliny the Elder (6.36.200–201). On the basis of these passages, Paletin constructed a conflated account of two fertile islands lying forty days' sail to the west of Gades (Cadiz). They were discovered by storm-driven Carthaginian merchants, whose brief attempt at colonization of these "Hesperides" was aborted when the Carthaginian authorities abruptly forbade settlement, fearing that the attractive new colony might drain population from Carthage itself and preferring to keep them in reserve as a possible refuge in time of danger. "Let no one doubt," Paletin urged, "that these two Hesperides islands are those that we call Española and Cuba (or Fernandina)."[67] Paletin's identification of these islands with the Hesperides, as well as his notion that the Carthaginians had visited the New World, were derived, as we shall see in the next chapter, from Gonzalo Fernández de Oviedo, acidly dubbed by Las Casas "el primero imaginador desta sotileza," though we shall see that it was not the Carthaginian visit that primarily interested Oviedo about the early history of these Antillean "Hesperides."[68] Paletin was manifestly lacking in eagerness to give Oviedo credit here, but there is no doubt about his familiarity with the chronicler's controversial chapter.[69]

But Paletin was not content to rest the Carthaginian discovery of the Indies upon this pastiche of classical literary sources. With manifest pride, he proclaimed: "And now I wish to say what I have seen"—or, as the Latin version more grandly put it: "Now, however, let us bring forth what we have witnessed in this matter over the course of ten years—what our own hands have handled."[70] He then proceeded to offer a valuable, if still relatively neglected, account of the Spanish exploration of the ruins of Chichén Itzá ("Cicinisa") during the unsuccessful attempt of Francisco Montejo the Younger in 1532–33 to found Ciudad Real amid the remains of the old Mayan city. Paletin penned here a vivid account of the decorated towers and buildings of the ruined city—even supplying a rough diagram of the layout of the principal structures. It was in this astonishing site that, amid reliefs of armies of bearded warriors sporting "axes like [those of the] Amazons," Paletin and his comrades made a startling discovery:

And on the top of those towers there are two kinds of letters, and none of our men could understand them, for they were neither Latin, Greek, nor Hebrew. Rather, in my opinion and judgment those letters were from Africa, from the Carthaginians. They are there today, and Your Majesty can find out what language they are in. . . . At that time, some of us, the most curious ones, marveling at such buildings, many times individually asked those Indians when those ruined old houses and cities were constructed. All of them were in agreement with each other and said that they knew from their ancestors over many years past that there came bearded men to those regions by ship from very distant lands, "just as you came—and they resembled you. They founded those cities and lived in them for some years. But afterward, as time passed, ships and people stopped coming from that land, and when our ancestors saw this, they began to wage war against them. And so, harrying them with war and famine they killed and exterminated them, leaving their cities deserted and abandoned, which are now broken and ruined by the passage of many years." It is obvious here that everything agrees: the histories, the location of the land, the distance of those regions from Europe and Africa, and the remains of the buildings.[71]

And in the corresponding passage in the Indiana Latin version, Paletin insisted "without any hesitation" [absque ulla hesitatione] that not only were the inscriptions in Punic, but "the shapes or sculpted images of the men are of Carthaginian soldiers."[72]

More than Marineo Sículo with his meager treasure of a single Roman coin found in Darién, more even than those amateur art historians in Cuba in 1517 who, we may recall, pronounced the little golden ducks and fish acquired by Hernández de Córdoba in Yucatán to be the work of refugees from Titus's destruction of Jerusalem, Vinko Paletin deserves the dubious honor of inaugurating that tenacious parahistorical tradition of interpreting American "finds" as evidence that the Old World had known of the New centuries before Columbus or even the Norsemen. Paletin displaying his impressive, if mysteriously acquired, grasp of Punic epigraphy to his bemused fellow conquistadors on the temples of Chichén-Itzá in the 1530s was a worthy forerunner to the likes of Cyrus Gordon, Barry Fell, and Ivan Van Sertima in our own time.

If Paletin's classical sources (borrowed from Oviedo) put the Carthaginians in possession of Cuba and Santo Domingo, and his autoptic experience established them on the mainland as well, it was a simple enough matter to transfer these distant Punic dominions into the worthy hands of the Romans. Alas, though the Spanish version of his treatise assumes this step, it presents it in characteristically truncated form. Remnants of the original full argument here can plausibly be retrieved from the Indiana Latin version, where Paletin cited what he called "the saddest law of nations: that everything belonging to the defeated passes into the power of the victor *(omnia victi cedunt in ius victoris)*," a principle supported, he claimed, by Jesus' words at Luke 11:21–22. Accordingly, "whatever was the legal authority of the monarchies and republics and kingdoms that came into the power of the Roman Empire, all of those jurisdictions entered into the power of the Roman Empire."[73] Therefore, as the Spanish version puts it, the Indies "belonged first to the Romans and the Carthaginians" [fueron primero de los rromanos y cartaginenses].[74]

Thus, Paletin used both classical and autoptic authority to bring the Indies into the Roman Empire, a feat that critics of the Roman model from Soto in 1535 to Vera Cruz in 1554 had confidently written off as impossible. All that remained for him was to transfer these overseas dominions of ancient Rome into the jurisdiction of the modern kings of Spain. Again, the fact that the "emperor of the Romans" had presided over the conquests of Mexico and Peru was irrelevant, for neither the Spanish monarchs who sponsored the initial discovery nor the current king to whom Paletin was dedicating his treatise were Roman emperors. The institution that effected the required transfer of jurisdiction from the ancient Romans to the modern Spaniards was not the Holy Roman Empire, but the papacy:

The Catholic Monarchs were beyond all other Christian princes girded with the zeal of spreading the faith, and they devoted every effort and made expenditures for the discovery of those regions with Cristóbal Colón as captain, and the Supreme Pontiff is the chief judge of all princes, and it was definitely for this reason that he conveyed those lands that belonged to the Roman Empire to the jurisdiction of the kings of Spain to legitimately discover them and subject them to their rule and bring those Indians to the Catholic Church. Thus, by reason of this ancient right they have justly and legitimately occupied and now hold those regions and provinces, and have subjugated them and are currently subjugating them.[75]

The origin of the pope's authority to effect this transfer of Rome's temporal dominions to the kings of Spain is the subject of the four remaining *conclusiones* of the Spanish version of Paletin's treatise. The first of these ("tercera conclusión") is a very short summary of the claim that, in accord with Christ's words at Matt. 28:18 ("All power in heaven and earth has been given me"), Christ during his time on earth assumed "temporal rule over all men, both believers and nonbelievers," in support of which this abbreviated version airily refers to "todos los santos doctores y teólogos." Paletin proceeded to argue that Christ passed this sweeping temporal authority on to his successors the popes, though the pagan emperors, insofar as they ruled justly, were to be regarded and obeyed as vice regents of God ("quarta conclusión"). Still, "the Roman Empire and any other worldly kingdom remained subject to the jurisdiction and verdict of the Supreme Pontiff," whose temporal authority was principally designed to facilitate the conversion of unbelievers ("quinta conclusión"). Thus, Paletin alleged that Pope Sylvester ordered Constantine to make idolatry punishable by death. And on the same principle Alexander VI had entrusted the New World to the kings of Spain in order that the natives might be converted. Here, complaining about Las Casas's highly selective citations of the 1493 bull *Inter cetera*, Paletin supplied a Spanish translation of the entire bull, a candid reading of which, he added, would suffice to prove that Las Casas was mistaken in asserting that there was no papal mandate to subjugate the Indians before attending to their conversion. Perhaps the apostles could convert peoples by peaceful means—they had divine Grace and the gift of languages—but we ordinary mortals need to conquer infidels first, then convert them. And finally, in the "sixth conclusion," Paletin returned more specifically to the "Roman title" and affirmed (to cite the heading) that "the Supreme Pontiff may, with just cause, transfer the right that belonged to the Roman Empire to any other Christian prince or king."[76] Unfortunately, the argument here is truncated. After a renewed assertion of the temporal power of the pope by virtue of Christ's role as judge of all the living and the dead, the discussion trails off without specifically alluding to the Roman Empire at all. But the specific thesis that the fuller version would have offered is clear enough from the heading of the conclusion and from the entire progress of Paletin's argument throughout this third question.

The contention that upon his Incarnation Christ assumed the temporal authority of earthly governments and then bequeathed that dominion to St. Peter and his successors—an authority particularly to be exercised over infidels for their own ultimate spiritual good—was most indissolubly associated with Hostiensis, though it goes back to the English canonist Alanus Anglicus at the beginning of the thirteenth century.[77] We have seen the argument deployed in support of Spanish dominion in the Indies at the expense of invalid native dominions in the fragmentary treatise René Acuña has attempted to identify as the *De debellandis Indis* of Vasco de Quiroga. But it may well have been a most unlikely precursor who inspired Paletin to concoct his specific argument that Christ's temporal authority over the Roman Empire had passed through Peter and his successors to Pope Alexander VI, who then bestowed it upon the kings of Spain as a reward for their evangelical foresight in sponsoring Columbus's voyages of discovery. Though Vinko Paletin repeatedly insisted that his treatise was designed to rebut the writings of Bartolomé de las Casas, his eccentric defense of the "Roman title" betrays uncanny echoes of those very writings—at least of the *Treinta proposiciones muy jurídicas,* a treatise included, along with the *Brevísima relación,* in the cycle of treatises that Las Casas published without license in Seville in 1552. There is, we may recall, no doubt about Paletin's familiarity with the *Thirty Propositions,* for he explicitly mentioned them in his treatise, though in a different connection. It is also possible that he looked into the elaboration of some of those propositions published by Las Casas early in 1553 as the *Tratado comprobatorio.*

True enough, Las Casas was far from sharing Paletin's admiration for the Romans, and both he and his bête noire Oviedo would surely have been outraged by Paletin's attempt to make the Indies part of the ancient Roman Empire. And yet it is hard not to be struck by the convergences between Paletin's argument here and Las Casas's delicate—or tortured—"juridical" argument in the two treatises. Both Dominicans emphasized (1) the pope's temporal power to effect a transfer of Roman imperial authority for the promotion of spiritual goals thanks to his status as vicar of Christ, who had inherited the dominion of the world upon his Incarnation; (2) the pious efforts of the Catholic Monarchs to discover new lands for Christian evangelization; and (3) the pope's laudable decision to exercise his right of transferring Roman imperial prestige in the Indies to the Catholic Monarchs and their descendants as a reward for their evangelical initiative. It is true that Las Casas claimed that it was only Roman imperial prestige *(dignidad)* that the pope could and did transfer, while Paletin more forthrightly chose to speak of a transfer of Rome's legal title *(derecho)*, but this minor divergence scarcely obscures the fundamental similarity of their strategies. It is particularly interesting that both Paletin and Las Casas—or, rather, Paletin with the help of Las Casas—devised a way of channeling the numinous power of the ancient Roman Empire into the Spanish title to the Indies while largely bypassing the role or even the existence of the contemporary "Roman Empire." Las Casas was eager to downplay the Roman Empire of his day because he wished to avoid getting sucked into the pro-Roman propaganda of the toadies whom he labeled "Caesariani," a fate that he regretfully observed that Vitoria had failed to avoid. He was determined to be as cautious as possible when applying to the Spanish king's New World dominion the Roman "dignidad imperial" that the pope "found among the heathens." Paletin, on the other hand, bypassed the Holy Roman Empire because it had become irrelevant— and in so doing it had thrown into sharper relief its original irrelevance at the time of the Catholic Monarchs. But though both Dominicans ignored the contemporary Roman Empire, they both reached back— Las Casas gingerly, Paletin enthusiastically—to the dignifying power of the ancient Roman Empire as one source of Spanish jurisdiction in the Indies.

Paletin's construction of a "Roman title" in the third question of his treatise was, then, pregnant with ironies. For one thing, he boldly derived from Las Casas's own writings a key argument he hoped would contribute to their decisive discrediting. Second, Paletin crafted his pro-Roman case by using the ideas of two men, Oviedo and Las Casas, who not only cordially detested each other but who were also, in their different ways and for their different purposes, passionate "anti-Romanists." For these reasons—to say nothing of his pioneering account of Chichén Itzá—Vinko Paletin deserves more attention and credit than he has so far received. He was, in his modest way, a polemicist of genius.

But surprising as Paletin's argument and its source may have been, a further surprise awaits us when we examine the Indiana copy of the Latin version of his treatise. We have already seen that the first proposition of this Latin manuscript parallels—and vastly supplements—the first conclusion of the Spanish version: an encomium on the superior justice of the Roman Empire among all monarchies of the unbelievers. But where the Spanish manuscript proceeds to devote five subsequent *conclusiones* to supporting the claim that the modern Spaniards had inherited the ancient Romans' unconscious title to the lordship of the Indies, the Latin version at Indiana University offers a single "secunda propositio." Startlingly, that proposition turns out to be a firm *rejection* of the idea that the Romans ever possessed, even unwittingly, a New World dominion! And what the Romans did not themselves possess they could not, of course, bequeath to any other empire.

Paletin began this proposition by acknowledging at once the lordship of the ancient Romans over Europe, Africa, and Asia. "But a doubt occurs concerning the West Indies, which they call the New World, and which many maintain was unknown to earlier ages." He proceeded to state the contrary possibility—that is, the very assumption on which the Spanish version (and what seems to have been its earlier, fuller Latin model) was based. On the basis of the law of war that "everything belonging to the conquered passes into the hands of the victor," perhaps the Romans could have inherited these regions from another empire. It was on this principle, after all, that they had acquired the territories of Alexander's successors—as, earlier, the Macedonians themselves had acquired the Persian Empire, and as the Persians and Medes had acquired the Assyrian Empire. In order to acquire a title to the New World, however, the Romans would have had to conquer an empire that possessed those regions. In a startling volte-face from his argument in the Spanish version, Paletin now decided that this had not in fact been the case.

> But to return to the question about the so-called new Indies of the Ocean Sea, with which we are now concerned: did they come into the jurisdiction of the Roman Empire or not? To achieve clarity in this matter, I say that those regions were known at another time by our

people [i.e. inhabitants of the Old World], but the Romans had no jurisdiction over them. The fact that they did not have it I prove thus: no state, kingdom, or empire came into the Roman Empire that had such a jurisdiction in those areas, nor did the Romans themselves discover them by themselves. If, on the other hand, they could have had this jurisdiction from any other source, it would have been from the jurisdiction of the Carthaginian state, which was conquered and defeated by the Romans by the right of a just war, and thus all of its jurisdictions ceded to the right of Rome. But even though those regions were discovered by the Carthaginians, and they possessed some jurisdiction over them for a period of time, by the time that Carthage was defeated the Carthaginians had no longer any authority in those regions. Therefore those western lands did not cede and come into the power of the Roman Empire.[78]

The fact that this conclusion renders the Carthaginian discovery and short-lived settlement of Cuba, Hispaniola, and Yucatán strictly irrelevant to the question of the Roman title to the Indies did not at all deter Paletin from proceeding to offer a very full account of the ancient evidence for the Carthaginian discoveries in the far west. In fact, his version of this now irrelevant history of ancient Europeans in America is considerably fuller in this Latin version than in the Spanish version in which it actually serves the argument. This is a strong indication that the Latin revision of this question in the Indiana manuscript incorporates large fragments of an original Latin version. (Similarly, the whole of the first proposition of this third question is clearly another such chunk, though it, too, has become irrelevant to the new, revised argument.) It will come as no surprise that Paletin could not resist retaining his remarkable account of the things he saw and heard at Chichén Itzá with the expedition of Francisco Montejo el Mozo. But while the Spanish version immediately followed this personal narrative with the ringing conclusion that those American regions "belonged first to the Romans and the Carthaginians" [fueron primero de los rromanos y cartaginenses] and were passed on to the kings of Spain by the pope, the inheritor of the temporal power of the Roman Empire, the revised Latin version offered, again, precisely the opposite conclusion:

Since all the aforementioned events occurred before Carthage was captured by the Romans, the jurisdiction over the Indies could not devolve upon the Roman Empire, nor was it upon this ground that in the time of the Catholic Monarchs the Supreme Pontiff had the right to grant them to the kings of Spain; rather, it is by the authority of Christ and his vicar and not by the title of the Roman Empire that they accepted that jurisdiction.[79]

These final words of the Indiana Latin version of the treatise's third question signal a complete abandonment of the defense of the Roman title and a retreat to the fallback position of Hostiensis that "with the coming of Christ every office and all governmental authority and all lordship and jurisdiction was taken from every infidel . . . and granted to the faithful through him who has the supreme power and who cannot err."[80]

Our examination of Vinko Paletin's use of the Roman Empire in his defense of Spanish sovereignty in the New World has been predicated upon—and has attempted to confirm—the assumption that this treatise went through at least three versions. Paletin seems first to have composed a Latin version around 1557, and it was this version that circulated in the New World and that the royal *cédula* of 1560 ordered confiscated.[81] The Spanish translation, dated 1559, was an abbreviated version of the Latin. Undaunted by the *cédula,* Paletin attempted to have both versions printed in Venice around 1564, but though the Venetian Council of Ten granted permission, the project came to naught. At some later date, Paletin appears to have undertaken a revision of the Latin version, and it is a copy of this that is in the Lilly Library at Indiana University. Since this manuscript offers fuller, but substantially similar versions of the first, second, and fourth questions handled by the Spanish text, it stands to reason that it is here faithful to the original Latin version. Turning to the third question, on the "Roman title," we find that, while the Indiana Latin manuscript does at certain points offer fuller versions of what we find in the 1559 Spanish translation, the differences are radical, and the conclusions are precisely the opposite. Since the extensive scholarly and autoptic argument for Carthaginian discovery and settlement of the New World—present in both versions, though fuller in the Latin—is of genuine relevance only to the argument advanced by the Spanish translation (and presumably also by the original Latin version), there can be little doubt that the Indiana copy is a later revision of the earlier Latin version and does not reflect some preliminary state of Paletin's treatise. The fact that the Indiana manuscript is missing the last two questions may be a further argument that this was a projected revision. Perhaps it was left incomplete at Paletin's death in the early 1570s.

Why, though, would Paletin have decided to revise his third question and to retract his earlier, distinctively ingenious claim that the Romans had acquired dominion over Cuba, Hispaniola, and Yucatán from the Carthaginians? A simple answer might be that further reflection—and perhaps readers' comments—forced him to accept the fact that the Carthaginians' abandonment of their settlement in the far west, explicitly noted by the ancient sources, made it impossible to continue to maintain that the Romans had unwittingly inherited this dominion as a result of the Punic Wars. This is of course possible, though normally those who devise arguments as curious and clever as that of Paletin tend not to abandon them so readily in the face of mere inconvenient evidence. Perhaps, instead, his revision is a testimony to the power of the ultimately triumphant weight of theological and juristic opinion against the notion of a Roman "world monarchy," either ancient or modern. While Las Casas's anti-Roman sentiments are unlikely to have moved him, Paletin may eventually have become impressed with the arguments advanced by Domingo de Soto in his magisterial *De iustitia et iure,* first published in 1553, revised in 1556, and increasingly widely circulated and cited.

Paletin's retreat from the defense of ancient Roman "world monarchy" would thus have the effect of making his book less eccentric—and hence more likely to be published. It is interesting to note that such a retreat would also have brought Paletin's treatise more into line with the work that, after all, inspired the way he framed his entire defense of Spanish dominion in the Indies: Vitoria's *Relectio de Indis* (first published in 1557). The "second state" of Paletin's treatise would have offered views on the Romans that were fundamentally harmonious with those of the revered Salamantine master. Like Paletin, Vitoria assumed the justice of the ancient Roman Empire. Like Paletin, Vitoria found ancient Roman precedent for the Spanish exploitation of wars of defensive alliance in generating an overseas empire. Like Paletin (after his second thoughts, that is), Vitoria nevertheless denied that the Romans were "lords of all the world." But though Paletin may have decided to promote his treatise by making it more "juridically correct," he could not bring himself to evict his now-irrelevant Carthaginian material. In particular, he remained understandably eager to tell of what he had seen with his own eyes in the New World—his account of Chichén Itzá is, after all, his surest claim to what fame he has—and there was simply no other plausible place for it in this treatise than in the now moot discussion of the "Roman title." However we may explain Paletin's fascinating digression, his account of what he saw—or thought he saw—in the ruins of the great Mayan city reminds us once again of the vivid presence of the ancient Mediterranean in the mental worlds of the first generations of those who experienced and evaluated the Spanish conquest of the New World.

Juan de Solórzano Pereira: From Roman Tyranny to Legitimate Dominion

Not surprisingly, both the celebration and the rejection of Roman imperialism as a model for Spanish behavior in the New World became increasingly irrelevant after Charles V's abdication of the imperial throne in 1556. Nevertheless, several scholars have recently drawn attention to the role of the Roman model in a widely influential "postmortem" on the debate of the Indies by the distinguished lawyer and Councilor of the Indies, Juan de Solórzano Pereira (1575–1654).[82] In his Latin treatise *De Indiarum iure* (1629 and 1639) and in a Spanish adaptation entitled *Política indiana* (1648), Solórzano attempted to establish (in the words of the subtitle of the Latin work) "the just discovery, acquisition and retention of the western Indies." These works, Mario Góngora has noted, "enjoyed an unrivaled prestige in the official and legal circles in the Indies for a century and a half."[83] Reviewing more than a century of debate, Solórzano, whose own contention was that the papal donation of 1493 was the only secure title for Spanish dominion in the Indies, vigorously rejected earlier attempts to use the Roman model to confer legitimacy upon the Spanish conquest.

In the teeth of those who appealed to Augustine on the supposed benefits of Roman rule for backward subjects, Solórzano cast Augustine's own observation that the Romans would have had greater success had they tried to spread the benefits of civilization by peaceful means (*De civ. D.* 5.17).[84] While he did allude elsewhere to the familiar prooftexts for Rome's supposedly God-given imperial jurisdiction, Solórzano found the civilizing mission of the Romans considerably less successful than that of the Spaniards: "It is obvious beyond any need for proof how much the Spaniards excel the Romans, and that they have passed on to the Indians much more useful and healthy laws, customs, arts and many other things for living a truly human and civilized life."[85] As for the argument that Roman lordship over the "whole world" granted legitimacy to Spanish conquests conducted under the aegis of Charles V as Roman emperor, Solórzano countered that "by far the truer and safer opinion is that of those others who deny that the Roman emperor can have any right *(ius)* in the lands and provinces of the unbelievers, particularly in those barbarian lands discovered by the Spanish, for the Roman Caesars neither possessed them, nor did they even have any knowledge of them."[86]

But though he rejected Roman precedent for the Spaniards' *acquisition* of the New World, Solórzano was perfectly content to invoke Roman exempla for Spanish *retention* of the Indies. In a formulation that undercut the urgency of establishing the justice of Roman—and implicitly also Spanish—conquests, Solórzano argued that

> when people inherit a dominion that is imperfect or acquired with less than complete legitimacy, it suffices that they confirm it and purge its defects, especially when the peoples possessed don't object and there has intervened a long space of time, in the course of which even tyranny turns into perfect and legitimate monarchy, as happened with that of the Romans and others of the main monarchies known in the world.[87]

Thus, the justice of Roman—and, even more, of Spanish—imperial government canceled out, over "a long space of time," any lingering doubts about the justice of the initial acts of conquest themselves (a point anticipated by Juan de Torquemada in his 1467 *Opusculum ad honorem Romani imperii*).[88] This even allowed Solórzano to turn back to Augustine's supposed encomium of Roman imperial rule to bolster the case for Spanish appropriation of precious metals and Indian labor to work the mines.[89] Similarly, he supported the Spanish claim to treasures from Indian tombs by an appeal to a Roman precedent in two phases: (1) the pagan empire's plundering of the tombs and holy places of conquered territories and (2) the Christianized empire's appropriation of pagan treasures. And he followed this with the startling Roman precedent of the extraction of swallowed jewels from the bodies of those slain in the fall of Jerusalem—yet another, somewhat bizarre, contribution to the history of the motif of the fall of Jerusalem in the conquest of the New

World.⁹⁰ In addition, David Brading has drawn attention to Solórzano's positive appeals to Roman rule in Spain as a model for Spanish policy in the Indies. Thus, the Roman practice of concentrating the Spanish population in towns validated similar Spanish policies in the Indies, while the Roman imposition of Latin in Spain showed greater administrative wisdom than the decision of church councils to preach in the native languages of the Indians.⁹¹ This enthusiastic assessment of the Roman presence in Spain stands in sharp contrast to the anti-Roman Iberian patriotism of Cano, Las Casas, and Morales that we shall be investigating in the next chapter.

A century's distance from the controversy that had been heated by the flames or embers of the conquest of the Indies allowed Solórzano to play both sides of the Roman road. He was able to join the sixteenth-century Dominicans in resisting the attraction of the Romans as conquerors, and, since the passions of the conquest had receded into the past, he could also cheerfully proceed to invoke them as exemplary imperial administrators. Ultimately, then, Solórzano's real contribution to the career of the Roman model in the controversy of the Indies was his use of it to help nail the lid on the coffin of the entire debate by shifting to a new focus, one "no longer on acquisition but rather on that which has been acquired."⁹² Viewing both Roman and Spanish conquests across a "long space of time" [largo curso de tiempo] as unassailable faits accomplis, Solórzano was able simultaneously to defend the legitimacy of Spanish sovereignty in the New World and to accept, with a shrug of indifference, ultimately irrelevant denunciations of the messy realities of the Romans' and Spaniards' respective wars of conquest.

CHAPTER FIVE

Romans and Iberians / Spaniards and Indians

The last three chapters have explored the surprising prominence of the model of ancient Roman imperialism in the Spanish controversy over the justice of the conquest and retention of the New World, from Domingo de Soto's Salamanca lecture of 1535, through the famous debate between Sepúlveda and Las Casas in Valladolid in 1550–51, and on to the skirmishing of the next decade. The final chapters of this book will focus on two of the richest and most fascinating classical dimensions to the controversy of the Indies, though both, as we shall see, repeatedly escaped the confines of the university lecture halls in which that controversy was formally conducted.

In this chapter, we shall explore the provocative suggestion that the Spanish conquest of the Indies disturbingly recapitulated the horrors of the Roman conquest of Spain in the second century B.C. This analogy owed its power to a growing, but by no means widely self-evident, assumption that the ancient Iberians whom the Romans subjugated were fundamentally the same people as modern Spaniards. In turn, the deployment of this parallel in the discourse of the conquest of the New World helped intensify that same "Iberian patriotism" that had suggested the analogy in the first place. This tale of two conquests was, then, both product and producer of a strong sense of *hispanidad,* a consciousness of long-term ethnic unity and continuity in the Iberian Peninsula. Thus, an argumentative strategy designed to induce Spaniards to empathize with the sufferings of their New World subjects made its own contribution to a sharpening perception of the European past. But though this appeal to the ancient history of the Iberian Peninsula was most deftly employed by the Dominicans Melchor Cano and Bartolomé de las Casas in their polemical struggle against the conquistadors and their chroniclers and apologists, we shall see how a powerful identification with the pre-Roman Iberian peoples also found expression in the writings of others who discussed or alluded to the conquest of the Indies—most notably, in the "anti-Romanism" of that industrious chronicler Gonzalo Fernández de Oviedo and in the revisionist historiography of Ambrosio de Morales.

Cano and Las Casas on the Roman Conquest of Spain as a Precedent for the Spanish Conquest of the New World

When the eminent Dominican theologian Melchor Cano in a lecture hall at the University of Alcalá in 1546 attacked the use of the Roman Empire as a model for Spanish dominion in the New World, he singled out two manifestly unjust Roman wars of imperial expansion.[1] Both were well suited for use in the controversy of the Indies, and both were seized upon and developed by Bartolomé de las Casas, who entered the controversy promptly upon his return to Spain the year after Cano's lecture.

One of these acts of Roman aggression was the acquisition of Judaea in 63 B.C., a state that, Cano maintained, "was not attacked because of any defect in government, for they had received from God a government better than that of the Romans." Las Casas appealed to this unjust Roman war of conquest in his *Historia de las Indias,* a massive work begun in 1527 and revised and expanded during the years of the controversy over Sepúlveda's *Democrates secundus.* In book 3, chapter 122, his subject was what we now tend to identify as one of the decisive factors in the conquest of Mexico: Cortes's shrewd exploitation of the hatred of the Tlaxcalteca for their Aztec overlords. We should recall that in his 1539 Salamanca *Relectio de Indis* Vitoria had compared this New World incident, his only specific example from the Indies, with the method by which the Romans expanded their empire. Vitoria had presented both the particular Spanish instance and the general Roman practice as confirmations of the "seventh just title," the *causa sociorum et amicorum,* that could plausibly be urged to justify Spanish wars of conquest in the Indies. Like Vitoria, Las Casas suggested that Cortés acted like a Roman in Tlaxcala, and like Cano, he was drawn to the example of Pompey in Judaea. After citing Aristotle (*Pol.* 5.11) on the habit tyrants have of exploiting or creating factionalism in a state, Las Casas added,

In this same way the Roman captain Pompey, having been sent by the Roman people against Tigranes king of Armenia, upon learning that there were factions and dissensions between two parties whose heads were the brothers Aristobulus and Hyrcanus, each of whom wished to be sole ruler in Jerusalem, recognized that the time was ripe to invade the city, enter it by force, subject it tyrannically, and make it tributary to the Roman Empire. And this is what he did. And after that time and in that unjust and tyrannical way Judaea and its inhabitants, the Jews, lost their liberty.[2]

This negative assessment of the actions of Pompey is strikingly absent from the main ancient source Las Casas employed here, Josephus, one of his favorite historians (the very first words of the *Historia de las Indias* are "Josepho aquel ilustre historiador y sabio"). Not only did Josephus lay the blame for the Jews' loss of liberty squarely and solely upon the shoulders of Aristobulus and Hyrcanus, but he also insisted that after the fall of Jerusalem Pompey behaved with a restraint "worthy of his excellence."[3]

Now, it is true that Las Casas rather uncharacteristically went on to admit that there was a *good* Roman model that Cortés might have followed had he so chosen: Titus Quinctius Flamininus's liberation of the Greek city-states from Macedonian domination and his proclamation of the "freedom of the Greeks" in 196 B.C.[4] But Pompey's negative exemplum was the one that best illustrated the grim realities of the Roman precedent for what Vitoria offered as the supposedly just *causa sociorum et amicorum*. It is interesting to note that Pompey, the villain of Las Casas's historical parallel, was mentioned several times in the *Verdadera historia* of Bernal Díaz del Castillo as a worthy ancient competitor for modern Spaniards achieving unprecedented deeds in the New World.[5]

In addition to being a corrective to Vitoria's positive appeal to the general model of Roman imperialism, Las Casas's use of the Roman conquest of Judaea was also a deftly distorted echo of another historical parallel offered as a model by those who participated in or wrote laudatory accounts of the conquest of Mexico. His historical analogy establishes these parallels: (1) Cortés imitates Pompey; (2) the Aztecs and the Tlaxcalteca echo the warring factions of Aristobulus and Hyrcanus; (3) the city of Jerusalem, unjustly attacked and tyrannically subjugated, recalls the climactic consequence of Cortés's adroit exploitation of native animosities: the fall of the great city of Tenochtitlan. Now, we have noted earlier the widespread appeal by the conquistadors and their publicists to a later, much more famous Roman siege of Jerusalem as a model for the siege and destruction of Tenochtitlan. In this analogy, the Roman exemplar for Cortés was Titus, in pagan eyes "the darling of the human race,"[6] and in Christian eyes the instrument of God's vengeance against the recalcitrant Jews. Not only did the fall of Jerusalem to the Romans in A.D. 70 supply a benchmark against which the preeminence of the Spaniards' achievement could be decisively established, but, as we have seen, the analogy also served the gratifying function of suggesting a parallel between the losers: both were people who rejected both the authority of the emperor and the divinity of Christ. By diverting attention from the fall of Jerusalem in A.D. 70 to that of 63 B.C., and by presenting both Jews and Indians as innocent victims of unjust imperial aggression, Las Casas clearly hoped to neutralize the power of the "canonical" model for the fall of Tenochtitlan.

But it was Las Casas's use of Cano's other specific citation of Roman imperial misbehavior, their conquest of Spain, that constituted what was perhaps his subtlest and most powerful attack on Roman imperialism as a model for Spanish behavior in the Indies.[7] To judge by the preserved summary of his *relectio,* Cano had contented himself with the implicit parallel between Roman hunger for Spanish gold and Spanish hunger for Indian gold. To support this identification of greed as a motivation for Roman imperialism he cited 1 Macc. 8:3, which records that Judas Maccabaeus, seeking allies against the Seleucids, was impressed by what the Romans had done in Spain, where "they had gained possession of mines of silver and gold," though Cano appears to have suppressed the next phrase: "and they took possession of the whole place through their good judgment and perseverance *(consilio suo et patientia)."* Las Casas's shrewd exploitation of this historical instance in his Latin *Apologia* occurs within the context of a discussion of the supposed right of so-called civilized peoples to subjugate so-called barbarians—in this case, the third category of barbarians, primitive peoples with no real states, rulers, or laws. Las Casas pointed out that in fact, long before the Indians learned of the existence of the Spaniards, they had had *res publicae* with excellent laws, religion, and institutions. They inhabited cities and were governed by laws "that in very many matters surpass our own"—a kind of comparison that will be our main concern in the last chapter of this book. Turning next to the question of the illiteracy of the New World natives, an important weapon in the arsenal of those who argued for the inferiority of these "barbarians," Las Casas turned to the Roman conquest of Spain, citing Justin's *Epitome* (bk. 44) of the *Historiae Philippicae* of Pompeius Trogus, a Gallo-Roman of the time of Augustus:

> Now if they are to be subjugated by war because they are ignorant of polished literature, let Sepúlveda hear Pompeius Trogus: "Nor could the Spaniards submit to the yoke of a conquered province until Caesar Augustus, after he had conquered the world, turned his victorious armies against them and organized that barbaric and wild people *(populum barbarum et ferum)* as a province, once he had led them by law to a more civilized way of life." Now see how he called the Spanish people barbaric and wild. I would like to hear Sepúlveda, in his cleverness, answer this question: Does he think that the war of the Romans against the Spanish was justified in order to free them from barbarism? And this question also: Did the Spanish wage an unjust war when they vigorously defended themselves against them? Next, I call the Spaniards who plunder that unhappy people torturers. Do you think that the Romans, once they had subjugated the wild and barbaric people of Spain *(subjugata effera et barbara hyspanie gente)* could with secure right divide all of you *(vos omnes)* among themselves, handing over so many head of both males and females as allotments to individuals? And do you then conclude that the Romans could have stripped your rulers of their authority and consigned all of you, after you had been deprived of your liberty, to wretched labors, especially in the search for gold and silver lodes and mining and refining the metals? And if the Romans finally did that, as is evident from Diodorus, would you not judge that you also have the right to defend your freedom, indeed your very lives by war? Sepúlveda, would you have permitted Saint James to evangelize your own people of Córdoba in that way?[8]

Las Casas here intensified Cano's criticism of the Romans' exploitation of Spain's mineral wealth by an appeal to a passage in one of his favorite classical historians, Diodorus Siculus, a passage he cited twice in the *Historia de las Indias*. These appeals to Diodorus allowed him to offer impeccably "classical" proof—proof hitting close to home for Spanish readers—that his accounts of the horrors of labor in the mines of the Indies were not "something made-up and excessively exaggerated" [cosa fingida y demasiadamente exagerada].[9] Now, while it is cer-

tainly true that Diodorus recorded that after the Roman conquest of
Spain entrepreneurs from Italy flocked to the Spanish mines, worked
them with "a multitude of slaves," and took home vast wealth
"through their greed" (5.36.4), he nevertheless pointed out that all of
these mines had originally been opened "by the money-hunger of the
Carthaginians" (5.38.2). Las Casas, who had no intention of being dis-
tracted from his obsessive animus against the Romans, conveniently
overlooked this. In any case, the Romans' exploitation of Iberian mineral wealth was only part of his brief against Roman rule in Spain. At
least as important was their enslavement of much of the population and
their abrogation of the political sovereignty of the native Spanish rulers.
All three of these issues, we recall, had been central to the controversy
of the Indies since Vitoria's relection and even before.

In this remarkable passage from the *Apologia,* largely paralleled in
the summary of the Valladolid debate published in 1552, Las Casas
managed to score several telling points with deft economy. First, he
forced his Spanish readers—and, in the Valladolid debate, listeners—to
put themselves in the picture of what their countrymen were doing in
the New World by visualizing the remarkably similar plight of their
ancestors when *they* were being brutally subjugated, deprived of political autonomy, robbed, enslaved, sent to the mines. Indeed, he glided
effortlessly from Rome's Iberian victims of the second century B.C. to a
startlingly immediate, repeated "all of you" [vos omnes]—softened
somewhat in Domingo de Soto's summary to "nuestros pasasdos los
españoles" and "nuestros abuelos."[10] And lest modern Spaniards
assume that the New World natives were barbarians fit only to be subjects and wards—if not slaves—of "superior" Europeans, Las Casas
reminded his audience that the ancient Spaniards whom the Romans
conquered so unjustly were, if anything, fitter candidates for barbarian
status than the Amerindians, many of whom had evolved political institutions that rivaled or surpassed those of modern Europeans. As for the
Romans, far from being fit cultural ancestors and models for modern
Spaniards, they were the brutal oppressors of ancient Spaniards. This
indictment of Roman behavior in Spain gave special point and resonance to Las Casas's equation of the Romans with those later oppressors of the Iberian Peninsula, the Moors, a point he was fond of making. Decent Spaniards needed to realize that they had far more in
common with the Indians of the New World than with those proto-
Moors, the Romans of the Old World.

Las Casas and the Perennial Question of Hispanidad

But Las Casas's expansion of Cano's citation of the Roman conquest of Spain was more than simply a clever assault upon the application of the model of Roman imperialism to Spanish behavior in the Indies. It was at the same time a contribution to a controversy that has haunted Spanish historiography—and indeed Spanish political and cultural life—from the Middle Ages to the present. The questions at issue were—and remain—fundamental and highly charged: What is Spain? How long has it existed? Who are the Spanish people? As Julián Marías noted in his *España inteligible* (Understanding Spain), at the beginning of a chapter entitled "What Is Spain?": "We are in Spain today. If we go back two centuries, three, five, obviously we are still in Spain. If we go further, if we go back a thousand years, things are less clear."[11] If what Marías calls "the invention of the Spanish nation" was a process that began—and even then only tentatively—with the unification of the kingdoms of Castile and Aragón in the reign of the Catholic Monarchs, the nature and even existence of "Spain" and "Spaniards" before 1479 becomes a potently delicate conundrum—though in fact the question of Spanish national identity has persisted, perhaps even intensified, over the past five hundred years.[12]

This debate over the true meaning of *hispanidad* has both a spatial and a temporal dimension—or perhaps one might more accurately say that the question has a sequence of spatial dimensions layered historically up through the temporal dimension. That is, every period of "Spanish history" has displayed some version of the tension between unity and localism in landscape, cultures, languages, and political structures. Examples of the larger units among which these tensions have played out are the pre-Roman Iberian tribes; the Roman provinces of Spain and their mixtures of Iberian and Italian populations; the Visigothic elite and the "sub-Roman" *Hispani;* the Christian and Moorish kingdoms of the medieval Iberian Peninsula; and the regions that have comprised the various forms taken by "modern Spain" since the Reconquest. Far from diminishing over the centuries, these tensions actually intensified in mid- to late-twentieth-century Spain. On the one hand, the great historian Ramón Menéndez Pidal, in the influential preface to his *Historia de España* (1947), insisted upon the fundamental unity of the inhabitants of the Iberian Peninsula and denounced localism as a "diseased accident" [accidente morboso], a view promoted by the nationalist ideology and centralized political structure of Franco's Spain and its hostility to such manifestations of *localismo* as minority dialects.[13] On the other hand, the Constitution of 1978 established a decentralized "State of the Autonomies" (Estado de las Autonomías), based on the principle of autonomous governments in Spain's "regions and historic nationalities," a political shift reflected also in the growing interest recent Spanish historians have shown in the historical diversity of the regions of the Iberian Peninsula.[14] Paralleling this growing interest in Spanish regional history is a heightened awareness among scholars that even in the reign of Charles V the sense of a shared Spanish identity was often surprisingly feeble.[15]

The temporal aspect to this debate over *hispanidad* has been of most concern to those who have insisted upon or at least assumed the existence in their own time of a more or less unified "Spanish people" (not necessarily organized into a full-scale nation-state, however). For these "unitarians," the question inevitably arises: how far back does this "Spanish people" extend in time? Who "counts" historically as Spanish, and who is to be regarded as an interloper, or at least a marginal presence? Spanish historians of the twentieth century expressed sharply and passionately contrasting views on this question. At one extreme, the towering figure of Ramón Menéndez Pidal could serenely open his study of "the Spaniards in history" with an account of the basic traits of "the Spanish character" that draws upon such authors as the Gallo-Roman Pompeius Trogus and the Hispano-Roman Seneca. In his view, not only does the modern Spaniard's supposed ability to "withstand the disturbing temptations to greed and self-indulgence" owe much to the "instinctive influence of Seneca," but the Stoicism of Seneca itself "owed a great deal to the fact that he sprang from a Spanish family."[16] (Oddly, Menéndez Pidal failed to add that Marcus Aurelius, too, was of "Spanish" stock.) Toward the other end of the spectrum, Américo Castro tirelessly reiterated his conviction that it is meaningless to speak of "Spaniards" before the Reconquest. Not only did Castro challenge the advocates of an "eternal Spain," but he also enthusiastically affronted those who have insisted upon a kind of European *limpieza de sangre* in the veins of "true Spaniards," for Castro insisted that the Spanish people were forged in the smithy of the contact, conflict, and coexistence or "shared lives" [convivencia] of three diverse but ultimately inseparable peoples: the Christians, the Jews, and the Moors.[17]

The twentieth-century debate over *hispanidad* was intense, and it has itself become an object of historical analysis.[18] In addition, the history of the concept of Spain in the Middle Ages has been extensively studied, notably by José Antonio Maravall.[19] Remarkably little attention has been paid, however, to the phase of this debate that coincided with the Spanish discovery and conquest of the Indies. This is surprising, for the interaction between the encounter with the New World and the continuing debate over Spanish identity is a fascinating historical phenomenon, and one of its most remarkable chapters is precisely the attempt of Las Casas to forge a link of shared feeling between modern Spaniards and Amerindians via the pre-Roman Iberian "Spaniards."[20] Naturally, his strategy of creating empathy for the American "other" required his listeners and readers to acknowledge a sense of genetic identity with the "barbarians" who lived in Spain seventeen centuries earlier. It needs to be emphasized here that Las Casas was by no means relying on his compatriots' automatic recognition of such a kinship. Rather, he was making a contribution to the creation of that recognition, a contribution to an expansion of what Américo Castro has labeled "the historical 'we'" [el "nosotros" de las historias].[21]

There were, after all, other attractive choices for a sixteenth-century Spaniard in the market for ancestors. The Visigoths spring to mind as natural candidates, for, as Castro has noted, "down into the seventeenth century, 'to have Gothic ancestry' *(ser de los godos)* was a seal of glory for Spaniards."[22] In particular, the chroniclers and other functionaries of the royal courts had long celebrated the supposed royal Gothic ancestry of their patrons.[23] Thus, in 1243 the chronicler Rodrigo Jiménez de Rada, archbishop of Toledo, wrote an influential version of an already traditional "Gothic" interpretation of Spanish history in his significantly titled *Historia de rebus Hispaniae sive Historia Gotica,* a chronicle that began with a search for ancestors of the Spanish kings in Scandinavia and Scythia. Both there and in a supplement, the *Historia Romanorum,* Jiménez de Rada celebrated the Goths not as invaders of Spain but as the saviors of *infelix Hispania,* victim of successive waves of exploitative interlopers, most recently and most egregiously the Romans.[24] Two centuries later, one of the great writers of fifteenth-century Spain, Fernán Pérez de Guzmán (c. 1378–1460?), began his *Generaciones y semblanzas* with the declaration that King Enrique III of Castile was "descended from the very ancient and distinguished generation of the Gothic kings and, particularly, from the glorious and Catholic prince Recared, king of the Goths in Spain."[25]

This "neo-Gothic" tradition continued to play a vigorous role in the reign of Charles V, as we can see from a writer mainly concerned with the Indies, the indefatigable Gonzalo Fernández de Oviedo. In the proem to book 38 of his *Historia general y natural de las Indias* (in fact, the only chapter in book 38, the concluding book of part 2), Oviedo passed on an amazing new "fact" that he had learned from "Olao the Goth" (i.e. Olaus Magnus, whose *Carta Marina* was published in Venice in 1539): the northern part of Labrador is connected to Europe. Oviedo proceeds to offer this encomium to the nation of the man who offered this revelation: he is

> a native of those areas and provinces from which emerged those famous Goths who conquered so much of the world, and among other kingdoms made themselves lords of Spain. And in Spain up to the present day there endures in the royal house of Castile the Gothic succession and lordship of those Goths, for His Caesarean Majesty and his predecessors descend from that ancestry, etc.[26]

A couple of generations later, an even more startling celebration of the Goths as the truest original Spaniards appeared in the *Florida* (1605) of Garcilaso de la Vega, son of a Spanish conquistador and an Inca princess. Recounting Hernando de Soto's furtive and hasty burial in a hollow log in the Mississippi, Garcilaso was inspired to develop an elaborate parallel with the burial of Alaric the Visigoth in 410. Shortly after "having sacked the imperial city of Rome—which was the first sack since it became an empire and autocracy," Alaric was laid to rest in the river Basentus near Consentia (Cosenza) in southern Italy. Not only were both Alaric and De Soto great leaders whose bodies were consigned to rivers far into foreign territory they had courageously invaded; they were in fact heroes of kindred blood, "for these Spaniards are descendants of those Goths," and, indeed, "the nobility of these Spaniards of ours and the nobility found in all of Spain today derives without any question from those Goths."[27]

The attractions of the Goths as prominent Spanish ancestors are obvious.[28] To begin with, emerging from humble and obscure origins, they had rapidly demonstrated their superiority to the once formidable Roman legions and had dared to sack the imperial city itself. Then, in the endlessly imitated words of Isidore of Seville, "the most flourishing people of the Goths, . . . after many victories all over the world, eagerly

seized you [Spain] and loved you *(rapuit et amavit)"* and created there
the first independent united kingdom in the Iberian Peninsula, however
unstable it soon proved to be.[29] And finally, the Visigoths' defeat at the
hands of the Moors inspired the chiefs of the Reconquest to regard
themselves as avengers of Christian Spanish ancestors who had been
oppressed by invading infidels.

Bartolomé de las Casas, however, appears to have shown no interest
in the Goths as Spanish ancestors. References to Goths in his writings
seem to be sparse, but there are two that reveal a distinct alienation
from the "the Gothic mirage." In book 1, chapter 15 of his *Historia de
las Indias,* in the course of an argument that we shall be examining
before long in another connection, Las Casas offered a potted history of
Spain, which "almost from its first settlement was oppressed and
afflicted by tyrants, such as the family of Geryon, . . . and afterward the
Romans . . . and, as time went on, by the Vandals and the Goths, and
finally by the Moors and barbarians [Berbers]."[30] Here the Goths
appear simply as one among many groups of oppressors of the Spanish
people, a history of oppression initiated, it is true, by native tyrants
whom Las Casas met in the fanciful pages of Giovanni Nanni and his
spurious Berosus.[31]

Las Casas offered a more extended—and still more negative—discussion of the Goths in the epilogue (or alternative conclusion) to his
Apologética historia, his massive defense of the Amerindian cultures.[32]
His subject here was, once again, the question of the meaning of the
word *barbarian.* One category of barbarians is recalcitrant infidels,
those who have been exposed to Christianity but have chosen to reject
it, often supplementing their rejection with persecution of Christians.
Among the "chief enemies of our sacred faith," Las Casas wrote, were
the Sarmatians and Goths, whom his sources regarded as either a single
group or as at least near neighbors. Constantine warred against them
"in favor and defense of the Christian religion and divine worship, for
they persecuted the faith and the Roman people." Las Casas proceeded
to cite the "Tripartite History" (i.e. the Latin conflation and abridgment of the three late antique Greek ecclesiastical historians Socrates,
Sozomen, and Theodoret of Cyrrhus) for a characterization of the
Goths as "a people prone and inclined to wars" and a terror to other
tribes, only capable of being subdued by the Romans. They often provoked the Romans to warfare, for "many times the Goths were most
troublesome to the Romans and on occasion they destroyed Rome."

We detect here no hint of that pride in the Gothic invasions that is so
marked in the chroniclers who celebrated the "neo-Gothic thesis."
Instead, Las Casas actually went so far as to declare the Roman wars
against the Goths just—an unprecedented concession on his part. "And
so it is apparent that Constantine justly waged war against them, either
for the sake of the faith that they fought against [and here he cites the
"Tripartite History" to remind his readers that the Goths of this period
were Arian heretics] or because they were troublesome and hostile to
the Romans." Remarkably, Las Casas here passed over in silence the
supposed fact that these Goths were the ancestors of the Spanish kings
and nobles of the Reconquest and beyond. From the point of view of his
polemical purpose here, there was not the slightest reason for such a
silence. On the contrary: an attack on the supposed ancestral Goths as
simply a horde of troublesome, heretical, persecuting barbarians would
have superbly suited his customary strategy in the *Apologetic History,* a
massive and sustained attack on what we have come to call "Eurocen-
trism." The fact that he did not in fact allude to them as Spanish ancestors is a testimony to the seriousness with which Las Casas took his
identification of the pre-Roman Iberians as "nuestros abuelos."

Another set of attractive ancestors for some sixteenth-century
Spaniards were the Romans. The most enthusiastic publicist of this
view was, predictably perhaps, an Italian—or at least a Sicilian. Lucio
Marineo Sículo (1444?–1533?) arrived in Spain in 1484 and taught Latin
at Salamanca for twelve years until he was summoned to the court of
the Catholic Monarchs to teach Latin to young nobles and assume the
duties of chronicler and, later, chaplain to Ferdinand. He quickly set
himself the task of composing historical encomia of the Spanish people
in mellifluous Latin prose. Around 1492 appeared his *De Hispaniae
laudibus,* and his collected historical works were published in 1530
under the title *De rebus Hispaniae memorabilibus,* which appeared in
Spanish translation at Alcalá in 1539. For Marineo Sículo, the Romans
in Spain were great civilizers who built to last—and they built not only
roads and bridges, but also the great families of Spain:

> Whatever there is that is noteworthy in Spain, we must not doubt was
> the work of the Romans. For they were very powerful and very gen-
> erous *(liberalissimi)*—especially in Spain, where they stayed so very
> many years. Thus, if we shall say that several noblemen of Spain have
> taken their origin from the Romans, we shall probably not be wrong.
> For there are in Spain many settlements of Roman patricians.[33]

We shall soon see that Marineo Sículo's attribution of much of the glory of Spain to the Roman presence aroused the ire of Fernández de Oviedo—as did a surprising claim he made about the "true" discovery of the Indies—but the writings of this eloquent and highly placed humanist clearly offered many Spaniards in the time of Charles V a chance to feel more like "natural" subjects of the reigning "emperor of the Romans." It goes without saying, however, that Bartolomé de las Casas would have been profoundly unsympathetic to the notion of Romans as ancestors of modern Spaniards, however much the behavior of some of those Spaniards in the Indies may have recalled that of the Romans at their worst.

Taking the next step back in history, Las Casas joined a number of other Spaniards of his day and earlier in settling upon the pre-Roman Iberian tribes, the "barbarian" victims of the purportedly "superior" Romans, as the most authentic ancestors of modern Spaniards. Nor was it only in the Valladolid debate that Las Casas displayed this "Iberian patriotism." Indeed, he had determined upon the identity of modern Spaniards with early Iberians even before he developed his anti-Roman views. As early as October 15, 1535, in his *Carta a un personaje de la corte,* he had insisted that the Indians of the present day "are what we were in Spain *(lo que fuimos en España)* before St. James's disciples converted us."[34] Similarly, in the *Octavo remedio* of 1541–42, he wrote: "Who of our ancient ancestors *(nuestros antiguos padres)* would have been saved, or who of us left alive, if before the faith was preached to them they had been punished for the idolatry and other sins committed in their infidelity?"[35]

Las Casas's equation of modern Indians and ancient Spaniards in the *Carta a un personaje de la corte* was manifestly inspired by a celebrated letter to the pope written by his friend and fellow Dominican Julián Garcés (1447–1542) apparently just a few months earlier.[36] Appointed bishop of Tlaxcala in 1527, Garcés entered into friendly association with Las Casas immediately upon his arrival in the New World. It seems that it was in the spring or summer of 1535 that his wrote his famous letter to Pope Paul III urging him to ignore any reports that might reach his ears asserting the intellectual inferiority and lesser humanity of the Indians of New Spain, even if those claims were to come from missionaries eager to blame the results of their own laziness on the shortcomings of their native flocks.[37] This eloquent and powerful document, carried directly to the pope by Bernardino de Minaya and

printed in Rome in 1537, is commonly credited with helping to inspire
the bull *Sublimis Deus* (1537), in which Paul III strongly endorsed the
full capacity of the Indians to be thoroughly instructed in the path of
salvation. One of the indications Garcés offered of the intellectual capa-
bilities of the Indians was the rapidity with which their youths were
learning Latin. In fact, the bishop, himself famous for the Latin style
that he had learned from Nebrija at Salamanca, claimed that Indian
youths were writing Latin "more elegantly than our boys" [nostris
pueris elegantius]. The Latinity of the native youths of New Spain will
prove of interest to us at the end of this chapter. For now, however, it is
the use Garcés made of the Christianization of "barbarian" Spain to
defend the "barbarians" of New Spain that concerns us. In words that
strikingly anticipate those of Las Casas's *Carta a un personaje de la
corte,* Garcés declared of the Indians: "We cast barbarism and idolatry
in their teeth, as though we had ancestors who were any better, right on
up to the time the blessed apostle James preached to them." And he proceeded to cite the *Punica* (1.225–28) of Silius Italicus (whom he mistakenly assumed to be a native of Italica in the Iberian province of Baetica)
on the supposed "feritas Hispanorum," in particular their propensity to
commit suicide upon sensing the onset of old age. Like Las Casas before
his encounter with Sepúlveda's use of the Roman model, Garcés did not
exploit the anti-Roman potential of this appeal to the early Iberian
"patres" of modern Spaniards. Rather, he observed that Spain under
Roman rule produced "so many soldiers, so many very famous generals, whom Rome even made use of as emperors," apparently under the
impression that the most prominent Hispano-Romans were of pure
native Iberian stock.

In the decade after the debate in Valladolid, Las Casas intensified his
portrait of the barbarism of the early Iberians in his massive
Apologética historia. Thus, he declared that "we ourselves in our ancestors" [nosotros mismos en nuestros antecesores]—a striking formulation of the identity of modern Spaniards with ancient Iberians—"were
much worse, both in irrationality and disordered government and in
vices and brutal customs throughout the whole breadth of our Spain."
Indeed, so frustrated was St. James by his lack of success with what
Justin, in the passage cited also in the Valladolid debate, termed Spain's
"fierce and most barbaric people" that he soon returned to Jerusalem.[38]
Similarly, earlier in the *Apologética historia* Las Casas maintained that
the good government of native rulers on Hispaniola showed that in this

respect "these peoples maintained an extraordinary advantage over the most ancient Spaniards *(los españoles antiquísimos),*" who never acquired a competent leader against "las guerras tiránicas de los romanos" until Viriathus came along.[39] Elsewhere in the *Apologética historia,* attempting to counter European horror at New World human sacrifice, Las Casas claimed that "our Spaniards" [los nuestros españoles] surpassed the "French" (i.e., the ancient Gauls) by choosing as sacrificial victims their own children.[40] Even though he adduced this ethnographic detail as proof of a superior "natural intelligence" among the Iberian peoples in that they offered a supremely valuable gift to their gods (acknowledging, however, that they were influenced by the Carthaginians in this), by alluding here and elsewhere to Iberian human sacrifice Las Casas was attempting to inspire in his Spanish readers a chastened sense of shared humanity between the New World natives and the ancient—and hence also the modern—"Spaniards." Similarly, in his defense of the Indians' consultation of soothsayers, he pointed out that in pagan times ("en tiempo de la gentilidad") "our country of Spain" [nuestra patria España] was not immune to "these errors and this blindness," as Strabo pointed out.[41] Whether the ancient Iberians were just like the Indians or "much worse," Las Casas's argumentative strategy depended heavily upon his fellow Spaniards' willingness to accept those Iberians as their closest of kin, as virtually themselves with no alienating gap or significantly diluting admixture.

Early Iberians as "Spaniards": The Career of a Topos from Alfonso X to Charles V

Though the passionate Dominican's identification of the early Iberians as the true *antepasados* of modern Spaniards was by no means the standard assumption in the Spain of his day, his position was neither eccentric nor in fact really new. Here we need to make a brief survey of the halting, spasmodic growth of medieval and early modern Spanish recognition of the early Iberians as their ancestors, with special emphasis upon the link that sometimes existed between this identification and a negative view of ancient Roman imperialism.

The unfinished *Estoria de Espanna* (commonly known as the *Primera crónica general de España*), commissioned by Alfonso X in the 1270s, is famous both for its celebration of "la nobleza de los godos" and for that obsession with Roman history for which we have cited it in chapter 2. But in his prologue Alfonso declared that his intention in commissioning this work was to let people know "the beginning of the Spaniards and by what peoples Spain was mistreated; that they might know of the battles Hercules of Greece waged against the Spaniards and the massacres the Romans committed among them."[42] Similarly, the sufferings inflicted upon Spain by the invading Moors were presented as a renewal of the horrors of the Roman conquest: "Spain, which had earlier been wounded by the sword of the Romans, but then had been healed and helped to recovery by the medicine and virtue of the Goths, was now shattered, for her offspring were laid low and killed."[43] Thus, in a work first printed five years before Cano's relection, we find Iberian victims of Roman aggression presented as "Spaniards" in good standing, and a continuity of Spanish identity is assumed to link pre-Roman Iberians with post-Roman Goths across the gap of an invasion and occupation by the common enemy of both, the Romans. And yet, the Alphonsine history begins its account of the Roman conquest of Spain with an encomium of the Romans as wise, well-led, and patient imperialists—"the best rulers in the world" [los meiores cabdiellos del mundo]—and emphasizes that "they did not acquire Spain through force of arms, but through the friendship that they established with some of them."[44] It was above all the *amor* that Scipio Africanus bestowed upon the Spanish people that proved the Romans' most efficient tool of imperial conquest. Though the chronicle acknowledges that his successors failed to sustain Scipio's respect and love for the Spaniards, its accounts of the resulting Spanish revolts against Roman rule, the career of Viriathus, and the siege of Numantia (chaps. 39–48) are notably short on Hispanic patriotism and, despite a recognition of Roman severity and even perfidy, short as well on pronounced anti-Roman sentiment. Indeed, a pro-Spanish tone is much more evident in the Roman work that served as a major source for the Alphonsine account of these events, Florus's *Epitome*.[45]

The fifteenth century saw a fuller and more consistent development of views of Spanish history that looked back to the early Iberians and regarded the Romans as brutal aggressors. Toward the middle of that century, Alvar García de Santa María (Alfonso de Cartagena, 1384–1460), bishop of Burgos, in his *Anacephaleosis regum Hispaniae*, celebrated the kingdom of Castile as "one of the oldest in the world" and offered a jaundiced view of the Romans as simply the last in a long sequence of those who had tyrannically occupied Spain ("tyrannice occupantibus") until they were finally driven out by "exercitus nobilis militiae Gothorum."[46] Not surprisingly, his brief account of Alaric passes over the destruction inflicted on the city of Rome and focuses (as did Augustine's *City of God*, for that matter) on the scrupulosity with which the Goths protected those who took sanctuary in the churches.[47] Thus, Santa María reaffirmed the "neo-Gothic" thesis advanced by Jiménez de Rada two centuries earlier.

Santa María's distinguished pupil, Rodrigo Sánchez de Arévalo (1404–70), bishop of Palencia and *referendarius* (petitions secretary) to Popes Pius II and Paul II, offered an even more critical view of the Roman invaders in his *Compendiosa historia hispánica*. Written and printed in Rome in 1470 ("the first work of Spanish humanism to appear in print"), this work was a passionately patriotic Spanish response to Italian prejudice against the "Gothic barbarism" of Spain.[48] A deft use of a classical allusion in its dedication to Enrique IV, king of Castile, gave a hint of the chronicle's anti-Roman bias. Just as Sallust had complained that the fame of the Athenians was unjustly greater than that of the Romans simply because the Athenians had been blessed with more eloquent publicists and literary self-promoters, the very same thing, Arévalo claimed, could be said about the doings of the Spaniards. While keeping slyly close to Sallust's actual wording, Arévalo proceeded to lump the deeds of Sallust's own Romans along with those of the Greeks and the Persians as unduly inflated in the historical record.[49] This diminishment of Roman glory became more intense in Arévalo's *laus Hispaniae* in part 1, chapter 4, where a distinct gloating tone was sounded in his account of Roman reversals in the conquest of Spain:

How often were Roman armies and generals cut down? How often were they captured after having entered upon a base alliance? How often were they finally almost reduced to desperation? When new generals were appointed, the Spaniards took up arms with renewed bravery, until Rome could find no one who was eager to go to Spain. For, as Livy and Eutropius say, in the six hundredth year after the founding of the city, so great a fear of the Celtiberians invaded Rome that there was not a single soldier or general out of the whole people who dared to go to Spain. The next year, it is true, Metellus was sent to Celtiberia, but he campaigned unsuccessfully. His successor Quin-

tus Pompeius and finally also Quintus Scipio, who fought against Vir-
itathus (who was waging war against the Roman people), returned
inglorious.[50]

In a treatise usually referred to as *De monarchia orbis*, written in
Rome probably early in 1467 to exalt the temporal sovereignty of the
pope at the expense of the Holy Roman emperor, Arévalo vigorously
denied the legitimacy of the pagan Roman Empire, which served as the
supposed foundation of its self-styled latter-day successor. Not only
had the empire persecuted the church, but it had no lawful jurisdiction
over the territories whose political dominions it had violently and
tyrannically usurped. Turning to specific examples, Arévalo lodged
another indictment against the Roman invaders of Spain as not only
timorous warriors but also as tyrants motivated by "pride and ambition
to dominate and eagerness for earthly glory" [superbia et ambitione
dominandi et aviditate gloriae mundanae]. Thus, the "famous and
noble Gothic people" were simply obeying God's command to "free the
one who suffers injury and violence" when they drove the Romans from
Spain.[51] Even more enthusiastically than Jiménez de Rada, Alfonso X,
and Alfonso de Santa María, Sánchez de Arévalo embraced two Spanish ancestors who shared the Romans as enemies: the pre-Roman Iberians and the post-Roman Visigoths. Just as medieval chroniclers saw the
Reconquest as vengeance for the Moorish conquest of the Visigothic
kingdom, so Arévalo saw the Visigothic conquest of Spain as itself
vengeance for the earlier Roman subjugation of the *prisci Hispani*. It is
also worth noting that this papal paladin's assault on the prestige of the
Roman Empire was so extreme that it triggered an immediate response
in a treatise by his countryman Cardinal Juan de Torquemada, the
Opusculum ad honorem Romani imperii et dominorum Romanorum, a
defense of the justice and political wisdom of the Romans. Arévalo
swiftly counterattacked with his *Clypeus monarchiae ecclesiae*, in
which, anticipating Domingo de Soto a century later, he appealed to the
authority of Augustine to establish the fundamental illegitimacy of
Roman rule.[52]

During the reign of Charles V scattered hints of this assumption of
modern Spaniards' kinship with pre-Roman Iberians continued to surface. A striking early instance was offered by Martín Fernández de
Enciso, a lawyer who was prominently, though maladroitly, involved in
the settlement of the Isthmus of Darién. Upon his return to Spain, he

published in 1519 his *Suma de geografía*, which Boies Penrose called "not only a cornerstone in the history of navigational literature, but the earliest printed American coastal pilot as well."[53] In the dedicatory epistle Enciso told the emperor that those who called him a descendant of the Goths were mistaken, for he was in fact descended from the native kings of Spain, a greater people than the Goths, for they won what the Goths later lost.[54]

The widely imitated Antonio de Guevara, author of the famous "Villano del Danubio," reflected this "Iberian patriotism," though with characteristic inconsistency. At the end of the Comunero Revolt early in Charles's reign, Guevara extolled Don Antonio de Zuñiga as "a new Viriathus among the Spaniards," glossing the latter as "this illustrious man" [este ilustre varón], first a herdsman, then a highwayman, "and afterward he was an emperor and sole defender of his country *(emperador y de su patria único defensor),*" a man whom the Romans themselves admitted was a tough enemy to beat.[55] In another of these artful *Epístolas familiares,* one dated 1524 and addressed to the marquis of Pescara, Guevara argued that success in warfare depends on the justice of one's cause, and he supported his thesis by adducing the Romans' difficulties in conquering Numantia:

> Never were the Romans so badly handled and humiliated in the war of Asia or that of Africa as they were in the siege of Numantia; and that was neither through a lack of resources in attacking her nor was it because the city was very strong, but because the Romans had no reason for the war, while the Numantines had a great reason to defend themselves.[56]

Here, for a moment at least, we may catch an echo of the fictitious speech of Guevara's Danubian peasant before the Roman Senate.

On the other hand, in a much fuller account of the fall of Numantia in yet another of his *Epístolas familiares,* Guevara did not markedly appeal to "Iberian patriotism."[57] Though he did contrast the strong communal ethos and the fierce independence of the Numantines with the Romans' baser motivation of envy of the city's good fortune, and he clearly took pride in the exaggerated claim, made also in letter 1.11, that no people ever matched the Numantines in the damage they did to the Romans, Guevara nevertheless emphasized the barbarity of the besieged Celtiberians, characterizing both their nocturnal "hunts" of

Roman prey and their final self-immolation as "cosas monstruosas." It is especially striking that he never once referred to the Numantines as "Spaniards," and indeed he even idiosyncratically claimed that the city was founded by the Romans and named after its founder, the second king of Rome, Numa Pompilius! Furthermore, in his other works Guevara preferred to focus on the Hispano-Romans as worthy ancestors and models. Thus, in his *Reloj de príncipes* he offered as a reason for selecting Marcus Aurelius as a model for Charles V the fact that "he was a native of my country *(natural de mi patria),*" and in the same vein he began his *Década de Césares* with adulatory lives of two emperors whose Spanish origin he emphasized, Trajan and Hadrian.[58] Thus, while the influential Antonio de Guevara did offer some hints of the nascent identification with the pre-Roman Iberians, he seemed more at home with the Hispano-Romans as suitably glorious ancestors for modern Spaniards.

Rather like Guevara, none other than Juan Ginés de Sepúlveda was torn between his admiration for the Romans and the appeal of the nascent proto-Iberian patriotism. In the *Democrates secundus,* immediately after citing the Romans as a particular instance of the general truth that it is just for the wise, good, and humane to rule over those who are unlike themselves, Sepúlveda proceeded to deliver an encomium on the Spaniards as a people similarly distinguished for their *prudentia et ingenium.* He also praised their bravery, a virtue superlatively demonstrated by Spanish warriors in antiquity, "as once upon a time in the Numantine war and in those waged under the leadership of Viriathus and Sertorius, when great armies of the Romans were routed by a small band of Spaniards and sent under the yoke."[59] Nevertheless, despite his willingness to celebrate and appropriate Iberian valor in the face of Roman imperialism, the rest of Sepúlveda's contribution to the venerable genre of the *laus Hispaniae* displays his eagerness to establish kinship also with Hispano-Romans like Lucan and the Senecas—not to mention such surprising compatriots as Averroes and Avempace! Like those more recent Spaniards who so irritated Américo Castro, Sepúlveda appears to have assumed that anyone born within the boundaries of modern Spain was a fellow "Spaniard."

Another, rather more emphatic, assertion of the kinship of valiant pre-Roman Iberians with contemporary conquistadors surfaced in the last years of Charles's reign. In the preface to his 1555 Italian translation of Pedro Cieza de León's *Cronica del Perú,* the Spanish diplomat

Agustín de Cravaliz placed Spanish exploits in the New World in the context of the long history of valor displayed by Spaniards against their invaders: "The Spaniards, from the earliest times we know of them, have made use of arms, first among themselves, then against the Carthaginians, the Romans, the Goths, and most recently against the Moors." Lucia Binotti notes that "Cravaliz's unconditional praise of Spain in the past led directly to praise of her providential destiny in the present, as exemplified by her triumphs in Italy and the New World," a lesson especially tailored for an Italian audience.[60] Cravaliz, it will be noted, posits a direct link between modern Spaniards and ancient Iberians, with both Romans and Goths viewed as gloriously resisted invaders, not as contributors to Spanish ethnicity. This view of Spanish history strikingly accords with that of Las Casas, though the Dominican, it is true, viewed the Iberian ancestors less as glorious resisters than as hapless victims of these successive waves of invaders.

The "Iberian Patriotism" and "Anti-Romanism" of Gonzalo Fernández de Oviedo

A more complex set of appeals to pre-Roman Spanish history in the discourse of the conquest of the New World was fashioned by none other than Las Casas's bête noire, Gonzalo Fernández de Oviedo. For the chronicler, as for the Dominican, the early Iberians were indisputably genuine Spaniards. One striking indication of Oviedo's assumption is his invocation of ancient Iberian prowess in the encomium on Cortés in book 33 of the *Historia general y natural de las Indias*. Here, amid the much fuller comparison of Cortés with Julius Caesar discussed in the first chapter of this book, Oviedo noted that the deeds of the conquistador frequently reminded him of that Iberian hero whom we have seen celebrated also by Guevara and Sepúlveda: "Captain Viriathus, one of us Spaniards *(nuestro español)*, and an Extremaduran" (like Cortés).[61] Even the specific point of comparison that reveals Viriathus's inferiority to Cortés, the much more constricted stage upon which he acted, serves obliquely to celebrate the supposed Spanish patriotism of the Iberian brigand and warlord, for his exploits were performed "within Spain, in his homeland" [dentro de España, en su patria].

But a much fuller and more complicated expression of Oviedo's "proto-Iberian patriotism," coupled with a more pronounced anti-

Roman bias, is the dedication to Charles V of the second part of his chronicle, published in Córdoba in 1557, the year of his death.[62] This passage is of considerable interest, for it combines the conquistadors' topos of "besting the ancients" with a criticism of Roman imperial rule paralleling that of the Dominicans (of which Oviedo may well have been aware from the 1552 publication of the summary of the Valladolid debate). Oviedo began this epistle with the claim that the deeds of the Spaniards in the New World had far surpassed not only those of earlier Spaniards, but also those of classical conquerors like Alexander the Great, limited as they had been to but a single hemisphere, and even those of legendary heroes such as Theseus and Jason (no match for Magellan, whose voyage Oviedo was about to recount at the beginning of book 20). But the bulk of the epistle is devoted to the attempt to convince his *Cesárea Majestad* of the inferiority of the ancient Romans not only to himself and his enterprising subjects but also to his own Gothic ancestors and his subjects' Iberian ancestors.[63]

To begin with, there was the question of ethnic ancestry. The Romans erred in selecting the traitor Aeneas as their most distinguished ancestor, when there was "another worthier, greater, better, nobler, more famous and respectable origin that can be attributed to them," for the Phrygians (i.e., Trojans) were derived from the Iberian "Brigos," who took their name from Brigo, fourth king of Spain. (Oviedo's source for this was the notorious "Berosus"—not the genuine Hellenistic Babylonian historian, but the spurious document concocted by the pro-Spanish fifteenth-century Dominican forger of texts, Giovanni Nanni, a.k.a. Annius of Viterbo.)[64] This is one way of dealing with the prestige of the Romans: turn them into descendants of very ancient Spaniards! But leaving aside such prehistory, Oviedo wrote,

> let us return to the Romans, from whom, according to some biased modern Italian historians who fancy they are bestowing honor on Spain, our Spanish ancestors received the art of war and the habit of political life and other honorable customs, improving the roughness and ignorance of Spain. I deny this, for it is all false and uttered by men of little credit and no authority, and the truth is the exact opposite. For, although some of their captains and warlords and consuls came to Spain and, thanks not to superior effort but to superior luck, subjugated the greater part of it, they didn't devote themselves to the virtues those authors mention so much as they did to martyring

Christians and teaching people to endure their tyranny and to practice idolatry as they did, in abhorrence at which many holy Spanish
virgins and martyrs, friends of God, took up for their merits the celes-
tial seats that Lucifer and his followers lost.

Oviedo proceeded to catalog many of these saintly Spaniards, *nuestros
naturales,* who "suffered countless torments for not wanting to follow
or accept Roman rites and idolatries."

Subsequently, Oviedo continued, "those who threw the Romans out
of Spain were Goths," and from the Gothic kings Charles can trace his
descent *por derecha línea.* Furthermore, Oviedo claimed that Count
Julián, the traitor who invited the Moors to invade Spain in revenge for
King Roderick's seduction of his daughter, was a pure-blooded Roman
("romano, y de su origen"). The majority of both Christian and Arabic
accounts of the Moorish conquest of Spain identified Count Julián as a
Goth.[65] Oviedo's Romanization of him evidently derived from the idiosyncratic account offered by Canciller Pedro López de Ayala
(1332–1407) in his *Crónica del Rey Don Pedro,* year 2, chapter 18, where
it is asserted that the count "no era de linage Godo, sinó de linage de los
Césares, que quiere decir, de los Romanos."[66] Ayala's chronicle was
printed by the house of Cromberger, Oviedo's own publisher, in Seville
in 1542. In the context of Oviedo's diatribe, Julián's Roman origin suggests a clever variation on the Alfonsine chronicle's suggestion that the
Moorish invasion was a renewal of the woes brought upon Spain by the
Romans. Fortunately, however, this second Roman destruction of
Spain was soon counteracted by the initiation of the Reconquest by
Pelayo, "godo y sancto." Strongly echoing Arévalo, Oviedo proceeded
to declare that "Spain ought to glory much more in her Goths and in
her own native Spaniards than in the benefits and industry of the
Roman race or their help or customs and the small usefulness and great
labors and evils that followed for Spain," a palpable hit at Marineo
Sículo. He then gloated over the defeats that the Romans had suffered
at the hands of the Goths, in particular the sack of Rome by Alaric.
Thus, Oviedo debunked the once powerful "Roman model" of Charles
V as he boldly edited the Romans out of Spanish ethnic and cultural
genealogy and heralded the dual Gothic and Iberian identity of modern
Spaniards. "Goths and Spaniards are those who have discovered these
our Indies," he insisted. And yet, we should not fail to note that Oviedo

was careful to attack the Romans primarily for their idolatry—a trait they shared with the Indians, after all!—and for the inflation of their military reputation, punctured by Goths both ancient and modern. For Oviedo, Roman *tiranía* was above all a dramatic pagan religious persecution providentially generating Spanish saints, rather than a brutal and exploitative imperialism that might awaken awkward echoes of Las Casas's very differently motivated anti-Roman tirade in Valladolid— though it is true that in one passage early in the chronicle Oviedo had contrasted the Catholic Monarchs' supposed care in sending to Hispaniola settlers of noble blood with the Romans' habit of filling their provinces with "shepherds" and "rapers of Sabine women."[67]

"Godos son y españoles los que estas nuestras Indias hallaron." Oviedo's succinct and ringing application of anti-Roman Iberian patriotism to the conquest of the New World gained polemical and propagandistic specificity in two widely separated but explicitly linked passages elsewhere in his massive chronicle. One, in the unpublished second part, was an angry attack on the writer whose glowing account of the Romans in Spain had clearly been on Oviedo's mind when he denounced those "modern Italian historians who fancy they are bestowing honor on Spain" by attributing the origin of Spanish greatness to the beneficence of the Roman invaders.[68] This was, of course, the Sicilian immigrant humanist Lucio Marineo Sículo, who, not content with exalting the Roman contribution to Spanish culture, announced the following arresting discovery in book 19 of his *De rebus Hispaniae memorabilibus:*

> There is something extremely worthy of mention and most deserving to be known that I shall not pass over in silence, especially since it has been neglected, as far as I can tell, by others. In a certain region said to be on the mainland [i.e., Tierra Firme, near Darién], whose bishop was Juan de Quevedo, men digging the earth in search of gold found a coin marked with the name and image of Augustus Caesar. Juan Rufo, archbishop of Cosencia, got hold of it and sent it as a remarkable object to Rome, to the pope. This fact has indisputably robbed the glory from the sailors of our time, who used to boast that they sailed there before all others, since through the evidence of this coin it is certain that the Romans once reached the Indies.[69]

This anecdote managed to stimulate comment for over a century.[70] Juan de Castellanos (1522–1607), conquistador turned priest and poet, attacked it contemptuously in his massive poem *Elegías de los varones ilustres de Indias* (1589).[71] However gratifying to non-Spaniards it may have been, the poet found the story utterly devoid of plausibility. If the Romans had truly settled the region, why had only one solitary coin been found—and this, he claimed, a silver coin in a region of gold mines? And how could Roman historians have neglected to record so glorious an episode in their national history? In any case, Castellanos asserted, the whole incident was a hoax *(burla)*: two Italians confessed on their deathbeds that they had "planted" the coin. In 1604 the eminent neo-Stoic Justus Lipsius, labeling the discovery of the coin a "silly story," likewise declared it to be a hoax in his *Physiologiae stoicorum.* Lipsius had returned to the Catholic fold in 1591, was appointed a royal historian by Philip II in 1595, and fawningly dedicated this book to Pedro Enríquez, Conde de Fuentes, former governor of the Spanish Netherlands.[72] No doubt Lipsius was happy to be able to denounce a story that robbed Spain of one of its greatest glories. Similarly, as late as 1648, the lawyer and councilor of the Indies Juan de Solórzano Pereira believed that it was necessary to denounce the story as "cosa sin substancia, y faláz," manifestly designed to diminish "la gloria de España."[73]

But no one surpassed Oviedo in despising this story. It was bad enough that Marineo Sículo had revealed himself as "mal informado" about the history of Spain, especially when he attempted to concoct genealogies linking prominent Spanish families with the Romans. It was worse that he had dared to intrude upon the history of a part of the world he had never visited—or perhaps, as Oviedo sarcastically opined, "he came to the Indies in his dreams"—and that he had made absurd errors about the most elementary facts, attributing, for example, the expedition of 1492 to one "Pedro" Colom with thirty-five ships. Even more absurd was his presumption in daring to write about Darién "not as a cosmographer but as a writer of romances *(novelero),*" for this just happened to be a region that Oviedo knew from firsthand experience. Indeed, Oviedo had been in Darién as inspector of mines at the very time when miners allegedly unearthed that coin, and so he would have been one of the first to hear of such a "find," had there been any such thing. But what especially infuriated Oviedo was the fact that Marineo Sículo made no attempt to disguise his intention of writing "in contempt of the Spaniards and the Admiral Don Cristóbal Colom, and he wishes to give the prize to the Romans." Not content with attributing Spanish achievements on the Iberian Peninsula to the Roman invaders, this Italian was trying to hijack the glory of one of modern Spain's most famous exploits and bestow it upon Augustus Caesar.

Another way of looking at Marineo's anecdote, as Giuliano Gliozzi has pointed out, is to note that he was attempting to transfer the glory of the discovery of the New World from Columbus and his heirs to the reigning "emperor of the Romans," the successor of the man whose face and name were on that dubious coin. When the Latin version of Marineo Sículo's book appeared (1530; repr. 1533), the Colón family's struggle to retain the rights and privileges that had been so liberally accorded the Admiral was entering its final stages. Columbus's daughter-in-law, María de Toledo, returned to Spain in 1529 to plead the family's case, if possible before the emperor himself. Marineo Sículo's story of the Roman coin thus served to promote not only its inventor's Italian cultural chauvinism but also the Spanish Crown's attempt to retrieve the overly generous privileges it had granted the Colón family. The Sicilian was betting on the winning horse, for on September 8, 1536, the emperor confirmed the decision taken by the Council of the Indies earlier that year to order the Colón family to renounce the title of Viceroy, the privilege of nominating officials in the New World, and the impressive revenues they had pulled in (which had included the tenth part of the gross receipts from the Indies).[74]

Accordingly, Oviedo's reference to Marineo Sículo's attempt to slight "the Spaniards and the Admiral Don Cristóbal Colom" was plausible enough. The exaltation of the ancient Romans at the expense of the modern Spaniards served Marineo's personal agenda as Italian cultural missionary in Spain, while the slight to the Admiral was an attempt to participate in a currently fascinating power struggle. But as Oviedo's further words reveal, he himself had played a remarkably similar game around the same time, one that found him concocting his most famous—or notorious—case for pre-Roman "Iberian patriotism."

> Neither did the Romans ever know of these regions, nor did the Sicilian find such a thing recorded. But the Spaniards *did* [know of these regions] before any Romans existed, for, as I have said, these islands are the Hesperides, named after Hesperus, who was the twelfth king of Spain, . . . 603 years before the city of Rome was founded, and 1,658 years before the Incarnation of Christ. All of this is more fully stated in book 2, chapter 3 of the first part of this *General History of the Indies.*[75]

Clearly, Marineo had stepped on Oviedo's toes not only by writing about the Indies, but more particularly by trying to float a rival "foundation myth" to compete with Oviedo's own contribution to the currently lively game of transferring the glory of the discovery from Columbus to the Spanish Crown.

The earlier passage to which Oviedo referred his readers is to be found in the segment of the chronicle that was published by Juan Cromberger in Seville in 1535, the year before the claims of the Columbus family were finally rejected. Having in the preceding chapter debunked a rival anti-Colón story, that of a Portuguese pilot who on his deathbed informed Columbus of lands he had found in the far west, Oviedo countered with his claim that these territories "had been known of and possessed by the kings of Spain in ancient times."[76] True, he also accepted the idea that the Antilles had been visited by the Carthaginians as well, following an account in the pseudo-Aristotelian *De admirandis in natura auditis* (more commonly known as *De mirabilibus auscultationibus*), which Oviedo knew through the *Vitae regularis sacri ordinis predicatorum* of Theophilus of Ferrara. (We have seen that this passage from Pseudo-Aristotle was an important part of Vinko Paletin's odd 1559 argument that the Romans had inherited the New World from the Carthaginians. Some twenty years later it achieved the distinction of being airily rejected as evidence of pre-Columbian contact by Montaigne in his essay "Des Cannibales.")[77] According to this story, Carthaginian merchants discovered an uninhabited and marvelously fertile island in the far western reaches of the Atlantic. They began to settle it, but the Carthaginian senate squelched the project lest the mother city experience a population drain. This island Oviedo identified as either Hispaniola or Cuba. But he was more interested in "another, greater origin of these parts: I hold these Indies to be those famous islands the Hesperides, so called from the twelfth king of Spain, named Hesperus." After a digression in which he appealed to Isidore of Seville on the ancient practice of naming kingdoms after their founders, Oviedo turned to "Berosus"—that is, again, the fabricator from Viterbo, Giovanni Nanni. As we have seen that he would do in his dedication of the second part of the chronicle to Charles V, Oviedo seized with particular glee upon the claim of "Berosus" that the Phrygians took their origin from Spain and their name from Brigo, the fourth king of Spain. This of course meant that "the Trojans originated from the

Spanish 'Brigians,'" and so in turn the Romans were ultimately Spanish in origin. Oviedo proceeded to claim that "Berosus's" ancient Spanish king Hesperus was identical to the brother of Atlas, about whom Oviedo had read in another fifteenth-century source, the commentary on Eusebius's *De temporibus* by Alonso de Madrigal (1400?–1455), alias "El Tostado." These brothers, according to "El Tostado," journeyed to Africa, where Atlas claimed a kingdom in the northwest (Mauritania/Morocco), and Hesperus took the adjacent "Fortunate Isles," which the poets named the Hesperides after him. Oviedo, however, rejected this identification of the Hesperides with the "Islas Fortunadas," which he took to be the Canaries. Pliny the Elder, Julius Solinus (an early-third-century geographer heavily dependent upon Pliny), and Isidore of Seville had located the Hesperides forty days' sail west of the "Gorgades," which Oviedo identified as the Cape Verde Islands. It followed, then, that the Hesperides occupied by Hesperus were "nuestras Indias." Accordingly, Oviedo concluded that "3,193 years ago Spain and her king Hesperus ruled these islands or Indies-Hesperides, and so, with most ancient right, . . . God returned this lordship to Spain after so many centuries." Thus, when the Catholic Monarchs sent Columbus forth at the very moment they were acquiring Granada and Naples, they were simply reclaiming a long-lost territory of their ancestors. Spanish kings had claimed this territory not only centuries before the reign of the Roman emperor whose portrait graced Marineo Sículo's coin, but centuries before anyone ever heard of the Romans—who were in any case simply Spaniards at a couple of removes.

Oviedo's gratifying theory came to the attention of the emperor at the end of 1533, two years before the first part of the chronicle appeared in print, and Charles expressed a lively interest in it.[78] Not only could it join Marineo Sículo's Roman coin tale in the brief against the Colón family, but it could prove a handy alternative to overdependence on the potentially revocable papal donation of 1493.[79] Naturally, the implications of Oviedo's Hesperides story did not escape Columbus's illegitimate son Ferdinand, who, writing soon after Oviedo's story circulated, noted with alarm that "some persons assign great value and importance to these fantasies, to the prejudice of the honor and glory of the Admiral."[80] Sidestepping "Berosus," Ferdinand applied withering scrutiny to Oviedo's reading of the ancient sources on the Hesperides. After all, in addition to his willful intent to deceive, "Oviedo knew no Latin" and was relying on misleading translations. Another emphatic rejection of

Oviedo's identification of the Hesperides with the Antilles appeared in the *Historia general de las Indias* of Francisco López de Gómara, chaplain and encomiast of Cortés.[81] Though no supporter of the claims of the Colón family, Gómara was not eager to see the glory of modern Spaniards preempted by Oviedo's ancient Iberians. Accordingly, he insisted that the Hesperides were simply the Cape Verde Islands. Nevertheless, Gómara himself could not resist detecting the Indies in classical texts, for he persuaded himself that they were Plato's Atlantis, the name of which he derived not from Atlas but from the Nahuatl word for water, *atl.*

But an even more passionate and detailed assault upon Oviedo's fantasy of a prehistoric Iberian dominion in the Indies came from his cordial enemy Bartolomé de las Casas, who devoted two substantial chapters of the *Historia de las Indias* (bk. 1, chaps. 15–16) to its demolition.[82] The second of these chapters need not detain us. It is a barrage of objections both to the notion that the Hesperides could have been the Indies (Las Casas favored the Azores or the Cape Verde Islands) and the suggestion that the name *Hesperides* was derived from "Berosus's" Spanish king Hesperus. The more likely eponym was Hesperus the evening star, whose setting in the west sufficiently accounted for the name of these western lands. More interesting are the arguments Las Casas offered in chapter 15 against the contentions that Columbus had ancient predecessors and, more specifically, that it was the ancient Iberian kings who discovered and briefly ruled over these regions—a claim Las Casas attributed to "noxious flattery of our illustrious kings." Las Casas offered four arguments against these claims. The first is an *argumentum ex silentio:* given the classical references to lesser feats of discovery, it scarcely stands to reason that an exploit of this magnitude would not have been recorded by at least one Greek or Roman author. Next, there is the implausibility of the idea that in the seventeenth millennium B.C. even the Greeks could have pulled off such a feat of navigation, to say nothing of the much more backward Spaniards—yet another reminder by Las Casas of the "barbarian" level of early Iberian culture. Then there is the fact that "Berosus" (whose authenticity Las Casas accepted and, indeed, later defended against the doubts of Juan Luis Vives) indicated that Hesperus ruled Spain for only ten years, not time enough to discover and become lord of the Indies.[83]

Las Casas's fourth argument against the pre-Columbian Iberian discovery of the New World takes us back once again to his anti-Roman obsession, specifically to his interest in early Spain as a victim of the imperialism of the Romans, among other invaders. Far from being a plausible candidate for the imperial ventures of Oviedo's prehistoric fantasies, early Spain was itself, Las Casas pointed out, the long-suffering object of such wars of conquest. "Almost from the time of her first settling, she was oppressed and afflicted by tyrants."[84] First there were the legendary tyrants Geryon and his three sons ("Berosus" is, again, the source here), then Phoenician settlers, then the Carthaginians, the Romans, the Vandals, the Goths, and the Moors. We have noted earlier how this passage demotes the Goths from the status of the truest and noblest Spanish ancestors to that of mere walk-ons in the Iberian Peninsula's long-playing pageant of invasion and oppression by foreigners. We should by now scarcely be surprised to find the Romans playing precisely the same role in this list. With formidable oppressors and exploiters like the Romans, Goths, and Moors, "Spain had no time or interval to rule over foreign peoples, especially not such distant regions." If news of the Indies *had* reached ancient Spain, it would have come to the notice of the people currently dominating Spain, and that people would have effected the conquest of the New World. "And if any people who ruled Spain had acquired knowledge and lordship of those kingdoms, it is obvious that it would have been the Romans, but no such thing is recorded of them." As proof of the Romans' ignorance of the New World, Las Casas offered two stories. One, taken from Albertus Magnus's *De natura locorum,* claimed that when Augustus ordered his census of the whole world, messengers traveling on ships supplied by the kings of Egypt (not that there were any such in the time of Augustus!) and Ethiopia found that once they hit the equator further progress became impossible either by land or sea, and so they turned back. The other story was Plutarch's account of Sertorius's idea of seeking refuge in the Fortunate Isles (the Canaries), whose existence had just come to his notice. If Plutarch here alluded to the nearby Canaries as a remarkable new discovery, "how much more obscure and hidden would these Indies of ours have been to the Romans and to the whole world over there?" This insistence on the Romans' failure to discover the New World seems unnecessary in the context of Las Casas's assault on Oviedo's Hesperides theory. Perhaps it was designed as a side-swipe at Marineo Sículo's story of the coin of Augustus excavated at Darién. If so, Las Casas clearly recognized the affinity between the rival claims of Oviedo's Iberian and Marineo's Roman anticipations of

Columbus's discovery. In any case, he now restated his fourth argument against Oviedo's fantasy, sharpening the anti-Roman tone: "If the Romans, who ruled Spain and many other provinces and who were industrious *(no eran negligentes)* at dominating foreign lands and in recording their own deeds, had no notice of [the Indies], . . . then it is wrong to make guesses and flatter Spain and peddle to her rulers things that never happened."[85]

Despite his sharply expressed contempt for Oviedo's equation of the Indies with the Hesperides and his claim that they had recently been restored to the descendants of those who had discovered and occupied them over three millennia earlier, Las Casas shared certain fundamental assumptions with the prolific historian and naturalist. Both men loathed the Roman Empire and regarded its extension to Spain not as a source of later Spanish glory or as a contribution to the formation of the Spanish people, but as an unjust alien intrusion. And both looked to the pre-Roman Iberian peoples as "true" Spaniards—though Oviedo, like Sánchez de Arévalo before him, enthusiastically embraced the Goths as a second set of worthy ancestors, especially for the Spanish royal houses. Oviedo and Las Casas also, of course, both applied their anti-Roman "Iberian patriotism" to the timely and hotly debated question of the legitimacy of the Spanish presence in the New World.

But the differences between their brands of anti-Roman Iberian patriotism are as significant as the similarities. Oviedo's Iberian ancestors were the denizens of medieval legend, enshrined in the pages of Rodrigo Jiménez de Rada and the Alphosine chronicle, resurrected in the late-fifteenth-century fabrications of Giovanni Nanni, and recycled yet again during the reign of Charles V in the fanciful official chronicle of Florián de Ocampo. These glorious prehistoric Iberians were conveniently indistinct figures ideally suited for transformation into bold master mariners and conquerors of distant lands—fit ancestors and forerunners of the conquistadors whose exploits in those very same distant lands Oviedo chronicled with such admiration. The Iberian ancestors to whom Las Casas appealed, on the other hand, were figures of much sharper historical verisimilitude, for they fell within the ken of respectable ancient historians recording genuine historical events of the second, not the seventeenth, century B.C. And while Oviedo's legendary Iberian explorers and conquerors foreshadowed the modern Spanish conquistadors, displacing the Roman models so often employed and so often challenged in the discourses of the conquest, Las Casas's Iberian ancestors resembled the Indians of the New World in being "barbarian" victims of a "civilizing" mission undertaken by a self-styled "superior" imperialist power.

Cano, Las Casas, and Ambrosio de Morales

We have now surveyed attempts made by early- and mid-sixteenth-century Spaniards—even by some publicists of the conquistadors—to reach back to the early Iberians as ancestors, and we have noted that Julián Garcés, first bishop of Tlaxcala, attempted to use the pre-Roman Iberian "barbarians" to elicit respect in modern Spaniards for the "barbarians" of New Spain. But it remained for Cano and especially Las Casas to link this conception of Spanish ethnicity to an anti-Roman animus pioneered by fifteenth-century chroniclers like Santa María and Sánchez de Arévalo and to suggest that the sufferings of "our ancestors the Spaniards" [nuestros pasados los españoles] at the hands of the Romans should sensitize modern Spaniards to their own countrymen's behavior toward the Indians.

To what extent were Cano and Las Casas directly influenced by the negative presentation of the Roman conquest of Spain in certain fifteenth-century chronicles? A survey of the voluminous writings of Las Casas, at least, does not reveal any explicit debt to Santa María or Arévalo. He did, however, allude to another fifteenth-century contributor to the "proto-Iberian model" in yet another subversion of Roman prestige in the *Apologia*. Insisting in chapter 33 that cannibalism was not historically restricted to "savages," Las Casas noted that this shocking practice had surfaced in the illustrious Spanish city of Numantia, whose citizens, "oppressed by extreme hunger during a siege by Scipio, ate human corpses. This event was reported by the Bishop of Gerona in these words: 'Besieged and driven in the end by hunger to eat human flesh, the people of Numantia offered to surrender to Scipio if he would give them humane treatment.'"[86] This bishop of Gerona, the Catalan chronicler Joan Margarit (ca. 1421–84), devoted the ten books of his *Paralipomenon Hispaniae* to the history of Spain up to the time of Augustus, thus contributing to the concept of a Spanish ethnicity antedating the Visigothic kingdom.[87] Though Margarit thus contributed to the growth of "Iberian patriotism," his lifelong association with Italian humanists did not generally allow him to be harshly critical of the

Roman conquerors of Spain. Nevertheless, Las Casas cleverly exploited his chronicle not only to demonstrate that "Spaniards," too, have feasted on human flesh (he also cited a more recent case of shipwrecked Spaniards in Cuba), but also to get in yet another dig at the savagery of those Roman conquerors who had reduced ancient Spaniards to this grim act.

If the fifteenth-century chroniclers, then, do not seem to have been the direct source for Cano's and Las Casas's pro-Iberian, anti-Roman argumentative strategy, a contemporary historian may well have played a key role in their deft use of early Spanish history, though the date of the publication of his work would seem at first to discourage such a connection. In 1574 Philip II's official court historian Ambrosio de Morales published in Alcalá the first volume of his continuation of Florián de Ocampo's chronicle of Spanish history, picking up the account with the conclusion of Roman operations against the Carthaginians in Spain in 206 B.C.[88] Morales's narrative in books 6 and 7 of the Roman conquest of Spain, the war against Viriathus, and the Numantine War reveals an eloquent and passionate intensification of both the feeling of kinship with the ancient Iberians and the hostility toward the Roman invaders that we have seen pioneered by Santa María and Sánchez de Arévalo in the previous century. He thus differed markedly from the chronicler whose work he was commissioned to extend. True, Ocampo had likewise assumed the identification of modern Spaniards with pre-Roman Iberians, a continuity over time that he had emphasized by the biological metaphor of labeling the pre-Roman period "the childhood of our Spain" [la niñez de nuestra España], but it appears that his account of the Roman conquest, had he lived to write it, would have been relatively benign, for in his prologue he linked the Romans with the Visigoths as "teachers and tutors" of the "adolescence" of the Spanish people, and he claimed that Romanization allowed the Spaniards to live like "true human beings" [verdaderos hombres].[89]

Morales's attitude to the Roman invaders, on the other hand, was relentlessly and proudly hostile. Book 7 opened with the declaration that in 198 B.C. the Romans had cast aside all pretense of being in Spain to aid the Spaniards:

From this point onward they fought in Spain for no other object than to subjugate it and make it their own. Now they could no longer say that they were protecting us, but that they were conquering and dominating us. And thus from this point onward this chronicle will relate nothing but the Romans giving us orders, warring with us to make us their vassals, extracting cruel tributes from us, enriching themselves with our treasures, and placing upon us a yoke that became heavier each day so that the subjugation might be the more complete.[90]

Especially striking here is the repeated emphasis upon *us (-nos, nosotros)*, a use of what Castro termed the "historical 'we'" that is strongly reminiscent of Las Casas's references to the Roman conquest of Spain. In accord with this programmatic declaration, Morales proceeded to devote the seventh and eighth books of his chronicle to a stark contrast between Roman greed and cruelty and Spanish heroism and love of freedom.

Readers attuned to the history of Spanish doings in the Indies would have been particularly struck by Morales's account of an embassy sent by "los miserables Españoles" in 169 B.C. to the Roman Senate to complain of the praetors' "tiranía y avaricia" (bk. 7, chap. 28). This chapter, an artful amplification of the rather bare account of this embassy offered by Livy (43.3), develops a pattern of motifs that would have been especially resonant for a mid-sixteenth-century Spanish reader: oppression of natives by brutal and greedy conquerors, an appeal over the heads of the exploiters to a higher authority in the imperial capital, the passing of ameliorative laws, and the prompt invalidation of those well-intentioned new laws by "special interests and unjust favors, by which the powerful customarily evade the force of laws and their rigorous punishments."[91] This highly colored chapter, which concludes with Morales's extended denunciation of "the injustice of the Romans and the tyranny with which they wore out poor Spain," is an unmistakable parable for the promulgation and almost immediate subversion of the New Laws of 1542.

Morales's celebration of the valor and nobility of the Iberians and his denunciation of Roman imperialism dominates his account of "the valor of Viriathus and his great deeds."[92] But if this brigand who became "the Romulus of Spain" offered Morales a rare opportunity to compose an encomium of a particular Iberian hero, he reserved his most intense patriotic fervor for a collective hero: the population of the city of Numantia. While Antonio de Guevara's earlier account of the final siege of this Celtiberian city did not, as we have seen, markedly solicit its readers' sense of identification with these victims of the Romans, Morales's account aggressively established the Numantines in the pantheon of Spanish national heroes. At the beginning of book 8, Morales introduced "the war of the Romans against our Numantines" with the ringing claim that "now the history of Spain reaches the highest point of glory and fame that it could reach in those times," for the terrible humiliations and reversals the Romans endured before the fall of that city were a testimony to "the great force and valor of our people."[93] This last phrase, "los nuestros," strikingly absent from Guevara's account, recurs insistently in that of Morales.

In their accounts of the siege of Numantia, Morales noted, the Romans themselves were constrained to give such glory to "los nuestros" that not even latter-day Spaniards could give them more. Similarly, the Romans could not deny the injustice of their involvement in this conflict—Florus in fact went so far as to call it Rome's most unjust war.[94] "And so," Morales concluded, "it seems that God allowed our people to carry out for some time the punishment that so unjust a cause merited." Not only did the Romans lack valid justification for this war, but individual Roman commanders in Spain were motivated solely by "ambition for glory and fame, desire for a triumph, or hunger for wealth, with no thought for the growth and authority of their republic."[95] Morales has here characteristically applied to *all* Roman commanders in Spain words that Appian had used to criticize *some* (τινες, *Roman History* 6.13.80). And Scipio Aemilianus, who presided over the city's fall, "was very harsh and terrible by nature," which did not prevent him from being at heart a coward who "had always feared an engagement with the Numantines."[96] By contrast, the Celtiberian father who bade his daughter's two suitors to sally forth and bring him the right hand of a Roman displayed the "attitude of a true Spaniard and Numantine" [pensamiento de verdadero Español y Numantino].[97] The self-immolation of the last surviving Numantines, labeled a "cosa monstruosa" by Guevara, inspired this funerary encomium from Morales: "Thus perished by her own hands the never defeated Numantia, a city distinguished among all those in the world," after having held out so long against "the Roman people, who fought with the resources of the whole world"—a dig at the Romans' supposed claim to be "lords of the whole world."[98]

When he moved on to a survey of the Iberian provinces of the Roman Empire, Morales did not, it is true, tend to sustain this anti-

Roman tone, and he proved happy enough to grant distinguished Hispano-Romans the proud title of "españoles." Thus, he entitled chapter
28 of book 9 "El Emperador Trajano, Español," and he proclaimed,
echoing Ruiz de Mota, that "Spain may very properly take pride in the
fact that of the three emperors she gave to Rome, two of them were
such that she never had better ones."[99] And since Trajan "was a
Spaniard and such an excellent prince, it will be fair and most fitting to
this history to recount his life at length." No doubt one reason for
Morales's willingness to celebrate Roman rule in Spain, despite his passionate denunciation of how that rule was acquired, was that Roman
Spain had left him an impressive set of architectural monuments and
inscriptions, and he prided himself on his industrious inspection of
these physical remains. Indeed, his diligent search for Roman inscriptions and other antiquities throughout Spain gave "his history of
Roman Spain an entirely new look," Sabine MacCormack has noted,
"because the course of his narrative was no longer bound by what the
ancient historians had said or failed to say."[100] Accordingly, the center-
piece of his account of that great "Spaniard" Trajan was a detailed survey of the high-span bridge over the Tagus at Alcántara and its inscriptions. Still, despite his strong proprietary interest in Roman Spain as an
antiquarian, he could nevertheless prove capable of viewing Roman
rule as an alien imposition upon a more authentic Spanish substratum.
Accordingly, he approvingly cited Orosius's claim that after the barbarian takeover of the peninsula at the beginning of the fifth century A.D.
"many Spaniards were more content with the free poverty in which they
now lived than with the prosperous and tribute-burdened servitude that
they had endured under the Romans."[101]

Morales's patriotic account of the Roman conquest of Spain not
only influenced later historians, it soon inspired a classic of Spanish literature, Cervantes's play *El cerco de Numancia,* written in the early or
mid 1580s.[102] In hailing victims of imperial conquest as the true Spanish
ancestors, both Morales and Cervantes implicitly undercut their modern compatriots' perception of themselves as glorious and justified conquerors of an overseas empire. This tension between ancient Spanish
imperial victims and modern Spanish imperial conquerors would have
inevitably inspired readers to invest those freedom-loving ancient
Spaniards with the lineaments of the contemporary inhabitants of the
New World. In fact, Willard F. King has plausibly argued that Cervantes modeled several scenes and certain Numantine characters and

customs of his drama not only on Morales's account, but also on passages in Alonso de Ercilla's remarkable epic of the rebellion of the Araucanian Indians of Chile, *La Araucana*.[103] Similarly, we have noted the likelihood that Morales himself was thinking of the New World as he composed his account of the Roman conquest of Spain, so even when Cervantes was dependent upon this impressive historical narrative, he was encountering resonances from across the Atlantic.

Morales, then, shared with Melchor Cano and Bartolomé de las Casas a hatred for Roman imperialism and a strong identification with the Romans' Iberian victims as authentic Spaniards, and all three were aware that ancient history was being disturbingly replayed on a distant stage, with the descendants of victims now taking the role of imperialistic oppressors. Could Morales have been influenced by the great Dominicans? That conclusion seems suggested by the fact that the historian had apparently been a student of Cano's at Alcalá at the very time when the latter was delivering his pronouncement on the question of the Indies.[104] It is at first tempting to suppose that around 1546 Cano—soon seconded by Las Casas upon his return to Spain in 1547—inspired Morales to develop that anti-Roman Iberian patriotism which would bear final fruit in 1574. But when Morales became Cano's student in 1543, he was already about thirty (having shortly before left—or been expelled from—the monastery of San Jerónimo near Córboda after imitating Origen's gruesomely literal interpretation of Matthew 19:12), and he himself stated in the prologue to his history, "I could truthfully affirm that I do not remember a period in my life from the beginning of my humanistic studies when I did not have this desire and intention of writing of the history and antiquities of Spain." He proceeded to record that he had originally abandoned his project of writing the early history of Spain when Florián de Ocampo, with considerable exaggeration, informed him at Alcalá that he had himself already written "the whole ancient history of Spain up to the Goths."[105] Since this conversation will presumably have taken place before Ocampo began to publish his history in 1544, we can see that Morales had already been immersing himself in the history of pre-Roman Spain and the Roman conquest several years before his teacher and friend Melchor Cano employed the historical exemplum of the Romans in Spain to castigate Spanish behavior in the Indies, a use of the exemplum that was in complete accord with the identification with the early Iberians and the condemnation of the Romans that Morales would explicitly develop in the books of his history published in 1574. Accordingly, it is perfectly possible that it was Cano and Las Casas who were indebted to Morales for this clever debating point and act of historical revaluation, not the other way around. In any case, it is hard not to imagine lively discussions of early Spanish history between Cano and Morales in the mid-1540s. It is perhaps no coincidence that Cano in his posthumously published and incomplete magnum opus *De locis theologicis* (Salamanca, 1563) expressed views on the writing of history that would have been very congenial to Morales. Cano advocated an historiography founded on sober and patient research, not on the novelistic fantasies that appealed to Morales's predecessor Florián de Ocampo.[106] It stands to reason that Las Casas, upon his arrival in Spain in 1547 and his immediate immersion into the Sepúlveda affair, would have found that Cano and Morales had developed in collaboration a markedly unromantic, gritty perspective on early Spanish history that was ready and waiting for his own deft use.

"In Discovering America Europe Had Discovered Itself"

In a stimulating and influential lecture delivered at Queen's University, Belfast, in 1969, J. H. Elliott considered "the uncertain impact" of the discoveries in the New World upon sixteenth-century European intellectual life. He argued that as news of strange lands and people began to cross the ocean, "mental shutters" came down, and most Europeans, faced "with so much to see and absorb," tended to "retreat to the half-light of their traditional mental world." In exculpation of this resistance to the new, Elliott suggested that it was hardly "a matter for surprise, for the attempt of one society to comprehend another inevitably forces it to reappraise itself."[107] The present chapter has proposed a qualification of Elliott's thesis, but also a confirmation of his recognition that a serious encounter with the cultural "Other" does inevitably precipitate changes in how one views one's own culture.

Since Elliott's groundbreaking Wiles lectures, scholars have increasingly recognized that a more acute awareness of the appearance and customs of the inhabitants of the New World influenced many Europeans' conception of their own ancestral past. Indeed, in a characteristically suggestive aside, Elliott himself had noted that the ideas of Las Casas and José de Acosta about the cultural evolution of the New

World peoples "had implications for the history of Europe which did not go entirely unnoticed," for it became increasingly apparent "that the ancestors of modern Europeans had once been like the present inhabitants of America."[108] In his fascinating 1989 study *Ancient Britons and the Antiquarian Imagination*, the archaeologist and historian of antiquarianism Stuart Piggott explored "the way in which the early antiquaries were influenced in their concept of the ancient Briton by their new knowledge of peoples of a culture which had no European counterparts and was far less sophisticated, technologically and socially, than anything they had previously encountered."[109] Piggott especially emphasized the visual impact of actual Indians exhibited in England. Thus, the eminent antiquarian William Camden recalled that the Eskimo women whom he saw in Bristol in 1577 were "painted about the eyes and balls of the cheek with a blue colour like the ancient Britons." And both John White, artist of the 1585 Virginia expedition, and the immigrant Huguenot Jacques Le Moyne offered visual reconstructions of ancient Picts and Britons to accompany their drawings of New World natives. When Theodor de Bry printed engravings of some of these Pictish portraits in his lavish *America* of 1590, he stated that he was including them "to showe how that the Inhabitants of the great Bretannie have bin in times past as sauvage as those of Virginia."[110] Piggott also aptly cited Robert Burton's preface to his 1621 *Anatomy of Melancholy*: "See but what Caesar reports of us, and Tacitus of those old Germans; they were once as uncivil as they in Virginia."[111]

More recently, Peter Burke has discussed the contribution of knowledge of the New World to the "rewriting of world history."[112] In particular, he has emphasized the way "in which the discovery of America affected ideas of world history . . . by changing the image of the early inhabitants of Europe, or at least by making it more vivid and more precise."[113] In addition to the material on early Britons cited above from Piggott (to which Burke adds Samuel Purchas's neat rhetorical question, "Were not Caesar's Britons as brutish as Virginians?"), Burke offers some parallels from the Continent. While Marc Lescarbot in his *History of New France* (1609) compared the natives of the New World to Tacitus's Germans, Philip Cluverius in his *Ancient Germany* (1616) reversed the current of cultural comparison by finding parallels for the nakedness and the religious practices of the ancient Germans in the Amerindians of recent report. Thus, Burke argues, an interesting "circularity" occurred: "After the American Indians had been perceived in terms of

European 'barbarians,' the tables were turned and the barbarians viewed in terms of the Indians. America thus offered a pristine, indeed a primitive, vision of European antiquity."[114] Burke proceeds to suggest that this may well have played a role in the vogue of the "primitive" that began in Europe in the late seventeenth century with Lafitau and Vico and would reach its apogee in the Romantic movement.

As we have now seen, the contribution made by a growing knowledge of the inhabitants of the New World to a vivid awareness of the "barbarian" ancestors of modern Europeans occurred considerably earlier in Spain than in the other European countries discussed by Piggott and Burke. Furthermore, we have seen that in Spain this recognition of the ancient "self" in the distant "other" went well beyond a fleeting ethnographic juxtaposition and mirroring of two societies that, though remote in time and place, appeared to reveal startling similarities. Rather, this perception of a cultural kinship was put to work within a polemically driven narrative of violent cultural conflict and of imperial conquest and exploitation, both ancient and contemporary. Not only were modern Spaniards asked to recognize that their ancient Iberian ancestors were no less "barbaric"—and sometimes, as we shall soon see, rather more so—than the modern Amerindian peoples, but it was no less important to become unflinchingly aware of their parallel fates at the hands of brutal and greedy invaders. Thus, the forging of a link between modern Spaniards and Amerindians by way of a more vivid identification of modern Spaniards with ancient Iberians was accompanied by a double estrangement. On the one hand, the better sort of modern Spaniards needed to distance themselves from—or, better yet, control and alter—the actions and attitudes of the majority of their compatriots in the Indies. On the other hand, they needed to banish from their inherited repertoire of cultural models those speciously attractive culture heroes, the ancient Romans—even if the reigning king of Spain *was* "emperor of the Romans." True enough, indications of this dethronement of the supposedly exemplary Romans had begun in the historiography of Spain—and France as well—some decades before Columbus set sail. But it was in the context of the "controversy of the Indies" that this powerful identification of modern Spaniards with ancient Iberians as victims of brutal aggression and exploitation came most powerfully into its own. Indeed, the hitherto neglected role of Ambrosio de Morales, the first Spanish historian fully worthy of the name, in this debate over the justice of the conquest and the nature of its victims helped insure that a conception of the Spanish past charged with a sense of anguish over key events in the Spanish present would play a substantial role in the continuing history of Spanish historical self-consciousness, *hispanidad.*

"In discovering America Europe had discovered itself." J. H. Elliott offered that arresting formulation to indicate one way in which the discovery of America *did* have an impact upon the minds of early modern Europeans: in giving them a sense of pride in the accomplishment itself, quite apart from what they learned or failed to learn about the New World. "The military, spiritual and intellectual conquest of the New World made [Europe] aware of its own power and achievements."[115] This awareness, of course, helps to account for the conquistadors' own challenges to the exemplarity of the Romans. But as we have seen in the present chapter, there is yet another sense in which Europe had "discovered itself" in the process of discovering America. In the polemically adept arguments Bartolomé de las Casas employed in the Valladolid debate, Spaniards gazing across the Atlantic at the New World would have not only caught uncanny echoes of their own cultural past, but would also have witnessed a troubling reenactment of the fate of their ancestors.

Aztec Latinists Encounter Spanish Pagan Victims of Roman Imperialism

But what of the Indians? Were they ever introduced to the heady idea that they shared the nature and destiny of their conquerors' own ancestors? One might not expect evidence of such a fascinating scenario to have been preserved. But we are fortunate in having a brief, tantalizing hint of some Mexican Indians' awareness of what they shared with their imperial masters, a hint offered by a witness who, while unabashedly biased against the Indians, seems unlikely to have fabricated this evidence in toto. This witness was the encomendero and notary Jerónimo López, who came to Mexico with the Narváez expedition of 1520. López was assigned an encomienda near Tula in the northern Valley of Mexico, but he spent much of his time in Mexico City, where he acted in a number of official capacities.[116] One of his favorite pastimes was sending chronicles of his grievances and pet peeves directly to his "Sacra Cesárea Católica Majestad." A typically lengthy example is the letter he

sent the king on February 25, 1545, written shortly after his return from
Spain as a member of a deputation sent by encomenderos of New Spain
to protest the implementation of the New Laws.[117] Much of this letter is
a defense of the encomienda system conducted via dark warnings about
the growing danger of the insubordination of an Indian people "fond of
new things and disturbances and changes."[118] López placed much of the
blame for the restlessness and unreliability of formerly docile and self-
effacing natives at the doorstep of the friars, who urged the Indians to
stop showing *veneración* to the Spaniards, most of whom, they claimed,
were after all nothing but "*maceguales,* which means 'common people,'
since the lords had stayed in Spain."[119]

Among the most dangerous weapons that these forerunners of "liberation theology" were supplying the Indians, according to López, was
a knowledge of the Spanish present and past. Instead of preaching the
doctrine of Christ, they have, he complained, been teaching about "our
qualities and conditions *(calidades e condiciones)*" and have even gone
so far as to inform the Indians "about the wars and troubles that Your
Majesty has with France and the Turks." Nor did the friars content
themselves with keeping the Indians abreast of the potentially embar-
rassing realities of contemporary Spanish politics. No less subversive
was the fact that they were giving many of them

> the elegance of the Latin language, making them read various kinds of
> exact knowledge *(ciencias)* from which they have come to know the
> whole beginning of our history *(todo el principio de nuestra vida)* and
> where we come from and how we were subjugated by the Romans
> and converted from paganism to the faith and everything else that has
> been written about this, all of which inspires them to say that we too
> came from the pagans and were subjects and defeated and subjugated
> and were subjects to the Romans and revolted and rebelled and were
> converted to baptism so very many years ago and are not even yet
> good Christians, we who demand that they convert in so short a time.
> There are many Indians who have studied and are studying this sort
> of thing, and the friars in both the country districts and in Mexico
> City give them opportunities to preach, and they speak and preach
> what they like about these and other things that take their fancy.[120]

There can be little doubt that López was primarily complaining—
not for the first time—about the Franciscan project of training promising Nahua noble youths at the Colegio de Santa Cruz de Tlatelolco,

inaugurated with great fanfare on January 6, 1536.[121] Fray Bernardino de Sahagún, who took upon himself the brunt of the Latin instruction in the first years of the college, recalled some years later:

> The Spaniards and the members of the other religious orders who learned of this laughed a great deal and made fun of us, confident that no one would prove able to teach such an incompetent people. But after we had worked with them for two or three years, they came to understand all the subjects in the art of grammar and to speak and understand Latin and even to write [Latin] heroic verses.[122]

In the early years of this remarkable establishment instruction was permitted only in Latin and Nahuatl—Spanish was apparently forbidden in the classroom—and Motolinía told with satisfaction of a student who trounced a newly arrived priest in a dispute over Latin grammar.[123] If Jerónimo López was one of those who laughed at the idea of Nahua youths becoming proficient in the study of Latin, his derision soon turned to alarm when he learned that they "speak Latin as elegantly as Cicero," and in a letter of October 20, 1541, he dutifully alerted the king to "the dangers that could follow from the Indians studying sciences."[124]

The cantankerous *escribano's* complaint of 1545 implies that for some years before Cano's relection of 1546 and Las Casas's presentation to the junta of theologians in Valladolid in 1550 certain Franciscans in Mexico City had been familiarizing young Nahua nobles with the parallels between ancient Spaniards and their own people, both in way of life and in historical experience. Like the Nahuas before the conquest, the ancestors of their Spanish conquerors were "pagans" *(gentiles)*— though López did not explicitly say that the friars compared the two peoples specifically as "barbarians" as well. Like the Nahuas, the ancient Spaniards had been defeated and subjugated by an imperialist power, a point that López repeated with sputtering indignation. While Cano and Las Casas designed this parallel to elicit the sympathy of decent Spaniards for the sufferings of startlingly similar "neighbors," López implied that the friars' students were internalizing this set of historical echoes as a reassuring revelation of the vulnerability of their conquerors (who had once been cowering victims themselves) and perhaps even as a precedent for insubordination or resistance (for the ancient Spaniards, too, had been rebellious imperial subjects).

Note also how the verbs of López's tirade signal an escalation of the outrages he nervously reported to the king. First, thanks to the priests, the Indians would *read (leer)* Latin accounts of ancient Spanish history, then they would go on to *say (decir)* openly what conclusions they had drawn from their reading, and finally, thanks again to the perilously indulgent friars, they would even be given the chance to *preach (predicar)* to their fellow Indians the exciting new perspective that they had acquired on their conquerors.[125] López's overheated claim about the preaching of Indian students reflects the fears of many critics of the Colegio de Santa Cruz de Tlatelolco—and the hopes of some of its founders—that this native elite was in fact being trained for the priesthood, an impression no doubt heightened by the cassock-like *hopas* that the students wore and the quasi-monastic daily routines that the friars imposed upon them.[126] It soon became apparent, however, that opposition to the ordination of Indians was too intense for this hope— or fear—to be realized in the foreseeable future, a fact confirmed by the Synod of 1555, which forbade the ordination of Indians, mestizos, and blacks. But López, writing ten years before that "final" decision, clearly felt that his alarmist scenario of learned Indians "preaching" about the skeletons in the closet of Spanish history would sound sufficiently plausible to the ears of the emperor—or whomever López realistically expected to read his enormous letters.

It is a pity that Jerónimo López neglected to tell us what Latin histories of the Roman conquest of Spain the friars were assigning their Indian students to read. An inventory of the library of Santa Cruz de Tlatelolco conducted in 1572 listed sixty-one volumes, none of which manifestly dealt with the Roman wars in Spain, apart from some references to the siege of Numantia in the Plutarchan lives of the Gracchi. One entry is intriguing, but its promise is illusory. This reads "Item, otro libro llamado Apiano de beliz."[127] The book in question was apparently a Latin translation of the *Roman History* of Appian, a Greek historian of the Antonine period. The sixth book of Appian's history remains to this day our fullest and most vivid account of the unedifying story of the Roman conquest of Spain, and it accordingly became a major source for the narrative of Ambrosio de Morales. Our suspicion that this volume was López's "smoking gun" may well be intensified when we learn that, in the course of a second inventory in November of 1574, Fray Bernardino de Sahagún included the Appian among nine volumes that he labeled "inútiles," and it was offered for sale at one peso, four reals.[128] One might suppose that Appian's history—along with "dos libros del Nuevo Testamento"!—had become too controversial a book to keep around. Unfortunately, a closer look at the publication record of Appian's fragmentary history reveals that this was not, after all, the book that had aroused López's suspicions in 1545. Book 6 of Appian's history did not appear in Latin until the edition of Caelius Secundus Curio, printed in Basel in 1554. Still, it is plausible that it was indeed this edition, with its extensive account of the Roman conquest of Spain, that was listed in the 1572 inventory and sold as "useless" two years later. The inventory, we recall, listed the title of the work as *De bellis (de beliz)*, and it stands to reason that the scribe, a man of dubious Latinity (witness his reference to a work entitled *Contentus mundi!*), would have recorded only the first couple of words of the title. The title of the 1554 Basel translation was *De bellis punicis liber. . . ,*" whereas earlier Latin translations of Appian had title pages beginning *Romanae historiae* (1477, 1495) or *De civilibus Romanorum bellis* (1529, 1538). Thus, while the copy of Appian that earned a temporary stay on the shelves of the library of Santa Cruz de Tlatelolco may well have fleshed out the Nahua youths' knowledge of the Roman conquest of Spain, it was not what they were reading when the irascible notary complained to the king in 1545. That volume had apparently disappeared—perhaps in response to López's complaints?—by 1574. The attrition rate in this library appears indeed to have been remarkable: eleven books recorded in the 1572 inventory were reported as lost in the inventory of 1574.[129] Conceivably the missing account of the Roman conquest of Spain was that of the *Compendiosa historia hispanica* of Rodrigo Sánchez de Arévalo, printed in Rome by Ulrich Hahn in 1470. We have noted above Arévalo's emphasis upon the aggression of the Romans—and the determined resistance of the Iberians. But this was likely to be a rare volume, and in fact no book that old was recorded on any of the surviving inventories of the library of the college.[130]

It is obvious that Jerónimo López's agitated account of the Spanish history lessons of Aztec youths tells us at least as much about the anxieties of the encomenderos of New Spain as it does about the actual aims and practices of the Franciscan friars or the thoughts and feelings of their Nahua students. But his complaint is persuasive testimony that Cano and Las Casas were not the first to discern behind the pageant of Spain's conquest of the New World the shadows of Rome's conquest of Spain. It is naturally tempting to suspect that the Franciscans' "subversive" curriculum at Santa Cruz de Tlatelolco in the mid-1540s may have influenced the formidable Dominicans in their own polemical use of this striking historical parallel shortly thereafter. But there are problems with such an assumption. To begin with, there is the fact that, as we have seen, Las Casas appears not to have developed his animus against the Roman Empire before he left the New World for the last time in early 1547, two years after López indicated that the Franciscans' students had been for some time thinking about the implications of the parallels between the ancient Roman masters of Spain and the modern Spanish masters of New Spain. It is also unlikely that Las Casas in Chiapas would have been in close touch with the Franciscans who were engaged in the impressive educational experiment in Tlatelolco. After all, on the question of higher education for the Indians the Dominicans of New Spain found themselves, for once, on the same side as the encomenderos, as the words of Sahagún quoted above indicate. In fact, only a few months before Jerónimo López sent his complaint to the emperor, the Dominican provincial Domingo de la Cruz and Fray Domingo de Betanzos had sent him their own list of objections to the Franciscans' project (May 5, 1544).[131] Their argument against teaching the natives Latin was rather less ingenious than that of López: they complained that highly educated Indians would make less learned priests look bad!

So it appears that we are faced with two independent developments of the highly charged parallel between the fate of ancient Iberian victims of Rome and that of Indian victims of Spanish adventurers who liked to boast that their own wars of conquest had dwarfed those of the Romans. If the two religious orders' appeals to the Roman conquest of Spain were indeed independent, that would in itself demonstrate how natural it was for Spanish critics of the conquest to interpret the astonishing events of the past few decades in the New World in the light of the ancient history of the Iberian Peninsula. Both Franciscans educating native youths and Dominicans disputing the justice of the conquest of the New World discovered in the distant story of Rome's subjugation of Spain a simultaneously domesticating and disturbing resonance for the new and strange dramas playing out in America. At the same time, these pedagogical and disputational strategies constituted acts of historical imagination bearing witness to a growing tendency among sixteenth-century Spaniards to become more poignantly aware of the identity, way of life, and sufferings of their own remote ancestors.

CHAPTER SIX

Romans and Indians

Augusta Emerita was, as its name implies, a veterans' settlement *(colonia)* established in the reign of Augustus.[1] Strategically situated at the confluence of the Guadiana and Albarregas rivers, it soon evolved into the most important town in the province of Lusitania. It boasted an amphitheater, a circus, a theater, two main aqueducts, and many impressive temples and public buildings. After the Roman loss of Spain, Emerita remained an important town under Visigothic rule, and while its importance did decline subsequently, Mérida (as it came to be called) has never ceased to be inhabited, and it is today an important center for textiles and leather in the province of Badajoz, Extremadura. By the end of the twentieth century, some fifty-five thousand people inhabited this town, whose street plan still reflects that of the original Roman *colonia* and whose Roman ruins, among the most impressive in Spain, draw thousands of visitors each year.

But there is another Mérida, also visited, or at least passed through, by tourists in quest of impressive ancient ruins. This Mérida, the capital of the Mexican state of Yucatán, has a population roughly ten times that of its Spanish eponym. What accounts for their shared name? It is not that the original Spanish conquistadors of Yucatán were Extremeños, however prominent men from that "wildest part of Castile" undoubtedly were in the early years of the conquest of the Indies.[2] The Montejo family, which presided over the long and difficult subjugation of the Mayan region, was from Salamanca, and Salamancas and Valladolids proliferated predictably in their wake. But when, early in 1542, Francisco Montejo the Younger founded, upon his father's orders, a new settlement to serve as the administrative capital of Yucatán, he fixed upon the name Mérida not in order to impose a nostalgically familiar name upon an exotic site, but in quest of a name that would, while staying patriotically Spanish, echo the American site itself.

235

According to a report submitted by the town council to the Council of the Indies in 1579, "The name Mérida was given to this city by the Spaniards when it was founded because they found well-constructed buildings of rough stone and mortar with many moldings similar to those that the Romans had made in Mérida in Spain."[3] Mérida in Yucatán thus differs strikingly from common examples of classical toponymic practice in Anglophone North America. While Athens, Georgia, reflects the cultural aspirations of southern planters, and Utica, New York, named for the site of the noble suicide of Cato the Younger, expresses the passion for political liberty of Yankee farmers, Mérida was named, apparently without grudging hesitation, in honor of the Mayan builders of the ancient city of T-hó, near whose ruins the new city was laid out.

Nor was this the first time that the architectural achievements of Mesoamerican Indians inspired Spaniards to think of Roman Mérida. In 1518, the expedition of Juan de Grijalva, on which Francisco de Montejo served as a captain, stopped at an island off the Tabascan coast that they named the Isla de Sacrificios. Here, according to the account of the chaplain Juan Díaz, they found "some very large buildings of mortar and sand and part of an edifice of the same material as that of an old arch in Mérida."[4] A Latin version of Díaz's account elaborated on this a bit: "Disembarking we saw many different buildings, among which were ruins of aqueducts very similar to those in the city of Mérida in Spain."[5]

It was even possible for conquistadors to deem New World architecture superior to that of the Romans. Thus, Pedro Sancho, secretary to Francisco Pizarro, declared that the ruins of Roman Spain failed to supply adequate analogies for the walls and houses of Cuzco:

> The Spaniards who see them say that neither the bridge of Segovia nor any other of the edifices which Hercules or the Romans made is so worthy of being seen as this. The city of Tarragona [Roman Tarraco] has some works in its walls made in this style, but neither so strong nor of such large stones.[6]

This is, in part, an example of that topos of "besting the ancients" that our first chapter traced in the writings of the conquistadors and their publicists. Here the conquistadors' superiority to the Romans is put at one remove: they have defeated a modern Indian people who had themselves surpassed those famous architects, the Romans.[7] At the same time, however flattering a Spanish reader might find such a passage, it is hard to deny that the conquistadors who gazed upon the walls of Cuzco, just as those who declared that the markets of Tlatelolco surpassed those "in Constantinople and all of Italy and Rome," were expressing a genuine sense of awe at the achievements of these amazing civilizations.[8]

It will not do, then, to say that the conquistadors would have automatically agreed with their eloquent champion Juan Ginés de Sepúlveda when he classified the New World natives as Aristotle's "natural slaves," as homunculi who are "as inferior to Spaniards as children to adults, women to men, . . . and finally I would almost say monkeys to human beings."[9] On the contrary, such facile contempt is understandably absent from accounts by conquistadors like those who had gazed upon the temples, squares, and markets of Tenochtitlan ("like the enchantments recounted in the book of Amadís"), who had then barely escaped from that city with their lives in the harrowing "Noche Triste," and who had strained every nerve and muscle to return to it, besiege it, and finally destroy it as utterly as the Romans once destroyed Jerusalem.[10] When such Spaniards as these searched for Old World analogues to their Indian adversaries, they instinctively reached back to the formidable and impressive foes of their fathers and grandfathers. Accordingly, as we noted in the first chapter, they viewed the conquest of the New World—at moments, at least—as virtually an extension of the *Re*conquest of Spain from the Moors. Thus, in a querulous chapter of his *Historia verdadera*, Bernal Díaz del Castillo claimed for the conquistadors rewards equivalent to those of the knights who had fought against the Moors.[11] And Cortés's chaplain and chronicler Francisco López de Gómara, we may recall, declared that "the conquest of the Indians began when that of the Moors was finished, so that Spaniards might always war against infidels."[12] But the conquistadors were also, as we have now seen, occasionally willing to compare the natives of the New World with Old World competitors more prestigious than the Moors: the ancient Romans.[13]

Oviedo's Romans and Indians

Despite the conquistadors' understandable respect for their native adversaries, Sepúlveda was able to bolster his comparison of the natives

of the New World to children, women, and even monkeys by an appeal
to the adventurers' most prolific and enthusiastic propagandist, Gonzalo Fernández de Oviedo.[14] In a note appended to that notorious comparison, Sepúlveda cited book 5, chapter 3, of Oviedo's *Historia general
y natural de las Indias,* a passage that has always occupied a special
place in the brief against "the racist historian Oviedo," author of a
book that served as a "rich source of xenophobic and racist judge-
ments" (Tzvetan Todorov).[15] Citing this chapter in evidence, David
Brading has declared that "nothing is more shocking in Oviedo to the
modern reader than his open denigration of the native inhabitants of
the New World."[16]

Upon closer inspection, however, the passage cited by Sepúlveda
proves ill designed for reassuring its readers that Spanish dominion in
the Indies was justified by the manifest superiority of the conquerors to
the conquered. In this chapter Oviedo set himself the task of explaining
how the population of Hispaniola had plummeted from the million
inhabitants it boasted at the time of the arrival of Columbus to five hundred or so in 1535.[17] His first explanation for this demographic disaster
reads like a passage from the writings of Bartolomé de las Casas: "Since
the mines were so rich, and the avarice of men so insatiable, some
worked the Indians excessively, and some did not give them the food
that they ought to have." True, Oviedo did immediately proceed to
"blame the victims," for he claimed that the disappearance of the
inhabitants of Hispaniola was also due to the fact that "this people is by
nature lazy and depraved, little inclined to work, melancholic, cowardly, of low and evil inclinations, and of little memory or constancy."[18]
Why, the precipitous drop in population was even partly due to the
Indians' tendency to commit suicide not only to avoid work but also
simply "for the fun of it" [por su pasatiempo]. But Oviedo also admitted the destructive role of disease, especially smallpox, and he went on
to note the disruptive effect of the frequent transfers of population as
the Indian communities were passed "from one greedy man to
another." The next moment, however, he veered back into a denunciation of the Indians themselves, insisting that God was clearly punishing
these "gentes salvajes e bestiales" for their many sins, including
sodomy. Indicating his awareness that the Dominicans and Franciscans
had made the depopulation of the Antilles a matter of earnest discussion in Spain, he recorded that he himself had furnished testimony on

these matters before the Council of the Indies. Finally, he closed this chapter with an attempt at "balance."

> As for me, I do not absolve the Christians who have enriched themselves or enjoyed the labor of the Indians, if they have maltreated them or not done their part for their salvation. And yet do I want to think that it was without any guilt on the part of the Indians that God has punished them and almost wiped them out of these islands, since they were so depraved, sacrificing to the Devil and performing the rites and ceremonies that will be mentioned below.[19]

Like many scholars of our own day, Las Casas depended heavily upon this chapter for his charge in the *Historia de las Indias* that Oviedo was guilty of slandering the reputation of the New World natives and thereby encouraging his readers to "think no more of killing them than of killing bedbugs." Though the extract that he cited from Oviedo does include the passage accusing many Spaniards of "insatiable avarice" [codicia insaciable], a phrase Las Casas was to use in the preface to his own *Brevísima relación,* the Dominican preferred to see the chapter as a single-minded assault on the good name of these "naked and unarmed peoples," and he shored up his charge with another notorious passage in Oviedo's history, from the proem to book 5, in which the chronicler attributed the slowness and incompleteness of the Christianization of the Indians partly to their possession of skulls so thick that prudent Spaniards refrained from using their swords on them lest their blades shatter! But Las Casas's main argument here against the "racism" of Oviedo brings us once again to the complexity and contradictions of the chronicler's views of the Indians—and it is here that the ancient history of the Old World comes into play.

Las Casas insisted that the only failing that Oviedo could really make "stick" against all of the pre-Columbian Amerindian peoples was the ineluctable charge of infidelity. But if all the Indian peoples were pagans before the arrival of the Spaniards, "Oviedo ought to consider his own ancestors *(abuelos)* and the whole world before the Son of God came to it and dispelled the shadows of ignorance." Here we see once again Las Casas's familiar habit of reminding a Spaniard that his own ancient ancestors were once little different from modern Indians. "Furthermore," he went on,

it wouldn't have hurt him to have considered—since he claimed to be
a serious historian and well read in Pliny, even though he had to read
him in Italian and not Latin—that these Indian peoples were not
among the first to eat human flesh . . . nor to sacrifice men to idols, as
he claims above in chapter 9 of book 6.[20]

But the fact is, Oviedo's point in chapter 9 of book 6, a brief extract of
which Las Casas quoted in this attack on him, was unambiguously
designed to make precisely the point that Las Casas insisted he ought to
have considered, though it is true that Oviedo was patriotically reluctant to adduce the habits of the ancient Spaniards. As the heading to the
chapter phrases it, Oviedo here "proves that in other parts of the world,
among the ancients, sacrifices were practiced where men were killed
and offered to their gods, and likewise in many places people were
accustomed to eat human flesh, and today it is done in many parts of
the mainland and some islands of these Indies."[21] Oviedo did claim that
the abominations of the Indians assure us that "it is not without reason
that God allows them to be destroyed," but he proceeded to challenge
his readers, "What are we to make of the fact that in the middle of the
world, or in the best part of it—that is, in Italy and Sicily—there were
those who were called Cyclopses and Laestrygonians?" Furthermore,
the ancient Gauls were notorious for human sacrifice, a practice that
came to an end only during the reign of Tiberius. "And no less guilty of
this were the Britons"—or English *(ingleses),* as Oviedo anachronisti-
cally called them. Lest modern Frenchmen or Englishmen take offense
at the chronicler's claims, he insisted that it was "Pliny, not I" who
vouched for their accuracy (in books 7.2.9 and 30.3.12–13).
    In a passage Oviedo later added to this chapter for his projected
revision of the chronicle, he zeroed in on the ancient Romans as anthro-
pophagous fellows of the modern Indians. Again relying on his favorite
Roman rival, Pliny (bk. 28.2.4), he related in loving detail the supersti-
tious belief of many Romans in the medicinal value of drinking the
blood of gladiators, preferably warm from the wound of a still-breath-
ing specimen. Some Roman valetudinarians, Pliny averred, would even
"seek out the leg marrow and the brains of babies." And some learned
Greeks went so far as to expatiate upon the different tastes of various
body parts, right down to nail parings! So the Romans of the first century A.D., with a little help from empirically inquisitive Greeks, did their
bit to demonstrate that "not only the Indians are guilty of this crime."

Thanks to Pliny's lurid information, Oviedo was able to come very close to making a point dear to the heart of Las Casas: that the Greeks and the Romans, far from having earned the right to label other peoples barbarians, were themselves capable of shocking displays of genuine barbarism. Furthermore, we can see here that Oviedo made his own contribution to the project of interpreting New World "abominations" in the context of Old World parallels, an exercise in that "comparative ethnography" Las Casas himself was to undertake at exhaustive length in his *Apologética historia sumaria*.[22]

Another chapter surprisingly foreshadowing Las Casas's *Apologética historia* is Oviedo's account of "este gran príncipe Montezuma" and his capital city of "Temisitlán" (Tenochtitlan) in part 2, book 33, chapter 46, a portion of the work not published until modern times. In general, Oviedo offered here an impressively favorable account of the Aztec ruler's way of life and the city in which he enjoyed it. True, he compared the obeisance required of those who came into Montezuma's presence with that of "the Moors of Granada," a relatively neutral instance of the common comparison of Aztecs and Moors. But Oviedo also noted that the Aztec lord's disdain for buying and selling recalled what Lucian said of Alexander the Great, Hannibal, and Scipio, "los tres capitanes más excelentes de los antiguos."[23] Turning to religious beliefs and practices, a subject that was to preoccupy Las Casas, Oviedo reached instinctively for Roman parallels in order to help his reader make sense of Aztec religion.[24] The war god to whom Montezuma offered sacrifice was like the Roman Mars, the maize divinity resembled Ceres, and so on. To his four or five principal gods Montezuma offered more than five thousand people each year. It is true that he did so, Oviedo claimed, on the advice of two demons who reportedly spoke to the Indians in their temples, but this is what demons have done to "many peoples over many years, and even today they do it throughout the world." For a modern example Oviedo chose a group of male and female witches and heretics from his own ancestral Asturias, the followers of one Fray Alonso de Mella from the cliff of Amboto. As for the European past, he wrote,

> what are we to say of those famous Romans and of their temples, which were founded with neither more nor less sanctity than the errors and absurdities of these Indians, since they made a god and its temple for everything that took their fancy, as Romulus did when he

ordained a temple for Jupiter and gave it the name Jupiter Feretrius, where were offered the arms and standards of the enemy kings and captains whom they had killed.

After citing other instances from Livy of the Romans' habit of inventing new divinities and promptly building new temples for them, Oviedo turned to Roman superstitions that paralleled those of the Aztecs.

> How subject to haruspices and fortune-tellers they were! And how fond of prophecy they were, and how obedient to vanities founded upon religiosity and false sanctimony. I want to say that if we look at the affairs of the ancient pagans in this matter, we have to consider them just as profane and diabolical as those of our Indies.

Despite Oviedo's reputation—industriously spread by Las Casas—as a slanderer of the Indians, his strategy here was oddly similar to what was soon to be Las Casas's own, both in the debate in Valladolid and in the subsequent *Apologética historia* (itself an expansion of material delivered in Valladolid). Like Las Casas, Oviedo was here attempting to exonerate the Aztecs, to defend them against the charge of religious barbarism. In their religious beliefs and superstitions, at least, they were no worse—though, it is true, no better—than the ancient Romans. We shall see that Las Casas would claim that the Aztecs *were* better than the Romans in their religious beliefs and practices, but the important thing to note here is that both Oviedo and Las Casas drew upon their oddly similar, if very differently motivated, anti-Roman feelings in order to render the inhabitants of the New World less odd, less repulsive, less "barbaric" to readers accustomed to admire and even emulate the most spectacular pagans of the Old World. While Oviedo found the Spanish conquistadors superior to their ancient Roman counterparts, he found their Indian adversaries in some respects the equals of those Romans—if not in cultural achievements, then at least in religious errors.

It is tempting to assume that Oviedo's intermittent respect for the New World natives, and accordingly his willingness to compare them favorably to the ancient Old World, increased as his chronicle came to deal with the more advanced Mesoamerican cultures such as those of the Aztecs and Incas. In fact, however, such flattering or at least exculpatory comparisons made their appearance even when Oviedo was discussing less spectacular Indian societies. For example, in part 3, book

42, chapter 11, he prefaced his account of the harvest festivals of Nicaragua with a reference to the similar festivals of "los antiguos," in which they gave pleasure to themselves and honor to their gods. "Well, then," he concluded, "if such a custom obtained in antiquity, among people of such great intelligence, then it is not surprising that the Indians do it."25 Later in this chapter he mentioned the many gods of the Nicaraguan Indians, to whom they sacrificed men and boys, either out of reverence or gluttony (for they were fond of human flesh). This Nicaraguan polytheism inspired Oviedo to "suppose that they imitate the ancient idolaters and pagans who made Ceres the goddess of abundance, and Mars the god of battles, and Neptune the god of the sea and the waters, and Vulcan the god of fire, etc."26 And at the end of this chapter Oviedo declared that if the Indians were idolaters, the making of idols began with the impeccably classical Prometheus, and even the people God originally chose as his own were all too capable of falling into this error. Accordingly, "it does not seem to me that those bestial Indians are so worthy of blame," although he conceded that they will join the ancient idolaters of the Old World in "la eterna condenación."27

The following chapter, on the sexual customs of the Indians of Nicaragua, makes rather complicated appeal to Roman paganism. The fact that these Indians operated virtual houses of prostitution, complete with "madams" ("madres del burdel"), was not so shocking, for Spaniards tolerated such establishments themselves in order to obviate worse sins. But these Indians did sink lower in that they also practiced homosexual prostitution. Worse still, the Nicaraguan Indians practiced a custom that surpassed in depravity any that Oviedo had ever heard of: an annual nocturnal festival in which women were granted sexual license with no subsequent punishment. He insisted that this was worse than what Livy told of the Roman women seduced into the Bacchanalian scandal of 186 B.C., for they, at least, were duly punished. On the other hand, Oviedo added with serene inconsistency, bad as the Nicaraguan ritual was, what Livy told of the crime wave accompanying the notorious Roman incident was unmatched in the New World. "Not even among the Indians do I know of or have heard of so heretical, filthy, diabolical, savage, or vicious a malady as that which, as I have said, occurred once in Rome."28

While Oviedo's accounts of the Aztecs and of the less advanced Nicaraguans did not make it into print in his own day, his surprisingly favorable and very full treatment of ritual behavior by the supposedly backward people of Hispaniola, complete with a dignifying Roman parallel, occurred relatively early in the portion of his chronicle printed in 1535 and reprinted in 1547. This is his account of the ritual songs and dances called *areitos* in chapter 1 of book 5, immediately after the notorious proem that informs us of the propensity of Indian skulls to shatter Spanish swords. Oviedo introduced this chapter with a declaration that, as an historian, he had from the moment he first set foot in the Indies made it his business to learn

> in what manner or form the Indians recall things about their origin and ancestors, and if they have books, or by what vestiges and signs they keep from forgetting the past. And in this island, so far as I have been able to learn, only their songs, which they call areitos, are their book or memorial that lasts from people to people, from parents to children, and from those living to those in the future.[29]

This seems at first a classic expression of the Spanish tendency to gauge the cultural level of the New World natives by their degree of remoteness from alphabetic writing, for "people without letters were thought of as people without history, and oral narratives were looked at as incoherent and inconsistent."[30] Thus, Pedro de Gante, one of three Flemish Franciscans who arrived in New Spain in August 1523, harshly assessed the Nahuas as "a people without writing, without letters, without written characters, and without enlightenment about anything."[31] It would be natural to assume that Oviedo, too, was questioning the full humanity of the Antilleans on the basis of their lack of a writing system.

Not so, however. After a brief digression on Antillean idolatry and divinatory practices (the latter he excused by citing Pliny's contention that this fraudulent art, native to Persia, "has had the greatest reputation in the whole world and in all periods"), Oviedo turned to an encomium of the illiterate historians of Hispaniola, who

> had a good and noble manner of keeping alive the things of the past, and this was in their songs and dances, which they call areito, which is the same thing that we call "dancing while singing" *(bailar cantando)*. Livy [7.2] says that the first dancers came to Rome from Etruria, and they arranged their songs by fitting the words to the dancers' movements. They did this in order to forget their grief over the deaths in the plague, the year Camillus died; and I say that this is

likely to have resembled the areitos, or songs-in-a-ring *(cantares en corro)* of these Indians.

Thus, the streets of the Roman Republic in the fourth century B.C. would have presented the inquisitive visitor with a festive spectacle perfectly analogous to the performances that natives of the Antilles—and Tierra Firme, as Oviedo proceeded to add—staged for religious festivals, victory celebrations, and simply for amusement ("por su pasatiempo").

Oviedo proceeded to describe the antiphonal singing and carefully choreographed movements of the Antillean areito, which he likened to "a very orderly contredanse" [un contrapás muy ordenado] and to the dances of Spanish and Flemish peasants—comparisons he had offered for the rowdier areitos of Tierra Firme as early as 1526 in his *Sumario de la natural historia de las Indias*.[32] Turning to the social function of these areitos as a means of keeping the past alive, he wrote:

> And those songs remained in their memories, serving the function of books, and in this way they recited the genealogies of their caciques and the kings or lords whom they had had, and the deeds they had done, and the bad or good weather that they had had or were having; and other things that they wanted to be communicated to children and grown-ups and to be well known and engraved in their memories. And for this aim these areitos are maintained, so that especially their famous victories in battle not be forgotten.[33]

To emphasize this point, Oviedo turned again to modern unlettered Europeans. "Let the aforesaid not appear to the reader as a lot of savagery *(mucha salvajez),* for the same thing is practiced in Spain and Italy." One needed only think of the popular ballads of contemporary Spain, which were the history texts for "those who do not read." To illustrate his point, Oviedo mentioned several specific historical events, from the early days of the Reconquest to the present, that were known to the bulk of the population of Spain only through "romances e canciones." What is arresting here is his practice of referring to specific examples of such Spanish songs as "another ballad or areito" [otro cantar o areito], an astonishing appropriation of an American word to label an analogous European cultural phenomenon, precisely the opposite of the customary habit of describing New World practices with Old

World vocabulary and a sharp jolt to our expectations of Spanish cultural chauvinism.

Though many modern scholars tend to make much of the cultural chasm that Spaniards posited between literate Europe and the illiterate New World, Oviedo went out of his way here to demonstrate how the Antilleans, supposedly the most primitive of the American peoples, could be said to have employed the same strategies of "record keeping without letters" as the earliest Romans and the humblest—and most numerous—inhabitants of modern Spain and Italy.[34] In fact, his surprisingly positive evaluation of the record-keeping function of the areitos of Hispaniola was not unprecedented. The European world had been introduced to these songs and dances in 1516, with the publication in Alcalá of the first three *Decades on the New World* by the Italian humanist Peter Martyr. In the eighth chapter of the third decade, he informed Pope Leo X,

> Your Holiness will be puzzled as to how simple people recall stories of their origins *(principia)* from remote generations, seeing that they do not understand any sort of writing. It is the custom among them from the beginning that, especially in the royal houses, the Boitii, i.e., the wise men, instruct their children in learning things by heart. In that teaching they put special emphasis upon two things: one, the general origin and succession of things; the other, the particular famous deeds done in peace and war by parents, grandparents, great-grandparents, and all other ancestors. They have these teachings composed in verses in their language. These they call areitos. And like a guitar-player *(citharoedus)* among us, they conduct their areitos with drums crafted in their fashion and they lead in their circular dances singing. The drum is called *maguey,* and they have amatory areitos, and they have plaintive ones, and ones that stir men up to battle, with individual styles as befits the subject matter. They also make use of leapings, in which they are much more agile than our people, for there is nothing they work harder at; and they are naked, and they don't care about costumes. In the areitos, they have from their ancestors a prophecy of the arrival of our people, and in these dances they thunder forth their ruin in groans, as in elegies.[35]

It is plausible that Oviedo owed his approving tone and his emphasis upon the social function of the areitos to this passage (it was perhaps not a coincidence that he had mentioned those *boitii* or *buhití* in this same chapter), but he expanded upon it in such a way as to make this material his own. For Peter Martyr's fleeting use of a European analogy ("uti citharoedus apud nos") became in Oviedo's chronicle a sustained exercise in comparative ethnography informed by something very like a theoretical insight about how pre- and subliterate cultures keep important memories alive. In this social endeavor so appealing to a historian such as Oviedo, the similarities among archaic Romans, rustic Spaniards, and Caribbean natives mattered far more than their differences.[36]

Oviedo's bold collocation of Antillean areitos with the Etruscan dances introduced into fourth century B.C. Rome shows that the chronicler was willing to compare American with Greco-Roman cultural phenomena in the earliest stratum of his "general and natural history," the edition of 1535. We have already noted that material that Oviedo wrote for the second and third parts of the chronicle sustained this comparison by locating Roman analogues for Aztec and Nicaraguan religious beliefs and practices. In addition, several chapters that Oveido added for his projected second edition of part 1, especially certain of the forty chapters of "depósitos" added to the original thirteen chapters of book 6, reveal that as time went on Oviedo thought more deeply about the meaning of such parallels, for these passages are manifestly more than mere embellishment or advertisements of their author's erudition.

Chapter 49, by far the longest of the "deposits" added to book 6, is a diverse and peculiar essay that seems at the beginning likely to contribute little to the reader's understanding of the Indies. Oviedo's aim here was to demonstrate the thesis that "some things appear new because they are very old and forgotten."[37] In support of this thesis, he offered a number of strikingly similar stories about events widely separated in time and place. For example, the self-abnegating loyalty Prince Ferdinand showed to his young nephew Juan II of Castile was foreshadowed by the Spartan Lycurgus's loyalty to his unborn nephew, son of the late king Polydectes. Similarly, pantomimed Machiavellian advice sent by the abbot of San Ponce to King Ramiro of Aragon recapitulated Livy's account of similar advice conveyed by Tarquin the Proud to his son—and Oviedo would have been delighted to learn that Livy's story was itself a clone of the *logos* of Thrasybulus's message to Periander in book 5 of Herodotus. After having taken up more than half of the chapter with such paired stories, Oviedo explained that his point had been to diminish the impression of newness and strangeness natural to Spaniards encountering or hearing of New World cultural phenomena for the first time. Thus, a Spaniard shocked to see severed heads hanging from trees or capping posts around houses in Tierra Firme needed to recall the heads of the seventy sons of Ahab that Jehu displayed at the gates of Jezreel (2 Kings 10). Similarly, ancient accounts of virgins sent to serve as sacred prostitutes in Cyprus should cushion the shock of finding the same custom in America, especially Nicaragua. Thus, records of classical and biblical antiquity revealed that the apparent "newness" of the "New World" was often the product of European cultural amnesia, for many of the mores of the natives of America had been familiar enough to the cultural ancestors of their scandalized conquerors.

Oviedo then turned from customs to inventions. Classical authors attributed viticulture to Dionysus, and the Bible nominated Noah, but the Indians nevertheless mastered the art of making fermented beverages from corn, yucca, and so forth, even though "they never heard of Pliny or Columella." Cicero attributed the invention of mirrors to Asclepius, but the Indians did not need "to learn to make mirrors from other peoples," Oviedo asserted, "for they make very fine ones of pearl in New Spain and in other parts of Tierra Firme," while the silver ones fashioned by the Indians of Peru "were among the finest of all, for I have seen some of those I am mentioning." Pliny credited Thrason with the art of building walls, but in fact wall building, both in wood and stone, was "very common and customary and ancient in the world." (Less common, it is true, were the shrewdly grown "living walls" of Tierra Firme, "a thing very strange and noteworthy"—living and carefully tended trees that formed a wall that was "the strongest that can be imagined," as many Spanish soldiers learned from bitter firsthand experience.) Pliny also asserted that Daedalus invented woodworking and the saw, but the Indians invented a remarkable saw made from strands of cotton, henequen, or pita fiber that, when used with grains of sand, could even cut iron—"and it was necessity that taught them this." The particular necessity in question was none other than that of liberating themselves from European chains. Oviedo thus cited as proof of the Indians' freedom from classical precedents a device that they invented to free themselves from much more literal attempts by Europeans to confine them! Finally, Oviedo cited Plutarch on Theseus as the supposed inventor of social stratification, while the Indies independently displayed the very same kind of hierarchical societies.

All of these independent American inventions drove Oviedo to this sweeping conclusion:

> I suspect that nature is the guide of the arts, and it is not without reason that the Florentines are accustomed to say, in their vernacular proverb, "The whole world is like home" [quasi-Hispanicized as *Tuto il mondo e como a casa nostra*]. And it seems to me, in truth, that when we wonder at seeing many things used among these peoples and savage Indians, our eyes are seeing in them the very same thing, or nearly so, that we have seen or read about of other nations of our Europe and of other parts of the world that are well educated.[38]

It is true that the example that he chose as one final proof of this claim somewhat undercut his point about nature or necessity as the source of independent inventions, for he compared the snake of Asclepius with the stone serpent in the house of Atahualpa in Cajamarca, and he proceeded to derive both of these "pagan" snakes from the serpent of Genesis. "And he who doubts my suspicion should recall that the same Devil who introduced idolatry to the ancients has sown that same damned idolatry among these Indians." Here, it is not simply nature or necessity that caused the "new" in the New World to resemble the "old" in the Old World; it is the work of that old enemy who appeared to the first humans as a snake and thus keeps reappearing in that guise. Nevertheless, Oviedo's main point remained the same. The inhabitants of the Indies were part of the larger world, and a candid look at their customs and inventions should encourage European observers to find more evidence of shared humanity than of the forbiddingly alien. It may be "fallen" humanity that one sees in the New World, but the same is true of the people who inhabit the pages of Pliny and Plutarch.

As an earlier "depósito" (chap. 45) makes clear, Oviedo owed his replacement of classical inventors with "human genius and necessity" to a chapter in the recently published (1540) miscellany of Pedro de Mexía, the *Silva de varia lección* (pt. 2, chap. 24). Oviedo was delighted to be able to support Mexía's theory of multiple inventions of the same practice by contributing New World instances. Thus, though Pliny attributed the bow and arrow to Scythes, son of Zeus, and others attributed it to Perseus (as putative ancestor of the Persians), Oviedo could proclaim:

I see that in these Indies of ours—which is no less ancient a land in its creation, nor are its people more recent than those inventors mentioned above—in many regions over here the Indians are commonly archers, and it cannot be proved, nor should one believe, that they learned it from Scythes or Perseus.[39]

Nor did they learn navigation from Icarus (pace Pliny), nor did they derive their slings from the Mallorcans (pace Vegetius). Furthermore, Oviedo added, the Indians of the Río de la Plata invented a weapon called the *guaranía* that was unfamiliar to Christians, Moors, and "los antiguos" alike. Oviedo had devoted an earlier "depósito" (chap. 35) to this device, a smooth rock attached to a long hempen cord that deftly trussed up its animal or human targets after being hurled with an accuracy that no Spaniards who tried their hand at it could match. Not only had the Indians invented something unknown to the ancients, but, Oviedo suggested, they may actually have come up with one common invention before the Greco-Roman world did. Probably at the same time as he composed the "depósitos" for book 6, he appended a new conclusion to chapter 2 of the same book, his discussion of the famous Antillean ceremonial ballgames.

> This ballgame, or invention of a similar pastime, Pliny attributes to King Pyrrhus, of whom these peoples had no information. So Pyrrhus should not take pride in this skill until we know who was the true first teacher of such a game, since these peoples must be more ancient than Pyrrhus.[40]

In addition to parallel inventions and social customs, the so-called New World was also capable of offering startling reincarnations of celebrated stories of classical antiquity. A striking example is yet another "depósito" to book 6, chapter 41, which Oviedo opened by cheerfully admitting "how much I enjoy the comparisons that I can apply from good authors" to this American subject matter. Take for instance the heartwarming account Valerius Maximus offered of the marital devotion of Cornelia and Tiberius Gracchus. That story called to Oviedo's memory the time when he was *capitán de justicia* in Santa María del Antigua in Darién and had to order the hanging of the rebel chief "Capitán Gonzalo." Oviedo was deeply moved by the noble speech of

Gonzalo's wife, who begged to die, along with her children, at the side
of her husband. Indeed, so moved was our chronicler that he wished he
could have spared the rebel's life. It is especially intriguing that this
account of paired classical and American exempla of marital love comes
just a couple of pages after a chapter (chap. 39) that Oviedo devoted to
an encomium of his own wife, Margarita de Vergara, for whom he likewise offered a classical parallel, if an odd one: just as Antonia, daughter
of Drusus, was never (according to Pliny) known to spit, the same was
true of "Margarita mía," whose untimely death devastated the chronicler. A famous Roman couple, a Panamanian rebel and his wife, and the
marital bliss of the historian himself all combine to validate the Floren-
tine proverb Oviedo cited with approval in chapter 49: "The whole
world is like home."

Oviedo's admitted delight in classical "comparaciones" for Indian
customs and inventions goes well beyond the desire of an autodidactic,
perhaps even (if we trust Las Casas) Latin-less chronicler to embellish
his text and "market" it to a sophisticated European readership. The
claim that "the new is the forgotten old" and the idea that necessity and
human ingenuity account for similar devices and customs in widely separated regions implicitly rest upon a very important assumption about
the place of the New World in the grand scheme of things. Indeed, as we
have just seen Oviedo implying in chapter 45 of book 6, he regarded it
as quite inaccurate to refer to these newfound lands as "the New
World" in the first place. Thus, there is much to be said for Antonello
Gerbi's claim that "in general Oviedo sees the New World as the com-
plement and not the antithesis of the Old. The two 'worlds' are a single
world, finally aware of its own oneness."[41] Indeed, Gerbi went on to
note that Oviedo was "reluctant to use the term 'New World,'"
confining his use of it almost exclusively to "phrases where the
courtier's voice is uppermost," or where he was eager to trumpet his
own dignity as chronicler.[42] Gerbi argued that Oviedo viewed the mainland of the Indies as a second half of the globe, new only in the sense
that the ancients had not known it—leaving, of course, the Antilles out
of the account, for it was, we recall, Oviedo's contention that the
ancients (at least the ancient Spaniards) *had* known these, as the Hesperides. Hence Oviedo's fascination with the contention—"una cosa
muy nueva"—of the Swedish geographer Olaus Magnus ("Olao
Gotho") that America and Europe were joined in the far north, and so,

since Europe, Asia, and Africa were also joined, it followed that "we can say that the whole world is one and the same land and coastline."[43] To cite more of Gerbi's perceptive account of Oviedo's assumptions:

> If he cites the ancients it is to make the things of the Indies more easily believable, to show that they are possible, that in fact they are in the nature of things, that they are not at all in contradiction with Pliny's science. In other words he quotes the Latin authors to prove the consubstantial oneness of the New World and the most ancient antiquity. The yearning of the Renaissance for totality and harmony is fully and clearly expressed in this immense embrace. . . . Nature is all one, in Oviedo's Indies and Pliny's Rome.[44]

In fact, Gerbi claimed, Oviedo's assumption that American natural and human phenomena were, however distinctive, still part and parcel of the larger world occasionally emboldened him to reverse the current of comparison and hint that "American reality serves to illustrate the ancient texts and make them more credible and rational, to reinforce tradition with empirical observation."[45] As an example, Gerbi offered Oviedo's comparison of the Caribbean custom of cementing alliances by partaking of human flesh with Catiline's attempt to solemnize his conspiracy with a ritual drinking of blood (bk. 27, chap. 5). "I know perfectly well that Catiline did not know that the Indians do thus in their confederations, nor do they know who Catiline was; but the one account we have in writing, and the other is certain and attested over here."[46] As we have seen, another example of this use of New World phenomena to illuminate those of the Old World is Oviedo's discussion of the Antillean areitos and their ancient Roman and modern Spanish counterparts.

Although our investigation of Oviedo's placement of New World phenomena within the armature of Greco-Roman antiquity confirms Gerbi's reading of Oviedo's text as a demonstration of "the oneness of the terraqueous globe," it should be admitted that other scholars have preferred to accentuate passages in which Oviedo marveled at the wonders of the New World as indications of the undeniable and astonishing *difference* of the newly discovered lands. "Marvelous are the works of God, and the living things are very different in the diverse areas and parts of the world," he declared in the proem to book 13.[47] Even more frequently cited is this proud claim: "What I have said cannot be learned in Salamanca, Bologna, or Paris."[48] Such passages have led several fine scholars to ignore or dismiss the kinds of parallels that we have been discussing and the assumptions that underlie their use. Thus, J. H. Elliott has written: "Nor could classical learning be of any great value in interpreting the phenomena of a part of the world of which it had remained unaware. Here, as Fernández de Oviedo never tired of pointing out, there was no substitute for personal experience."[49] In a more extended discussion of Oviedo as an embodiment of "the autoptic imagination," Anthony Pagden has argued that for Oviedo,

> once the immediate attachments which, in the first instance, had bound the old to the new had been loosened, there simply was nothing *but* America. . . . [Oviedo's text] offers very little that would have been immediately familiar to the contemporary reader, skilled as he was in moving from citation to citation in reading a narrative in terms of the references it provided him, and of the network of inferences that those references suggested in their turn. Oviedo, by contrast, is, as he so often says, only seeking to describe what he has seen and known. In place of all those other texts, therefore, he offered only a stream of claims to autoptic authenticity.[50]

While it should by now be obvious that Pagden's contention is a considerable overstatement, it is not hard to see how he could be led to take this position. For one thing, we need to admit readily that Oviedo was far from achieving—or intending to achieve—theoretical consistency in his massive work, a work that underwent a long process of addition and revision before it was, as Paul Valéry once maintained of serious poems, not so much finished as abandoned. In addition, it was an important part of the argument of our first chapter that Oviedo did indisputably feel a certain agonistic anxiety toward the Old World—both for the sake of his subject matter and on his own account as author. Just as Cortés vastly eclipsed the glory of Julius Caesar, and just as the "honorable merchant" Francisco Hernández surpassed Ulysses simply by returning home to Spain to be best man at a friend's wedding, so Oviedo had surpassed his main classical model, Pliny the Elder, for, he boasted, "I am not writing with the authority of any historian or poet, but as an eyewitness, for the most part, of what I will discuss here."[51] Indeed, in the proem to book 13, he insisted that he went beyond Pliny not only as an eyewitness of many new kinds of fish, but even as what we might call a palate-witness, "having eaten the majority of them."[52] Thus, in his comparison of Caribbean cannibal alliance-sealing with the blood-drinking initiation ritual of the Catilinarian conspirators, Oviedo hinted at a kind of superiority for his New World material based upon its authenticity as something widely and recently observed and hence "certain and verified" [cierto e averiguado], whereas the Roman story was implicitly demoted as merely "written" [escripto]. Similarly, what "El Tostado" (Alfonso de Madrigal) offered in his account of Thracian human sacrifice was largely "fabula" and "ficción," while what Oviedo himself could supply from his New World experience was "verdad."[53] And in the proem to book 31, Oviedo contrasted the "pluma," the "ingenio," and the "auctoridad" of Homer to the solid "materia" that he himself was offering his readers.[54]

Thus, when Oviedo chose, as at times he indisputably did, to accentuate the distinctiveness, even oddity of New World phenomena, he did so primarily in order to burnish his own reputation as the official chronicler—and, in a sense, the intellectual proprietor—of the Indies.[55] At moments like these, one may indeed endorse Kathleen Myers's detection of "a tension between empiricism and written authorities" in Oviedo's work.[56] On those far more numerous occasions, however, when he strove—unsystematically enough, it is true—to understand and interpret Amerindian societies, he was more inclined to bring the New World and the Old World, especially the ancient Mediterranean, into a mutually illuminating relation, to inscribe the New World into *world* history. He was, as we have seen, unwilling to follow Pliny and other classical authorities in honoring legendary Greeks as the true inventors of customs and devices shared by the Old and New Worlds, but Oviedo's principal aim here was to deploy this apparent rejection of classical prestige and authority in order to bolster his impressive attack on what we now call "diffusionism" as an explanation for cultural similarities across wide distances. Nevertheless, he insisted, even though New World phenomena were not *derived* from Old World prototypes, the inevitable joint operation of "human genius and necessity" (Pedro Mexía's phrase) in every part of the inhabited world insured that classical—and modern—European parallels were perfectly valid and illuminating aids to understanding what struck many Spaniards as unsettlingly alien practices in the Indies. Oviedo employed such parallels to help potentially disoriented European readers grasp the principle that "some things appear new because they are very old and forgotten."

That is, classical parallels could help Europeans negotiate the "shock of the new" by enabling them to realize that ancient Europe, especially the Greco-Roman world, as well as subliterate modern European communities, exhibited cultural products of "human genius and necessity" that strikingly echoed the apparent anomalies of New World societies.

Once again, as with Las Casas's use of the Roman invasion of Spain, we see how a strategy of discourse designed to throw a conceptual bridge across the gulf separating the Old World from the New had the effect of "bringing home" to modern Europeans aspects of Europe's own past—as well as at times facilitating a deeper, more sympathetic understanding of that vast segment of modern European cultural life that fell below the normal threshold of refined awareness. Thus, a Spaniard reading in Oviedo about the "very orderly contredanse" of the Antillean areitos would not only discover a new perspective on early Roman culture, but would also learn to appreciate the social function of those areitos of modern Spain, the ballads of illiterate peasants. Oviedo's classical parallels for Indian cultural phenomena thus bolstered his contention that, despite wide expanses of both time and space, "the whole world is like home."

The Superiority of the Indians to the Romans in the Apologética historia of Bartolomé de las Casas

Fernández de Oviedo, then, usually employed parallels between classical and Amerindian cultures in order to establish the right of the peoples of the New World to take their place, humble though that place might be, among the other descendants of Adam and Noah, notwithstanding numerous cultural peculiarities that this diligent thaumatographer was only too happy to record. To a certain extent, much the same could be said of many pages penned by one of his most ardent detractors, Bartolomé de las Casas, for his *Apologética historia sumaria* represented, in the words of J. H. Elliott, "an extraordinarily ambitious attempt to embrace the peoples of the New World within a global survey of human civilization."[57] But Las Casas far surpassed Oviedo both in the almost obsessive thoroughness of his cultural comparisons and in the equally obsessive venom that he directed at the classical world, especially at the Romans. Oviedo, too, as earlier chapters demonstrated, was scarcely an enthusiastic encomiast of the ancient Romans, but his "anti-Romanism" was much more pronounced when it was modern Spaniards, rather than Aztecs or Incas, who were being measured against the classical world.[58]

We have seen that Las Casas compared the Romans with the Indians in two parts of his *Apologia*, the text that seems our closest approximation to his presentation before the junta in Valladolid in 1550. Chapters 34–37 attempt to deflect condemnation of American human sacrifice by establishing that the custom was part of the *ius gentium* and thus practiced by virtually all peoples at one time or another—not excluding those self-styled missionaries of civilization, the ancient Romans. In addition, in the fifth chapter of the *Apologia*, which appears to have been an addition to the material he presented in Valladolid, Las Casas targeted the Romans as excellent examples of his fourth kind of barbarian: pagans whose ignorance of "the mysteries of Christian philosophy" left them exposed to the "barbarism of vice." While the same might be said of the Indians of the New World, Las Casas's intention here was less to suggest a comparison of the two cultures than it was to defuse Spanish denunciations of the "heathen" practices and beliefs of the Indians by excoriating instead those of the ancient Greeks and, especially, the Romans. This allowed him to resurrect the vivid and passionate attacks Augustine and Lactantius launched upon the "heinous vices and detestable practices, . . . the shameful games and hateful sacrifices" of the Romans, who thereby showed the world that "they far outdistanced all other nations in insensitivity of mind and barbarism."

It is likely that this vitriolic addition to his remarks at Valladolid (where he had apparently not offered paganism as one definition of barbarism) was a spillover from the major project that seems to have occupied much of his time in the 1550s, the *Apologética historia sumaria*. Though this work remained unpublished until recent times, it did circulate in manuscript, and its influence has been detected in later works, notably those of the Augustinian Jerónimo Román and the Franciscans Jerónimo de Mendieta and Juan de Torquemada.[59] In addition, as we have noted in chapter 3, Las Casas apparently read an early version of this work before the junta in Valladolid, and so its arguments and many of its details achieved a kind of publicity even though the formal book remained unpublished.

Designed as an antidote to the slanders hurled at the natives of the New World, this "brief defensive history" was no mere attempt to show

that Amerindian cultures deserved to be compared with those of classical antiquity. Rather, it aimed to demonstrate that "in following the
rules of natural reason [the Indians] have surpassed the world's most
prudent peoples, such as the Greeks and the Romans, by a wide margin
(con no chico exceso)," and its juxtaposition of societies was designed
to reveal the "advantage and superiority" [ventaja y exceso] that the
New World civilizations had displayed over those of the ancient
Mediterranean.[60] Though Las Casas frequently compared Greek and
even Egyptian culture with that of the Amerindians, it was Roman culture that he subjected to the most withering abuse. His animus against
the Romans as inappropriate models for Spaniards in the Indies was
such an overmastering obsession that contempt for Roman practices
and beliefs reverberated throughout the many pages of comparative
ethnology that constitute the bulk of this vast "unread masterpiece."[61]

Though often denounced as a loose baggy monster of a book, the
Apologética historia does have a generally clear overall structure. The
first section (twenty-two chapters) describes and extols the physical setting within which the New World societies had grown to their pre-
Columbian telos. The favorable climate of Hispaniola is presented first
and most fully, and its features conducive to human rationality are sum-
marily extended to the rest of the New World. The rest of the book is a
demonstration that the inhabitants of these comfortable lands reveal a
rational capacity that confirms Cicero's contention in book 1 of *De leg-
ibus* that human beings the world over share a fundamental nature
informed by reason, or, as Las Casas famously phrased it, "all the
nations of the world are men *(todas las naciones del mundo son hombres)*, and there is one definition of all humans, and that is that they are
rational."[62] The second section (seventeen chapters), following naturally upon the geographical survey of the first book, applies to the Indians six essential qualities—or *causas naturales*—by virtue of which
humans enjoy this rationality: the influence of the stars and planets; the
effects of climate; the constitution of bodies and sense organs; the
clemency of the seasons; and adequate subsistence. The inhabitants of
the New World, he claims, enjoy all of these qualifying requirements.

The third—and by far the longest—section (224 chapters) is a sustained refutation of the claim that the Indians fall into the third category of barbarians Las Casas had identified in the debate in Valladolid
and at the beginning of the Latin *Apologia* (a survey of meanings of
"barbarian" that he recapitulated in the concluding chapters of the

Apologética historia). Drawn largely from passages in Aristotle's *Politics* and Aquinas's commentary upon it, this definition refers to barbarians "in the strict sense" [simpliciter], men whom Aristotle called "slaves by nature since they have no natural government and no political institutions . . . , nor do they have a ruler."[63] Since Mair and Sepúlveda had deployed Aristotle's category of the "natural slave" against the Indians, it made superb strategic sense for Las Casas to lay down an Aristotelian formulation upon which to construct his defense of the Indians against the charge of being sub-civilized barbarians "naturally" meriting enslavement. No longer content to dismiss Aristotle as "a pagan burning in Hell" (his slur of 1519), Las Casas now respectfully proffered the six essential elements (μέρη) of the true state that the philosopher established in book 7 of the *Politics* (1328b). These elements, with their corresponding social classes, are: a supply of food (farmers), crafts (craftsmen), weapons (soldiers), money (the wealthy), divine worship (priests), and a means of deciding what is profitable and fair (governmental and judicial authorities). Las Casas's massive third section surveys the societies of the New World in accord with each of these elements and classes, with an inevitable focus on the Aztecs and Incas. In each case, faithful to the promise of the "Argumento," Las Casas was eager to demonstrate that in meeting this classical definition of the true state, the Indians had equaled or surpassed the Greco-Roman civilizations from whose womb that definition had come forth.

Since Amerindian—especially Aztec—religion offered the most luridly effective support for Sepúlveda's contention that the New World natives flagrantly violated the laws of nature, Las Casas shrewdly chose religious beliefs and practices—Aristotle's fifth prerequisite for "prudencia política"—as the sphere for his boldest demonstrations of the decided superiority of New World societies to the civilizations of the Greeks and Romans.[64] Indeed, he devoted well over half the third section (chaps. 71–194) to aspects of religious life: divination, idolatry, magic and prodigies, gods, temples, priests, and ritual. Normally, Las Casas treated each of these sub-divisions of religion in three sections: Old World examples, New World examples, and a comparison of the two. Understandably enough, it is ritual *(culto)* that receives the fullest treatment: chapters 143–94, nearly a fifth of the entire *Apologética historia.*[65] And nearly half of this discussion of *culto* is a very detailed account of Old World pagan rituals and festivals, especially Roman rituals, drawing upon a wide variety of ancient sources, as well as some contemporary antiquarians.

But the Romans come in for rough handling well before that long concluding onslaught on their disgusting rituals. For example, the bulk of chapter 86 is a deflection of attacks upon Amerindian idolatry by means of a gleeful retelling of Josephus's account of a scandal during the reign of Tiberius, when a virtuous Roman matron named Paulina was hoodwinked by a spurned lover, the equestrian Decius Mundus, who appeared to her, with the connivance of priests of Isis, in the guise of the god Anubis (Joseph. *AJ* 18.66–80). We might at first find the story implausible, Las Casas observes, "but taking into account other great blindnesses and brutish errors indulged in by the Romans, who presumed to govern the world *(que el mundo presumieron de regular)*, we mustn't be amazed at this great piece of foolishness."[66] Las Casas is here echoing his dig at the Romans in the fifth chapter of the Latin *Apologia* (probably written not long before) where he argued that the disgusting religious practices of the Romans undercut their fitness "to enact laws for other nations," as well as their right to label other peoples barbarous. Interestingly enough, Josephus and Las Casas had a similar motive for telling this lurid story. Just as Las Casas was trying to deflect criticism of New World idolaters by showing the depths to which even the famous Romans could sink because of their idolatry, so Josephus told his story at such length in order to lessen the impact of the much shorter account of four Jewish swindlers in Rome whose misdeeds precipitated Tiberius's expulsion of the Jews from the city (18.81–84). But while Josephus, careful as always not to offend Roman readers, intended the story of Paulina to evoke indignation at "the insolent acts of the priests in the temple of Isis," Las Casas focused on the Roman ethnicity of Paulina and Decius Mundus and thus added this story to his stockpile of anti-Roman ammunition.

Chapters 103–27 juxtapose and then compare the gods of Old World polytheism with those of the Indians. The Old World gods come first here, and they receive three times as much space as the New World divinities (though we should admit that mention of Vulcan inspires a long digression on volcanoes that offers some relief from the indictment of classical polytheism). Not only are Greco-Roman divinities the main recipients of abuse here, but it is Roman gods in particular who are singled out. Thus, at the beginning of chapter 105, Las Casas ridiculed "the

multitude of the gods that, with such dense blindness, insane paganism—and most especially Roman paganism—fabricated and invented
and adored."⁶⁷ Drawing enthusiastically upon the sarcastic chapters in
The City of God that Augustine devoted to the likes of the goddess Pertunda (the wedding night "Thrustress") and Cloacina (whom one might
term Our Lady of the Sewers), Las Casas invited his readers to gauge
"how much insensibility of ignorance the most wise Romans possessed."⁶⁸ Not only did they elevate undignified concepts to divine status, but they also deified unworthy humans. Thus, the emperor Hadrian
turned his dead catamite Antinous into a god, an act that allows us to
gauge "the 'prudence' and vileness and most dull-witted darkness of the
intellects of the unhappy Romans." Servius's reference, meanwhile, to
the deification of the divine inventor of fertilizer inspires Las Casas to
exclaim: "¡Oh bestiales romanos!"⁶⁹

It is true that the Romans could not be blamed for the invention of
polytheism—it was the Egyptians and Phoenicians who passed it on to
the Greeks and Romans, Las Casas claimed—but it took hold "muy
principalmente" among the Romans, among whom it acquired greater
strength than ever, and it was all the more blameworthy among them
"because they fancied themselves wiser than other peoples."⁷⁰ This
spotlight on the special culpability of the Romans in the evolution of
Old World paganism took on a further meaning a little later, when Las
Casas effected his transition to the polytheism of the New World. Here,
remarkably though fleetingly, he suggested that Old World paganism
may well have been the source of Amerindian polytheism, "which they
may have received and inherited from those ancient idolaters, as is
probable at least to a large extent," though he also admitted the possibility of independent invention.⁷¹ Las Casas did not provide a precise
scenario for this diffusionist hypothesis; it is a brief, tantalizing parallel
to his suggestion, based on reports of crosses on Cozumel, that Christian missionaries may once have reached Yucatán centuries before
Columbus.⁷² But his aim here is less to provide a serious account of cultural development than an exoneration of the American polytheists and
a further dig at the Romans.

Chapter 127 presents Las Casas's case for the manifest superiority of
New World conceptions of divinity to those of the Greeks and Romans.
Again, as so often elsewhere in his references to the classical world, it is
the Romans who came in for particular opprobrium, for "to tell the
truth, with reference to divinities, one can't find in those who have writ-

ten on the subject that the Greeks were as irrational as the Romans."
For while the Greeks worshiped "only human beings and their statues,"
the Romans worshiped "vile inanimate objects." But if the Greeks surpassed the Romans in this respect, "these Indian peoples have surpassed
both Greeks and Romans in choosing for gods, not mortals who were
sinful, criminal, and infamous, but virtuous men," culture heroes like
Quetzalcóatl.[73] Furthermore, those Indians who worshiped only the sun
or fountains proved easier to attract to the Christian faith than were the
pagans of Old World with their multitude of gods and idols. Central to
this chapter is Las Casas's contention that a people's natural conception
of divinity, unassisted by Grace, is the highest and truest indication of
the extent of their participation in natural human rationality. Since the
Indians in their choice of divinities surpassed the Greeks, who in turn
surpassed the Romans, then it follows that "these Indian peoples have
shown and continue to show that they are and have been of much better rational judgment and are more respectable and prudent than the
Greek and Roman peoples."[74]

In his comparison of European and American priests, Las Casas
excoriated the Roman *epulones*, the college of priests whose job it was
to invite the gods to a banquet *(lectisternium)* at which the priestly hosts
drank themselves silly, thus offering us proof of "how deceived and
mocked and possessed by the demons the Romans were through their
lack of true knowledge of God."[75] Several chapters later, when forced to
admit the existence of similar drunken feasts among the Indians of New
Spain and Honduras, he not only referred back to the Roman *epulones*
for comparison, but he again floated his diffusionist gambit, arguing that
the prevalence of wild banquets among "los antiguos gentiles" implied
that "from them these Indians of ours must have inherited it."[76] There
were also among the Romans three orders of priests who "fulfilled and
perfected the blindness and most vile insensibility of that people who
presumed to give laws to the world and govern it." These "bestial and
abominable priests" were the infamous Galli, the self-castrating priests
of Cybele, to whom Las Casas was only too happy to return in the cul-
mination of his attack on Roman rituals. Slanderers of the Indians
needed to keep these Galli in mind, he insisted, for they offered a sober-
ing lesson in comparative ethnography. "We really ought to contemplate
this so that we shall not be astonished at what we find of such absurdities among these Indian peoples," though in fact "in many respects they
did not have such ugly practices as this and many others."[77]

Rituals and sacrifices supplied the richest scope for Las Casas's comparison of ancient European and modern American paganism (chaps. 143–94). Just as no people lacks a sense of a divinity who can offer aid, he observed, so no people lacks the belief that thanks are owed to that divinity for that help, even though no thanks can ever truly suffice. But the precise nature of the thanks offered has differed markedly from one people to another—it is a matter of positive (conventional), not natural, law. Las Casas proceeded to discuss the ritual purifications with which ancient Europeans prepared for their sacrifices, ascetic practices ranging from fasts and ablutions all the way to the self-castration of the Galli—this time cited as proof of piety, not perversity. So impressed was he by the seriousness with which the ancients took such preparations that he suggested that many Christian priests could take a lesson from their pagan counterparts. Citing Flavio Biondo's *De Roma triumphante* on the preparatory confessions of sins by pagan priests "just as we prepare ourselves by confession for receiving or administering sacraments," Las Casas concluded chapter 143 with a complaint that many Christian priests failed to take their preparations for the Eucharist as seriously as pagan priests approached a sacrifice.[78] This point recurs several times in this long section on *culto*, but most emphatically in the discussion of New World ritual practices.

The general discussions of ancient Old World inanimate and animal sacrifices in the next two chapters show a similar, rather surprising impartiality, a reason for which becomes clear at the end of chapter 145, where Las Casas admitted that he had lifted all of this material from the industrious Seventeenth Syntagma ("De sacrificiis") of Lilio Gregorio Giraldi's recent *De deis gentium* (Basel, 1548).[79] But before long Las Casas's inveterate distaste for the Romans broke through, significantly in a passage that harks back to his passionate opposition to the use of the Roman Empire as a model for Spanish policies and behavior in the Indies. Discussing pagan sacrifices to the major gods in chapter 148, he noted that it was "principalmente" the Romans who offered sacrifices to Mars. Why so? Obviously, they were inspired by "the natural inclination that they recognized in themselves to overrun and harass the world with wars and battles."[80] But the Romans' pious attention to Mars was rivaled by one other ancient European people: "Our Spaniards also were extremely devoted to Mars, more than any other nations." Perhaps Las Casas intended here to suggest that the modern Spaniards' unfortunate similarity to the ancient Romans had roots in

Iberian antiquity. In any case, ancient Spanish sacrifices to Mars, as attested by Strabo, open the next chapter as well.

With his account of sacrifices to Bacchus in chapters 151 and 152, Las Casas continued to reach his customarily brisk anti-Roman stride. After an account of Greek sacrifices to Dionysus based on material in Pausanias (one of Las Casas's favorite sources in this long account of ancient rituals), he turned to Augustine (*City of God* 7.21) for support for his contention that in Roman Italy this "bestial god" was worshiped with "more pomp and more blindness and vileness and less shame" than in Greece. In Lavinium, for example, a large phallus was carried around in his honor and crowned by supposedly respectable matrons. "What greater bestiality and foulness could any nation have?"[81] Nastiness of this order obviously merited a full chapter of its own, and Las Casas accordingly devoted chapter 152 to Livy's famous account of the first outbreak of the Dionysiac epidemic in Rome in 186 B.C. (bk. 39.8–19). But in chapter 153 Las Casas returned to the irresistible image of Roman matrons adorning an idol's phallus, this time that of the egregious Priapus. "This was affirmed to be a most respectable act and an expression of the highest religious duty among that Roman or Italian people of such renown." From Rome, the rites of Priapus radiated outward, infecting even the Jews.[82] Roman veneration of Bacchus and Priapus, coupled with their unparalleled devotion to Berecynthia (Cybele), whom they honored "with such shameless, degrading, and abominable feasts, ceremonies, rites, and sacrifices," impressively indicated that "there has been no nation in the whole world so forsaken and abandoned by God" (chap. 158).[83] And while they feebly attempted to prettify the worship of Cybele by absurdly claiming that she was a virgin, Las Casas insisted that they deserved no credit for the honesty with which they honored the human prostitute Flora with "divine" honors that perfectly suited her true nature. Augustine's *City of God* aptly offered the dances of naked prostitutes at the Roman Floralia as a demonstration of the "philosophy and theology and wisdom of the Romans" (chap. 160).[84]

But the most ancient and widespread ritual act in the Old World was precisely the one that aroused the greatest disgust among Europeans who learned of New World religion: human sacrifice. Las Casas devoted two full chapters to his contention that "no nations—or almost none—have been found in the world that have not sacrificed men."[85] Predictably, he seized upon Lactantius's claim that "our Latins and

Romans" were guilty of this practice. Especially arresting is Lactantius's insistence that the Romans' reputation for pursuing the "liberal
arts" meant that they were more wicked for practicing human sacrifice
than were ignorant barbarians, who had the excuse of lacking such cultural refinement. As we have seen, Las Casas was himself very fond of
this notion that it was precisely the Romans' unparalleled reputation
for civilization that made their ill-hidden barbarism all the more repre-
hensible. This allowed Las Casas to reconcile a possible contradiction in
his argument. If human sacrificers in the New World were simply par-
ticipating in a worldwide custom, as Las Casas claimed, then why might
one not offer the same excuse for the Romans? The answer is simple.
While the inhabitants of the New World had been subjected to outra-
geous slander for over half a century—calumny that Las Casas designed
the entire *Apologética historia* to counteract—the Romans had enjoyed
for many centuries an undeserved reputation for civilized behavior—a
"civility" that they themselves had assumed they were entitled to
impose upon others by force of arms. Again, we find that Las Casas's
animus against the Romans was stoked by his keen sense of the lingering power of the Roman model in a world that needed to outgrow such
insidious influences.

   Another antipagan tract of the Constantinian era, Eusebius of Caesarea's *De evangelica praeparatione,* supplied Las Casas with a handy
survey of Mediterranean societies that practiced human sacrifice, culminating in a claim that human sacrifice was regularly perpetrated in
the very city of Rome up to the time that paganism ceased to be the state
religion: "Who is unaware that in the great city itself—I think Eusebius
means the city of Rome—the Latins sacrifice men in the ceremonies for
Jupiter?"[86] Still, despite his eagerness to blacken the reputation of the
Romans with a reference to the rites of Jupiter Latiaris, Las Casas cannot be accused of harboring simple and straightforward views on the
explosive subject of human sacrifice. In the next chapter (162), it is true,
he duly recorded Lactantius's outrage over instances of the sacrifice of
"innocent children," a practice that the North African apologist excoriated as a "plague upon the human race." But at this moment, just when
one might expect our Dominican to second with glee Lactantius's
attack upon Old World religious practices, he startlingly forced his
readers to look at child sacrifice from the unfamiliar standpoint of the
sacrificers themselves.

But they could reply to Lactantius that the piety that is owed to God is greater than that owed to one's own blood, for given the fact that those who offered that sacrifice of their children believed, albeit mistakenly, that they were offering it to the true God, to whom that and more is owed by men, ... then it follows that they could reply to Lactantius that they did no wrong in offering their children to God or the gods.[87]

Las Casas seems here to have realized the danger of his attack upon Old World ritual practices: such rites could inconveniently call to the reader's mind those of the New World. Accordingly, he proceeded to invoke his famous defense of human sacrifice, even if this meant letting Old World pagans off the hook for a moment. But not for long. A couple of pages later he turned to a hostile account of early Iberian human sacrifice. While those who lived along the Duero appear to have offered human sacrifice on their own initiative, the Andalusians—"the simplest and most peaceful nation," our Dominican from Andalusia labeled them—were corrupted by the Carthaginians, who induced them to adopt their own custom of infant sacrifice. But Las Casas conscientiously admitted that he had no ancient source for the introduction of human sacrifice into Andalusia; he was following the chronicle of Florián de Ocampo, who claimed to be using ancient evidence that Las Casas could not locate. Similarly, Alfonso X had attributed Iberian human sacrifice to the "Almunites."

Chapter 164 is a grab bag of material on Greco-Roman festivals and their survivals in modern Europe—the latter a fascinating preoccupation to which we shall return—concluding with an expression of weariness from having to record "so many absurdities in a people who showed such great presumption to rule and give orders to the world."[88] Then, in the final chapter expressly devoted to Old World rituals, Las Casas returned to the proposition with which he had initiated this long discussion of *culto:* the devotion pagans paid to their gods should be a model for the piety of Christians. As a classical example of such devotion, he gave most of this chapter over to the inviolable secrecy of certain Greco-Roman rites, notably the Eleusinian Mysteries, which resisted the curiosity of the early Christian apologists. But even more impressive heathen models of ritual scrupulosity were supplied by the inhabitants of the New World, and it is to their rituals that the next seventeen chapters (166–82) are devoted. A recurring point here is the way in which the rituals of the New World demonstrated through grueling fasts and even more spectacular self-mortification a penitential piety that put Europeans to shame, even though "they had far fewer sins than we do."[89]

His survey of New World rituals concluded, Las Casas offered three chapters of reflections on religious views and practices dictated by natural reason, showcasing once again his bold defense of human sacrifice. Since Aristotle insisted that the well-ordered state must have a formal mechanism for attempting to pay our ultimately unpayable debt of gratitude to divinity, it follows that the more pious a people is, the more precious will be the gifts it offers to what it regards as divine. Thus, it is nobler to sacrifice animals than plants, and it is better to offer the finer animals than the viler ones, and, finally and ineluctably, it is nobler to sacrifice humans than animals.[90] The belief shared by all societies that the performance of ritual gratitude to the gods is essential to the well-being of the state helps explain the Romans' persecution of the early Christians, whose defiance of the ancestral gods seemed to undermine the Roman state—a notably rare attempt by Las Casas to see things from the Roman point of view. This is followed by the breathtaking argument concluding chapter 184: since the Devil has sown into human nature the conviction that earthly felicity depends upon proper sacrifice to the gods, it follows that those peoples who have offered up human lives to their putative deities "have provided for them more abundantly and properly in accord with natural reason, and were more prudent in looking after the welfare . . . of the commonweal than those who did not perform or allow others to perform human sacrifices."[91]

Accordingly, he proceeded in the next chapter to bestow a prize in Old World religiosity upon the "French" (i.e., the Gauls) with their mass sacrifices in wicker structures. Still, while the human bulk of the Gallic offerings was impressive, when it came to the intrinsic value of human offerings it was the Carthaginians who held the "advantage" [ventaja] over other nations, for they sacrificed their own children. Not that "nuestra gente o nación española" was far behind (*muy atrás*—still this peculiar language of spiritual contest), for they sacrificed hecatombs of human victims, including their own firstborn, a practice they had learned from the Carthaginians, "and so in the noble concept and most fitting estimation which they had of the gods, and consequently in using rational judgment more prudently than other peoples, we may almost compare them to the Carthaginians."⁹² Whereas earlier (chap. 162) he had suggested that the Carthaginians had corrupted some of the Iberian nations with their shocking practices, now he argued that they could not have taught them so well had their pupils not already been so well endowed with natural reason!

The conclusion to this entire lengthy investigation of rituals in the Old and New Worlds is an explicit comparison of the two systems under eight categories: preparations for festivals and sacrifices; the multitude of offerings to the gods; the value of these offerings; the suffering endured by celebrants in the course of the rituals; the care with which rituals are carried out; the avoidance of indecency; ceremonies approximating Easter; and number of festivals.⁹³ Chapters 186–91 present the case for Indian superiority in all these areas, with the possible exception of the last, for Las Casas dared not claim that the inhabitants of the New World organized more festivals than the Romans. Finally, chapters 192–93 gave Las Casas his last extended opportunity to indulge in passionate invective against ancient Mediterranean, especially Roman, religious practices. After a blanket declaration that God humbled the vainglorious Romans by allowing them to wallow "in the most vile and absurd things, remote from any good rational judgment," he insisted that the Indians, especially those of New Spain, showed "infinite superiority" to the Greeks and Romans in each of the eight categories of comparison. Thus, the preparations that the ancients made for sacrifices (notwithstanding claims to the contrary in chapter 185) were no different from those of the "most barbaric and worse than bestial men, men we keep locked up in lunatic asylums." As for the value of their offerings to their gods, recollection of what they offered to Bacchus, Priapus, Cybele (Berecynthia), and Venus will sufficiently display their "prudencia y juicio." Thus, the Greeks, so celebrated for their moral philosophy, offered their daughters for ritual prostitution—witness the one thousand virgins offered up at a time at the temple of Aphrodite in Corinth. But even more vile were the offerings of the Romans, whose matrons brought Cybele libations of urine and the incense of farts. More degrading still were the Galli's offerings of their own severed genitals, consummate proof that "those Indians of ours were one hundred thousand times ahead of the Greeks and Romans . . . in the preciousness and value of their sacrifices." In comparison with rituals for such divinities as the prostitute-turned-goddess Flora, the drunken Bacchus, and the obscene Priapus, the sacrifices of the New World displayed no *vileza* and nothing not conformable to reason.

But it was the mood in which they approached and carried out their festivals that most decisively demonstrated the Indians' superiority to the Romans. The Aztecs and other New World natives prepared for their sacrifices in an utterly appropriate mood of "dolor y penitencia," with heroic fastings, sleep deprivation, and mortifications of the flesh. As Las Casas had emphasized in his discussion of the rituals of the Indians of New Spain, "those Indians whom we have so despised have surpassed us a thousandfold in their fasts and penitence and devotion and fervor for their gods."[94] Thus, the supposed barbarians of the New World not only showed their full participation in natural reason; they also offered lessons in penitential piety for the Europeans of the Counter-Reformation. In his formal comparison of the tone of American rituals with that of Greco-Roman festivals in chapter 192, Las Casas insisted that none of the historical records known to him revealed

> such sufferings and voluntary torments and fasting and vigils and such horrible and severe penitence, with wailings and groanings, endured for their gods; but as for the Greeks and the Romans, all their sacrifices and festivals were nothing but pleasures, delights, merrymakings, lewd displays, and all sorts of sensual delights. . . . As to the ceremonies that the Romans practiced, they were of all the peoples in the world the most vile, most debased, most impure, and most irrational.[95]

The next chapter sustains this vituperative assault upon the obscene frivolity of Greco-Roman rituals, of the "insensible and abusive blindness, dishonor, and bestiality of those so eminent peoples who then possessed the world," a charge driven home by one of the Dominican's favorite mental images: Augustine's description of respectable Roman matrons garlanding a huge phallus drawn through the streets on a float.[96]

Aside from the enjoyment Las Casas manifestly experienced in chronicling the religious enormities of the Roman Empire, he did not want his readers to forget that he had a serious aim in resurrecting this material with such relish. In chapter 159, he had stated his aim in this way:

> I believe that what I have said about the cult and ceremonies of this mother of the gods Berecynthia (or the "good goddess") and about

those through which those most unspeakable gods Bacchus and Priapus were served and venerated, honored and feasted by so many peoples, especially the Greeks and the Romans, people considered so wise in the world, may suffice to insure that we should not reasonably regard with astonishment or dismay the gods, ceremonies, and sacrifices of all the other peoples, no matter how ugly and dishonorable, bestial and abominable they may be.[97]

This justification for locating classical parallels occurred to many in the sixteenth century. We have seen that Oviedo observed that the Romans were so addicted to haruspices and fortune-tellers that "if we look at the affairs of the ancient pagans in this matter, we have to consider them just as profane and diabolical as those of our Indies" (bk. 33, chap. 46). Similarly, in his widely read *Historia natural y moral de las Indias* (1590), the Jesuit José de Acosta declared in a prologue introducing his discussion of New World religion:

If anyone will be astonished by any rites and customs of the Indians and will despise them as stupid and silly, or detest them as inhuman and diabolical, let him see that among the Greeks and the Romans, who ruled the world, the very same things—or things similar or sometimes even worse—were found, as one will be able to learn not only from our [i.e., Christian] authors Eusebius of Caesarea, Clement of Alexandria, Theodoretus of Cyrene, and others, but also from their own writers, such as Pliny, Dionysius of Halicarnassus, and Plutarch.[98]

These three independent passages all display what Fermín del Pino, referring to Acosta, has called "the aseptic virtue that the classical model possesses for inhibiting the natural reaction of rejection that would be automatic without it."[99]

But while Las Casas's attack upon Greco-Roman religion was designed primarily to deflect or neutralize criticism of New World religious conceptions and practices, it is impossible to miss the persistent undertone of a more aggressive purpose. It was not only the cultural prestige of Greco-Roman civilization that needed to be undermined in order to enhance the reputation of the slandered natives of the New World; it was also their ill-gotten glory as "lords of the world" that attracted the Dominican's ire. Thus, in his final summary in chapter 194 of "this whole long and prolix discourse" on comparative religion, Las

Casas insisted that he had demonstrated the superiority of American religious rituals to those of the Greeks and the Romans, who "were lords and governors—or took it upon themselves to be lords and governors—of the world."[100] There can be little doubt that Las Casas attacked the Romans not only because of their use as cultural benchmarks for all subsequent civilizations, but also because of the role they had been made to play in the debate over the justice of the conquest—especially in the *Democrates secundus* of Juan Ginés de Sepúlveda. After all, unlike those who invoked the juristic principle of the Roman emperor, ancient or modern, as "lord of the world," Sepúlveda's use of the Romans was largely cultural and "humanistic": the Romans owed their empire to their cultural superiority to their subjects, and the Spaniards should follow in their footsteps—not as "legal" inheritors of a world empire, but as worthy emulators of worthy cultural models. Accordingly, Las Casas's demolition of the cultural prestige of the Romans in the *Apologética historia,* foreshadowed already in his contribution to the debate in Valladolid, was not only an antidote to calumnies against the cultural level of the American natives, but also another blow at a disreputable model for Spanish imperial rule.

Las Casas the Antiquarian and "Pagan Survivals" in the Old World and the New

The merest glance at Las Casas's comparison of Greco-Roman and Amerindian religion would suffice to confirm Anthony Pagden's claim that the *Apologética historia,* along with the *Apologia,* offers a "programme for comparative ethnology."[101] But we have now seen that these chapters also consistently sustain Las Casas's obsessive preoccupation with the baleful power of the model of ancient Roman imperialism in the debate over the conquest of the New World. There is, however, a further dimension to these chapters—nearly half the whole huge volume, we should note. In addition to their potential contribution to anthropological speculation and to the ethics of colonial rule, they are also an impressive exercise in classical antiquarianism. Had the book been published in its time, it would not only have given its Spanish readers a considerable amount of new and exotic information, much of it gathered from missionary friars and other eyewitnesses, about the societies of the New World; it would also have offered a rich, if incorrigibly biased, fund of knowledge about the ancient Mediterranean.

Not surprisingly, few modern readers—or, more frequently, consulters—of the *Apologética historia* have shown much patience with this ancient European material, intent as they have been upon mining the text for its information about New World peoples. Thus, a standard survey of Las Casas's life and writings laments that "unfortunately, . . . he added a whole mass of extraneous data. . . . Nowadays this material is unreadable."[102] A classical scholar may beg to differ.[103] While no one will be so bold as to credit Las Casas with original research into Greco-Roman culture in general and religious life in particular, it is hard to withhold from him a frank respect—at times even astonishment—at the breadth of his reading in classical primary sources and in Renaissance antiquarian scholarship. It would have been natural enough for him to rely primarily upon the passionate attacks upon Greco-Roman religious life in such works as Augustine's *City of God* and Lactantius's *Divine Institutes,* and we have seen that he did, in fact, make extensive use of these works. As Sabine MacCormack has aptly observed, Las Casas enthusiastically "reinvigorated the ancient Christian apologetic against the persuasive power and moral corruption of Mediterranean paganism."[104] But his knowledge of the primary sources was by no means restricted to what he could find in patristic writers or postclassical compendia.

One of the most impressive aspects of this "extraneous" account of ancient European religious life is Las Casas's extensive use of classical authors who were not yet firmly established in the early modern Greco-Roman canon. For instance, one of his favorite sources for ancient geographical and ethnographical data was Herodotus. Though Valla's Latin translation had been available in print since 1474, the "father of history" did not seriously begin to live down his ancient reputation for unreliability and downright mendacity until Henri Estienne published his *Apologia pro Herodoto* in 1566, the year Las Casas died.[105] Arnaldo Momigliano made the intriguing suggestion that the rise in status Herodotus began to experience in the second half of the sixteenth century was facilitated by accounts of the New World, for these reports

> showed that one could travel abroad, tell strange stories, enquire into past events, without necessarily being a liar. One of the standard objections against Herodotus had been that his tales were incredible.

But now the study of foreign countries and the discovery of America revealed customs even more extraordinary than those described by Herodotus.[106]

The scores of Herodotean citations in the *Apologética historia* support Momigliano's suggestion that an increasing awareness of Amerindian customs contributed to the rehabilitation of the testimony of the Greek historian. Las Casas also made extensive use of a later work that was Herodotean both in its ethnographic focus and in its studied use of the Ionic dialect: *De dea Syria,* Lucian of Samosata's vivid account of the worship of Atargatis at Hierapolis, featuring the ever-fascinating self-castration of the Galli.[107] More surprising is Las Casas's extensive use of the guidebook to Greece by Pausanias (second century A.D.). This priceless source of information about Greek religious sites and the traditions associated with them was not fully available in Latin until the very years of the Valladolid debate. (Abraham Loescher's Basel edition appeared in 1550, and Romulo Amaseo's Latin translation first appeared in Florence in 1551.)[108] Las Casas clearly wasted little time before divining the usefulness of this work for documenting the life of the pagan Mediterranean. For example, in a chapter devoted to Diana, he reproduced much of Pausanias's account of the religious life of the city of Patrai in northwestern Peloponnese, in particular its highly idiosyncratic festival of the Laphria, in honor of Artemis, climaxing in a stampede and immolation of wild animals.[109] We shall soon see what Las Casas did with the help of a rather more out-of-the-way passage in Pausanias.

Scarcely less impressive is Las Casas's use of some of the most authoritative antiquarian studies of the Renaissance. We have already noted that he quickly seized upon the 1548 *De deis gentium* of Lilio Gregorio Giraldi, whom Jean Seznec has called "one of the great figures of humanism."[110] The *Apologética historia* also reveals at least a nodding familiarity with the work of the great fifteenth-century antiquarian Flavio Biondo, with three references to his last work, *De Roma triumphante* (1452–59), an ambitious survey of several aspects of Roman culture, including religious life. More surprising—and considerably more baffling to Las Casas's modern editors—are two references to Wolfgang Lazius's recently published *Reipublicae Romanae in exteris provinciis constitutae commentarii* (Basel, 1551), a work characterized by William McCuaig as "an enormous compilation of Austrian antiquities, together with what would now be called *limes* studies."[111] Not only is this not the sort of thing one might readily imagine even our industrious Dominican consulting, but it is sufficiently obscure that all three editors of the *Apologetic History* printed the author's name as "Uvolegango" and threw up their hands at his true identity.[112] Las Casas drew upon book 10 of Lazius's work "De Ludis" for information about the Roman Saturnalia and about admission to the rites of Eleusinian Demeter.

Thus, had the *Apologética historia* managed to see the light in its own time, Las Casas's impressive command of both ancient and modern sources on Greco-Roman culture, especially religion, would have earned him a worthy place in the history of the popularization of knowledge about that "old new world" whose discovery preceded, prepared for, and accompanied the discovery of the cultures of America. Seen in this light, the book is an impressive monument to these two inextricably intertwined projects of discovery and "invention." But there is another, largely neglected dimension to Las Casas's impressive and thorough, if also impressively and thoroughly hostile, account of the religious life of Greco-Roman paganism: his fascination with the idea that the poisonous effects of ancient Roman paganism lived on in modern Europe.[113] For his polemically driven survey of ancient Roman religious customs repeatedly suggested that these rituals and festivities were not simply of safely antiquarian interest; they still lurked beneath the surface of European life well over a millennium after the triumph of Christianity.

We should admit at once that Las Casas did not regard every modern echo of a pagan practice as profoundly troubling, for he seems to have assumed that many of the analogues were as likely to have been coincidental as genetic. Especially likely to be coincidental, he implied, were official rituals of the Catholic Church that seemed analogous to practices of Roman paganism. Thus, the vestal virgins were shorn "like nuns in our Christianity."[114] And citing Flavio Biondo's claim that pagan priests uttered confessions before handling sacred things, Las Casas observed that this was "just as we use confession to prepare to receive or give the sacraments."[115] In an even more positive appeal to ancient paganism, he suggested that Pausanias's story of the punishment Artemis inflicted in Patrai upon a priestess and her lover who had sacrilegiously coupled in her temple offered an instructive hint for Christians of the wrath that their own God would inflict upon those who violate nuns or who otherwise show disrespect for sacred space or office.[116] In addition, the Roman practice of prefacing a sacrifice with a call for a reverent silence *(favete linguis)* was echoed when a Catholic priest would announce the reading of a lesson with the words "Jube, Domine, benedicere."[117]

Las Casas occasionally ventured to suggest that certain Catholic rituals did not merely resemble pagan practices but actually continued them. Thus, in the Feralia or Parentalia, part of the *februa* (purifications) of the eponymous month of February, it was the custom for families to gather at their ancestral tombs with torches and candles to pray for the repose of the souls of their dead, "and this custom has remained to our day, as is clear on All Saints' Day and that which we call the Day of the Souls."[118] In his discussion of a similar placatory offering for the dead, the funeral feast known as the *silicernium*, Las Casas claimed that this custom proved so tenaciously embedded in Rome and the rest of Italy in the years after the official Christianization of the empire that the popes succeeded in eradicating it only by channeling its spiritual energy into the Feast of the Chair of St. Peter (February 22).[119] A richer presentation of this kind of official Catholic appropriation and neutralization of a pagan ritual occurs in the chapter on the worship of Ceres and Diana (chap. 154). Advancing ever more deeply into the "labyrinth" of "the blind madness of paganism," our Dominican drew attention to the Roman practice of lighting candles or lamps for Ceres.

> From this is believed to have come about in the Christian Church the custom of the candles on the Day of Nuestra Señora Candelaria [i.e., Candlemas, Feb. 2] in order to uproot the survivals *(para desarraigar las reliquias)* of the superstition and rites that the pagans observed in their idolatry. Others believe that it takes its origin from the festivals that the Romans called the "segillarian" games or feasts [i.e., the Sigillaria, the last days of Saturnalia, when friends exchanged candles], about which we shall speak further on and which they celebrated right around that time of the month of February with the same ritual.[120]

Not only is this passage intriguing testimony to the fact that Las Casas was familiar with more than one speculation about the pagan origins of Candlemas, it is also remarkable for advancing a distinctly benevolent interpretation of the survival of pagan practices. The candles and lamps lit for Ceres had been co-opted and exorcized, as it were, and reestablished harmlessly in the Catholic liturgical year. This passage may even have a bearing on the question of missionary strategies in the New World. In signaling his implicit approval of the accommodationist policy of the early church in this instance, he may be gently suggesting that a similar approach might at times be advisable in the New World.[121]

But it was the survivals (*vestigios, rastros, reliquias* are his terms) of Roman paganism in the popular customs of modern Europe that especially interested—and troubled—Las Casas. Some of these survivals he noted briefly and relatively neutrally. Thus, discussing the Roman Ambarvalia and Amburbium, apotropaic processions with sacrificial animals around fields or city walls, he commented that "even today some part—and perhaps a large part—of this superstition remains among us."[122] It was the Romans' custom to decorate the temple of Flora with flowers on the first of May, "and we see practically everybody observing the survivals *(reliquias)* of these rites on the first of May, bringing carnations, roses, and other flowers in their hands."[123] In addition, in honor of Janus and the beginning of the year, Romans presented friends and relatives with ripe figs, dates, and honey, as well as coins, "whence seems to have come the custom of children asking for a gift *(aguinaldo)* on New Year's Day."[124] And it was from the offerings to Maia, mother of Mercury, that "there have remained in our times the *mayas* that our children make."[125] The *mayas* of Las Casas's day were "May queens," girls adorned as brides and stationed at house doors to ask passersby for money.[126]

Las Casas more emphatically condemned another common—perhaps universal—children's custom in the course of his account of the ancient worship of Venus. In a rather garbled paraphrase of a passage in book 2 of Pausanias, he claimed that at Sikyon two virgin priestesses offered Aphrodite dolls of linen and wool in order to stay chaste—"or perhaps for the opposite reason," he cynically interjected. "And today we see clearly the vestige of this idolatrous practice, for we see our little girls, almost as soon as they are born, take delight in the dolls that we give them—and this is a practice which we shouldn't observe, for there are other toys that could give them pleasure."[127] It is intriguing that in these very years the identification of dolls with idolatry was being made in circles far removed from that of Las Casas, but the idolatrous religion under attack there was not ancient Roman paganism but the supposed modern paganism of the Roman Catholic Church. Thus, the Protestant Heinrich Bullinger wrote caustically in 1529: "Indeed, in our places of worship, what are representations of the Virgin mother and the other

gods and goddesses but huge dolls *(puppae)*? Are they set up by barbarians?"[128] We shall return to this Protestant tradition of attacks on
Catholic "pagano-papalism."

The richest conglomeration of European pagan survivals Las Casas
identified and denounced is to be found in chapter 164, a survey of various Roman festivals. Referring to the mock kings and magistrates presiding over the Saturnalia, he suggested that "a vestige *(vestigio)* of this
appears to have remained among us Christians, in the custom of
installing the *obispillos* in the cathedrals for St. Nicholas' Day."[129]
These *obispillos*, "little bishops," were choirboys dressed like bishops
and allowed to mimic their sacral actions.[130] He then proceeded to the
Saturnalia custom of exchanging gifts *(strenae)*,

> which we today exchange under the name of *aguinaldos* [New Year's
> gifts], and thus there remains today in the days from Christmas to
> Epiphany the vestige and trace *(vestigio y rastro)* of those festivals
> among the Christians, and today as I write I see the banquets and par-
> ties that people throw for one another with great regularity.

He went on to mention the Sigillaria, the last days of Saturnalia, noting
that while the pagan custom of giving little dolls (the *sigilla*) was no
longer observed, "people still put faces and figures on breads and fruit-
cakes, a practice that is derived from those ancient bad habits *(resabios
antiguos)*." Similarly, referring to the lascivious cross-dressing dancers
of the Roman festival of Tibicines, Las Casas recalled that

> the memory and vestige of those [dances] I have witnessed in the days
> when, during the year 1507, I went from these Indies to Rome. From
> Epiphany to Shrovetide many singers and instrumentalists would get
> together and enter the houses of rich folk, where they would play
> their instruments and sing sweetly and afterward ask for their New
> Year's gifts. Other games and representations were performed in
> Rome by the maskers, who represented extremely profane and vile
> scenes of antiquity in front of a large assembly of people, and this
> happened for the whole time between Christmas and Shrovetide. In
> these practices little profit is derived for that which God demands of
> us, his Christians.[131]

It is tempting to imagine the twenty-two-year-old encomendero, fresh
from witnessing areitos in Cuba, presented with the spectacle of star-

tlingly similar "pagan" singers and dancers in the streets of the very center of Christendom.

If modern "pagans" might at certain seasons disconcertingly dance their way through the streets of Catholic Rome, in certain more peripheral regions of Europe a deeper danger might be poised to spring forth, lurid testimony that the suppressed spiritual energies of ancient Roman paganism might still be powerful enough to erupt in an alarming recrudescence of heathen beliefs and rituals. As mentioned above, chapter 152 of the *Apologética historia* is largely given over to quotation and paraphrase of Livy's account (39.8–19) of the spread of Bacchic secret associations from the Greek cities of southern Italy to the city of Rome in 186 B.C. Despite Livy's narrative of the Roman senate's ruthless suppression of this cult, Las Casas dwelt on the secret rituals themselves as evidence for "the irrationality and great bestiality of the Greeks and Romans, who have passed for wise."[132] After supplementing Livy's famous account with other Bacchic information culled from Pausanias, Plutarch, Herodotus, and others, Las Casas concluded the chapter with the revelation that "this plague-festival of those Bacchanals appears to have been reborn *(renovado)* in Bohemia"—that is, in the emergence of the Hussite sect of the "Pikardi" or "Adamites" toward the end of the second decade of the fifteenth century. Here Las Casas translated and appropriated much of chapter 41 of the *Historia boiemica* of Aeneas Sylvius Piccolomini, the future Pope Pius II, who had witnessed these "Adamites" as a papal ambassador to Bohemia.[133] Especially shocking to Piccolomini—and to Las Casas—were the spurious weddings of the "Pikardi," in which couples unblessed by the church were told to "go forth and multiply." Lest one suppose that this "pagan revival" had died out over a century earlier, Las Casas concluded this chapter with an appeal to the vastly popular 1520 treatise *De omnium gentium moribus* of Johann Boemus (bk. 3, chap. 11), which claimed that this heresy persisted still, albeit secretly, in certain parts of Bohemia. Las Casas cited Boemus's lurid account of the love feasts of the Pikardi, "where they put out all the lights and all stay in the dark, with no respect or reverence for elders or minors, nor for married or unmarried, nor for widows or virgins—they all circulate and mate." Our Dominican was duly impressed at "how similar these celebrations are to the ancient Bacchanals, the rites and festivals that were offered to Bacchus through the blindness of the Greeks and Latins and even the Romans themselves."[134] How similar, rather, to the lurid charges made against the early Christians by the Romans![135] Be that as it may, Las Casas adopted with relish Boemus's comparison of the Pikardi to the Bacchants, and so we have here a vivid expression of the conviction that Greco-Roman paganism lingered in modern Europe not only as supposedly harmless "survivals" in popular festivities or even the doll-play of little girls, but also as a full-blown—if for the time being sub rosa— revival of one of the most disturbing pagan cults.

Las Casas was by no means unique in his eagerness to identify "pagan survivals" in early modern Europe.[136] By the 1550s the detection of such cultural ghosts was being pursued with considerable gusto, and the search would intensify in the later years of the century and on into the next. But the vast majority of those who were determined to reveal the "heathen" customs of their contemporaries were Protestants unmasking what Luther termed "the pagan servitude of the Church." Thus, John Calvin claimed that Catholics not only devised their ceremonies in imitation of the Mosaic law, but also "have partly taken their pattern from the ravings of the Gentiles."[137] Pierre Viret (1511–71), friend of Calvin and chief pastor of Lausanne, asserted that Catholic rituals for the dead were "borrowed from the infidels and pagans. . . . For what purpose do all those lights serve but to declare that we are the successors of the pagans, who similarly used torches and candles at the burials and funerals of their dead."[138] In the next century the Protestant attack on "pagano-papalism" continued unabated. John Milton, for example, repeatedly denounced the early church's dangerous strategy of making "the old Christians Paganize, while by their scandalous and base conforming to heathenism they did no more . . . but bring some Pagans to Christianize."[139] And Thomas Hobbes concluded chapter 46 of part 4 of *Leviathan* with a nasty, short catalog of "old empty bottles of Gentilism, which the doctors of the Roman Church . . . have filled up again with the new wine of Christianity," a packaging error that Hobbes predicted would soon shatter the bottles. "The heathens had also their *aqua lustralis,* that is to say, *holy water.* The Church of Rome imitates them also in their *holy days.* They had their *bacchanalia;* and we have our *wakes,* answering to them. They, their *saturnalia;* and we our *carnivals,*" and so on. A late but widely read specimen of this genre was Conyers Middleton's *Letter from Rome, Showing an Exact Conformity between Popery and Paganism* (1729), a book admired by Thomas Jefferson.[140] Indeed, examples of this venerable Protestant polemical tradition may be found to this day.[141]

Just as it was natural for Protestants to exploit what they saw as lurking "paganism" in Catholic Europe, so it is not surprising that Catholics tended to be less than eager to assist them in this polemical project. Thus, Las Casas's habit of unmasking vestiges of Roman paganism in modern Spain and Italy calls for explanation. But first it will be illuminating to consider the writings of three Catholic antiquarians who did, in fact, draw attention to parallels between Greco-Roman and modern Catholic religious practices. Two of them, Flavio Biondo and Polydore Vergil, were cited in the *Apologética historia,* albeit not in this context. Though the treatise of the other, Guillaume du Choul, appeared while Las Casas was in the midst of his project and does not seem to have come to his attention, it nonetheless offers interesting parallels and contrasts to the Dominican's own strategy.

No account of Renaissance antiquarianism fails to give pride of place to the impressive pioneering achievements of the papal secretary Flavio Biondo (1392–1463).[142] Encouraged by the reception of his *Roma instaurata,* an architectural and archaeological survey of the ancient city of Rome (1444–46), he extended his researches to the rest of Roman Italy in the *Italia illustrata* of 1454. But it was Biondo's last book, *Roma triumphans* (1452–59), a survey of Roman social and political institutions and "the most significant Renaissance work on Roman history prior to the 1550's," which attracted the attention of Las Casas.[143] The first two of the treatise's ten books are devoted to religion, and it is these books that Las Casas cited in the *Apologética historia.*[144] Biondo did not often allude to what one would call modern "survivals" of Roman religious life, though he did suggest that the pagan priest's call for reverent silence *(favete linguis)* is preserved *(servatur)* by the priest officiating at a mass when he focuses attention on the lection by intoning *iube, domine, benedicere.*[145] More often, Biondo referred in passing to similarities between pagan and Christian religious and parareligious phenomena without implying any direct descent. Thus, when discussing Roman associations of laymen assigned to gods and deified emperors, he compared them with modern religious sodalities, specifically the Teutonic Knights in Germany and the Order of St. James in Spain.[146] Discussing the Roman Saturnalia, Biondo remarked: "And yet the things we do in the same month for the Nativity celebrations of our God Christ are very similar."[147] And in an apparently humorous aside he noted that it was fitting that the shacks of modern prostitutes were to be found near the site where the Romans celebrated the scandalous

Floralia.[148] A more sustained parallel between pagan and Christian Rome forms the resounding conclusion to the entire treatise.[149] Here, after describing the progress of an ancient Roman triumph through the streets of the capital, Biondo suggested that there is an impressive similarity between ancient consuls and the modern pope, between the senators and the cardinals, between the *magister militum* and the Holy Roman emperor—and so on for other dignitaries ancient and modern. Rising aloft on the wings of this fancy, he went so far as to propose that the modern *ecclesiastica res Romana* preside over the reconquest of ancient Rome's errant provinces—particularly those currently under the yoke of the Turks and Saracens. Perhaps Biondo was inspired by the antique pageantry attending Frederick III's progress to his imperial coronation in Rome in 1452—and no doubt he was also agitated by the fall of Constantinople the following year.[150] Apart from this rousing finale of Roman revival, however, Biondo's parallels between Roman antiquity and modern European life seem to have been intended to make ancient practices more vivid and familiar to a modern reader, rather than to affirm a genetic relationship.[151]

Markedly different is the case of another widely read antiquarian compendium consulted by Las Casas: the *De inventoribus rerum* of Polydore Vergil (ca. 1470–1555). In 1521 this Italian humanist and priest supplemented the three books of his 1499 treatise with five books on the origins of the rituals and customs of the Catholic Church, in which he identified a large number of the practices of his own day as survivals of ancient Roman religion.[152] While Polydore Vergil's attitude toward these pagan survivals was complex, two main tendencies do emerge. When discussing a popular custom that had attached itself to the fringes of an official religious sacrament or feast day, his attitude tended to be hostile. Thus, certain ancient Roman funerary customs were kept alive in modern Europe, especially Italy, "with an almost mad zeal."[153] Similarly, he turned to Vergil and Juvenal to explain the fact that in modern times "churches on feast days and houses celebrating weddings are adorned with tapestries; doors are hung with laurel, ivy, and other festive leaves, and thresholds are decorated with crowns and strewn with flowers," and he added that Pope Martin "both mentions and forbids these same customs."[154] And when modern Europeans celebrate New Year's, May Day, and the like, they "solemnly imitate those same ancients in singing and dancing," even though Pope Zacharias had threatened excommunication for anyone observing such pagan customs.[155]

But when "pagan survivals" could be detected in official Catholic ritual, Polydore Vergil tended to view them not as worrisome vestiges but as strategic adaptations of pagan practices crafted by the wisdom of early pontiffs and church fathers.[156] Thus, in a letter prefacing these additional books he declared his intention to show

> that the church fathers, in accepting a fair number of those practices acted piously and sensibly, for, eager to lead still barbarous peoples to the practice of true piety, they judged that they ought to be attracted by the seasonings of gentleness, for they did not utterly abhor or abolish their customs, but improved them, in order that no danger be created for religion if they were to accept too little or change too little.[157]

Las Casas, we may recall, had similarly suggested that the *silicernium* of Saturnalia had been diverted into the Feast of the Chair of St. Peter (chap. 151) and the Cerealia into Candlemas (chap. 154).

Some of Polydore Vergil's examples of strategically borrowed ecclesiastical practices are startlingly bold. Thus, countering those who maintained that nuns did not antedate the time of Jerome, he insisted that "it is clear that first the apostles and then our popes introduced the religious orders of women on the model of the vestal virgins *(exemplo Vestalium Virginum)* so that both sexes might serve God in chastity."[158] Las Casas himself compared the shearing of the vestal virgins with the cropping of the locks of nuns "en nuestra cristiandad," and we have seen that he had invoked the privileges of the vestals as a supposedly persuasive parallel for Christian clerical immunity in a treatise composed in Mexico in 1546.[159] But Polydore Vergil's hypothesis of strategic imitation of pagan customs as the origin of Christian nuns and his attribution of that custom to the apostles themselves surely pushed the limits of acceptable speculation. It will come as no surprise that the phrase "exemplo Vestalium Virginum" was removed from editions of *De inventoribus rerum* when the book began to encounter difficulties with the Holy Office.

Another strategic borrowing from pagan cult by the leaders of the Christian Church, according to this remarkable volume, was nothing short of the very words that gave the Mass its name. When Catholic priests dismissed their congregations with the formula "Ite, missa est," their voices echoed the accents of pagan priests, for it was Polydore Vergil's contention "that our priests borrowed it from the customs and practices of the ancients."[160] Also startling are Polydore Vergil's claims that the Roman Lupercalia was one origin of the Christian confraternities of flagellants, and that Christian sodalities were explicitly modeled on Roman *sodalitates* (religious fraternities).[161] Similarly, the papal establishment of regular periods of fasting was borrowed from the Romans, and so, once again, the Christian pontiffs "changed the empty rites of the ancients to the true practice of piety."[162]

It is interesting to see how close Polydore Vergil came in such passages to the emerging Protestant polemical tradition of thrashing "pagano-papalism." Both Protestants and Polydore Vergil emphasized the Catholic hierarchy's deliberate retention of pagan elements, particularly during the Constantinian period. But while Protestants excoriated the decision to compromise with pagan practices in order to fish for souls, Polydore Vergil praised the wisdom of this strategy, always emphasizing that the pagan customs adopted were markedly improved in the process. But why would a Catholic author choose to identify and discuss such borrowings and survivals in the first place? Here, surely, the subject of his book as a whole was the determining factor. *De inventoribus rerum* is, after all, a book about how things came to be. Given that the inventors of customs and devices in the first three books were, more often than not, the Greeks and Romans, it can scarcely be surprising to find them taking their place alongside the Jews in the last five books as the originators of Christian customs as well, both official and popular. In time, inevitably, many of these passages fell afoul of the Holy Office, and later editions of the still popular book deleted them. No less inevitably, Protestant publishers printed editions of the full text—or even polemically intensified versions, such as the English translation perpetrated by Thomas Langley in 1546.[163]

Three and a half decades after Polydore Vergil published his expanded edition of *De inventoribus rerum,* and during the very years Las Casas was hard at work on his *Apologética historia,* the Lyonnais nobleman and coin collector Guillaume du Choul published his attractively illustrated *Discours de la religion des anciens Romains* (1556).[164] A pioneering attempt to extract antiquarian information from coins and medals, the *Discours* also offered bold comparisons of Roman religious life with religious practices in contemporary Catholic Europe. Given the escalating clashes between Catholics and Calvinists in the Lyon of the 1550s, casual readers of Du Choul's treatise have assumed that he was a Calvinist, but an attentive examination of his text leaves little doubt that he was at least a nominal Catholic and decidedly non-Calvinist in his view of the religious rituals of his day.[165] Thus, his unusual, even eccentric book is worth comparing with the even more unusual and eccentric project of Las Casas, even though there is no hint that Du Choul's *Discours* came to the Dominican's attention.

Of the twenty-three specific pagan-Christian parallels in Du Choul's book, nineteen are straightforward analogues of the sort "Ancient Roman practice X resembles modern Christian practice Y." Usually he signaled these parallels with a simple *comme nous faisons . . .* or with the adjective *semblable.* It seems plausible to assume that Du Choul primarily intended these parallels as illustrative, as ways of making Roman practices "come alive" for readers in mid-sixteenth-century Lyon. Perhaps the most noteworthy aspect of these analogues is the fact that each of them refers to strictly ecclesiastical matters: holy water fonts, priestly dress and tonsure, ritual procedures, and so forth. Thus, for example, Du Choul noted that new vestal virgins had their hair shorn "as do the nuns of today."[166] On the other hand, Du Choul never attempted to find any pagan parallel or source for the kind of parareligious custom that especially bothered Las Casas, despite the fact that such popular customs and celebrations were, as Natalie Zemon Davis has noted, highly developed in Lyon in this period.[167] This restriction to "official" religious life, be it pagan or Christian, may simply reflect the limitations of Du Choul's main source of evidence: the Roman coin collection of which he was so proud.

At moments, however, Du Choul was emboldened to suggest that contemporary Christian (Catholic) ceremonial practices not only echoed ancient rituals, but were in fact derived from paganism. A brief example of this occurs in his subsidiary discussion of Egyptian religion. The morning prayers of the Egyptian priests "have been followed by those of our Christian religion, who recite the office of the matins and still observe that which the Egyptians did."[168] Elsewhere, he suggested that "what the pagans did in their laughable superstitions we have transferred *(nous avons transferé)* to our Christian religion when we have our Agnus Dei figurines and bells consecrated and blessed so that they may take on the power to dispel storms and bad weather."[169] A more striking example appears a few pages earlier, at the end of his discussion of Roman sacrificial procedure.[170] After comparing the officiating Roman priest's concluding "I licet" with the "Ite, missa est" of a Catholic priest (recall here book 5, chapter 11 of Polydore Vergil's *De inventoribus rerum,* discussed above), our antiquarian proceeded to point out that these sacrifices were performed "in their temples and basilicas, which our people have taken over *(ont usurpé)* for the use of our religion." This was more than pragmatic adaptation of conveniently available architecture, however, for Du Choul went on to suggest that modern Christians appropriately emulated the Roman pagans in believing that divinity should be worshiped in suitably impressive buildings, "for there is nothing in which one should put more diligence, thought, hard work, and care than in building our temples well and in adorning them with triumphant and magnificent things; for the temple that is well served and adorned adds an ornament to the city where it is." Continuing in this distinctly non-Calvinist vein, he added that houses for God deserve at least as much magnificence as palaces and other human habitations, and that a fitting adornment to piety were "temples that delight our hearts and attract us with their grace and impressiveness, and the ancients affirmed that piety was honored when we visit our temples and pray to the gods." Not only were Christians right to appropriate the remains and designs of pagan buildings, but Christian Europe also quite fittingly inherited the entire pagan complex of grand religious display and civic pride.

Though these are the only passages in the body of Du Choul's treatise where he suggested that Christians had actually borrowed from pagan religious customs, the claim returns spectacularly in the concluding words of the treatise:

> And if we examine carefully, we shall recognize that many institutions of our religion have been taken and transferred *(ont esté prises & translatées)* from the ceremonies of the Egyptians and the pagans: such as the tunics and surplices, the tonsure of our priests, their inclinations of the head around the altar, the sacrificial pomp, the music of the temples, adorations, prayers and supplications, processions and litanies, and many other things that our priests take over *(usurpent)* in our rites, and they refer to one single God Jesus Christ that which the ignorance, false religion, and mad superstition of the pagans showed to their gods and to mortal men after their apotheosis.[171]

We find here a much bolder and more extensive suggestion of Christian borrowing from pagan practices than the corresponding passages in the body of the text had implied, and it is perfectly understandable that at least one scholar has concluded, on the basis of this passage, that Du

Choul's book was a salvo in "the Protestant assault" on Catholic "paganism."[172] But the antiquarian's tendency to identify Catholicism as "nostre religion," as well as his defense of magnificent church buildings, should disabuse one of that suspicion.

Du Choul was an intriguing and enigmatic scholar, whose fascination with pagan-Christian analogues and "pagan survivals" within Christianity begs for—and frustrates—explanation. Particularly when one takes into account the explosive nature of the community in which he wrote, his non-Protestant account of "pagano-papalism" is perplexing. But whatever his deeper motivations, strategies, and even confusions might have been, surely at least part of the answer to this puzzle is simply the well-known avocational hazard of all antiquarians: the tendency to view their discoveries as fundamentally *theirs*. This would be particularly true of an antiquarian such as Du Choul, who did in fact literally own his evidence, in the form of the coins that his book so lovingly reproduced.[173] These bits of metal, whose exploitation for antiquarian purposes Du Choul was hereby pioneering, revealed to his proprietary gaze a rich religious life that he inevitably came to think of as his own—indeed, he could refer to ancient Roman religious functionaries as "nos Pontifes & ministres des Dieux" and could easily slip into the first person when claiming that the pagans "affirmed that piety was honored when we visit our temples and make sacrifices to the gods"—and, hence, comparison to familiar Catholic rituals would have seemed perfectly natural.[174] Du Choul's interest in pagan survivals, then, reveals him as a true son of the Renaissance in his eagerness to reach across the centuries that separated him from his beloved Romans and to experience an intense feeling of cultural and even spiritual kinship with the classical age.

As early- to mid-sixteenth-century Catholic excavators of Catholic "pagan survivals," Polydore Vergil and Guillaume du Choul offer rare and illuminating parallels for Las Casas's recurrent identification of ghosts of Roman paganism haunting the Europe of his day. Both antiquarians had powerful incentives for laying bare such practices and thereby risking the charge of corroborating Protestant controversialists. Polydore Vergil was nudged in this direction by the internal imperative of his chosen subject, for his book was an account of the origins of customs and institutions, and the extension of his investigation to the origins of religious practices in modern Europe easily led this well-read humanist to find here, too, the spectral presence of classical antecedents. Guillaume du Choul, proud collector of numismatic windows onto Roman antiquity, was eager to invite his contemporaries to shift their gaze from the lethally complicated France of his day to an alternative religious world, at once fascinatingly alien and reassuringly familiar. We might expect, then, that Las Casas, too, had strong incentives to play the risky game of finding vestiges of Roman paganism lurking under the practices of modern Catholic Europe. One obvious motive would be the intense anti-Roman bias generated in him by Sepúlveda's detested *Democrates secundus*. But Las Casas's religious archaeology is likely to have been inspired also by yet another polemical project.

While Las Casas was unusual among sixteenth-century Catholics in displaying so keen an interest in "pagan survivals" in modern Europe, a nervous preoccupation with far more urgently worrisome "vestiges" haunted many of his fellow clerics in the New World. Indeed, we may thank this fear for some of the most informative Spanish accounts of Amerindian life and customs. Thus, the Franciscan Bernardino de Sahagún opened the prologue to his massive *Historia general de las cosas de Nueva España* with the trope that a good doctor must first understand the nature of the disease he aims to cure—the disease here being, of course, the entire body of "heathen" customs the book proceeded to chronicle so thoroughly.

> The sins of idolatry and idolatrous rites and idolatrous superstitions and auguries and false beliefs and idolatrous ceremonies have not yet utterly passed away. In order to preach against these things, and even to know that they exist, one must know how they practiced them in the time of their idolatry, for it is our ignorance of this that allows them to perform many idolatrous acts in our presence without our knowing it.[175]

Sahagún's 1585 treatise *Arte adivinatoria* zeroed in on the supposedly expurgated Nahua soothsaying calendar, the *tonalpohualli,* as a screen behind which native paganism could pursue its immemorial subterranean existence, for in their minds the natives "have not left off holding their gods as gods, nor rendering them services, offerings, and celebrations on the sly."[176] Similarly, the Dominican Diego Durán, writing his *Book of the Gods and Rites* in the mid-1570s, declared that his "intention was and is to alert priests to the omens and idolatries of these peoples . . . for although it is true that the Indians are aware of God now and are Christians, who could deny that among a thousand good ones there are a hundred bad who still keep their bad habits *(resávios)*, like ill-broken colts?"[177] It was this fear that was later to inspire the notorious *Extirpación* of seventeenth- and eighteenth-century Peru.[178]

Those who attempted to counter these suspicions of lingering native idolatry could, of course, venture a categorical denial. Thus, the Franciscan Toribio de Benavente ("Motolinía") confidently insisted that "wherever the teaching and Word of Christ have reached, there has not remained a bit [of idolatry] known or needing to be taken into account."[179] True enough, Motolinía went on, certain Spaniards, motivated by religious zeal and by a hefty dose of greed, were able to locate and confiscate Indian idols, but what they were handed were not objects of living worship but freshly disinterred figurines that the Indians themselves would have preferred to have left rotting in the ground. Why, in some cases Indians were so pressured to hand over idols that they had to resort to making new ones simply to have something to surrender and thus get the Spaniards off their backs![180]

Las Casas attempted a very different strategy. Rather than replicate his old rival Motolinía's attempt to give the lie direct to those who scented native "pagan survivals," he adopted the simple expedient of never once mentioning in all the seventeen chapters of the *Apologética historia* devoted to New World ritual the mere possibility of a survival of the ancient practices. On the contrary, he often made a point of claiming that in many ways the precontact Indians had in fact anticipated Catholic rituals. Thus, the inhabitants of Hispaniola offered choral responses to the prayers of their priests, "as when we answer 'amen,'" while the habit of some Florida Indians of extending their hands to the sun and touching their faces "resembles what the inhabitants of Galicia do at Communion, for they raise their hands when they adore the Host and then touch their faces."[181] Indeed, speaking of a Totonac ritual once performed in Chiapas ("our bishopric"), he went so far as to suggest that the shared consumption of a mixture of rubber, seeds, and the blood of three sacrificed boys was practiced "in the manner of Communion" [a semejanza de comunión].[182] In addition, as noted above, he repeatedly offered the precontact fasts and ceremonies of mortification as not only parallel to Catholic practices but in fact worthy models for Christian piety.

But while Las Casas repeatedly suggested that native rituals had anticipated Christianity and thus paved the way for its acceptance, he never openly admitted the possibility of the survival of the old ways underneath or alongside the new. If one were determined to find crypto-pagans in the mid–sixteenth century, he insinuated, the place to look would not be New Spain or Peru but Spain and Italy! Rather than attempting to scrape out the last motes of precontact New World "heathenism," modern Europeans should attend to the pagan beams in their own eyes. While Aztec human sacrifice, for example, was safely a thing of the past, the rites of the Roman Flora, that apotheosized prostitute, were still unwittingly celebrated by modern Europeans. Why, every Spanish girl playing with a doll was keeping alive the practice of Sicyonian maidens offering idols to their lascivious Aphrodite! Here, then, we have a further explanation, in addition to his settled aversion to the Romans, for Las Casas's dangerous game of pointing out pagan survivals in modern Europe. Coordinated with his silence about surviving heathen practices in the New World, Las Casas's detection of lingering paganism in Catholic Europe was calculated to defuse suspicions about the orthodoxy of the freshly converted pagans across the Atlantic.

Indians versus Romans as Empire Builders and Warriors: Las Casas, the Inca Garcilaso de la Vega, Alonso de Ercilla, and Gerónimo de Vivar

An early modern admirer of the classical world could well have objected that ancient Roman religious beliefs and practices offered unworthily safe targets for Las Casas's attacks. After all, despite Polybius's claim that Roman religious attitudes constituted the principal superiority of their constitution (*Histories* 6.56.6), few postclassical champions of Rome would have singled out Roman religious beliefs and rituals as the most admirable and exemplary aspects of their civilization. Accordingly, Las Casas was aware that he needed to demonstrate the superiority of at least some New World natives on terrain more advantageous to the Romans: the acquisition and administration of an empire. And since empire building was predicated upon martial valor, another specialty of the Romans, it was inevitable that ancient Romans would find themselves competing with modern Indians as warriors—though Las Casas, for his own reasons, proved less eager than some other observers to referee this particular contest.

But let us begin with a tenaciously exemplary product of Roman imperialism that indeed both followed and facilitated the movement of victorious troops, but that also served panegyrists as the epitome of the blessings of the Pax Romana.[183] Among the most enduringly impressive monuments to the Romans' administration of a far-flung empire are the remains of the network of roads that held that empire together. A Spaniard, of course, would have been especially struck by the remains of the Via Augusta, which stretched from the Pillars of Hercules to the Pyrenees, where it joined the Via Domitia. The latter then passed through Gaul and led on to Italy and Rome, thus forming "a crucial link between the most Romanized areas of Spain and the capital of the empire."[184] Near the end of the last (chap. 262) of his sixty-two chapters demonstrating the ease with which New World societies met Aristotle's sixth and last requirement for civilized life, the administration of well-ordered states, Las Casas adduced the superiority of the Incas to the Romans in the imperial art of road building:

> Then there is the astonishing nature *(monstruosidad)* of the aforesaid roads—I term it thus because this is the most remarkable thing, a most extraordinary work, a product, in my view, of the greatest genius in this species of construction that the world has ever seen. The most excellent of them, the road from the mountains to the plains, runs at least six hundred or even eight hundred leagues, and they say that it goes on to the provinces of Chile, that is to say, over eleven hundred leagues. What road, what skill, what most ingenious structures have these roads not surpassed? In the opinion of any people on earth they would be judged superior to all other heroic works and would be deemed even more worthy than the seven man-made wonders of the world. I have seen in Spain and Italy some fragments of the road that they say the Romans built from Spain to Italy, but it is all a despicable thing *(asco es todo)* in comparison with the aforementioned road of these peoples and this land.[185]

This suggestively rich passage constitutes an interesting variation on a strategy of persuasion frequently employed by those two cordial enemies Fernández de Oviedo and Las Casas: an assertion of authority based on autopsy. Usually, the strategy depends upon what the author has seen with his own eyes in the New World, a privileged fund of first-hand experience denied to armchair students of the Indies.[186] In this instance, however, Las Casas was inspired to compensate for his lack of autoptic authority concerning a New World phenomenon—he never visited Peru, though not for lack of trying—by appealing to his inspection of an Old World, ancient Roman artifact, the Via Augusta and Via Domitia. And what did this direct experience reveal? In the first instance, of course, it would have suggested ancient Rome's attempt to link Spain to Italy—Las Casas's "Roman imperial theme" in its technological aspect. But no less clear to Las Casas's critical gaze was the ultimate failure of the Roman project. All that was left for the Dominican's inspection was "some fragments" [algunos pedazos] of this would-be umbilical cord linking Spain to her imperial mother-city. But the failure of the Romans was not simply an inability to enjoy Jupiter's promise of "imperium sine fine." The surviving fragments of this road are sufficient to establish that the original structure was a jerry-built embarrassment from the very beginning—*asco es todo,* a very strong phrase indeed.[187] Thus, even in a case where circumstances prevented Las Casas from appealing to autopsy to establish the superiority of the New World cultures, he deftly and imperturbably employed it to establish the inferiority of the "classical" civilizations of the Old World.

Though Las Casas was perfectly capable of concocting this denigration of Roman roads on his own initiative, two earlier works might have given him an additional nudge. One was the second volume of the *Crónica del Perú* by the prolific chronicler Pedro de Cieza de León. When Cieza died around the age of thirty-four in 1554, the year after the first volume of his chronicle was published in Seville, he left the remaining three volumes unpublished—they would not see print until the nineteenth century. But in his will he expressed the desire that, should his executors fail to publish these volumes, they should send the manuscript "to the bishop of Chiapas at the court and give it to him with the said charge that he print it."[188] Though this command does not appear to have been carried out, it certainly implies a close connection between these two men in Seville between 1552 (when Las Casas established residence there) and 1554, and it is probable that Cieza was relying on an interest in his manuscripts that Las Casas would not surprisingly have exhibited while laboring on his *Apologética historia.*[189] Chapter 63 of the second volume (which is now generally known as *Del señorío de los Incas*) offers an account of the construction, upon the orders of Guayna (Huaina) Capac, of the road from Cuzco to Quito with a link to the road to Chile—that is, the same linked roads whose *monstruosidad* we have just seen Las Casas celebrating. Like Las Casas, Cieza singled out for unfavorable comparison the Roman Via Augusta in Spain.

Oh, what great feat can be mentioned of Alexander or of any of the powerful kings who ruled the world—did they order such a road as this built, or even come up with the provisions which were found on this road? The road the Romans built which passed through Spain was nothing *(no fué nada)* in comparison with this.[190]

But there is also the tantalizing possibility that Las Casas's denigration of the Roman road from Spain to Italy was a fleeting dig at a recently printed celebration of Roman rule in Spain, the 1539 Spanish translation of Marineo Sículo's *De rebus Hispaniae memorabilibus*. In support of his claim in book 4 that "whatever is ancient and worthy of being remembered in Spain today was built by the Romans," Marineo offered the bridge at Alcántara and, of course, the great Roman roads.[191] And in a parenthetical remark not found in the Latin version we read that "some fragments that remain of this road are in Italy, for that is where it began." The phrase "algunos pedazos," offered in the Spanish version of Marineo Sículo's book as neutral testimony to the once impressive length of this road, resurfaces in Las Casas's account as a surviving proof of the contemptible paltriness of Roman imperial technology when compared with the feats of the road builders of the Inca empire.

But how did Incas and Romans acquire these vast territories linked by such ambitious roads? Chapter 251 of the *Apologética historia* traces the growth of the Inca empire against the background of a schematic history of Rome's rise to dominion in the Mediterranean. Rather vaguely appealing to Livy, Augustine, and Orosius, Las Casas offered an account of Roman expansion in three phases: (1) an initial period of unjust attacks on neighbors or provocations of attacks by them; (2) a period when "the unjust wars some nations initiated against them became the excuse for them, fighting in their own defense, to conquer and subjugate them so that they might not presume to rise up against them"; and finally (3) a phase when, "after they were already powerful, avarice and the ambition to extend their empire . . . generated very unjust wars."[192] To elucidate the central phase of Roman expansion through relatively just wars, he cited book 4, chapter 15, of the *City of God*, a chapter in which Augustine acidly suggested that the Romans' exploitation of the wickedness of their neighbors should have suggested to them that they worship Injustice as a goddess alongside the cult of Victory. For once less critical of the Romans than Augustine, Las Casas observed that a by-product of the just imperial wars of the Romans was that the resulting reputation of the Romans for valor, power, and good government generated even more allies and subjects. As an example, he noted that "Judas Maccabaeus, having heard the news of the virtues and the great power of the Romans, sent ambassadors so he could join in friendship with them." Las Casas neglected to mention that one of the reports that had particularly impressed Judas was of the Roman seizure of Spain with its gold and silver mines, a reference that we have seen Melchor Cano taking out of context in order to denounce Roman imperial avarice!

Las Casas then presented the imperial conquests of the Inca Pachacuti (Pachacutec) as approximating this second phase of Roman empire-building, the phase of expansion through justified wars. And yet the empire inherited and expanded by Pachacuti was "more just and upright" [más justo y recto] than that of the Romans, for the Inca was able to build upon a first phase that had not been sullied by the unjust aggression and provocation that had characterized the beginnings of Roman expansion. Upon this nobler basis and before launching his own just wars of conquest, Pachacuti wisely set about solidifying Inca imperial rule first by "ordering and adjusting religious matters." Establishing a cult of the sun, converting palaces into temples to the new divinity, and styling himself "son of the Sun," Pachacuti launched a program of religious and moral reform manifestly more respectable than that which Rome's second king, Numa Pompilius, owed to the advice of his supposedly divine consort, the nymph Egeria. Indeed, guided solely by natural illumination, this great Inca reformer "gives a sterling, imitable example to Catholic kings and emperors"! But his genius as imperial statesman was not confined to religious policy; this "good and most prudent king next devoted himself to ordering what was fitting for the government and common good of his kingdoms and to polishing and burnishing all his republics with a beautiful, a perfect (insofar as was possible without faith in the true God), and a new manner of public order *(policia)*." The key to this political revitalization was the establishment of a new civic order in Cuzco as a model for the rest of the Inca empire. Vital to this project was the division of the imperial capital into several districts, thereby facilitating both effective supervision of the populace by government officials and a productively healthy spirit of competition *(envidia virtuosa)*.

A striking parallel to Las Casas's comparison of Inca empire-building with that of the Romans, with a similar focus on the importance of the imperial capital, is to be found in the first part of the *Royal Commentaries of the Incas,* which the complex mestizo historian, the Inca Garcilaso de la Vega (1539–1616), published in Lisbon in 1609.[193] In his description of the imperial city of Cuzco in book 7, chapter 8, he derided the justly short-lived Spanish rechristening of Cuzco as "New Toledo," for Toledo and Cuzco failed to resemble each other in the least. A more appropriate Old World sister city for Cuzco was ancient Rome.

> For Cuzco in relation to her empire was another Rome in relation to hers, and the one can thus be compared to the other, for they resembled each other in the most noble respects: first and foremost, in having been founded by their first kings; secondly, in the many diverse nations which they conquered and subjected to their empire; thirdly, in the large number of such good and truly excellent laws which they established for the government of their states; and fourthly, in producing so many and such excellent men and raising them with good civic and military teachings.[194]

Up to this point, Garcilaso scrupulously maintained parity between ancient Rome and that "otra Roma" in Peru (an epithet for Cuzco he used also in the prologue to the *Comentarios reales*), much as Las Casas had toyed with the idea that Incas and Romans resembled each other in their methods of expanding their empires. Suddenly, though, like Las Casas, he revealed the crucial superiority of one over the other, but the winner this time was ancient Rome—or so, at least, an unwary reader might be tricked into supposing. Expanding on the fourth point of comparison, the education of so many excellent youths, Garcilaso admitted, with a touch of ironic bitterness, that "here Rome had the advantage over Cuzco—not in having brought them up better—but in being luckier *(mas venturosa)* in having attained the art of writing and having by this means made her sons immortal." In a deflation of Rome rather subtler than any perpetrated by Las Casas, Garcilaso ironically conceded the advantage *(ventaja)* to the Romans through no natural superiority of their own, but strictly through their good luck in having become literate and thereby able to publicize themselves efficiently. Garcilaso here indulged himself in some general reflections on the rival claims of the pen and the sword. Whether skill in the one contributed more to the state than prowess in the other, and whichever owed the greatest debt to the other, ancient Rome was enviably and indisputably blessed with an abundance of distinguished wielders of both. And in Julius Caesar the Romans could boast a single paragon in both spheres of activity—a point anticipated by Bernal Díaz del Castillo, who fancied himself a rival to Caesar as chronicler of his own martial exploits, as well as veteran of even more battles.

Abruptly Garcilaso pulled himself away from these topoi on "los de las armas" and "los de las plumas" and sorrowfully acknowledged

> the ill luck of our country *(la desdicha de nuestra patria):* for although it had sons distinguished in arms, and of great judgment and understanding, and very able and capable in learning *(ciencias)*, the fact that they did not have writing meant that they did not leave behind the memory of their great deeds and penetrating thoughts, and so both deeds and thoughts perished with their state. Only a few of their deeds and utterances remain, having been entrusted to a feeble tradition and wretched teaching of words by fathers to sons—which itself has been lost with the entry of the new people and the change to alien lordship and government—as always tends to happen when empires are destroyed and change hands.

Garcilaso expressed here a more pessimistic view of the worth of oral tradition than Oviedo had expressed with regard to the Antillean areitos or Cieza de León (echoed by Las Casas) in referring to the "romances y villancicos" through which the Incas preserved the memory of their kings.[195] But this brief expression of despair soon gave way to his recollection of the very mission that this entire magnificent chronicle embodies: "Stimulated by the desire to preserve the ancient traditions of my country—those few that have remained—I have devoted myself to the overwhelming task . . . of recording its ancient polity until it came to an end." Accordingly, he buckled down at last to the task of offering an account of this "other Rome," Cuzco, his country's "mother and mistress," lest its ancient glory pass into oblivion. It was Garcilaso's mission, then, single-handedly to repair his motherland's cultural gap by mastering the grand old Roman art of immortalizing on paper the memories of an entire people.

But Garcilaso's rich and moving comparison of Cuzco to Rome reveals yet another shrewd rhetorical strategy. The idea that the Incas excelled at deeds but lacked the self-promoting advantage of the written word was a clever adaptation to the New World of a topos that had been current in Spain for some time: the lament that the Romans' success in trumpeting their own glory constituted a proleptic diminution of the fame properly due to the exploits of the Spaniards in the Reconquest—and, later, in her various foreign and overseas ventures. Like Garcilaso's encomium of the inhabitants of Cuzco, this "lament" was in fact a boast, a celebration of Spain as a land of doers rather than writers. This pride in Spanish "activismo" appears to have surfaced first in the fifteenth century, in the writings of Juan de Mena, Rodrigo Sánchez de Arévalo (whose use of it we have discussed in the previous chapter), Fernán Pérez de Guzmán, Fernando de Pulgar, and the author of *Los hechos del condestable don Miguel Lucas de Iranzo*—and even in Montalvo's preface to *Amadís de Gaula*. In the sixteenth century it cropped up, as J. A. Maravall has noted, in "writers beyond counting."[196] It is quite possible that this industriously employed topos may have played a role in the development of the conquistadors' "superiority complex" vis-à-vis the Romans, their resentment that their greater deeds and harder work still received less glory in contemporary Europe than the relatively modest achievements of those master self-publicists the Romans. Ironically, this topos was itself of Roman provenance. In chapter 8 of his *Bellum Catilinae*, Sallust offered the greater fame of Athenian than Roman deeds as proof of the truism that

> luck rules in every area *(fortuna in omni re dominatur)*. The deeds of the Athenians, in my opinion, were sufficiently splendid and distinguished, but nonetheless somewhat less so than reported by publicity *(fama)*. But since very talented writers arose there, the deeds of the Athenians are celebrated throughout the world as preeminent. Thus the excellence of those who performed the deeds has a reputation matched by the ability of famous intellects to extol those deeds. But the Roman people never had that opportunity, for each of their most intelligent men was extremely busy; nobody exercised his intellect without exercising his body; and each of the best people preferred to act rather than to use words, to have his fine deeds praised by others rather than to recount the deeds of others.

Notice how emphatically Garcilaso sustained Sallust's insistence that this supposed superiority of the one culture to the other was a matter of luck, *fortuna*. Rome was not naturally superior to Cuzco; she was "luckier" [mas venturosa] than the civilization whose "desdicha" the mestizo historian lamented—and hoped to ameliorate. In cleaving so closely to the classical model here, Garcilaso scored a particularly deft hit against Spanish readers who had grown so used to reading smug appropriations of Sallust's words to promote "the idea that the Spaniards preferred to perform great deeds than to write about them."[197]

But Garcilaso was not the first to appropriate this topos for the natives of the New World. Four decades earlier it had surfaced in an investigative report drafted in accord with a royal *cédula* by a conscientious and impressively compassionate judge and royal official. Reflecting and intensifying the Crown's ambivalence over the actions and power of the encomenderos of New Spain, Alonso de Zorita composed his *Brief and Summary Relation of the Lords of New Spain* between 1566 and 1570, after a stay of some ten years in New Spain. Roughly in the middle of this substantial report, Zorita paused to reflect on the habit of many Spaniards—even those who, like Cortés himself, should have known better—of referring to the natives of New Spain as "barbarians."[198] Such calumniators of the Indians should realize that "there are among them some good Latinists and well-educated men"—a reference to the Colegio de Santa Cruz de Tlatelolco, even though its most impressive days were already over.[199] In a strikingly Lascasian tone, Zorita proceeded to ridicule the Greeks and Romans for denigrating the manifestly civilized Egyptians, to whom they owed so much, significantly singling out for censure a Hispano-Roman writer: "Martial called the Egyptians barbarians in the first of his epigrams because their language, customs, and idolatry differed from those of the Romans. The Romans and Greeks called peoples of different speech 'barbarians' for the same reason."[200] So modern Spaniards had simply adopted a bad classical habit. Zorita then interjected a comparison of the Indians of New Spain with the common folk of old Spain, for those who deride the New World natives as simple-minded barbarians because Spanish entrepreneurs manage to make a profit selling them worthless junk should realize that "we could also call the Spaniards barbarians in this sense, for at the present day, even in the best-governed cities, little toy swords and horses, and brass whistles, and little wire snakes, and castanets with bells are sold in the streets." Then, after reminding his readers once more of the "good Latinists and musicians" [buenos latinos y músicos] to be found among the present-day Indians of New Spain, Zorita drew explicitly upon Sallust's famous remark in order to drive home a flattering comparison of the Indians with the ancient Romans:

> From what has been told above we may also judge whether these Indians, who observed their laws so strictly as to impose the most rigorous penalties on their own sons, were at all inferior to the famous Romans and other ancient peoples in justice and government, or less ingenious in justifying their wars. Whoever considers the question maturely must conclude that they were the equals of the ancients in all respects, or fell but little short of the ancients in their achievements. But just as Alexander envied Achilles in that Achilles had a Homer to sing his feats, so the Indians could envy the ancients for having many excellent historians to celebrate their exploits. As Sallust observes, and as St. Jerome remarks in his life of St. Hilarion, the lives of the virtuous have only the fame and influence that is in the power of writers of genius to grant them. The picture writings in which the Indians recorded their history are either damaged or lost, and the only persons who have seriously attempted to study them are a small number of religious.[201]

The interest in the preconquest Indians' rigorous punishment of their own children appears to have been something of a topos in sixteenth-century Spanish accounts of native culture: Cieza de León, for instance, emphasized it in the first part of his *Crónica del Perú*, published in Seville in 1553.[202] In the context of an explicit comparison with the ancient Romans, it inevitably reminds one of Lucius Junius Brutus presiding over the execution of his own treasonous sons, a powerful exemplum of inflexible rectitude ambiguously celebrated by Vergil (*Aen.* 6.817–23) and condemned as unnaturally harsh by Augustine (*City of God* 3.16). The anecdote of Alexander's jealous tears over Achilles' luck in having attracted the lyre of Homer was a familiar story in antiquity, told by Cicero *(Arch.* 10: "O fortunate adulescens . . ."), Plutarch (*Alex.* 15.8), and Arrian (*Anab.* 1.12), and it enjoyed wide vogue in the Middle Ages and Renaissance. Zorita was surely not the first to pair it with Sallust's pseudolament, but his application of both to the Mesoamerican Indians was deft and effective.

But as Fortuna would have it, around the very time that Zorita wrote these words, a population of New World natives surpassed the luck of Alexander by attracting a latter-day Homer—in the unlikely guise of a Spanish conquistador who fought against them. To add to the surprise, these lucky Indians were not empire- and city-builders like the Aztecs and the Incas; rather, they were remote and supposedly primitive inhabitants of Spain's colonial frontier in Chile. Four years after the Spanish settlement of Concepción in 1549 and the fatal discovery of gold shortly thereafter, the Araucanian Indians rose up against their new masters in a revolt stunningly inaugurated by the crushing defeat of the Spaniards at Tucapel, the death of the governor Pedro de Valdivia, and the sack of Concepción. When the young courtier (former page of Prince Philip), soldier, and poet Alonso de Ercilla (1533–94) arrived in Chile in 1557, Spanish setbacks persisted, but in November of that year the fortunes of the Indians declined sharply with the battles of Las Lagunillas and Millarapue. Ercilla served for two years in the ongoing struggle against the rebels, exploiting pauses in the battles and skirmishes to scribble down the first major poem written by a European in America: the romantic epic *La Araucana,* which began to appear in print in 1569, after Ercilla had returned to high society and diplomatic missions in Spain. (Parts 2 and 3 appeared in 1578 and 1589.)

The first two stanzas of this intriguing poem profess to establish a delicate balance between praise of "the valor, the deeds, and the prowess of those brave Spaniards" who sought to subjugate the Araucanians and commemoration of the "very remarkable doings *(cosas . . . harto notables)* of people who obey no king, memorably bold undertakings that rightly deserve to be celebrated *(temerarias empresas memorables / que celebrarse con razón merecen)."* True, Ercilla proceeded to declare that the worthiness of these Indians served "to exalt the Spaniards, for the victor is not more esteemed than the vanquished is held in high regard *(pues no es el vencedor más estimado / de aquello en que el vencido es reputado)."*[203] But undermining this avowed patriotic aim is the frequently astonishing fervor of Ercilla's admiration for the Araucanians' valor and their passion for liberty—and his powerful condemnation of the cowardice and avarice of their Spanish foes.[204] Noting that Ercilla nostalgically "assimilates the Araucanians with a feudal nobility already becoming outmoded in Europe," David Quint suggests that the poem projects onto the New World the contemporary European "crisis of the aristocracy." At the same time, Quint argues, Ercilla's poetics reflect a defeat of the Roman "victors' epic" (Vergil's *Aeneid*) at the hands of the Roman "losers' epic" (Lucan's *Pharsalia*), with the help of Italian romance and its implicit hostility to imperialis-

tic "linearity."[205] For our present purposes, what is especially interesting is the way Ercilla's respect for the Araucanian "other," however
covertly "Eurocentric" that respect may be, aligns him at certain key
moments with Las Casas's strategy of celebrating the New World
natives, not the Spanish conquistadors, as the superiors of the ancient
Greeks and Romans.[206]

Before inspecting the classical armature of Ercilla's Araucanians, we
need to register the significance of the preeminent virtue for which he
honored them. As the great Venezuelan scholar and poet Andrés Bello
noted in 1841 in a pioneering essay on Ercilla's epic, "the concepts on
which he dwells most lovingly are those of Araucanian heroism."[207] In
his prose preface Ercilla offered a forthright defense of this disconcerting preoccupation:

> And if it seems to anyone that I reveal myself as somewhat inclined to
> the side of the Araucanians, treating their affairs and acts of bravery
> (valentías) at greater length than barbarians deserve, nevertheless, if
> we wish to look at their upbringing, customs, and manner of waging
> and training for war, we will see that many peoples have not proved
> superior to them, and there are few who have defended their land
> with such constancy and firmness against enemies as fierce as the
> Spaniards. And indeed it is cause for wonder that the Araucanians—
> not possessing more than twenty leagues of territory, without having
> within that territory a single developed settlement, nor a wall, nor a
> moated house (casa fuerte) for their defense, nor even defensive arms
> (since the weary war and the Spaniards have wasted and consumed
> them), and not living in a rugged terrain, and surrounded by three
> Spanish towns and with two fortresses in their midst—have won back
> and maintained their liberty with unadulterated valor and stubborn
> determination (con puro valor y porfiada determinación).[208]

Despite the natives' fearful losses, mere boys had stepped forward to
avenge their fallen fathers, and finally, "even the women are coming to
the war and, fighting often as men, they give themselves up to death
with great courage." All of which testifies to "the valor of these peoples,
worthy of more praise than I could give them in my verses."

What is important to bear in mind here is the centrality of the question of the bravery or cowardice of New World natives in the debate
over their true status in the human family and the proper way of treating them. In a pair of important articles, Rolena Adorno has argued

that "the conceptualization of the Amerindian as warrior was as important as (and certainly more widespread than) the theorization of the Amerindian as natural slave."[209] Thus, Sepúlveda offered as decisive proof of the natural inferiority of the Indians the claim that they were "so sluggish and timid that they could scarcely endure the hostile sight of our men, and often many thousands of them would flee, scattering in womanish flight *(muliebri fuga)* before very few Spaniards."[210] Any lingering doubts that Indians were "slaves by nature" should be dispelled by the Aztecs' frightened admission of the Spaniards into Tenochtitlan, the arrest of Montezuma in the heart of his own capital, and Cortes's subsequent seizure of the city "with the help of such a small number of Spaniards and a few natives."[211]

Adorno, following a suggestion of Demetrio Ramos, has argued that in his later Latin account of the conquest (*De rebus Hispanorum ad novum terrarum orbem Mexicumque gestis*—also called *De orbe novo*—written 1553–58) Sepúlveda executed a startling "about-face" and "described the conduct of the Mexica during the final defense of Tenochtitlan . . . in terms that recalled the valor of the ancient Numantian defense against the Romans."[212] This goes too far. Sepúlveda was no Ercilla. It is true that in one passage, the only one cited by Adorno, Sepúlveda did admit that "our people realized that they had to deal with men of no womanish spirit *(muliebri animo)* but rather brave men who despised death."[213] But this was Sepúlveda's editorial interpretation inserted into what was essentially his Latinization of Cortés's own account of the reluctance with which his men initially greeted a request for aid from the beleaguered city of Cuauhnahuac (Cuernavaca). The appeal had arrived immediately after a demoralizing repulse by the Mexica of an assault upon Tenochtitlan in the course of which Cortés himself had been terrifyingly, if temporarily, captured, and Sepúlveda was accordingly forced to offer the ferocity of the Aztec defense as an explanation for the Spaniards' moment of hesitation before accepting the appeal from Cuauhnahuac. Advancing into his account of the siege and fall of Tenochtitlan, however, Sepúlveda emphasized less the bravery and patriotism of the defenders of the doomed city than their—and especially their leader's—"blind and stupid obstinacy and dazed disorientation" [caeca et stulta pertinacia et stupor]—language quite similar to that he had used of the Aztecs in the *Democrates secundus (stupor,* for example, appeared there too).[214] Cuauhtémoc consistently comes across in this account as stubborn, dazed, and downright mad, led fatally astray not so much by "pride and arrogance as by shock and mental disturbance" [non superbia et arrogantia . . . sed stupore ac perturbatione animi], finally jumping into the canoe in which he was soon caught not because he seriously hoped to escape but because he was "at his wit's end and out of his mind" [inops consilii . . . et alienata mente].²¹⁵ These judgments are strictly those of Sepúlveda; they are his editorializing additions to Cortés's impressively restrained account. Not that Cortés recorded admiration for his adversaries in this climactic siege; rather, his account reflects a no doubt genuine sense of perplexity at the intransigence of Mexica resistance and a frustration over the destruction of the city that he had hoped to seize relatively intact. A striking contrast to Cortés's frustration and Sepúlveda's contempt is the account of Bernal Díaz del Castillo, who consistently presented the Aztecs as formidable opponents and attributed to Cortés a chivalrous compliment to the defeated ruler for having proved "tan valiente."²¹⁶ But perhaps Bernal Díaz's most impressive tribute to the bravery of the Aztecs was his frank admission that he faced each encounter "with loathing and grief in my heart, and I would have to urinate one or two times and entrust myself to God and His Blessed Mother."²¹⁷

Predictably enough, the views of Las Casas on Indian valor forthrightly countered those of Sepúlveda. Relatively early in the *Apologética historia* (chap. 33), sustaining the venerable Hippocratic project of correlating ethnic characteristics with climate, he argued that most of the American Indians, being inhabitants of a region blessed with a generally temperate climate, were able to enjoy both the intellectual vigor of inhabitants of warm climates and the "courage and boldness" [esfuerzo y animosidad] of northerners. Supplementing this theoretical argument, Las Casas appealed to "what we see through our own experience": for though virtually naked and equipped with weapons that "are, at least in comparison to ours, like children's toys," they have repeatedly dared to attack invaders "so brave and so ferocious and so well armed with iron that one of our men disembowels with his sword five hundred of them in an hour." Horrific encounters in which natives have defended their "lives, countries, and liberty" against mounted Spaniards, each of whom "kills with a lance a thousand in a quarter of an hour," have sufficiently demonstrated that these peoples are "bold to the highest degree and of great courage."²¹⁸ Yes, they have proved timid at times, but this is not a sign of innate cowardliness. It is, rather, a phenomenon occurring *per accidens* as a result of the debilitating and unprecedented shock of "the great and extreme cruelties we have inflicted upon them" and the fear they have acquired through their experience of appalling servitude. "And this would be enough to make not only them but even the Scipios servile and cowardly"—an uncanny anticipation of a passage in Montaigne's "Des coches," in which he noted the effect upon naked peoples of "the thunderings and lightnings of our cannons and harquebuses which would be capable of confounding Caesar himself had he been caught unawares with as little experience of them."²¹⁹ Like Las Casas, Montaigne insisted that in "hardiesse et courage" the modern Indians were worthy of being compared "to the most famous examples from antiquity." In "Des Coches," he was thinking primarily of the Aztecs and Incas, but in "Des cannibales" (bk. 1, essay 31) he had praised the valor of the Brazilians, whose fortitude in defeat reminded him of the Spartans at Thermopylae. Montaigne's celebration of Indian bravery in war in fact outdid that of Las Casas, for the Dominican had no intention of creating impressions that might undermine his more usual habit of comparing brutal Spaniards and helpless Indians to "hungry wolves tearing apart these most gentle sheep."²²⁰

While Las Casas argued that the greatest Roman heroes, placed in the demoralizing situation of the Amerindians, would have appeared no less cowardly, Ercilla, beginning his epic in these same years during breaks from firsthand experience of Araucanian valor, felt entitled to insist that these obstinate Indians had unequivocally proved superior to Roman heroes. Perhaps the most impressive instance of this praise appears in canto 3, at the moment when Ercilla introduced Lautaro, the main Araucanian hero of the first stage of the revolt. This young man, a groom of the Spanish commander Pedro de Valdivia, turned on his master in the heat of a battle his fellow Araucanians were manifestly losing. Implicitly defying his Spanish readers' discomfort with this rebellious "page" *(paje),* Ercilla presented Lautaro's seemingly suicidal charge as an exploit so impressive that it inspired Fortune to change her mind and turn the tide of battle. But the act of this "bárbaro muchacho" not only routed the Spaniards, it also put to flight the heroes of "antigua escritura," particularly the heroes of the Roman Republic (with the Spartan hero of Thermopylae thrown in for good measure):

> Neither the two Publii Decii who sacrificed their lives for their beloved country, nor Curtius, nor Horatius, nor Scaevola, nor Leonidas gave so distinguished a display, nor those who have attained

great fame through the sword in wars so bitterly fought: Furius, Mar-
cellus, Fulvius, Cincinnatus, Marcus Sergius, [Q. Publius] Philo,
Scaeva, and Dentatus.
 Tell me: what did these famous men do that could equal the deed
of this barbarian *(bárbaro)*? What undertaking, what battle did they
take on that did not offer at least some hope? To what risk or dangers
did they expose themselves to which the thirst for ruling did not
inspire them, and in which they were not aided by the great profits
that make the timid bold?[221]

 Beatríz Pastor Bodmer has argued that Ercilla's use of such classical
comparisons, through which American Indians were "assimilated into
Western history and dignified according to European cultural and ideological codes," was part of his strategy of a general "Europeanizing" of
his Indians in order to persuade his readers of the full humanity of "the
other."[222] Ercilla's claim that Lautaro had not merely equaled but actually surpassed the heroes of antiquity could be simply one variety of this
domestication: a non-European allowed to play the familiar medieval
and Renaissance game of "topping" classical precedents—what E. R.
Curtius termed *Überbietung*.[223] But Lautaro's defeat of classical models
has another dimension, for Ercilla not only asserted that the heroes of
ancient Rome fell short of the Araucanian hero in valiant and self-
sacrificing patriotism, but they were also tainted by "thirst for ruling"
[sed del reinar] and by the profit motive ("intereses grandes"), failings
shared by many of the Spaniards in Ercilla's epic. Indeed, this third
canto opened with a passionate denunciation of "the insatiable avarice
of mortals," for "avarice was the cause of so great a war and the total
destruction of this land."[224] Thus, in the powerful introduction of the
principal native hero of the first part of his poem, Ercilla managed to
link the three anti-Roman strategies we have seen at work in the discourse of New World conquest. Like his fellow conquistadors in Mexico, Ercilla asserted that the valor of the heroes of ancient Rome had
been dwarfed by heroic exploits performed in the New World, but he
joined the conquistadors' Dominican opponents not only in attacking
the motivations of Roman imperialism, but also in declaring that the
Romans had been surpassed not by the conquistadors but by those
native adversaries whose customary designation as *bárbaros* gives off a
markedly ironic ring in Ercilla's astonishing epic.
 Shortly after demoting Roman heroic exempla below a youth whom
most Spanish readers would have abominated as a murderous traitor,

Ercilla proceeded to claim that the rebel sack of Concepción, too, topped a classical precedent. Here, though, it was the ferocity, not the valor, of the natives that was at issue. Now, it was not generally difficult for those who derided the timidity of the Indians to excoriate in their next breath their cruelty in battle—or, in the case of human sacrificers and cannibals, after battle. As Rolena Adorno observed of such Janus-faced portrayals of the Aztecs, "both these depictions . . . were manifestations of the same phenomenon: the surrender to appetite instead of the exercise of reason, . . . to savagery instead of restraint."[225] Ercilla, however, chose to communicate the fury of the Indians not by invoking their innate "savagery," but by comparing them to the most famous of all classical sackers of cities: "Not with as much harshness did the Greek people enter the settlement of Troy, scattering Phrygian blood and living flame, . . . as did the barbarians, blind with wrath, vengeful-ness, and fury, . . . ruin, destroy, and lay waste. . . ."[226] True enough, the vindictive rage of the victorious Araucanians surpassed that of the vil-lains of one of Ercilla's main classical models, Vergil's *Aeneid,* and it must also be admitted that he soon compared their delight at seeing the city in flames to that of Nero watching Rome burn. But an epic luster still clings here to Ercilla's presentation of the deeds of these remote "barbarians." Far from being dismissed as subhumans lacking in ratio-nal self-control, they are compared to Homer's heroes (though not Vergil's!).

But even after the fortunes of the Araucanians began to turn, Ercilla continued to dignify them with classical parallels. Thus, at the end of the second part (published in 1578), he recorded how, after the reverses at Las Lagunillas and Millarapue, the rebels were driven by "el amor de la patria" to sacrifice their farms in a "scorched earth" strategy, behav-ior comparable to "the distinguished deeds of the ancients" [las hazañas de antiguos señaladas].[227] A list of Roman patriotic suicides (and one legendary Athenian, the self-sacrificing king Codrus) ensues, culminat-ing in "El Uticense," Cato the Younger, hero of that great Roman "loser's epic" so well known to Ercilla, Lucan's *Pharsalia.* "Well, this Araucanian people deserves to enter into this company," the poet declared. Similarly, after the failure of the Araucanian assault on the fort at Penco and the flight of the wounded chief Tucapel, the stubborn search of the "unhappy beautiful barbarian woman" [infelice bárbara hermosa] Tegualda for the body of her husband merited her inclusion in a roster of classical, especially Roman, heroines (canto 21).[228] Lía

Schwartz Lerner and Beatríz Pastor Bodmer are surely right to stress the "essentially literary character of Ercilla's heroines"—they do indeed "recall the person and values of the 'lady' in the literature of chivalry" even more strongly than their menfolk resemble the heroes of chivalric romance.[229] And yet the probably fictional Tegualda's insertion into the ranks of the heroines of antiquity ("Bien puede ser entre éstas colocada / la hermosa Tegualda") emphatically contributes to Ercilla's project of conferring classical dignity upon a very real group of New World natives.

The accelerating decline of the Araucanian revolt, in the third and last part of the poem (published in 1589), inspired what is surely Ercilla's most sustained and intriguing complex of classical models for his heroic New World natives, and here too the ancient models and the Indian parallels are remarkable women—and one of them, as we shall see, can no longer be dismissed as nothing but a chivalric fiction. Cantos 32–33 present the Spaniards' ruthless hunt for the fleeing and disguised Caupolicán, the leader of the revolt, after the Spanish victory at Cañete. The poet introduced this hunt for scampering fugitives, in which he had himself vigorously participated, by singing the praises of the "excelente virtud" of "clemencia" that the Spaniards were so enthusiastically ignoring. Extrapolating from the hunting down of these fugitives to the whole history of the Spanish presence in Chile, Ercilla lamented that breaches in "the laws of war" have diminished the "hoped-for fruit" of this land, for the expeditions and conquests carried out there were accompanied by "enormous atrocities never before witnessed" [crueldades enormes nunca vistas]. And yet it was through this now spectacularly neglected virtue of clemency "that Rome became so powerful and conquered more peoples than by the sword" [por ella Roma fué tan poderosa, / y más gentes venció que por la espada].[230] The positive view of Roman imperial expansion here reminds us that Ercilla did not in fact sustain the critical view of Roman imperial expansion hinted at in canto 3, where it was implied that the Romans had been no less inspired by lust for domination and greed than modern Spaniards. Most of the Roman references in Ercilla's epic are in fact implicitly laudatory. While the poet tended to call in the Romans in order to dignify the Indians, unlike Las Casas he did not consistently assume that the honor of the Indians had to be erected on the razed ruins of that of the Romans.

But before Ercilla recorded the capture of Caupolicán, he developed at great length a pair of stories that featured two women, one Indian, one classical, and also himself as the purported discoverer of the first woman and the oral chronicler of the second. Much as he had claimed in canto 20 to have discovered the heroic Tegualda in her battlefield search for her husband, so now our courtier-conquistador-poet claimed to have led his troop of horsemen into the hiding place of another exemplary widow of an Araucanian hero, the wounded Lauca.[231] So devoted was Lauca to her husband, an exemplar of "rare courage and valor" [esfuerzo raro y valentía], that she was at his side when he died and herself took a bullet in the side, followed by a sword stroke too clumsily delivered by a well-meaning Spaniard who attempted to honor her wish to join her husband. Lauca reportedly entreated Ercilla to "use your pity with me, sir, by completing here and now the job that the soldier left unfinished thanks to his feeble arm." Consoling her and enlightening her as to the impiety of her request, Ercilla left behind an Indian ally to tend her wounds and began to ride back to the fort with his troop. As they rode, they fell into a conversation about "the faith and constancy of Indian women" [la fe de las Indias y constancia]. It is intriguing to recall here the way Gonzalo Fernández de Oviedo had similarly mused, in a passage in his chronicle not published in Ercilla's day, on the "grande amor" for her rebel husband demonstrated by another Indian woman, the wife of the condemned "Capitán Gonzalo" of Darién, a rebel whom Oviedo was willing enough to admit was "muy valiente."[232] Like Lauca, Gonzalo's wife displayed her nobility in a moving speech in which she declared her earnest desire to accompany her husband in death—or, better yet, to take his place. And just as Oviedo offered for this devoted marital pair the classical parallel of Cornelia and Tiberius Gracchus, so Ercilla, as a character in his own poem, suggested to his fellow cavalrymen that "not even chaste Elissa Dido preserved her faith to her husband with such rigor" as had the Araucanian Lauca.

Anticipating the natural puzzlement of many a reader, a young soldier promptly protested that Vergil's *Aeneid* demonstrated that Dido did not, in fact, maintain her fidelity to the murdered Sichaeus; rather, she entered upon a disastrous affair with Aeneas. Though other impressively well-read soldiers seconded this young man, Ercilla serenely informed them that "since the Mantuan wished to dignify his flourishing Aeneas," from whom "César Augusto Octaviano" boasted descent, he "treated Dido inhumanely, defaming her unjustly and falsely," thereby implanting a slander among "the rude, ill-informed common people" [el rudo común mal informado]. Accordingly, for the rest of this canto and the beginning of the next, by far the longest digression in the poem (102 octaves!), Ercilla expounded to his cavalrymen—and his readers—the "true," pre-Vergilian story of Dido: how she left Tyre after her husband fell victim to her brother's greed, how she tricked her brother into letting her assemble a fleet, then tricked several prominent Tyrians into accompanying her on a search for a new homeland, how she then tricked the African natives to sell her more territory than they had bargained on, how she was, for a change, herself tricked by her own people to consent to marriage with the Libyan king Iarbas, and how, finally, she returned to the role of successful trickster in evading marriage by means of a spectacularly staged suicide, thus staying true to her first husband after all.²³³ Though modern readers may be as startled by this version as Ercilla's men supposedly were, his "true" tale of Dido is in fact an embellishment of a genuinely pre-Vergilian version, that of the Greek Sicilian historian Timaeus (ca. 350–260 B.C.), which passed into the Middle Ages and Renaissance in the version of Justin's *Epitome* of Pompeius Trogus, a fourth-century text based on the work of a historian of the reign of Augustus. (The story was also familiar to Tertullian, who wittily remarked in chapter 13 of his *Exhortation to Chastity* that Dido preferred to burn than to marry!) As María Rosa Lida de Malkiel industriously demonstrated some years ago, this non-Vergilian story of Dido had a surprisingly extensive vogue in Renaissance Spain.²³⁴

The anti-Vergilian story of Dido, suggested by the exemplary marital fidelity of the wounded Lauca, is immediately followed by Ercilla's account of yet another Araucanian heroine. When the Spaniards capture and bind the disguised rebel chief Caupolicán, they are at first unaware of the identity of their prisoner. Suddenly, though, a captured woman clutching a small boy appears, indignantly mocks Caupolicán's bound "feminized right hand" [afeminada diestra], and contemptuously reveals his identity—and her own, for this is none other than his wife, Fresia. She proceeds to berate him for evading "una breve muerte honrada" and concludes by abandoning their son to him: "Raise him, raise him yourself, you who have changed that brawny body into the female sex, since I don't want the title of mother of a base son of a base father." With this, "angry and furious," she casts her son from her and rejects entreaties to pick him up again. The captors have to find a surrogate mother for him from among the captives before proceeding on their way. Thus, at a moment when an Araucanian hero of the epic, hitherto habitually denominated "el gran Caupolicán," proves disappointingly "feminized," the gender vacuum is immediately filled by his "masculinized" wife.

The episodes of Lauca and Fresia were thus carefully crafted to form the side panels of a triptych whose huge central panel is devoted to the impeccably ancient, if non-Vergilian, Dido, an exemplum of womanly heroism shedding classical dignity not only upon Lauca, the explicit *comparanda*, but also upon Fresia. A skeptical reader can be forgiven for suspecting that Lauca owes her existence solely to classical antiquity and to the Spanish poet's desire to give extensive poetic form to the analogous "true story" of Dido.[235] But any similar doubts about Fresia are no longer plausible, now that we have unexpected confirmation of the fundamental historicity of this episode in the prose chronicle of another eyewitness to the events of the Araucanian revolt, the *Crónica y relación copiosa y verdadera de los Reinos de Chile* (1558) of Gerónimo de Vivar (or Bibar), a work whose relatively recent appearance has reopened the question of the value of Ercilla's poem as an historical document.[236] But what is most arresting here is the fact that, just as Ercilla placed Fresia's act right after the story of the spectacularly noble Dido, so Vivar chose an ancient parallel for the captured chieftain's here unnamed wife. Indeed, he chose another heroic Carthaginian woman! As lieutenant Alonso de Reynoso was leading back the captured Araucanian chief, whom Vivar calls Teopolican,

> he happened to encounter a woman who was the wife of Teopolican, and she was carrying a year-old child. And since she did not expect that Teopolican would come along in captivity, when she saw him she began to say to him: "What's this? Are you Teopolican, the valiant man who used to say that no Christian could be taken whom you didn't have to kill, and they raised you up as general of the land—you who have now thus let yourself be captured by the Spaniards? And does it seem right to you that you go along bound, and that I have the son of a man as cowardly as you?" And she threw the child down a cliff, and it died. This indeed seems to me great spirit and courage *(grande ánimo y esfuerço)* in a woman, something we can compare with that good Carthaginian woman who threw herself with her two children into the fire because her husband had negotiated with the Romans. And so Teopolican was taken to the city and impaled. And so perished that bad Indian, so great an enemy to the Spaniards.[237]

The "buena mujer cartajinesa" to whom Vivar alluded here was the wife of Hasdrubal, the main general in the Third Punic War, which ended in the destruction of Carthage: the fullest account of her story is that of Appian (8.19.131). Perhaps the fact that Hasdrubal's wife killed her children inspired Vivar to record that Teopolican's wife killed her son. Ercilla's Fresia, we recall, simply refused to continue mothering the child.

Gerónimo de Vivar's chronicle, perhaps "the most valuable document of the history of America discovered in recent years," offers us three other impressive classical parallels for the astonishing valor and martial skills of the Araucanian rebels.[238] And it is especially striking that these parallels return us to the link between the early Iberians and the New World natives that we saw the Dominicans developing in the context of the controversy of the Indies. Shortly before his account of the outbreak of the revolt, Vivar devoted a chapter (104) to the war-making habits and weapons of the Araucanians of the province of Concepción. He began with an explanation of their surprisingly effective prowess as warriors, assisted by a dignifying classical parallel:

> This people had from ancient times engaged in wars against each other, for they were all divided into factions, one group of lords fighting another. When they come forth to fight, they come in their squadrons in such good order and concert that it seems to me that they wouldn't have come forth in better order if they had been accustomed to making war with the Romans.[239]

The suggestion that these contemporary Araucanians might resemble the most formidable of Rome's enemies surfaces again, with sharper specificity and deeper resonance, near the end of this chapter:

> And they go to war covered in war paint *(envixados)*. In this, in the stratagems *(ardiles, i.e., ardides)* that they practice in war, and in their order and manner of fighting, they seem to me to be Spaniards when they were conquered by the Romans *(ser españoles quando eran conquistados de los rromanos)*. And in fact they are in the latitude *(grados y altura)* of our Spain.[240]

Here, as in the writings of Las Casas, we see a bold equation of modern Indians with the Iberian victims of Roman imperial expansion, though Vivar emphasizes less the Iberians' sufferings than their worthiness as formidable adversaries of the supposedly more "civilized" war machine fielded by the Romans. Also reminiscent of Las Casas is Vivar's hint that similarities between Araucanian and early Iberian war-making skills and customs owed something to the equidistance of Spain and Chile from the equator, an appeal to the venerable tradition of positing a correlation between ethnic characteristics and climatic conditions that Las Casas, writing around this very time, was invoking so often in the *Apologética historia*—including chapter 33, where he insisted that the climate and latitudes of the Indies constituted no inhibition to the martial virtues of their natives. (Of course, it is highly unlikely, to say the least, that Vivar would have had access to Las Casas's manuscript. But we should remember that the Dominican's parallel between the ancient Spaniards and the modern Indians had been in print, in the version offered in Domingo de Soto's summary of the Valladolid debate, since 1552.)

Vivar's other comparison of Araucanian warriors with ancient Iberians confronting Roman imperial expansion appears in the chapter (133) that he devoted to the Spanish victory in a battle fought in the province of Millarapue in November 1557. In language strikingly reminiscent of Ercilla's, he recorded that the Araucanians were led here by Teopolican, "an Indian very aggressive and warlike *(velicoso y guerrero)*," and that both sides in the momentous conflict fought bravely—"the Spaniards to defeat them, the Indians to defend their country" [los españoles por los vençer, y ellos por defender su patria].[241] Suddenly Vivar zeroed in on the vivid vignette of an Indian (apparently the figure whom Ercilla celebrated as "Galvarino" in cantos 22–23 and 25–26 of *La Araucana)* who had lost his hands upon the orders of the late Valdivia, holding up his stumps, eloquently exhorting his "hermanos" to avoid his fate, and marching out in front of a squadron, determined to do with his teeth what he could no longer do with his hands. "I wanted to record this here," Vivar adds, "for they did not seem to me the thoughts of Indians but of those ancient Numantines who defended themselves against the Romans." We noted in the last chapter the centrality of the siege of Numantia to that assertion of the identity of modern Spaniards and pre-Roman Iberians that intensified in the fifteenth and sixteenth centuries, culminating in the vividly patriotic accounts of the siege in the history of Ambrosio de Morales and the *Numancia* of Cervantes. We also noted that the accounts of Morales and Cervantes very likely hinted at the experiences of the Indians invaded by the "neo-Roman" Spaniards. In fact, Cervantes's play seems to have been influenced by Ercilla's

Araucana, an epic that, incidentally, graced the shelves of that connoisseur of heroic deeds, Don Quixote.[242] On the other hand, we have also
seen that in his notorious *Democrates secundus* Juan Ginés de
Sepúlveda had cited the valor of the ancient Spaniards in the Numantine war as a validation of the fitness of modern Spaniards to rule the
manifestly inferior peoples of the Indies. Writing a decade later than
Sepúlveda, Gerónimo de Vivar may have been the first to suggest that
the truest modern parallels for the besieged Numantines were not the
Spanish conquistadors but their Indian victims, a parallel later made
powerfully implicit by Morales and Cervantes (quite independently of
Vivar, of course). Thus, Vivar's invocation of the siege of Numantia is
in itself powerful and quite possibly original. But its impact in its narrative context is shockingly intensified by the stark sentence that immediately and abruptly follows, recording the fate of the valiant handless
Indian: "And here he was captured, and the governor ordered him
thrown to the dogs." From heroic Numantine to hapless dogfood: what
more jolting juxtaposition could be imagined to epitomize the fate of
Indians fighting valiantly and desperately "por defender su patria"?

Despite these three arresting ancient comparisons for the Araucanian
rebels, classical allusions are not in fact particularly frequent elsewhere
in Vivar's chronicle, though the few that do surface offer impressive testimony to the learning of this apparently not especially distinguished
conquistador-chronicler. Recounting Valdivia's *entrada* into the Valley
of Copiapo, Vivar noted that the natives of this region had once held a
fortress for a year and a half against the Inca Guayna Capac, "a second
Alexander the Great" [otro segundo Alexandre].[243] An appeal to
Alexander is conventional enough in conquistador narratives—five, for
example, occur in the *Historia verdadera* of Bernal Díaz del Castillo.
What is, of course, remarkable about Vivar's allusion is its application
not to a conquistador but to a native empire-builder. Slightly earlier in
his account of this *entrada* Vivar did compare a Spanish capitán to a
figure from classical history. It is a much more recherché parallel than
the Alexander reference, and it has understandably perplexed Vivar's
most recent editor. Relating how Valdivia invited some hostile Indians to
visit his camp and sit down to share a meal with him, he remarked that
the *adelantado* was acting "with as much shrewdness as Bias practiced
with Alyattes in order to free his country from siege."[244] Vivar was alluding here to the ruse Thrasybulus, tyrant of Miletus, employed against the
invading Median king Alyattes. In order to disguise the food shortage in

his city, Thrasybulus ordered that all public and private stores of grain, including his own, be collected in the public square and that the citizens put on an impressive show of feasting and merrymaking timed to coincide with the expected arrival of Median ambassadors. True, Vivar confused Thrasybulus of Miletus with Bias of Priene, but the slip may, paradoxically, be a testimony to his learning. For the original and best source for the story of Thrasybulus and Alyattes is Herodotus (bks. 21–22), and Herodotus did proceed to tell another, unrelated story about Bias of Priene a couple of pages later (1.27). This suggests that Vivar did not derive his allusion from a chrestomathy but from Herodotus himself. (In addition, it is noteworthy that Vivar made a deft allusion to a work known to relatively few Spaniards of his day: Dante's *Purgatorio*.)[245] Thus, his literary citations, infrequent though they were, betray a surprising level of culture in a man whose narrative otherwise makes few pretensions to literary art and gives few hints that its author was a man of distinguished background.

Not only are Vivar's literary allusions impressive hints of the breadth of his reading, they are also striking in the use to which he put them. Whereas a chronicler like Bernal Díaz del Castillo, composing the final version of his work around this same time, employed classical allusions to dignify the conquistadors and their exploits, we have seen that Vivar did so only once, and then not to celebrate Spanish valor but to adorn an instance of shrewdness *(astuçia)* worthy of the Greeks. Otherwise, the classical parallels serve, as in Ercilla's epic, to dignify the military prowess or exemplary bravery of the natives, especially the Araucanian rebels. It is worth emphasizing here the relative rarity of such comparisons between ancients and Indians in the chronicles of the deeds of the conquistadors. Acts of desperate valor would, it is true, on rare occasions elicit such comparisons. Thus, in a document reporting events in the conquest of regions of Nueva Granada (modern Colombia), the autoptic author recorded that in November 1541 certain Indian skirmishers—most notably one who, armed only with a sword fashioned from a palm tree, wounded one Spaniard of a pair he attacked—were "unsurpassed by the Romans in their deeds" [romanos en sus hechos no hicieron más].[246] A similar Roman dignity was shed on another Indian monomachist by Pedro Pizarro, cousin of Francisco, in his *Relación del descubrimiento y conquista del Perú*, completed in 1571 (though not published until the nineteenth century). In his account of the revolt of Manco Inca in 1535 (chap. 19), he recorded how the

Spaniards, besieged in Cuzco, staged a counterattack on a multilayered fortress held by the rebels. When they reached the top level, they encountered "an *orejón* [Inca nobleman] who indeed could have been written about among the Romans *(que çierto se pudiera escrevir entre los rromanos),*" for he ran valiantly back and forth, warding off Spanish attackers and killing up to thirty slackers on his own side before leaping to his death.[247] And in his 1610 epic poem *Historia de la Nueva México,* Gaspar Pérez de Villagrá compared the destroyed citadel of Acoma to "aquella gran Numancia trabajosa"—calling to mind Vivar's comparison of the Araucanians at the battle of Millarapue to "aquellos antiguos numantinos quando se defendian de los rromanos."[248]

Against such scattered comparisons of uncommonly valiant Indians with Romans or with the Romans' formidable Iberian opponents, the relative frequency of such parallels in the writings of Ercilla and Vivar on the Araucanian revolt is remarkable, to say the least, as is both writers' general avoidance of classical parallels for the conquistadors. The influence of Vivar's chronicle on Ercilla's poem—or, for that matter, vice versa—cannot be entirely ruled out, and José Durand, for one, has assumed that it is "probable" that Ercilla knew and used Vivar's manuscript.[249] If so, Ercilla is highly unlikely to have read the complete manuscript, for Vivar recorded that he laid down his pen on December 14, 1558, and it was precisely at this year's end that Ercilla was exiled from Chile. While it is likely enough that the two men were acquainted and could well have shown each other drafts of their works in progress, it is no less plausible that the main factor that led both Spaniards to turn to ancient history to characterize the Araucanian rebels was nothing less than the fundamentally unprecedented tenacity, valor, and martial skill with which these Indians defended their liberty. As J. H. Parry and Robert G. Keith have emphasized, "It must be remembered that most of the Spaniards who came to Chile had never encountered Indians who were able to stand up to Spanish cavalry in battle or to offer any kind of protracted resistance to conquest, though under the right circumstances they might inflict temporary defeats on them."[250] In fact, though both Ercilla and Vivar recorded the eventual predominance of the Spaniards in pitched battles in the field, control of areas beyond the environs of the main settlements remained insecure. Indeed, "the Indians were not effectively conquered in this part of Chile until the nineteenth century."[251] It seems only fair to say that these liberty-loving rebels, noted for their orderly and highly effective manner of waging war, simply earned themselves an incontrovertible place alongside the exemplars of classical history—including, for Vivar, the valiant Iberian ancestors of the modern Spaniards. Just as the ruins of the Mayan town of T-ho inspired Francisco Montejo the Younger to name the newly founded capital of Yucatán after the Hispano-Roman city of Mérida, so the valor and the passion for liberty of the Araucanian rebels made them seem in Vivar's eyes "to be Spaniards when they were conquered by the Romans." One did not have to be an ally of Las Casas to admit that the Indians of the New World could be worthy competitors of the culture heroes—or national ancestors—of classical antiquity.

Comparisons of New World natives with the most famous peoples of antiquity, especially the Romans, served varied functions, as we have seen. For the supposedly "anti-indigenist" chronicler Gonzalo Fernández de Oviedo, such parallels enabled him to inscribe the cultural practices and artifacts of the New World into world culture and world history. While Oviedo did often choose to emphasize the oddity of the Indies and the Indians, thereby heightening his own unique glory as the interpreter of a world unknown to the likes of Pliny the Elder, he persistently felt the tug of a contrary domesticating impulse, reassuring his readers that the Indies were not located in another world, that Antillean *areitos*, Roman and Etrurian songs and dances, and the *romances y canciones* of modern Spanish peasants were all fundamentally similar cultural phenomena. Just as "we can say that the whole world is one and the same land and coastline" (preface to book 37), so we can say that ancient Romans and modern Indians were both denizens of the same cultural continuum.

Bartolomé de las Casas conducted, as we have seen, an altogether more systematic and sustained comparison of classical European and modern Indian cultures—to the point where Anthony Pagden could call the *Apologética historia* "a programme for comparative ethnology."[252] But Pagden's phrase, apt as it is, should not blind us to the fact that Las Casas's project was not conducted in a spirit of anthropological detachment. Rather, it was a polemically fueled juxtaposition of cultures frankly and single-mindedly designed to demolish the libel of Indian inferiority. If some Spaniards excoriated the Indians as servants of the Devil, then it was incumbent upon their defender to remind his readers, in the spirit of the church fathers at their most vitriolic, that when one needed to identify Devil-worshipers few candidates had more sterling credentials than the ancient Romans, those savage pagan persecutors of the nascent Christian religion. A modern scholar professionally devoted to the study of classical antiquity may be forgiven for feeling that Las Casas ultimately replaced the libels against the New World natives with a scarcely less shrill set of libels against the Greco-Roman world. Be that as it may, the sustained vehemence of the Dominican's attacks upon the ancients—the Romans, above all—surely calls for an explanation that goes beyond his worthy desire to devise a bold strategy to dignify the cultural level of the American Indians. The answer surely lies in the extensive and intensive deployment of the model of Roman imperialism in the controversy of the Indies. In particular, it was Sepúlveda's cultural, rather than juristic, use of the Roman precedent, his exaltation of the Romans as model warriors and rulers rather than as legators of imperial dominium, that surely kindled in Las Casas the passion with which he pursued his project of demolishing the cultural exemplarity of the Romans for modern Spaniards. Indeed, far from imitating the ancient Romans, modern Europeans needed to be vigilantly alert to the survivals of Roman religious practices in the culture of their own time and place. Rather than suspect the Christianized Indians of the New World of clinging to pagan practices under the veneer of the new religion, professedly Christian Europeans needed to be made aware of the extent to which they themselves kept Roman paganism alive not only in the remote villages but even in the cities of modern Europe. Indeed, paganism was alive in the city of Rome itself, where Las Casas witnessed maskers, manifest inheritors of the obscenely cross-dressing Tibicines of ancient Rome, representing "extremely profane and vile scenes of antiquity in front of a large assembly of people." Why, many a Spaniard who suspected that the Indians of the New World were slyly persisting in the worship of their ancestral devils was himself guilty of handing his little daughters pagan idols in the form of speciously innocuous dolls! Thus, Las Casas's polemical purposes in the *Apologética historia* drove him to make an idiosyncratic contribution to the early modern search for pagan survivals in European culture, a search more commonly pursued by Protestants denouncing "paganopapalism" than by his fellow Catholics.

    If the juxtaposition of New World and Greco-Roman religious life was one of the richest and most astonishing comparative projects in the Spanish discourse of the conquest, scarcely less varied and vigorous was the representation of the Indians as warriors worthy of comparison with the Romans—and with the Romans' most formidable enemies. After all, both religion and martial behavior were central issues for the assessment of the cultural level of the Indians—and hence of their status as fully human beings. Virtually as popular as the characterization of Indians as Devil-worshiping human sacrificers was their contradictory reputation as both womanish cowards and fiendishly cruel warriors. Those who sought to rehabilitate the martial reputation of the New World natives did so with a variety of aims and from a variety of backgrounds of status and experience, but all found the ancient history of the Mediterranean useful for their purposes. For Las Casas, the Indians were by nature warriors as worthy as the Scipios of Rome—but even the Scipios would have blanched before the terrors of modern technological superiority. (On other occasions, of course, it suited the Dominican's purpose to extol the lamblike passivity of the Indians.) For Alonso de Ercilla, the Araucanian rebels of Chile were at least the equals of the Romans in martial valor and skill and in their fierce devotion to their "patria," and their women deserved to be celebrated alongside Virginia, Cloelia, and Cornelia. In part, the classical dignity Ercilla bestowed upon his Araucanians served to magnify the bravery of the Spaniards who faced them, but no reader of this unsettling work can fail to be persuaded of the sincerity of Ercilla's conviction that the rebels whom he encountered in his relatively brief sojourn in Chile were the true heroes of his epic and worthy competitors of the heroes of ancient Rome. His fellow soldier in this bitter campaign, Gerónimo de Vivar, independently delivered a similar blow to European cultural pride, but the ancient heroes to whom Vivar compared the Araucanians were not the Roman paragons of Ercilla's epic, but the Romans' noblest victims—especially the Spaniards who tenaciously resisted the Roman invaders. And that remarkable product of both Indian and European civilizations, the Inca Garcilaso de la Vega, could maintain that Rome and Cuzco resembled each other "in the many and diverse nations that they conquered and subjugated," and also "in producing so many and such excellent men and raising them with good civic and military teachings."[253]

We are left, then, with the versatility of classical antiquity, especially ancient Rome, for sixteenth-century Spaniards struggling to grasp and to communicate what at first must have struck them as the incorrigibly alien reality of the societies of the New World. While it was Bartolomé de las Casas, the passionate Dominican "apostle to the Indians," who most intensely exploited the comparison of classical and Indian cultures, even conquistadors were able to admit, on occasion at least, the validity of such parallels. Just as the Romans were on hand as positive or negative models for the claims and behavior of the Spanish conquerors of the Indies, so too were they obligingly available as cultural foils allowing the natives of the New World to take on a dignity that could simultaneously affirm and qualify the Eurocentric pride of their conquerors—or could even, in the bitter invective of Las Casas, subject that pride to an unrelenting barrage of attacks upon its classical foundations.

Conclusion

Bernal Díaz del Castillo tells us that when Francisco Vázquez Coronado, overcome with longing for his uncommonly virtuous and beautiful bride Beatríz de Estrada, abandoned his search for the Seven Cities of Cíbola, some of the soldiers in his company quipped that he was trying "to imitate *(remedar)* Ulysses, the Greek captain, who feigned madness while at Troy in order to go and enjoy his wife Penelope."[1] Though this story is apparently unattested in classical traditions about Odysseus/Ulysses, some members of the rank and file *(soldados,* not *capitanes)* of Coronado's company—if we are to believe Bernal Díaz—deftly devised a telling parallel between a uxorious conquistador and a famous "capitán greciano." It is also Bernal Díaz who assures us that at the very moment of the consummation of the siege of Tenochtitlan, when Cortés stood at last face to face with the captive Cuauhtémoc, his first act was to tell the last Aztec *tlatoani's* squabbling captors the story—also not precisely a version attested in any ancient source—of the dispute between Marius and Sulla over the credit for capturing Jugurtha.[2]

Such stories offer us vivid glimpses into what J. H. Elliott has called the "mental world" of the conquistadors.[3] Whether or not Coronado's men or Cortés actually uttered the classical parables Bernal Díaz put into their mouths, the chronicler clearly assumed that his readers would find such allusions in such startlingly nonclassical surroundings perfectly natural. Similarly, the Inca Garcilaso de la Vega assumed that readers of his lively chronicle *Historia de la Florida* would not be at all surprised to learn that Hernando de Soto's company included "many Spaniards well read in history" [muchos españoles leídos en historias] who had likened the Indians of Florida to classical models. In their view, Garcilaso claimed, Floridan chiefs seemed to have served under "the most famous captains of Rome when she ruled the world with arms," while eloquent native youths "appeared to have studied in

318

Athens when she flourished in moral letters."⁴ And the poet Alonso de
Ercilla has left us the piquant picture of a troop of Spanish cavalrymen
returning from an engagement with the formidable Araucanian rebels,
passing the time by arguing over the question of what, exactly, was the
"true" story of Dido, queen of Carthage.⁵ And speaking of Carthaginians, let us not forget Vinko Paletin, a Dalmatian adventurer in Yucatán
in the company of Francisco Montejo el Mozo in 1532, informing his
comrades that the reliefs that met their puzzled gaze in the ruins of
Chichén-Itzá bore inscriptions in Punic and representations of Carthaginian soldiers.⁶

Such classical vignettes embedded into narratives of the conquest
suggest the ease with which references to the ancient Mediterranean
may have surfaced in the Spaniards' quotidian encounter with the New
World, and not just in the chroniclers' programmatic assertions of the
conquistadors' superiority to the heroes of antiquity. Further testimony
to the Greco-Roman presence in the conquest is the extraordinary
energy and time that Alonso de la Vera Cruz expended in attacking the
"Roman title" for Spanish dominion in the Indies before an audience of
young clerics during the first academic year of the University of Mexico
(1554-55).⁷ Vera Cruz clearly suspected that many encomenderos hop-
ing to receive the sacrament of confession were confident that the
ancient Roman Empire's claim to world dominion constituted a basis
for Spanish sovereignty in America that guaranteed them an unclouded
conscience, and the learned professor of theology was determined that
his pupils disabuse them of this comforting fancy. No doubt several of
these aging encomenderos fondly recalled the spectacular festival staged
in Mexico City in 1539 in honor of the emperor's visit to France, when
they had participated in or witnessed games "like those they used to
perform in Rome when the consuls and captains who had won battles
used to enter in triumph"—games orchestrated by "a Roman knight
named Luis de León, a man said to be a descendant of the patricians, a
native of Rome."⁸ And these same old soldiers had long been used to
hearing—and saying—how their exploits had surpassed those of the
Romans—as, for instance, Francisco de Aguilar, conquistador turned
repentant Dominican, remembered "all" of his comrades doing back in
the heady years of the conquest of New Spain.⁹ But even among some
of the children of the conquistadors' native foes the Romans seem to
have achieved a highly charged presence, for at the Colegio de Santa
Cruz de Tlatelolco, founded by the Franciscans early in 1536, Latin-

speaking Aztec youths were apparently being instructed in the headily dangerous history of the brutal Roman conquest of Spain. Writing to the emperor in 1545, the outraged notary Gerónimo López noted that these privileged native youths were learning that their conquerors' ancestors had themselves been "subjects of the Romans and revolted and rebelled," as well as being heathens who took their own good time converting to Christianity.[10]

If classical anecdotes and allusions followed the routes of the American *entradas* of the conquistadors, the ancient Mediterranean's most sustained rebirth in the discourse of the conquest occurred in the lectures of the great Dominican theologians and jurists of Salamanca and Alcalá, in the treatises of those eloquent enemies Sepúlveda and Las Casas, and in the chapel of the Colegio de San Gregorio in Valladolid, where those two colorful adversaries presented their passionately conflicting views on the justice of the conquest. As we have seen, the role of the Roman Empire in the controversy of the Indies was considerably more extensive than that of the classical concept that has received much more scholarly attention: Aristotle's doctrine of the natural slave. It has also become clear that the debate over the relevance of the Roman Empire consistently reached beyond the juridical question of modern Spaniards' inheritance of the Roman Empire's supposed world sovereignty to a searching reconsideration of Roman imperialism as a historical and cultural phenomenon, as a vital and, for better or worse, profoundly influential chapter in the history of Europe—and particularly in the history of Spain. No less probing a reassessment of Roman civilization were the exercises in polemical ethnography that juxtaposed classical—especially Roman—civilization and the societies of the New World.

It is natural—and, within limits, sound and illuminating—to regard classical allusions in the writings of the conquistadors and their publicists, appeals to the Roman Empire in the debate over Spanish sovereignty overseas, and comparisons of modern Indians with ancient Greeks and Romans as instances of the frequently noted habit of early modern Europeans, when faced with the "shock of the new" in America, to fall back on comfortable ancestral European intellectual grids, to see America and themselves on American ground through the distorting lenses of the classical past. But our exploration of the persistent and ubiquitous presence of ancient Rome in the Spanish experience of the New World has repeatedly revealed a more intriguing—and increasingly debated and studied—phenomenon: the intellectual impact of the New World upon the Old.

Again and again, Spaniards' application of Greco-Roman patterns and perspectives to the New World inspired a revaluation of the classical interpretive framework itself. Far from providing stable models and yardsticks in a disorientingly alien world, the ancient Romans' imperial ventures, arts of governance, and cultural achievements proved limited, inadequate, irrelevant, sometimes even downright dangerous. Thus, through the very act of transplanting ancient cultural models to the New World, sixteenth-century Spaniards found themselves revising their conception of their identity as inheritors of Greco-Roman civilization. When the "other" is interpreted and "domesticated" by an appeal to the familiar, there is always the risk that the current will be reversed and that the familiar will be "defamiliarized" by the conceptually unruly "other." At least, such was often the fate of the ancient Romans in the discourse of the Spanish conquest of the New World.

Thus, we have seen that the conquest of the Indies was attended by several assaults upon the exemplars of classical antiquity—Roman exemplars above all. The conquistadors saw their own conquests—especially their destruction of the Aztec empire—as exploits that put Roman imperial glory in the shade, for no Roman general had ever faced and overcome challenges to match those that they themselves had so dazzlingly met. For that matter, no Roman general had had to travel nearly so far in order simply to come face to face with his foes, and no Roman, consequently, had been forced to rely on such unnervingly remote sources of support and supply. We may recall, for example, Fernández de Oviedo's insistence that a merchant of Santo Domingo who traveled to Spain and back in order to attend a friend's wedding had proved himself a greater hero than Ulysses.

The critics of the conquistadors—especially Dominican critics—agreed that ancient Rome had become an inadequate model, but for distinctly different reasons. They passionately insisted that the model of Roman imperialism was an utterly inappropriate guide for the behavior of Christians in the New World—not just obsolete, but profoundly treacherous for the health and fate of one's soul. Rome's "right" was founded solely upon "might"—*ius erat in armis,* as Domingo de Soto succinctly put it—and the tyranny of the Romans' imperial rule made them little different from those "heathen" tyrants of modern Europe, the Turks. Nor did the cultural achievements of the ancient Romans survive unscathed their use as a yardstick for the attainments of the advanced civilizations of the New World. Thus, Bartolomé de las Casas argued at excessive and obsessive length that the Aztecs and Incas had surpassed the Romans "by no small margin" [con no chico exceso].[11] In particular, the obscenity and frivolity of Roman religious ceremonies implied a cultural level far below that indicated by the dignity of Aztec religious rituals and by the awesome solemnity of their sincere and pious desire to offer in sacrifice to their gods the most valuable gift in the world: human life. But even a less advanced Indian society could elicit a reassessment of Roman cultural exemplarity from a man who was no priest, but a courtier-conquistador-poet who encountered these "primitives" on the field of battle, for Alonso de Ercilla's romantic epic *La Araucana* presents the Araucanian rebels of the Chilean frontier as worthy competitors to the heroes of ancient Rome.

But if the Spanish experience of the New World could call into question the Greco-Roman heritage of modern Europe, it could also cast a new light on the peoples whom the Romans had violently brought within their empire—especially the early Iberians, who were now increasingly being recognized as the truest ancestors of modern Spaniards. Rather than strive to emulate or surpass Roman conquerors, Las Casas and his friends argued, Spaniards should instead identify with the Iberian victims of Roman imperialism—victims whom Las Casas urged his Spanish audience to regard as "your ancestors" or, more starkly and simply, "you." After all, the Indians in the New World "are what we were in Spain before St. James's disciples converted us," as Las Casas phrased it in 1535, seconded by an influential letter Julián Garcés sent around this time to Pope Paul III.[12] And fifteen years later, during his famous debate with Sepúlveda in Valladolid, Las Casas informed his audience that the Indians of the New World had the same right to resist imperial aggression as did "your ancestors" when the Romans came to enslave them, abolish their native dominions, and appropriate their mineral wealth.[13] This was, of course, very close to the kind of history lesson Gerónimo López accused the Franciscans of teaching their elite corps of Aztec youths in the Colegio de Santa Cruz de Tlatelolco. And this kind of parallel occurred later to a conquistador-chronicler of the Araucanian revolt, Gerónimo de Vivar, who remarked that his foes "seem to me to be Spaniards when they were conquered by the Romans," and who elsewhere compared the valor of the rebels at the battle of Millarapue (Nov. 1557) to that of "those ancient Numantines who defended themselves against the Romans."[14] In fact, the two most influential sixteenth-century accounts of the siege and fall of Numantia, those of the history of Ambrosio de Morales and of Cervantes's drama *El cerco de Numancia,* drew palpable energy from the parallel between ancient Iberians and modern Indians, and we have seen that Morales may well, at an early stage of his career, have played a pioneering role in the development of this parallel.

Not only did some Spaniards thus come to see their own ancestors as virtually brethren of the Indians of the New World, as fellow heathen "barbarians" subjected to brutal imperial conquest and exploitation, but certain features of contemporary European and especially Spanish life could take on a surprisingly alien cast when viewed in the light of the encounter with the people of the New World. Thus, Spaniards who found the ways of the Amerindians inaccessibly outlandish could be reminded that Spain herself harbored her own "Indians," particularly among the peasant classes.[15] Accordingly, Francisco de Vitoria, in his enormously influential *Relectio de Indis* delivered at the University of Salamanca in 1539, assured his listeners that the apparent inferiority of the American Indians was largely the result of "bad and barbarous education," not nature, and as proof of this he offered the fact that many of the *rustici* of Spain seem "little different from brute animals."[16] Similarly, the royal judge Alonso de Zorita, writing a report on the Indians of New Spain in the late 1560s, said that those who mock the Indians for buying the worthless trinkets offered them by Spanish peddlers should realize that "we could also call the Spaniards barbarians in this sense, for at the present day, even in the best-governed cities, little toy swords and horses, and brass whistles, and little wire snakes, and castanets with bells are sold in the streets."[17] A few years later, in the mid-1570s, the Franciscan Diego Durán offered a partial defense of the superficiality of the faith of the Indian converts of New Spain by pointing out that "in Spain there are people as uncouth and coarse," and in fact in some of the remoter regions of Castile "men's minds are extraordinarily brutish and rude (especially in matters of religious instruction), much more so than these natives."[18] And Juan de Castellanos, in his immense poem *Elegías de varones ilustres de Indias,* published in 1589, presented none other than Christopher Columbus, homeward bound from his first voyage, assuring his sailors that the backwardness of the inhabitants of the Antilles was paralleled by that of the illiterate common folk of Italy, France, and Spain: "Look at your nearest neighbors—look at the rusticity of the mountain: if they are so dull-witted today, what would they be like if they were thus forgotten for centuries?"[19] An earlier and even more impressive instance of this "Indianization" of Europe is the remarkable chapter that the supposed "anti-Indianist" Fernández de Oviedo devoted to a demonstration that the *areitos* of the Caribbean were not savage and meaningless jumpings and shoutings but rather "a good and noble manner of keeping alive the things of the past," precisely paralleled not only by the dances that the early Romans imported from Etruria, but also by the *cantares* of modern Spain and Italy.[20] Characterizing such European ballads as history texts "for those who do not read," Oviedo proceeded to cite examples of Spanish "romances e canciones" that possessed reasonably accurate historical content, introducing each one as "another ballad or areito," an arresting equation of Spanish and Caribbean terminology to describe a European phenomenon.

But the most sustained reexamination of European popular culture in the light of the experience of the Indies occurred in the massive *Apologetic History* of Las Casas—and it was none other than the ancient Romans who allowed him to reveal the lingering backwardness of the common people of modern Spain and Italy, and of many of their "betters," too. Eager to deflect from the New World natives the common charge of crypto-paganism, Las Casas was inspired to harness his habitual anti-Roman polemical energies to an exposé of the "survivals" *(vestigios, reliquias, rastros)* of ancient Roman paganism in the villages and cities of modern Europe—indeed, in the very heart of the Christian world, in the Roman streets where in 1507 he witnessed carnival maskers keeping alive the lascivious dances of the ancient Tibicines as they "represented extremely profane and vile scenes of antiquity."[21] If Las Casas had managed to get his unwieldy manuscript into print, he might have induced at least some Spanish readers to worry less about the Indians of the New World persisting in their ancestral beliefs and rites and to cast a more critical eye upon their own habit of giving their daughters dolls, thereby keeping alive pagan practices that Pausanias recorded in the Roman Empire of his day.[22] Thus, a sensitivity to charges of lurking paganism in the New World could inspire a search for disturbing evidence of the very same phenomenon in Christian Europe.

The alienation that both the conquistadors and their harshest critics increasingly experienced from the Greco-Roman foundations of European civilization may be regarded as a harbinger and anticipation of the "creole patriotism" that eventually—and inevitably—took root in Spanish America. A famous symbolic moment in the growth of this later development neatly illustrates the dethronement of the classical European past in favor of a distinctly American self-conception.[23] When the Conde de Paredes arrived in Mexico City in 1680 as the new viceroy of New Spain, he was greeted by the astonishing sight of an ornate wooden triumphal arch, ninety feet high and fifty feet wide, complete with Corinthian columns and recessed niches for statues. Such imitations of Roman triumphal arches were a common sight in early modern Europe, and they tended to be adorned with statues and scenes from classical mythology and history, thereby shedding a Roman dignity upon the arch's honorand. We may recall yet again the elaborate imitation of a Roman triumph staged in Mexico City in 1539. What the newly arrived Conde de Paredes saw in that same city a century and a half later, however, when he gazed up at this arch designed by the eccentric Mexican intellectual Carlos de Sigüenza y Góngora, was a series of painted panels beginning with the Aztec tribal god Huitzilopochtli and proceeding to portray in order the entire sequence of the eleven Aztec emperors, along with inscriptions indicating the virtues supposedly embodied by each. In effect, the new Spanish viceroy was being invited to ground his administration in the consciousness of an *American*, not a European—and Roman—tradition of imperial rule. As Elizabeth Boone has noted, Sigüenza y Góngora thus "succeeded in replacing the classical age of the Mediterranean world with the classical (Aztec) age of Mexico."[24] The sixteenth-century Spaniards of America who have claimed our attention in this book did not go so far as to graft their sense of their cultural identity onto the stock of the native heritage of the New World. But their repeated and sustained challenges to the exemplarity of Europe's classical tradition call dramatic attention to their growing conviction that what they had performed and witnessed in lands undreamed of by their ancestors left them, as Perry Miller said of the Puritans of New England, "alone with America."[25]

Notes

Introduction

1. Michel de Montaigne, *Essays*, trans. Donald Frame (Stanford: Stanford University Press, 1958), bk. 3, chap. 6, p. 695; French text: *Essais*, ed. Alfred Thibaudet (Paris: Gallimard, 1950), 1019–20. Montaigne's essay was first published in 1588.

2. Earlier studies contributing to an understanding of the Roman model in the three spheres covered by this book will be indicated in the notes. The only relatively comprehensive study of the Roman model in the Spanish encounter with the New World appears to be Jaime González Rodríguez, *La idea de Roma en la historiografía indiana* (Madrid: Consejo Superior de Investigaciones Científicas, 1981), a useful and often perceptive book, though careless in its citation of sources. Despite its title, it offers some discussions of the Roman theme in the nonhistoriographical writings of Las Casas and Sepúlveda, though he neglects the contributions of other participants in the "controversy of the Indies," such as Vitoria, Soto, and Cano. González appends a useful anthology of primary passages (151–200). While the present study inevitably intersects with that of González at a number of points, our approaches and primary sources tend to be quite different. The fact that González's unduly neglected book came to my attention only when this study was virtually complete leads me to echo Wolfgang Haase's lament that there is no standard bibliography on the classical tradition in the New World ("America and the Classical Tradition," in *The Classical Tradition and the Americas*, ed. Haase and Meyer Reinhold, vol. 1, pt. 1 [Berlin: Walter de Gruyter, 1994], xxvi n. 44). Unwittingly confirming his own point, Haase himself omitted González's study from his own survey of the literature.

3. See, for example, Howard Mumford Jones, *O Strange New World* (New York: Viking, 1964), chap. 1, "The Image of the New World"; J. H. Elliott, *The Old World and the New, 1492–1650* (Cambridge: Cambridge University Press, 1970), esp. 23–25, 41–42; Anthony Grafton, with April Shelford and Nancy Siraisi, *New Worlds, Ancient Texts: The Power of Tradition and the Shock of Discovery* (Cambridge: Harvard University Press, 1992); Jean-Pierre Sánchez, *Mythes et légendes de la conquête de l'Amérique* (Rennes: Presses Universitaires de Rennes, 1996).

4. For an attempt to locate an "anticlassical tradition" in the early U.S. Republic, see Meyer Reinhold, *Classica Americana: The Greek and Roman Heritage in the United States* (Detroit: Wayne State University Press, 1984), 116–41. But see Carl J. Richard, *The Founders and the Classics: Greece, Rome, and the American Enlightenment* (Cambridge: Harvard University Press, 1994), passim, but esp. p. 4.

5. The current debate over the impact exerted upon the Old World by the discovery and conquest of the New World received its main stimulus from J. H. Elliott's rich little book *The Old World and the New*. Two important volumes of papers delivered at conferences convened to assess the issues raised by Elliott's book are Fredi Chiappelli, ed., *First Images of America: The Impact of the New World on the Old*, 2 vols. (Berkeley and Los Angeles: University of California Press, 1976); and Karen Ordahl Kupperman, ed., *America in European Consciousness, 1493–1750* (Chapel Hill: University of North Carolina Press, 1995). Both collections contain interesting comments by J. H. Elliott himself.

Chapter 1

1. Francisco López de Gómara, *Historia general de las Indias*, ed. Jorge Gurría Lacroix (Caracas: Biblioteca Ayacucho, 1979), 1:7. Gómara's association with Cortés began after the latter's return to Spain; he never visited the New World himself.

2. For the text of Velázquez's instructions, see René Jara and Nicholas Spadaccini, eds., *1492–1992: Re/discovering Colonial Writing*, Hispanic Issues 4 (Minneapolis: Prisma Institute, 1989), 412–13 (Eng.), 451 (Span.). For the conquistadors' obsession with Amazons, see Irving A. Leonard, *Books of the Brave* (Cambridge: Harvard University Press, 1949), 36–64; Martín de Riquer, "California," in *Homenaje al Profesor Antonio Vilanova*, ed. Adolfo Sotelo Vázquez and Marta Cristina Carbonell (Barcelona: Universidad de Barcelona, 1989), 1:581–99; Luis Weckmann, *The Medieval Heritage of Mexico*, trans. Frances M. López-Morillas (New York: Fordham University Press, 1992), 46–52, 55–59; K. March and K. Passman, "The Amazon Myth and Latin America," in Haase and Reinhold, *Classical Tradition*, 285–338.

3. Hernán Cortés, fourth letter, October 1524, in *Cartas de relación*, ed. Manuel Alcalá, 16th ed. (Mexico City: Porrúa, 1992), 184; Eng. trans. in Cortés, *Letters from Mexico*, trans. and ed. Anthony Pagden (New Haven: Yale University Press, 1986), 298–300; see also 502 n. 21.

4. Quoted in Leonard, *Books of the Brave*, 49, who contends that by "istorias antiguas" Cortés was referring to the conquistadors' beloved knightly romances, particularly Montalvo's *Sergas de Esplandián*. But it seems unlikely that the respectably educated Cortés would use this term when thinking primarily of a romance published just fourteen years earlier.

5. General discussions of classical models for the exploits of the conquistadors are Winston A. Reynolds, "Hernán Cortés y los heroes de la antigüedad," *Revista de Filología Española* 45 (1962): 259–71; José Antonio Maravall, *Antiguos y modernos: La idea de progreso en el desarrollo inicial de una sociedad* (Madrid: Sociedad de Estudios y Publicaciones, 1966), esp. 438–41; J. A. Rodríguez Barbón, "Bernal Díaz, ¿'idiota y sin letras'?" in *Studia hispánica in honorem R. Lapesa II*, ed. D. Alonso et al. (Madrid: Gredos, 1974), 89–104; Juan Gil Fernández, "El libro greco-latino y su influjo en Indias," in *Homenaje a Enrique Segura Covarsí, Bernardo Muñoz Sánchez, y Ricardo Puente Broncano*, ed. José María Álvarez Martínez et al. (Badajoz: Departamento de Publicaciones

de la Excelentísima Diputación, 1986), 61–111, esp. 99–107; Sánchez, *Mythes et légendes*, vol. 1, chap. 17, "L'épopée de la *conquista* (briefer version in "Myths and Legends in the Old World and European Expansionism on the American Continent," in Haase and Reinhold, *Classical Tradition*, 212–13). An unpersuasive attempt to identify echoes of the *Odyssey* in Bernal Díaz's *Historia verdadera* is Yolanda Fabiola Orquera, *Los castillos decrépitos* (Tucumán: Universidad Nacional de Tucumán, 1996), 163–66. Manuel Alcalá's comparative studies are not remarkably illuminating: *César y Cortés* (Mexico City: Editorial Jus, 1950) and "César y Cortés frente al enemigo," in *Actas del Primer Congreso internacional sobre Hernán Cortés* (Salamanca: Ediciones Universidad de Salamanca, 1986), 17–26. Eberhard Straub has argued, implausibly, that Cortés was inspired by Caesar's *De bello gallico* not only in the composition of his *Cartas de relación*, but also in the actual conduct of his campaign in Mexico: *Das Bellum Iustum des Hernán Cortés in México* (Cologne: Böhlau, 1976), chap. 4 , "Cortés und Caesar," esp. 101–23.

    6. Bernal Díaz del Castillo, *Historia verdadera de la conquista de la Nueva España*, ed. Joaquín Ramírez Cabañas, 14th ed. (Mexico City: Porrúa, 1986), chap. 19, pp. 32–33. Cf. a similar passage in chap. 193, p. 515. See J. González's discussion of Bernal Díaz's classical references (*La idea de Roma*, 60–63).

    7. Bernal Díaz, *Historia verdadera*, chap. 59, p. 99. For Cortés's possible classical inspirations for scuttling the ships (notably Agathocles and Julian the Apostate), see Fernando Soler Jardón, "Notas sobre la leyenda del incendio de las naves," *Revista de Indias* 9, nos. 31–32 (1948): 537–59. Francisco Cervantes de Salazar had Cortés utter Caesar's Rubicon *mot* upon beginning his second march on Tenochtitlan: *Crónica de Nueva España*, ed. Manuel Magallón, Biblioteca de Autores Españoles (subsequently abbreviated BAE), vol. 245 (Madrid: Atlas, 1971), bk. 5, chap. 39, p. 108.

    8. Miguel de Cervantes Saavedra, *El ingenioso hidalgo Don Quijote de la Mancha*, ed. Francisco Rodríguez Marín, rev. ed. (Madrid: Atlas, 1948), pt. 2, chap. 8, 4:183–84.

    9. "Algunas respuestas de Bernardino Vázquez de Tapia," January 23, 1529, doc. 93 in *Documentos cortesianos*, ed. José Luis Martínez, vol. 2: *1526–45*, pt. 4: *Juicio de Residencia* (Mexico City: Universidad Nacional Autónoma de México, Fondo de Cultura Económica, 1991), 42. See J. H. Elliott, "The Mental World of Hernán Cortés," in *Spain and Its World, 1500–1700* (New Haven: Yale University Press, 1989), 32. Caesar's habit of quoting the lines from the *Phoinissai* is mentioned by Cicero in *De officiis* 3.21.82, a passage quoted in turn by Suetonius, *De Vita Caesarum* 1.30.5. Though he suspects that the quotation "enjoyed some currency among sixteenth-century Spaniards," Elliott remarks that "it would not be surprising if at some stage in his life Cortés had read Suetonius on Caesar." Cortés's familiarity with Suetonius is implied by Bernal Díaz's claim that as he signed the execution order for mutineers at Veracruz he quoted Nero's remark in similar circumstances that it would be better not to know how to write (*Historia verdadera*, chap. 57, p. 97), an allusion, as Juan Gil has noted ("El libro greco-latino," 101–2), to Suetonius 6.10.2. The Borgia motto *aut Caesar aut nihil* was later cited with approval by the far less ambiguously rebellious conquistador

Lope de Aguirre in his sarcastic letter to the Dominican provincial Francisco de Montesinos, August 1561, cited by the chronicler Francisco Vásquez. See Elena Mampel González and Neus Escandell Tur, eds. *Lope de Aguirre, Crónicas, 1559–1561* (Barcelona: Editorial 7½, Ediciones Universidad de Barcelona, 1981), 242 (reading, with the editors, "César o nihil" for the text's unintelligible "cesa un hil").

    10. Bernal Díaz, *Historia verdadera*, chap. 69, pp. 119–20. Cortés's own account of his speech in his *Segunda Relación* does not mention the Romans, but he does promise the grumblers, in addition to the heavenly reward due to those who fight against "the enemies of our faith, . . . greater honor and renown than any generation before our time" (*Cartas de relación*, 40, *Letters from Mexico*, 63).

    11. Bernal Díaz, *Historia verdadera*, chap. 129, p. 267.

    12. Francisco López de Gómara, *Historia de la conquista de México* (1552), ed. J. Ramírez Cabañas (Mexico City: Editorial Pedro Robredo, 1943), chap. 83, 1:250; trans. Lesley Bird Simpson, *Cortés: The Life of the Conqueror by His Secretary* (Berkeley and Los Angeles: University of California Press, 1964), 171. See Reynolds, "Hernán Cortés," 260, on echoes of Gómara's comparison in the poets Juan Zapata (1566) and Gabriel Lasso de la Vega (1594). Oddly, this is the only classical parallel in Gómara's history of the conquest of Mexico (see Reynolds, 259). J. Gil, who missed this passage, suggested that by avoiding classical parallels Gómara was complying with Cortés's concern to deflect ill will ("El libro greco-latino," 104–5), a contention that might be supported by the absence of self-promoting classical comparisons in Cortés's own *Cartas de relación*.

    13. Gómara, *Historia general de las Indias*, chap. 65, 1979 ed., p. 99.

    14. Francisco Cervantes de Salazar, dedication to *Diálogo de la dignidad del hombre*, in *Obras*, ed. Francisco Cerdá y Rico (Madrid: Antonio de Sancha, 1772), n.p.

    15. Cf. Fernández de Oviedo: "I don't doubt that Hernando Cortés was ignorant of Vegetius and Cato and other excellent authors who wrote on the art of war, but I affirm and believe that the talent of this captain in the business of war was such that he was naturally born to teach many others what ought to be done in war." *Historia general y natural de las Indias*, ed. Juan Pérez de Tudela Bueso, BAE vol. 120 (Madrid: Atlas, 1959), bk. 33, chap. 20, p. 98.

    16. Bernal Díaz, *Historia verdadera*, chap. 122, p. 240 (Guidela); chap. 162, p. 403 (Narváez to Garay).

    17. Jorge Manrique, *Coplas de Don Jorge Manrique por la muerte de su padre*, beginning of stanza 27, lines 313–18; Manrique, *Poesía*, ed. Jesús-Manuel Alda Tesán, 10th ed. (Madrid: Cátedra, 1985), 161. This poem is one of the most widely anthologized in Spanish literature. That Bernal Díaz was quoting Manrique has been noted by Juan Gil, "El libro greco-latino," 100.

    18. E. R. Curtius, "Jorge Manrique und der Kaisergedanke," *Zeitschrift für romanische Philologie* 52 (1932): 146–47. Curtius's article is a thorough discussion of the two "Kaiserstrophen."

    19. Manrique, *Coplas*, stanzas 29, lines 337–39, and 40, lines 479–80; *Poesía*, 162, 167.

20. Bernal Díaz, *Historia verdadera*, prefatory paragraph, xxxv.

21. Bernal Díaz, *Historia verdadera*, chap. 212, p. 593. In the concluding chapters of his chronicle Bernal Díaz repeatedly insisted upon his mission to insure that "the glory of all not be referred to one captain alone" (chap. 205, p. 573), and he particularly resented the way Cortés's *Cartas de relación* exalted his own reputation at the expense of that of his men: see esp. chap. 205, p. 560 ("he gives all the honor and glory of our conquests to himself and makes no mention of us"); chap. 210, p. 585; chap. 212, p. 593.

22. This characterization of Julius Caesar comes from Bernal Díaz's first draft of chap. 212. It can be found in a footnote to the Ramírez Cabañas edition, p. 592.

23. Juan Gil, "El libro greco-latino," 104.

24. Fray Francisco de Aguilar, *Relación breve de la conquista de la Nueva España* (Mexico City: Porrúa, 1954), 65.

25. On Bernal Díaz's resentment and the "atmosphere of dissatisfaction" of the conquistadors generally, see Ramón Iglesia, *Cortés, Columbus, and Other Essays* (Berkeley and Los Angeles: University of California Press, 1969), 72–77. Elsewhere in this collection Iglesia makes some suggestive remarks about the "popularism" of Bernal Díaz's chronicle (38–49). For a more recent discussion of Bernal Díaz's disgruntlement, see Mauricio Parra, "Alienación y marginalidad discursiva en la *Historia Verdadera de la Conquista de la Nueva España*," *Romance Language Annual* 3 (1992): 550–53. Parra argues that Bernal Díaz's chronicle offers us "the 'other face' or, better, the other voice of the conquest" and compares his resentment with that of his notorious contemporary, Lope de Aguirre (553).

26. Bernal Díaz's 1539 "probanza de méritos y servicios" is reprinted in *Historia verdadera*, 615–31 (opposition of Villalobos: 616; Cortés's letter in support: 619–20).

27. Testimony of Juan Rodríguez Cabrillo de Medrano, in support of the *probanza* of Bartolomé Becerra, in Bernal Díaz, *Historia verdadera*, 647.

28. Bernal Díaz, prologue to *Historia verdadera*, xxxv. The sensitive question of the inheritability of the encomiendas is clearly implicit here.

29. Bernal Díaz, *Historia verdadera*, chap. 212, p. 593.

30. Ibid., chap. 207, p. 577. For part of this passage I have adopted the translation of Lesley Bird Simpson in Iglesia, *Columbus, Cortés*, 74–75.

31. Bernal Díaz, *Historia verdadera*, chap. 89, p. 163.

32. Ibid., chap. 97, p. 189.

33. See David A. Brading, *The First America: The Spanish Monarchy, Creole Patriots, and the Liberal State: 1492–1867* (Cambridge: Cambridge University Press, 1991), chap. 14, "Creole Patriots." On p. 293 he notes that the resentment of the creole patriots "in part . . . derived from the conquerors, from men such as Bernal Díaz del Castillo, who charged that the Crown had failed to reward their heroic services with adequate recompense." See also Anthony Pagden, "Identity Formation in Spanish America," in *Colonial Identity in the Atlantic World, 1500–1800*, ed. N. Canny and Pagden (Princeton: Princeton University Press, 1987), 51–93, esp. 51–58; and José Durand, *La transformación social del conquis-*

tador, 2d ed. (Lima: Nuevos Rumbos, 1958), chap. 6, "La ambición de nobleza," 88–98.

34. The pair "cudicia y ambición" appears in both the argument and the prologue of Las Casas's most widely read book, *Brevísima relación de la destrucción de las Indias*, in *Tratados de Fray Bartolomé de las Casas*, ed. Lewis Hanke and Manuel Giménez Fernández, vol. 1 (Mexico City: Fondo de Cultura Económica, 1965), 5 and 13. The longer passage quoted comes from his introduction to the summary account of his dispute with Sepúlveda, "Argumento de la presente obra," *Aquí se contiene una disputa*. . . , in *Tratados*, 1:223. See González Rodríguez, *La idea de Roma*, 78–79, for Las Casas's attack on the deadly mixture of greed and ambition among the Romans. See also Ramón Menéndez Pidal, "¿Codicia insaciable? ¿Ilustres hazañas?" in *España y su historia*, vol. 2 (Madrid: Minotauro, 1957), 114–26, where Bernal Díaz's Renaissance competition with the ancients is defended against the assaults of Las Casas, "el más agriado hombre del mundo" and a cultural traitor to his native Spain.

35. Stuart B. Schwartz, "New World Nobility: Social Aspirations and Mobility in the Conquest and Colonization of Spanish America," in *Social Groups and Religious Ideas in the Sixteenth Century*, ed. Miriam Usher Chrisman and Otto Gründler, Studies in Medieval Culture 13 (Kalamazoo: Medieval Institute, Western Michigan University, 1978), 28. Speaking more specifically of the conquistadors of Mexico City, Bernard Grunberg has recently concluded that most "did not profit much from their participation in the conquest as a whole. . . . Many ended their days in poverty, encumbered by debts. A better share in colonial life came to the second generation, the sons and daughters of the conquistadores, because of the labors of their fathers" ("The Origins of the Conquistadores of Mexico City," *Hispanic American Historical Review* 74 [1994]: 283).

36. Ernst Robert Curtius, *Europäische Literatur und lateinisches Mittelalter*, 6th ed. (Bern: Francke, 1967), 171–74, trans. Willard Trask as *European Literature and the Latin Middle Ages* (New York: Pantheon, 1953), 162–65.

37. Peter Martyr, *De orbe novo decades octo*, 5.8, in Petrus Martyr de Angleria, *Opera*, ed. Erich Woldan (Graz: Akademische Druck- und Verlagsanstalt, 1966), 194 (photographic reprint of 1530 ed.): "En rem Romano populo, quando illustrius res illorum vigebant, non facilem."

38. For Oviedo's death, see Juan Pérez de Tudela Bueso, "Vida y escritos de Gonzalo Fernández de Oviedo," introduction to his edition of the *Historia general y natural de las Indias*, vol. 1, BAE vol. 117 (Madrid: Atlas, 1959), clxvi. For Oviedo's attempt to get his revised and completed history printed, see Daymond Turner, "The Aborted First Printing of the Second Part of Oviedo's *General and Natural History of the Indies*," *Huntington Library Quarterly* 46 (1983): 105–25.

39. López de Gómara, *Annals*, quoted from Turner, "Aborted First Printing," 111, who does not find Gómara's claims plausible.

40. Oviedo, *Historia general*, bk. 33, chap. 20, BAE vol. 129, 97. I have adopted, and slightly modified, L. B. Simpson's translation of this passage, from his translation of Ramón Iglesia's essay on Oviedo in Iglesia, *Columbus, Cortés*, 226–27. Book 33 was part of part 2 of Oviedo's history, not published until the mid–nineteenth century.

41. See Oviedo, *Historia general*, bk. 46, chap. 15, BAE vol. 121, 84. When the first part of Oviedo's history was republished by Juan de Junta in Salamanca in 1547, several copies were bound together with a reissue of Jerez's *Conquista del Perú*. See Turner, "Aborted First Printing," 119. Turner notes that the Library of Congress copy is printed this way. So is the copy in the Bancroft Library at the University of California.

42. Franciso de Jerez (Xeres), *Verdadera relación de la conquista del Perú*, ed. José Luis Moure, in *Crónicas iniciales de la conquista del Perú*, ed. Alberto M. Salas, Miguel A. Guérin, and José Luis Moure (Buenos Aires: Plus Ultra, 1987), 148. Note particularly the echo of Jerez's phrase "en tierras sabidas y proveídas de mantenimientos usados" in Oviedo's "en provincias e partes pobladas e proveídas."

43. For Oviedo and Cortés, see Antonello Gerbi, *Nature in the New World*, trans. Jeremy Moyle (Pittsburgh: University of Pittsburgh Press, 1985), 315–16; Iglesia, *Columbus, Cortés*, 221–23. For Oviedo's miffed feelings over Cortés's lack of cooperation, see *Historia general*, chap. 33, proem, BAE vol. 120, 8.

44. Gerbi, *Nature in the New World*, 258–63. For an illuminating, though in my opinion overstated, investigation of Oviedo's fascination with the new and strange, see Anthony Pagden, *European Encounters with the New World* (New Haven: Yale University Press, 1993), 56–68.

45. Oviedo, *Historia general*, bk. 7, chap. 1, BAE vol. 117, 229.

46. Ibid., bk. 13, proem, BAE vol. 118, 56.

47. Ibid., bk. 1, BAE vol. 117, 8.

48. Ibid.

49. Compare also Cervantes de Salazar's 1546 encomium of Cortés, emphasizing his conquest of "tan gran espacio de tierra . . . sin ayuda de rei alguno." See note 14 in this chapter.

50. Oviedo, *Historia general*, bk. 33, chap. 20, BAE vol. 120, 98.

51. Jaime González-Rodríguez, "El antiromanismo de Gonzalo Fernández de Oviedo," *Revista de Indias* 43, no. 171 (1983): 335–42; Ramón Iglesia, ""Bernal Díaz and Popularism in Spanish Historiography," in *Columbus, Cortés*, 38–49.

52. Iglesia, *Cortés, Columbus*, 41, citing Oviedo, *Historia general*, bk. 16, chap. 7, BAE vol. 118, 96.

53. Oviedo, *Historia general*, bk. 18, proem, BAE vol. 118, 183.

54. Ibid., bk. 33, proem, BAE vol. 120, 7.

55. Ibid., bk. 29, chap. 34, BAE vol. 119, 355.

56. Oviedo, *Historia general*, bk. 30, proem, BAE vol. 119, 357. Oviedo's language here is strikingly echoed in a recent study on the social background and aspirations of the conquistadors of Mexico: "They were primarily men who tried to find what they could not obtain in their native country" (Grunberg, "Origins of the Conquistadores," 282).

57. Oviedo, *Quinquagenas* II, no. 198, "Vanidad nobiliaria en Indias," in *Las memorias de Gonzalo Fernández de Oviedo*, ed. Juan Bautista Avalle-Arce (Chapel Hill: North Carolina Studies in the Romance Languages and Literatures, Department of Romance Languages, 1974), 1:374. See also no. 199, "Abusos del título de *don* en Indias," 375–76.

58. See Oviedo, *Historia general,* bk. 26, chap. 1, BAE vol. 119, 62. (Oviedo chooses here to disguise the fact that the proposal was his.)

59. For example, López de Gómara duly noted that "the ship *Argo* of Jason, which they put in the stars, sailed very little in comparison with the ship *Victoria*" (*Historia general de las Indias,* chap. 98, 1979 ed., 150). For other instances, see Gerbi, *Nature in the New World,* 269–71.

60. Oviedo, *Historia general,* bk. 20, chap. 1, BAE vol. 118, 228. Cf. bk. 6, chap. 40, BAE vol. 117, 199, where the *Victoria* wins the contest of the five great ships of history, the others being Noah's Ark, the *Argo,* the ship of the Egyptian king Sisore, and Columbus's flagship.

61. Ibid., bk. 31, proem, BAE vol. 119, 363.

62. Narváez vs. the ancients: ibid., bk. 35, chap. 3, BAE vol. 120, 299; Alonzo Zuazo: bk. 50, chap. 10, BAE vol. 121, 322. Cf. bk. 47, chap. 6, BAE vol. 121, 148: the disastrous return of Diego de Almagro from Chile, during which Oviedo lost his only son, compared to the less impressive story of the Argonauts.

63. The term "process of democratization" [proceso de democratizatión] is found in Iglesia, *Columbus, Cortes,* 48.

64. Oviedo, *Historia general,* bk. 31, proem, BAE vol. 119, 363.

65. An extended survey of Oviedo's debt to classical sources, especially Pliny, is Bruno Rech, "Zum Nachleben der Antike im spanischen Überseeimperium: Der Einfluss antiker Schriftsteller auf die *Historia general y natural de las Indias* des Gonzalo Fernández de Oviedo," *Spanische Forschungen der Görresgesellschaft* 31 (1984): 181–244. See also Gerbi, *Nature in the New World,* esp. 386–87, and see index under "Pliny"; Pagden, *European Encounters,* 59–68; Karl Kohut, "Humanismus und Neue Welt im Werk von Gonzalo Fernández de Oviedo," in *Humanismus und Neue Welt,* ed. Wolfgang Reinhard, Mitteilung 15 der Kommission für Humanismusforschung, Deutsche Forschungsgemeinschaft (Weinheim: VCH, 1987), 65–88. For Oviedo's classical allusions in his account of Peru, see Sabine MacCormack, "Conversations across Time and Space: Classical Traditions in the Andes" (forthcoming), sec. 1.

66. Oviedo, *Historia general,* bk. 2, chap. 1, BAE vol. 117, 13.

67. Ibid., bk. 1, BAE vol. 117, 11.

68. Ibid., bk. 13, chap. 2, BAE vol. 118, 57. Bruno Rech acutely notes: "Das ist die Ironie eines Mannes, der die See wirklich kennt, gegenüber einem Stubengelehrten, der nur nach Sekundärquellen gearbeitet hat" ("Zum Nachleben der Antike," 199).

69. For a cogent discussion of such "discourses of privileged vision," see Pagden, *European Encounters,* chap. 2, "The Autoptic Imagination."

70. Oviedo mentions Pliny's death in the eruption of Vesuvius in a footnote to bk. 39, chap. 2, BAE vol. 120, 343. His account of his ascent of Masaya is chap. 5 of bk. 42, BAE vol. 120, 390–98.

71. Pagden, *European Encounters,* 66–68; Oviedo, *Historia general,* bk. 18, proem, BAE vol. 118, 182.

72. Oviedo, *Historia general,* bk. 47, chap. 6, BAE vol. 121, 148.

73. Quoted from Pagden, *European Encounters,* 39.

74. Cortés, *Letters from Mexico,* 158; *Cartas de relación,* 96.

75. Cortés, *Letters from Mexico*, 337; *Cartas de relación*, 205. Padgen's phrase "principle of attachment" is the title of chap. 1 of *European Encounters*.

76. Tzvetan Todorov, *The Conquest of America*, trans. Richard Howard (New York: Harper and Row, 1984), 87, 83, 86. Todorov's contrast of the improvisatory skills of the conquistadors with the Aztecs' "submission of the present to the past" owes something, as he notes on p. 256, to Stephen Greenblatt's "Improvisation and Power," in *Literature and Society*, ed. Edward Said (Baltimore: Johns Hopkins University Press, 1980) 57–99, but also to chap. 5 of Octavio Paz, *Labyrinth of Solitude*, trans. L. Kemp (New York: Grove Press, 1961), esp. 93–94, and even to William H. Prescott's *History of the Conquest of Mexico* (1843; Boston: Mackay, 1892). See Inga Clendinnen, "'Fierce and Unnatural Cruelty': Cortés and the Conquest of Mexico," *Representations* 33 (1991): 65–100, esp. 66.

77. Bernal Díaz, *Historia verdadera*, chap. 156, pp. 369–70. For the Guatemala manuscript's "una contienda ni más ni menos que ésta," the early printed editions read "otra contienda de la misma manera que esta." See the edition of Carmelo Sáenz de Santa María (Madrid: Consejo Superior de Investigaciones Científicas, 1982), 660. For the principals of the Roman quarrel, the text printed by Ramírez Cabañas reads, nonsensically, "Mario Cornelio y Sila."

78. Hugh Thomas, *Conquest* (New York: Simon and Schuster, 1993), 525–26.

79. Prescott, *History of the Conquest*, 3:180 n. 24.

80. Thomas suggests as sources Plutarch's life of Marius and, less plausibly, an unknown ballad (*Conquest*, 525 and 754 n. 61). But neither in his "Marius" (chap. 32) nor his "Sulla" (chap. 3) did Plutarch mention the triumphal squabble that is the central feature of Bernal Díaz's anecdote. Nor did Plutarch mention the "patrician vs. novus homo from Arpinum" angle, details an irregularly educated old soldier like Bernal Díaz is unlikely to have added to the anecdote on his own. Nor is Bernal Díaz's anecdote any more closely paralleled by the other ancient historians who mentioned Sulla's capture of Jugurtha: Sallust, Appian, the Periochae of Livy, Valerius Maximus, Florus, Festus, Eutropius, the author of "De viris illustribus," and Orosius.

81. Bernal Díaz, *Historia verdadera*, 370. The grant of a coat of arms to Cortés preserved in the Harkness Collection of the Library of Congress mentions not seven kings, but "three gold crowns on a black field," representing the three kings of Tenochtitlan with whom Cortés had to deal: Montezuma, Cuitláhuac, and Cuauhtémoc: *The Harkness Collection in the Library of Congress: Manuscripts concerning Mexico: A Guide*, with selected transcriptions and translations by J. Benedict Warren (Washington, D.C.: Library of Congress, 1974), 42–43.

82. Bernal Díaz referred to Medina del Campo as a "noble e insigne villa" in *Historia verdadera*, chap. 1, p. 1. He compared it to Tlatelolco in chap. 92. 171.

83. At her death, María Rosa Lida de Malkiel left unpublished a massive study of the theme of the fall of Jerusalem in Spanish literature. The fullest exposition of this material in print is her posthumous monograph *Jerusalén: El tema literario de su cerco y destrucción por los romanos* (Buenos Aires: Faculdad de Filosofía y Literaturas Hispánicas Dr. Amado Alonso, 1972). A brief discussion of the conquistadors' use of the motif is on pp. 111–12. See also Juan Gil, "El libro

greco-latino," 93–95, and David Hook, "The Legend of the Flavian Destruction of Jerusalem in Late Fifteenth-Century Spain and Portugal," *Bulletin of Hispanic Studies* 65 (1988): 113–28. See also Eduardo Subirats, *El continente vacío: La conquista del Nuevo Mundo y la conciencia moderna* (Mexico City: Siglo Veintiuno, 1994), 55 n. 6. While the fall of Jerusalem usually served as the "type" of the fall of Tenochtitlan, the Augustinian Antonio de la Calancha, in a history of his order published in Barcelona in 1638, offered it as the model for the Spanish destruction of the Inca government-in-exile in Vilcabamba in 1571; see Sabine MacCormack, "*Ubi Ecclesia?* Perceptions of Medieval Europe in Spanish America," *Speculum* 69 (1994): 78–79.

84. Bernal Díaz, *Historia verdadera*, chap. 156, p. 370. The reference to the silence succeeding the din of a *campanario* is on p. 369. It may be that Bernal Díaz read about the siege of Jerusalem in the religious romance *La estoria del noble Vaspasiano enperador de Roma*, printed by Juan Vázquez in Toledo sometime between 1491 and 1494: so Lida de Malkiel, *Jerusalén*, 111, and Hook, "Legend of Flavian Destruction," 116.

85. Cortés, *Letters from Mexico*, 159, *Cartas de relación*, 96.

86. Pagden, in Cortés, *Letters from Mexico*, 482 n. 119.

87. Motolinía, *Historia de los Indios de la Nueva España*, ed. Georges Baudot (Madrid: Castalia, 1985), first treatise, chap. 1, pp. 118–19.

88. Oviedo, *Historia general*, bk. 33, chap. 30, BAE vol. 120, 151–52.

89. Cortés, *Letters from Mexico*, 159, *Cartas de relación*, 96.

90. See the translation of the Nahuatl "Destruction of Jerusalem" by Marilyn Ekdahl Ravicz, *Early Colonial Religious Drama in Mexico: From Tzompantli to Golgotha* (Washington, D.C.: Catholic University of America Press, 1970), 181–209. See also Hook, "Legend of Flavian Destruction," 113–16.

91. For a stimulating recent account of this festival, emphasizing its "hidden transcripts," both native and Franciscan, see Max Harris, *Aztecs, Moors, and Christians* (Austin: University of Texas Press, 2000), 132–47. Harris does not draw attention to resonances with the Roman siege of Jerusalem. The account offered by Motolinía is in *Historia de los Indios*, second treatise chap. 15, pp. 202–15. Harris leans toward Edmundo O'Gorman's suggestion that the author of the account was a "resident friar of Tlaxcala," Motolinía himself not having been in the area in June (134, 266 n. 11). See also Richard Trexler, "We Think, They Act: Clerical Readings of Missionary Theatre in Sixteenth Century New Spain," in *Understanding Popular Culture*, ed. Steven L. Kaplan (Berlin: Mouton, 1984), 189–227, esp. 208–10. He argues that this play, like other pageants staged in New Spain in this period, was an example of a "theater of humiliation," conjuring "a world safe for Hispanicism."

92. Motolinía, *Historia de los Indios*, 205–6.

93. See Harris, *Aztecs, Moors, and Christians*, 137–39.

94. Oviedo, *Historia general*, bk. 33, chap. 31, BAE vol. 120, 152.

95. Bernal Díaz, *Historia verdadera*, chap. 6, p. 13.

96. See Giuliano Gliozzi, *Adamo e il nuovo mondo* (Florence: Nuova Italia, 1976), chap. 2, "Gli ebrei nel Nuovo Mondo," 49–110.

97. Diego Durán, *The History of the Indies of New Spain*, trans. Doris Hey-

den (Norman: University of Oklahoma Press, 1994), 3–11. For the relationship between the Roldán manuscript and Duran's history, see Gliozzi, *Adamo e il nuovo mondo*, 49–61.

98. For the battle cry "Santiago y a ellos," see Bernal Díaz, *Historia verdadera*, chap. 142, p. 305. See Weckmann, *Medieval Heritage of Mexico*, 111–13 and 115 n. 20. Gómara implied that Santiago put in a spectral appearance early on in Cortés's expedition at the battle against the Tabascans at Cintla (*Cortés*, chap. 20, p. 47), but Bernal Díaz ironically noted, "I, a poor sinner, was unable to see him" (*Historia verdadera*, chap. 34, p. 56). Cortés referred to Aztec temples as *mesquitas* in his second letter, *Cartas de relación*, 64. See Weckmann, 107–8. The idea that the conquistadors saw the conquest of the Indies as a later phase of the Reconquista is a topos of conquest scholarship. See, for example, Américo Castro, *The Spaniards: An Introduction to Their History*, trans. Willard F. King and Selma Margaretten (Berkeley and Los Angeles: University of California Press, 1971), 175–76; Peggy Liss, *Mexico under Spain, 1521–1556: Society and the Origins of Nationality* (Chicago: University of Chicago Press, 1975), 19–30; Octavio Paz, *El ogro filantrópico* (Barcelona: Seix Barral, 1979), 31; Anthony Pagden, "*Ius et Factum:* Text and Experience in the Writings of Bartolomé de las Casas," *Representations* 33 (1991): 155–56; Thomas, *Conquest*, 293. Thomas notes that the very word *conquistador* "was one used by the Castilian victors against Islam." For illuminating hints of how the organization and procedures of Spanish *entradas* in the New World were in fact indebted to those of bands of warriors in the Reconquest of Spain, see Mario Góngora, *Studies in the Colonial History of Spanish America* (Cambridge: Cambridge University Press, 1975), 1–3. Pagden, on the other hand, argues that "economically, politically and militarily the conquest of America had more in common with the Spanish wars in Italy than it had with the recovery of the peninsula. But ideologically the struggle against Islam offered a descriptive language which allowed the generally shabby ventures in America to be vested with a seemingly eschatological significance" (*Lords of All the World* [New Haven: Yale University Press, 1995], 74). A brief but stimulating dissent to the Reconquest-conquest model is Charles Gibson's article "Reconquista and Conquista," in *Homage to Irving A. Leonard*, ed. R. Chang-Rodríguez and D. A. Yates (East Lansing: Latin American Studies Center, Michigan State University, 1977), 19–28. Somewhat rigidly restricting himself to the level of official royal claims and propaganda, Gibson argues that the attitudes implied by the term *reconquista* (itself of eighteenth-century vintage) would have only come into play where there was at least a plausible pretence of recovering supposedly former Spanish Visigothic territory (notably in North Africa) held by Moslems. In America, at most only "some derivative attributes of Reconquista survived" (26). He also argues that the "Reconquest mentality" would have been highly attenuated in the New World because "not only different individuals but different generations were involved" (20). This ignores what one might call the "epigonoi complex," the desire of sons and grandsons to match the exploits and share the glory of their celebrated forbears.

99. Cortés, *Letters from Mexico*, 63, *Cartas de relación*, 40.

100. López de Gómara, *Historia general de las Indias*, dedication to Charles V (Madrid: Espasa-Calpe, 1932), 1:5.

101. Oliver Dunn and James E. Kelly Jr., eds., *The Diario of Christopher Columbus' First Voyage to America, 1492–1493, Abstracted by Fray Bartolomé de las Casas* (Norman: University of Oklahoma Press, 1989), 17–18, 291. See Todorov, *The Conquest of America*, 50.

Chapter 2

1. A fine account "controversy of the Indies" is Anthony Pagden, *The Fall of Natural Man: The American Indian and the Origins of Comparative Ethnology*, 2d ed. (Cambridge: Cambridge University Press, 1986). See also three books by Lewis Hanke: *The Spanish Struggle for Justice in the Conquest of America* (Philadelphia: American Historical Association, 1949); *Aristotle and the American Indians* (Bloomington: Indiana University Press, 1959); *All Mankind Is One* (De Kalb: Northern Illinois University Press, 1974). A succinct summary of the major texts in the controversy is Mauricio Beuchot, *La Querella de la conquista: Una polémica del siglo XVI* (Mexico City: Siglo Veintiuno, 1992). Useful collections of essays are Juan Friede and Benjamin Keen, eds., *Bartolomé de las Casas in History* (De Kalb: Northern Illinois University Press, 1971); and Demetrio Ramos et al., eds., *La ética en la conquista de América*, Corpus Hispanorum de Pace, vol. 25 (Madrid: Consejo Superior de Investigaciones Científicas, 1984). See also Brading, *The First America*, 79–101; Luis N. Rivera, *A Violent Evangelism: The Political and Religious Conquest of the Americas* (Louisville: Westminster/John Knox Press, 1992), esp. 200–216; Luciano Pereña Vicente, *La idea de justicia en la conquista de América* (Madrid: Mapfre, 1992), with an annotated bibliography on pp. 263–77 and a useful chronological chart of the years 1493–1585 on pp. 279–98; and Gustavo Gutiérrez, *Las Casas: In Search of the Poor of Jesus Christ*, trans. Robert R. Barr (Maryknoll: Orbis, 1993), with a very full bibliography on pp. 627–68. The fullest account of the theological debate remains the learned, if jingoistic, work of Venancio D. Carro, *La teología y los teólogos-juristas españoles ante la conquista de América*, 2 vols. (Madrid: Publicaciones de la Escuela de Estudios Hispano-Americanos de la Universidad de Sevilla, 1944). A stimulating recent discussion that acknowledges the importance of the model of Roman imperialism in the debate is Pagden's *Lords of All the World*. See also González Rodríguez, *La idea de Roma*. A promising subject for future research would be a comparison of Spanish appeals to the "Roman model" with those of other colonizing powers in the New World. Patricia Seed offers an excellent preliminary sketch for such a project in *Ceremonies of Possession in Europe's Conquest of the New World* (Cambridge: Cambridge University Press, 1995), 180–84.

2. See Marie Tanner, *The Last Descendant of Aeneas: The Hapsburgs and the Mythic Image of the Emperor* (New Haven: Yale University Press, 1993), esp. 98–109.

3. For the imperial claims of Alfonso VI and Alfonso VII, see R. B. Merriman, *The Rise of the Spanish Empire in the Old World and the New*, vol. 1: *The*

Middle Ages (New York: Macmillan, 1918), 89–91. See also Percy Ernst Schramm, "König Alfonso X. el Sabio (1252–84), deutscher Gegenkönig. Ein Beitrag zur spanischen 'Kaiseridee,'" in Schramm, *Kaiser, Könige und Päpste: Gesammelte Aufsätze zur Geschichte des Mittelalters,* vol. 4, pt. 1 (Stuttgart: Anton Hiersemann, 1970), 378–81. A literary account of the "nationalspanische Geschichtstradition" of an equation of Spanish and Roman Imperial dignity is Ernst Robert Curtius, "Jorge Manrique und der Kaisergedanke." In a brief account of the imperial pretensions of Alfonso VI and VII, Pagden notes that "there was little to match this in either France or England" (*Lords,* 41).

4. For Vincentius Hispanus, see Gaines Post, *Studies in Medieval Legal Thought: Public Law and the State, 1100–1322* (Princeton: Princeton University Press, 1964), 482–93.

5. Charles F. Fraker, "Alfonso X, the Empire, and the *Primera crónica*" (orig. 1978), reprinted in *The Scope of History* (Ann Arbor: University of Michigan Press, 1996), 155–69. For an account of Alfonso X's imperial ambitions, see Schramm, *Kaiser, König und Päpste,* 383–419.

6. Merriman, *Rise of Spanish Empire,* 91. Merriman proceeds to note that "when the imperial dignity was finally revived under Charles V, it was bound to arouse many stirring memories, and the glories which the Spaniards had never ceased to associate with it went far to reconcile them to the government of a foreign dynasty."

7. Juan de Mena, *Laberinto de fortuna,* CCXXX (line 1834) and CXLII (line 1131), ed. John G. Cummins, 4th ed. (Madrid: Cátedra, 1990), 161 and 121. Victor Frankl claimed that de Mena "introduce en la visión histórica española un motivo enteramente nuevo, de inaudita fecundidad política y de amplísimas consecuencias históricas e histroiográficas: el 'Romanismo' o 'Latinismo.' . . . Pero ante todo introduce Juan de Mena este 'Romanismo' en la visión histórica a causa de una nueva idea política de suma pujanza, a saber, el nacionalismo español de definida orientación imperialista, que entraña no sólo el programa de la unidad de España y la concentración de todas sus energías en la Reconquista, sino también el del dominio universal de su rey y la sucesión del mismo en el Imperio romano, indentifcándose, en cierto sentido, Roma y España." *El "Antijovio" de Gonzalo Jiménez de Quesada y las concepciones de realidad y verdad en la época de la contrarreforma y del manierismo* (Madrid: Ediciones Cultura Hispánica, 1963), 214–15.

8. I owe these citations to José Antonio Maravall, "El concepto de monarquía en la edad media española," reprinted in his *Estudios de historia del pensamiento español,* vol. 1 (Madrid: Ediciones Cultura Hispánica, 1983), 67–85.

9. See Ramón Menéndez Pidal, "Idea imperial de Carlos V" (1940), in *España y su historia,* 2:91–107; and Frances A. Yates, "Charles V and the Idea of the Empire," in *Astraea: The Imperial Theme in the Sixteenth Century* (London: Routledge and Kegan Paul, 1975), 1–28. For the recurrent contention that Charles V was, as Roman emperor, "lord of the whole world," see Pagden, *Lords;* and Franz Bosbach, *Monarchia universalis: Ein politischer Leitbegriff der frühen Neuzeit* (Göttingen: Vanderhoeck and Ruprecht, 1988), chap. 3, "Die Univer-

salmonarchie Karls V.," 35–63. Bosbach has made an extensive survey of the tracts and speeches promoting this idea inherited from medieval jurists.

10. See Marcel Bataillon, *Erasmo y España*, trans. Antonio Alatorre, 2d ed. (Mexico City: Fondo de Cultura Económica, 1966), 231–32; in French, *Érasme et l'Espagne*, 2d ed. (Geneva: Droz, 1991), 248–49.

11. John M. Headley, "The Hapsburg World Empire and the Revival of Ghibellinism," *Medieval and Renaissance Studies*, vol. 7, ed. S. Wenzel (Chapel Hill, 1978), 93–127. The text of Mota's speech may be found in *Cortes de los antiguos reinos de León y de Castilla*, vol. 4 (Madrid: La Real Academia de la Historia, 1882), 293–98. The quoted passage is on p. 295. See also Bosbach, *Monarchia universalis*, 54–56, for a brief compendium of Gattinara's formulations. For the topos of Spain as mother of emperors, see Agustín Redondo, *Antonio de Guevara (1480?–1545) et l'Espagne de son temps* (Geneva: Droz, 1976), 470. It goes back to Pacatus's panegyric to Theodosius and was picked up in the thirteenth century by Lucas de Tuy in his *Chronicon Mundi* ("Hispania Romae dedit imperatores strenuos").

12. Miguel de Ulzurrum (Michael Ulcurrunus), *Catholicum opus imperiale regiminis mundi*. I have used the edition published in vol. 16 of *Tractatus universi iuris* (Venice: Zilettus, 1584–86), 103v–130r. For a brief discussion of Ulzurrum's treatise, see José Antonio Maravall, *Carlos V y el pensamiento del renacimiento* (Madrid: Instituto de Estudios Políticos, 1960), 173–76.

13. Ulzurrum, *Catholicum opus imperiale*, part 2, third principal question, secs. 24–25, 50, 59, fols. 117v, 119r, 119v.

14. Ibid., 2.3, secs. 21–22, fol. 117v.

15. Ibid., secs. 18–19, fol. 117v; see also secs. 37 and 42, fol. 118v; also the addendum attacking Oldradus, secs. 20–21, 32, 34, fols. 122v, 123r.

16. Ibid., 2.3, sec. 47, fol. 119r.

17. Ibid., untitled addendum on Oldradus, sec. 32, fol. 123r. This was the foundation legend of the church of S. Maria in Aracoeli on the Capitoline Hill in Rome. See the twelfth-century pilgrim manual *Mirabilia Urbis Romae*, pt. 2, chap. 1. See also Gregorovius, *History of the City of Rome in the Middle Ages*, trans. Annie Hamilton (London: G. Bell, 1902), vol. 4, pt. 2, pp. 472–74. I owe this information to a personal communication from Edwin P. Menes.

18. Ulzurrum, *Catholicum opus imperiale*, secs. 33–34, fol. 123r.

19. Ibid., secs. 50–51, fol. 124r.

20. Ibid., part 2, Second principle question, secs. 67 and 72, fols. 114v–115r.

21. Innocent IV, *Quod super his*, translated in Brian Tierney, *The Crisis of Church and State: 1050–1300* (Englewood Cliffs, N.J.: Prentice-Hall, 1964), 155.

22. Ulzurrum, *Catholicum opus imperiale*, part 2, second principle question, sec. 98, fol. 116r.

23. Ibid., third principle question, sec. 90, fol. 121r.

24. I derive my information about Arredondo y Alvarado's chronicle from Pagden, *Lords*, 42. I have not been able to examine this work at first hand.

25. Lodovico Ariosto, *Orlando Furioso*, ed. Dino Provenzal (Milan: Rizzoli, 1955), canto 15, stanza 26, 2:11. The next stanza refers to Cortés's conquest of Mexico.

26. Roy Strong, *Splendour at Court: Renaissance Spectacle and Illusion* (London: Weidenfeld and Nicolson, 1973), 81–82. Chapter 3 offers a well-illustrated account of the pageants of Charles V (pp. 79–119). Cf. Erwin Panofsky's suggestion that the Roman *hasta* with which Titian supplied Charles in the great equestrian portrait celebrating the Battle of Mühlberg in 1547 was meant to call to mind the ancient ritual of the Profectio Augusti (*Problems in Titian, Mostly Iconographic* [New York: New York University Press, 1969], 86).

27. Bernal Díaz, *Historia verdadera*, chap. 201, pp. 544–45. Max Harris suggests that this festival took place during carnival week (Lent began on February 19, 1539) (*Aztecs, Moors, and Christians*, 125). For recent discussions of the festivities, which included a pageant in which Cortés retook Rhodes from the Turks, see Harris, 123–31 and Patricia Lopes Don, "Carnivals, Triumphs, and Rain Gods in the New World," *Colonial Latin American Review* 6 (1997): 17–40. Luis de León Romano probably owed his festival plans less to his supposed descent from the ancient Romans than from his recollections of Charles V's triumphal entry into Rome in 1536. See Robert Ricard, *Études et documents pour l'histoire missionnaire de l'Espagne et du Portugal* (Louvain: Aucam, 1931), 161–68.

28. Posthumous editions brought Mexía's chronicle forward, via other hands, to the reign of Charles V (e.g. the 1561 edition cited by Pagden, *Lords*, 231) and even beyond.

29. Antonio de Guevara, *Libro aúreo de Marco Aurelio*, ed. Raimond Foulché-Delbosc, *Revue hispanique* 76, no. 169 (1929): 13. This is not a reprint of any of the published versions of the *Libro aúreo*, but an edition of the manuscript in the Escorial. There is a possibility that this is the MS Guevara presented to the king in 1524. In any case, Foulché-Delbosc maintains that "sa belle exécution permet du moins de supposer qu'il fut offert à quelque personnage d'un rang élevé" (5).

30. See the passage cited from the preface to the *Reloj de príncipes* in Joseph R. Jones, *Antonio de Guevara* (Boston: Twayne, 1975), 54–55.

31. For the manuscript and printed history of the *Libro aúreo* and the *Reloj de príncipes*, see the appendix to Redondo's authoritative *Antonio de Guevara*, 465–71, 523–26, 757–60.

32. The significance of this has been noted by Maravall, who argues that this "utopian" touch implies that "el autor considera una imagen del Imperio muy diferente de la que ha condenado" *(Carlos V,* 201).

33. Guevara, *Libro aúreo*, 119. The episode of the "Villano" occupies chapters 31–32 of the work, pp. 118–26.

34. Guevara, *Libro aúreo*, 121.

35. I am using the text of the *Reloj* version of the "Villano" as reprinted in Guillermo Díaz-Plaja, ed., *Antología mayor de la literatura española*, vol. 2: *Renacimiento* (Barcelona: Editorial Labor, 1958), 617–25. The passage on Rome's "civilizing mission" is on pp. 621–22.

36. I have cited the *Reloj* version from Díaz-Plaja, 623. Cf. *Libro aúreo*, 123.

37. The relevance of the "Villano" to the New World was emphasized in a widely reprinted article by Américo Castro, "Antonio de Guevara: Un hombre y un estilo del siglo XVI," originally published in 1945. I have used the reprint in

Castro's *Hacia Cervantes,* 3d ed. (Madrid: Taurus, 1967), 86–117; see esp. 97–98. Castro was anticipated by René Costes, *Antonio de Guevara: Son oeuvre* (Bordeaux: Feret, 1926), 1:60–62. See also Asunción Rallo Gruss, *Antonio de Guevara en su contexto renacentista* (Madrid: Cupsa, 1977), 133–38; and González Rodríguez, *La idea de Roma,* 47–49, 104. Redondo's extensive treatment of this question is *Antonio de Guevara,* 661–90.

38. Guevara, *Libro aúreo,* 120, where the reading "que ni la mar nos pudo valer en sus abismos, ni la tierra segurar en sus cuevas" is preferable to the reading of the *Reloj,* "que ni la mar vos pudo valer en sus abismos, ni la tierra vos pudo asegurar en sus campos" (618). See Redondo, *Antonio de Guevara,* 666 n. 459; and Castro, "Antonio de Guevara," 107–8 n. 2.

39. See Redondo, *Antonio de Guevara,* 664–66.

40. Pedro de Córdoba, cited by Nicolás Sánchez-Albornoz, in *Cambridge History of Latin America,* ed. Leslie Bethell, vol. 2 (Cambridge: Cambridge University Press, 1984), 12. In addition, Redondo (*Antonio de Guevara,* 685 n. 551) cites Las Casas's 1542 *Octavo remedio* on infanticide, abortion, and abstention from marital intercourse among the Indians of Cuba (*Obras escogidas,* ed. Juan Pérez de Tudela Bueso, vol. 5, BAE vol. 110 [Madrid: Atlas, 1972], 103–4).

41. Marcel Bataillon, "Vasco de Quiroga et Bartolomé de las Casas," in *Études sur Bartolomé de las Casas* (Paris: Centre de Recherches de L'institut d'études Hispaniques, 1965), 229–30. Bataillon has been followed by Redondo, *Antonio de Guevara,* 501 n. 205, and 662 n. 40; and Silvio Zavala, *Por la senda hispana de la libertad* (Madrid: Mapfre, 1992), 221. The abbreviation V.M., which Bataillon takes to mean "Vuestra Merced," was taken by the first editor of the text to be "Vuestra Majestad" (*Documentos inéditos del Archivo de Indias,* vol. 10, 1868, 333), and this persuaded René Costes (*Antonio de Guevara,* 1:61), Américo Castro ("Antonio de Guevara," 97), and Rallo Gruss (*Antonio de Guevara,* 134 n. 14) that the document was addressed to the emperor. In his introduction to an edition of the *Información en derecho,* Carlos Herrejón Peredo does not mention the possibility of Charles being the addressee. While he does cite Bataillon's thesis, he ventures only to affirm that it was probably addressed to a member of the Consejo de Indias: *Información en derecho del licenciado Quiroga* (Mexico City: Secretaría de Educación Pública, 1985), 12–13.

42. Vasco de Quiroga, *Información en derecho,* chap. 2, sec. 6, p. 58.

43. Hayward Keniston, ed., *Libro de la vida y costumbres de Don Alonso Enríquez de Guzmán,* BAE vol. 126 (Madrid: Atlas, 1960), 162.

44. André Chastel, *The Sack of Rome, 1527,* trans. Beth Archer (Princeton: Princeton University Press, 1983), 36.

45. Alfonso de Valdés, *Diálogo de las cosas ocurridas en Roma* (Madrid: Espasa-Calpe, 1956), 14.

46. See Bataillon, *Erasmo y España,* 383.

47. Guevara, *Libro aúreo,* 123; *Reloj* (in Díaz-Plaja), 620. For the length of the most violent phase of the 1527 sack of Rome, see Gregorovius, *History of Rome,* vol. 8, pt. 2, p. 593; and Ludwig Pastor, *History of the Popes from the Close of the Middle Ages,* vol. 9 (St. Louis: Herder, 1910), 416 (and n. 1). The Visigothic sack of Rome in 410, on the other hand, lasted three days.

48. Guevara, *Reloj* (in Díaz-Plaja), 621.

49. Pedro Mexía, *Silva de varia lección*, ed. Antonio Castro, vol. 1 (Madrid: Cátedra, 1989), 442. For Mexía's use of Guevara, see Pilar Concejo, *Antonio de Guevara: Un ensayista del siglo XVI* (Madrid: Ediciones Cultura Hispanica, Instituto de cooperación iberoamericana, 1985), 39–41.

50. Cervantes, *Numancia*, ed. Robert Marrast, 2d. ed. (Madrid: Cátedra, 1990), 56, lines 485–88.

51. Guevara, *Libro aúreo*, 216.

52. Guevara, *Reloj*, bk. 3, chap. 16, cited by Redondo, *Antonio de Guevara*, 660; and Ricardo del Arco y Garay, *La idea de imperio en la política y la literatura españolas* (Madrid: Espasa-Calpe, 1944), 161. Maravall (*Carlos V*, 200) misleadingly implies that this passage was found in the *Libro aúreo*. In fact, he was citing Cromberger's 1532 edition of the *Reloj (Libro de Marco Aurelio con el Reloj de príncipes*, fol. clviii).

53. The claim that God "quiere que un emperador solo sea monarcha y señor del mundo" is in Guevara, *Reloj*, bk. 1, chap. 18. It is cited by Redondo, *Antonio de Guevara*, 587, Maravall, *Carlos V*, 197 (where, again, it is misleadingly attributed to the *Libro aúreo*); and J. A. Fernández-Santamaría, *The State, War, and Peace: Spanish Political Thought in the Renaissance 1516–1559* (Cambridge: Cambridge University Press, 1977), 264 (where it is misleadingly attributed to *Vida*, but in fact he was using the same 1532 edition of the *Reloj* as Maravall). See Maravall, 200–203, for Guevara's remarkable juxtaposition of the theoretical doctrine of the emperor's lordship of the world with a passionate rejection of wars of conquest. This supplies an important corrective to Fernández-Santamaría's presentation of Guevara as "a partisan of the imperial idea" little different from Ulzurrum (261).

54. Brading, *The First America*, 1.

55. Hanke, *Aristotle*, 37.

56. Menéndez Pidal's fullest attack on Las Casas was *El Padre Las Casas: Su doble personalidad* (Madrid: Espasa-Calpe, 1963). See also "Vitoria y Las Casas," the title essay in his collection *El Padre Las Casas y Vitoria, con otros temas de los siglos XVI y XVII*, 2d ed. (Madrid: Espasa-Calpe, 1953), 9–48. I have taken his phrase "el más agriado hombre del mundo" from his essay "¿Codicia insaciable? ¿Ilustres hazañas?" 116.

57. Gutiérrez, *Las Casas*.

58. Las Casas, *Historia de las Indias*, bk. 3, chap. 3; from the abridged translation by Andrée M. Collard, *History of the Indies* (New York: Harper, 1971), 183. Cf. Spanish edition by Miguel Angel Medina, in *Obras completas*, ed. Paulino Castañeda Delgado (Madrid: Alianza Editorial, 1994), 5:1760.

59. Las Casas, *Historia de las Indias*, bk. 3, chap. 3, 5:1760; *History of the Indies*, 183.

60. Las Casas, *Historia de las Indias*, bk. 3, chap. 4, 5:1761–62; *History of the Indies*, 184.

61. The likely contribution of Las Casas to his text of Montesinos's Advent sermon is assessed by Antonio García y García, "El sentido de las primeras denuncias," in Ramos et al., *La ética en la conquista*, 70–73. In light of other indi-

cations, García particularly suspects any challenges to the justice of the conquest, for Montesinos's focus appears to have been on the encomienda.

62. Response of Ferdinand (probably drafted by Fonseca) to Diego Columbus, in J. H. Parry and Robert G. Keith, *New Iberian World,* 5 vols. (New York: Times Books, 1984), 2:313. A useful short account of the aftermath of Montesinos's sermon is chap. 2 of Hanke's *Spanish Struggle for Justice,* 23–36.

63. Las Casas, *Historia de las Indias,* bk. 3, chap. 12, 5:1802–3.

64. A translation of the Laws of Burgos is in Parry and Keith, *New Iberian World,* 1:336–47. The passage forbidding Spaniards to call Indians "dogs" is on p. 343 (article 24).

65. Patricia Seed, "'Are These Not Also Men?' The Indians' Humanity and Capacity for Spanish Civilisation," *Journal of Latin American Studies* 25 (1993): 640.

66. Ibid., 634.

67. Las Casas, *Historia de las Indias,* bk. 3, chap. 5, 5:1768.

68. Daniel Deckers, "La justicia de la conquista de América. Consideraciónes en torno a la cronología y a los protagonistas de una controversia del siglo XVI muy actual," *Ibero-Amerikanisches Archiv* 18 (1992): 331–66; see esp. pp. 346–59.

69. For the career and works of Domingo de Soto, see Juan Belda Plans, *La escuela de Salamanca* (Madrid: Biblioteca de Autores Cristianos 2000), 399–500. Soto's *Relectio de dominio* was first published in a critical edition, with introduction and facing Spanish translation, by Jaime Brufau Prats in 1964 (Universidad de Granada). A perusal of scholarship on the controversy of the Indies reveals the neglect of De Soto's seminal relection. For example, though Anthony Pagden does include it in the bibliography to *The Fall of Natural Man,* he in fact cites only *De iustitia et iure* in the text, and he lists Soto among several Dominicans whose pronouncements show that "in the years which followed the delivery of *De Indis* the justice of the Spanish conquests and the nature of the American Indian formed a staple part of any discussion on the nature and origin of human societies or on the rule of law" (107). Similarly, Mauricio Beuchot, though he does acknowledge Soto's priority, places his summary of *De dominio (Querella de la conquista,* 41–50) after a much fuller discussion of Vitoria. In addition, he devotes much of his discussion of Soto's relection to the question of slavery, though Soto did not in fact consider slavery in relation to the conquest of the Indies at all. While Gustavo Gutiérrez correctly maintains that "Soto intervened in questions of the Indies before Vitoria did," he supports this with the claim that Soto "quite early" wrote a book on the subject, the lost *De ratione promulgandi Evangelium* (*Las Casas,* 505 n. 15). But Soto mentioned this lost treatise as being "ready" *(paratum)* at the end of pt. 4, question. 4, art. 2 of *De iustitia et iure* (p. 307). This implies that this was in 1553 a recent work Soto intended to print soon, thus obviating the necessity to deal with the question of the Indies explicitly in *De iustitia et iure.* In a later footnote Gutiérrez more correctly noted that Vitoria was anticipated by Soto, "who some years earlier, in 1535, had presented his *relección De Dominio,* in which he deals with the question of the Indies" (576 n. 11), though he does not indicate that he has actually read Soto's relection, which he

does not cite in his extensive bibliography. One scholar who has more adequately emphasized the priority of Soto is, not surprisingly, the first editor of the *De dominio:* J. Brufau Prats. See his collection of earlier articles published as *La escuela de Salamanca ante el descubrimiento del nuevo mundo* (Salamanca: Editorial San Estéban, 1989), esp. chap. 5, "Domingo de Soto y su relección 'De Dominio'" (repr. from *Anuario de la Asociación Francisco de Vitoria* 16 [Madrid, 1965–66], 117–44), and also chap. 8, "Revisión de la primera generación de la escuela salamantina," 151–69, esp. 152 (repr. from Ramos et al., *La ética en la conquista,* 383–412). In addition to the four codices of Soto's relection described by Brufau Prats on pp. 20–33 of his edition, another copy has been discovered in the Fernán Nuñez Collection in the Bancroft Library of the University of California at Berkeley by Thomas M. Izbicki. See Izbicki, "Salamancan Relectiones in the Fernán Nuñez Collection," *Studia Gratiana* 29 (1998): 489–500.

70. Brufau Prats dates Soto's *De Dominio* between February 28 and June 23, 1535. See the introduction to his edition, 54–57.

71. For an illuminating treatment of the importance of the concept of *dominium* in the controversy of the Indies, see Anthony Pagden, *Spanish Imperialism and the Political Imagination* (New Haven: Yale University Press, 1990), chap. 1. See esp. pp. 16–17 for the use of the term *dominium* by the "School of Salamanca." Here he draws attention to the influential formulation of *dominium* offered by Soto in his mature *De iustitia et iure,* but this was all anticipated nearly twenty years earlier in the *Relectio de dominio* (which Pagden does not cite).

72. Soto, *De dominio,* 74, 78.

73. Ibid., 138. For the supposed "world dominion" of the emperor, see Pagden, *Lords;* and Bosbach, *Monarchia universalis.*

74. The appeal to the statue of Daniel 2 in the attempt to justify Spanish dominion in the Indies in fact antedated the reign of Charles V. Around 1512–14, the royal jurist Juan López de Palacios Rubios, author of the notorious "Requerimiento," wrote a defense of Ferdinand's claim to the Indies in which he invoked the statue of Daniel in order to posit a succession of world monarchies culminating in the Roman Empire at the time of Augustus. With the birth of Christ, Palacios Rubios argued, world dominion passed to Christ and hence to the pope, who was thus entitled to pass dominion of the Indies on to the Catholic Monarchs. See the translation by Agustín Millares Carlo, *De las Islas del mar Océano* (Mexico City: Fondo de Cultura Económica, 1954), 79–80.

75. Soto, *De dominio,* 144. Pagden *(Lords,* 38) observes that, while the Romans themselves harmonized an awareness of lands beyond the imperial frontier with an assumption that the true *orbis terrarum* coincided with their political and cultural dominion, "later writers tended to be far more literal-minded, and were consequently more troubled by the degree of fit—or evident lack of it— between the Roman world and *the* world itself." (Pagden does not cite Soto's *De dominio* in this book.)

76. Soto, *De dominio,* 148. David A. Brading rightly observes that "in the debate over the Conquest of the Indies, the *City of God* was as influential a text as Aristotle's *Politics.*" See *Prophecy and Myth in Mexican History* (Cambridge: Center for Latin American Studies, Cambridge University, 1984), 7–27, and "The

Two Cities: St. Augustine and the Spanish Conquest of America," *Revista portugeusa de filosofía* 44, no. 1 (1988): 99–126.

77. "Aquinas," *De regimine principum ad regem cypri,* ed. Joseph Mathis, 2d ed. (Turin: Marietti, 1948), bk. 3, chaps. 4–6, pp. 41–44.

78. For Ptolemy of Lucca and his complicated attitude toward the Romans, see Charles Till Davis, "Roman Patriotism and Republican Propaganda: Ptolemy of Lucca and Pope Nicholas III" and "Ptolemy of Lucca and the Roman Republic," reprinted in his *Dante's Italy, and Other Essays* (Philadelphia: University of Pennsylvania Press, 1984), 224–89.

79. Soto, *De dominio,* 150.

80. Marinus "considered that the Romans had no universal right to empire because they had established their dominion through force of arms, so that the empire was essentially a merely *de facto* power" (J. P. Canning, "Law, Sovereignty, and Corporation Theory, 1300–1450," in *Cambridge History of Medieval Political Thought, c. 350–c. 1450,* ed. J. H. Burns [Cambridge: Cambridge University Press, 1988], 465).

81. Anthony Pagden and Jeremy Lawrance, eds., *Political Writings,* by Francisco de Vitoria (Cambridge: Cambridge University Press, 1991), xiii. For a recent account of Vitoria's career and teachings, see Belda Plans, *La escuela de Salamanca,* 252–61, 313–98.

82. For the influence of Vitoria's views and the placement of his students, see Luciano Pereña, "La escuela de Salamanca y la duda indiana," in Ramos et al., *La ética en la conquista,* 291–344; and Agueda Rodríguez, "Discípulos de la Universidad de Salamanca en América," in Ramos et al., *La ética en la conquista,* 499–549.

83. Vitoria's reputation as a pioneer of international law was given currency in the English-speaking world by the inclusion of his *relectiones* on the Indies in the "Classics of International Law" series published by the Carnegie Institution in the early decades of the twentieth century and by the publication of James Brown Scott's influential *The Spanish Origin of International Law,* pt. 1: *Francisco de Vitoria and His Law of Nations* (Oxford: Clarendon Press, 1934). For a recent attempt to present Vitoria as "fundador del derecho internacional," see Belda Plans, *La escuela de Salamanca,* 379–93.

84. Vitoria, letter to Miguel de Arcos, *Political Writings,* appendix A, 331–33. The original text, in a mixture of Spanish and Latin, is printed as appendix 1 in Vitoria, *Relectio de Indis,* ed. L. Pereña and J. M. Pérez Prendes, Corpus Hispanorum de Pace (hereafter abbreviated CHP), vol. 5 (Madrid: Consejo Superior de Investigaciones Científicas, 1967), 137–39. Unless otherwise indicated, all subsequent citations of the *Relectio de Indis* are to this edition. Though this text prints the date "8.a novembre 1534" as part of the manuscript, T. Urdánoz maintained that "el texto de la carta no expresa el año en que fué escrita" (Vitoria, *Obras,* ed. Teófilo Urdánoz [Madrid: Editorial Católica, 1960], 505–6 n. 30). Despite the letter's apparent treatment of the events in Peru as recent, Urdánoz argued for a much later date: 1545 (pp. 505–6 and also p. 57)—the letter's mention of the vacancy of the archbishopric of Toledo would suit either 1534 or 1545. Urdánoz believed that the later date was preferable because it did away with the "larga fase

de silencio y reserva" that would have to be posited between the earlier date and the *Relectio de Indis* of 1539. This argument has impressed a number of scholars: the letter's discoverer Beltrán de Herédia (according to Urdánoz), Carro, Pérez Fernández, and, most recently, Gutiérrez (*Las Casas*, 585 n. 59). For information on Arcos's copy of Soto's *De dominio*, see Brufau Prats's edition, 23–24.

85. The relevant passages from "On the Evangelization of Unbelievers" are translated in Vitoria, *Political Writings*, appendix B, 339–51 (Indians' *dominium rerum*, 349; sins against nature, 347).

86. R. Agostino Iannarone, "Génesis del pensamiento colonial en Francisco de Vitoria," an introductory essay to the CHP edition of *Relectio de Indis*, xxxiv. Iannarone quotes here the whole of the relevant passage from Vitoria's *In II-II, p. 62, a, I, n. 28*

87. The best English translation of these relections is Vitoria, *Political Writings*, 231–327. The now standard Latin texts with Spanish translations are in the CHP series, vol. 5, *Relectio de Indis*, and vol. 6, *De iure belli*, ed. L. Pereña, V. Abril, C. Baciero, A. García, and F. Maseda (Madrid: Consejo Superior de Investigaciones Científicas, 1981). Subsequent citations of *De iure belli* are to this edition. Latin texts may also be found in *De Indis et De iure belli relectiones*, ed. Ernest Nys (Washington D.C.: Carnegie Institute, 1917). In addition to the introductions and appendices of the Pagden and Lawrance translations and the CHP editions, useful discussions are Carro, *La teología*, 2:9–254; Maravall, *Carlos V*, 248–62; Fernández-Santamaría, *State, War, and Peace*, 58–119; Quentin Skinner, *The Foundations of Modern Political Thought*, vol. 2 (Cambridge: Cambridge University Press, 1978), 135–73; Pagden, *Fall of Natural Man*, 64–108; James Muldoon, *Popes, Lawyers, and Infidels: The Church and the Non-Christian World, 1250–1550* (Philadelphia: University of Pennsylvania Press, 1979), 143–52.

88. Vitoria, *Relectio de Indis*, praeludium, 2.

89. Ibid., 1.1, p. 13.

90. Ibid., 1.15, p. 29.

91. Ibid., 2.1, p. 34

92. Ibid., 2.2, p. 36. Cf. Soto, *De dominio*, 140.

93. Biographical note by Pagden and Lawrance in Vitoria, *Political Writings*, 355.

94. Vitoria, *Relectio de Indis*, 2.2, pp. 37–38. The reference to Augustine presents a difficulty. Vitoria seems to be referring to *De civ. D.* bk. 18, chap. 2 (not 20, *pace* Pereña and Pérez Prendes), where Augustine said that the great empires, including that of the Romans, did not come about "sine Dei providentia." This, however, would seem to support precisely that "correction" of Augustine which Vitoria offers immediately after his citation of him: "sed quod providentia divina factum est, etc." Pereña and Pérez Prendes finesse this problem by simply transposing the Augustine quotation to the appropriate location in their translation: "sino que, como dice asímismo muy bien San Agustín, plugo a la Divina Providencia . . ." (38). Pagden and Lawrance hew closer to the transmitted text ("and Augustine says the same thing"), but they inexplicably substitute CD 3.10 as the citation, a chapter on Rome's early expansion by violent means, with no hint of any sort of approval by the Christian God (Vitoria, *Political Writings*, 254).

95. Vitoria, *Relectio de Indis*, 3.17, pp. 95–96. The early printed editions of Vitoria's relections refer to book 3 of *De civ. D.* here. Like Pagden and Lawrance, I have followed the correction to book 5 of Simon's 1696 Frankfurt edition (p. 406—photographically reproduced in Nys's edition, 266). It will be recalled that Soto, who anticipated all of Vitoria's authorities here, had cited the fifth book of *De civ. D.* It should also be noted here that when Vitoria appealed to the Roman Empire for confirmation of the justice of aiding allies, he was no longer paraphrasing Cajetan but offering his own observation. See the text of Cajetan's gloss in Aquinas, *Opera Omnia*, vol. 8 (Rome: Ex Typographia Polyglotta S.C. de Propaganda Fide, 1895), 314b. For an interesting discussion of the concept of alliance as central to the French project of establishing political possession of New World territories, see Seed, *Ceremonies of Possession*, 63–65.

96. Vitoria, *Relectio de Indis*, 3.1, p. 77.

97. Ibid., 3.11, p. 90.

98. Ibid., 3.12, p. 91.

99. Ibid., 3.13, pp. 92–93.

100. Ibid., 3.14, pp. 93–94.

101. For this resolution of the apparent inconsistency between the fifth illegitimate title and the fifth just title, see Carro, *La teología*, 2:166–67.

102. Vitoria, *Relectio de Indis*, 3.15, pp. 94–95.

103. Ibid., 3.17, pp. 97–98.

104. See Jonathan Barnes, "The Just War," in *Cambridge History of Later Medieval Philosophy*, ed. Norman Kretzmann, Anthony Kenny, and Jan Pinborg (Cambridge: Cambridge University Press, 1982), 771–84, esp. 778. See also Frederick H. Russell, *The Just War in the Middle Ages* (Cambridge: Cambridge University Press, 1975), 65–66.

105. Carro, *La teología*, 2:164. Carro presumably meant that the principle of sociability came into play here as underlying the common cause of Spaniards and Tlaxcalteca. So Ramón Hernández interprets this passage, citing a lecture course on Aquinas in which Vitoria defended going to war on behalf of allies on the basis that "friends are one with ourselves," "La hipótesis de Francisco de Vitoria," in Ramos et al., *La ética en la conquista*, 368–69. (As in his relection, Vitoria was following here Cajetan's commentary on *Summa Theologica* 2, 2, q. 40, art. 1: "amici et socii unum censentur.") Similarly, Urdánoz, one of the few commentators who did not attempt to sweep the seventh just title under the carpet, maintained that the conditions Vitoria placed upon such an alliance (just war, explicit request for aid) constituted "las leyes de la amistad y caridad rectamente entendidas" (Vitoria, *Obras*, 633). Urdánoz's celebration of the "charity" of aiding the oppressed may indeed reflect Vitoria's underlying assumptions, but this does not emerge self-evidently from the rather laconic phrasing of the published relection. Another, briefer attempt to ground this title in "sociability" is Gutiérrez, *Las Casas*, 339. But Gutiérrez prefaces this fleeting gesture with the admission that "the seventh title is a case apart."

106. Muldoon, *Popes, Lawyers, and Infidels*, 150. More recently, Paulino Castañeda Delgado has attempted to deal with the problem by assuming that Vitoria could scarcely go against "toda la tradición teológica," and in any case he

insisted that the war in question be a just one: "La ética en la Conquista de América," in *De conquistadores y conquistados: Realidad, justificación, representación*, ed. Karl Kohut (Frankfurt am Main: Vervuert, 1994), 77. A much fuller discussion of the seventh title is Manuel M. Martínez, "Las Casas on the Conquest of America," in Friede and Keen, *Las Casas in History*, 325–28. Martínez's main focus here is on Las Casas's rejection not only of Vitoria's seventh title, but also of his supposedly "pro-Roman" stance.

107. Vitoria, *De iure belli*, 96.

108. Ibid., 202–6.

109. Scott, *Francisco de Vitoria*, 241.

110. The traditional medieval orthodoxy of Vitoria's views on the law of war will be apparent from a consultation of Barnes, "The Just War"; Russell, *Just War*; and M. H. Keen, *The Laws of War in the Late Middle Ages* (London: Routledge and Kegan Paul, 1965).

111. Hence Luis Rivera complains: "In general this treatise is disappointing. It attempts to establish particular norms for justice in the wars against the indigenous peoples of the New World, but it forgets them completely in the course of its treatise" (*A Violent Evangelism*, 289 n. 25).

112. Vitoria, *De iure belli*: Spain vs. France: see esp. 146, 148, 160, 190; Turks and Saracens: 166, 168, 176.

113. L. Pereña offers a full account of Vitoria's preoccupation with the European situation in his introduction to this relection (Vitoria, *De iure belli*, 29–63).

114. Vitoria, *De iure belli*, 85.

115. Ibid., 176.

116. Ibid., 182.

117. Ibid., 200.

118. Ibid., 196.

119. "At some moments . . . we shall be perplexed as to what Vitoria's position really is." So, not unjustly, Gutiérrez, *Las Casas*, 334.

120. Pereña argues that, while Vitoria rejected the imperialist pretensions of the late Gattinara, he "nunca . . . cuestionó la legitimidad de la conquista," and in fact his relections of 1539 were not intended to attack the emperor but rather to offer justification for his dominion in the Indies against the attacks of François I of France ("La escuela de Salamanca," 299; also, "La tesis de la paz dinámica," intro. to his ed. of *De iure belli*, 49–50). Straub insists that Vitoria's "discovery" of the law of nations was designed "um Spaniens Ansprüche auf Amerika zu sichern" (*Das Bellum Iustum*, 42 n. 28). Rivera claims that "one of Vitoria's central objectives is the theoretical and theological justification for Spanish hegemony over the New World" (*A Violent Evangelism*, 82). Deckers derives from Vitoria's relections the powerful impression of "un esfuerzo sutil y sofisticado de legitimación del dominio español en las Indias" ("Justicia de la conquista," 356). Rolena Adorno argues that Vitoria in his "dubious" eighth "legitimate title" anticipated Sepúlveda in basing Spanish dominion on the natural incapacity of the Indians ("Los debates sobre la naturaleza del Indio en el siglo XVI: Textos y contextos," *Revista de estudios hispánicos* 19 [1992]: 47–66, esp. 54–57). Gutiérrez announces, "The final conclusion is clear: Spanish sovereignty in the Indies is

legitimate, and the wars waged against the Indians are justified" (*Las Casas*, 342). A little later he offers a somewhat more nuanced view: "Those who armed themselves with Vitoria's idea ["sociability"] in order to defend their interest in the Indies could therefore make use of certain ambiguities, vacillations, and perplexities in the Master's writings" (344).

121. Note Pagden's argument that "Gattinara's universalist ambitions did not, as so many historians have claimed, die with him" (*Lords*, 44). For an interpretation of Vitoria as less impressed with imperial propaganda than I am claiming, see Maravall, *Carlos V*, 248–63, in a chapter entitled "La oposición a la idea imperial." Maravall argues that Vitoria's "profunda y fuerte conciencia de universalidad . . . se levanta frente a los intentos de interpretaciones 'imperialistas' en torno a Carlos V" (261). With respect to the claim that the emperor was "lord of the world," this is surely correct. But Vitoria was not immune to the prestige of the Roman model.

122. See Vitoria, "On Civil Power," in *Political Writings*, 20. This reference to Roman history was omitted from the earliest printed editions of Vitoria's relections. Pagden and Lawrance characterize it as a "satirical reference to the Roman imperial and republican constitutions, with its evident allusion to contemporary humanist eulogies of antique liberty" (in Vitoria, *Political Writings*, 20 n. 20).

123. Gutiérrez, *Las Casas*, 346, cf. 348–49; Las Casas, *Apologia*, ed. with Spanish translations by Angel Losada (Madrid: Editora Nacional, 1975), chap. 56, MS p. 238; Engl. trans. *In Defense of the Indians*, by. Stafford Poole (1974; repr. De Kalb: Northern Illinois University Press, 1992), 341.

124. Maravall, *Carlos V*, 262.

125. Charles V's letter to the prior of San Esteban in Salamanca is printed as appendix 5 to the CHP ed. of *De Indis*, 152–53. Gutiérrez insists that "the letter unmistakably alludes to Vitoria (and to Domingo de Soto, who addressed the topic before Vitoria did). Attempts to dissimulate this reaction on the part of the king and to see a smooth-as-silk relationship between these two personages are in vain" (*Las Casas*, 348). Prominent among those attempting to minimize the irritation of "el magnánimo emperador" is Urdánoz, in Vitoria, *Obras*, 55–57, 506.

126. The relevant segments of the sketchy, often macaronic student notes of Carranza's lectures are printed, with facing Spanish translation, by L. Pereña in his *Misión de España en América* (Madrid: Consejo Superior de Investigaciones Científicas, 1956), 38–57.

127. Carranza, in Pereña, *Misión*, 42/43.

128. Carranza, in Pereña, *Misión*, 46/47.

129. Carranza, in Pereña, *Misión*, 50/51.

130. Carranza, in Pereña, *Misión*, 40/41. The Latin text is also printed in Juan de la Peña, *De bello contra insulanos: Intervención de España en América: Escuela española de la Paz, Segunda generación, 1560–1585: Testigos y fuentes*, ed. L. Pereña, V. Abril, C. Baciero, A. García, J. Barrientos, and F. Maseda, vol. 1, CHP 9 (Madrid: Consejo Superior de Investigaciones Científicas, 1982), 553. This text prints "et" for "im[m]o" in the quoted passage. I have followed Pereña's earlier text on grounds of sense alone; I have not been able to consult the original MS.

131. Cano's "Quaestio 40 de bello" is printed (Latin text only) in Vitoria's *De iure belli*, 323–42. The Roman model is on p. 340. For Cano's career and writings, see Belda Plans, *La escuela de Salamanca*, 501–750.

132. Cano's *Relectio de dominio Indorum* is printed, with facing Spanish translation, in Pereña, *Misión*, 90–147. A more recent edition of the Latin text only is printed in Peña, *De bello contra insulanos* (to be referred to below as CHP 9), 555–81. While this is usually referred to as a relection, Pereña has more recently referred to it as a portion of an unpublished 1545–46 *Tratado de iustitia et iure*: see the appendix "Fuentes académicas indianas" to *La ética en la conquista de América*, CHP vol. 25 (Madrid: Consejo Superior de Investigaciones Científicas, 1984), 668.

133. Cano, *De dominio Indorum*, in Pereña, *Misión*, 106 (= CHP 9, 561).

134. Pereña, *Misión*, 76. Cano's opinion of Sepúlveda's dialogue was solicited in 1547. It is doubtful that he saw it before that.

135. Sepúlveda, *Democrates secundus*, ed. Angel Losada (Madrid: Consejo Superior de Investigaciones Científicas, 1951), 64; see also p. 58.

136. Vitoria, *Relectio de Indis*, 3.11, 90.

137. Ibid., 3.17, 97.

138. Ibid., 3.9, 87.

139. Ibid., 3.14, 94.

140. I do not understand Pagden's argument that Cano did in fact take issue with Vitoria on theoretical grounds here (*Spanish Imperialism*, 23).

141. Cano, *De dominio Indorum*, in Pereña, *Misión*, 142 (= CHP 9, 579).

142. Gutiérrez, *Las Casas*, chap. 3, pp. 67–95; quoted passages on p. 85; passage from *De thesauris* (fol. 132v) discussed on p. 88.

143. Cano, *De dominio Indorum*, in Pereña, *Misión*, 144 (= CHP 9, 580).

144. Covarrubias, "De iustitia belli adversos indos," from his *Relectio in regulas peccatum*, in Vitoria, *De iure belli*, 362–63 (the relevant section of the relection forms appendix 3, pp. 343–63).

145. The text of Covarrubias printed in Pereña, *Misión*, 228, implies that Cajetan's gloss on Aquinas adduced the Roman Empire as confirmation. The edition of Aquinas with Cajetan's notes cited by Pereña offers no reference to the Romans: Aquinas, *Opera Omnia*, 8:314b. Pereña's 1981 text, however, removes this implication. (Note esp. the change from *defendit* to *defenditur*.)

146. Cano, *De dominio Indorum*, in Pereña, *Misión*, 94–96 (= CHP 9, 556).

147. Cano, *De dominio Indorum*, in Pereña, *Misión*, 96 (= CHP 9, 557).

148. Cano, *De dominio Indorum*, in Pereña, *Misión*, 110 (= CHP 9, 563–64).

149. Cano, *De dominio Indorum*, in Pereña, *Misión*, 112 (= CHP 9, 564). I am following Pereña's 1982 CHP text ("tempore enim Sti. Lucae") rather than his 1956 *Misión* text ("tempore enim Octavii"). This same point had been made by Juan de Torquemada in his *Opusculum ad honorem Romani imperii et dominorum Romanorum*, in Hubert Jedin, "Juan de Torquemada und das Imperium Romanum," *Archivum Fratrum Praedicatorum* 12 (1942): 269–70.

150. Cano, *De dominio Indorum*, in Pereña, *Misión*, 116 (= CHP 9, 566). Again, I am following Pereña's 1982 CHP text. The most significant difference is the reference to the Persians ("cum Persis," 1982, vs. "cum ipsis," 1956).

151. Cf. Soto, *Relectio de dominio:* limitations of Roman rule: 144, 152; practical impossibility of world empire: 142 (ref. to Aristotle's "non est melior quanto maior," as in Cano), 144–46.

152. I have omitted a short, obscure passage here that seems to allude again to Cano's point that the Roman Empire acquired legitimacy as time passed. Pereña's two editions offer widely divergent texts here, and without an opportunity to study the original manuscript, I must leave the question of the precise meaning open. The 1956 text reads: "neque in hoc faciunt fideliter, sed cum est lex sancita et ab optima politia ut romana servata tempore Augusti esset iusta." The 1982 text substitutes for the last four words: "tunc Augustinus existimavit esse iusta."

153. See Pagden's reference to the way "Charles V himself somewhat wearily protested to Pope Paul III in 1536 that 'some say that I wish to be Monarch of the world, but my thoughts and deeds prove that the contrary is true'" (*Lords,* 42).

154. The relevant extract of the *Relectio de insulanis* of Domingo de las Cuevas and Juan de Salinas is printed as appendix 10 of the Pereña and Pérez Prendes edition of Vitoria's *Relectio de Indis,* 196–218. The precise date of their relection does not appear to be known, but since Cuevas taught at Alcalá 1544–48, and I am arguing that he accepted Cano's 1546 anti-Roman correction of Vitoria, I would date the relection to 1546–48.

155. I am drawing my information about the career of Domingo de las Cuevas from Pereña's appendix 4 to his edition of Vitoria's *De iure belli,* 375–76.

156. Santa Cruz's relection no longer exists. The date 1536–39 was proposed by Beltrán de Heredia; see Vitoria, *Political Writings,* 339 n. 2. Could Santa Cruz's relection have been produced in reaction to Domingo de Soto's *Relectio de dominio* of 1535?

157. The phrase "vel in rebelli" in Pereña's text (200) needs to be corrected to *vel iure belli.*

158. Cuevas and Salinas, in Vitoria, *Relectio de Indis,* pp. 216–17.

159. Pagden and Lawrance, introduction to Vitoria, *Political Writings,* xvii. I owe the reference to sixteenth-century reprints of Soto's treatise to Bernice Hamilton, *Political Thought in Sixteenth-Century Spain* (Oxford: Clarendon Press, 1963), 190. I have used a reprint of the 1556 edition of Soto, *De iustitia et iure* (Madrid: Instituto de estudios políticos, 1968). This offers a photographic reprint with facing translation by Marcelino González Ordóñez and an introduction by Venancio D. Carro.

160. Soto, *De iustitia et iure,* bk. 4, question 4, art. 2, 4:303–7.

161. Ibid., 303b, 306b.

162. Ibid., 307b.

163. See the discussion of the lost *De ratione promulgandi Evangelium* in Brufau Prat's edition of the *De dominio,* 46–47. Hamilton suggested that "a fragment in the Vat. Lib. (Cod. ottob. lat. 782) may be a part of it" (*Political Thought,* 190). For this fragment, see Brufau Prats, 38–39.

164. Soto, *De iustitia et iure,* 4:305b.

165. Ibid., 4:306a; cf. *De dominio,* 150.

166. Soto, *De iustitia et iure,* 4:306b.

167. The fullest edition of Peña's pronouncements on the matter of the Indies is Peña, *De bello contra insulanos,* CHP 9. The texts by Peña occupy pp. 135–495:

Latin, with facing Spanish translations. I have derived my information about Peña's career from Pereña's introduction, 59–61. See also Ramón Hernández Martín, "La escuela dominicana de Salamanca ante el descubrimiento de América," in *Los domínicos y el nuevo mundo*, vol. 1 (Madrid: Deimos, 1988), 127–32. (Pagden appears to be mistaken in identifying Peña as "a pupil of Soto" [*Spanish Imperialism*, 30].) The second volume contains much useful material on the "second generation" of the "School of Salamanca," but despite its title page, it has nothing further by Juan de la Peña. A rather different, shorter version of Peña's 1559–60 lecture is printed in Pereña, *Misión*, 268–305.

168. Peña, *De bello contra insulanos*, question 2, pt. 1, sec. 2, p. 176; cf. Vitoria, *Relectio de Indis*, 51.

169. Peña, *De bello contra insulanos*, question 2, pt. 3, sec. 10, p. 204.

170. Ibid., sec. 29, 254–56.

171. Las Casas, *Historia de las Indias*, bk. 3, chap. 122, 5:2290–91 (misidentified by González Rodríguez, *La idea de Roma*, 68 n. 240).

172. Arthur Young, cited in Pagden, *Lords*, 73.

Chapter 3

1. Las Casas knew of Sepúlveda's ideas not through the dialogue *Democrates secundus* but through the shorter *Apologia* published in Rome in 1550. Sepúlveda was not allowed to inspect the actual text Las Casas read before the Valladolid junta, but had to content himself with Domingo de Soto's summary.

2. Las Casas, *Defense of the Indians*, 9.

3. Soto, *De Dominio*, 164.

4. Las Casas, *Aquí se contiene una disputa*, 261.

5. Cano to Sepúlveda, 1549, cited in P. Vicente Beltrán de Heredia, *Domingo de Soto: Estudio biográfico documentado*, Biblioteca de Teólogos Españoles, vol. 20 (Salamanca, 1960), 245.

6. Angel Losada, *Fray Bartolomé de las Casas a la luz de la moderna crítica histórica* (Madrid: Tecnos, 1970), 276; Bataillon, *Érasme et l'Espagne*, 1:457.

7. For Sepúlveda's life and career, see Angel Losada, *Juan Ginés de Sepúlveda a través de su "Epistolario" y nuevos documentos* (1949; repr. Madrid: Consejo Superior de Investigaciones Científicas, 1973); and Aubrey F. G. Bell, *Juan Ginés de Sepúlveda* (Oxford: Clarendon Press, 1925).

8. Bell's claim (*Juan Ginés de Sepúlveda*, 4) that Sepúlveda spent his time at Carpi in the company of Musurus seems implausible; the Cretan had left Carpi to become professor of Greek at Padua in 1503: see Deno John Geanakoplos, *Greek Scholars in Venice* (Cambridge: Harvard University Press, 1967), 133. Similarly, Pagden *(Fall of Natural Man*, 109) is mistaken in assuming that Sepúlveda associated with Aldus Manutius at Carpi; the Venetian printer had died in February 1515, several months before Sepúlveda's arrival in Italy. Both errors appear to stem from careless reading of the prologue to Sepúlveda's *Antapologia pro Alberto Pio* (quoted in Bell, 63–64), where Aldus and Musurus are listed among learned habitués of the court of Carpi, without any implication that Sepúlveda actually met them there.

9. We should note, however, that the years of his association with Alberto

Pio coincided with the prince of Carpi's shift of allegiance to the House of Valois upon the accession of Charles V, after several years of siding with the imperial camp during the reign of Maximilian.

10. For Zúñiga's quarrel with Erasmus, see J. J. Mangan, *Life, Character, and Influence of Desiderius Erasmus*, vol. 2 (New York: Macmillan, 1927), 34–42, and Bataillon, *Erasmus y España*, 91–96, 115–22. For Pio's quarrel with Erasmus, see Myron P. Gilmore, "Erasmus and Alberto Pio, Prince of Carpi," in *Action and Conviction in Early Modern Europe: Essays in Memory of E. H. Harbison*, ed. Theodore K. Rabb and Jerrold E. Siegel (Princeton: Princeton University Press, 1969), 299–318. For an account of Sepúlveda's involvement in these disputes, see Losada, *Juan Ginés de Sepúlveda*, 74–81.

11. See Mangan, *Desiderius Erasmus*, 353–54, where much of Sepúlveda's letter to Erasmus is printed.

12. Las Casas, *Apologia*, chap. 27, MS pp. 125–125v. See Losada's discussion of this passage in *Las Casas*, 275–77: he asserts that it allows us to consider Las Casas "un erasmista español."

13. A useful discussions of Sepúlveda's ideas in the context of those of Erasmus and Vives is Fernández-Santamaría, *State, War, and Peace*, 120–236; for Vives, see also Brading, *The First America*, 82–83.

14. I owe these references to Erasmus's *Adagia* to James D. Tracy, *The Politics of Erasmus* (Toronto: University of Toronto Press, 1978), 37.

15. Ibid., 27.

16. Ibid.

17. Ibid., 142–43 n. 37.

18. Juan Luis Vives, *Pompeius fugiens*, trans. Lorenzo Riber, in *Obras completas*, vol. 1, (Madrid: Aguilar, 1947), 584.

19. Vives, *Pompeius fugiens*, 587; cf. 589, "César, pestilencia de todo el mundo."

20. Vives, *Pompeius fugiens*, 589.

21. See Brading, *The First America*, 82.

22. I have used the text of *Ioannis Genesii Sepulvedae Cordubensis . . . opera, quae reperiri potuerunt omnia* (Cologne: Birkmann, 1602), 310–39.

23. Sepúlveda, *Gonsalus*, 324.

24. Ibid., 326, 333.

25. Ibid., 321–22.

26. Ibid., 317–18.

27. I have used the Spanish translation of *De concordia et discordia in humano genere* by Lorenzo Riber, in Vives, *Obras completas*, 2:75–253. A useful account of this treatise is Fernández-Santamaría, *State, War, and Peace*, 49–56 and 144–50.

28. Vives, *De concordia et discordia*, 98.

29. Ibid., 98–99.

30. Ibid., 103.

31. Sepúlveda, *Gonsalus*, 319.

32. Cf. Vives's note on Augustine, *City of God* 8.9, for his nostalgia for a supposed pre-Carthaginian and pre-Roman era of peace and virtue among the Iberian peoples (Everyman ed. of *City of God*, 423–24).

33. Vives, *De concordia et discordia*, 104.

34. A modern Spanish translation is available in *Tratados políticos de Juan Ginés de Sepúlveda*, trans. Angel Losada (Madrid: Instituto de Estudios Políticos, 1963), 127–304. See Fernández-Santamaría, *State, War, and Peace*, 172–88, for a discussion of this dialogue.

35. Fernández-Santamaría, *State, War, and Peace*, 185.

36. Sepúlveda, *Democrates primus*, in *Opera*, 396 (where it goes under the title *De militaris disciplinae honestate*): "ergo quae Fabricii, Reguli, Attilii, Cincinnati, ac Cn. Scipionis summorum virorum frugali et modesta paupertate creverat cum maxima gloria, eadem Crassi, Pompeii ac Caesaris ambitiosis opibus turpiter est labefactata. (Cf. Sepúlveda, *Tratados políticos*, 252.) Vives, *De concordia et discordia*, bk. 3, p. 150; cf. *Pompeius fugiens*, ibid., 1:587–89.

37. New Laws, cited in Hanke, *Spanish Struggle for Justice*, 92.

38. Sepúlveda, "Proposiciones temerarias, escandalosas y heréticas que notó el doctor Sepúlveda en el libro de la conquista de Indias. . . ," in A. Fabié, *Vida y escritos de Fray Bartolomé de las Casas*, vol. 2 = vol. 71 of *Colección de documentos inéditos para la historia de España* (Madrid: Ginesta, 1879), 336. According to Anthony Pagden, this document "has some claim to derive from a writing or writings by Sepúlveda although it was evidently composed after his death" ("The 'School of Salamanca' and the 'Affair of the Indies,'" *History of Universities* 1 [1981]: 107–8 n. 157). The document identifies Sepúlveda's abettor as both archbishop of Seville and president of the Council of the Indies. This appears to mean García de Loaysa, who held both offices in 1543. Pagden prefers Fernando de Valdés, who succeeded García de Loaysa as archbishop of Seville, though he does not appear ever to have served as president of the Council of the Indies: "The 'School of Salamanca,'" 88 (where "1533" should read "1543") and *Fall of Natural Man*, 109–10; cf. Losada, *Juan Ginés de Sepúlveda*, 198.

39. Las Casas, *Apologia*, MS p. 2; *Defense of the Indians*, 8.

40. The standard edition is Juan Ginés de Sepúlveda, *Democrates segundo, o de las justas causas de la guerra contra los indios*, Latin text with facing Spanish translation by Angel Losada (Madrid: Consejo Superior de Investigaciones Científicas, 1951). The passing reference to encomiendas is on p. 122. There appears to be no English translation as yet. A useful short account of Sepúlveda's argument is offered by Pagden, *Fall of Natural Man*, 109–18, and a longer commentary on the work may be found in Teodoro Andrés Marcos, *Los imperialismos de Juan Ginés de Sepúlveda en su Democrates Alter* (Madrid: Instituto de Estudios Políticos, 1947), 89–247. Illuminating attempts to situate Sepúlveda in the broader context of the political thought of the time of Charles V are Maravall, *Carlos V*, 297–311, and Fernández-Santamaría, *State, War, and Peace*, 163–236.

41. Sepúlveda, *Democrates secundus*, 17.

42. Page references for these four *causae* in Sepúlveda, *Democrates secundus*, are (1) 19–33 (quoted passage on p. 19); (2) 39–61; (3) 61–64; (4) 64–83, with a recapitulation on 83–85.

43. Mair's text is cited, with discussion, in Pagden, *Fall of Natural Man*, 38–41.

44. Vitoria, *Relectio de Indis*, 1.1, 1.16, pp. 13, 31.

45. This was cited by Aquinas in *De regimine principum*, bk. 2, chap. 9; Aquinas was in turn cited by Cano in his presentation of the "natura servus" argument in *De dominio Indorum*, CHP 9, 556.

46. Arist. *Pol.* bk. 1, chap. 3, 1254a28ff.; Sepúlveda, *Democrates secundus*, 20.

47. Arist. *Pol.* bk. 1, chap. 3, 1256b21ff. (my translation); Sepúlveda refers to this in *Democrates secundus*, 19 and 22 (despite the latter's false reference of "Polit. 1 c. 5"). Unlike Rackham (Loeb translation), Sepúlveda took the antecedent of the relative clause "which ought to be used . . ." (ἣ δεῖ χρῆσθαι . . .) to be 'the art of hunting' (ἡ θηρευτική). I believe that Sepúlveda was right about this.

48. Vitoria, *Relectio de Indis*, 1.16, p. 31.

49. Sepúlveda, *Democrates secundus*, 30 ("sub tributo serviant"); 120 ("temporis progressu cum iidem fuerint humaniores facti . . ."); 29 ("cum aliqua victricis gentis, sed multo maiore devictorum barbarorum commoditate").

50. Pereña (*Misión*, 76) and Lewis Hanke (*Aristotle*, 31) assumed that Cano was attacking Sepúlveda in 1546, but I do not know on what basis. He never explicitly alluded to him, nor was the Aristotelian passage that he cited ("by nature a slave and a barbarian are the same thing," 1252b9) cited by Sepúlveda, though it would certainly have been apt.

51. Sepúlveda, *Democrates secundus*, 31–32. For another discussion of Sepúlveda's views on the Romans, see González Rodríguez, *La idea de Roma*, chap. 4, especially 69–75 and 98–100.

52. Sepúlveda, *Democrates secundus*, 32. In his *De regno et regis officio*, published in Lérida in 1571, Sepúlveda again dragooned book 5 of *De civ. D.* into service to support an application of the model of Roman imperialism to Spanish conquests in the New World. This time, however, he scaled back his distortion of Augustine's views from tendentious glossing to mere truncation and omission. See Sepúlveda, *Tratados políticos*, 34–35.

53. Sepúlveda, *Democrates secundus*, 32–33. This "bella digresión sobre la gloria," as Angel Losada terms it (32 n. 26), is found only in the fullest of the MSS of the *Democrates secundus*, that of the Biblioteca de la Academia de Historia in Madrid.

54. Ibid., 33.

55. Ibid., 34.

56. Ibid., 85.

57. Ibid., 95–96.

58. I am assuming that the marginal citations of Augustine were meant to gloss the reference to the moderation of the Romans, amplifying the text's "ut testatur Augustinus." Losada lumps these citations together with references to Aristotle and Cicero on the proper end of war. This might suit the letter to Boniface, but not *City of God* 5.12 and 13 or the letter to Marcellinus.

59. Sepúlveda, *Democrates secundus*, 122.

60. See *Democrates secundus*, 36.

61. See J. H. Parry, *The Spanish Seaborne Empire* (New York: Knopf, 1966), 149: "Sepúlveda wished to interpose permanently between the Crown and the

Indians a benevolent aristocracy, who might exercise at first hand a paternal authority which the Crown could not easily exert at a distance, and who would be entitled to use Indian labour in reward for their services. The feudal implications of this proposal . . . made it unacceptable to a royal government always suspicious of aristocratic pretensions." Cf. Liss, *Mexico under Spain*, 31–47. Liss suggests that Sepúlveda failed to secure royal support because of "two principal discretionary errors. . . . These were that he had the bad sense to undercut the prevailing theory of religious mission by emphasizing only the Spanish civilizing one, and that he wrote of New World dominion by the Spanish nation when more prudent men referred to that of the monarch" (41).

62. See the conflicting accounts of Beltrán de Heredia, *Domingo de Soto*, 237–51, and Jaime González Rodríguez, "La junta de Valladolid convocada por el emperador," in Ramos et al., *La ética en la conquista*, 199–227. In addition, the Salamantine scholar Teodoro Andrés Marcos supplied many previously unpublished documents relative to the universities' condemnation of the dialogue and the subsequent debate, in *Los imperialismos de Sepúlveda*, 15–83.

63. Cano to Sepúlveda, cited in Beltrán de Heredia, *Domingo de Soto*, 244. (A fairly full account of the Sepúlveda-Cano feud is offered on pp. 241–49.)

64. Las Casas, *Apologia*, chap. 56, MS p. 238, trans. p. 375; cf. *Defense of the Indians*, 341.

65. Cano, from the proem to bk. 12 of *De locis theologicis* (Salamanca, 1563), quoted in Pagden, " 'School of Salamanca,' " 97 n. 18.

66. On these Spanish summaries, see Losada, *Juan Ginés de Sepúlveda*, 206; Losada located two of them in the Bibliothèque Nationale in Paris. A Latin summary, virtually identical to the 1550 *Apologia* minus the last six pages, is in the Biblioteca Nacional in Madrid. It was published by Fabié, *Vida y escritos*, 2:311–29.

67. See the beginning and end of the letter to Philip that precedes Las Casas's Latin *Apologia*: Losada trans., 115, 119; *Defense of the Indians*, 17, 22.

68. Quoted in Hanke, *All Mankind Is One*, 67.

69. Las Casas had already characterized Aristotle thus ("el Filósofo era gentil y está ardiendo en los infiernos") as early as 1519, in the presence of Charles V, at the meeting of the Council of the Indies in Barcelona. See Las Casas, *Historia de las Indias*, bk. 3, chap. 149, 5:2413.

70. In addition to chapter 4 of González Rodríguez's *Idea de Roma* (64–116; esp. 64–69, 78–81, and 93–106), some useful observations and citations are to be found in Ramón Menéndez Pidal, "Vitoria y Las Casas," esp. 42–47; Martínez, "Las Casas on Conquest," esp. 326–28; and Bruno Rech, "Las Casas und die Kirchenväter," *Jahrbuch für Geschichte von Staat, Wirtschaft und Gesellschaft Lateinamerikas* 17 (1980): 1–47, esp. 36–37. See also G. Gutiérrez, *Las Casas*, 533 n. 25.

71. Las Casas, "Representación al Emperador Carlos V," in *Obras escogidas*, 124. In a "Memorial de remedios," also penned in 1542, when Las Casas searched the past for examples of "tiranos y crueles y robadores" to compare with contemporary Spanish conquistadors, rather than classical antecedents he offered the biblical Nimrod (ibid., 120).

72. Las Casas, *Historia de las Indias,* bk. 1, chap. 154, 4:1136.
73. Las Casas, *Brevísima relación,* 5. I have quoted the English translation by Nigel Griffin, *A Short Account of the Destruction of the Indies* (London: Penguin, 1992), 3.
74. Helen Rand Parish and Harold E. Weidman, *Las Casas en México: Historia y obra desconocidas* (Mexico City: Fondo de Cultura Económica, 1992). This volume consists of a full discussion by Rand Parish of the treatise and the circumstances of its composition, an edition of the Latin text with Spanish translation by both scholars, and thirty appendices of related material, much of it previously unpublished.
75. Ibid., 153. I wonder if *indita* might not be a misreading of the more natural *insita.*
76. Ibid., 154.
77. Ibid., 154–55. For an annotated text and translation of Symmachus's third *relatio,* see R. H. Barrow, *Prefect and Emperor: The Relationes of Symmachus,* A.D. 384 (Oxford: Oxford University Press, 1973), 34–47.
78. See Monico Melida González-Monteagudo, "El Padre Las Casas y Valladolid," in *Estudios sobre política indigenista española en América,* vol. 1 (Valladolid: Universidad de Valladolid, 1975), 9–27.
79. Bernal Díaz, *Historia verdadera,* chap. 211, pp. 587–89.
80. For the dating of these two treatises see Henry Raup Wagner and Helen Rand Parish, *The Life and Writings of Bartolomé de las Casas* (Albuquerque: University of New Mexico Press, 1967), 277–78, where a date of 1549 is proposed for both. Conclusive proof that these treatises antedate at least April 1551 is Las Casas's reference to both of them in his twelfth reply to Sepúlveda's corresponding objection, not only in the version he prepared for publication in 1552 (see *Tratados,* 427, 433, 439 for references to the *Treinta proposiciones,* and 435 for a reference to the *Tratado comprobatorio*), but also in the draft that apparently served as the text of his presentation to the second session of the Valladolid junta in April 1551: see Las Casas, *Tratado de Indias y el Doctor Sepúlveda,* ed. M. Giménez Fernández (Caracas: Academia Nacional de la Historia, 1962), 250, 252, 260. It is true that Las Casas noted at the end of the *Treinta proposiciones* that forty-nine years had passed since his first arrival in the Indies (499), and near the beginning of the *Tratado comprobatorio* he boasted of "more than fifty" years of familiarity with the Indies (921). Figuring from 1502 (the date of his first arrival), this would yield 1551 and 1552 or later, but these are likely to be dates supplied as Las Casas was readying these treatises for their publication in 1552 and 1553, respectively.
81. Las Casas, *Aquí se contienen treinta proposiciones muy jurídicas,* in *Tratados,* 481–83. The restriction of the *Tratado comprobatorio* to these two propositions is stated in *Tratados,* 919.
82. Las Casas, *Treinta proposiciones,* 485.
83. Las Casas, *Tratado comprobatorio del imperio soberano y principado universal que los reyes de Castilla y León tienen sobre las indias,* in *Tratados,* 921. For Las Casas's equation of the conquistadors with Moors and Turks, see Alain Milhou's articles "De la 'destruction' de l'Espagne à la 'destruction' des Indes:

Notes sur l'emploi des termes 'destroyr, destruir, destruymiento, destrución, destroydor, destruidor' de la 'Primera Crónica General' à Las Casas," in *Mélanges à la mémoire d'André Joucla-Ruau* (Aix-en-Provence: Université de Provence, 1978), 907–19, esp. 916–17 (where he suggests that Las Casas was inspired by chronicles that treated the fall of Spain to the Moors, especially Florián de Ocampo's 1541 publication of Alfonso X's *Primera crónica general*), and "De la destruction de l'Espagne à la destruction des Indes: Histoire sacrée et combats idéologiques," in *Études sur l'impact culturel du Nouveau Monde,* Séminaire Interuniversitaire sur l'Amérique Espagnole Coloniale (Paris: L'Harmattan, 1981, 1983), 1:25–47 and 3:11–54 (esp. 31–32: the "Moorish" behavior of the Spaniards raises the threat of a second divinely ordained fall of a sinful Spain). While Milhou implies that Las Casas's earliest use of this topos was in the *Brevísima relación* of 1542, already in his 1531 *Carta al Consejo de Indias* he referred to Indians committing suicide to avoid a tyranny "more Turkish than Christian" (*Obras escogidas*, 5:49).

84. Las Casas, *Treinta proposiciones,* 479.

85. Anthony Pagden has recently claimed that "Las Casas was one of the few to endorse . . . both the validity of the Papal Bulls and the emperor's claim to universal sovereignty" (*Lords,* 52). But the only document he cites in support of this supposed endorsement of the emperor's world dominion, the *De regia potestate* (apparently ca. 1564), offers only a very hedged reference to this idea. In question 1, sec. 3 he insisted that the power of both emperor and king is a power of jurisdiction, not a direct *dominium* over the properties of their subjects. "And it is only to this extent that the emperor is called lord of the world." *De regia potestate, o derecho de autodeterminación,* 1.3.3, ed. Luciano Pereña, J. M. Pérez-Prendes, Vidal Abril, and Joaquín Azcarraga, CHP 8 (Madrid: Consejo Superior de Investigaciones Científicas, 1969), 24. As we shall soon see, Las Casas directly attacked the idea of the emperor's world lordship in chapter 21 of the *Apologia.*

86. Las Casas, *Tratado comprobatorio,* 1125. Despite Las Casas's claim that he was limiting the *Tratado comprobatorio* strictly *(solamente)* to the seventeenth and eighteenth of the *Treinta proposiciones,* he did expand upon the sixteenth as well (1127–29).

87. Las Casas, *Tratado comprobatorio,* 1133.

88. Ibid., 1105.

89. Ibid., 1127.

90. Las Casas, *Treinta proposiciones,* 481.

91. Speaking of the *Treinta proposiciones* and the *Tratado comprobatorio,* Gutiérrez acutely notes that "we are dealing with a limit case. . . , a text whose circumstances—the attacks of which he has been the object—move Las Casas to yield as far as he possibly can to the opinion current in his age" (*Las Casas,* 369).

92. Las Casas, *Tratado comprobatorio,* 1191–93; cf. Gutiérrez, *Las Casas,* 377–82.

93. See Las Casas's argument in the *Tratado comprobatorio,* 1101–33.

94. Las Casas emphasizes the importance of this "translatio imperii" in both treatises (*Tratados,* 481, 1129).

95. Cortés, *Segunda relación,* ed. Alcalá, 31; *Letters from Mexico,* 56. For

discussions of Cortés's words here, see R. Menéndez Pidal, "Idea imperial de Carlos V," 2:91–107, esp. 106–7; and Victor Frankl, "Imperio particular e imperio universal en las *Cartas de relación* de Hernán Cortés," *Cuadernos Hispanoamericanos* 55 (1963): 443–82, esp. 443–59. (Frankl's arguments for a later Cortesian concept of universal empire *según la tradición gibelina*, 459–82, are very strained.)

96. Pagden, *Spanish Imperialism*, 32.

97. Pagden, *Lords*, 32.

98. Pagden claims that "Las Casas was one of the few to endorse . . . both the validity of the Papal Bulls and the emperor's claim to universal sovereignty" (*Lords*, 52). This is, at best, imprecisely stated, as we have seen. In contrast to the universal temporal authority of the pope in matters pertaining to the faith, Las Casas underlined the geographical limits of the emperor's power at *Tratado comprobatorio*, 1015: "ni el emperador en cuanto emperador fuera del Imperio, ni los reyes fuera de sus reinos pueden ejercer un quilate de jurisdición en parte alguna regularmente."

99. See Weckmann, *Medieval Heritage of Mexico*, 332.

100. This *cédula* of Philip II is printed in *Información sobre los tributos que los Indios pagaban a Moctezuma, Año de 1554* (Mexico City: Porrúa, 1957), 19–23. I owe this reference to Weckmann, *Medieval Heritage of Mexico*, 331. Weckmann implies that the *cédula* explicitly refers to Moctuzuma's territory as an "imperio," but this is not the case.

101. This characterization of the *Tratado comprobatorio* is that of Wagner and Parish, *Bartolomé de las Casas*, 174. Parallels for the *cédula's* phrases "universal señorío" and "señor universal" will be found throughout the two treatises. See, for example, "universales señores" in the *conclusión primera* and "soberano, imperial e universal principado y señorío" in the *conclusión segunda* of the *Tratado comprobatorio*, both in *Tratados*, 925.

102. My account of the Valladolid junta in this and the following paragraph is especially indebted to the pair of articles by Silvio Zavala and Angel Losada, "Aspectos formales de la controversia entre Sepúlveda y Las Casas. . . ," *Cuadernos americanos* 212 (1977): 137–61. Earlier scholars' views are clearly laid out here, and questions about our manuscript evidence for Las Casas's contributions are addressed. I have also profited from Hanke's *All Mankind Is One* and Jean Dumont's *La vraie controverse de Valladolid* (Paris: Criterion, 1995). See Dumont, 15–26, for an evocative account of the setting of the debate, both the city of Valladolid and the chapel of the Colegio de San Gregorio.

103. Sepúlveda (?), "Proposiciones temerarias," 338.

104. Sepúlveda (?), "Proposiciones temerarias," 338, implied that the first session adjourned after the judges received copies both of Soto's summary and of Sepúlveda's twelve objections, and this account is followed by Hanke in *All Mankind Is One*, 68. I prefer the reconstruction of Manuel Giménez Fernández, who assumed that the need to afford Soto time to abridge Las Casas's manuscript and Sepúlveda time to draft responses necessitated the adjournment of the junta to a second session, at the beginning of which both Sepúlveda's objections and

Las Casas's replies would have been presented. See Zavala and Losada, "Aspectos formales," 138.

105. Our knowledge of the second session is somewhat conjectural. An acute study that—unusually—concentrates on the second session is V. Abril Castelló, "La bipolarización Sepúlveda-Las Casas y sus consecuencias: La revolución de la duodécima réplica," in Ramos et al., *La ética en la conquista*, 229–88. Abril is, in turn, indebted to the documents published by Giménez Fernández in Las Casas, *Tratado de Indias*.

106. These "Postreros apuntamientos que dio Sepúlveda en la congregación" are printed in Las Casas, *Tratado de Indias*, 29–31. See also the "Proposiciones temerarias," 338.

107. Las Casas, *Apologia* and *Defense of the Indians*.

108. Hanke, Giménez Fernández, and Losada all assumed that Las Casas read a Latin manuscript against Sepúlveda's main arguments, switching later to a Spanish manuscript on Indian culture and customs (see Zavala and Losada, "Aspectos formales," 137–40). But the "Argumento" of the *Aquí se contiene una disputa* clearly seems to imply that the document that Las Casas read in Valladolid was the document he had composed "en romance" in response to a Spanish version of Sepúlveda's *Apologia* (*Tratados*, 223). For the date of the Latin version, see Poole's preface to *Defense of the Indians*, xx–xxi. He settles on a date "sometime in 1552 or early 1553."

109. Las Casas, *Defense of the Indians*, 362.

110. Las Casas, *Aquí se contiene una disputa*, 283.

111. A succinct statement of Losada's position is Zavala and Losada, "Aspectos formales," 152–61.

112. Las Casas, *Apologia*, chap. 36; *Defense of the Indians*, 234.

113. Ibid., *Apologia*, chap. 4; *Defense of the Indians*, 43.

114. Las Casas, *Aquí se contiene una disputa*, 375–77.

115. Las Casas, *Apologia*, chap. 4; *Defense of the Indians*, 43.

116. Ibid., *Apologia*, chap. 5; *Defense of the Indians*, 49.

117. Ibid., *Apologia*, chap. 5; *Defense of the Indians*, 50.

118. Ibid.

119. Ibid.; citing Lactantius, *Divine Institutes*, bk. 1, chap. 20.

120. Las Casas, *Apologia*, chap. 1; *Defense of the Indians*, 28–29.

121. Las Casas, "Octava réplica," in *Aquí se contiene una disputa*, 375.

122. Las Casas, *Apologia*, 100v; *Defense of the Indians*, 151.

123. Las Casas, *Apologia*, 101; *Defense of the Indians*, 152. See the previous chapter for the refutation of the Roman emperor's lordship of the whole world by Las Casas's fellow Dominicans Soto, Vitoria, Carranza, and Cano. See also the first chapter of Pagden's *Lords of All the World*, though he does not discuss this chapter of Las Casas's *Apologia*.

124. A useful study of the phrase is James Muldoon, "Extra ecclesiam non est imperium," *Studia Gratiana* 9 (1966): 553–80; see 578–79 for the position of Hostiensis.

125. Cited in Gutiérrez, *Las Casas*, 497 n. 18.

126. Las Casas, *Tratado comprobatorio,* 1087. Further on in this treatise, however, Las Casas noted that he had composed a Latin treatise absolving Hostiensis of the "heresy" of this blanket slander of unbelievers; rather, he claimed, the canonist was thinking primarily of the Muslim enemies of Christendom (1093, 1177). He alluded to this treatise also in chapter 15 of the *Apologia,* 76–76v; *Defense of the Indians,* 118–19.

127. Las Casas, *Apologia,* chap. 34, p. 154; *Defense of the Indians,* 224.

128. Ibid., chap. 34, p. 153v; *Defense of the Indians,* 223.

129. So Cichorius, as cited in F. C. Babbitt's Loeb edition of the *Moralia,* vol. 4 (Cambridge: Harvard University Press, 1936), 125 note b.

130. Dionysius of Halicarnassus, *Roman Antiquities,* bk. 1, chap. 24.1, trans. E. Cary (Cambridge: Harvard University Press, 1937), 76–77.

131. It is interesting to compare this account of the story from Dionysius of Halicarnassus in chapter 36 of the *Apologia* with the fuller translation/paraphrase offered in chapter 161 of the *Apologética historia sumaria,* ed. Vidal Abril Castelló, Jesús A. Barreda, Berta Ares Queija, and Miguel J. Abril Stoffels, in *Obras completas* (Madrid: Alianza Editorial, 1992), 8:1126–27. In the latter account, Las Casas does acknowledge the difference between the foreign Pelasgians and the Italian "Aborigines," but he "improves" Dionysius by explicitly interpolating the Aborigines into the human sacrifice story alongside the Pelasgians. This time, however, he does not claim that the custom spread from here throughout the world.

132. Las Casas, *Apologia,* chap. 52, p. 223v; *Defense of the Indians,* 321.

133. Ibid., *Apologia,* chap. 52; *Defense of the Indians,* 325. (This passage is misidentified by González Rodríguez, *La idea de Roma,* 67 n. 237).

134. Las Casas, *Apologia,* 225v; not rendered in Poole's translation. The reference is to *De iustitia et iure,* bk. 4, question 2, art. 2; the discussion of Augustine and the Roman Empire that we discussed in the last chapter was bk. 4, question 4, art. 2.

135. A difficulty here is that the Latin text states that Las Casas hoped to offer this fuller treatment "below" *(infra).* Since he was nearly at the end of this long manuscript, *infra* does not make much sense, unless he intended to tuck this discussion into part 2 of the *Apologia,* the ancestor, according to Losada, of the *Apologética historia.* True enough, we shall see that the Romans have an extensive role to play in that later work, but there does not seem to be a plausible place in such a project for the kind of work that Las Casas envisioned here. Perhaps this is an argument for considering that Las Casas did not himself compose the Latin version of the *Apologia,* though he probably did supervise it (his handwriting seems to appear only on the first page). *Infra* may have been a misleading translation of "en otra parte" *vel sim.* The parallel word in chap. 21 for the proposed treatise on Ulzurrum was *alibi.*

136. Las Casas, *Apologia,* chap. 58, p. 242v; *Defense of the Indians,* 347.

137. Bartolomé de la Vega, in Las Casas, *Apologia,* 102 (he does not provide the original [?] Latin text); *Defense of the Indians,* 5.

138. Vega, in Las Casas, *Apologia,* 101; *Defense of the Indians,* 3.

Chapter 4

1. Miguel de Arcos, *Parecer mío sobre un tratado de la guerra que se puede hacer a los indios*, in *Cuerpo de Documentos del siglo XVI sobre los derechos de España en las Indias y las Filipinas*, ed. Agustín Millares Carlo and Lewis Hanke (1943; repr. Mexico City: Fondo de Cultura Económica, 1977), 3–9.

2. Lewis Hanke, *La lucha por la justicia en la conquista de América* (Buenos Aires: Editorial Sudamericana Historia, 1949), 355–56 (in his introduction to the first publication of the MS Hanke had proposed Bernardo de Arévalo as the unnamed bishop [Millares Carlo and Hanke, *Cuerpo de documentos*, xviii]). See also Hanke, *Aristotle*, 78–79; Bataillon, "Vasco de Quiroga," esp. 232–38 (also in *Estudios sobre Bartolomé de las Casas* [Barcelona: Ediciones Península, 1976], 267–79, esp. 273–79).

3. Luis Rivera has called attention to the rarity of Arcos's position here: he "was one of the few who allowed himself certain critical references to Roman [i.e. papal] corruption" (*A Violent Evangelism*, 278–79 n. 5).

4. Arcos, *Parecer mío*, 7.

5. Arcos, *Parecer mío*, 8. For the *Gamaliel,* see David Hook's articles "The *Auto de la destruición de Jerusalén* in Relation to Its Source," *Bulletin of Hispanic Studies* 51 (1974): 335–45, and "Legend of Flavian Destruction."

6. Arcos, *Parecer mío*, 8.

7. Louis H. Feldman, *Josephus and Modern Scholarship, 1937–1980* (Berlin: De Gruyter, 1984), 41–42.

8. Vasco de Quiroga, *De debellandis Indis: Un tratado desconocido*, ed. with extensive introduction by René Acuña (Mexico City: Universidad Nacional Autónoma de México, 1988). An impressionistic discussion of this treatise in Fernando Gómez, *Good Places and Non-Places in Colonial Mexico* (Lanham, University Press of America, 2001), 181–205.

9. For a text of this letter and a discussion of it, see Bataillon, "Vasco de Quiroga," 225–38.

10. Benno Biermann, "Don Vasco de Quiroga und seine Schrift *De debellandis Indis*," *Neue Zeitschrift für Missionswissenschaft* 22, no. 3 (1966): 189–200.

11. Benno Biermann, "Don Vasco de Quiroga y su tratado *De Debellandis Indis* (II)," *Historia Mexicana* 72, no. 18 (1969): 615–22, esp. 620.

12. Quiroga, *De debellandis Indis*, 34–50. Quiroga alluded to the earlier treatise in chap. 2, sec. 19 of the *Información en derecho*, pp. 63–64.

13. Arcos, *Parecer mío*, 9.

14. Ibid., 8.

15. See J. M. de Bujanda, *Index des livres interdits*, vol. 5: *Index de l'Inquisition espagnole, 1551, 1554, 1559* (Geneva: Droz, 1984), 251, 599.

16. See Clive Griffin, *The Crombergers of Seville* (Oxford: Clarendon Press, 1988), 124, 125 n. 109.

17. Silvio Zavala, "En busca del tratado de Vasco de Quiroga, *De debellandis Indis*," *Historia Mexicana* 68, no. 17 (1968): 485–515; "En torno del tratado *De debellandis Indis* de Vasco de Quiroga," *Historia Mexicana* 72, no. 18 (1969): 623–26; "Algo más sobre Vasco de Quiroga," *Historia Mexicana* 151, no. 38

(1989): 533–49 (including a brief response from Acuña); "Adición sobre Fray Miguel de Arcos," *Historia Mexicana* 154, no. 39 (1989): 555–61.

18. Quiroga, *De debellandis Indis*, 176–77 (= Madrid MS, Muñoz collection, fol. 205r). See 220–21 n. 208 for Paulus de Castro and the original text of this passage.

19. Alonso de la Vera Cruz, *The Writings of Alonso de la Vera Cruz*, vols. 2 and 3: *Defense of the Indians: Their Rights*, Latin text with English translation by Ernest J. Burrus (Rome: Jesuit Historical Institute, 1968). For the life of Vera Cruz, I have relied on Burrus, 2:9–15, and Prometeo Cerezo, "Influencia de la Escuela de Salamanca en el pensamiento universitario americano," in Ramos et al., *La ética en la conquista*, 551–96, esp. 556–66.

20. Vera Cruz, *Defense of the Indians*, "testis sum oculatus," doubt 1, par. 44, 2:108; anecdote, doubt 4, par. 222, 2:182.

21. "Magistrum meum, Theologorum sui temporis facile principem," cited by Burrus, in ibid., 2:63.

22. "Until new evidence comes to light, I think that the answer must remain in the realm of conjecture. At present, we must be content with noting the striking similarities" (Burrus, in ibid., 2:65).

23. Vera Cruz, *Defense of the Indians*, doubt 1, 2:422–23. His discussion of this *causa* occupies paragraphs 840–55 in Burrus's numbering (422–29).

24. Ibid., doubt 11, pars. 842–47, 2:422–27.

25. Vera Cruz appealed to book 18 of Augustine's *City of God* here, rather than to book 3 as the manuscripts of Vitoria appear to have done. The latter was probably a slip for book 5, which Simon's 1696 Lyons edition printed, followed by many modern editors. Perhaps Vera Cruz recognized that book 3 was a false reference, so he turned back to the other "Roman passage" in the *Relectio de Indis,* where the reference was to book 18, and simply substituted that. Burrus, not noticing this earlier reference in the *De Indis* and also committed to the curious assumption that Vera Cruz could not actually have had the *De Indis* in front of him before 1557, opined that "Vera Cruz got his references mixed up," for he could find nothing in book 18 of the *City of God* to support Vera Cruz's remarks here. True, book 5 would have been a better reference, but book 18 chap. 22 was surely close enough for Vera Cruz to adopt from the earlier passage in Vitoria. Presumably, Vera Cruz's reference to "Aquinas's" *Opusculum XXII* was a misreading for the *Opusculum XXI* of Vitoria's text.

26. Vera Cruz, *Defense of the Indians*, doubt 11, pars. 848–55, 2:426–29.

27. Ibid., doubt 7, par. 343, 2:228–29.

28. Ibid, par. 359, 2:234–35.

29. I have emended the text of Burrus's translation from "badly throughout" to "badly thought-out" for *inconsiderata.*

30. Vera Cruz, *Defense of the Indians*, doubt 7, pars. 363–83, 2:234–41.

31. Ibid., par. 381, 2:240–41.

32. Ibid., par. 382, 2:240–41.

33. Ibid., par. 408, 2:250–51.

34. Ibid., par. 380, 2:238–41.

35. The citation of the Golden Rule and Prov. 22:28 against Roman imperial

rule seems to be indebted to Oldradus's *Consilium*. See Ulzurrum, in *Tractatus universi iuris*, 122.

36. Vera Cruz, *Defense of the Indians*, doubt 7, par. 433, 2:262–63. I have modified Burrus's translation somewhat.

37. Ibid., par. 424–30, 2:258–61.

38. Ibid., par. 432, 2:260–61.

39. Burrus, introduction to ibid., 2:63 n. 121.

40. Vera Cruz, *Defense of the Indians*, vol. 2, doubt 10, par. 666, 2:354–55; my translation.

41. Marineo Sículo, *De rebus Hispaniae memorabilibus*, bk. 19, in Schottus, *Hispaniae illustratae*, 479. The Spanish text quoted by Oviedo kept close to the Latin *constat* with *consta*: Oviedo, *Historia general*, bk. 29, chap. 30, BAE vol. 119, 330.

42. The full treatise is available only in the Spanish translation of 1559 in the bilingual (Spanish/Serbo-Croatian) edition of Franjo Šanjek and Mirjana Polić-Bobić, *Rasprava o pravu i opravdanosti rata što ga španjolski vladari vode protiv naroda Zapadne Indije (1559) / Tratado del derecho y justicia dela guerra que tienen los reyes de España contra las naciones dela Yndia Ocidental (1559)* (Zagreb: Nakladni zavod Globus, 1994). This contains extensive introductory material, notes, and bibliography by Šanjek; the transcription of the Spanish text and the translation into Serbo-Croatian are the work of Polić-Bobić. The original MS is in the Colección Salazar y Castro, N 75, fl. 68 112, Real Academia de la Historia, Madrid. Extracts and summary of this Spanish version were first published by Millares Carlo and Hanke in *Cuerpo de documentos*, 11–37. Unfortunately, it often appears that the text offered by Polić-Bobić is less reliable than the abbreviated version of Millares Carlo and Hanke. For example, in a key passage on the "Roman title" Polić-Bobić absurdly prints "camino de Yndia" when the context clearly calls for "camino de un dia" (156; contrast Millares Carlo and Hanke, 29), and on p. 158 (fol. 93r) Polić-Bobić prints "aquellas tierras pertenescian al Romano ynperio traspasado en el derecho de los rreyes de España," where the Millares Carlo text more plausibly places a *que* after *tierras* and offers *traspasó* for *traspasado* (31).

43. I am drawing here on Šanjek's introduction to the edition of the Spanish version, where he brings together material that he had presented in a number of earlier articles in Serbo-Croatian. See also Hanke's introduction to Millares Carlo and Hanke, *Cuerpo de documentos*, xix–xxi.

44. "Il desiderio di veder cose varie e quasi incredibili," from the prologue to his Italian translation of Pedro de Medina's *Arte de navegar* (Venice, 1554), cited by Šanjek, 18.

45. The dates of Paletin's sojourn in the New World are not entirely certain. In the Latin version of his treatise he claimed that he left Santo Domingo for New Spain in 1530 and stayed for ten years (63v–64r), and Šanjek notes that he alluded to a ten-year stay also in the prologue to his translation of the *Arte de navegar* (*Rasprava*, 18). Since Dominican documents record that he left New Spain for Europe in 1546, Šanjek assumes that he must have in fact arrived in 1535/36 and participated in the pacification of Yucatán in 1537/41 (*Rasprava*, 18, 66 n. 36, cf.

chart on 258). But Paletin was explicit about being present when Francisco Montejo el Mozo made his failed attempt to found a city in the ruins of Chichén Itzá. The Latin treatise dates this to 1532, and the Spanish translation dates it to 1533, and these dates fit the historical reality of the venture of Montejo el Mozo. See Chamberlain, *The Conquest and Colonization of Yucatán, 1517–1550* (Washington, D.C.: Carnegie Institution, 1948; repr. New York: Octagon, 1966), chap. 7: "Montejo the Younger and Ciudad Real de Chichén Itzá, 1532–33," 132–49.

46. This discussion will assume that Vinko Paletin personally composed both the Latin and the Spanish versions. This is assumed by Šanjek and Polić-Bobić, but it is not entirely certain. For one thing, though Paletin spent a long time in Spain and the Spanish New World, it is perfectly possible that he may have found it trying, back home in Korčula, to turn so long a treatise into Spanish. Also, for what it is worth, the Madrid manuscript does not appear to be in the same hand as a letter by Paletin to Philip II. Compare the writing under Paletin's sketch of the layout of the buildings of Chichén Itzá in Šanjek and Polić-Bobić, 159, with the extracts from Paletin's letter to Philip II of Sept. 15, 1564, on p. 35. The possibility that the Spanish version is a free adaptation of the Latin original by a second party to whom Paletin farmed out the manuscript cannot be entirely excluded.

47. Šanjek, *Rasprava*, 12–14, 64 nn. 1 and 4.

48. Millares Carlo and Hanke, *Cuerpo de documentos*, xx; cf. Šanjek, *Rasprava*, 14, 64 n. 10.

49. Šanjek, *Rasprava*, 14, 64 nn. 8 and 9.

50. On p. 16 of his introduction, Šanjek declared that Francesca Cantú of the University of Rome had discovered "la versión latina integral del tratado," but he has since stated categorically that "la seule version latine est celle du manuscrit de la Indiana University" (personal communication, June 21, 2002). The Indiana MS, entitled *Tractatus de iure et iustitia belli quod habent reges Castellae et Legionis in regionibus occidentalis Indiae, quam quidam novum appellant orbem,* is in the Spanish History Mss. Collection, but Šanjek refers to it by its name from an earlier collection: Phillips 11789. This was the manuscript of which Antonin Zaninovic, OP (1879–1973) was for some years preparing an edition (see Hanke, *Aristotle and the American Indians,* 145, n. 22, and *All Mankind is One,* 148, n. 28), a project which Stjepan Krasic, OP, apparently inherited, though also without bringing it to completion. I wish to acknowledge the courtesy of the Lilly Library, Indiana University, for permission to examine and cite this manuscript.

51. For example, in question 3, on the "Roman title," the Latin version offers a very full "first proposition," an encomium of the patriotism, justice, and benevolence of Roman rule (53r–57r), while the Spanish version offers a two-sentence summary of the conclusion, wearily waving off the reader with "y quien mas largamente lo quisiere ver vea las historias" (91v, 154). Similarly, the Spanish version of question 4, on the title of wars of alliance (98v–101r, 178–86), shears away all of the specific historical exempla, many of them from Roman history, offered by the Latin version (69r–78r). Šanjek inexplicably refers to the Latin version of this question as "una respuesta parcial"; in fact, it is the Spanish version that is truncated. But, again, it should be borne in mind that in the third question,

where the two versions diametrically diverge, the Spanish version again seems, at certain points, to be an abridgment of a longer version—perhaps a first Latin version.

52. The first reference in the Spanish text to the unnamed "obispo" is in the programmatic "Principio," on p. 69v (*Rasprava*, 86); in the Latin version the offender was a mere "cuiusdam" (3r). The reference to "quel obispo de Chiapa" is in the discussion of the Roman title on 97r, 174; and Las Casas is at last explicitly named at 103v, 196. For other patent references to Las Casas in the Spanish version, see the index to the Šanjek edition.

53. Paletin's references to the *Treinta proposiciones* are at 74r/98 of the Spanish version and 12v of the Latin MS.

54. *Tractatus*, 4v. I take the reference to "litteras latinas" to refer to a familiarity with European script, not a dig at the classical learning of the students of the Colegio de Santa Cruz de Tlatelolco.

55. See Paletin, first question, Latin version, 8r–49v; Spanish version, 71v–89v/92–146; for the specific claim that the conquistadors "non fuisse tiranos," see the Latin version, 44v; Spanish, 88v/142 ("no fueron tiranos").

56. Ibid., Latin version, xxx–45r; Spanish version, 79r–89r/114–42.

57. Paletin's account of the Cholula affair is on 37r–39v of the Latin version; 85v–86v/132–38 of the Spanish version, with references to Las Casas's "libellus infamatorius" on 39v of the Latin; 86v/136 of the Spanish version. Bernal Díaz's account is chapter 83 of the *Historia verdadera*, 43–51, with a reference to Las Casas on p. 150.

58. Paletin, Latin, 33v; Spanish, 83v/128. For Las Casas's claim that Cortés sang "Mira Nerón de Tarpeya / a Roma cómo se ardía, etc." during the massacre at Cholula, see *Brevísima relación*, 71; *Short Account*, 47.

59. Paletin, Latin, 46r; Spanish, 89r/144.

60. Ibid., Latin, 46v.

61. Ibid., Latin 48r; cf. Spanish, 89v/144–45.

62. Ibid., Latin, 70r; cf. Spanish, 99r/180. Šanjek's note (250 n. 185) inexplicably assumes that Paletin was referring here to "the Roman civil wars that ended with the destruction of the Republic."

63. Paletin, Latin, 76r, 77v–78r; Spanish, 100r/182.

64. Ibid., Spanish, 91v/154.

65. Ibid., Latin, 53r–57v.

66. Ibid., Spanish, 91v/156; the *segunda conclusión* as a whole is 91v–93r/156–58.

67. Ibid., Spanish, 92r/156.

68. Las Casas, *Historia de las Indias*, 3:411. Oviedo's Hesperides-Indies theory is bk. 2, chap. 3, of the *Historia general*, BAE vol. 117, 17–20.

69. For example, Paletin followed Oviedo in explaining that modern voyages to the Indies often take less than forty days because of improvements in navigation since antiquity: Paletin, Spanish, 92r/156, cf. Latin, 63r; Oviedo, *Historia general*, bk. 2, chap. 3, BAE vol. 117, 19.

70. Paletin, Spanish, 92r/156; Latin, 63v.

71. Ibid., Spanish, 92v–93r/158; cf. Latin, 66r–67v. In the first sentence quoted Polić-Bobić prints "ni eran latinas ni griegas ni arabicas," but Muñoz offered "hebraicas" for the last word (Hanke and Millares Carlo, *Cuerpo de documentos*, 30), and this is confirmed by the corresponding passage in the Indiana Latin version, "Ebreae," 66r.

72. Paletin, Latin, 66r.

73. Ibid., 58r.

74. Ibid., Spanish, 93r/158.

75. Ibid., Spanish, 93r/158. I am following Muñoz's transcription of the manuscript here rather than Polić-Bobić's.

76. Ibid., Spanish, 98r/ 176.

77. See Muldoon, *Popes, Lawyers, and Infidels*, 16–18.

78. Paletin, Latin, 58v–59r.

79. Ibid., Latin, 68r.

80. Hostiensis, cited in Muldoon, *Popes, Lawyers, and Infidels*, 16.

81. It is worth mentioning again that Franjo Šanjek no longer stands by his earlier claim (*Rasprava*, 16) that a complete Latin version (the original Latin version, it was tempting to hope), has come to light.

82. James Muldoon's illuminating, if overambitiously titled, *The Americas in the Spanish World Order: The Justification for Conquest in the Seventeenth Century* (Philadelphia: University of Pennsylvania Press, 1994) is a full analysis of the second book ("just acquisition") of *De Indiarum iure*. His main discussions of the model of the Roman Empire in the acquisition of Spain's New World empire are on pp. 47–48, 64, 144–53. Discussions of the Roman model in the *Política indiana* are Juan Pérez de Tudela Bueso, "*La política indiana* y el político Solórzano," in *Homenaje a D. Ciriaco Pérez-Bustamante*, vol. 3 (Madrid: Consejo Superior de Investigaciones Científicas, 1970), 103–5, 111; Pagden, *Spanish Imperialism*, 33–35; Brading, *The First America*, 219–20.

83. Góngora, *Studies in Colonial History*, 62.

84. Solórzano Pereira, *De Indiarum iure*, 2.8.125 (Lyon: Laurentius Anisson, 1662), 1:176; cf. Muldoon, *Americas*, 64.

85. Solórzano Pereira, *De Indiarum iure*, 2.7.72–76, 1:176–77; cf. Muldoon, *Americas*, 47–48.

86. Solórzano Pereira, *De Indiarum iure*, 2.21.38, 1:308; cf. Muldoon, *Americas*, 149–50.

87. Solórzano y Pereyra, *Política indiana*, bk. 1, chap. 11.19, ed. Francisco Ramiro de Valenzuela, BAE vol. 252 (Madrid: Atlas, 1972), 111–12. See Pérez de Tudela, "El político Solórzano," 111; and Pagden, *Spanish Imperialism*, 34.

88. For Torquemada, see Jedin, "Juan de Torquemada," 270.

89. Solórzano, *Politica indiana*, bk. 2, chap. 15.25, BAE vol. 252, 266.

90. Ibid., bk. 6, chap. 5.22 and 30, BAE vol. 255, 342–43.

91. Brading, *The First America*, 219–20, citing *Politica indiana*, bk. 2, chaps. 24.29 and 26.14.

92. Solórzano, *Política indiana*, bk. 1, chap. 11.20, BAE vol. 252, 112.

Chapter 5

1. Cano, *De dominio Indorum*, 110 (= CHP 9, 563–64).

2. Las Casas, *Historia de las Indias*, bk. 3, chap. 122, 5:2289. The widespread assumption that Las Casas was of converso ancestry might add some special poignancy to this lament of the Jews' loss of liberty.

3. Joseph. *AJ* 14.34–79: see p. 77 for Josephus's blame of the brothers, p. 72 for Pompey's exemplary restraint. Cf. also Joseph. *BJ* 1.127–58. For Josephus as a model for Las Casas's own writing of history, see the prologue to the *Historia de las Indias*, 3:327–28, 335–36.

4. Las Casas, *Historia de las Indias*, 5:2290–91.

5. In chapters 19, 129, and 193 of the *Historia verdadera*, pp. 33, 267, 515, Bernal Díaz links Pompey with Julius Caesar as a great Roman general surpassed by Cortés.

6. The phrase is that of Suetonius: "amor et deliciae generis humani" (*Tit.* chap. 1).

7. One of the most valuable contributions of González Rodríguez's *La idea de Roma en la historiografía indiana* is his demonstration of the importance of Spanish views of the Roman conquest of Spain for the controversy of the Indies. See especially pp. 8–36 (several references to attitudes toward the Roman conquest in medieval chroniclers, a discussion, like the present one, deeply indebted to the work of R. B. Tate), 65–67 (Las Casas's use of the Romans in Spain in the Valladolid debate), and several other scattered references passim. While the present discussion confirms his insistence upon the power of this historical precedent, it is our contention that the Dominicans' use of this particular "Roman model" also constituted a significant contribution to a growing identification with the pre-Roman Iberians as the "true" ancestral Spaniards. In addition, González appears to have been unaware of the role of Melchor Cano and Ambrosio de Morales in the development of the motif of the Romans in Spain.

8. Las Casas, *Apologia*, chap. 4; I have used Poole's translation, *Defense of the Indians*, 43.

9. Diod. Sic. 5.35–38: see esp. 36.3–4 and 38.1–2. Las Casas misidentified this as bk. 6, chap. 9 both in the *Apologia* and in *Historia de las Indias*, bk. 2, chap. 13, 4:1350 (a passage mistakenly assigned to the *Apologetic History* by González Rodríguez, *La idea de Roma*, 66), and bk. 3, chap. 10, 5:1791–92, where the phrase cited in the text is found. In a later article González mistakenly assigned to chapter 40 of the *Apologetic History* a passage virtually identical to Losada's translation of the passage in chapter 4 of the *Apologia* ("El antiromanismo de Oviedo," 341–42 n. 33). For Las Casas's familiarity with, and predilection for, the history of Diodorus, see Bruno Rech, "Las Casas und die Autoritäten seiner Geschichtsschreibung," *Jahrbuch für Geschichte von Staat, Wirtschaft und Gesellschaft Lateinamerikas* 16 (1979): 30–41. To see how the precedent of Roman mines in Spain could be "defanged" to provide an innocuous or even positive model for Spanish mines in the Indies, see Oviedo, *Historia general*, bk. 2, chap. 12, BAE vol. 117, 47. Before the Spaniards arrived, Oviedo notes, the Indi-

ans had only picked up surface minerals, "and similarly the Spaniards didn't have the experience that the ancient Asturians, Lusitanians, and Galicians got in the working of the mines in those provinces in Spain, whence the Romans got great treasures." What Las Casas would label "trabajos infernales" (*Historia de las Indias,* bk. 3, chap. 10, 5:1791) Oviedo could blandly label "esperiencia"! Closer to Las Casas's comparison of Roman Spanish and Spanish American mines is José de Acosta's *Historia natural y moral de las Indias* (1590), bk. 4, chap. 8, where he noted that just as Pliny tells us the Romans chose to exploit Spanish mineral wealth in order to save their own Italian population, so the modern Spaniards, despite their native mineral resources, chose to exploit the Indies. Fermín del Pino curiously regards this "equivalence" of ancient Romans and modern Spaniards as an expression of "el profundo espíritu nacionalista que late en el Renacimiento español" ("Culturas clásicas y americanas en Acosta," 346).

10. Las Casas, *Aquí se contiene una disputa,* 375–77.

11. Julián Marías, *Understanding Spain,* trans. Frances M. López-Morillas (Ann Arbor: University of Michigan Press, 1992), 13. (The Spanish edition, *España inteligible,* was published in 1990.)

12. Marías, *Understanding Spain,* chap. 13, "Invention of the Spanish Nation," 143–58.

13. Ramón Menéndez Pidal, preface to *Historia de España,* 3d ed (Madrid: Espasa-Calpe, 1963), ix–ciii, esp. sec. 4, "Unitarismo y localismo," li–lxx. The heading "Localismo como accidente morboso" is on p. lxx. This important essay is available in an English translation by Walter Starkie as *The Spaniards in Their History* (London: Hollis and Carter, 1950); see esp. 177–203.

14. See Horst Pietschmann, "El problema del 'nacionalismo' en España en la edad moderna. La resistencia de Castilla contra el emperador Carlos V," *Hispania* 52, no. 180 (1992): 83–106, esp. 85–86. See also Peter Linehan's engaging and illuminating survey of modern Spanish historians' views of the Gothic and medieval periods in *History and the Historians of Medieval Spain* (Oxford: Oxford University Press, 1993), chap. 1, "Ways of Looking Back."

15. See, in addition to Pietschmann, Helmut Koenigsberger, "Spain," in *National Consciousness, History, and Political Culture in Early-Modern Europe,* ed. Orest Ranum (Baltimore: Johns Hopkins University Press, 1975), 144–72; and I. A. A. Thompson, "Castile, Spain, and the Monarchy: The Political Community from *Patria Natural* to *Patria Nacional,*" in *Spain, Europe, and the Atlantic World: Essays in Honour of John H. Elliott,* ed. R. Kagan and G. Parker (Cambridge: Cambridge University Press, 1995), 125–59. In contrast to the common view that in the early modern period Castile imposed unity on the rest of Spain, Thompson maintains that Castile itself lacked a clear sense of itself as a coherent unit. Indeed, it was "this relative weakness of a Castilian sense of identity" that facilitated "its immersion in a broader Spanish national sentiment," insofar as such a sentiment was indeed felt (137–38).

16. Menéndez Pidal, *Spaniards in Their History,* 120–21.

17. Américo Castro's vigorous historiographical polemic on the Spaniards' "consciousness of their own collective identity" was conveniently encapsulated in a posthumous edition of reworkings of earlier studies, *Sobre el nombre y el quién*

de los españoles (Madrid: Taurus, 1973), where the phrase just quoted appears on p. 173. A much fuller Spanish exposition of his viewpoint is *La realidad histórica de España*, rev. ed. (Mexico City: Porrúa, 1962). An earlier stage is available in English as *The Structure of Spanish History*, trans. Edmund L. King (Princeton: Princeton University Press, 1954), the first seven chapters of which were later reworked as *The Spaniards*. C. Sánchez-Albornoz's passionate response to Castro is *España: Un enigma histórico*, 2 vols. (Buenos Aires: Editorial Sudamericana, 1956).

18. See, for example, Simon Barton, "The Roots of the National Question in Spain," in *The National Question in Europe in Historical Context*, ed. Mikuláš Teich and Roy Porter (Cambridge: Cambridge University Press, 1993), 106–27, esp. 107–12; E. Inman Fox, "Spain as Castile: Nationalism and National Identity," in *The Cambridge Companion to Modern Spanish Culture*, ed. David T. Gies (Cambridge: Cambridge University Press, 1999), 21–36.

19. José Antonio Maravall, *El concepto de España en la edad media* (Madrid: Instituto de Estudios Políticos, 1954). See also Diego Catalán, "España y su historiografía: De objeto a sujeto de la historia," introductory essay to Menéndez Pidal, *Los Españoles en la historia*, 2d ed. (Madrid: Espasa-Calpe, 1985), esp. 9–49. Also helpful are R. B. Tate's studies of fifteenth-century Spanish historiography, to which I shall be referring shortly.

20. Given the lively controversy over *hispanidad* and given also the complex tribal picture of pre-Roman Spain, it is a tricky business to find a noncontroversial and nonmisleading single word for the pre-Roman, non-Carthaginian inhabitants of the Iberian Peninsula. In this book I have settled for the term *pre-Roman Iberians* or simply *Iberians*, as used by William V. Harris in *The Cambridge Ancient History*, 2d ed., vol. 8 (Cambridge: Cambridge University Press, 1989), 118–42.

21. A. Castro, "The Historical 'We,'" in *An Idea of History: Selected Essays of Américo Castro*, trans. and ed. Stephen Gilman and Edmund L. King (Columbus: Ohio State University Press, 1977), 313–34. The article appeared in Spanish as "El 'nosotros' de las historias," *Revista de Occidente*, 2d ser. 2, no. 15 (1964): 259–82; and it was revised as "El 'nosotros' de las historiables colectividades humanas," in *Sobre el nombre*, 188–208.

22. Castro, *Structure of Spanish History*, 76 (= *Realidad histórica de España*, 163).

23. See Maravall, *Concepto de España*, chap. 6, "La tradición de la herencia goda." See also Catalán, "España en su historiografía," 16–30; and Castro, *Realidad histórica de España*, 163–66, and *Structure of Spanish History*, 76–80.

24. For Rodrigo Jiménez de Rada, see Linehan, *History and Historians*, esp. 313–412. See also Maravall, *Concepto de España*, 339–41, 357–58; Diego Catalán, "España en su historiografía," 28–30; González Rodríguez, *La idea de Roma*, 12–14.

25. Fernán Pérez de Guzmán, *Generaciones y semblanzas*, ed. J. Dominguez (Madrid: Espasa-Calpe, 1954), 11.

26. Oviedo, *Historia general*, proem to bk. 38, BAE vol. 120, 330.

27. Garcilaso de la Vega, *Historia de la Florida*, in *Obras completas*, ed.

P. Carmelo Sáenz de Santa María, vol. 1, BAE vol. 132 (Madrid: Atlas, 1965), 463, 464.

28. The persistence of the celebration of the Goths persisted well into the next century; see the 1645 *Corona gótica, castellana y austríaca* of Diego de Saavedra Fajardo (BAE vol. 25). On the other hand, certain Spanish champions of the Greco-Roman world did view the Goths in a more negative light, as culture-wrecking barbarians. See Maravall, *Antiguos y modernos*, 292, for references to Juan de Arfe (1535–1603), Felipe de Guevara (d. 1564), and Fernando de Herrera (d. 1597), who criticized "esos bárbaros de godos" (Guevara's phrase) for destroying Roman culture in Spain—especially, for Arfe and Guevara, the fine arts and architecture.

29. Isidore of Seville, prologue to *Historia de regibus Gothorum, Wandalorum et Suevorum*. I have used the translation of Kenneth Baxter Wolf in *Conquerors and Chroniclers of Early Medieval Spain* (Liverpool: Liverpool University Press, 1990), 82.

30. Las Casas, *Historia de las Indias*, bk. 1, chap. 15, 3:417.

31. For the role of Nanni and "Berosus" in Spanish historiography, see Julio Caro Baroja, *Las falsificaciones de la historia (en relación con la de España)* (Barcelona: Seix Barral, 1992), 47–78.

32. Las Casas, *Apologética historia sumaria*, epilogue, chap. 267, ed. Edmundo O'Gorman (Mexico City: Universidad Nacional Autónoma de México, Instututo de Investigaciones Históricas, 1967), 2:649–50; *Obras completas*, 8:1587–88.

33. Sículo, *De rebus Hispaniae memorabilibus*, bk. 4, p. 318. The work as a whole occupies pp. 291–517.

34. Las Casas, *Carta a un personaje de la corte*, October 15, 1535, *Obras escogidas*, 5:65. See Gutiérrez, *Las Casas*, 88.

35. Las Casas, *Octavo remedio*, 5:82.

36. Important accounts of the career of Garcés, his association with Las Casas, and the role of his letter to Paul III in the genesis of the bull *Sublimis deus* are Lewis Hanke, "Pope Paul III and the American Indians," *Harvard Theological Review* 30 (1937): 65–102; and A. Lobato Casado, "El obispo Garcés, O.P., y la bula *Sublimis Deus*," in *Los dominicos y el nuevo mundo*, 741–95. See also P. Mariano Cuevas, *Historia de la Iglesia en México*, 5th ed. (Mexico City: Editorial Patria, 1946), 1:373–79; Gutiérrez, *Las Casas*, 303 and 561–62 nn. 3, 6, and 7; Rand Parish and Weidman, *Las Casas en México*, 21; Carlos Sempat Assadourian, "Hacia la *Sublimis Deus*: Las discordias entre los dominicos indianos y el enfrentamiento del franciscano padre Tastera con el padre Betanzos," *Historia Mexicana* 47, no. 187 (1998): 465–536, esp. 474–75. Lobato Casado prints a photographic copy of the 1537 printing of Garcés's letter on pp. 769–84, with following Spanish translation, 785–92. Juan Solórzano Pereira included the entire letter in his 1629/39 *De Indiarum iure*, bk. 2.8.66 (Lyons: Anisson, 1662), 1:184–88. A widely available, but highly unreliable, edition of the letter is P. Francisco Javier Hernaez, *Colección de bulas, breves y otros documentos relativos a la Iglesia de América y Filipinas* (Brussels: Vromant, 1879; repr. Vaduz: Kraus, 1964), 1:56–62.

37. Though Garcés claimed in his letter to have had ten years' experience of the Indians (text in Lobato Casado, "El obisbo Garcés," 775), the consensus is that he wrote the letter in 1535: Hanke, "Pope Paul III," 70; Lobato Casado, 755; and esp. Sempat Assadourian, "Hacia la Sublimis Deus," 475 n. 16, who draws attention to Garcés's reference to Minaya as currently Dominican prior of the city of México, a post in which the vicar general Betanzos had apparently installed his associate Pedro Delgado before August 24, 1535.

38. Las Casas, *Apologética historia sumaria,* bk. 3, chap. 263, *Obras completas,* 8:1574–75.

39. Las Casas, *Apologética historia,* bk. 3, chap. 198, *Obras completas,* 8:1285.

40. Las Casas, *Apologética historia,* bk. 3, chap. 189, *Obras completas,* 8:1246.

41. Las Casas, *Apologética historia,* bk. 3, chap. 79, *Obras completas,* 7:672. Another passage in this book in which Las Casas spoke slightingly of the ancient Iberians was in chap. 47, where the full humanity of Indians who lived scattered lives without settlement was vindicated by an appeal to the pre-Roman Italians and to the "grande y ruda simplicidad" of the ancient inhabitants of "nuestra España" (*Obras completas,* 7:533).

42. Alfonso X, *Primera crónica general de España,* ed. R. Menéndez Pidal (Madrid: Gredos, 1955), 1:4. The reference to "the nobility of the Goths" quoted in the text follows shortly after this passage on the same page. For this chronicle's use of the term *español,* see Castro, *Sobre el nombre,* 72–81. While he notes that the chronicle tends to distinguish pre-Roman and Roman-period *españoles* from later *godos* and the still later *cristianos* of the Reconquest, Castro argues that the Alfonsine adoption of the Provençal-derived *español* as a vernacular equivalent for the Latin *Hispani* ultimately proved to have "disastrous consequences for Spanish historiography," and that it helped inspire "the absurd legend that the subjects of Charles V were as much Spaniards as those who fought against the Carthaginians and the Romans before the birth of Christ" (79–80).

43. Alfonso X, *Primera crónica,* chap. 559, p. 312.

44. Alfonso X, *Primera crónica,* chap. 23, p. 18. Alfonso's praise of the Roman's intelligence and patience may have been inspired in part by the claim in 1 Macc. 8.3 that they acquired Spain "consilio suo et patientia." For a discussion of this passage in particular and of the views of Rome taken in the Alfonsine chronicles generally, see Charles F. Fraker, *The Scope of History* (Ann Arbor: University of Michigan Press, 1996), 101–13, esp. 104–5.

45. On the chronicle's view of Scipio's policy of *amor,* see Charles Fraker, "Scipio, and the Origins of Culture: The Question of Alfonso's Sources," *Dispositio* 10 (1987): 15–27, reprinted in *The Scope of History,* 114–31. The chronicle's reference to Scipio's successors is at the beginning of chap. 39, p. 26. For Florus's view of the Romans in Spain, see in particular his account of the siege of Numantia, *Epitome,* 1.34, which abounds in celebrations of Celtiberian valor, anticipating the tone of Ambrosio de Morales's patriotic account published in 1574, to be discussed below. "Numantia quantum Carthaginis Capuae Corinthi opibus inferior, ita virtutis nomine et honore par omnibus, summumque, si viros aestimes,

Hispaniae decus" (1.34.1); "Macte fortissimam et meo iudicio beatissimam in ipsis malis civitatem! etc." (1.34.16–17). Alfonso's chroniclers austerely deny themselves this encomiastic coloring of these events that would loom so large in later Spanish patriotic historiography and literature.

46. Alfonso García de Santa María, *Anacephaleosis*, in Schottus, *Hispaniae illustratae*, 251. The whole work occupies pp. 246–91 of Schottus's collection. For an acute discussion of Santa María, see Robert B. Tate, "The *Anacephaleosis* of Alfonso García de Santa María," in *Hispanic Studies in Honour of I. González Llubera*, ed. Frank Pierce (Oxford: Dophin Book Co., 1959), 387–401, Span. trans. in his *Ensayos sobre la historiografía peninsular del siglo XV* (Madrid: Gredos, 1970), 55–73. French chroniclers of the fifteenth century appear to have fostered a similar discovery of the Gauls as ancestors of the French people, either alongside or in place of Trojan or Frankish ancestors, coupled with an animus against the Romans as invaders and oppressors. See Colette Beaune, *The Birth of an Ideology: Myths and Symbols of Nation in Late-Medieval France*, trans. Susan Ross Huston (Berkeley and Los Angeles: University of California Press, 1991), 333–45. She notes that "by 1480 a Frenchman was almost certain to boast of Gallic ancestors he would not have known he had around 1400" (342). See also Claude-Gilbert Dubois, *Celtes et Gaulois au XVIe siècle: Le développement littéraire d'un mythe nationaliste* (Paris: Vrin, 1972).

47. Alfonso García de Santa María, *Anacephaleosis*, chap. 9, p. 255.

48. See Richard H. Trame, *Rodrigo Sánchez de Arévalo, 1404–1470: Spanish Diplomat and Champion of the Papacy* (Washington, D.C.: Catholic University of America Press, 1958). See also Robert B. Tate, "Rodrigo Sánchez de Arévalo (1404–1470) and His *Compendiosa Historia Hispánica*," *Nottingham Medieval Studies* 4 (1960): 58–80, repr. in *Ensayos*, 74–104; and Jeremy N. H. Lawrance, "Humanism in the Iberian Peninsula," in *The Impact of Humanism on Western Europe*, ed. Anthony Goodman and Angus MacKay (London: Longman, 1990), 229; the quoted phrase comes from here.

49. Sánchez de Arévalo, *Compendiosa historia hispánica*, in Schottus, *Hispaniae illustratae*, 121. Arévalo's history occupies pp. 120–246 of Schottus.

50. Arévalo, *Compendiosa historia*, pt. 1, chap. 4, pp. 125–26.

51. This treatise was known more formally as *De origine ac differentia principatus imperialis ac regalis*. Tate's citation from this latter (fol. 54r) is the source of my quotations from the treatise: see *Ensayos*, 104 and n. 43. For accounts of this treatise and the political circumstances to which it was responding see Trame, *Rodrigo Sánchez de Arévalo*, 151–56, and J. H. Burns, *Lordship, Kingship, and Empire: The Idea of Monarchy, 1400–1525* (Oxford: Clarendon Press, 1992), 85–91.

52. For Arévalo's controversy with Torquemada, see Trame, *Rodrigo Sánchez de Arévalo*, 156–59; and Jedin, "Juan de Torquemada" (includes an edition of Torquemada's treatise).

53. Boies Penrose, *Travel and Discovery in the Renaissance, 1420–1620* (New York: Atheneum, 1962), 120.

54. For Enciso, see Maravall, *Concepto de España*, 357, citing 3d ed. of 1546.

55. Antonio de Guevara, *Libro primero de las epístolas familiares*, ed. José María de Cossío (Madrid: Aldus, 1950), 56–67, letter 1.7.

56. Guevara, *Epístolas familiares*, 1.11, 80.1.

57. Guevara, *Epístolas familiares*, 1.5 (addressed to Don Alonso Manrique, archbishop of Sevilla and Don Antonio Manrique, duke of Nájara), 37–47. For an account of this letter that unduly stresses the pro-Iberian, anti-Roman elements, see Rachel Schmidt, "The Development of *Hispanitas* in Spanish Sixteenth-Century Versions of the Fall of Numancia," *Renaissance and Reformation/Renaissance et Réforme* 19 (1995): 28–31. Schmidt argues that Guevara was presenting Numantia as a "utopia" destroyed by the "greed, obstinacy, and envy" of Scipio.

58. Guevara, general prologue to *Reloj*, quoted in Arco y Garay, *La idea de imperio*, 27–28; Joseph R. Jones, ed., *Una década de Césares* (Chapel Hill: University of North Carolina Press, 1966).

59. Sepúlveda, *Democrates segundo*, ed. Losada, 34. Sepúlveda had anticipated this identification with Iberian resistance to Roman invasion as early as his *Cohortatio ad Carolum V ut . . . bellum suscipiat in turcas*, published in Bologna in 1529. Here, as an incentive to Charles to attack the simultaneously menacing and insignificant Turks, Sepúlveda adduced the patriotically inspiring "glory of Numantia," when "4,000 Spaniards held out for fourteen years against an army of 40,000 . . . brave Roman soldiers." But this is a brief *praeteritio* appended to a much more extensive presentation of the model of Greek, Macedonian, and especially Roman victories over feeble Asiatics and followed by yet another appeal to emulate the Romans, "men of great military knowledge and experience and conquerors of the whole world." See Sepúlveda, *Tratados políticos*, 17–23. González Rodríguez has also drawn attention to Sepúlveda's rather rare exaltations of the primitive Spaniards at the expense of the Romans (*La idea de Roma*, 55 n. 210).

60. Lucia Binotti, "Cultural Identity and the Ideologies of Translation in Sixteenth-Century Europe: Italian Prologues to Spanish Chronicles of the New World," *History of European Ideas* 14, no. 6 (1992): 769–88. The passage cited from Cravaliz and Binotti's quoted comment on it are on p. 780.

61. Oviedo, *Historia general*, bk. 33, chap. 20, BAE vol. 120, 97.

62. Oviedo, *Historia general*, pt. 2, dedicatory epistle to Charles V, BAE vol. 118, esp. 212–14. For discussions of the anti-Roman tone of this epistle, see Jaime González Rodríguez, "El antiromanismo de Gonzalo Fernández de Oviedo," *Revista de Indias* 43 (1983): 335–42, esp. 337–39, and also *La idea de Roma*, 49–52. See also Rech, "Zum Nachleben der Antike," 238–39: "Die Identität Spaniens wird somit radikal von Rom getrennt." This epistle and book 20 were the only sections of part 2 published until all three parts appeared in 1851–55. Oviedo's strong interest in the history of Spain is attested by two unpublished MSS: the *Catálogo real de España* of 1532 (Biblioteca de Escorial) and *Epílogo real, imperial y pontifical* of 1535 (Biblioteca Nacional de Madrid). Oviedo alludes to the former in the dedicatory epistle, p. 214. Though these MSS do not seem to have been studied extensively, a brief indication of their contents may be found in González Rodríguez, "La significación de las Indias para la historia de España según Oviedo," in *América y la España del siglo XVI*, ed. Francisco de Solano y Fermín del Pino, vol. 1 (Madrid: Consejo Superior de Investigaciones Científicas,

1982), 77–84. A useful short discussion of Oviedo's "Iberian nationalism," and of his prejudice against the Romans, is Gerbi, *Nature in the New World,* 267–69.

63. When Oviedo wrote this dedicatory epistle, he appears to have been unaware that Charles had ceded the imperial crown to his brother Ferdinand on August 23, 1556—hence his continued use of the phrase *Cesárea Majestad.* In any case, Charles's transfer of the crown was not formally ratified by the prince-electors until February 1558.

64. For the importance of Nanni's forgeries in early modern Spain, see Caro Baroja, *Las falsificaciones,* 49–78. For a more general account of Nanni, see Anthony Grafton, *Forgers and Critics: Creativity and Duplicity in Western Scholarship* (Princeton: Princeton University Press, 1990).

65. For example, the Alfonsine chronicle declared that Julián "vinie de grand linnage de partes de los godos" (Alfonso X, *Primera crónica,* chap. 554, ed. R. Menéndez Pidal, 307).

66. López de Ayala, *Crónica del Rey Don Pedro,* year 2, chap. 18, in *Crónicas de los reyes de Castilla,* vol. 1, ed. Cayetano Rosell, BAE vol. 66 (1875; repr. Madrid: Atlas, 1953), 421. Juan Menéndez Pidal conjectured that López de Ayala was indebted to a lost source used also by two fifteenth-century chroniclers, Arcipreste Rodríguez de Almela (who added, for good measure, that Julián was of the family of Julian the Apostate!) and Lope García de Salazar, *Leyendas del ultimo rey godo* (Madrid: Tipografía de la Revista de archivos, bibliotecas y museos, 1906), 128.

67. Oviedo, *Historia general,* bk. 3, chap. 12, BAE vol. 117, 84.

68. Ibid., bk. 29, chap. 30, BAE ed., vol. 119, 329–30.

69. Sículo, *De rebus Hispaniae memorabilibus,* bk. 19, pp. 478–79. I have translated the Latin of the 1530 edition; Oviedo offered the passage in its 1539 Spanish translation, 330. A useful discussion of the "Roman coin" story and its afterlife is packed into a footnote in Gliozzi's *Adamo e il nuovo mondo,* 271–72 n. 72.

70. See Gliozzi's note, *Adamo e il nuovo mondo,* 271–72 n. 72, for references to Lipsius and Solórzano Pereira. He was apparently unaware of Castellanos's attack on the story. He also cites a reference to the "find" in Stephen Batman's 1582 commentary on the *De proprietatibus rerum* of Bartholomaeus Anglicus: *Batman upon Bartholome* (London, 1582), 250r. Ricardo del Arco y Garay also cites the offended rejection of Marineo Sículo by Camilo Borrell in his *De regis catholici praestantia,* a work written around 1580 but not published until 1611 (*La idea del imperio,* 433). Arco y Garay also notes that chap. 19 of Marineo's book was removed from the later printings (434 n. 18).

71. Castellanos, *Elegías de varones ilustres de Indias,* pt. 1, elegy 1, canto 6, stanzas 9–13, BAE vol. 4, 9th ed. (Madrid: Atlas, 1944), 19.

72. Lipsius, *Physiologiae stoicorum,* in *Opera omnia* (Vesalilae, 1675), 4:862; as cited by Gliozzi, *Adamo e il nuovo mondo,* 271 n. 72. See Mark Morford, *Stoics and Neostoics: Rubens and the Circle of Lipsius* (Princeton: Princeton University Press, 1991), 99.

73. Solórzano Pereira, *Política indiana,* bk. 1, chap. 6, BAE vol. 252 (Madrid: Atlas, 1972), 67.

74. See J. B. Thacher, *Christopher Columbus*, vol. 3 (New York: Putnam, 1904), 627.

75. Oviedo, *Historia general*, bk. 29, chap. 30, BAE vol. 119, 330.

76. Ibid., bk. 2, chap. 3, BAE vol. 117, 17-20.

77. Montaigne, "Des cannibales," in *Essais*, bk. 1, chap. 31, pp. 241-42.

78. So Gliozzi, *Adamo e il nuovo mondo*, 17, citing an article by Bataillon; cf. Gerbi, *Nature in the New World*, 271.

79. Charles Gibson suggested that Oviedo may also have intended his Hesperides/Indies theory to tap into the prestige of the Reconquest. Oviedo's suggestion that Hesperus had passed through North Africa before setting sail westward would have bolstered recent Spanish claims to the former province of Mauritania Tingitana as a region once held by the Visigothic kings. Accordingly, "Oviedo's historical reconstruction would have made America too a part of the Reconquista" ("Reconquista and Conquista," 26). Anthony Pagden has apparently misunderstood Gibson to be attributing to Oviedo a theory that the Indians "might be the remnant of a Visigothic diaspora" (*Fall of Natural Man*, 37; *Lords*, 39). Not only did Oviedo offer no hint of such a thing, but he seems never to have attempted to account for the origin of the Indians: see Alberto M. Salas, *Tres cronistas de Indias* (Mexico City: Fondo de Cultura Económica, 1959), 124-25 n. 25. Similarly mistaken is Lee Eldridge Huddleston's assumption that Oviedo's Hesperides/Indies equation was designed as an "argument for a Spanish origin for the inhabitants" (*Origins of the American Indians* [Austin: University of Texas Press, 1967], 20).

80. Fernando Colón, *The Life of the Admiral Christopher Columbus by His Son Ferdinand*, trans. Benjamin Keen (New Brunswick, N.J.: Rutgers University Press, 1959), chap. 10, p. 29. This book was published in Italian in 1571. Its original Spanish version, composed not long before the author's death in 1539, was lost.

81. Gómara, *Historia general de las Indias*, chap. 220, 1932 ed., 2:249. See Gliozzi, *Adamo e il nuovo mondo*, 19.

82. Las Casas, *Historia de las Indias*, bk. 1, chaps. 15-16, 3:410-28.

83. Las Casas's defense of Nanni and "Berosus" against Vives is in the *Apologética historia*, bk. 3, chap. 108, in *Obras completas*, 7:819-21.

84. Las Casas, *Historia de las Indias*, bk. 1, chap. 15, 3:414.

85. Ibid., 3:418.

86. Las Casas, *Apologia*, chap. 33; trans. Poole, *Defense of the Indians*, 220.

87. On Margarit, see R. B. Tate, "The *Paralipomenon Historiae* of Joan Margarit, Cardinal Bishop of Gerona," *Bulletin of the John Rylands Library* 34 (1951): 137-65, also in his *Ensayos*, 123-50. See also Lawrance, "Humanism," 230-31: "He had no interest in the Gothic theory, which had been appropriated by the Castilians, and turned by preference to the Ibero-Roman period."

88. The combined chronicle of Ocampo and Morales was later published in ten volumes as *Corónica general de España* (Madrid: B. Cano, 1791), and this is the edition I have used. For Morales's life and his qualities as an historian, see Enrique Redel, *Ambrosio de Morales, Estudio biográfico* (Córdoba: Diario, 1908); and Benito Sánchez Alonso, *Historia de la historiografía española*, vol. 2

(Madrid: Consejo Superior de Investigaciones Científicas, 1950), 25–30. Both emphasize Morales's impressive critical treatment of written sources, as well as his use of archaeological, epigraphic, and numismatic evidence. See also Sabine MacCormack, "History, Memory, and Time in Golden Age Spain," *History and Memory* 4 (1992): 38–68. She observes that in Morales's work "the history of the Roman Empire came to be anchored in one of that Empire's provinces, in a specific landscape and in a specific chronology capable of being documented not just with ancient texts but with the records of everyday life" (47). Morales's historical method appears to have had its own impact upon the study of the Indies, for J. H. Elliott notes that the mestizo historian Garcilaso de la Vega "seems to have derived his scholarly interest in the proper spelling of Quechua words from his membership of a circle of Córdoba *savants,* who had learned . . . from Morales to employ literary, topographical and philological evidence in their study of Spanish antiquities" (*Old World and New,* 36).

89. Florián de Ocampo, *Corónica general,* prologue, 1:xx and xi. For Ocampo's "Iberian patriotism" and his tendency to find Spaniards everywhere in the pre-Roman Mediterranean, see Américo Castro, *The Spaniards,* 23 (or *Realidad histórica de España,* 3–4). Castro approvingly cites Georges Cirot's suggestion that "the spectacle of Spanish conquest in the New World must have given Ocampo the idea that 'Spaniards' in the times of Atlas, the Sicanians, the Siculians, and other mythical characters had been adventurers and colonizers."

90. Ambrosio de Morales, *Corónica general,* bk. 7, chap. 1.1, 3:195.

91. Ibid., bk. 7, chap. 28.3, 3:294.

92. Morales's account of the war of Viriathus occupies chaps. 44–53 of bk. 7, 3:348–82. The quoted phrase is from his concluding encomium on the Lusitanian hero, p. 381.

93. Ibid., bk. 8, chap. 11.1, 4:1. The final phases of the Numantine War occupy the first ten chapters of bk. 8, and this evidently served as Cervantes's principal inspiration and source for his patriotic pageant, the *Numancia.* See Willard F. King, "Cervantes' *Numancia* and Imperial Spain," *Modern Language Notes* 94 (1979): 200–221, esp. 202–7, a useful discussion of the patriotic bent of Morales's chronicle. While we have already seen the inaccuracy of King's claim that "in it for the first time the Celtiberians are brought to the fore as the original Spaniards," she still deserves credit for having drawn attention to the important but relatively neglected question of the sixteenth-century Spaniards' conceptions of their ethnic identity and origin.

94. Morales, *Corónica general,* bk. 8, chap. 1, 2. Cf. L. Annaeus Florus, *Epitomae libri II,* 1.34.3, "non temere, si fateri licet, ullius causa belli iniustior."

95. Morales, *Corónica general,* bk. 8, chap. 4, 4:17.

96. Ibid., chap. 10, 4:43. Both quoted phrases are inserted in a passage that is otherwise taken over directly from Appian (15.95).

97. Ibid., chap. 3, 4:13.

98. Ibid., chap. 10, 4:45.

99. Ibid., bk. 9, chap. 18, 4:515.

100. MacCormack, "History, Memory, and Time," 47.

101. Morales, *Corónica general*, bk. 11, chap. 13.4, 5:361. His reference is to Orosius, *Libri septem adversus paganos* 7.41.

102. Cervantes, *Numancia*. Studies of Cervantes's play against the background of Morales's history are King, "Cervantes' *Numancia*"; and Schmidt, "Development of *Hispanitas*."

103. King, "Cervantes' *Numancia*," 207–16.

104. See Redel, *Ambrosio de Morales*, 78–80.

105. Morales, *Corónica general*, prologue, 3:vii–viii.

106. See Ernest Grey, *Guevara, a Forgotten Renaissance Author* (The Hague: Nijhoff, 1973), 45–51.

107. Elliott, *Old World and New*, chap. 1, "The Uncertain Impact."

108. Ibid., 50.

109. Stuart Piggott, *Ancient Britons and the Antiquarian Imagination: Ideas from the Renaissance to the Regency* (London: Thames and Hudson, 1989), 73. See the section "The Impact of America," 73–86.

110. Ibid., 76–77.

111. Ibid., 85. Cf. the Everyman edition of Burton (London: Dent, 1932), 1:86. Note that Burton, having projected the New World onto the Old, proceeded to project the Old back onto the New when he suggested that the cultural progress made by the inhabitants of Britain and Germany offered hope that enlightened imperial rule might help achieve similar results among the Virginia Indians and the "wild Irish."

112. Peter Burke, "America and the Rewriting of World History," in Kupperman, *America in European Consciousness*, 33–51.

113. Ibid., 42.

114. Ibid., 44.

115. Elliott, *Old World and New*, 53.

116. A handy summary of López's career is Robert Himmerich y Valencia, *The Encomenderos of New Spain, 1521–1555* (Austin: University of Texas Press, 1991), 183.

117. This letter is printed in its entirety in Francisco del Paso y Troncoso, ed., *Epistolario de Nueva España 1505–1818*, vol. 4 (Mexico City: Porrúa, 1939), letter no. 236, 150–79. An extract, including our passage, is available in English translation in Parry and Keith, *New Iberian World*, 3:446–53. Though López sailed to Spain with the encomenderos' delegation on June 17, 1544, he was back in New Spain by the time he wrote this letter "desta gran cibdad de México" (179). See Lesley Byrd Simpson, *The Encomienda in New Spain*, rev. ed. (Berkeley and Los Angeles: University of California Press, 1950), 139.

118. López in *Epistolario*, 161.

119. Ibid., 163.

120. Ibid., 169; my translation.

121. For accounts of the Colegio de Santa Cruz de Tlatelolco (sometimes called the Colegio de Santiago Tlatelolco), see Robert Ricard, *The Spiritual Conquest of Mexico*, trans. Lesley Byrd Simpson (Berkeley and Los Angeles: University of California Press, 1966), 217–35; and José María Kobayashi, *La educación como conquista* (Mexico City: El colegio de México, 1974), 292–407. For an

account of Latin instruction at the colegio, see Ignacio Osorio Romero, *La enseñanza del Latín a los indios* (Mexico City: Universidad Nacional Autónoma de México, 1990), xxii–xlv.

122. Bernardino de Sahagún, *Historia general de las cosas de Nueva España*, from the "Relación del autor digna de ser anotada" interjected between chapters 27 and 28 of book 10 (Mexico City: Porrúa, 1956, repr. 1989), 583. Cited also in Ricard, *Spiritual Conquest of Mexico*, 226.

123. For the languages of instruction, see Osorio Romero, *La enseñaza del latín*, xxiii; and Ricard, *Spiritual Conquest of Mexico*, 224. I am not sure what Walter Mignolo has in mind when he asserts that at the colegio "Castilian was used, although Nahuatl and Latin were taught" (*The Darker Side of the Renaissance: Literacy, Territoriality, and Colonization* [Ann Arbor: University of Michigan Press, 1995], 53). His footnote refers to Ricard and Kobayashi, but without specific references. Nor do I understand his assertion on p. 347 n. 58, that Latin instruction at the colegio "was limited . . . in time (after 1560, under Philip II)." Ricard cites Motolinía's anecdote on p. 224.

124. Jerónimo López quoted in Mariano Cuevas, *Historia de la iglesia en México*, 1:439.

125. The translation offered in *New Iberian World* attributes this "preaching" solely to the friars: "The friars who are in this land and in Mexico say and preach anything they want about those things." But the Spanish seems inescapably to mean that the priests gave their students "turns" at preaching: "los frailes la tierra adentro y en México les dan veces de predicar: dicen e predican lo que quieren destas cosas e otras que se les antoja."

126. See Ricard, *Spiritual Conquest of Mexico*, 219.

127. The inventories of 1572 and 1574 are recorded in *Códice Mendieta: Documentos Franciscanos. Siglos XVI y XVII* (México, 1892), 2:255–57; the entry on Appian is on p. 255. See also Miguel Mathes, *Santa Cruz de Tlatelolco: La primera biblioteca académica de las Américas* (Mexico City: Secretaría de relaciones exteriores, 1982), 32. Mathes appears to have assumed that this was a book with the title *Apiano de Beliz*—perhaps a long-lost cousin of *Amadís de Gaula*?!

128. *Códice Mendieta*, 2:262; cf. Mathes, *Santa Cruz de Tlatelolco*, 33.

129. *Códice Mendieta*, 2:261; cf. Mathes, *Santa Cruz de Tlatelolco*, 34.

130. See the table in Mathes, *Santa Cruz de Tlatelolco*, 81.

131. See Ricard, *Spiritual Conquest of Mexico*, 226.

Chapter 6

1. See the entry on Augusta Emerita by Luis G. Iglesias in *The Princeton Encyclopedia of Classical Sites*, ed. Richard Stillwell (Princeton: Princeton University Press, 1976), 114–16.

2. See Thomas, *Conquest*, 152, on the role of Extremeños among the chief men of the expedition of Cortés, himself an Extremeño. The phrase "wildest part of Castile" is on p. 117.

3. *Relación que hizo el cabildo de la ciudad de Mérida á su Magestad, el 18 de Febrero de 1579*, quoted in Juan Francisco Molina Solís, *Historia del des-*

cubrimiento y conquista de Yucatán (Mérida de Yucatán: Caballero, 1896), 632 n. 2; Eng. trans. in *New Iberian World*, 3:517.

4. Juan Díaz, *Itinerario*, Eng. trans. Henry R. Wagner in *The Discovery of New Spain in 1518 by Juan de Grijalva* (New York: Cortés Society, 1942), 77. The original Spanish version of Díaz's account has been lost; Wagner translated an Italian translation. The Mérida of Venezuela, founded in 1549, owes its name not to the Roman ruins of Mérida, but to the Caballeros de Mérida, the military order to which the Extramaduran town was entrusted after the Reconquest. See José Antonio Calderón Quijano, *Toponimia española en el Nuevo Mundo* (Seville: Caja San Fernando, 1988), 173–74 (and see 172–73 for an entry on Mérida in Yucatán).

5. *Provinciae sive regiones in India Occidentali noviter repertae in ultima navigatione*, translated by Wagner in *Discovery of New Spain*, 64.

6. Pedro Sancho, *An Account of the Conquest of Peru*, trans. Philip Ainsworth Means in *Documents and Narratives concerning the Discovery and Conquest of Latin America*, vol. 2 (New York: Cortés Society, 1917), 156. An illuminating discussion of Inca-Roman architectural parallels in Sancho, Cieza de León, et al. is Valerie Fraser, *The Architecture of Conquest: Building in the Viceroyalty of Peru, 1535–1635* (Cambridge: Cambridge University Press, 1990), 27–35. She argues, however, that Spanish observers ultimately tended to find the Incas inferior to the Romans because of their puzzling failure to invent the arch. Had they made this discovery, one anonymous early-seventeenth-century writer commented, "they would have outshone all the nations of the world" (quoted by Valerie Fraser, *The Architecture of Conquest: Building in the Viceroyalty of Peru, 1535–1635* [Cambridge: Cambridge University Press, 1990], 34).

7. Thus, Anthony Grafton, alluding to López de Gómara's analogy between Aztec codices and Egyptian hieroglyphics, noted that "the Indians were at once so barbarous as to deserve conquest and so splendid as to endow their Spanish conquerors with unimaginable glory" (*New Worlds, Ancient Texts*, 138).

8. The reaction of well-traveled conquistadors to the markets of Tlatelolco was recorded by Bernal Díaz, *Historia verdadera*, chap. 92, p. 173. See the same chapter for Díaz's surprised claim that the great plaza of Tlatelolco was larger than the Plaza Mayor of Salamanca (172). He also compared the markets of Tlatelolco with those of his own hometown, Medina del Campo, one of the great fair towns of early modern Europe—burned to the ground, ironically enough, in the Comunero Revolt less than a year after its native son participated in the fall of Tenochtitlan (171).

9. Sepúlveda, *Democrates secundus*, ed. Angel Losada, 33; the word *homunculi* appears on p. 35. The phrase about apes and men was erased in the Madrid MS, and Losada removed it from the text and interred it in the app. crit. But see Pagden, *Fall of Natural Man*, 233 n. 45. Sepúlveda's application of Aristotle's category of "natural slaves" to the New World natives should not be taken to mean that he championed the literal enslavement of those who willingly accepted Spanish rule. See J. A. Fernández-Santamaría, "Juan Ginés de Sepúlveda on the Nature of the American Indians," *Americas* 31 (1975): 434–51, and *State, War, and Peace*, 196–236. Fernández-Santamaría suggests that Sepúlveda's habit

of praising ancient Roman imperialism implicitly belies the widespread assumption that he urged the enslavement of the Indians, for the Romans did not enslave the "inferior" peoples whom they conquered (see *State, War, and Peace*, 190–91, 218, 225, 227 n. 94). The same point is made by Francisco Castilla Urbano, "Juan Ginés de Sepúlveda: En torno a una idea de civilización," *Revista de Indias* 52 (1992): 345–46. For useful discussions of Sepúlveda's inconsistencies or "oscillations" on the nature of the Indians, see Alejandro Lipschutz, *El problema racial en la conquista de América, y el mestizaje*, 2d ed. (Santiago de Chile: Andrés Bello, 1967), 89–94; and Vidal Abril Castelló, "Bipolorización Sepúlveda–Las Casas," in Ramos et al., *La ética en la conquista*, 229–88, esp. 274–79.

 10. Díaz, *Historia verdadera*, chap. 87, p. 159.

 11. Ibid., chap. 207, pp. 577–78.

 12. López de Gómara, *Historia general de las Indias*, dedication to Charles V, 1979 ed., 1:8.

 13. Illuminating accounts of Spanish comparisons between the New World natives and the classical world are Benjamin Keen, *The Aztec Image* (New Brunswick, N.J.: Rutgers University Press, 1971), 71–137, and John F. Moffitt and Santiago Sebastián, *O Brave New People* (Albuquerque: University of New Mexico Press, 1996), chap. 5 "The Influence of Classical Models on the Renaissance Image of the American Indian." See also Michael T. Ryan, "Assimilating New Worlds in the Sixteenth and Seventeenth Centuries," *Comparative Studies in Society and History* 23 (1981): 519–38. Ryan notes that one of the main ways Renaissance Europeans devised to assimilate the natives of the New World into their mental horizons was to recognize them "immediately and unselfconsciously as pagan peoples. . . . The most obvious and immediate consequence of the identification of exotic peoples as pagans was the possibility of comparisons with pagan antiquity" (525–26). While Ryan proceeds to treat Las Casas's *Apologética historia sumaria* simply as a catalog of classical/Indian comparisons, Sabine MacCormack has more acutely drawn attention to how "Las Casas' advocacy of Amerindian religions endowed his reading of the ancient and venerable texts that had guided and inspired European scholars for centuries with novelty and dramatic tension. . . . His comparisons between the pagan gods and cults of pre-Christian Europe and those of the Americas reinvigorated the ancient Christian apologetic against the persuasive power and moral corruption of Mediterranean paganism" (*Religion in the Andes: Vision and Imagination in Early Colonial Peru* [Princeton: Princeton University Press, 1991], 207). See also Pagden, *Fall of Natural Man*, chap. 6, "A Programme for Comparative Ethnology, (1) Bartolomé de las Casas." J. A. Maravall places Las Casas's Greco-Roman vs. Amerindian agon in the context of the medieval and Renaissance debate over "ancients vs. moderns," with the New World natives assuming the surprising role of surrogate "moderns" (sometimes even explicitly referred to as *modernos* in the *Apologética historia*) (*Antiguos y modernos*, 446–49).

 14. Sepúlveda, *Democrates secundus*, ed. Losada, 33 n. 89.

 15. Todorov, *The Conquest of America*, 166, 151. There have been some scholars, however, who have admitted the complexity of Oviedo's views about the Amerindians and have drawn attention to his use of classical parallels. See

especially Gerbi, *Nature in the New World*, 129–423 passim, but especially 263–67; Salas, *Tres cronistas de Indias*, 121–24; Manuel Ballesteros Gaibrois, *Gonzalo Fernández de Oviedo* (Madrid: Fundación universitaria española, 1981), 201–32; Stephanie Merrim, "The Apprehension of the New in Nature and Culture: Fernández de Oviedo's *Sumario*," in Jara and Spadaccini, *1492–1992*, 166–99, esp. 186–87 (where, unfortunately, her misreading of Oviedo's theory of the Indies as the Hesperides leads her to assume that for Oviedo the Indians were "lapsed Spaniards").

16. Brading, *The First America*, 40. True, on the next page Brading does admit: "In all fairness to the memory of Oviedo, it should be noted that in the later, unpublished sections of his chronicle, he inserted more favourable comments on Indian character and quality," a fact that Brading attributes to the evolution of the conquest itself, as it moved on from the Antilles to the more advanced civilizations of the mainland. We shall soon see, however, that Oviedo expressed respect for some aspects of Caribbean Indian life in the earliest strata of his book.

17. Oviedo, *Historia general*, bk. 3, chap. 6, BAE vol. 117, 66–67. The BAE edition gives for "now" the date 1548, which reflects Oviedo's later revision of the manuscript. The 1547 edition, which appears to be a virtually unaltered reprint of the 1535 edition, gives 1535 as the current date for the figure of five hundred natives still on Hispaniola. Daymond Turner calls these first two editions "substantially identical" (*Gonzalo Fernández de Oviedo y Valdés: An Annotated Bibliography* [Chapel Hill: University of North Carolina Press, 1966], 8).

18. Oviedo, *Historia general*, bk. 3. chap. 6, BAE vol. 117, 67. I have adapted the translation of Brading, *The First America*, 40. (Brading oddly renders "de poco trabajo" as "of little faith.")

19. Oviedo, *Historia general*, bk. 3, chap. 6, BAE vol. 117, 69.

20. Las Casas, *Historia de las Indias*, bk. 3, chap. 143, 5:2389. For his use of the phrase "codicia insaciable" in the *Brevísima relación*, see *Tratados*, 21.

21. Oviedo, *Historia general*, bk. 6, chap. 9, BAE vol. 117, 167. This heading appeared in the 1547 edition, and I am assuming that it was also present in the 1535 version.

22. I am assuming, with Edmundo O'Gorman, that Las Casas composed the *Apologética historia* between the years 1552 and 1559. See the "Estudio preliminar" to his edition of the work, xxi–xxxvi. As for Oviedo, I am following the conclusion of Daymond Turner that "in 1548 he . . . made the final entries in the *Historia general . . . as we now know it*" (*Gonzalo Fernández de Oviedo y Valdés*, xv).

23. Oviedo, *Historia general*, bk. 33, chap. 45, BAE vol. 120, p. 220.

24. Ibid., 221.

25. Ibid., bk. 42, chap. 11, BAE vol. 120, 413.

26. Ibid., 419.

27. Ibid., 421.

28. Ibid., chap. 12, BAE vol. 120, 421–22.

29. Ibid., bk. 5, chap. 1, BAE vol. 117, 112.

30. Mignolo, *Darker Side*, 3.

31. Pedro de Gante, cited in ibid., 45.

32. Oviedo, *Sumario de la natural historia de las Indias,* ed. Juan Bautista Avalle-Arce (Salamanca: Anaya, 1963), 50.

33. Oviedo, *Historia general,* bk. 5, chap. 1, BAE vol. 117, 114.

34. The phrase "record keeping without letters" is from the title to the third chapter of Mignolo's *Darker Side of the Renaissance,* a book that fails to discuss Oviedo's fascinating chapter on the Antillean areitos, though Mignolo did refer briefly to this passage in his article "La colonización del lenguaje y de la memoria: Complicidades de la letra, el libro, y la historia," in *Discursos sobre la "invención" de América,* ed. Iris M. Zavala (Amsterdam: Rodopi, 1992), 208, and in what is essentially an English version of the same article, "On the Colonization of Amerindian Languages and Memories: Renaissance Theories of Writing and the Discontinuity of the Classical Tradition," *Comparative Studies in Society and History* 34 (1992): 320. In both versions, Mignolo misidentifies the chapter as book 1, chap. 1.

35. Peter Martyr (Pietro Martire d'Anghiera, Petrus Martyr de Angleria), *De orbe novo decades octo,* decade 3, chap. 8, fol. xlix, p. 130. Peter Martyr had employed a rather fanciful classical analogy for the areitos in decade 1, chap. 5 (fol. xii, p. 58), where the thirty dancing wives of a cacique allegedly caused Spanish viewers to imagine that they were beholding "dryades formossissimas aut nativas fontium nymphas." While he did not actually call the dance of these "nymphs" areitos, Las Casas did so in describing the same scene (*Historia de las Indias,* bk. 1, chap. 114, 3:964).

36. Perhaps Oviedo's comparison of New World songs with Spanish peasant ballads inspired Pedro Cieza de León to compare Inca songs in honor of dead rulers with Spanish "romances y villancicos" and also to label them "cantares" (*Del señorío de los Incas,* ed. Alberto Mario Salas [Buenos Aires: Ediciones Argentinas "Solar," 1943], chaps. 11, 12, pp. 74–78. See Sabine MacCormack, "History and Law in Sixteenth-Century Peru," in *Cultures of Scholarship,* ed. S. C. Humphreys (Ann Arbor: University of Michigan Press, 1997), 285–91. She suggests that "when Spaniards in Peru listened to 'old men' and 'wise men' reciting Inca traditions, the experience was not altogether alien." Similarly, Las Casas referred to the "romances y cantares" in which the Incas preserved the memories of the deeds of their kings (*Apologética historia,* chap. 250, ed. O'Gorman, 2:573; *Obras completas,* 8:1520).

37. Oviedo, *Historia general,* bk. 6, chap. 49, BAE vol. 117, 216, cf. 211.

38. Ibid., 218.

39. Ibid., chap. 45, BAE vol. 117, 205.

40. Ibid., chap. 2, BAE vol. 117, 146. This paragraph was not in the first or second editions, though the comparison of Antillean ballgames with games in Lombardy and Naples was there from the start (BAE ed. 145).

41. Gerbi, *Nature in the New World,* 258.

42. Ibid., 259.

43. Oviedo, *Historia general,* bk. 38, proem, BAE vol. 120, 330 "una cosa muy nueva," 334 ("todo el mundo podemos decir que es una mesma tierra e costa"). Cf. Gerbi, *Nature in the New World,* 262.

44. Gerbi, *Nature in the New World*, 263–64.

45. Ibid., 267.

46. Oviedo, *Historia general*, bk. 27, chap. 5, BAE vol. 119, 149; cf. Gerbi, *Nature in the New World*, 267.

47. Ibid., bk. 13, proem, BAE vol. 118, 56.

48. Ibid., bk. 2, chap. 9, BAE vol. 117, 39.

49. Elliott, *Old World and New*, 40.

50. Pagden, *European Encounters*, 60, 68. Cf. Kathleen A. Myers, "Imitation, Authority, and Revision in Fernández de Oviedo's *Historia general y natural de las Indias*," *Romance Languages Annual* 3 (1992): 423–30, esp. 426.

51. Oviedo, *Historia general*, bk. 2, chap. 1, BAE vol. 117, 13.

52. Ibid., bk. 13, proem, BAE vol. 118, 56.

53. Ibid., bk. 6, chap. 9, BAE vol. 117, 168.

54. Ibid., bk. 31, proem, BAE vol. 119, 363.

55. See Merrim on Oviedo's self-presentation in the 1526 *Sumario* ("Apprehension of the New," 190–91): "Exalting himself through the exaltation of his material, Oviedo makes knowledge his commodity, his stepping stone to power and *fama*."

56. Myers, "Imitation, Authority, and Revision," 526.

57. Elliott, *Old World and New*, 48.

58. See González Rodríguez, "El antiromanismo de Oviedo."

59. For Román's familiarity with Las Casas's book, see Rolena Adorno, "Censorship and Its Evasion: Jerónimo Román and Bartolomé de las Casas," *Hispania* 75 (1992): 812–27, esp. 818–20; and MacCormack, *Religion in the Andes*, 245–46. For Mendieta and Torquemada, see O'Gorman's introduction to his edition of the *Apologética historia*, 1:xxxv–vi. For a brief comparison of the views of Las Casas and Torquemada, see Keen, *The Aztec Image*, 182–84.

60. Las Casas, *Apologética historia sumaria*, "argumento de toda ella," *Obras completas*, 6:286.

61. Elliott, *Old World and New*, 48.

62. Las Casas, *Apologética historia*, chap. 48, ed. O'Gorman, 1:257; *Obras completas*, 7:536.

63. Las Casas, *Apologia*, chap. 2, Poole trans., 33. Cf. *Apologética historia*, chap. 265, *Obras completas*, 8:1582.

64. Sepúlveda's main attack on Indian religious practices in the *Democrates secundus* is on pp. 39–61 of the Losada edition. See also his *Apologia* (Rome, 1550), photographically reprinted in Sepúlveda and Las Casas, *Apologia*, ed. Losada, p. Aiiii: "Isti barbari implicati erant gravissimis peccatis contra legem naturae," particularly the sins of idolatry and human sacrifice, the same sins for which God commanded the extermination of the Canaanites. In his 1571 treatise *De regno et regis officio*, Sepúlveda offered Indian religious abominations as "proofs of their savage life, comparable to that of beasts" (*Tratados políticos*, 35). For illuminating remarks on Las Casas's comparison of classical and Amerindian religious beliefs and practices, see MacCormack, *Religion in the Andes*, 235–40.

65. For Las Casas's special interest in matters of ritual, see Sabine MacCor-

mack, "Limits of Understanding: Perceptions of Greco-Roman and Amerindian Paganism in Early Modern Europe," in Kupperman, *America in European Consciousness*, 124–25 n. 35.

66. Las Casas, *Apologética historia*, chap. 86, *Obras completas*, 7:706.

67. Ibid., chap. 105, *Obras completas*, 7:801.

68. Ibid., *Obras completas*, 7:803 (Pertunda and Cloacina); chap. 117, *Obras completas*, 7:855 ("insensibilitad de ignorancia").

69. Ibid., chap. 114. *Obras completas*, 7:842, 844.

70. Ibid., chap. 118, *Obras completas*, 7:858.

71. Ibid., chap. 120, *Obras completas*, 7:869.

72. Ibid., chap. 123, *Obras completas*, 7:882–83. He also alludes to Portuguese claims of evidence of the apostle Thomas's visit to Brazil.

73. Ibid., chap. 127, *Obras completas*, 7:898.

74. Ibid., *Obras completas*, 7:899.

75. Ibid., chap. 135, *Obras completas*, 7:935–36.

76. Ibid., chap. 180, *Obras completas*, 8:1205.

77. Ibid., chap. 135, *Obras completas*, 7:937–38.

78. Ibid., chap. 143, *Obras completas*, 7:971.

79. Ibid., chap. 145, *Obras completas*, 7:979.

80. Ibid., chap. 148, *Obras completas*, 7:989.

81. Ibid., chap. 151, *Obras completas*, 7:1006–7.

82. Ibid., chap. 153, *Obras completas*, 7:1017.

83. Ibid., chap. 158, *Obras completas*, 7:1038.

84. Ibid., chap. 160, *Obras completas*, 7:1049.

85. Ibid., chap. 161, *Obras completas*, 8:1124.

86. Eusebius's source was the Neoplatonist Porphyry's vegetarian treatise *De abstinentia*. But the charge of supposed libations to Jupiter Latiaris of gladiators' blood shed in the Feriae Latinae had long been a staple of early Christian antipagan propaganda: Justin, 2 *Apol.* 11.12.5; Tert. *Apol.* 9.5; Min. Fel. *Oct.* 30.4.

87. Las Casas, *Apologética historia*, chap. 162, *Obras completas*, 8:1129.

88. Ibid., chap. 164, *Obras completas*, 8:1144.

89. Ibid., chap. 173, *Obras completas*, 8:1175 (specifically on the Indians of Cholula). Cf. chap. 169, *Obras completas*, 8:1162 (New Spain generally); chap. 172, *Obras completas*, 8:1171 (Tlaxcala); chap. 174, *Obras completas*, 8:1176 (genital mutilation in New Spain displaying "mil ventajas" to Christian penitence).

90. Ibid., chap. 183, *Obras completas*, 8:1215–17.

91. Ibid., chap. 184, *Obras completas*, 8:1223.

92. Ibid., chap. 185, *Obras completas*, 8:1225.

93. The programmatic list in ibid., chap. 188 (*Obras completas*, 8:1240) has a ninth category, sacred perpetual fires, but he never in fact discussed this, and at the beginning of chap. 192 (*Obras completas*, 8:1257) he refers to "aquellas ocho cosas."

94. Ibid., chap. 174, *Obras completas*, 8:1176.

95. Ibid., chap. 192, *Obras completas*, 8:1259.

96. Ibid., chap. 193, *Obras completas,* 8:1262.

97. Ibid., chap. 159, *Obras completas,* 7:1044.

98. José de Acosta, *Historia natural y moral de las Indias,* bk. 5, "Prologo a los libros siguientes," ed. Francisco Mateos, BAE vol. 73 (Madrid: Atlas, 1954), 139.

99. Fermín del Pino Díaz, "Culturas clásicas y americanas en Acosta," in *América y la España del siglo XVI,* ed. Francisco de Solano and Fermín del Pino (Madrid: Consejo Superior de Investigaciones Científicas, 1982), 357–58.

100. Las Casas, *Apologética historia,* chap. 194, *Obras completas,* 8:1266.

101. Pagden, *Fall of Natural Man,* title of chap. 6.

102. Wagner and Parish, *Bartolomé de las Casas,* 203.

103. In addition to the present account, see a paper by Geoffrey Eatough, "In Defense of the Amerindian: Bartolomé de las Casas's Classical Strategies," in *The Reception of Classical Texts and Images,* ed. Lorna Hardwick and Stanley Ireland, pt. 2 (Milton Keynes: Open University, 1996), 153–73.

104. MacCormack, *Religion in the Andes,* 207. See also Rech, "Las Casas und die Kirchenväter."

105. See Arnaldo Momigliano, "Herodotus in the History of Historiography," in *Studies in Historiography* (New York: Harper and Row, 1966), 139.

106. Ibid., 137.

107. See esp. Las Casas, *Apologética historia,* chap. 159, *Obras completas,* 7:1044–47; cf. also chap. 191, *Obras completas,* 8:1255, and chap. 192, *Obras completas,* 8:1258. See also Bruno Rech, "Bartolomé de las Casas und die Antike," in Reinhard, *Humanismus und Neue Welt,* 191–93. Rech's assumption that the *Dea Syria* is pseudo-Lucianic does not agree with the current consensus: see C. P. Jones, *Culture and Society in Lucian* (Cambridge: Harvard University Press, 1986), 41.

108. See the essay on translations of Pausanias by George B. Parks in Paul O. Kristeller and F. Edward Cranz, eds., *Catalogus Translationum et Commentariorum: Mediaeval and Renaissance Latin Translations and Commentaries: Annotated Lists and Guides,* vol. 2 (Washington, D.C.: Catholic University of America Press, 1971), 215–20.

109. Paus. 7.18–21; Las Casas, *Apologética historia,* chap. 155, *Obras completas,* 7:1025–27.

110. See Jean Seznec's account of Giraldi's work in *The Survival of the Pagan Gods* (Princeton: Princeton University Press, 1953), 230–47.

111. William McCuaig, *Carlo Sigonio: The Changing World of the Late Renaissance* (Princeton: Princeton University Press, 1989), 58 n. 170. Las Casas cites Lazius in chap. 164 (*Obras completas,* 8:1139) and chap. 165 (*Obras completas,* 8:1146).

112. In their note to the former passage, the editors of the *Obras completas* confess: "No hemos podido identificar a este autor" (8:1594). Jesús-Angel Barreda concludes his introductory essay on "Documentación bibliográfica de la *Apologética*" with a lament over his inability to identify this author, though he did successfully recognize "Uvolegango" as *Wolfgang* (6:220). The credit for the correct identification of this author belongs to Brian Ogilvie, then a graduate stu-

dent at the University of Chicago, who replied to a query I posted to the Classics List (Linda Wright, owner) in December 1996.

113. Given the standard neglect of the classical material in the *Apologetic History*, it is perhaps not surprising that Las Casas's interest in "pagan survivals" has seldom attracted notice. Two scholars who have mentioned this in passing are Teresa Silva Tena, "El sacrificio humano en la *Apologética historia*," *Historia mexicana* 16, no. 63 (1967): 352–53; and Eatough, "Defense of the Amerindian," 166–67. It is striking that Michael Ryan, in an article treating Las Casas in considerable detail, acutely drew attention to the growing interest in European pagan survivals in the sixteenth and seventeenth centuries ("Assimilating New Worlds," 526) but failed to note that Las Casas himself participated in— even helped pioneer—this trend.

114. Las Casas, *Apologética historia*, chap. 116, *Obras completas*, 7:849.

115. Ibid., chap. 143, *Obras completas*, 7:971.

116. Ibid., chap. 155, *Obras completas*, 7:1027.

117. Ibid., chap. 164, *Obras completas*, 8:1142.

118. Ibid., 8:1144; cf. chap. 150, *Obras completas*, 7:1001.

119. Ibid., chap. 151, *Obras completas*, 7:1004. He cites as his source for this "la leyenda o historia de la misma fiesta de la cátedra."

120. Ibid., chap. 154, *Obras completas*, 7:1021. Cardinal Cesare Baronio (*Martyrologium Romanum* [1586], 87) claimed that Pope Gelasius I (492–96) established Candlemas at Rome in order to neutralize an attempt to revive Lupercalia.

121. A famous example of the "accommodationist" policy would be Pope Gregory the Great's letter to Abbot Mellitus on his departure for England, reproduced in Bede's *Ecclesiastical History*, bk. 1, chap. 30. An extensive study of the flexible approach to pagan customs in the early Middle Ages is Valerie I. J. Flint, *The Rise of Magic in Early Medieval Europe* (Princeton: Princeton University Press, 1991).

122. Las Casas, *Apologética historia*, chap. 148, *Obras completas*, 7:991.

123. Las Casas, *Apologética historia*, chap. 160, ed. O'Gorman, *Obras completas*, 7:1048.

124. Las Casas, *Apologética historia*, chap. 147, *Obras completas*, 7:984.

125. Ibid., 7:988.

126. So the entry on *maya* in the eighteenth-century *Diccionario de autoridades*, 3:517. The late-sixteenth-century dictionary of Covarrubias mentions a girl-boy couple, the *maya* and *mayo*, who chastely represent a bridal pair in a mock marriage bed (780).

127. Las Casas, *Apologética historia*, chap. 157, *Obras completas*, 7:1036. In chap. 74 (*Obras completas*, 7:649), Las Casas more benignly cited European children's dolls as proof of the universal human susceptibility to idolatry. See MacCormack, *Religion in the Andes*, 237.

128. Cited by Edward Snow, "'Meaning' in *Children's Games:* On the Limitations of the Iconographic Approach to Bruegel," *Representations* 2 (1983): 58 n. 39.

129. Las Casas, *Apologética historia*, chap. 164, *Obras completas*, 8:1139.

130. *Diccionario de autoridades*, s.v. *obispillo*.

131. Las Casas, *Apologética historia*, chap. 164, *Obras completas*, 8:1140–41. For this little-noted early visit of Las Casas to Rome, see O'Gorman, appendix 1 to his edition of the *Apologética historia*, 1:lxxxiii–lxxxiv. He suggests that this may have been the occasion on which Las Casas received full ordination.

132. Las Casas, *Apologética historia*, end of chap. 151, introducing the next chapter; *Obras completas*, 7:1007.

133. Though he also cited "Volaterano" (i.e., Rafaelle Maffei) and Nauclerus, Las Casas's account of the Pikardi was entirely drawn from Aeneas Sylvius Piccolomini, though he misunderstood his reference to a "certain Picard" [Piccardus quidam] to mean "a heretic named Pichardo." See *Historia Boiemica* (Basel: Petrus Perna, 1575), chap. 41, "De Adamitis haereticis," 37–38.

134. Las Casas, *Apologética historia*, chap. 152, *Obras completas*, 7:1013. Boemus, too, adduced Livy's account: "Est execrandus hic damnatae gentis ritus non multum diversus a bacchanalibus illis," etc., *Repertorium librorum trium . . . de omnibus gentium ritibus* (Augsburg: Grimm, 1520), lii.

135. See, for example, Minucius Felix, *Octavius* 9.6–7. See Norman Cohn, *Europe's Inner Demons* (New York: Basic Books, 1975), 1–74, for the history of Christian application of Roman anti-Christian slanders to their own heretics.

136. The fullest treatment I have found of the history of the identification of "pagan survivals" in early modern Europe is H. Pinard de la Boullaye, *L'étude comparée des religions* (Paris: Gabriel Beauchesne, 1922), vol. 1, chap. 4. Though itself a polemical account of a polemical genre, it is useful as a catalog of texts. Briefer accounts are Margaret T. Hodgen, *Early Anthropology in the Sixteenth and Seventeenth Centuries* (Philadelphia: University of Pennsylvania Press, 1964), 325–30 (to be used with caution); and Jonathan Z. Smith, *Drudgery Divine: On the Comparison of Early Christianities and the Religions of Late Antiquity* (Chicago: University of Chicago Press, 1990), 20–26. See also Peter Burke, *Popular Culture in Early Modern Europe* (New York: Harper and Row, 1978), 209–10. Burke alludes to Erasmus's labeling as "veteris paganismi vestigia" Sienese floats of rams, tortoises, and contrade totems that participated in the bullfights in the Campo (*Supputatio errorum in censuris Beddae*, in *Opera* [Leiden, 1706], col. 516). See also Ryan, "Assimilating New Worlds," 526: "Protestant critiques of Catholic 'paganism,' Catholic rebuttals, and a new sensitivity to the survival in rural Christianity of pagan beliefs and customs made analyses of pagan religion anything but neutral undertakings." As we have seen with Las Casas and will see with his contemporaries, it was by no means exclusively—or even primarily— rural Christianity that was discovered to be harboring pagan "ghosts."

137. Calvin, *Institutes of the Christian Religion*, bk. 4, chap. 10, n. 12, trans. Ford Lewis Battles, ed. John T. McNeill, Library of Christian Classics, vol. 21 (Philadelphia: Westminster, 1960), 1190.

138. Pierre Viret, cited by Hodgen (*Early Anthropology*, 328). I have adapted her quotation of a 1579 English translation of Viret's 1544 *Christian Disputations*.

139. John Milton, "Animadversions" (July 1641) in *Collected Prose Works*, vol. 1, Don M. Wolfe ed. (New Haven: Yale University Press, 1953), 689; cf. "On Reformation" (May 1641) in the same vol., p. 556; and "On Christian Doctrine"

(ca. 1658–60), bk. 2, chap. 4, in *Collected Prose Works,* vol. 6, ed. Maurice Kelley (New Haven: Yale University Press, 1973), 667.

140. For Conyers Middleton, see Hodgen, *Early Anthropology,* 328–29; and Smith, *Drudgery Divine,* 20–25.

141. For a vivid example, see the many color plates added to a recent edition of Ellen G. White's founding text of the Seventh Day Adventist movement: *The New, Illustrated Great Controversy* (DeLand, Fla.: Laymen for Religious Liberty, 1990).

142. For discussions of the writings and significance of Flavio Biondo, see Eric Cochrane, *Historians and Historiography in the Italian Renaissance* (Chicago: University of Chicago Press, 1981), esp. 34–40; Angelo Mazzocco, "Rome and the Humanists: The Case of Biondo Flavio," in *Rome in the Renaissance: The City and the Myth,* ed. P. A. Ramsey (Binghamton: Center for Medieval and Early Renaissance Studies, 1982), 185–95; Philip Jacks, *The Antiquarian and the Myth of Antiquity* (Cambridge: Cambridge University Press, 1993), 113–24.

143. Flavio Biondo, *De Roma triumphante libri decem* (Venice: Philippus Pincius Mantuanus, 1511). The quoted characterization of Biondo's *Roma triumphans* is that of McCuaig, *Carlo Sigonio,* 125.

144. Las Casas's references to Biondo's *Roma triumphans* occur in chap. 119 (*Obras completas,* 7:865), regarding purification by water near the Porta Capena; chap. 143 (*Obras completas,* 7:971), regarding the Roman practice of confessing sins before handling sacred things; chap. 165 (*Obras completas,* 8:1148), on secret rites conducted by soothsayers on the Capitol.

145. Biondo, *De Roma triumphante,* 26. Perhaps Las Casas was tacitly drawing upon Biondo when he cited the same parallel in *Apolgética historia,* chap. 164, as noted above.

146. Biondo, *De Roma triumphante,* 19.

147. Ibid., 22.

148. Ibid., 22.

149. Ibid., 133–34.

150. For Frederick III's progress through Italy, see Friedrich Heer, *The Holy Roman Empire,* trans. Janet Sondheimer (New York: Praeger, 1968), 125–26.

151. For a list of some further "Roman characteristics [that] persisted in numerous aspects of postclassical life," see Mazzocco, "Rome and the Humanists," 191.

152. The edition I will be citing is the 1563 Basel printing of Thomas Guarinus. It reflects the text before the cuts mandated by the Holy Office. A useful, though not always completely accurate, English version is now available: *Beginnings and Discoveries: Polydore Vergil's "De Inventoribus Rerum,"* trans. Beno Weiss and Louis C. Pérez (Nieuwkoop: De Graaf, 1997). Las Casas referred to Polydore Vergil's text four times, but only once to the supplemental books. In chap. 85 of the *Apologética historia* (*Obras completas,* 7:702), he referred to the discussion of priestly tonsure in book 4, chap. 8, of *De inventoribus rerum.*

153. Polydore Vergil, *De inventoribus rerum,* bk. 6, chap. 9, p. 443.

154. Ibid., bk. 5, chap. 1, p. 327.

155. Ibid., chap. 2, pp. 331–32.

156. Jonathan Z. Smith misleadingly asserts that the *De inventoribus rerum* concentrates on "Christian 'borrowing,' usually by the laity who were assumed to be prone to superstition" (*Drudgery Divine*, 21).

157. Polydore Vergil, *De inventoribus rerum*, preface to bk. 4, p. 242.

158. Ibid., bk. 4, chap. 13, p. 311.

159. Las Casas, *Apologética historia*, chap. 116, *Obras completas*, 7:849; *De exemptione sive damnatione*, in Helen Rand Parish and Harold E. Weidman, eds., *Las Casas en México: Historia y obra desconocidas* (Mexico City: Fondo de Cultura Económica, 1992), 154.

160. Polydore Vergil, *De inventoribus rerum*, bk. 5, chap. 11, p. 389.

161. Ibid., bk. 7, chap. 6, p. 508 (Luperci and flagellants): bk. 6, chap. 3, p. 419 *(sodalitates)*. The former passage, but not the latter, was later censored.

162. Polydore Vergil, *De inentoribus rerum*, bk. 6, chap. 3, p. 419.

163. For Langley's Protestant doctoring of Polydore Vergil's text, see Denys Hay, *Polydore Vergil* (Oxford: Oxford University Press, 1952), 66–69.

164. For Du Choul's interest in pagan parallels or survivals, see Smith, *Drudgery Divine*, 21 n. 35; and Hodgen, *Early Anthropology*, 327. For Du Choul's importance as an antiquarian and pioneer numismatist, see Margaret M. McGowan, *The Vision of Rome in Late Renaissance France* (New Haven: Yale University Press, 2000), 71–81; John Cunnally, *Images of the Illustrious* (Princeton: Princeton University Press, 1999), esp. 19, 141, 187–89; Francis Haskell, *History and Its Images* (New Haven: Yale University Press, 1993), 16; and Mathieu Varille, "Antiquaires lyonnais de la renaissance," *Revue du Lyonnais*, 1923, 453–60. Unfortunately, the best study known to me of Du Choul's importance for the history of antiquarianism remains unpublished: Brian W. Ogilvie, "On Numismatics and Antiquarian Method in the Sixteenth Century," a paper delivered to the Department of History, University of Chicago, March 28, 1993.

165. Margaret Hodgen appeared to imply that she regarded Du Choul as a Calvinist, for her brief remarks on his book follow a sentence that runs, "The literature supporting the Protestant assault [on Catholic "paganism"] was voluminous and circumstantial" (*Early Anthropology*, 327). Unfortunately, as Mathieu Varille pointed out, the life of Du Choul is "bien peu connue" ("Antiquaires lyonnais," 454).

166. Du Choul, *Discours de la religion des anciens Romains* (Lyon: Guillaume Rouillé, 1556), 220; cf. Las Casas, *Apologética historia*, chap. 116, *Obras completas*, 7:849.

167. Natalie Zemon Davis, "The Sacred and the Body Social in Sixteenth-Century Lyon," *Past and Present* 90 (1981): 40–70.

168. Du Choul, *Discours*, 309.

169. Ibid., 263. This remarkable passage proceeds to draw a parallel between pagan religious belief and central doctrines of Christianity. Why, he asks, were pagans skeptical of Christ's raising of Lazarus from the dead when Asclepius did the same thing, and why were they so slow to accept the Virgin Birth when their own goddess Vesta was "a virgin and mother of the gods."

170. Ibid., 305.

171. Ibid., 312.

172. Hodgen, *Early Anthropology*, 327. More oddly, she seems to enlist Polydore Vergil in the Protestant camp as well.

173. See Paula Findlen, "Possessing the Past: The Material World of the Italian Renaissance," *American Historical Review* 103 (1998): 83–114, esp. for the passion of Renaissance antiquarians for owning bits of antiquity. For them, the past was "an embodied presence" (95). She cites Lisa Jardine's claim that "the Renaissance . . . was a celebration of the urge to own" (*Worldly Goods: A New History of the Renaissance* [New York: Doubleday, 1996], 33–34).

174. The quoted passages are at Du Choul, *Discours*, 264, 305.

175. Sahagún, *Historia general de las cosas de Nueva España*, ed. Ángel María Garibay K., 7th ed. (Mexico City: Porrúa, 1989), 17. See Charles E. Dibble, "Sahagún's Appendices," in *The Work of Bernardino de Sahagún, Pioneer Ethnographer of Sixteenth-Century Aztec Mexico*, ed. J. Jorge Klor de Alva, H. B. Nicholson, and Eloise Quiñones Keber (Austin, Tex.: Institute for Mesoamerican Studies, 1988), 107–18. For a vivid account of Franciscans uncovering supposed pagan survivals and revivals in Yucatán in 1562, see Inga Clendinnen, *Ambivalent Conquests: Maya and Spaniard in Yucatán, 1517–1570* (Cambridge: Cambridge University Press, 1987).

176. Sahagún, *Arte adivinatoria*, cited in Walden Browne, "When Worlds Collide: Crisis in Sahagun's *Historia universal de las cosas de la Nueva España*," *Colonial Latin American Historical Review* 5, no. 2 (1996): 105.

177. Diego Durán, *Ritos y fiestas de los antiguos mexicanos* (Mexico City: Cosmos, 1980), chap. 21, p. 212.

178. On the Andean *Extirpación*, see Kenneth Mills, *Idolatry and Its Enemies: Colonial Andean Religion and Extirpation, 1640–1750* (Princeton: Princeton University Press, 1997); Nicholas Griffiths, *The Cross and the Serpent: Religious Repression and Resurgence in Colonial Peru* (Norman: University of Oklahoma Press, 1996).

179. Motolonía, *Historia de los Indios de la Nueva España*, ed. Georges Baudot (Madrid: Castalia, 1985), 254.

180. Ibid., 255.

181. Las Casas, *Apologética historia*, chap. 166, *Obras completas*, 8:1153; chap. 168, *Obras completas*, 8:1159.

182. Ibid., chap. 175, *Obras completas*, 8:1182. Elsewhere in this chapter and the following one he uses the verb *comulgar* to refer to this ritual, and he likens the officiating priests to a "pope" and "deacons."

183. See, for example, the "Roman oration" of the second century A.D. orator Aelius Aristides, oration 26, sec. 101: "you have spanned the rivers with all kinds of bridges and hewn highways through the mountains and filled the barren stretches with posting stations; you have accustomed all areas to a settled and orderly way of life." Trans. James H. Oliver, "The Ruling Power," *Transactions of the American Philosophical Society*, n.s. 43, pt. 4 (1953): 906.

184. John S. Richardson, *The Romans in Spain* (Oxford: Blackwell, 1996), 161.

185. Las Casas, *Apologética historia*, chap. 262, *Obras completas*, 8:1569–70. Compare the passage near the end of Montaigne's "Des coches": "Quant à la

pompe et magnificence. . . , ny Graece, ny Romme, ny Aegypte ne peut, soit en utilité, ou noblesse, comparer aucun de ses ouvrages au chemin qui se voit au Peru, dressé par les Roys du pays, depuis la ville de Quito jusques à celle de Cusco" (*Essais*, bk. 3, chap. 6, pp. 1024–25).

186. See Pagden, *European Encounters*, chap. 2, "The Autoptic Imagination."

187. Note an early-eighteenth-century gloss on the phrase "es un asco": "Modo de hablar con que se dá à entender que alguna cosa es súcia y provocativa à náusea: y tambien se usa de esta phrase quando está mal hecha, y tan toscamente executada, que cáusa fastidio y disgusto el verla. Lat. *Res foeda est; Nauseam movet*" (*Diccionario de autoridades*, 1:430).

188. Miguel Maticorena Estrada, "Cieza de León en Sevilla y su muerte en 1554," *Anuario de Estudios Americanos* 12 (1955): 669.

189. On the basis of the absence of any reference to Cieza's manuscripts in an inventory of Las Casas's papers made at the end of the sixteenth century, Maticorena argues that not only did Las Casas not receive them in accord with the will, but he was in fact completely unfamiliar with them (ibid., 632, 636). This does not follow, for Cieza's testamentary wish makes the most sense if we assume that he was already assured of Las Casas's interest in these manuscripts. On the other hand, Gustavo Gutiérrez is clearly overbold in assuming that Cieza's will implied "that the second and third parts of the *Crónica del Perú* had been sent to the bishop of Chiapa" (*Las Casas*, 611 n. 73). For another likely Lascasian echo of this unpublished work, note that Las Casas's reference to the "romances y cantares" of the Incas (*Apologética historia*, chap. 250) echoes Cieza's labeling of these Inca songs as "romances y villancicos" and "cantares" in chaps. 11 and 12 of the *Señorío*.

190. Pedro de Cieza de León, *Del señorío de los Incas*, chap. 63, p. 291. Already in the first, published version of his chronicle Cieza had claimed that this mountain road had "topped" a famous classical exemplum: that which "Hannibal made when he came down into Italy" (*Crónica del Perú*, chap. 37 [Bogotá: Revista Ximénez de Quesada, 1971], 151). In addition, in chapter 92, discussing the way the Incas gathered information about their provinces from the four roads radiating from Cuzco, Cieza compared the provinces (and implicitly the roads) of the Romans ("los antiguos") in Spain (330). For classical allusions and echoes in Cieza's writings, see MacCormack, "History and Law," 281–85, "The Incas and Rome," in *Garcilaso Inca de la Vega: An American Humanist*, ed. José Anadón (Notre Dame: University of Notre Dame Press, 1998), 9–10, and "History, Historical Record, and Ceremonial Action: Incas and Spaniards in Cuzco," *Cambridge Studies in Society and History* 43 (2001), esp. 332–34.

191. The Spanish translation of book 4 (fols. xx–xxi of the 1539 edition) is reprinted in the appendix to González Rodríguez, *La idéa de Roma*, 157–60; see esp. 158. For the Latin original, see Schottus, *Hispaniae illustratae*, 318. It is interesting that Cieza de León compared the carrying capacity of the rope bridge over the river Bilcas (Villca) at Uramarca with that of the Roman bridges at Alcántara and Córdoba. He later declared that the Roman bridge at Córdoba offered one of the few Iberian rivals to the stonework of the Coricancha, the Inca temple of the sun in Cuzco (*Del señorío de los Incas*, chap. 27, 151).

192. Las Casas, *Apologética historia,* chap. 251, *Obras completas,* 8:1525.

193. Garcilaso's views on the Roman model, which reflect his status as child of both victors and vanquished, merit further study. In the "Prologo a los indios mestizos y criollos" of the second part of the *Comentarios Reales,* the *Historia general del Perú,* Garcilaso likened the European assumption that the Indians are barbarians to the Greeks' and Romans' classification of the culturally backward Spaniards as barbarians, a slander belied by the brilliant role that the Spaniards proceeded to play in the Roman Empire. This assimilation of contemporary Indians to ancient Iberians recalls the strategy of Cano and Las Casas discussed previously. But earlier in this prologue Garcilaso was able to balance claims that the Incas equaled or surpassed the ancients with praise of their Spanish conquerors as "césares en felicidad y fortaleza" (BAE vol. 134, 11–12). Similarly, in book 1, chapter 2, he declares the superiority of the three conquistadors who planned the conquest of Peru to the Second Triumvirate. While this seems a simple instance of the motif of the conquistadors "defeating the Romans" discussed in the first chapter, Garcilaso injects into this motif the strong condemnation of Roman imperialism that we have seen the Dominicans developing in the mid–sixteenth century: "Our triumvirate merits as much fame, honor, and glory as the Romans deserve shame, hatred, and curses, for ours shall never be sufficiently praised . . . , nor the Romans sufficiently cursed for their wickedness and tyranny" (trans. Harold V. Livermore, *Royal Commentaries of the Incas and General History of Peru* [Austin: University of Texas Press, 1966], 2:636 = BAE vol. 134, 19). For classical echoes in Garcilaso, both explicit and implicit, see Claire Pailler and Jean-Marie Pailler, "Une Amérique vraiment latine: Pour une lecture 'Dumézilienne' de l'Inca Garcilaso de la Vega," *Annales ESC,* January–February 1992, 207–35; MacCormack, "The Incas and Rome"; and MacCormack, "Cuzco, Another Rome?" in *Empires: Perspectives from Archaeology and History,* ed. Susan E. Alcock, Terence N. C'Altroy, Kathleen D. Morrison, and Carla M. Sinopoli (Cambridge: Cambridge University Press, 2001), 419–35. A perceptive study that emphasizes Garcilaso's ambivalence about his dual heritage is David A. Brading, "The Incas and the Renaissance: *The Royal Commentaries* of Inca Garcilaso de la Vega," *Journal of Latin American Studies* 18 (1986): 1–23.

194. Inca Garcilaso de la Vega, *Comentarios reales de los Incas,* bk. 7, chap. 8, in *Obras completas,* ed. P. Carmelo Sáenz de Santa María, vol. 2, BAE vol. 133 (Madrid: Atlas, 1963), 255. Cf. Eng. trans., *Royal Commentaries,* 1:417. Cf. procm, 3, where Garcilaso identified himself as "natural del Cozco, que fue otra Roma en aquel Imperio."

195. Cieza de León, *Del señorío de los Incas,* chap. 11, p. 75; cf. Las Casas's reference to Inca "romances y cantares," *Apologética historia,* chap. 250, *Obras completas,* 8:1520.

196. Maravall, *Antiguos y modernos,* 274 n. 138. For the fifteenth-century examples, see Frankl, *El "Antijovio,"* 209–26. See also González Rodríguez, *La idea de Roma,* 22 n. 73, 28, 44, who, despite the subject of his book, fails to note New World applications of the topos.

197. The formulation is Maravall's ("la idea de que los españoles han preferido realizar grandes hazañas a escribirlas")—see previous note.

198. Alonso de Zorita, *Life and Labor in Ancient Mexico* (= *Breve y sumaria relación de los señores de la Nueva España*), trans. Benjamin Keen (New Brunswick, N.J.: Rutgers University Press, 1963), 168–74; Spanish text in J. García Icazbalceta, ed., *Nueva colección de documentos para la historia de México* (Mexico City: Francisco Díaz de León, 1891), 3:146–50.

199. Zorita, *Life and Labor*, 168; *Breve y sumaria relación*, 147.

200. Zorita, *Life and Labor*, 171; *Breve y sumaria relación*, 148.

201. Zorita, *Life and Labor*, 173–74; *Breve y sumaria relación*, 150.

202. Cieza de León, *La crónica del Perú*, chap. 44 , 179. Though Cieza did not mention any classical comparisons here, Sabine MacCormack suggests that "the cultivated sixteenth-century reader would here remember stories about the heroic severity of Rome's founding fathers," most notably Lucius Junius Brutus ("The Incas and Rome," 10; cf. "History and Law," 282).

203. Alonso de Ercilla, *La Araucana*, ed. Isaías Lerner (Madrid: Cátedra, 1993), canto 1, first two octaves, 77–78.

204. For a recent discussion of Ercilla's pro-Araucanian, anti-Spanish bias, see Beatríz Pastor Bodmer, *The Armature of Conquest: Spanish Accounts of the Discovery of America, 1492–1589* (Stanford: Stanford University Press, 1992), 207–75.

205. David Quint, *Epic and Empire: Politics and Generic Form from Virgil to Milton* (Princeton: Princeton University Press, 1993), 157–85. The passage cited on the Araucanians and European feudal nobility is on p. 174. For the claim that "Lucan meets and overlaps with Ariosto in the *Araucana,* and together they put up a fight against Virgil," see p. 182.

206. José Durand has argued that much of Ercilla's criticism of Spanish behavior, especially that of Valdivia, can be attributed to the poet's status as *chapetón* (newcomer) in the Indies and the slights that he endured from the long-time *indianos* or *baquianos* ("El chapetón Ercilla y la honra Araucana," *Filología* 10 [1964]: 113–34). Surely his close connections with the royal court would have exacerbated this friction.

207. Andrés Bello, *Selected Writings,* trans. Frances M. López-Morillas (Oxford: Oxford University Press, 1997), 45.

208. Ercilla, *La Araucana*, prologue, 69–70.

209. Rolena Adorno, "The Warrior and the War Community: Constructions of the Civil Order in Mexican Conquest History," *Dispositio* 14 (1989): 225; "The Colonial Subject and the Cultural Construction of the Other," *Revista de Estudios Hispánicos* 17–18 (1990–91): 149–65, esp. 149–56.

210. Sepúlveda, *Democrates secundus*, ed. Losada, 35.

211. Ibid., 36.

212. Adorno, "Warrior and War Community," 231. Cf. Demetrios Ramos Pérez, introduction to a Spanish translation of Sepúlveda, *De rebus Hispanorum: Los hechos de los españoles en el Nuevo Mundo* (Valladolid: Seminario americanista de la Universidad de Valladolid, 1976), 70: "Las cualidades de los naturales para el combate es, en efeto, uno de los aspectos que con mayor reiteración se menciona en la obra de Sepúlveda. Hasta tal extremo, que parece complacerse el autor en acentuar el carácter numantino de la defensa de Tenochtitlan."

213. Sepúlveda, *De orbe novo*, bk. 7.26.2, ed. A. Ramírez de Verger (Stuttgart: Teubner, 1993), 307.

214. Ibid., bk. 7.39.1, p. 322.

215. Ibid., bk. 7.43.4, p. 325; bk. 7.45.1, p. 326.

216. Bernal Díaz, *Historia verdadera*, chap. 156, p. 368. It is interesting that Montaigne, too, emphasized the courage of Cuauhtémoc, especially under torture after his capture ("Des coches," 1022–23).

217. Bernal Díaz, *Historia verdadera*, chap. 156, p. 372.

218. Las Casas, *Apolgética historia*, chap. 33, *Obras completas*, 6:433.

219. Montaigne, "Des coches," 1019.

220. See e.g., Las Casas, *Historia de Indias*, bk. 3, chap. 10, "lobos hambrientes despedazadores . . . destas ovejas mansísimas," *Obras completas,* 5:1788. Quint rightly faults as "one-sided and misleading" Todorov's claim that Las Casas always viewed the Indians as docile and meek (*Epic and Empire,* 392 n. 66).

221. Ercilla, *La Araucana,* canto 3, stanzas 43–44, pp. 149–50.

222. Pastor Bodmer, *The Armature of Conquest,* 244.

223. Curtius, *Europäische Literatur,* 171–74; *European Literature,* 162–65.

224. Ercilla, *La Araucana,* canto 3, stanzas 1 and 3, pp. 135–36. Ercilla's denunciation of Valdivia's *codicia* occupies the first six stanzas of this canto—as well as the concluding stanzas of the preceding canto.

225. Adorno, "Warrior and War Community," 229.

226. Ercilla, *La Araucana,* canto 7, octave 48, p. 248.

227. Ibid., canto 29, octaves 1–2, p. 783.

228. Ibid., canto 21, esp. first four octaves, pp. 587–88. This canto is also in the poem's second part, published in 1578.

229. Pastor Bodmer, *Armature of Conquest,* 229, 225; Lía Schwartz Lerner, "Tradición literaria y heroínas indias en *La Araucana,*" *Revista Iberoamericana* 38 (1972): 615–25.

230. Ercilla, *La Araucana,* canto 32, octave 1, p. 839.

231. Ibid., octaves 31–42, pp. 848–52.

232. Oviedo, *Historia general,* bk. 6, chap. 41, BAE vol. 117, 199–201.

233. Ercilla, *La Araucana,* canto 32, octaves 43–91, canto 33, octaves 1–54, pp. 852–85.

234. María Rosa Lida (de Malkiel), "Dido y su defensa en la literatura española," pt. 2, *Revista de Filología Hispánica* 4 (1942): 318–82. She discusses Ercilla's version on pp. 373–80.

235. Apropos of "Lauca," Frank Pierce charitably suggested that Ercilla "transforms what may have been a personal experience in the field into a pastoral elegy" (*Alonso de Ercilla y Zúñiga* [Amsterdam: Rodopi, 1984], 54).

236. Gerónimo de Vivar, *Crónica y relación copiosa y verdadera de los Reinos de Chile (1558),* ed. Leopoldo Saez-Godoy (Berlin: Colloquium Verlag, 1979). (The chronicle had first appeared in an edition dated 1966, though it did not become available immediately.) For the importance of this chronicle for establishing the historicity of Ercilla's account, see José Durand, "Caupolicán, clave historial y épica de 'La Araucana,'" *Revue de littérature comparée* 52 (1978): 367–89. Apparently unaware of Vivar's account, Lía Schwartz Lerner insisted,

"Fresia es, pues, también una figura heroica inventada por Ercilla" ("Tradición literaria," 625).

237. Vivar, *Crónica y relación*, fol. 207.20–31, p. 248.

238. The quoted characterization of Vivar's chronicle ("el más valioso documento de la historia de América encontrado en los últimos años") is that of its most recent editor, Leopoldo Sáez-Godoy, introduction, v.

239. Vivar, *Crónica y relación*, chap. 104, p. 182.

240. Ibid., 184. For *envixados*, a South American usage, see the *Diccionario de auroridades*, s.v. *enbixar*: "Pintar y teñir con Mínio o bermellón el rostro. Es voz Indiana. etc."

241. Vivar, *Crónica y relación*, chap. 133, pp. 241, 242.

242. For echoes of Ercilla's epic in Cervantes's play, see King, "Cervantes' *Numancia*," esp. 207–16. The curate's praise of the poem in *Don Quixote* is in pt. 1, chap. 6.

243. Vivar, *Crónica y relación*, chap. 15, p. 34.

244. Ibid., chap. 14, p. 32. In his note on this passage Sáez-Godoy confesses, "No he encontrado todavía referencias sobre esta pareja"—which may go to show that the conquistador-chronicler was better read in the classics than his modern editor.

245. When he recorded the questions fresh troops from Peru asked veterans of the war against the rebels, he compared the questions newly arrived souls in Purgatory asked Vergil and Dante at *Purg.* 2.59–60. No Spanish translations of *Purgatorio* were in print in 1555. See Werner P. Friedrich, *Dante's Fame Abroad: 1350–1850* (Chapel Hill: University of North Carolina Press, 1950), 21–55.

246. *Descripción de los pueblos de la provincia de Ancerma (1540–1541)*, in *Colección de documentos ineditos relativos al descubrimiento, conquista y colonización de los possessiones españoles en América y Oceania*, ed. Joachim F. Pacheco and Francisco de Cárdenas (Madrid: Manuel B. de Quirós, 1865), 3:408.

247. Pedro Pizarro, *Relación del descubrimiento y conquista del Perú*, ed. Guillermo Lohmann Villena (Lima: Pontificia Universidad Católica del Peru, 1978), chap. 19, p. 132.

248. Gaspar Pérez de Villagrá, *Historia de la Nueva México*, trans. and ed. Miguel Encinias, Alfred Rodríguez, and Joseph P. Sánchez (Albuquerque: University of New Mexico Press, 1992), canto 34, p. 296.

249. Durand, "Caupolicán," 370.

250. Parry and Keith, *New Iberian World*, 4:371.

251. Ibid., 4:372.

252. Pagden used this phrase as the title of two of the chapters of *The Fall of Natural Man*, one on Las Casas (6), one on Acosta (7).

253. Garcilaso de la Vega, *Commentaries reales*, bk. 7, chap. 8, in *Obras Completas*, vol. 2, 255.

Conclusion

1. Bernal Díaz, *Historia verdadera*, chap. 198, p. 538.

2. Ibid., chap. 156, pp. 369–70; see above, chap. 1.

3. See Elliott, "Mental World," 27–41.

4. Garcilaso de la Vega, *Historia de la Florida*, bk. 2, pt. 1, chap. 27, p. 314; see above, chap. 6.

5. Alonso de Ercilla, *La Araucana*, canto 32; see above, chap. 6.

6. Vinko Paletin, *Tractatus de iure et iustitia belli*, MS in Lilly Library, Indiana University, 66v; see above, chap. 4.

7. Vera Cruz, *Defense of the Indians*; see above, chap. 4.

8. Bernal Díaz, *Historia verdadera*, chap. 201, p. 544; see above, chap. 2.

9. Francisco de Aguilar, *Relación breve*, 65; see above, chap. 1.

10. Gerónimo López, in Francisco del Paso y Toncoso, *Epistolario de Nueva España*, letter 236; see above, chap. 5.

11. Las Casas, *Apologetica historia*, "Argumento," ed. O'Gorman, 1:4; *Obras completas*, 6:286; see above, chap. 6.

12. Las Casas, *Carta a un personaje de la cortes*, October 15, 1535, in *Obras escogidas*, 5:65; Garcés, letter to Paul III, reproduced in Lobato Casado, "El obispo Garcés," esp. 775–77; see above, chap. 5.

13. Las Casas, *Apologia*, chap. 4; cf. *Aquí se contiene una disputa*, 5:328; see above, chap. 5.

14. Vivar, *Crónica y relación*, chap. 104, ed. Saez-Godoy, 182; chap. 133, 242; see above, chap. 6.

15. Cf. Peter Mason, *Deconstructing America: Representations of the Other* (London: Routledge, 1990), chap. 2, "Popular Culture and the Internal Other," esp. pp. 60–63: "The Europeanisation of Amerindia and the Indianisation of Europe." Though our arguments support each other, our supporting details do not overlap.

16. Vitoria, *Relectio de Indis*, ed. Nys, 335: "etiam apud nos videamus multos rusticorum parum differentes a brutis animantibus."

17. Zorita, *Life and Labor*, 172; *Breve y sumaria relación*, 149.

18. Diego Durán, *Ritos y fiestas de los Indios de la Nueva España* (Mexico City: Cosmos, 1980), prologue, 69; trans. from *Book of the Gods and Rites and The Ancient Calendar* by Fernando Horcasitas and Doris Heyden (Norman: University of Oklahoma Press, 1971), 52. Durán singled out the inhabitants of the area near Sayago and Las Batuecas as especially unsophisticated, and he offered some examples of folk belief that might well interest students of early modern Europe.

19. Castellanos, *Elegías de varones ilustres de Indias*, part 1, elegy 1, canto 6, stanza 28, BAE vol. 4, 9th ed. (Madrid: Atlas, 1944), 20.

20. Oviedo, *Historia general*, bk. 5, chap. 1, BAE vol. 117, 113–16.

21. Las Casas, *Apologética historia*, chap. 164, ed. O'Gorman, 2:159; *Obras completas*, 8:1140–41.

22. Ibid., chap. 157; O'Gorman, ed., 2:119; *Obras completas*, 7:1036; cf. chap. 74, O'Gorman, ed., 1:386; *Obras completas*, 7:649.

23. For accounts of the triumphal arch designed by Sigüenza y Góngora, see Keen, *The Aztec Image*, 191–92; Brading, *The First America*, 362–63; Elizabeth H. Boone, *Incarnations of the Aztec Supernatural: The Image of Huitzilopochtli in Mexico and Europe* (Philadelphia: American Philosophical Society, 1989), 58–59.

24. Boone, *Incarnations*, 59. Keen notes that in his writings Sigüenza y Góngora "never lost an opportunity to compare Indian achievements with those of the Greco-Roman world, to the advantage of the former" (*The Aztec Image*, 190).

25. Perry Miller, *Errand into the Wilderness* (Cambridge: Harvard University Pres, 1956), 15.

Bibliography

Abril Castelló, Vidal. "La bipolarización Sepúlveda-Las Casas y sus consecuencias: La revolución de la duodécima réplica." In *La ética en la conquista de
América*, edited by Demetrio Ramos et al., 229–88. Madrid: Consejo Superior
de Investigaciones Científicas, 1984.
———. "Los derechos de las naciones según Bartolomé de las Casas y la Escuela
de Salamanca." Preliminary study to Las Casas, *Apologética historia sumaria*,
in *Obras completas*, 6:15–181. Madrid: Alianza, 1992.
Adorno, Rolena, "Censorship and Its Evasion: Jerónimo Román and Bartolomé
de las Casas." *Hispania* 75 (1992): 812–27.
———. "The Colonial Subject and the Cultural Construction of the Other."
Revista de estudios hispánicos 17–18 (1990–91): 149–65.
———. "Los debates sobre la naturaleza del Indio en el siglo XVI: Textos y con-
textos." *Revista de estudios hispánicos* 19 (1992): 47–66.
———. "The Warrior and the War Community: Constructions of the Civil Order
in Mexican Conquest History." *Dispositio* 14, nos. 36–38 (1989): 225–46.
Alcalá, Manuel. *César y Cortés*. Mexico City: Editorial Jus, 1950.
———. "César y Cortés frente al enemigo." In *Actas del Primer Congreso Inter-
nacional sobre Hernán Cortés*, edited by Alberto Navarro González, 17–26.
Salamanca: Ediciones Universidad de Salamanca, 1986.
Alfonso X. *Primera crónica general de España*. Edited by R. Menéndez Pidal.
Madrid: Gredos, 1955.
Andrés Marcos, Teodoro. *Los imperialismos de Juan Ginés de Sepúlveda en su
Democrates Alter*. Madrid: Instituto de Estudios Políticos, 1947.
Anon. *Descripción de los pueblos de la provincia de Ancerma (1540–41)*. In
*Colección de documentos ineditos relativos al descubrimiento, conquista y
colonización de los posesiones españoles en América y Oceanía, sacados, en su
mayor parte, del Real Archivo de Indias*, edited by Joachim F. Pacheco and
Francisco de Cárdenas, 3:389–415. Madrid: Manuel B. de Quirós, 1865.
Arco y Garay, Ricardo del. *La idea de imperio en la política y la literatura
españolas*. Madrid: Espasa-Calpe, 1944.
Arcos, Miguel de. *Parecer mío sobre un tratado de la guerra que se puede hacer
a los indios*. In *Cuerpo de Documentos del siglo XVI sobre los derechos de
España en las Indias y las Filipinas*, edited by Agustín Millares Carlo and
Lewis Hanke, 3–9. 1943; repr. Mexico City: Fondo de Cultura Económica,
1977.
Ariosto, Lodovico. *Orlando Furioso*. Edited by Dino Provenzal. 4 vols. Milan:
Rizzoli, 1955.

Ballesteros Gaibrois, Manuel. *Gonzalo Fernández de Oviedo*. Madrid: Fundación Universitaria Española, 1981.

Barbón Rodríguez, José Antonio. "Bernal Díaz del Castillo, ¿'idiota y sin letras'?" In *Studia Hispánica in honorem R. Lapesa*, edited by Dámaso Alonso et al., 2:89–104. Madrid: Editorial Gredos, 1974.

Barnes, Jonathan. "The Just War." In *The Cambridge History of Later Medieval Philosophy*, edited by Norman Kretzmann, Anthony Kenny, and Jan Pinborg, 771–84. Cambridge: Cambridge University Press, 1982.

Barton, Simon. "The Roots of the National Question in Spain." In *The National Question in Europe in Historical Context*, edited by Mikuláš Teich and Roy Porter, 106–27. Cambridge: Cambridge University Press, 1993.

Bataillon, Marcel. *Érasme et l'Espagne*. 2d ed. Geneva: Droz, 1991.

———. "Vasco de Quiroga et Bartolomé de las Casas." In *Études sur Bartolomé de las Casas*, 225–38. Paris: Centre de Recherches de L'institut d'études Hispaniques, 1965.

Beaune, Colette. *The Birth of an Ideology: Myths and Symbols of Nation in Late-Medieval France*. Translated by Susan Ross Huston. Berkeley and Los Angeles: University of California Press, 1991.

Belda Plans, Juan. *La escuela de Salamanca*. Madrid: Biblioteca de Autores Cristianos, 2000.

Bell, Aubrey F. *Juan Ginés de Sepúlveda*. Oxford: Clarendon Press, 1925.

Beltrán de Heredia, P. Vicente. *Domingo de Soto: Estudio biográfico documentado*. Biblioteca de Teólogos Españoles, vol. 20. Salamanca, 1960.

Beuchot, Mauricio. *La querella de la conquista: Una polémica del siglo XVI*. Mexico City: Siglo Veintiuno, 1992.

Biermann, Benno. "Don Vasco de Quiroga und seine Schrift De Debellandis Indis." *Neue Zeitschrift für Missionswissenschaft* 22, no. 3 (1966): 189–200.

———. "Don Vasco de Quiroga y su tratado De Debellandis Indis (II)." *Historia Mexicana* 72, no. 18 (1969): 615–22.

Binotti, Lucia. "Cultural Identity and the Ideologies of Translation in Sixteenth-Century Europe: Italian Prologues to Spanish Chronicles of the New World." *History of European Ideas* 14, no. 6 (1992): 769–88.

Biondo, Flavio. *De Roma triumphante*. Venice: Philippus Pincius Mantuanus, 1511.

Boemus, Johann. *Repertorium librorum trium . . . de omnibus gentium ritibus*. Augsburg: Sigismund Grimm, 1520.

Bonilla y San Martín, Adolfo. *Luis Vives y la filosofía del renacimiento*. 1904; repr. Madrid: Publicaciones de la Real Academia de Ciencias Morales y Políticas, 1981.

Boone, Elizabeth H. *Incarnations of the Aztec Supernatural: The Image of Huitzilopochtli in Mexico and Europe*. Philadelphia: American Philosophical Society, 1989.

Bosbach, Franz. *Monarchia universalis. Ein politischer Leitbegriff der frühen Neuzeit*. Schriftenreihe der historischen Kommission bei der bayerischen Akademie der Wissenschaften, vol. 32. Göttingen: Vandenhoeck und Ruprecht, 1988.

Brading, David A. *The First America: The Spanish Monarchy, Creole Patriots, and the Liberal State, 1492–1867.* Cambridge: Cambridge University Press, 1991.

———. "The Incas and the Renaissance: *The Royal Commentaries* of Inca Garcilaso de la Vega." *Journal of Latin American Studies* 18 (1986): 1–23.

———. *Prophecy and Myth in Mexican History.* Cambridge: Center for Latin American Studies, Cambridge University, 1984.

———. "The Two Cities: St. Augustine and the Spanish Conquest of America." *Revista Portuguesa de Filosofía* 44, no. 1 (1988): 99–126.

Browne, Walden. "When Worlds Collide: Crisis in Sahagun's *Historia universal de las cosas de la Nueva España.*" *Colonial Latin American History Review* 5, no. 2 (1996): 101–49.

Brufau Prats, Jaime. *La escuela de Salamanca ante el descubrimiento del Nuevo Mundo.* Facultad de Teología de San Estéban, Insituto Histórico Dominicano, Biblioteca de Teólogos Españoles 33. Salamanca: Editorial San Estéban, 1989.

Bujanda, J. M. de. *Index de l'Inquisition espagnole 1551, 1554, 1559: Index des livres interdits.* Vol. 5. Geneva: Droz, 1984.

Burke, Peter. "America and the Rewriting of World History." In *America in European Consciousness 1493–1750,* edited by Karen Ordahl Kupperman, 33–51. Chapel Hill: University of North Carolina Press, for the Institute of Early American History and Culture, 1995.

Burns, J. H. *Lordship, Kingship, and Empire: The Idea of Monarchy, 1400–1525.* Oxford: Clarendon Press, 1992.

Calderón Quijano, José Antonio. *Toponimia española en el Nuevo Mundo.* Seville: Caja San Fernando, 1988.

Canning, J. P. "Law, Sovereignty, and Corporation Theory, 1300–1450." In *Cambridge History of Medieval Political Thought, c.350–c.1450* , edited by J. H. Burns, 454–76. Cambridge: Cambridge University Press, 1988.

Cano, Melchor. *De dominio Indorum.* In Luciano Pereña Vicente, *Misión de España en América,* 90–147. Madrid: Consejo Superior de Investigaciones Científicas, 1956.

———. *De dominio Indorum.* In Juan de la Peña, *De bello contra insulanos: Intervención de España en América: Escuela española de la Paz, secunda generación, 1560–1585,* edited by L. Pereña, V. Abril, C. Baciero, A. García, J. Barrientos, and F. Maseda, 1:555–81. Corpus Hispanorum de Pace, vol. 9. Madrid: Consejo Superior de Investigaciones Científicas, 1982.

Caro Baroja, Julio. *Las falsificaciones de la historia (en relación con la de España).* Barcelona: Seix Barral, 1992.

Carranza, Bartolomé de. *Ratione fidei potest Caesar debellare et tenere indos novi orbis?* In Luciano Pereña Vicente, *Misión de España en América,* 38–57. Madrid: Consejo Superior de Investigaciones Científicas, 1956.

Carro, Venancio D. *La teología y los teólogos-juristas españoles ante la conquista de América.* 2 vols. Madrid: Publicaciones de la Escuela de Estudios Hispano-Americanos de la Universidad de Sevilla, 1944.

Cartagena, Alfonso de. See García de Santa María, Alfonso.

Castañeda Delgado, Paulino. "La ética en la Conquista de América." In *De con-*

quistadores y conquistados: Realidad, justificación, representación, edited by Karl Kohut, 68–81. America Eystettensia: Publikationen des Zentralinstituts für Lateinamerika-Studien der Katolischen Universität Eichstätt, Serie A: Kongressakten 7a. Frankfurt am Main: Vervuert, 1992.

Castellanos, Juan de. *Elegías de varones ilustres de Indias.* 9th ed. Biblioteca de Autores Españoles, vol. 4. Madrid: Atlas, 1944.

Castilla Urbano, Francisco. "Juan Ginés de Sepúlveda: En torno a una idea de civilización." *Revista de Indias* 52 (1992): 327–48.

Castro, Américo. *An Idea of History: Selected Essays of Américo Castro.* Translated and edited by Stephen Gilman and Edmund L. King. Columbus: Ohio State University Press, 1977.

———. "Antonio de Guevara: Un hombre y un estilo del siglo XVI." In *Hacia Cervantes,* 86–117. 3d ed. Madrid: Taurus, 1967.

———. *La realidad histórica de España.* 2d ed. Mexico City: Porrúa, 1962.

———. *Sobre el nombre y el quién de los españoles.* Madrid: Taurus, 1973.

———. *The Spaniards: An Introduction to Their History.* Translated by Willard F. King and Selma Margaretten. Berkeley and Los Angeles: University of California Press, 1971.

———. *The Structure of Spanish History.* Translated by Edmund L. King. Princeton: Princeton University Press, 1954.

Catalán, Diego. "España en su historiografía: De objeto a sujeto de la historia." In Ramón Menéndez Pidal, *Los Españoles en la historia,* 9–49. 2d ed. Madrid: Espasa-Calpe, 1985.

Cerezo, Prometeo. "Influencia de la escuela de Salamanca en el pensamiento universitario americano." In *La ética en la conquista de América,* edited by Demetrio Ramos et al., 551–96. Madrid: Consejo Superior de Investigaciones Científicas, 1984.

Cervantes Saavedra, Miguel de. *El ingenioso hidalgo Don Quijote de la Mancha.* Edited by Francisco Rodrígues Marín. Vol. 4. Madrid: Atlas, 1948.

———. *Numancia.* Edited by Robert Marrast. 2d ed. Madrid: Cátedra, 1990.

Cervantes de Salazar, Francisco. *Crónica de la Nueva España.* Edited by Manuel Magallón. Vol. 2. Biblioteca de Autores Españoles, vol. 245. Madrid: Atlas, 1971.

———. *Obras.* Edited by Francisco Cerdá y Rico. Madrid: Antonio de Sancha, 1772.

Chamberlain, Robert S. *The Conquest and Colonization of Yucatán.* Washington, D.C.: Carnegie Institution, 1948; repr. New York: Octagon, 1966.

Chastel, André. *The Sack of Rome, 1527.* Translated by Beth Archer. Princeton: Princeton University Press, 1983.

Cieza de León, Pedro. *La Crónica del Perú.* Bogotá: Ediciones de la Revista Ximénez de Quesada, 1971.

———. *Del Señorío de los Incas.* Edited by Alberto Mario Salas. Buenos Aires: Ediciones Argentinas "Solar," 1943.

Clendinnen, Inga. *Ambivalent Conquests: Maya and Spaniard in Yucatan, 1517–1570.* Cambridge: Cambridge University Press, 1987.

———. "'Fierce and Unnatural Cruelty': Cortés and the Conquest of Mexico." *Representations* 33 (1991): 65–100.

Cochrane, Eric. *Historians and Historiography in the Italian Renaissance.* Chicago: University of Chicago Press, 1981.

Códice Mendieta: Documentos franciscanos, siglos XVI y XVII. In *Nueva colección de documentos para la historia de México,* edited by Joaquín García Icazbalceta, vols. 4–5. Mexico City, 1892; repr. Nendeln: Kraus, 1971.

Cohn, Norman. *Europe's Inner Demons.* New York: Basic Books, 1975.

Columbus, Christopher. *The Diario of Christopher Columbus' First Voyage to America, 1492–1493. Abstracted by Fray Bartolomé de las Casas.* Edited by Oliver Dunn and James E. Kelly Jr. Norman: University of Oklahoma Press, 1989.

———. "Letter to the Sovereigns." In *Journals and Other Documents on the Life and Voyages of Christopher Columbus,* ed. Samuel Eliot Morison, 185–86. New York: Heritage Press, 1963.

Columbus, Ferdinand. *The Life of the Admiral Christopher Columbus by His Son Ferdinand.* Translated by Benjamin Keen. New Brunswick, N.J.: Rutgers University Press, 1959.

Concejo, Pilar. *Antonio de Guevara: Un ensayista del siglo XVI.* Madrid: Ediciones Cultura Hispánica, Instituto de cooperación iberoamericana, 1985.

Cortes de los antiguos reinos de León y Castilla. Vol. 4. Madrid: La Real Academia de la Historia, 1882.

Cortés, Hernán. *Cartas de relación.* Edited by Manuel Alcalá. 16th ed. Mexico City: Porrúa, 1992.

———. *Letters from Mexico.* Translated and edited by Anthony Pagden. New Haven: Yale University Press, 1986.

Costes, René. *Antonio de Guevara: Son oeuvre.* Bordeaux: Feret, 1926.

Covarrubias, Diego de. "De iustitia belli adversus indos." In *Relectio de iure belli, o paz dinámica: Escuela española de la Paz, Primera Generación 1526–1560,* edited by L. Pereña, V. Abril, C. Baciero, A. García, and F. Maseda, appendix 3, 343–63. Corpus Hispanorum de Pace, vol. 6. Madrid: Consejo Superior de Investigaciones Científicas, 1981.

Cuevas, Domingo de, and Juan de Salinas. *De insulanis.* In Vitoria, *Relectio de Indis, o libertad de los Indios,* edited and translated by L. Pereña and J. M. Pérez Prende, 196–218. Corpus Hispanorum de Pace, vol. 5. Madrid: Consejo Superior de Investigaciones Científicas, 1967.

Cuevas, P. Mariano. *Historia de la Iglesia en México,* 5th ed. Mexico City: Editorial Patria, 1946.

Cunnally, John. *Images of the Illustrious: The Numismatic Presence in the Renaissance.* Princeton: Princeton University Press, 1999.

Curtius, Ernst Robert. *Europäische Literatur und lateinisches Mittelalter.* 6th ed. Bern: Francke, 1967.

———. "Jorge Manrique und der Kaisergedanke." *Zeitschrift für romanische Philologie* 52 (1932): 129–51.

Davis, Charles Till. *Dante's Italy, and Other Essays.* Philadelphia: University of Pennsylvania Press, 1984.

Davis, Natalie Zemon. "The Sacred and the Body Social in Sixteenth-Century Lyon." *Past and Present* 90 (1981): 40–70.

Deckers, Daniel. "La justicia de la conquista de América. Consideraciónes en torno a la cronología y los protagonistas de una controversia del siglo XVI muy actual. " *Ibero-Amerikanisches Archiv* 18 (1992): 331–66.

Díaz del Castillo, Bernal. *Historia verdadera de la conquista de Nueva España.* Edited by Joaquín Ramírez Cabañas. 14th ed. Mexico City: Porrúa, 1986.

———. *Historia verdadera de la conquista de Nueva España.* Edited by Carmelo Sáenz de Santa María. 2 vols. Madrid: Consejo Superior de Investigaciones Científicas, 1982.

Díaz-Plaja, Guillermo, ed. *Antología mayor de la literatura española.* Vol. 2: *Renacimiento.* Barcelona: Editorial Labor, 1958.

Dibble, Charles E. "Sahagún's Appendices." In *The Work of Bernardino de Sahagún, Pioneer Ethnographer of Sixteenth-Century Aztec Mexico,* edited by J. Jorge Klor de Alva, H. B. Nicholson, and Eloise Quiñones Keber 107–18. Austin, Tex.: Institute for Mesoamerican Studies, 1988.

Don, Patricia Lopes. "Carnivals, Triumphs, and Rain Gods in the New World: A Civic Festival in the City of Mexico-Tenochtitlan in 1539." *Colonial Latin American Review* 6 (1997): 18–40.

Du Choul, Guillaume. *Discours de la religion des anciens Romains.* Lyon: Guillaume Rouillé, 1556.

Dubois, Claude-Gilbert. *Celtes et Gaulois au XVIe siècle: Le développement littéraire d'un mythe nationaliste.* Paris: Vrin, 1972.

Dumont, Jean. *La vraie controverse de Valladolid: Premier débat des droits de l'homme.* Paris: Criterion, 1995.

Durán, Diego. *History of the Indies of New Spain.* Translated by Doris Heyden. Norman: University of Oklahoma Press, 1994.

———. *Ritos y fiestas de los antiguos mexicanos.* Edited by Alfredo Chavero. 1880; repr. Mexico City: Cosmos, 1980.

Durand, José. "Caupolicán, clave historial y épica de 'La Araucana.'" *Revue de littérature comparée* 52 (1978): 367–89.

———. "El *chapetón* Ercilla y la honra Araucana." *Filología* 10 (1964): 113–34.

———. *La transformación social del conquistador.* 2d ed. Lima: Editorial Nuevos Rumbos, 1958.

Eatough, Geoffrey. "In Defence of the Amerindian: Bartolomé de las Casas's Classical Strategies." In *The Reception of Classical Texts and Images,* edited by Lorna Hardwick and Stanley Ireland, pt. 2, 153–73. Milton Keynes: Open University, 1996.

Elliott, J. H. "The Mental World of Hernán Cortés." In *Spain and Its World, 1500–1700.* New Haven: Yale University Press, 1989.

———. *The Old World and the New: 1492–1650.* Cambridge: Cambridge University Press, 1970.

———. "Renaissance Europe and America: A Blunted Impact?" In *First Images of America: The Impact of the New World on the Old,* edited by Fredi Chiappelli, 11–23. Berkeley and Los Angeles: University of California Press, 1976.

Enríquez de Guzmán, Alonso. *Libro de la vida y costumbres de Don Alonso*

Enríquez de Guzmán. Edited by Hayward Keniston. Biblioteca de Autores Españoles, vol. 126. Madrid: Atlas, 1960.

Ercilla y Zúñiga, Alonso de. *La Araucana.* Edited by Isaías Lerner. Madrid: Cátedra, 1993.

Fabié, A. M. *El padre Fray Bartolomé de las Casas, obispo de Chiapa.* 2 vols. Colección de documentos inéditos para la historia de España, vols. 70–71. Madrid: Miguel Ginesta, 1879; repr. Vaduz: Kraus, 1966.

Feldman, Louis H. *Josephus and Modern Scholarship, 1937–1980.* Berlin: De Gruyter, 1984.

Fernández de Oviedo, Gonzalo. *La hystoria de las Indias.* Salamanca: Juan de Junta, 1547.

———. *Historia general y natural de las Indias.* Edited by Juan Pérez de Tudela Bueso. 5 vols. Biblioteca de Autores Españoles, vols. 117–21. Madrid: Atlas, 1959.

———. *Quinquagenas.* In *Las memorias de Gonzalo Fernández de Oviedo,* edited by Juan Bautista Avalle-Arce. 2 vols. Chapel Hill: North Carolina Studies in the Romance Languages and Literatures, Department of Romance Languages, 1974.

———. *Sumario de la natural historia de las Indians.* Edited by Juan Bautista Avalle-Arce. Salamanca: Anaya, 1963.

Fernández-Santamaría, J. A. "Juan Ginés de Sepúlveda on the Nature of the American Indians." *Americas* 31 (1975): 434–51.

———. *The State, War, and Peace: Spanish Political Thought in the Renaissance, 1516–1559.* Cambridge: Cambridge University Press, 1977.

Findlen, Paula. "Possessing the Past: The Material World of the Renaissance." *American Historical Review* 103 (1998): 83–114.

Flint, Valerie I. J. *The Rise of Magic in Early Modern Europe.* Princeton: Princeton University Press, 1991.

Fox, E. Inman. "Spain as Castile: Nationalism and National Identity." In *The Cambridge Companion to Modern Spanish Culture,* edited by David T. Gies, 21–36. Cambridge: Cambridge University Press, 1999.

Fraker, Charles F. "Alonso X, the Empire, and the *Primera crónica.*" *Bulletin of Hispanic Studies* 55 (1978): 95–102.

———. *The Scope of History: Studies in the Historiography of Alfonso el Sabio.* Ann Arbor: University of Michigan Press, 1996.

Frankl, Victor. *El "Antijovio" de Gonzalo Jiménez de Quesada y las concepciones de realidad y verdad en la época de la contrarreforma y del manierismo.* Madrid: Ediciones Cultura Hispánica, 1963.

———. "Imperio particular e imperio universal en las *Cartas de relación* de Hernán Cortés." *Cuadernos Hispanoamericanos* 55 (1963): 443–82.

Fraser, Valerie. *The Architecture of Conquest: Building in the Viceroyalty of Peru, 1535–1635.* Cambridge: Cambridge University Press, 1990.

Friede, Juan, and Benjamin Keen, eds. *Bartolomé de las Casas in History.* De Kalb: Northern Illinois University Press, 1971.

Friedrich, Werner P. *Dante's Fame Abroad, 1350–1850.* Chapel Hill: University of North Carolina Press, 1950.

García de Santa María, Alfonso (Alfonso de Cartagena). *Anacephaleosis regum Hispaniae.* In *Hispaniae illustratae,* edited by Andreas Schottus, 246–91. Frankfurt am Main: Marnius, 1603–8.

García y García, Antonio. "El sentido de las primeras denuncias." In *La ética en la conquista de América,* edited by Demetrio Ramos et al., 67–115. Madrid: Consejo Superior de Investigaciones Científicas, 1984.

Garcilaso de la Vega, El Inca. *Comentarios reales de los Incas.* In *Obras completas,* edited by P. Carmelo Sáenz de Santa María, vols. 2–3. Biblioteca de Autores Españoles, vols. 133–34. Madrid: Atlas, 1963.

———. *La Florida.* In *Obras completas,* edited by P. Carmelo Sáenz de Santa María, vol. 1. Biblioteca de Autores Españoles, vol. 132. Madrid: Atlas, 1965.

———. *Royal Commentaries of the Incas and General History of Peru.* Translated by Harold V. Livermore. 2 vols. Austin: University of Texas Press, 1966.

Geanakoplos, Deno John. *Greek Scholars in Venice.* Cambridge: Harvard University Press, 1967.

Gerbi, Antonello. *Nature in the New World: From Christopher Columbus to Gonzalo Fernández de Oviedo.* Translated by Jeremy Moyle. University of Pittsburgh Press, 1985.

Gibson, Charles. "Reconquista and Conquista." In *Homage to Irving A. Leonard,* edited by Raquel Chang-Rodríguez and Donald A. Yates, 19–28. East Lansing: Latin American Studies Center, Michigan State University, 1977.

Gil Fernández, Juan. "El libro greco-latino y su influjo en Indias." In *Homenaje a Enrique Segura Covarsí, Bernardo Muñoz Sánchez, y Ricardo Puente Broncano,* edited by José María Álvarez Martínez et al., 61–111. Badajoz: Departamento de Publicaciones de la Excelentísima Diputación, 1986.

Gilmore, Myron P. "Erasmus and Alberto Pio, Prince of Carpi." In *Action and Conviction in Early Modern Europe: Essays in Memory of E. H. Harbison,* edited by Theodore K. Rabb and Jerrold E. Siegel, 299–318. Princeton: Princeton University Press, 1969.

Ginés de Sepúlveda, Juan. *Democrates segundo, o de las justas causas de la guerra contra los indios.* Latin text with translation by Angel Losada. Madrid: Consejo Superior de Investigaciones Científicas, 1951.

———. *Los hechos de los españoles en el Nuevo Mundo.* Translated by Demetrio Ramos Pérez. Valladolid: Seminario americanista de la Universidad de Valladolid, 1976.

———. *De orbe novo (De rebus Hispanorum ad novum terrarum orbem Mexicumque gestis).* Edited by Antonio Ramírez de Verger. Stuttgart: Teubner, 1993.

———. *Tratados políticos de Juan Ginés de Sepúlveda.* Translated by Angel Losada. Madrid: Instituto de Estudios Políticos, 1963.

———. *Opera, quae reperiri potuerunt omnia.* Cologne: Birkmann, 1602.

Ginés de Sepúlveda, and Bartolomé de las Casas. *Apología.* Latin texts with translations by Angel Losada. Madrid: Editora Nacional, 1975.

Gliozzi, Giuliano. *Adamo e il nuovo mondo: La nascita dell'antropologia come ideologia coloniale: Dalle genealogie bibliche alle teorie razziali (1500–1700).* Florence: Nuova Italia, 1977.

Gómara. See López de Gómara, Francisco.

Gómez, Fernando. *Good Places and Non-Places in Colonial Mexico: The Figure of Vasco de Quiroga (1470–1565)*. Lanham: University Press of America, 2001.

Góngora, Mario. *Studies in the Colonial History of Spanish America*. Cambridge: Cambridge University Press, 1975.

González Rodríguez, Jaime. "El antiromanismo de Gonzalo Fernández de Oviedo." *Revista de Indias* 43 (1983): 335–42.

———. *La idea de Roma en la historiografía indiana (1492–1550)*. Madrid: Consejo Superior de Investigaciones Científicas, 1981.

———. "La junta de Valladolid convocada por el Emperador." In *La ética en la conquista de América*, edited by Demetrio Ramos et al., 199–227. Madrid: Consejo Superior de Investigaciones Científicas, 1984.

———. "La significación de las Indias para la historia de España según Oviedo." In *América y la España del siglo XVI*, edited by Francisco de Solano and Fermín del Pino, 1:77–84. Madrid: Consejo Superior de Investigaciones Científicas, 1982.

Grafton, Anthony. *Forgers and Critics: Creativity and Duplicity in Western Scholarship*. Princeton: Princeton University Press, 1990.

Grafton, Anthony, with April Shelford and Nancy Siraisi. *New Worlds, Ancient Texts: The Power of Tradition and the Shock of Discovery*. Cambridge: Harvard University Press, 1992.

Gregorovius, Friedrich. *History of the City of Rome in the Middle Ages*. Translated by Annie Hamilton. Vol. 8, pt. 2. London: G. Bell, 1902.

Greenblatt, Stephen. "Improvisation and Power." In *Literature and Society*, edited by Edward Said, 55–99. Baltimore: Johns Hopkins University Press, 1980.

———. *Marvelous Possessions*. Chicago: University of Chicago Press, 1991.

Grey, Ernest. *Guevara, a Forgotten Renaissance Author*. The Hague: Nijhoff, 1973.

Griffin, Clive. *The Crombergers of Seville: The History of a Printing and Merchant Dynasty*. Oxford: Clarendon Press, 1988.

Griffiths, Nicholas. *The Cross and the Serpent: Religious Repression and Resurgence in Colonial Peru*. Norman: University of Oklahoma Press, 1996.

Grunberg, Bernard. "The Origins of the Conquistadores of Mexico City." *Hispanic American Historical Review* 74 (1994): 259–83.

Guevara, Antonio de. *Libro aúreo de Marco Aurelio*. Edited by Raimond Foulché-Delbosc. *Revue hispanique* 76, no. 169 (1929): 1–319.

———. *Libro primero de las epístolas familiares*. Edited by José María de Cossío. Madrid: Aldus, 1950.

———. *Una década de Césares*. Edited by Joseph R. Jones. Chapel Hill: University of North Carolina Press, 1966.

Gutiérrez, Gustavo. *Las Casas: In Search of the Poor of Jesus Christ*. Translated by Robert R. Barr. Maryknoll: Orbis, 1992.

Haase, Wolfgang. "America and the Classical Tradition." In *The Classical Tradition and the Americas*, vol. 1: *European Images of the Americas and the*

Classical Tradition, part 1, edited by Wolfgang Haase and Meyer Reinhold, v–xxxiii. Berlin: De Gruyter, 1994.

Hampe Martínez, Teodoro, ed. *La tradición clásica en el Perú virreinal*. Lima: Sociedad Peruana de Estudios Clásicos and Universidad Nacional Mayor de San Marcos, 1999.

Hanke, Lewis. *All Mankind Is One*. De Kalb: Northern Illinois University Press, 1974.

———. *Aristotle and the American Indians*. Bloomington: Indiana University Press, 1959.

———. "Pope Paul III and the American Indians." *Harvard Theological Review* 30 (1937): 65–102.

———. *The Spanish Struggle for Justice in the Conquest of America*. Philadelphia: American Historical Association, 1949.

Harris, Max. *Aztecs, Moors, and Christians: Festivals of Reconquest in Mexico and Spain*. Austin: University of Texas Press, 2000.

Harris, William V. "Roman Expansion in the West: III. Spain." In *The Cambridge Ancient History*, 8:118–42. 2d ed. Cambridge: Cambridge University Press, 1989.

Haskell, Francis. *History and Its Images: Art and the Interpretation of the Past*. New Haven: Yale University Press, 1993.

Hay, Denys. *Polydore Vergil: Renaissance Historian and Man of Letters*. Oxford: Oxford University Press, 1952.

Headley, John M. "The Hapsburg World Empire and the Revival of Ghibellinism." In *Medieval and Renaissance Studies*, vol. 7, edited by S. Wenzel. Chapel Hill, 1978.

Heer, Friedrich. *The Holy Roman Empire*. Translated by Janet Sondheimer. New York: Praeger, 1968.

Hernáez, Francisco Javier. *Colección de bulas, breves, y otros documentos relativos a la Iglesia de América y Filipinas*. Brussels: Vromant, 1879; repr. Vaduz: Kraus, 1964.

Hernández Martín, Ramón. "La escuela dominicana de Salamanca ante el descubrimiento de América." In *Los domínicos y el nuevo mundo: Actas del I Congreso Internacional sobre los domínicos y el nuevo mundo*. Madrid: Deimos, 1988.

———. "La hipótesis de Francisco de Vitoria." In *La ética en la conquista de América*, edited by Demetrio Ramos et al., 345–81. Madrid: Consejo Superior de Investigaciones Científicas, 1984.

Himmerich y Valencia, Robert. *The Encomenderos of New Spain, 1521–1555*. Austin: University of Texas Press, 1991.

Hodgen, Margaret T. *Early Anthropology in the Sixteenth and Seventeenth Centuries*. Philadelphia: University of Pennsylvania Press, 1964.

Höffner, Joseph. *La ética colonial española del siglo de oro*. Madrid: Ediciones Cultura Hispánica, 1957.

Hook, David. "The *Auto de la Destruición de Jerusalén* in Relation to Its Source." *Bulletin of Hispanic Studies* 51 (1974): 335–45.

———. "The Legend of the Flavian Destruction of Jerusalem in Late Fifteenth-Century Spain and Portugal." *Bulletin of Hispanic Studies* 65 (1988): 113–28.

Horcasitas, Fernando. *El teatro nahuatl.* Mexico City: Universidad Nacional Autónoma de México, 1974.

Huddleston, Lee Eldridge. *Origins of the American Indians: European Concepts, 1492–1729.* Austin: University of Texas Press, 1967.

Hughes, Dennis D. *Human Sacrifice in Ancient Greece.* London: Routledge, 1991.

Iglesia, Ramón. *Columbus, Cortés, and Other Essays.* Translated by Lesley Bird Simpson. Berkeley and Los Angeles: University of California Press, 1969.

Izbicki, Thomas M. "Salamancan Relectiones in the Fernán Nuñez Collection." *Studia Gratiana* 29 (1998): 489–500.

Jacks, Philip. *The Antiquarian and the Myth of Antiquity: The Origins of Rome in Renaissance Thought.* Cambridge: Cambridge University Press, 1993.

Jara, René, and Nicholas Spadaccini, eds. *1492–1992: Re/discovering Colonial Writing.* Hispanic Issues 4. Minneapolis: Prisma Institute, 1989.

Jardine, Lisa. *Worldly Goods: A New History of the Renaissance.* New York: Doubleday, 1996.

Jedin, Hubert. "Juan de Torquemada und das Imperium Romanum.' *Archivum Fratrum Praedicatorum* (Istituto storico domenicano di S. Sabina), 12 (1942): 247–78.

Jerez, Francisco de. *Verdadera relación de la conquista del Perú y provincia del Cuzco, llamada la Nueva Castilla.* Edited by José Luis Moure. In *Crónicas iniciales de la conquista del Perú,* edited by Alberto M. Salas, Miguel A. Guérin, and José Luis Moure, 147–252. Buenos Aires: Plus Ultra, 1987.

Jones, C. P. *Culture and Society in Lucian.* Cambridge: Harvard University Press, 1986.

Jones, Joseph. R. *Antonio de Guevara.* Boston: Twayne, 1975.

Keen, Benjamin. *The Aztec Image.* New Brunswick, N.J.: Rutgers University Press, 1971.

King, Willard F. "Cervantes' *Numancia* and Imperial Spain." *Modern Language Notes* 94 (1979): 200–221.

Kobayashi, José María. *La educación como conquista (empresa franciscana en México).* Centro de Estudios Históricos, n.s. 19. Mexico City: El Colegio de México, 1974.

Koenigsberger, Helmut. "Spain." In *National Consciousness, History, and Political Culture in Early-Modern Europe,* edited by Orest Ranum, 144–72. Baltimore: Johns Hopkins University Press, 1975.

Kohut, Karl. "Humanismus und Neue Welt im Werk von Gonzalo Fernández de Oviedo." In *Humanismus und Neue Welt,* edited by Wolfgang Reinhard, 65–88. *Mitteilung XV der Kommission für Humanismusforschung,* Deutsche Forschungsgemeinschaft. Weinheim: VCH, 1987.

Las Casas, Bartolomé de. *Apologia.* In Ginés de Sepúlveda and Bartolomé de las Casas, *Apología,* translated by Angel Losada. Madrid: Editora Nacional, 1975.

———. *Apologética historia sumaria.* Edited by Edmundo O'Gorman. 2 vols.

Mexico City: Universidad Nacional Autónoma de México, Instututo de Investigaciones Históricas, 1967.

———. *Apologética historia sumaria.* Edited by Vidal Abril Castelló, Jesús A. Barreda, Berta Ares Queija, and Miguel J. Abril Stoffels. 3 vols. In *Obras completas,* edited by Paulino Castañeda Delgado, vols. 6–8. Madrid: Alianza Editorial, 1992.

———. *In Defense of the Indians.* Translated by Stafford Poole. 1974; repr. De Kalb: Northern Illinois University Press, 1992.

———. *Historia de las Indias.* Edited by Agustín Millares Carlo. 3 vols. Mexico City: Fondo de Cultura Económica, 1951.

———. *Historia de las Indias.* 3 vols. Edited by Miguel Angel Medina, with introductory material by Jesús Angel Barreda and Isacio Pérez Fernández. In *Obras completas,* edited by Paulino Castañeda Delgado, vols. 3–5. Madrid: Alianza Editorial, 1994.

———. *History of the Indies.* Translated and abridged by Andrée M. Collard. New York: Harper, 1971.

———. *Obras escogidas.* Edited by Juan Pérez de Tudela Bueso. Vol. 5. Biblioteca de Autores Españoles, vol. 110. Madrid: Atlas, 1972.

———. *The Only Way.* Translated by F. P. Sullivan. Edited by Helen Rand Parish. New York: Paulist Press, 1992.

———. *De regia potestate, o derecho de autodeterminación.* Edited by Luciano Pereña, J. M. Pérez-Prendes, Vidal Abril, and Joaquín Azcarraga. Corpus Hispanorum de Pace, vol. 8. Madrid: Consejo Superior de Investigaciones Científicas, 1969.

———. *A Short Account of the Destruction of the Indies.* Translated by Nigel Griffin, with an introduction by Anthony Pagden. Harmondsworth: Penguin, 1992.

———. *Tratados de Fray Bartolomé de las Casas.* Edited by Lewis Hanke and Manuel Giménez Fernández. 2 vols. Mexico City: Fondo de Cultura Económica, 1965.

———. *Tratado de Indias y el doctor Sepúlveda.* Edited by Manuel Giménez Fernández. Fuentes para la Historia Colonial de Venezuela. Caracas, 1962.

Lawrance, Jeremy N. H. "Humanism in the Iberian Peninsula." In *The Impact of Humanism on Western Europe,* edited by Anthony Goodman and Angus MacKay, 220–58. London: Longman, 1990.

Leonard, Irving A. *Books of the Brave.* Cambridge: Harvard University Press, 1949.

Lerner, Lía Schwartz. "Tradición literaria y heroínas indias en *La Araucana.*" *Revista Iberoamericana* 38 (1972): 615–25.

Lida de Malkiel, María Rosa. "Dido y su defensa en la literatura española." *Revista de Filología Hispánica* 4 (1942): 209–52, 318–82.

———. *Jerusalén: El tema literario de su cerco y destrucción por los romanos.* Buenos Aires: Facultad de Filosofía y Letras, Instituto de Filología y Literaturas Hispánicas Dr. Amado Alonso, 1972.

Linehan, Peter. *History and the Historians of Medieval Spain.* Oxford: Oxford University Press, 1993.

Lipschutz, Alejandro. *El problema racial en la conquista de América, y el mestizaje.* 2d ed. Santiago de Chile: Andrés Bello, 1967.

Liss, Peggy. *Mexico under Spain, 1521–1556: Society and the Origins of Nationality.* Chicago: University of Chicago Press, 1975.

Lobato Casado. "El obispo Garcés, OP., y la bula 'Sublimis Deus.'" In *Los Domínicos y el nuevo mundo: Actas del I Congreso Internacional,* 741–95. Madrid: Deimos, 1987.

López de Ayala, Pedro. *Crónica del Rey Don Pedro.* Edited by Eugenio de Llaguno y Amirola. In *Crónicas de los Reyes de Castilla,* edited by Cayetano Rosell, 1:393–614. Biblioteca de autores españoles, vol. 66. 1875; repr. Madrid: Atlas, 1953.

López de Gómara, Francisco. *Cortés: The Life of the Conqueror.* Translated by Lesley Bird Simpson. Berkeley and Los Angeles: University of California Press, 1964.

———. *Historia de la conquista de México.* Edited by Joaquín Ramírez Cabañas. Mexico City: Pedro Robredo, 1943.

———. *Historia general de las Indias y Vida de Hernán Cortés.* Edited by Jorge Gurría Lacroix. Caracas: Biblioteca Ayacucho, 1971.

Losada, Angel. *Fray Bartolomé de las Casas a la luz de la moderna crítica histórica.* Madrid: Tecnos, 1970.

———. *Juan Ginés de Sepúlveda a través de su "Epistolario" y nuevos documentos.* 1949; repr. Madrid: Consejo Superior de Investigaciones Científicas, 1973.

———. "Observaciónes sobre 'La Apología' de Fray Bartolomé de las Casas." *Cuadernos Americanos* 212 (May–June 1977): 152–61.

MacCormack, Sabine. "Approaches to Historicization: Romans and Incas in the Light of Early Modern Spanish Scholarship." In *Aporemata: Kritische Studien zur Philologiegeschichte,* vol. 5, edited by Glenn W. Most, 69–101. Göttingen: Vandenhoeck and Ruprecht, 2001.

———. "Conversations across Time and Space: Classical Traditions in the Andes." forthcoming.

———. "Cuzco, Another Rome?" In *Empires: Perspectives from Archaeology and History,* edited by Susan E. Alcock, Terence N. D'Altroy, Kathleen D. Morrison, and Carla M. Sinopoli, 419–35. Cambridge: Cambridge University Press, 2001.

———. "History and Law in Sixteenth-Century Peru: The Impact of European Scholarly Traditions." In *Cultures of Scholarship,* edited by S. C. Humphreys, 277–310. Ann Arbor: University of Michigan Press, 1997.

———. "History, Historical Record, and Ceremonial Action: Incas and Spaniards in Cuzco." *Cambridge Studies in Society and History* 43 (2001): 329–63.

———. "History, Memory, and Time in Golden Age Spain." *History and Memory* 4 (1992): 38–66.

———. "The Incas and Rome." In *Garcilaso Inca de la Vega: An American Humanist,* edited by José Anadón, 8–31. Notre Dame: University of Notre Dame Press, 1998.

———. "Limits of Understanding: Perceptions of Greco-Roman and Amerindian Paganism in Early Modern Europe." In *America in European Consciousness, 1493–1750*, edited by Karen Ordahl Kupperman, 79–129. Chapel Hill: University of North Carolina Press, 1995.

———. *Religion in the Andes: Vision and Imagination in Early Colonial Peru.* Princeton: Princeton University Press, 1991.

———. "*Ubi Ecclesia?* Perceptions of Medieval Europe in Spanish America." *Speculum* 69 (1994): 74–100.

Mampel González, Elena, and Neus Escandell Tur, eds. *Lope de Aguirre: Crónicas, 1559–1561*, Barcelona: Editorial 7 1/2, Ediciones Universidad de Barcelona, 1981.

Mangan, John Joseph. *Life, Character, and Influence of Desiderius Erasmus of Rotterdam.* Vol. 2. New York: Macmillan, 1927.

Manrique, Jorge. *Poesía.* Edited by Jesús-Manuel Alda Tesán. 10th ed. Madrid: Cátedra, 1985.

Maravall, José Antonio. *Antiguos y modernos: La idea de progreso en el desarrollo inicial de una sociedad.* Madrid: Sociedad de Estudios y Publicaciones, 1966.

———. *Carlos V y el pensamiento político del renacimiento.* Madrid: Instituto de Estudios Políticos, 1960.

———. *El Concepto de España en la edad media.* Madrid: Instituto de Estudios Políticos, 1954.

——— "El concepto de monarquía en la edad media española." In *Estudios de historia del pensamiento español*, 1:67–85. Madrid: Ediciones Cultura Hispánica, 1983.

March, K., and K. Passman. "The Amazon Myth and Latin America." In *The Classical Tradition and the Americas*, vol. 1: *European Images of the Americas and the Classical Tradition*, edited by Wolfgang Haase and Meyer Reinhold, pt. 1, 285–338. Berlin: De Gruyter, 1994.

Marías, Julián. *Understanding Spain.* Translated by Frances M. López-Morillas. Ann Arbor: University of Michigan Press, 1992.

Marineo Sículo, Lucio. *De rebus Hispaniae memorabilibus.* In *Hispaniae illustratae*, edited by Andreas Schottus, 291–517. Frankfurt am Main: Marnius, 1603–8.

Martínez, José Luis, ed. *Documentos cortesianos*, vol. 2: *1526–1545*, pt. 4: *Juicio de Residencia.* Mexico City: Fondo de Cultura Económica, Universidad Nacional Autónoma de México, 1991.

Martínez, Manuel M. "Las Casas on the Conquest of America." In *Las Casas in History*, edited by Juan Friede and Benjamin Keen, 309–49. De Kalb: Northern Illinois University Press, 1971.

Martyr, Peter (Petrus Martyr de Angleria). *De orbe novo decades octo.* In *Opera*, edited by Erich Woldan. Facsimile of 1530 Alcalá ed. Graz: Akademische Druck- und Verlagsanstalt, 1966.

Mason, Peter. *Deconstructing America: Representations of the Other.* London: Routledge, 1990.

Mathes, Miguel. *Santa Cruz de Tlatelolco: La primera biblioteca académica de las Américas*. Mexico City: Secretaría de Relaciones Exteriores, 1982.

Maticorena Estrada, Miguel. "Cieza de León en Sevilla y su muerte en 1554." *Anuario de estudios americanos* 12 (1955): 615–74.

Mazzocco, Angelo. "Rome and the Humanists: The Case of Biondo Flavio." In *Rome in the Renaissance: The City and the Myth. Papers of the Thirteenth Annual Conference of the Center for Medieval and Early Renaissance Studies*, edited by P. A. Ramsey, 185–95. Binghamton, N.Y.: Center for Medieval and Early Renaissance Studies, 1982.

McCuaig, William. *Carlo Sigonio: The Changing World of the Late Renaissance*. Princeton: Princeton University Press, 1989.

McGowan, Margaret M. *The Vision of Rome in Late Renaissance France*. New Haven: Yale University Press, 2000.

Melida González-Monteagudo, Monico. "El Padre Las Casas y Valladolid." In *Estudios sobre política indigenista española en América*, 1:9–27. Valladolid: Universidad de Valladolid, 1975.

Mena, Juan de. *Laberinto de Fortuna*. Edited by John G. Cummins. 4th ed. Madrid: Cátedra, 1990.

Menéndez Pidal, Juan. *Leyendas del último rey godo: Notas é investigaciones*. 2d ed. Madrid: Tipografía de la Revista de Archivos, Bibliotecas y Museos, 1906.

Menéndez Pidal, Ramón. "¿Codicia insaciable? ¿Ilustres hazañas?" In *España y su historia*, 2:114–26. Madrid: Minotauro, 1957.

———. *El Padre Las Casas: Su doble personalidad*. Madrid: Espasa-Calpe, 1963.

———. *El Padre Las Casas y Vitoria, con otros temas de los siglos XVI y XVII*. Madrid: Espasa-Calpe, 1953.

———. *Los Españoles en la historia*. 2d ed. Madrid: Espasa-Calpe, 1985.

———. "Idea imperial de Carlos V." In *España y su historia*, 2:91–107. Madrid: Minotauro, 1957.

Merrim, Stephanie. "The Apprehension of the New in Nature and Culture: Fernández de Oviedo's *Sumario*." In *1492–1992: Re/Discovering Colonial Writing*, edited by René Jara and Nicholas Spaddacini, 165–99. Hispanic Issues 4. Minneapolis: Prisma Institute, 1989.

———. "'*Un mare magno e oculto*': Anatomy of Fernández de Oviedo's *Historia general y natural de las Indias*." *Revista de estudios hispánicos* 17 (1984): 101–19.

Merriman, R. B. *The Rise of the Spanish Empire in the Old World and the New*. Vol. 1: *The Middle Ages*. New York: Macmillan, 1918.

Mexía, Pedro de. *Silva de varia lección*. Edited by Antonio Castro. 2 vols. Madrid: Cátedra, 1989.

Mignolo, Walter. "La colonización del lenguaje y de la memoria: Complicidades de la letra, el libro y la historia." In *Discursos sobre la "invención" de América*, edited by Iris M. Zavala, 183–220. Amsterdam: Rodopi, 1992.

———. *The Darker Side of the Renaissance: Literacy, Territoriality, and Colonization*. Ann Arbor: University of Michigan Press, 1995.

———. "On the Colonization of Amerindian Languages and Memories: Renais-

sance Theories of Writing and the Discontinuity of the Classical Tradition."
Comparative Studies in Society and History 34 (1992): 301–30.

Milhou, Alain. "De la destruction de l'Espagne à la destruction des Indes: Histoire sacrée et combats idéologiques." In *Études sur l'impact culturel du Nouveau Monde*, 1:25–47, 3:11–54. Paris: L'Harmattan, 1981, 1983.

———. "De la 'destruction' de l'Espagne à la 'destruction' des Indes: Notes sur
l'emploi des termes 'destroyr, destruir, destruymiento, destrución, destroydor,
destruidor' de la 'Primera Crónica General' à Las Casas. In *Mélanges à la
mémoire d'André Joucla-Ruau*, 907–19. Aix-en-Provence: Université de
Provence, 1978.

Miller, Perry. *Errand into the Wilderness*. Cambridge: Harvard University Press,
1956.

Mills, Kenneth. *Idolatry and Its Enemies: Colonial Andean Religion and Extirpation, 1640–1750*. Princeton: Princeton University Press, 1997.

Moffitt, John F., and Santiago Sebastián. *O Brave New People: The European
Invention of the American Indian*. Albuquerque: University of New Mexico
Press, 1996.

Molina Solís, Juan Francisco. *Historia del descubrimiento y conquista de
Yucatán*. Mérida de Yucatán: Caballero, 1896.

Momigliano, Arnaldo. "Herodotus in the History of Historiography." In *Studies
in Historiography*, 127–42. New York: Harper and Rowe, 1966.

Montaigne, Michel de. *Complete Essays*. Translated by Donald Frame. Stanford:
Stanford University Press, 1958.

Morford, Mark. *Stoics and Neostoics: Rubens and the Circle of Lipsius*. Princeton: Princeton University Press, 1991.

Motolinía, Fray Toribio de Benavente. *Historia de los Indios de la Nueva
España*. Edited by Georges Baudot. Madrid: Castalia, 1985.

Muldoon, James. *The Americas in the Spanish World Order: The Justification for
Conquest in the Seventeenth Century*. Philadelphia: University of Pennsylvania Press, 1994.

———. "*Extra Ecclesiam non est Imperium*: The Canonists and the Legitimacy
of Secular Power." *Studia Gratiana* 9 (1966): 551–80.

———. *Popes, Lawyers, and Infidels: The Church and the Non-Christian World,
1250–1550*. Philadelphia: University of Pennsylvania Press, 1979.

Myers, Kathleen A. "Imitation, Authority, and Revision in Fernández de
Oviedo's *Historia general y natural de las Indias*." *Romance Languages
Annual* 3 (1992): 523–30.

Ocampo, Florián de, and Ambrosio de Morales. *Corónica general de España*. 10
vols. Madrid: B. Cano, 1791.

Ogilvie, Brian. "On Numismatics and Antiquarian Method in the Sixteenth Century." Paper delivered in the Department of History, University of Chicago,
March 28, 1993.

Orquera, Yolanda Fabiola. *Los castillos decrépitos, o la "Historia Verdadera" de
Bernal Díaz del Castillo (Una indagación de las relaciones entre cultura pop-
ular y cultura letrada)*. Tucumán: Facultad de Filosofía y Letras, Universidad
Nacional de Tucumán, 1996.

Osorio Romero, Ignacio. *La enseñanza del latín a los indios*. Mexico City: Universidad Nacional Autónoma de México, 1990.

Oviedo. See Fernández de Oviedo.

Pagden, Anthony. *European Encounters with the New World*. New Haven: Yale University Press, 1993.

———. *The Fall of Natural Man: The American Indian and the Origins of Comparative Ethnology*. 2d ed. Cambridge: Cambridge University Press, 1986.

———. "Identity Formation in Spanish America." In *Colonial Identity in the Atlantic World, 1500–1800*, 51–93. Princeton: Princeton University Press, 1987.

———. "*Ius et Factum*: Text and Experience in the Writings of Bartolomé de las Casas." *Representations* 33 (1991): 147–62.

———. *Lords of All the World: Ideologies of Empire in Spain, Britain, and France, c.1500–c.1800*. New Haven: Yale University Press, 1995.

———. "The 'School of Salamanca' and the 'Affair of the Indies.'" *History of Universities* 1 (1981): 71–112.

———. *Spanish Imperialism and the Political Imagination: Studies in European and Spanish-American Social and Political Theory, 1513–1830*. New Haven: Yale University Press, 1990.

Pailler, Claire, and Jean-Marie Pailler. "Une Amérique vraiment latine: Pour une lecture 'Dumézilienne' de l'Inca Garcilaso de la Vega." *Annales ESC* (1992): 207–35.

Paletin, Vinko. (Fr. Vicente Palatino de Curzola). *Rasprava o pravu i opravdanosti rata što ga španjolsi vladari vode protiv naroda Zapadne Indije (1559) / Tratado del derecho y justicia dela guerra que tienen los reyes de España contra las naciones dela Yndia Occidental (1550)*. Edited by Franjo Šanjek (introductory material, notes, and translation into Serbo-Croatian) and Mirjana Polić-Bobić (Spanish text). Zagreb: Nakladni Zavod Globus, 1994.

———. *Tractatus de iure et iustitia belli quod habent reges Castellae et Legionis in regionibus occidentalis Indiae, quam quidam novum appellant orbem*. Spain History MSS, Lilly Library, Indiana University.

———. *Tratado del derecho y justicia de la guerra que tienen los reyes de España contra las naciones de la India Occidental*. In *Cuerpo de documentos del siglo XVI sobre los derechos de España en las Indias y las Filipinas*, edited by Agustín Millares Carlo and Lewis Hanke, 13–37. 1943, repr. Mexico City: Fondo de Cultura Económica, 1977.

Panofsky, Erwin. *Problems in Titian, Mostly Iconographic*. New York: New York University Press, 1969.

Parish, Helen Rand, and Harold E. Weidman. *Las Casas en México: Historia y obra desconocidas*. Mexico City: Fondo de Cultura Económica, 1992.

Parks, George B. "Pausanias." In *Catalogus Translationum et Commentariorum: Medieval and Renaissance Latin Translations and Commentaries: Annotated Lists and Guides*, edited by Paul O. Kristeller and F. Edward Cranz, 2:215–20. Washington, D.C.: Catholic University of America Press, 1971.

Parra, Mauricio. "Alienación y marginalidad discursiva en la *Historia verdadera de la conquista de Nueva España*." *Romance Languages Annual* 3 (1992): 550–53.

Parry, John H. *The Spanish Seaborne Empire.* New York: Knopf, 1966.

Parry, John H., and Robert G. Keith. *New Iberian World: A Documentary History of the Discovery and Settlement of Latin America to the Early Seventeenth Century.* 5 vols. New York: Times Books, 1984.

Paso y Troncoso, Francisco del. *Epistolario de Nueva España 1505–1818.* Vol. 4. Mexico City: Porrúa, 1939.

Pastor, Ludwig. *History of the Popes from the Close of the Middle Ages.* Vol. 9. St. Louis: Herder, 1910.

Pastor Bodmer, Beatríz. *The Armature of Conquest: Spanish Accounts of the Discovery of America, 1492–1589.* Stanford: Stanford University Press, 1992.

Paz, Octavio. *The Labyrinth of Solitude.* Translated by Lysander Kemp. New York: Grove Press, 1961.

———. *El ogro filantrópico.* Barcelona: Seix Barral, 1979.

Peña, Juan de la. *De bello contra insulanos: Intervención de España en América: Escuela española de la Paz, secunda generación, 1560–1585.* Edited by L. Pereña, V. Abril, C. Baciero, A. García, J. Barrientos, and F. Maseda. 2 vols. Corpus Hispanorum de Pace, vols. 9 and 10. Madrid: Consejo Superior de Investigaciones Científicas, 1982.

Penrose, Boies. *Travel and Discovery in the Renaissance, 1420–1620.* New York: Atheneum, 1962.

Pereña Vicente, Luciano. "La escuela de Salamanca y la duda indiana." In *La ética en la conquista de América,* edited by Demetrio Ramos et al., 291–344. Madrid: Consejo Superior de Investigaciones Científicas, 1984.

———. *La idea de justicia en la conquista de América.* Madrid: Mapfre, 1992.

———. *Misión de España en América.* Madrid: Consejo Superior de Investigaciones Científicas, 1956.

Pérez de Tudela, Juan. "*La Política indiana* y el político Solórzano." In *Homenaje a D. Ciriaco Pérez-Bustamante,* 3:77–171. Madrid: Consejo Superior de Investigaciones Científicas, 1970.

Pérez de Villagrá, Gaspar. *Historia de la Nueva México, 1610.* Edited and translated by Miguel Encinias, Alfred Rodríguez, and Joseph P. Sánchez. Albuquerque: University of New Mexico Press, 1992.

Pierce, Frank. *Alonso de Ercilla y Zúñiga.* Amsterdam: Rodopi, 1984.

Pietschmann, Horst. "El problema del 'nacionalismo' en España en la edad moderna. Las resistencias de Castilla contra el emperador Carlos V." *Hispania 52,* no. 180 (1992): 83–106.

Piggott, Stuart. *Ancient Britons and the Antiquarian Imagination: Ideas from the Renaissance to the Regency.* London: Thames and Hudson, 1989.

Pinard de la Boullaye, H. *L'étude comparée des religions.* Paris: Gabriel Beauchesne, 1922.

Pino Díaz, Fermín del. "Culturas clásicas y americanas en la obra del Padre Acosta." In *América y la España del siglo XVI,* edited by Francisco De Solano and Fermín del Pino, 1:327–62. Madrid: Consejo Superior de Investigaciones Científicas, 1982.

———. "Humanismo renacentista y orígenes de la etnología: A propósito del P. Acosta, paradigma del humanismo antropológico jesuita." In *Humanismo y visión del otro en la España moderna: Cuatro estudios,* edited by Berta Ares, Jesús Bustamante, Francisco Castilla, and Fermín del Pino, 377–429. Madrid: Consejo Superior de Investigaciones Científicas, 1992.

Pizarro, Pedro. *Relación del descubrimiento y conquista del Perú.* Edited by Guillermo Lohmann Villena, with notes by Pierre Duviols. Lima: Pontificia Universidad Católica del Peru, 1978.

Post, Gaines. *Studies in Medieval Legal Thought: Public Law and the State, 1100–1322.* Princeton: Princeton University Press, 1964.

Prescott, William H. *History of the Conquest of Mexico.* 3 vols. 1843; Boston: Mackay, 1892.

Quint, David. *Epic and Empire: Politics and Generic Form from Virgil to Milton.* Princeton: Princeton University Press, 1993.

Quiroga, Vasco de [?]. *De Debellandis Indis.* Edited by René Acuña. Mexico City: Universidad Nacional Autónoma de México, 1988.

———. *Información en derecho del licenciado Quiroga sobre algunas provisiones del real consejo de Indias.* Edited by Carlos Herrejón Peredo. Mexico City: Secretaría de Educación Pública, 1985.

Rabasa, José. "Utopian Ethnology in Las Casas's *Apologética.*" In *1492–1992: Re/discovering Colonial Writing,* edited by René Jara and Nicholas Spadaccini, 263–89. Hispanic Issues 4. Minneapolis: Prisma Institute, 1989.

Rallo Gruss, Asunción. *Antonio de Guevara en su contexto renacentista.* Madrid: Cupsa, 1979.

Ramos, Demetrio, et al., eds. *La ética en la conquista de América.* Corpus Hispanorum de Pace, vol. 25. Madrid: Consejo Superior de Investigaciones Científicas, 1984.

Ravicz, Marilyn Ekdahl. *Early Colonial Religious Drama in Mexico: From Tzompantli to Golgotha.* Washington, D.C.: Catholic University of America Press, 1970.

Rech, Bruno. "Las Casas und die Antike." In *Humanismus und Neue Welt,* edited by Wolfgang Reinhard, 167–97. Mitteilung XV der Kommission für Humanismusforschung, Deutsche Forschungsgemeinschaft. Weinheim: VCH, 1987.

———. "Las Casas und die Autoritäten seiner Geschichtsschreibung." *Jahrbuch für Geschichte von Staat, Wirtschaft und Gesellschaft Lateinamerikas* 16 (1979): 13–52.

———. "Las Casas und die Kirchenväter." *Jahrbuch für Geschichte von Staat, Wirtschaft und Gesellschaft Lateinamerikas* 17 (1980): 1–47.

———. "Zum Nachleben der Antike im spanischen Überseeimperium: Der Einfluss antiker Schriftsteller auf die *Historia general y natural de las Indias* des Gonzalo Fernández de Oviedo (1478–1557)." *Spanische Forschungen der Görresgesellschaft* 31 (1984): 181–244.

Redel, Enrique. *Ambrosio de Morales, estudio biográfico.* Córdoba: Diario, 1908.

Redondo, Agustín. *Antonio de Guevara (1480?–1545) et l'Espagne de son temps: De la carrière officielle aux oeuvres politico-morales.* Geneva: Droz, 1976.

Reinhold, Meyer. *Classica Americana: The Greek and Roman Heritage in the United States.* Detroit: Wayne State University Press, 1984.

Reynolds, Winston. A. "Hernán Cortés y los heroes de la antigüedad." *Revista de Filología Española* 45 (1962): 259–71.

Ricard, Robert. *Études et documents pour l'histoire missionnaire de l'Espagne et du Portugal.* Louvain: Aucam, 1931.

————. *The Spiritual Conquest of Mexico.* Translated by Lesley Byrd Simpson. Berkeley and Los Angeles: University of California Press, 1966.

Richard, Carl J. *The Founders and the Classics: Greece, Rome, and the American Enlightenment.* Cambridge: Cambridge University Press, 1994.

Richardson, John S. *The Romans in Spain.* Oxford: Blackwell, 1996.

Riquer, Martín de. "California." In *Homenaje al Profesor Antonio Vilanova,* edited by Adolfo Sotelo Vázquez and Marta Cristina Carbonell, 1:581–99. Barcelona: Universidad de Barcelona, 1989.

Rivera, Luis N. *A Violent Evangelism: The Political and Religious Conquest of the Americas.* Louisville: Westminster/John Knox Press, 1992.

Rowe, John Howland. "Ethnography and Ethnology in the Sixteenth Century." *Kroeber Anthropological Society Papers* 30 (1964): 1–15.

————. "The Renaissance Foundations of Anthropology." *American Anthropologist* 67 (1965): 1–20.

Russell, Frederick H. *The Just War in the Middle Ages.* Cambridge: Cambridge University Press, 1975.

Ryan, Michael T. "Assimilating New Worlds in the Sixteenth and Seventeenth Centuries." *Comparative Studies in Society and History* 23 (1981): 519–38.

Sahagún, Bernardino de. *Historia general de las cosas de Nueva España.* Edited by Ángel María Garibay K. 1956, repr. Mexico City: Porrúa, 1989.

Salas, Alberto M. *Tres cronistas de Indias. Pedro Mártir de Anglería, Gonzalo Fernández de Oviedo, Fray Bartolomé de las Casas.* Mexico City: Fondo de Cultura Económica, 1959.

Sánchez, Jean-Pierre. *Mythes et légendes de la conquête de l'Amérique.* 2 vols. Rennes: Presses Universitaires de Rennes, 1996.

————. "Myths and Legends in the Old World and European Expansionism on the American Continent." In *The Classical Tradition and the Americas,* edited by Wolfgang Haase and Meyer Reinhold, vol. 1, pt. 1, 189–240. Berlin: De Gruyter, 1994.

Sánchez-Albornoz, Carlos. *España: Un enigma histórico.* 2 vols. Buenos Aires: Editorial Sudamericana, 1956.

Sánchez Alonso, Benito. *Historia de la historiografía española.* Vol. 2. Madrid: Consejo Superior de Investigaciones Científicas, 1950.

Sánchez de Arévalo, Rodrigo. *Compendiosa historia hispánica.* In *Hispaniae illustratae,* edited by Andreas Schottus, 120–246. Frankfurt am Main: Marnius, 1603–8.

Schmidt, Rachel. "The Development of *Hispanitas* in Spanish Sixteenth-Century Versions of the Fall of Numancia." *Renaissance and Reformation/Renaissance et Réforme* 19 (1995): 27–45.

Schramm, Percy Ernst. "König Alfonso X. el Sabio (1252–84), deutscher Gegenkönig. Ein Beitrag zur spanischen 'Kaiseridee.'" In *Kaiser, Könige und*

Päpste. Gesammelte Aufsätze zur Geschichte des Mittelalters, vol. 4, pt. 1, 378–419. Stuttgart: Anton Hiersemann, 1970.

Schwartz, Stuart B. "New World Nobility: Social Aspirations and Mobility in the Conquest and Colonization of Spanish America." In *Social Groups and Religious Ideas in the Sixteenth Century,* edited by Miriam Usher Chrisman and Otto Gründler, 22–37. Kalamazoo: Medieval Institute, Western Michigan University, 1978.

Scott, James Brown. *The Spanish Origin of International Law.* Pt. 1: *Francisco de Vitoria and His Law of Nations.* Oxford: Clarendon Press, 1934.

Seed, Patricia. " 'Are These Not Also Men?' The Indians' Humanity and Capacity for Spanish Civilization." *Journal of Latin American Studies* 25 (1993): 629–52.

———. *Ceremonies of Possession in Europe's Conquest of the New World, 1492–1640.* Cambridge: Cambridge University Press, 1995.

Sempat Assadourian, Carlos. "Hacia la *Sublimis Deus:* Las discordias entre los dominicos indianos y el enfrentamiento del franciscano padre Tastera con el padre Betanzos." *Historia Mexicana* 187, no. 47 (1998): 465–536.

Sepúlveda. See Ginés de Sepúlveda.

Seznec, Jean. *The Survival of the Pagan Gods: The Mythological Tradition and Its Place in Renaissance Humanism and Art.* Translated by Barbara F. Sessions. Princeton: Princeton University Press, 1953.

Silva Tena, Teresa. "El sacrificio humano en la *Apologética historia.*" *Historia Mexicana* 16, no. 63 (1967): 341–57.

Simpson, Lesley Byrd. *The Encomienda in New Spain.* Rev. ed. Berkeley and Los Angeles: University of California Press, 1950.

Skinner, Quentin. *The Foundations of Modern Political Thoughts.* Vol. 2: *The Age of Reformation.* Cambridge: Cambridge University Press, 1978.

Smith, Jonathan Z. *Drudgery Divine: On the Comparison of Early Christianities and the Religions of Late Antiquity.* Chicago: University of Chicago Press, 1990.

Snow, Edward. " 'Meaning' in Children's Games: On the Limitations of the Iconographic Approach to Bruegel." *Representations* 2 (1983): 26–60.

Soler Jardón, Fernando. "Notas sobre la leyenda del incendio de las naves." *Revista de Indias* 9, nos. 31–32 (1948): 537–59.

Solórzano Pereira, Juan de. *De Indiarum iure.* Lyon: Laurentius Anisson, 1662.

———. *Política indiana.* Edited by Francisco Ramiro de Valenzuela. 4 vols. Biblioteca de Autores Españoles, vols. 252–55. Madrid: Atlas, 1972.

Soto, Domingo de. *De iustitia et iure.* 1566; rpt. Madrid: Instituto de Estudios Políticos, 1967–68.

———. *Relección "De Dominio."* Edited by Jaime Brufau Prats. Granada: Universidad de Granada, 1964.

Straub, Eberhard. *Das Bellum Iustum des Hernán Cortés in México.* Beihefte zum Archiv für Kulturgeschichte, vol. 11. Cologne: Böhlau, 1976.

Strong, Roy. *Splendour at Court: Renaissance Spectacle and Illusion.* London: Weidenfeld and Nicolson, 1973.

Subirats, Eduardo. *El continente vacío: La conquista del Nuevo Mundo y la conciencia moderna.* Mexico City: Siglo Veintiuno, 1994.

Tanner, Marie. *The Last Descendant of Aeneas: The Hapsburgs and the Mythic Image of the Emperor.* New Haven: Yale University Press, 1993.

Tate, Robert B. *Ensayos sobre la historiografía peninsular del siglo XV.* Madrid: Gredos, 1970.

Thacher, John Boyd. *Christopher Columbus.* 3 vols. New York: Putnam, 1903–4.

Thomas, Hugh. *Conquest: Montezuma, Cortés, and the Fall of Old Mexico.* New York: Simon and Schuster, 1993.

Thomas, Keith. *Religion and the Decline of Magic.* New York: Scribner's, 1971.

Thompson, I. A. A. "Castile, Spain, and the Monarchy: The Political Community from *Patria Natural* to *Patria Nacional.*" In *Spain, Europe, and the Atlantic World: Essays in Honor of John H. Elliott,* edited by Richard L. Kagan and Geoffrey Parker, 125–59. Cambridge: Cambridge University Press, 1995.

Tierney, Brian. *The Crisis of Church and State: 1050–1300.* Englewood Cliffs, N.J.: Prentice-Hall, 1964.

Todorov, Tzvetan. *The Conquest of America.* Translated by Richard Howard. New York: Harper and Row, 1984.

Tracy, James D. *The Politics of Erasmus: A Pacifist Intellectual and His Political Milieu.* Toronto: University of Toronto Press, 1978.

Trame, Richard H. *Rodrigo Sánchez de Arévalo, 1404–1470: Spanish Diplomat and Champion of the Papacy.* Washington, D.C.: Catholic University of America Press, 1958.

Trexler, Richard. "We Think, They Act: Clerical Readings of Missionary Theatre in Sixteenth Century New Spain. In *Understanding Popular Culture: Europe from the Middle Ages to the Nineteenth Century,* edited by Steven L. Kaplan, 189–227. Berlin: Mouton, 1984.

Turner, Daymond. "The Aborted First Printing of the Second Part of Oviedo's *General and Natural History of the Indies.*" *Huntington Library Quarterly* 46 (1983): 105–25.

————. *Gonzalo Fernández de Oviedo y Valdés: An Annotated Bibliography.* Chapel Hill: University of North Carolina Press, 1966.

Ulzurrum [Ulcurrunus, Ulçurrum], Miguel de. *Catolicum opus imperiale regiminis mundi.* In *Tractatus universi iuris,* 16:104–30. Venice: Zilettus, 1586.

Valdés, Alfonso de. *Diálogo de las cosas ocurridas en Roma.* Edited by José F. Montesinos. Madrid: Espasa-Calpe, 1956.

Varille, Mathieu. "Antiquaires Lyonnais de la renaissance." *Revue du Lyonnais,* 1923, 453–60.

Vázquez Vera, Josefina Zoraida. *La imagen del Indio en español del siglo XVI.* Cuadernos de la Facultad de Filosofía, Letras y Ciencias 16. Veracruz: Universidad Veracruzana, 1962.

Vera Cruz, Alonso de la. *The Writings of Alonso de la Vera Cruz.* Edited and translated by Ernest J. Burrus. 5 vols. Rome: Jesuit Historical Institute, 1968–76.

Vergil, Polydore. *Beginnings and Discoveries: Polydore Vergil's "De Inven-*

toribus Rerum." Translated and edited by Beno Weiss and Louis C. Pérez. Nieuwkoop: De Graaf, 1997.

———. *De inventoribus rerum.* Basel: Thomas Guarinus, 1563.

Verrazzano, Giovanni da. *The Voyages of Giovanni da Verrazzano, 1524–1528,* edited by Lawrence C. Wroth. New Haven: Yale University Press, 1970.

Vitoria, Francisco de. *De Indis et de iure belli relectiones.* Edited and translated by Ernest Nys. Classics of International Law. Washington D.C.: Carnegie Institute, 1917.

———. *Obras: Relecciones teológicas.* Edited by Teófilo Urdánoz. Biblioteca de Autores Cristianos. Madrid: Editorial Católica, 1960.

———. *Political Writings.* Edited by Anthony Pagden and Jeremy Lawrance. Cambridge: Cambridge University Press, 1991.

———. *Relectio de Indis, o libertad de los Indios.* Edited and translated by L. Pereña and J. M. Pérez Prendes, with introductory essays by V. Beltrán de Heredia, R. Agostino Iannarone, T. Urdánoz, A. Truyol, and L. Pereña. Corpus Hispanorum de Pace 5. Madrid: Consejo Superior de Investigaciones Científicas, 1967.

———. *Relectio de iure belli, o paz dinámica: Escuela española de la Paz, Primera Generación 1526–1560.* Edited by L. Pereña, V. Abril, C. Baciero, A. García, and F. Maseda. Corpus Hispanorum de Pace 6. Madrid: Consejo Superior de Investigaciones Científicas, 1981.

Vivar, Gerónimo de. *Crónica y relación copiosa y verdadera de los Reinos de Chile (1558).* Edited by Leopoldo Saez-Godoy. Bibliotheca Ibero-Americana: Veröffentlichungen des Ibero-Amerikanischen Instituts, vol. 27. Berlin: Colloquium Verlag, 1979.

Wagner, Henry Raup. *The Discovery of New Spain in 1518 by Juan de Grijalva.* New York: Cortés Society, 1942.

Wagner, Henry Raup, with Helen Rand Parish. *The Life and Writings of Bartolomé de las Casas.* Albuquerque: University of New Mexico Press, 1967.

Weckmann, Luis. *The Medieval Heritage of Mexico.* Translated by Frances M. López-Morillas. New York: Fordham University Press, 1992.

Wolf, Kenneth Baxter. *Conquerors and Chroniclers of Early Medieval Spain.* Liverpool: Liverpool University Press, 1990.

Yates, Frances A. "Charles V and the Idea of the Empire." In *Astraea: The Imperial Theme in the Sixteenth Century,* 1–28. London: Routledge and Kegan Paul, 1975.

Zavala, Silvio. "Adición sobre Fray Miguel de Arcos." *Historia Mexicana* 154, no. 39 (1989): 555–61.

———. "Algo más sobre Vasco de Quiroga." *Historia Mexicana* 151, no. 38 (1989): 533–49.

———. "En busca del tratado de Vasco de Quiroga, *De Debellandis Indis.*" *Historia Mexicana* 68, no. 17 (1968): 485–515.

———. "En torno del tratado *De Debellandis Indis* de Vasco de Quiroga." *Historia Mexicana* 72, no. 18 (1969): 623–26.

———. *Por la senda hispana de la libertad.* Madrid: Mapfre, 1992.

Zorita, Alonso de. *Breve y sumaria relación de los señores de la Nueva España.* In *Nueva colección de documentos para la historia de México,* edited by Joaquín García Icazbalceta, 3:150. Mexico City: Francisco Díaz de León, 1891.

———. *Life and Labor in Ancient Mexico.* Translated by Benjamin Keen. New Brunswick, N.J.: Rutgers University Press, 1963.

Index

Index of Modern Scholars

References are to authors of books and articles cited, not editors or texts or collections.

Printed and bound by CPI Group (UK) Ltd, Croydon, CR0 4YY

09/06/2025

14685643-0001